Cumulative Paperback Index

R. Reginald

Has

Also

Written

STELLA NOVA: *Contemporary Science*

Fiction Authors

Cumulative Paperback Index
1939-1959

A Comprehensive Bibliographic Guide to
14,000 Mass-Market Paperback Books of
33 Publishers Issued under 69 Imprints

by

R. Reginald

and

M. R. Burgess

Gale Research Company   Book Tower   Detroit, Michigan 48226

**Library of Congress
Cataloging in Publication Data**

Reginald, R
   Cumulative paperback index, 1939-1959.

   1. Bibliography--Paperback editions. I. Burgess, M. R.,
joint author. II. Title.
Z1033.P3R4   018'.4   73-6866

Dedicated to my parents, who made it all possible;
to my three brothers, Steve, Mark, and Scott; and
to the best of friends, Liz Fishman and Doug Menville

THANK YOU: Doug Menville, Joanne Burger, Art Nelson, Mark Owings, Lyn Young, A. Stephens, Don Tuck.

Crosby Library of Gonzaga University, Doheny Library of University of Southern California, California State College-San Bernardino Library, the Library of the University of California at Los Angeles, University of Redlands Library, State Library of California.

Bond Street Book Store (Steve Edrington and Jim McDonald), Hollywood; Inland Book Store (Dean Gilbert), Spokane; Clark's Old Book Store (Jerome Peltier), Spokane; Art's Book Shop (Art Papadopolo), San Bernardino; ABC Book Service, Hollywood; Sunset-Vine Bookmart (Al and Joe Saunders), Hollywood; Bartlett Street Book Store, Medford; Cosmopolitan Book Store (Eli Goodman), Los Angeles; Thieves' Market (Mickey Starr), Medford; Acres of Books, Long Beach; Family Book Store, Glendale; Pacific Book Store, Los Angeles; Collectors Book Store, Hollywood; D-J Book Search Service (Dorothy and John Bright), San Bernardino.

Ace Publishing Corporation (Donald Wollheim); Ballantine Books, Inc. (Betty Ballantine and Eleanor Budris); Popular Library, Inc. (Joseph Johnston and Sheila Levine); Berkley Publishing Corporation (Thomas A. Dardis and Nancy Kaminski); Manor Books, Inc. (Donald A. Schrader); New American Library, Inc. (Sidney Kramer and Peter Gruenthal); Pyramid Publications, Inc. (Matthew Huttner and Norman Goldfind); Fawcett World Library (Roger Fawcett and Edmund Pendergast); Doubleday & Company, Inc. (John T. Sargent and Walter Freese); Bantam Books, Inc. (Arthur May and Oscar Dystel); Pocket Books, Inc. (Helen Dworkin and Herbert Alexander); Avon Book Division, The Hearst Corporation (Peter M. Mayer and Alice Bosk); Dell Publishing Company, Inc. (George T. Delacorte, Walter B. J. Mitchell, Jr., and Eva Bayne).

California State College-San Bernardino Faculty Development Funds.

The professional appearance of this book is due primarily to the excellent work of our long-suffering typist, Mrs. Linda Evans, who for three months spent her night and weekend hours sitting in front of a keyboard when she could have been doing much more pleasant tasks. For her patience, accuracy, and sense of duty, our deepest gratitude.

CONTENTS

Introduction

The CUMULATIVE PAPERBACK INDEX is a continuing bibliography of the American mass-market paperback. It includes pocket-sized, paper-bound books distributed in the United States through newsstand outlets and other mass-market channels. Volume I covers the period from the release of the first ten Pocket Books in June, 1939, through the end of 1959.

The following materials are not included: books published by firms located outside the continental United States; paper-bound publications distributed primarily through bookstores or by mail; and paperbacks issued by companies specializing in erotica. Subsidiary lines published by companies already qualifying for inclusion are generally included.

Arrangement

The CPI is divided into three sections: an author index, a title index, and the publisher specifications section, which provides an informational and statistical survey of each of the companies covered. The main entry is the author entry, which gives author, title, publisher, stock number, publication date, and price, in that order. The title section lists titles and authors only.

Library of Congress filing rules are followed, except that names or words beginning in Mc-are arranged in strict alphabetical order. Since the CPI indexes stock numbers, titles may be listed more than once in the author section. Duplicate titles are arranged in chronological order, and are indicated by seven-space lines. Anonymous works are filed in both the author and title sections by title. Books authored by corporate authors are considered anonymous publications. Paperbacks with three or more individual authors are listed under the first name only.

No attempt has been made to identify pseudonyms, or to provide an author's full name or dates. In general, names are recorded as they appear on the books, except that titles or honorifics are not included, and minor variations in nicknames are ignored. Authors will be found under the commonest variants of their names. Additional information is provided when necessary for identification. Certain classical authors of Greek and Roman times are recorded under the forms established by the National Union Catalog. To assist in identification, authors listed in the title section may have the initial letters of their surnames underlined when the beginnings of the names are not obvious.

A certain lack of consistency in the capitalization of titles reflects the varying standards of the NUC, as well as the inherent difficulties in identifying proper names in some types of materials. The western novel provides some particularly noteworthy examples. In general, words or names are left in lower case unless 1) they are capitalized in some other source, or 2) they are obviously the name of some person, place, or event.

Minor variations in stock numbers are not separately recorded. Series or numbers not covered include: the 2000 number series of Pocket Books, Inc. (regarded as a haphazard reissue series); variations in price prefix letters for certain publications of the New American Library (Signet, Signet Key, and Mentor Books); the 1300-1500 series of Dell Books (a reissue series); Popular Library publications with suffixed reissue letters; Avon Books numbered above G-2002, or above T-500; Ballantine Books publication number F1; and any similar anomalies. For a complete record of the stock numbers included in this book, please see the publisher specifications section.

In the author section, publisher entries have been abbreviated to a maximum of four spaces (please see the abbreviations list). Publication dates are shortened to the last two digits of the year (from 39-59). Unverified dates (and occasionally other information) are underlined. Unnumbered books are indicated by the letters "nn". Books whose stock numbers are not known are labelled "unk". Stock numbers which were assigned to paperbacks, but which did not actually appear on the books themselves, are listed in parentheses.

As is customary in a book of this sort, a small number of check entries have been randomly scattered throughout the text. Since no real names have been employed for this purpose, the legitimate user should not experience any difficulties. A complete list of the bogus entries will be provided to anyone who has obtained written permission to use the book's material.

Specifications Section

The CPI indexes by author and title a manuscript originally arranged by publisher and publisher stock number. The Publisher Specifications Section is a statistical summary of the information contained in the unpublished stock number index, plus some additional data concerning the physical appearances of the books, and a chronological survey of company addresses and imprints. The material is arranged by publisher and publisher imprint, as indicated in the master abbreviations list. In most cases, the information is drawn entirely from original sources, that is, from the books themselves.

Each entry includes the following: publisher, name of parent company, addresses (listed in chronological order, with dates), stock number spans (with dates of usage), book heights, color of the stains applied to the outer three edges of the firm's publications, types of stock numbering systems used, price codes, and total books issued or recorded. In addition, informational notes may be appended after the list of stock numbers. Exceptions to price codings are noted underneath the list of code letters or numbers, in parentheses. Uncertain dates are indicated with question marks. A small "x" after a date indicates that the series or address to which it refers continued through the end of the time span covered by this edition of the CPI (1959).

Mass market paperbacks have been published in two basic sizes. The smaller height, averaging 16cm, was introduced by Pocket Books in 1939, and for many years served as the standard size for all paperbacks. However, Penguin (and its successor, New American Library) pioneered a taller version which averaged 17 1/2cm in height, and this format gradually gained acceptance in the 1950's, particularly for higher-priced books. By the 1960's, it had become the predominate form, and during the latter part of that decade the smaller size died out completely. The two forms are listed herein as "small" and "large". Firms using both sizes are indicated by "mixed".

Pocket also initiated the practice of dyeing the outer edges of its publications with a uniform identifying color. Most of its competitors followed suit, each company having its own distinctive stain. A few firms either did not adopt the practice, or used it selectively, leaving some imprints uncolored to resemble large-sized quality paperbacks. Unstained books are listed as "blank". Companies using a variety of colors are indicated by "mixed".

Various methods have been developed to number American paperbacks. The simplest method, the consecutive number system, was first used by Pocket Books, Inc. in June of 1939. Pocket numbered its first ten releases consecutively from 1-10; the second ten received numbers 11-20, and so on, into infinity. Most of the other paperback companies followed Pocket's lead, although not all firms started their numbering with "1". Some initiated their systems with odd numbers, such as Graphic's "11", or Gold Medal's "99". Bantam Books was the first company to add prefixed letters to its stock numbers to indicate different price levels. Its first 35¢ title, published in February, 1950, was numbered A760. The practice soon became widespread.

The second system was initiated by Avon Books in February, 1951. The price series method lumps together all books having the same cover price, and numbers each group from some base number. In Avon's case, its first 50¢ title was given the number 1001, and the second 1002; the third was called G1003. Every 50¢ title published thereafter was numbered consecutively from G1003. 35¢ books had their own series, beginning with AT51, and 25¢ books continued to be numbered from the original series, which eventually reached 878 before expiring. As new price levels were introduced, new number series were started for each, with appropriate identifying letters. A number of the larger companies, including Dell and Pocket, eventually adapted the system to their own use.

The third system has received very limited use in America. Bantam Books experimented with a subject-oriented numbering system in 1948-49, numbering each western, for example, consecutively from 200, each mystery from 300, and so on. It proved impractical, and was abandoned after a year's use. Airmont Books revived the subject series method in January, 1962, and Vega Books also experimented with a similar system in the mid-1960's. Both lines were short-lived: Vega disappeared in 1966 and Airmont dropped all but its classic series in 1964.

The final system is the computer alphabetic method, pioneered by Dell in June, 1962. Basically, Dell reserved a span of numbers from 0000-9899. As each book was released, a computer was used to determine statistically where within the span of the 9900 numbers the publication would fall if it were arranged in alphabetical order by title with every other book that Dell would publish. Hence, a book called Abe Lincoln received a number near the beginning of the span (0001); another title, The Young Lovers, was numbered 9856, near its end. The numbers were assigned for the life of the book, regardless of price changes. As time passed, one defect of the system became obvious: after large amounts of numbers had been used, books tended to get out of sequence, as gaps in the span were filled in. Consequently, Welcome to the Monkey House, for example, received the number 9478, well beyond What Time Collects at 9452. Such anomalies seem to be inherent in the system.

Sources

The primary sources of information were, in order of importance: 1) the books themselves, with their advertisements; 2) the paperback publishers, either from stock catalogs or internal company records; 3) Publishers' Weekly, including the "Weekly Record" section, periodic forecasts of scheduled publications, reviews, and advertisements; 4) Paperbound Books in Print; 5) Catalog of Copyright Entries; 6) National Union Catalog and similar publications; 7) other miscellaneous items, including genre bibliographies, general trade news, library or collection catalogs, etc.

The CPI could not have been completed without the generous assistance of a large number of mass market publishers, including: Ace Books, Ballantine Books, Popular Library, Berkley Books, Manor Books, New American Library, Pyramid Books, Fawcett Publications, Doubleday and Company, Bantam Books, Pocket Books, Avon Books. Many of these firms provided lists of their publications and all made vigorous efforts to answer every question posed. In addition, several used paperback stores went far beyond the normal courtesies, and not only opened up their stock rooms, but even made special searches for obscure materials. Much gratitude, then, to Art's Book Shop of San Bernardino, The Sunset-Vine Bookmart in Hollywood, Clark's Old Book Store in Spokane, the ABC Book Service in Hollywood, Bond Street Book Store in Hollywood, and the Thieves' Market of Medford, Oregon. Credit should also go to three libraries that provided much assistance: the Doheny Library of the University of Southern California, the State Library of California in Sacramento, and the California State College, San Bernardino Library. Finally, special thanks to fellow bibliographer Mark Owings for his assistance in a time of need, and to a close friend, Doug Menville, who allowed free access to his collection, and who also lent a good pair of eyes.

One last source needs to be mentioned. This book could not have been undertaken without access to the Author's personal library of 8000 paperbacks. The collection provided a basic background grid against which each successive piece of information could be laid, and was in itself a unique and vital reference tool. Without it, the book would have required a much longer period of time to complete.

A bibliography is never finished. One can only hope to come close. Anyone having additional information, or wishing to make corrections, is urged to contact the Author through Gale Research Company. Sources will be fully credited in future editions. It is anticipated that the next volume of the CPI, covering the period 1960-69, will be available around 1977.

Abbreviations

Ace	Ace Books		Ment	Mentor Books (New American Library)
Avon	Avon Books		Mon	Monarch Books
AvnF	Avon Fantasy Novels		MonB	Monarch Human Behavior Series
Ball	Ballantine Books		NL	Novel Library
Ban	Bantam Books		nn	unnumbered book
BanB	Bantam Biographies		Nov	Novel Selections
BanC	Bantam Classics		PB	Pocket Books, Inc.
Bard	Bard Books (Avon)		PBA	Pocket Books Art Series
Bart	Bart House		PBJr	Pocket Book Juniors
Berk	Berkley Books		PBL	Pocket Library (Pocket)
BH	Bleak House (Parsee)		Pel	Pelican Books (New American Library)
BK	Black Knight (Ideal)		PelM	Pelican-Mentor (New American Library)
Bond	Bonded Mysteries		Pen	Penguin Books (New American Library)
BPLA	Bantam Publications, L.A.		PenG	Penguin Guides (New American Library)
Card	Cardinal Editions (Pocket)		PenN	Penguin-Signet (New American Library)
Chek	Checkerbooks		PenS	Penguin Specials (New American Library)
Com	Comet Books (Pocket)		Perm	Permabooks (Pocket)
Crst	Crest Books (Fawcett)		Phan	Phantom Mysteries
Dell	Dell Books		Pnnt	Pennant Books (Bantam)
DelF	Dell First Editions		Pony	Pony Books
DelL	Dell Laurel Editions		Pop	Popular Library/Popular Books
DelT	Dell 10¢ Series		Prem	Premier Books (Fawcett)
Dmnd	Diamond Books (Berkley)		Prmb	Permabooks
Eag	Eagle Books (Popular Library)		Pyr	Pyramid Books
Egle	Eagle Books (New American Library)		PyrR	Pyramid Royals
Eton	Eton Books (Avon)		RC	Red Circle Books (Lion)
Gal	Galaxy Books		RCL	Readers-Choice Library
GC	Green Circle (Ideal)		RS	Red Seal Books (Fawcett)
GD	Green Dragon (Ideal)		Sig	Signet Books (New American Library)
GM	Gold Medal Books (Fawcett)		SigC	Signet Classics (New American Library)
Graf	Graphic Books		SigK	Signet Key Books (New American Library)
Han	Handi-Books		SML	Saint Mystery Library
HanW	Handi-Book Westerns		Sup	Superior Reprints
HH	Hangman's House (Parsee)		unk	stock number unknown
Hill	Hillman		WSP	Washington Square Press (Pocket)
Inf	Infantry Journal		Zen	Zenith Books
Lion	Lion Books/Lion Library			

Note: names in parentheses indicate firms under which imprints are listed in the Publisher Specifications Section.

Publisher Specifications

Ace

Ace Books, Inc.   1952-x
(A. A. Wyn, Inc.)
  23 West 47th Street
  New York 36, New York

Publications:
  D-1 - D-411   10/52-x
  (includes 224 doubles)

Bk. height: small
Edge color: yellow orange
No. system: consecutive number
Price code:
  S=25¢, D=35¢, G=50¢
  (D-293/50¢)

Total books published: 635

Avon

Avon Book Company   1941-1945
  432 Fourth Avenue
  New York 16, New York
New Avon Library   1945-1948
Avon Publishing Company, Inc.   1948-1951
  119 West 57th Street
  New York 19, New York
Avon Publishing Company, Inc.   1951-1953
Avon Publications, Inc.   1953-1959
Avon Book Division, Hearst Corp.   1959
  575 Madison Avenue
  New York 22, New York
Avon Book Division   1959-x
The Hearst Corporation
  959 Eighth Avenue
  New York 19, New York

Publications:
  (1)-(40), 41-864   11/41-x
  nn (one book)   1943
  T-2   unknown
  AT51 - AT-70, T-71 - T-378   1/53-x
  1001-1002, G1003 - G-1040   2/51-x
  G-2001 - G-2002   1959?
  V-2031   1959?

Bk. height: small (25¢), mixed
  (other prices)
Edge color: red (25¢), yellow
  orange (other prices)
No. system: price series
Price code:
  no number=25¢, no letter=25¢,
  AT=35¢, T=35¢, G=50¢, V=75¢
  (388/35¢, 1001-1002/50¢)

Total books published: 1235

--- --- --- --- --- --- ---

Avon Fantasy Novels

Publications:
  1-2   4/50

Bk. height: small
Edge color: red
No. system: consecutive number
Price code:
  no letter=25¢

Total books published: 2

--- --- --- --- --- --- ---

Avon Bard

Publications:
  1 - T-06   7/55-x

Bk. height: small
Edge color: variously blank,
  yellow orange
No. system: consecutive number
Price code:
  no letter=35¢, T=35¢
  (2/50¢)

Total books published: 6

--- --- --- --- --- --- ---

Eton

Eton Books, Inc.   1951-1953
  575 Madison Avenue
  New York 22, New York

Publications:
  101-103, ET104-E132   1/51-9/53
  ET51   1952?

Bk. height: mixed
Edge color: red (1951), yellow
  orange (1951-53)
No. system: consecutive number
  (1951-52), price series
  (1952-53)
Price code:
  no letter=25¢, E=25¢, ET=35¢

Total books published: 31

Ballantine

| Ballantine Books, Inc.
404 Fifth Avenue
New York 18, New York | 1952-1956 |
| Ballantine Books, Inc.
101 Fifth Avenue
New York 3, New York | 1956-x |

Publications:
  1-264, 268-269, 265K-267K,
  269K-350K, 352K-F356K   11/52-x

Bk. height: large
Edge color: orange
No. System: consecutive number
Price code:
  no letter=35¢, F=50¢, S=75¢
  (26, 34, 48, BSF320/50¢)

Total books published: <u>347</u>

Bantam

| Bantam Books, Inc.
1107 Broadway
New York 10, New York | 1945-1950 |
| Bantam Books, Inc.
23 West 45th Street
New York 36, New York | 1950-x |

Publications:
  1-158   11/45-7/50
  200-214, 227, 250-262, 300-320,
  350-366, 400-427, 450-477,
  500-507, 550-557   2/48-1/50
  A-1 - A-5   6/48-2/52
  nn (two books)   9/50
  700-F1932, 1934-A1961, A1964,
  A1966-F1968, A1970-A1978,
  F1980-1984, A1986-A1992,
  S1995-2002, F2004-S2013,
  F2015-A2017, A2020-A2021,
  A2024, 2031, F2033-A2036,
  A2060, A2063, A2070, A2073   7/49-x

Bk. height: small (1945-53),
  large (1953-x)
Edge color: red (25¢), yellow
  (other prices)
No. system: consecutive number
  (subject variant, 1948-49)
Price code:
  no number=35¢, no letter=25¢,
  A-=25¢, A=35¢, F=50¢, S=75¢

Total books published: <u>1557</u>

Bantam Biographies

Publications:
  FB400-FB418   1/56-9/58

Bk. height: large
Edge color: yellow
No. system: consecutive number
Price code:
  FB=50¢

Total books published: <u>18</u>

Bantam Classics

Publications:
  AC1-FC52   9/58-x

Bk. height: large
Edge color: blank
No. system: consecutive number
Price code:
  AC=35¢, FC=50¢, SC=75¢, NC=95¢

Total books published: <u>50</u>

Pennant

Publications:
  P1-P79   6/53-7/55

Bk. height: large
Edge color: steel blue (1953-
  55), red (1955)
No. system: consecutive number
Price code:
  P=25¢

Total books published: <u>66</u>

Bantam Publications

| Bantam Publications, Inc.
Pacific Mutual Building
Los Angeles, California | ?1940-1943? |

Publications:
  18, 21-28
  number unknown (8 books)   ?1940-1943?

Bk. height: small
Edge color: blank
No. system: consecutive number
Price code:
  no letter=10¢

BANTAM PUBLICATIONS (cont.)

Total books recorded: 17

Bart House

Bartholomew House, Inc.   1944-1947
    205 East 42nd Street
    New York 17, New York

Publications:
    (1)-(2), 3-39?   1944-1947
    101-103?   1946-1947

Bk. height: small
Edge color: blank (1944),
    burgundy (1944-1946),
    blank (1947)
No. system: consecutive number
Price code:
    no letter=25¢

Total books recorded: 40

Berkley

Berkley Publishing Corporation   1955-x
    145 W. 57th Street
    New York 19, New York

Publications:
    101-112   3/55-4/55
    313-386   5/55-2/59
    G-1 - G294   6/55-x

Bk. height: small (1955-59),
    large (1959-x)
Edge color: steel blue (25¢,
    1955), burgundy (25¢, 1955-
    59), yellow green (other
    prices, 1955-59), red (1959-x)
No. system: consecutive number
Price code:
    no letter=25¢, G=35¢, BG=50¢,
    S=75¢

Total books published: 377

    ---   ---   ---   ---   ---   ---   ---

Berkley Diamond

Publications:
    D2001-D2020   8/59-x

Bk. height: small
Edge color: yellow green
No. system: consecutive number
Price code:
    D=35¢

Total books published: 20

Bonded Mysteries

Anson Bond Publications, Inc.   1946-1947
    913 N. La Cienega Boulevard
    Hollywood 46, California

Publications:
    1-16?   ?5/46-2/47?

Bk. height: small
Edge color: blank
No. system: consecutive number
Price code:
    no letter=25¢

Total books recorded: 16

Checkerbooks

Checkerbooks, Inc.   1949
    1 East 42nd Street
    New York 17, New York

Publications:
    1-10?   10/49-12/49?

Bk. height: large
Edge color: blank
No. system: consecutive number
Price code:
    no letter=15¢

Total books recorded: 10

Dell

Dell Publishing Company, Inc.   ?1943-1948
    149 Madison Avenue
    New York 16, New York
Dell Publishing Company, Inc.   1948-1958
    261 Fifth Avenue
    New York 16, New York
Dell Publishing Company, Inc.   1958-x
    750 Third Avenue
    New York 17, New York

Publications:
    1-1008   ?1/43-x
    nn (two books)   1947
    D101-D294, D296-D311, D313-
      D323, D325-D331   1/52-x
    F50-F90, F94-F95   4/53-x
    X1   3/59-x

Bk. height: small
Edge color: steel blue (1943-49),
    blue (25¢, 1949-1957; all

DELL (cont.)

    prices, 1957-x), orange brown
    (other prices, 1952-53),
    yellow (other prices, 1953-57)
No. system: price series
Price code:
    no number=25¢, no letter=25¢,
    D=35¢, F=50¢, X=75¢

Total books published: 1281

    ---   ---   ---   ---   ---   ---   ---

Dell 10¢ Books

Publications:
    1-36   1/51-12/51

Bk. height: small
Edge color: blank
No. system: consecutive number
Price code:
    no letter=10¢

Total books published: 36

    ---   ---   ---   ---   ---   ---   ---

Dell First Editions

Publications:
    1E-2E, D3-FE100   9/53-4/56
    103-109, A110-A193   4/56-x
    B101-B133, B135-B143, B148,
    B152   4/56-x
    C101-C108   9/56-x

Bk. height: small
Edge color: blue (25¢, 1953),
    red (25¢, 1954-55?), yellow
    (other prices, 1953-1957),
    blue (25¢, 1956?-1957; all
    prices, 1957-x)
No. system: consecutive number
    (1953-56), price series
    (1956-x)
Price code:
    no letter=25¢, A=25¢, D=35¢,
    B=35¢, F=50¢, FE=50¢, C=50¢

Total books published: 243

    ---   ---   ---   ---   ---   ---   ---

Dell Laurel Editions

Publications:
    LB110-LB134   11/57-x
    LC101-LC128, LC130-LC140   5/57-x
    LX101-LX106, LX108-LX116,
    LX120   4/58-x

    LY101-LY102   3/59-x

Bk. height: small
Edge color: blue
No. system: price series
Price code:
    LB=35¢, LC=50¢, LX=75¢, LY=95¢

Total books published: 81
_____

Fawcett

Fawcett Publications, Inc.   1949-x
    (Fawcett Place)
    Greenwich, Connecticut
listed variously as:
Fawcett World Library
    67 West 44th Street
    New York 36, New York

    ---   ---   ---   ---   ---   ---   ---

Gold Medal

Publications:
    99-s946   5/49-x

Bk. height: large
Edge color: yellow (1949-50),
    orange (1950-53), yellow
    (1953-x)
No. system: consecutive number
Price code:
    no letter=25¢, G=35¢, S=35¢,
    s=35¢, D=50¢, d=50¢
    (184, 192, 198/35¢)

Total books published: 848

    ---   ---   ---   ---   ---   ---   ---

Red Seal

Publications:
    7-29   4/52-4/53

Bk. height: large
Edge color: blue
No. system: consecutive number
Price code:
    no letter=35¢

Total books published: 23

    ---   ---   ---   ---   ---   ---   ---

Crest

Publications:
    114-344   9/55-x

FAWCETT - CREST (cont.)

Bk. height: large
Edge color: red orange
No. system: consecutive number
Price code:
  no letter=25¢, s=35¢, d=50¢,
  t=75¢

Total books published: 231

    ---   ---   ---   ---   ---   ---   ---

Premier

Publications:
  s12-d86   9/55-x

Bk. height: large
Edge color: red orange
No. system: consecutive number
Price code:
  s=35¢, d=50¢

Total books published: 75

Galaxy

Galaxy Publishing Corporation   1958
The Guinn Company, Inc.
  421 Hudson Street
  New York 14, New York

Publications:
  32-35   1958
  (continuation of a digest-
   sized series)

Bk. height: small
Edge color: red (32-33),
  yellow (34-35)
No. system: consecutive number
Price code:
  no letter=35¢

Total books published: 4

Graphic

Graphic Publishing Company, Inc. 1949-1950?
  22 Bond Street
  New York 12, New York
Graphic Publishing Company, Inc. ?1950-1955
  181 Boulevard
  Hasbrouck Heights, New Jersey
Graphic Publishing Company, Inc. 1956-1957
  240 West 40th Street
  New York, New York

Publications:
  11-157   Sp/49-5/57
  G101, G201-G223   1952-5/57

Bk. height: small
Edge color: mixed (1949-1954),
  red (25¢, 1954-57), red
  orange (other prices)
No. system: price series
Price code:
  no letter=25¢, G=35¢

Total books published: 170

Handi-Books

Quinn Publishing Company, Inc.   ?1943-1945
  745 Fifth Avenue
  New York 22, New York
Quinn Publishing Company, Inc.   1945-1951
  Kingston, New York

Publications:
  ?12-139?   1943-1951

Bk. height: small
Edge color: blank (1943-44),
  blue (top edge only, 1944-45),
  blank (1945-51), red (1951)
No. system: consecutive number
Price code:
  no letter=15¢ (12-53),
  20¢ (54-?), 25¢ (?-139)

Total books recorded: 124

    ---   ---   ---   ---   ---   ---   ----

Handi-Book Westerns

Publications:
  1-4   1947?

Bk. height: small
Edge color: blank
No. system: consecutive number
Price code:
  no letter=20¢?

Total books published: 4

Hillman

Hillman Periodicals, Inc.   1943-?
  1476 Broadway
  New York 18, New York
Hillman Periodicals, Inc.   1948-x
  535 Fifth Avenue
  New York 17, New York

HILLMAN (cont.)

Publications:
```
1 (Hillman Detective Novel)    1943
?1-48?                         1948-1951?
nn (two books)                 1948, 1952
?100-105                       ?2/57-4/57
106-129                        6/59-x
```

Bk. height: small
Edge color: yellow (1943), red
  (1948-52), mixed (1957), red
  orange (1959-x)
No. system: consecutive number
Price code:
  no letter=25¢ (1943-57), no
  number=25¢, no letter=35¢
  (1959-x)
  (105/35¢, 106/50¢)

Total books recorded: 69

Ideal

```
Ideal Distributing Company     ?1944-1947?
  480 Lexington Avenue
  New York 17, New York
```

--- --- --- --- --- --- ---

Black Knight Mysteries

Publications:
```
26, 31
number unknown (7 books)       ?1946-1947?
```

Bk. height: small
Edge color: blank
No. system: consecutive number
Price code:
  no letter=25¢

Total books recorded: 9

--- --- --- --- --- --- ---

Green Circle

Publications:
```
number unknown (one book)      ?1946
```

Other information unknown.

Total books recorded: 1

--- --- --- --- --- --- ---

Green Dragon

Publications:
```
number unknown (5 books)       ?1944-1947?
```

Other information unknown.

Total books recorded: 5

Infantry Journal

```
The Infantry Journal           1945
  Washington, D. C.
```

Publications:
```
J101-J102?                     6/45-7/45?
```

Bk. height: small
Edge color: red
No. system: consecutive number
Price code:
  J=25¢

Total books recorded: 2

Lion

```
Lion Books, Inc.               1949-1951
  Empire State Building
  New York 1, New York
Lion Books, Inc.               1952-1954
  270 Park Avenue
  New York, New York
Lion Books, Inc.               1954-1957
  655 Madison Avenue
  New York 21, New York
```

Publications:
```
8-11, 14-233                   11/49-1/55
LL 1 - LL 175 (Lion Library)   7/54-4/57
```

Bk. height: small (1949-54),
  mixed (1954-57)
Edge color: mixed (1949-53),
  yellow (1953-57)
No. system: consecutive number
Price code:
  no letter=25¢, LB=25¢, LL=35¢
  (LL 67, LL 114, LL 121, LL 136
  /50¢)

Total books recorded: 392

--- --- --- --- --- --- ---

Red Circle

```
Select Publications, Inc.      1949
  Empire State Building
  New York 1, New York
```

Publications:
```
1-7, 12-13                     1949-12/49
```

Bk. height: small

LION - RED CIRCLE (cont.)

Edge color: green
No. system: consecutive number
Price code:
  no letter=25¢

Total books published: <u>9</u>

Monarch

Monarch Books, Inc.   1958-x
  Derby, Connecticut

Publications:
  101-142   10/58-x
  K50-K52   11/58-x

Bk. height: large
Edge color: red
No. system: price series
Price code:
  no letter=35¢, K=50¢

Total books published: <u>44</u>

--- --- --- --- --- --- ---

Monarch Human Behavior Series

Publications:
  MB501-MB503   7/59-x

Bk. height: large
Edge color: red
No. system: consecutive number
Price code:
  MB=35¢

Total books published: <u>3</u>

New American Library

Penguin Books, Inc.   ?1942-1948
  245 Fifth Avenue
  New York 16, New York
New American Library of World   1948-1950
  Literature, Inc.
  245 Fifth Avenue
  New York 16, New York
New American Library of World   1950-x
  Literature, Inc.
  501 Madison Avenue
  New York 22, New York

--- --- --- --- --- --- ---

Penguin

Publications:
  501-651, 653-654   3/42-12/47
  652, 655-657, 659, 661
  (Penguin Signet)   1/48-2/48

Bk. height: mixed (1942-45),
  large (1945-x)
Edge color: blank (1942-44),
  red (1944-48)
No. system: consecutive number
Price code:
  no letter=25¢

Total books published: <u>159</u>

--- --- --- --- --- --- ---

Signet

Publications:
  658, 660, 662-668, 670-671,
   674, 679 (Penguin Signet)   3/48-6/48
  669, 672-673, 675-678, 680-
   1715, T1717-D1740, Q1742-
   1744, D1746-1750   7/48-x

Bk. height: large
Edge color: red (25¢, 1948-54;
  all prices, 1954-x), yellow
  orange (other prices, 1950-54)
No. system: consecutive number
Price code:
  no letter=25¢, S=35¢, suffixed
  AB=50¢, D=50¢, T=75¢, Q=95¢

Total books published: <u>1080</u>

--- --- --- --- --- --- ---

Penguin Specials

Publications:
  S201-S240   3/42-7/45?

Bk. height: small
Edge color: blank (1942-44),
  red (1944-45)
No. system: consecutive number
Price code:
  S=25¢

Total books recorded: <u>32</u>

--- --- --- --- --- --- ---

Pelican

Publications:
  P1-P24   1/46-1/48
  P25 (Pelican Mentor)   2/48

NEW AMERICAN LIBRARY - PELICAN (cont.)

Bk. height: large
Edge color: red
No. system: consecutive number
Price code:
  P=25¢ (P1-P16), P=35¢ (P17-P25)

Total books published: 25

--- --- --- --- --- --- ---

Mentor

Publications:
  M26-M29 (Pelican Mentor)   3/48-6/48
  M30-MD265, MD267-MD268, MD270-
  MD279, MT287   8/48-x

Bk. height: large
Edge color: red (35¢, 1948-54;
  all prices, 1954-x), yellow
  orange (other prices, 1952-54)
No. system: consecutive number
Price code:
  M=35¢, Ms=50¢, MD=50¢, MT=75¢
  (MD247/75¢)

Total books published: 253

--- --- --- --- --- --- ---

Penguin/Signet Guides

Publications:
  G1-G2   7/47-1949

Bk. height: large
Edge color: unknown
No. system: consecutive number
Price code:
  G=25¢ (G1), G=35¢ (G2)

Total books published: 2

--- --- --- --- --- --- ---

Signet Key

Publications:
  K300-KD365, Ks367-KT373   1/54-x

Bk. height: large
Edge color: red
No. system: consecutive number
Price code:
  K=25¢, Ks=35¢, KD=50¢, KT=75¢

Total books published: 73

--- --- --- --- --- --- ---

Signet Classics

Publications:
  CD1-CD10   8/59-x

Bk. height: large
Edge color: blank
No. system: consecutive number
Price code:
  CD=50¢

Total books published: 10

--- --- --- --- --- --- ---

Eagle

Eagle Books, Inc.   1947
  270 Madison Avenue
  New York, New York

Publications:
  E3   11/47

Bk. height: large
Edge color: blank
No. system: consecutive number
Price code:
  E=25¢

Total books published: 1

Novel Library

Novel Publications   1948
  4600 Diversey Avenue
  Chicago, Illinois
Diversey Publishing Corporation 1948
  4600 Diversey Avenue
  Chicago, Illinois
Diversey Publishing Corporation 1948-1950
  119 West 57th Street
  New York 19, New York

Publications:
  1-46?   1948-1950

Bk. height: small
Edge color: blue (1948), red
  (1948-50)
No. system: consecutive number
Price code:
  no letter=25¢

Total books recorded: 46

Novel Selections

Novel Selections, Inc.   unknown
  New York, New York

NOVEL SELECTIONS (cont.)

Publications:
  51   unknown

Bk. height: small
Edge color: red
No. system: consecutive number
Price code:
  no letter=25¢

Total books recorded: 1

Parsee

Parsee Publications   ?1946-1948?
  122 East 42nd Street
  New York 17, New York

--- --- --- --- --- --- ---

Bleak House

Publications:
  number unknown (6 books)   ?1946-1948?

Other information unknown.

Total books recorded: 6

--- --- --- --- --- --- ---

Hangman's House

Publications:
  13, 17, 21
  number unknown (5 books)   ?1946-1947?

Bk. height: small
Edge color: blank
No. system: consecutive number
Price code:
  no letter=25¢

Total books recorded: 8

Permabooks (Doubleday and Company)

Doubleday and Company, Inc.   1951-1954
  Garden City, New York

Publications:
  P98, P102-P313   1/51-11/54
  P5, P7, P25, P65, P89 (reissues
    in paper of earlier hardcover
    line)   various
  (sold to Pocket 8/54)

Bk. height: small (1951-52),
  mixed (1952-53), large (1953-54)

Edge color: mixed
No. system: consecutive number
Price code:
  no letter=25¢, P=35¢,
  P + suffixed S=50¢
  (P294/75¢)

Total books published: 208

Phantom Mysteries

No imprint.

Publications:
  nn (one book)   unknown

Bk. height: small
Edge color: red
No. system: none
Price code:
  no number=25¢

Total books recorded: 1

Pocket

Pocket Books, Inc.   1939
  386 Fourth Avenue
  New York, New York
Pocket Books, Inc.   ?1939-1947
  Rockefeller Center
  1230 Sixth Avenue
  New York 20, New York
Pocket Books, Inc.   1947-1948
  Rockefeller Center
  1230 Avenue of the Americas
  New York 20, New York
Pocket Books, Inc.   1948-1951
  Rockefeller Center
  18 W. 48th Street
  New York 19, New York
Pocket Books, Inc.   ?1952-x
  (Rockefeller Center)
  (630 Fifth Avenue)
  New York 20, New York

Publications:
  1-1252, 1254-1261   6/39-x
  B70   1952

Bk. height: small
Edge color: red
No. system: consecutive number
Price code:
  no letter=25¢, B=35¢
  (650, 715, 720, 765, 788,
  890, 893/35¢)

Total books published: 1259

--- --- --- --- --- --- ---

POCKET (cont.)

Cardinal Editions

Publications:
    C-1 - C-353, C-355 - C-365,
     C-367 - C-368, C-370, C-372 -
     C-373, C-376, C-391   9/51-x
    GC-1 - GC-62, GC-65 - GC-77   1/53-x
    GC-750 - GC-753, GC-755 -
     GC-757   1956-x
    (GC-1954), GC-1955 - GC-1956 12/53-12/55

Bk. height: small
Edge color: yellow
No. system: price series
Price code:
    C=35¢, GC=50¢, GC (750 series)=
    75¢
    (C-57, C-60, C-71/50¢)

Total books published: 454

--- --- --- --- --- --- ---

Pocket Library

Publications:
    PL1-PL71   ?6/54-5/59
    PL500-PL525, PL544   ?1956-3/59
    PL750-PL751   9/58-11/58
    (superceded by Washington
     Square Press)

Bk. height: small (35¢, 50¢),
    large (75¢)
Edge color: yellow
No. system: price series
Price code:
    PL=35¢, PL (500 series)=50¢
    PL (750 series)=75¢
    (PL1-PL4, PL11-PL13, PL16-
    PL17, PL19, PL35/50¢)

Total books published: 97

--- --- --- --- --- --- ---

Comet

Publications:
    1-34   10/48-12/49
    (continued by Pocket Book Jrs.)

Bk. height: large
Edge color: red
No. system: consecutive number
Price code:
    no letter=25¢

Total books published: 34

--- --- --- --- --- --- ---

Pocket Book Jrs.

Publications:
    J-35 - J-77   1/50-12/51
    (continuation of Comet)

Bk. height: small
Edge color: red
No. system: consecutive number
Price code:
    J=25¢ (J-35 - J-67), J=35¢
    (J-68 - J-77)

Total books published: 43

--- --- --- --- --- --- ---

Pocket Library of Great Art

Published with:
Harry N. Abrams, Inc.
    New York, New York

Publications:
    A1-A24   10/53-1/55
    (series continued without
     Pocket)

Bk. height: large
Edge color: blank
No. system: consecutive number
Price code:
    A=50¢

Total books published: 24

--- --- --- --- --- --- ---

Permabooks

Permabooks   1954-1956
    45 Rockefeller Plaza
    New York 20, New York
Thereafter from Pocket Books, Inc.

Publications:
    M-1000   12/54
    M-1600   1954
    M-3001 - M-3123   2/55-12/58
    M-4001 - M-4136, M-4138 -
     M-4142, M-4145 - M-4153,
     M-4161, M-4168   2/55-x
    M-5000 - M-5014   2/55-x
    M-7500   1958-x
    (continuation of Permabooks,
     Doubleday and Company)

Bk. height: small (25¢, 35¢),
    mixed (other prices)
Edge color: yellow
No. system: price series

POCKET - PERMABOOKS (cont.)

Price code:
   M (1000 series)=35¢, M (1600
   series)=50¢, M (3000 series)=
   25¢, M (4000 series)=35¢, M
   (5000 series)=50¢, M (7500
   series)=75¢

Total books published: 292

---   ---   ---   ---   ---   ---   ---

Washington Square Press

Washington Square Press, Inc.   1959-x
   630 Fifth Avenue
   New York 20, New York

Publications:
   W1-W2, W4, W8, W10, W15, W22,
   W30, W38-W39, W99-W101, W115,
   W121, W550-W551, W561   6/59-x

Bk. height: small
Edge color: yellow
No. system: price series
Price code:
   W=35¢, W (500 series)=50¢

Total books published: 18

Pony

Stamford House   1945-1946
   Stamford, Connecticut
Stamford House   1946
   New York, New York

Publications:
   45-62?   12/45-6/46?

Bk. height: small
Edge color: yellow
No. system: consecutive number
Price code:
   no letter=25¢

Total books recorded: 16

Popular Library

(Popular Books)   1943
Popular Library
   45 West 45th Street
   New York, New York
Popular Library   ?1943-?
   11 East 39th Street
   New York 16, New York

Popular Library, Inc.   ?1948-1959
   10 East 40th Street
   New York 16, New York
Popular Library, Inc.   1959-x
   355 Lexington Avenue
   New York 17, New York

Publications:
   (1)-(4), 5-835   2/43-2/58
   G100-G398   2/52-x
   SP100, SP2-SP53   3/53-x
   PC300, PC400   4/57-x
   W400, W500, W600   4/57-x

Bk. height: small (1943-52),
   large (1953-x)
Edge color: blank (1943-?),
   green (?1948-x)
No. system: price series
Price code:
   no letter=25¢, G=35¢, SP=50¢,
   PC=mixed, W=75¢
   (SP100, SP3, W400/25¢;
   W500/35¢)

Total books published: 1191

---   ---   ---   ---   ---   ---   ---

Popular Library Eagle

Publications: 11/53-2/58
   EB1-EB104

Bk. height: large
Edge color: green
No. system: consecutive number
Price code:
   EB=25¢

Total books published: 104

Pyramid

Almat Publishing Corporation   1949-1952
   185 Madison Avenue
   New York 16, New York
Pyramid Books   1952-x
   444 Madison Avenue
   New York 22, New York

Publications:
   11-G468   Fall/49-x

Bk. height: small (1949-55),
   large (1956-x)
Edge color: mixed (1949-54),
   red (1954-56; 25¢, 1956-59),
   orange (other prices, 1956-59;
   all prices, 1959-x)

PYRAMID (cont.)

No. system: consecutive number
Price code:
  no letter=25¢, G=35¢, R=50¢
  (R188, R202, R207, R210, R211,
  R223, R232, R237, R243, R246,
  R256, R273, R281, R289, R300,
  R318, R330, R340/35¢)

Total books published: 457

---   ---   ---   ---   ---   ---   ---

Pyramid Royals

Publications:
PR10-PG26 3/56-x

Bk. height: large
Edge color: orange
No. system: consecutive number
Price code:
  PG=35¢, PR=50¢
  (PR10/95¢; PR11-PR12, PR14-
  PR16, PR19-PR20, PR23/35¢;
  PR21S/50¢)

Total books published: 17

Readers-Choice Library

The Readers-Choice Library 1950-?
St. John Publishing Company
  545 Fifth Avenue
  New York 17, New York

Publications:
  4, 7-8, 12 1950-?
  (some books in this series
   published in digest format)

Bk. height: small
Edge color: red
No. system: consecutive number
Price code:
  no letter=25¢

Total books recorded: 4

Saint Mystery Library

Great American Publications, Inc. 1959-x
  270 Madison Avenue
  New York 16, New York

Publications:
  118-125 8/59-x
  (also called 1-8 inside books)

Bk. height: small
Edge color: mixed
No. system: consecutive number
Price code:
  no letter=35¢

Total books recorded: 7

Superior Reprints

The Military Service Publishing
  Company 1944-1945
  Harrisburg, Pennsylvania

Publications:
  M637-M657 11/44-9/45

Bk. height: small
Edge color: red
No. system: consecutive number
Price code:
  M=25¢

Total books published: 21

Zenith

Zenith Books, Inc. 1958-x
  Rockville Centre, New York

Publications:
  ZB-1 - ZB-34 7/58-x

Bk. height: large
Edge color: yellow (1958),
  light blue (1959-x)
No. system: consecutive number
Price code:
  ZB=35¢

Total books recorded: 27

TOTAL NUMBER OF PUBLISHERS: 33

TOTAL NUMBER OF IMPRINTS: 69

TOTAL BOOKS RECORDED: 14,051

Author Index

A

AAF: the official guide.   PB   265   44   .25

AARON, SAM with James A. Beard
  How to eat better for
    less money.   Perm M-4065 57 .35

AARONS, EDWARD S.
  Assignment--Angelina.   GM   749   58   .25
  Assignment--Budapest.   GM   707   57   .25
  Assignment--Carlotta
    Cortez.   GM   834   59   .25
  Assignment--Helene.   GM   863   59   .25
  Assignment--Lili Lamaris. GM s911 59 .35
  Assignment--Madeleine.   GM   799   58   .25
  Assignment--Stella Marni. GM 666 57 .25
        .   GM   906   59   .25
  Assignment--suicide.   GM   621   56   .25
        .   GM   923   59   .25
  Assignment to disaster. GM 491 55 .25
        .   GM   895   59   .25
  Assignment--treason.   GM   568   56   .25
  Come back, my love.   GM   362   54   .25
  Escape to love.   GM   258   52   .25
  Girl on the run.   GM   424   54   .25
  The sinners.   GM   280   53   .25

ABBEY, EDWARD
  The brave cowboy.   PB   1185   57   .25

ABBEY, KIERAN
  Beyond the dark.   Dell 93   45   .25

ABBOT, ANTHONY
  About the murder of the
    circus queen.   Pop   159   48   .25
  About the murder of the
    night club lady.   GD   unk   46   .25
  The creeps.   Dell 88   45   .25
  Murder of a clergyman's
    mistress.   Pop   286   50   .25

ABBOTT, A. C.
  Branded.   Sig   1142   54   .25
  Wild blood.   GM   208   52   .25

ABBOTT, ANITA with Lisa Andors
  The home book of French
    cooking.   Crst s204   58   .35

ABELL, ELIZABETH
  American accent.   Ball 75   54   .35
with Joseph I. Greene
  First love.   Ban   503   48   .25
  Husbands and lovers.   Ban   742   49   .25
  Stories for here and now. Ban A914 51 .35
  Stories of sudden truth. Ball 19   53   .35

ABRAHAMS, ROBERT
  Death in one-two-three.   HH   unk   47   .25

ABZUG, MARTIN
  How cheap can you get?   Berk G-58   57   .35

ACKWORTH, ROBERT C.
  The moments between.   Hill 129   59   .35

ADAMS, CASWELL
  Fifty famous sports
    stories.   Pony 61   46   .25

ADAMS, CLEVE F.
  The black door.   Pop   426   52   .25
  Contraband.   Sig   902   51   .25
        .   Sig   1298   56   .25
  The crooking finger.   Dell 104   46   .25
  Murder all over.   Sig   765   50   .25
  No wings on a cop.   Han   112   50   .25
  The private eye.   Sig   850   51   .25
        .   Sig   1405   57   .25
  Sabotage.   Pen   522   43   .25
        .   Sig   936   52   .25
        .   Sig   1419   57   .25
  Shady lady.   Ace   D-115   55   .35
  Up jumped the devil.   Han   33   44   .15
  What price murder.   Pop   456   52   .25

ADAMS, CLIFFORD R. with Vance O. Packard
  How to pick a mate.   Dell 224   48   .25

ADAMS, CLIFTON
  The colonel's lady.   GM   230   52   .25
  Death's sweet song.   GM   483   55   .25
  The desperado.   GM   121   50   .25
  Gambling man.   GM   533   55   .25
  Law of the trigger.   GM   593   56   .25
  A noose for the
    desperado.   GM   168   51   .25
        .   GM   683   57   .25
  Outlaw's son.   GM   674   57   .25
  Two-gun law.   GM   422   54   .25
  Whom gods destroy.   GM   291   53   .25

ADAMS, FAY
  Appointment in Paris.   GM   228   52   .25
  Lili of Paris.   RS   19   52   .35
  To love, to hate.   GM   333   53   .25

ADAMS, FRANK R.
  Arizona feud.   Dell 413   50   .25

ADAMS, JOEY
  Cindy and I.   Pop   G371   59   .35
  The curtain never falls. Pop 285 50 .25
  From gags to riches.   Avon 202   49   .25
  Joey Adams' joke book.   Pop   504   53   .25
           Pop   G216   58   .35

Author/Title	Pub./Stock No.	Yr.	Price
ADAMS, JOEY (cont.)			
Strictly for laughs.	PB 1130	56	.25
ADAMS, JOHN PAUL			
The Avon book of puzzles			
for everybody.	Avon 295	51	.25
Girls--for men only.	Avon T-123	56	.35
Picture quiz book.	Pop 223	50	.25
Puzzles for everybody.	Avon 645	55	.25
We dare you to solve			
this!	Berk 376	57	.25
ADAMS, SAMUEL HOPKINS			
Canal town.	Dell F51	53	.50
Grandfather stories.	Sig D1503	58	.50
_____.	Sig D1627	59	.50
The Harvey girls.	Dell 130	46	.25
Night bus.	DelT 3	51	.10
Sunrise to sunset.	Ban A1107	53	.35
Tambay gold.	Dell 20	43	.25
ADDAMS, CHAS.			
Drawn and quartered.	Ban 37	46	.25
ADDIS, HUGH			
The dark voyage.	Han 37	45	.15
ADLER, ALFRED			
Understanding human			
nature.	Prem d52	57	.50
ADLER, EDWARD			
Living it up.	Ace S-114	55	.25
_____.	Ace D-399	59	.35
ADLER, IRVING			
How life began.	SigK Ks369	59	.35
Magic house of numbers.	SigK Ks361	58	.35
The stars.	SigK Ks364	58	.35
ADLER, POLLY			
A house is not a home.	Pop G140	54	.35
_____.	Pop SP36	59	.50
AGEE, JAMES			
A death in the family.	Avon G-1034	59	.50
AGETON, ARTHUR A.			
The jungle seas.	Sig S1200	55	.35
AHERNE, OWEN			
An affair to remember.	Avon T-182	57	.35
Man on fire.	Avon T-177	57	.35
AIKEN, HENRY D.			
The age of ideology.	Ment MD185	56	.50
AKUTAGAWA, RYUNOSUKE			
Rashomon and other			
stories.	BanC AC42	59	.35

Author/Title	Pub./Stock No.	Yr.	Price
ALARCÓN, PEDRO de			
The miller and the			
mayor's wife.	Avon 199	49	.25
ALBEE, GEORGE SUMNER			
Girl on the beach.	DelF 4	53	.25
_____.	DelF B131	59	.35
ALBERT, JAY			
The man from Stony			
Lonesome.	Ace D-144	56	.35
ALBERT, MARVIN H.			
Apache rising.	GM 696	57	.25
The bounty killer.	GM 760	58	.25
The law and Jake Wade.	GM 553	56	.25
_____.	GM 756	58	.25
Lie down with lions.	GM 519	55	.25
Party girl.	GM 808	58	.25
Pillow talk.	GM 918	59	.25
The reformed gun.	GM 856	59	.25
Renegade posse.	GM 826	58	.25
Rider from Wind River.	GM 902	59	.25
That Jane from Maine.	GM 846	59	.25
with T. R. Seidman			
Becoming a mother.	Prem d66	58	.50
ALBERT, SIM			
Vice girl.	Berk G244	59	.35
ALBRAND, MARTHA			
After midnight.	Dell 396	50	.25
Desperate moment.	Dell 651	53	.25
No surrender.	PB 247	44	.25
Wait for the dawn.	Dell 544	51	.25
ALCALDE, MIGUEL			
Love and idleness.	Prmb P93	51	.35
ALCOTT, LOUISA MAY			
Little men.	PB 75	40	.25
with Jean Francis Webb			
Little women.	Dell 296	49	.25
ALDISS, BRIAN W.			
No time like tomorrow.	Sig S1683	59	.35
Vanguard from Alpha.	Ace D-369	59	.35
ALDRICH, ANN			
We too must love.	GM s727	58	.35
We walk alone.	GM 509	55	.25
_____.	GM s774	58	.35
ALDRICH, BESS STREETER			
A lantern in her hand.	PB 470	47	.25
ALDRIDGE, JAMES			
The hunter.	Dell 657	53	.25

Author/Title	Pub./Stock No.	Yr.	Price
ALDRIDGE, JOHN W. with Vance Bourjaily			
discovery no. 1.	Card C-80	53	.35
ALEXANDER, DAVID			
The corpse in my bed.	Ace D-59	54	.35
Die, little goose.	Ban 1655	57	.25
The murder of Whistler's			
brother.	Ban 1736	57	.25
Murder points a finger.	Ban 1315	55	.25
Paint the town black.	Ban 1534	56	.25
Shoot a sitting duck.	Ban 1601	57	.25
Terror on Broadway.	Ban 1408	56	.25
ALGREN, NELSON			
The jungle.	Avon T-185	57	.35
	Avon T-324	59	.35
————.			
The man with the golden			
arm.	PB 757	51	.25
	Card C-31	53	.35
————.			
The neon wilderness.	Avon 222	49	.25
————.	Avon 424	52	.25
————.	Avon T-125	56	.35
Never come morning.	Avon 185	48	.25
————.	Avon 419	52	.25
————.	Avon T-108	55	.35
————.	Avon T-223	58	.35
A walk on the wild side.	Crst d157	57	.50
ALIANDRO, HYGINO			
The English-Portuguese			
pocket dictionary.	Card GC-750	56	.75
ALL about girls.	Avon 229	50	.25
————.	Avon 357	51	.25
————.	Avon 527	53	.25
ALLEN, EDWARD FRANK			
How to write and speak			
effective English.	Prem s13	55	.35
————.	Crst s284	59	.35
ALLEN, ERIC			
Hangtree country.	Pyr G329	58	.35
ALLEN, FRANCIS			
First come, first kill.	Ban 34	46	.25
ALLEN, FREDERICK LEWIS			
The great Pierpont			
Morgan.	BanB FB402	56	.50
Only yesterday.	Ban 27	46	.25
————.	Ban A1069	53	.35
————.	Ban F1620	57	.50
————.	BanC FC15	59	.50
ALLEN, H. WARNER with E. C. Bentley			
Trent's own case.	Pen 510	42	.25
ALLEN, HERVEY			
Action at Aquila.	PB 370	46	.25
Anthony Adverse in			
Africa.	Dell 283	49	.25
Anthony Adverse in			
America.	Dell 285	49	.25
Anthony Adverse in			
Italy.	Dell 281	49	.25
Bedford Village.	Dell D128	53	.35
The forest and the fort.	Dell D110	52	.35
ALLEN, JANE			
I lost my girlish			
laughter.	Avon 345	51	.25
ALLEN, JOHN HOUGHTON			
Southwest.	Ban 1167	53	.25
ALLEN, ROBERT S.			
Drive to victory.	Berk BG-90	57	.50
ALLEN, STEVE			
Fourteen for tonight.	Dell D172	56	.35
The girls on the 10th			
floor.	Pop G377	59	.35
ALLEN, T. D.			
Ambush at Buffalo			
Wallow.	Crst 152	56	.25
ALLINGHAM, MARGERY			
Black plumes.	Pen 534	44	.25
Death of a ghost.	Pen 503	42	.25
	Dell D234	58	.35
————.			
The fashion in shrouds.	PB 329	45	.25
Kingdom of death.	Bond 12	46	.25
More work for the			
undertaker.	PB 665	50	.25
The sabotage murder			
mystery.	Avon (29)	43	.25
The tiger in the smoke.	Dell 777	54	.25
Wanted: someone			
innocent.	Pony 56	46	.25
ALLISON, SAM			
Trouble on Crazyman.	Lion 183	53	.25
Wyoming war.	Lion LB 157	57	.25
ALLRED, GORDON T. with Yasuo Kuwahara			
Kamikaze.	Ball 244	58	.35
————.	Ball 317K	59	.35
ALMAN, DAVID			
World full of strangers.	Sig 803	50	.25
ALPERT, HOLLIS			
The summer lovers.	Ban A1954	59	.35
ALTH, MAX			
The wicked and the			
warped.	Berk G-161	58	.35

Author/Title	Pub./Stock No.	Yr.	Price
ALVAREZ, WALTER C.			
How to help your doctor help you.	Dell D146	55	.35
ALVER, DOUGLAS M.			
The little green men.	Ban 475	49	.25
The weird sisters.	Ban 457	48	.25
AMBERG, GEORGE			
Ballet.	Ment M42	49	.35
Ballet in America.	Ment Ms123	54	.50
AMBLER, ERIC			
Background to danger.	PB 286	45	.25
_____.	Dell D238	58	.35
Cause for alarm.	Pen 511	42	.25
A coffin for Dimitrios.	PB 232	43	.25
_____.	Dell D201	57	.35
Epitaph for a spy.	Pnnt P3	53	.25
_____.	Ban A1772	58	.35
Journey into fear.	PB 193	43	.25
Judgment on Deltchev.	PB 887	52	.25
The Schirmer inheritance.	Ban 1327	55	.25
State of siege.	Ban A1671	57	.35
The AMERICAN heritage reader.	DelF C101	56	.50
AMERICANS vs. Germans	PenS S209	42	.25
AMES, DELANO			
Murder begins at home.	Dell 552	51	.25
Nobody wore black.	Dell 579	52	.25
She shall have murder.	Dell 493	51	.25
AMES, LOUISE BATES with Frances L. Ilg			
Child behavior: Gesell Institute.	Dell D180	56	.35
_____.	DelL LC120	59	.50
AMES, ROBERT			
Awake and die.	GM 518	55	.25
The dangerous one.	GM 435	54	.25
The devil drives.	GM 269	52	.25
AMSBARY, MARY ANNE			
Caesar's angel.	Sig S1080	53	.35
ANDERS, CURT			
The price of courage.	Ban A1908	59	.35
ANDERSEN, U. S.			
Hard and fast.	Eag EB72	56	.25
The smoldering sea.	Card C-140	54	.35
ANDERSON, BRAD with Phil Leeming			
Marmaduke.	Pop 795	57	.25
Marmaduke rides again.	Mon 109	59	.35

Author/Title	Pub./Stock No.	Yr.	Price
ANDERSON, CLIFFORD			
The hollow hero.	Ace D-404	59	.35
ANDERSON, EDWARD			
Hungry men.	Lion 8	49	.25
_____.	Lion LL 51	55	.35
_____.	Pyr G456	59	.35
Thieves like us.	Berk G-130	58	.35
Your red wagon.	Ban 350	48	.25
ANDERSON, FRANK W. JR.			
Great flying stories.	DelL LB116	58	.35
ANDERSON, MARIAN			
My lord what a morning.	Bard T-05	58	.35
ANDERSON, OLIVER			
Maidens in the midden.	Avon 391	51	.25
ANDERSON, POUL			
Brain wave.	Ball 80	54	.35
The enemy stars.	Berk G289	59	.35
No world of their own.	Ace D-110	55	.35
Planet of no return.	Ace D-199	57	.35
The snows of Ganymede.	Ace D-303	58	.35
Star ways.	Ace D-255	57	.35
War of the wing-men.	Ace D-303	58	.35
War of two worlds.	Ace D-335	59	.35
We claim these stars.	Ace D-407	59	.35
ANDERSON, ROBERT			
Tea and sympathy.	Sig 1343	56	.25
ANDERSON, SHERWOOD			
Dark laughter.	PB 878	52	.25
Winesburg, Ohio.	Pen 585	46	.25
_____.	Sig 1304	56	.25
ANDERSON, THOMAS			
Your own beloved sons.	Ban A1570	57	.35
ANDERSON, WILLIAM R. with Clay Blair Jr.			
Nautilus 90 north.	Sig D1692	59	.50
ANDERTON, RUSS			
Tic-polonga.	Prmb 308	54	.25
ANDORS, LISA with Anita Abbott			
The home book of French cooking.	Crst s204	58	.35
ANDREWS, NED			
Cowdog.	PBJr J-56	50	.25
ANDREWS, ROBERT HARDY			
Great day in the morning.	Ace D-206	57	.35
ANDREYEV, LEONID			
Seven who were hanged.	Avon 655	55	.25

Author/Title	Pub./Stock No.	Yr.	Price
ANDRIOLA, ALFRED with Mel Casson			
Ever since Adam and Eve.	Sig 1361	57	.25
ANET, CLAUDE			
Ariane.	Sig 676	48	.25
Love in the afternoon.	Sig 1404	57	.25
ANTHOLZ, PEYSON			
All shook up.	Ace D-306	58	.35
ANTHONY, EDWARD with Frank Buck			
Bring 'em back alive.	PB 47	40	.25
ANTHONY, J. J.			
Marriage, sex and family			
problems and how to			
solve them.	Hill unk	49	.25
ANTHONY, JOSEPH			
The invisible curtain.	Ban A1760	58	.35
APPEL, BENJAMIN			
Alley kids.	Lion LB 116	56	.25
Brain guy.	Lion 39	50	.25
	Lion LL 151	57	.35
Dock walloper.	Lion 166	53	.25
The funhouse.	Ball 345K	59	.35
Hell's kitchen.	Lion 95	52	.25
	Berk G-152	58	.35
Life and death of a			
tough guy.	Avon T-101	55	.35
Plunder.	GM 266	52	.25
	GM s809	58	.35
The raw edge.	Dell F81	59	.50
Sweet money girl.	GM 385	54	.25
	GM s642	57	.35
Teen-age mobster.	Avon T-162	57	.35
APPEL, DAVID with Eugene Freeman			
The wisdom and ideas of			
Plato.	Prem s28	56	.35
	Prem d84	59	.50
APPELL, GEORGE C.			
Ambush hell.	Lion 199	54	.25
Gunman's grudge.	Lion 139	53	.25
	Lion LL 161	57	.35
The man who shot			
Quantrill.	PB 1232	59	.25
Massacre trail.	Perm M-3013	55	.25
Queen's own.	DelF 74	55	.25
Quick on the shoot.	Dell 892	56	.25
Ramrod.	Lion LL 57	55	.35
Shadow on the border.	Ball 185	57	.35
Three trails.	Perm M-3112	58	.25
APPLEBY, JOHN			
The arms of Venus.	Dell 663	53	.25
Barbary hoard.	Dell 751	54	.25
Grounds for murder.	Dell 994	58	.25

Author/Title	Pub./Stock No.	Yr.	Price
APRIL, JACK			
Feud at Five Rivers.	Pyr G239	57	.35
APULEIUS MADAURENSIS			
The golden ass of			
Apuleius.	Card C-62	52	.35
_____.	PBL PL6	54	.35
ARCHER, JULES with S. U. Lawton			
Sexual conduct of the			
teen-ager.	Berk G-2	55	.35
_____.	Berk G-200	59	.35
with Maxine Sawyer			
Sex life and you.	RC 1	49	.25
ARD, WILLIAM			
All I can get.	Mon 124	59	.35
Cry scandal.	Pop G236	58	.35
Deadly beloved.	Dell 991	58	.25
The diary.	Pop 477	53	.25
Don't come crying to me.	Pop 639	55	.25
A girl for Danny.	Pop 502	53	.25
Hell is a city.	Pop 756	56	.25
Mr. Trouble.	Pop 723	56	.25
No angels for me.	Pop 591	54	.25
The perfect frame.	Pop 416	52	.25
A private party.	Pop 569	54	.25
_____.	Pop G328	59	.35
You can't stop me.	Pop 526	53	.25
ARDEN, LEON			
The savage place.	Dell F64	58	.50
ARFELLI, DANTE			
The girl of the Roman			
night.	Berk G-113	58	.35
The unwanted.	Sig 984	53	.25
ARISTOTLE			
The Pocket Aristotle.	PBL PL519	58	.50
ARMITAGE, ANGUS			
The world of Copernicus.	Ment M65	51	.35
ARMSTRONG, CHARLOTTE			
Alibi for murder.	PB 1095	56	.25
The black-eyed stranger.	PB 880	52	.25
The chocolate cobweb.	PB 575	49	.25
A dram of poison.	Crst 191	57	.25
The innocent flower.	PB 427	47	.25
Mask of evil.	Crst 247	58	.25
Mischief.	PB 805	51	.25
Murder's nest.	PB 1058	55	.25
The unsuspected.	PB 444	47	.25
Walk out on death.	PB 1034	54	.25
ARMSTRONG, DONALD B. with Grace T. Hallock			
What to do till the			
doctor comes.	PB 220	43	.25

Author/Title	Pub./Stock No.	Yr.	Price
ARMSTRONG, LOUIS			
Satchmo.	Sig S1245	55	.35
ARNAUD, GEORGES			
Flesh and fire.	Avon 804	58	.25
The wages of fear.	Avon 531	53	.25
ARNO, PETER			
The new Peter Arno			
Pocket book.	PB 1087	55	.25
The Peter Arno Pocket			
book.	PB 417	46	.25
ARNOLD, A. F.			
How to play with your			
child.	Ball 105	55	.35
ARNOLD, ELLIOTT			
Blood brother.	Ban A918	51	.35
_____.	Ban F1500	56	.50
Everybody slept here.	Sig 735	49	.25
_____.	Pop 620	54	.25
Rescue!	Ban A1770	58	.35
The time of the gringo.	Ban F1379	55	.50
Two loves.	Sig 770	50	.25
Walk with the Devil.	PB 839	52	.25
ARNOLD, OREN			
The Wild West joke book.	Perm M-3081	57	.25
ARNOLD, PAULINE			
Rate yourself.	Perm M-4084	58	.35
ARNOTHY, CHRISTINE			
God is late.	Pop G226	58	.35
I am fifteen--and I			
don't want to die.	Eag EB95	57	.25
The ART of barbecue and			
outdoor cooking.	Ban F1775	58	.50
ARTHUR, BURT			
The buckaroo.	Sig 782	50	.25
The drifter.	Ace D-92	55	.35
Duel on the range.	Berk G242	59	.35
Gun play at the X-Bar-X.	Avon 785	57	.25
Gunsmoke in Nevada.	Sig 1443	57	.25
Killer's crossing.	Lion 168	53	.25
Outlaw fury.	Avon 770	57	.25
Return of the Texan.	Sig 1339	56	.25
Ride out for revenge.	Avon T-198	57	.35
Stirrups in the dust.	Sig 952	52	.25
	Sig 1697	59	.25
The Texan.	Sig 1135	54	.25
Thunder Valley.	Pop 425	52	.25
Trigger man.	Sig 822	50	.25
	Sig 1401	57	.25
_____.			
Trouble town.	Sig 866	51	.25
Two-gun Texan.	Lion 189	54	.25
_____.	Lion LB 85	56	.25
ARTHUR, ELLA BENTLEY			
My husband keeps telling			
me to go to hell.	Sig 1210	55	.25
ARTHUR, ERIC			
Invitation to dishonor.	Eton E117	52	.25
ARTHUR, MAX			
Death in the stacks.	Pop 829	57	.25
Gentlemen prefer corpses.	Ban 316	49	.25
_____.	Pnnt P70	54	.25
ARTZYBASHEFF, MIKHAIL			
The savage.	Lion unk	51	.25
ASBURY, HERBERT			
The Barbary coast.	PB 474	47	.25
_____.	Card C-251	57	.35
The French quarter.	PB 565	49	.25
_____.	Card C-195	55	.35
The gangs of New York.	Avon 263	50	.25
ASCH, SHOLEM			
The apostle.	Card GC-38	57	.50
Mary.	Card C-255	57	.35
Moses.	Card GC-43	58	.50
The Nazarene.	Card GC-36	56	.50
The prophet.	Card GC-49	58	.50
ASHABRANNAR, BRENT			
The stakes are high.	Pnnt P64	54	.25
ASHBROOK, HARRIETTE			
The purple onion mystery.	Pen 626	47	.25
ASHBURN, WADE			
Violent valley.	Pop G359	59	.35
ASHE, GORDON			
Drop dead!	Ace D-71	54	.35
You've bet your life.	Ace D-221	57	.35
ASHTON, BLAIR			
Deeds of darkness.	Ace D-314	58	.35
ASIMOV, ISAAC			
The caves of steel.	Sig S1240	55	.35
The currents of space.	Sig 1082	53	.25
The death dealers.	Avon T-287	58	.35
Earth is room enough.	Ban A1978	59	.35
The end of eternity.	Sig S1493	58	.35
I, robot.	Sig S1282	56	.35
The man who upset the			
universe.	Ace D-125	55	.35
The Martian way and			
other stories.	Sig S1433	57	.35
The naked sun.	Ban A1731	58	.35
The 1,000 year plan.	Ace D-110	55	.35
Pebble in the sky.	Ban A1646	57	.35
The rebellious stars.	Ace D-84	54	.35

Author/Title	Pub./Stock No.	Yr.	Price
ASIMOV, ISAAC (cont.)			
2nd foundation: galactic			
empire.	Avon T-232	58	.35
ASTRACHAN, SAM			
An end to dying.	Ban A1739	58	.35
ASWELL, JAMES			
The birds and the bees.	Sig 1121	54	.25
The midsummer fires.	Avon 247	50	.25
There's one in every			
town.	Sig 941	52	.25
	Sig 1314	56	.25
The young and hungry-			
hearted.	Sig 1166	55	.25
ASWELL, MARY LOUISE			
New short novels.	Ball 63	54	.35
ATHANAS, VERNE			
Maverick.	DelF A115	56	.25
The proud ones.	PB 936	53	.25
Rogue Valley.	PB 999	54	.25
ATHAS, DAPHNE			
The fourth world.	Pyr G267	57	.35
ATIYAH, EDWARD			
Murder, my love.	Avon 786	57	.25
The thin line.	Avon 510	53	.25
ATKINSON, D. T.			
Magic, myth and			
medicine.	Prem d69	58	.50
ATKINSON, ORIANA			
Her life to live.	Pop 307	51	.25
ATLEE, PHILIP			
The naked year.	Lion 188	54	.25
_____.	Lion LL 66	56	.35
ATTAWAY, WILLIAM			
Blood on the forge.	Pop 491	53	.25
Tough kid.	Lion unk	52	.25
_____.	Lion LB 77	56	.25
ATWATER, MONTGOMERY			
Ski patrol.	PBJr J-35	50	.25
AUCHINCLOSS, LOUIS			
The great world and			
Timothy Colt.	Ban F1722	58	.50
A law for the lion.	Sig S1143	54	.35
Sybil.	Sig 1004	53	.25
The unholy three and			
other stories.	Sig 1255	55	.25
Venus in Sparta.	Crst s320	59	.35

Author/Title	Pub./Stock No.	Yr.	Price
AUDETT, BLACKIE			
Rap sheet--my forty years			
outside the law.	Ban A1440	56	.35
AUERBACH, ARNOLD "RED"			
Basketball.	PB 933	53	.25
_____.	Card C-289	58	.35
AUGUST, JOHN			
Advance agent.	Pop 133	48	.25
The woman in the picture.	Pop 65	45	.25
AUGUSTINUS, AURELIUS			
The confessions of St.			
Augustine.	Card C-27	52	.35
_____.	PBL PL45	57	.35
AUSTEN, JANE			
Emma.	BanC FC10	58	.50
Pride and prejudice.	PB 63	40	.25
_____.	Card C-37	52	.35
_____.	PBL PL9	54	.35
_____.	DelL LC122	59	.50
Sense and sensibility.	DelL LC128	59	.50
AUSTIN, ALEX			
Great tales of city			
dwellers.	Lion LL 53	55	.35
Great tales of the Far			
West.	Lion LL 88	56	.35
The greatest lover in			
the world.	Hill 110	59	.35
War!	Sig S1478	57	.35
Wives and lovers.	Lion LL 111	56	.35
Women without men.	Lion LL 141	57	.35
AUSTIN, BRETT			
Gambler's gun luck.	Lion 20	50	.25
Rawhide summons.	Han 121	50	.25
AUSTIN, FRANK			
The return of the			
rancher.	Pop 784	56	.25
Triggerman.	Dell 636	52	.25
AUSTIN, GENE			
The secret brand.	Prmb 257	53	.25
Texan-killer.	Perm M-3001	55	.25
AUTHENTIC librettos of the			
grand opera.	Eton ET107	52	.35
The AUTHENTIC New			
testament.	Ment MD215	58	.50
AUTRY, GENE			
Gun smoke yarns.	Dell 217	48	.25
Western stories.	Dell 153	47	.25

Author/Title	Pub./Stock No.	Yr.	Price
AVALLONE, MICHAEL			
The case of the bouncing Betty.	Ace D-259	57	.35
The case of the violent virgin.	Ace D-259	57	.35
The crazy mixed-up corpse.	GM 718	57	.25
Dead game.	Perm M-3012	55	.25
The spitting image.	Prmb 289	54	.25
The tall Delores.	Prmb 244	53	.25
Violence in velvet.	Sig 1294	56	.25
The voodoo murders.	GM 703	57	.25
AVERBUCH, BERNARD with John Wesley Noble			
Never plead guilty.	Ball 141	56	.35
AVERY, A. A.			
Anything for a quiet life.	Ban 38	46	.25
The AVON all-American fiction reader.	Avon 1002	51	.50
AVON bedside companion.	Avon 109	47	.25
_______.	Avon 482	52	.25
_______.	Avon 603	54	.25
_______.	Avon T-367	59	.35
The AVON book of great mystery stories.	Avon (36)	43	.25
The AVON book of modern short stories.	Avon (15)	42	.25
AVON book of new stories of the great Wild West.	Avon 194	49	.25
The AVON ghost reader.	Avon 90	46	.25
The AVON mystery storyteller.	Avon 86	46	.25
The AVON story teller.	Avon 72	45	.25
AVON Webster English dictionary.	Avon G1007	52	.50
AXELROD, GEORGE			
Beggar's choice.	Ban 403	48	.25
Blackmailer.	GM 248	52	.25
The seven year itch.	Ban 1371	55	.25
Will success spoil Rock Hunter?	Ban A1653	57	.35
AYERS, RUBY M.			
Afterglow.	Dell 336	49	.25
AYMÉ, MARCEL			
The grand seduction.	Crst s250	58	.35

Author/Title	Pub./Stock No.	Yr.	Price
B			
BABCOCK, DWIGHT V.			
The gorgeous ghoul murder case.	Avon (30)	43	.25
	Avon 320	51	.25
A homicide for Hannah.	Avon 68	45	.25
_____.	Avon 332	51	.25
BABINGTON-SMITH, CONSTANCE			
Air spy.	Ball F307K	59	.50
BACCANTE, LEONORA			
Johnny Bogan.	Pop 423	52	.25
_____.	Pop G336	59	.35
BACHMANN, LAWRENCE			
Ten seconds to hell.	Crst s237	58	.35
with Hannah Lees			
Death in the doll's house.	Dell 122	46	.25
_____.	Dell 356	49	.25
BAD men and good.	Pop 610	54	.25
BAGBY, GEORGE			
Blood will tell.	Ban 1226	54	.25
The body in the basket.	Dell 904	56	.25
Coffin corner.	PB 736	50	.25
Cop killer.	Dell 997	59	.25
The corpse with sticky fingers.	Berk G-84	57	.35
Dead on arrival.	Ban 1197	54	.25
Dead storage.	Dell 949	57	.25
Drop dead.	Ban 1308	55	.25
Give the little corpse a great big hand.	Dell 848	55	.25
BAGNOLD, ENID			
National Velvet.	PB 66	40	.25
BAILEY, H. C.			
The best of Mr. Fortune stories.	PB 190	43	.25
The bishop's crime.	Pony unk	46	.25
A clue for Mr. Fortune.	Pony 52	46	.25
This is Mr. Fortune.	Bond unk	47	.25
The twittering bird mystery.	Bond 8	46	.25
BAILEY, JOHN			
The Saturday evening post cartoons.	Lion LL 58	55	.35
BAILEY, SETH			
The hand in the cobbler's safe.	Bart (1)	44	.25
BAILEY, TEMPLE			
The blue cloak.	Bart 31	46	.25

Author/Title	Pub./Stock No.	Yr.	Price
The pink camellia.	Dell 178	47	.25
Wallflowers.	Dell 245	48	.25
BAINTON, ROLAND H.			
Here I stand.	Ment MD127	55	.50
BAIRD, JACK			
Hot, sweet and blue.	GM 557	56	.25
BAKER, CHARLES JR.			
Blood of the lamb.	Dell 492	51	.25
BAKER, DENYS VAL			
A journey with love.	Crst 122	56	.25
Strange fulfillment.	Pyr G341	58	.35
BAKER, DOROTHY			
Trio.	Pen 604	46	.25
Young man with a horn.	Pen 561	45	.25
_____.	Sig 1088	53	.25
BAKER, LEDRU JR.			
...And be my love.	GM 183	51	.25
_____.	GM 841	59	.25
The cheaters.	GM 244	52	.25
The preying streets.	Ace S-122	55	.25
BAKER, RACHEL			
Sigmund Freud for everybody.	Pop 712	55	.25
BAKER, SAMM SINCLAIR			
Miracle gardening.	Ban A1746	58	.35
Murder--very dry.	Graf 135	56	.25
One touch of blood.	Graf 97	55	.25
BALCH, GLENN			
Blind man's bullets.	Ace D-208	57	.35
Grass greed.	Ace D-372	59	.35
Indian paint.	Com 31	49	.25
Tiger roan.	PBJr J-50	50	.25
BALCHIN, NIGEL			
Mine own executioner.	PenN 674	48	.25
The small back room.	Lion 31	50	.25
BALDWIN, BATES			
The sultan's warrior.	PB 884	52	.25
_____.	Pop G186	57	.35
Tide of empire.	Avon T-72	53	.35
BALDWIN, FAITH			
Alimony.	Dell 318	49	.25
Bride from Broadway.	DelT 5	51	.10
District nurse.	PB 456	47	.25
Enchanted oasis.	Dell 255	48	.25
For richer, for poorer...	Dell 574	52	.25
Give love the air.	PB 658	50	.25
The heart has wings.	Pony unk	46	.25

Author/Title	Pub./Stock No.	Yr.	Price
BALDWIN, FAITH (cont.)			
The heart remembers.	Dell 288	49	.25
.	Dell D317	59	.35
The high road.	Dell 445	50	.25
Honor bound.	Dell 116	46	.25
Hotel hostess.	Ban 411	48	.25
The incredible year.	Dell 532	51	.25
Love is a surprise!	Ban 455	48	.25
Manhattan nights.	Dell 475	51	.25
Marry for money.	Ban 471	50	.25
Medical center.	PB 380	46	.25
Men are such fools.	Dell 138	46	.25
The moon's our home.	Dell 368	50	.25
No private heaven.	PB 613	49	.25
The office wife.	PB 150	42	.25
Private duty.	PB 445	47	.25
Rehearsal for love.	PB 513	48	.25
Rich girl, poor girl.	Dell 196	47	.25
Self-made woman.	Dell 163	47	.25
Skyscraper.	Dell 236	48	.25
Week-end marriage.	Dell 73	45	.25
White collar girl.	PB 311	46	.25
White magic.	Sup M637	44	.25
Wife vs. secretary.	Dell 12	43	.25
.	DelT unk	51	.10
Woman on her way.	PB 603	49	.25
BALDWIN, JAMES			
Giovanni's room.	Sig S1559	59	.35
Go tell it on the mountain.	Sig 1138	54	.25
BALDWIN, LINTON			
Sinners' game.	Lion 227	54	.25
BALDWIN, MONICA			
The called and the chosen.	Sig D1601	58	.50
I leap over the wall.	Sig S1371	57	.35
BALLARD, (W)(ILLIS) T(ODHUNTER)			
Blizzard range.	Pop 638	55	.25
Chance Elson.	Card C-277	58	.35
Dealing out death.	Graf 18	49	.25
.	Graf 72	54	.25
Fury in the heart.	Mon 134	59	.35
Gunman from Texas.	Pop 735	56	.25
Guns of the lawless.	Pop 772	56	.25
High iron.	Pop 552	54	.25
Incident at Sun Mountain.	Pop 492	53	.25
Murder can't stop.	Graf 26	50	.25
.	Graf 65	53	.25
The package deal.	Ban A1600	57	.35
Rawhide gunman.	Pop 617	54	.25
.	Pop G255	58	.35
Roundup.	Eag EB83	57	.25
Saddle tramp.	Pop G249	58	.35
Say yes to murder.	Pen 566	45	.25
Trail town marshal.	Eag EB93	57	.25
Trigger trail.	Pop 680	55	.25

Author/Title	Pub./Stock No.	Yr.	Price
Trouble on the Massacre.	Pop G309	59	.35
Two-edged vengeance.	Pop 454	52	.25
.	Pop G320	59	.35
Walk in fear.	GM 259	52	.25
West of quarantine.	Pop 524	53	.25
with James C. Lynch			
Showdown.	Pop 476	53	.25
.	Pop G335	59	.35
BALLINGER, BILL S.			
The beautiful trap.	Sig 1134	54	.25
The body beautiful.	Sig 774	50	.25
.	Sig 1274	56	.25
The body in the bed.	Sig 730	49	.25
.	Sig 1243	55	.25
The darkening door.	Sig 1040	53	.25
Formula for murder.	Sig 1585	58	.25
The longest second.	Sig 1730	59	.25
Portrait in smoke.	Sig 897	51	.25
.	Sig 1321	56	.25
The tooth and the nail.	Sig 1319	56	.25
The wife of the red-haired man.	Sig 1494	58	.25
BALMER, EDWIN with Philip Wylie			
When worlds collide.	Dell 627	52	.25
BALZAC, HONORÉ de			
The best of Balzac.	Crst s220	58	.35
Droll stories.	Avon T-102	55	.35
Eugénie Grandet.	BanC AC17	59	.35
The girl with the golden eyes.	Avon 697	56	.25
Père Goriot.	Pyr G177	56	.35
.	PyrR PR21S	59	.50
Temptation in Paris.	Avon T-140	56	.35
Ten droll tales.	Hill unk	48	.25
BAMM, PETER			
The invisible flag.	Sig S1512	58	.35
BANKHEAD, TALLULAH			
Tallulah.	Dell D132	54	.35
BANKS, POLAN			
My forbidden past.	Pop 319	51	.25
BANKS, ROSIE M.			
Settlement nurse.	Perm M-4153	59	.35
Surgical nurse.	PB 1243	59	.25
BANNING, MARGARET CULKIN			
The clever sister.	Dell 381	50	.25
BANNON, ANN			
I am a woman.	GM d833	59	.50
Odd girl out.	GM s653	57	.35
Women in the shadows.	GM s919	59	.35
The BANTAM concise dictionary.	Ban 61	46	.25

Author/Title	Pub./Stock No.	Yr.	Price
BARBER, ROWLAND with John I. Day			
1953 racing almanac.	Dell 671	53	.25
with Rocky Graziano			
Somebody up there likes			
me.	Card C-210	56	.35
BARBER, W. A. with R. F. Schabelitz			
Drawn conclusion.	Pen 531	44	.25
Murder enters the			
picture.	Pen 542	44	.25
Pencil points to murder.	Pen 524	43	.25
BARBETTE, JAY			
Death's long shadow.	Ban 1349	55	.25
Final copy.	Ban 1076	53	.25
BARDON, MINNA			
The case of the			
bloodstained dime.	BH unk	46	.25
BARKER, RICHARD			
The fatal caress.	Dell 733	53	.25
BARKER, SHIRLEY			
Rivers parting.	Dell D107	52	.35
BARNARD, ALLAN			
Cleopatra's nights.	Dell 414	50	.25
The harlot killer.	Dell 797	54	.25
BARNARD, CHARLES N.			
A treasury of True.	Crst d256	58	.50
BARNES, MARGARET CAMPBELL			
The king's choice.	Dell 563	52	.25
BARNET, SYLVAN et al.			
Eight great comedies.	Ment MD216	58	.50
_____.	Ment MT287	59	.75
Eight great tragedies.	Ment MD195	57	.50
BARNETT, LINCOLN			
The universe and Dr.			
Einstein.	Ment M71	52	.35
_____.	Ment MD231	58	.50
BARNHART, CLARENCE			
The Thorndike-Barnhart			
handy pocket dictionary.	Prmb P130	52	.35
_____.	Ban F1299	55	.50
BARNS, GLENN M.			
Deadly summer.	Perm M-3114	58	.25
Masquerade in blue.	Ace S-142	56	.25
BARNWELL, J. O.			
Death rider.	Sig 1366	57	.25
BARON, ALEXANDER			
The golden princess.	Ban A1634	57	.35

Author/Title	Pub./Stock No.	Yr.	Price
Queen of the East.	Pop G243	58	.35
There's no home.	Sig 872	51	.25
BARON, STANLEY			
All my enemies.	Ball 3	52	.35
End of the line.	Ace S-91	55	.25
BARRETT, MICHAEL			
The golden lure.	Crst 153	56	.25
BARRETT, MONTE			
Smoke up the valley.	Pop 311	51	.25
_____.	Pop 630	54	.25
Sun in their eyes.	Pop 224	50	.25
_____.	Pop G137	54	.35
Tempered blade.	Pop 270	50	.25
_____.	Pop G207	57	.35
BARRETT, WILLIAM E.			
The left hand of God.	PB 924	53	.25
The sudden strangers.	Card C-247	57	.35
To the last man.	Pnnt P54	54	.25
BARRINGTON, LOWELL			
The bad one.	Pop 670	55	.25
BARRON, DAVE			
Desert cache.	Eag EB19	54	.25
BARRY, JACK			
Twenty-one.	Pyr G322	58	.35
BARRY, JOE			
The clean-up.	Han 63	47	.20
The fall guy.	Han 42	45	.15
Kiss and kill.	Ace D-47	54	.35
Three for the money.	Han 106	50	.25
The triple cross.	Han 52	46	.15
BARRY, PHILIP			
The Philadelphia story.	PB 102	41	.25
BARRYMORE, DIANA with Gerold Frank			
Too much, too soon.	Sig D1490	58	.50
BARTH, ALAN			
The loyalty of free men.	Card C-32	52	.35
BARTLETT, GEORGE H.			
Is marriage necessary?	Pel P18	47	.35
BARTLETT, JOHN			
The shorter Bartlett's			
Familiar quotations.	Prmb P205S	53	.50
_____.	Perm M-5002	55	.50
BARTLETT, SY with Beirne Lay Jr.			
Twelve o'clock high.	Ban 743	49	.25
BARTOLINI, ELIO			
La signora.	Lion LB 163	57	.25

Author/Title	Pub./Stock No.	Yr.	Price
BARTON, BRUCE			
The man nobody knows.	PB 40	40	.25
BARTON, JACK			
Ambush range.	Pop 708	55	.25
Brand of fury.	Pop 659	55	.25
Day of the .44.	Pop 793	57	.25
Gun in his hand.	Pop 768	56	.25
The mustangers.	Pop 826	57	.25
Texas rawhider.	Pop 498	53	.25
Trail of the damned.	Pop 611	54	.25
The untamed breed.	Pop G322	59	.35
The vengeance riders.	Pop 729	56	.25
BARUCH, BERNARD			
Baruch: my own story.	Card GC-52	58	.50
BASINSKY, EARLE			
The big steal.	Sig 1286	56	.25
Death is a cold, keen edge.	Sig 1351	56	.25
BASS, FRANK			
The angry land.	PB 1247	59	.25
BASSETT, JACK with Norman Monath			
Play it yourself.	Perm M-3054	56	.25
BASSING, EILEEN			
Home before dark.	Ban F1807	58	.50
BASSLER, ANTHONY			
Just what the doctor ordered.	Avon 227	49	.25
BASSO, HAMILTON			
The view from Pompey's Head.	Card C-229	56	.35
BAST, WILLIAM			
James Dean: a biography.	Ball 180	56	.35
BATCHELOR, PAULA			
The duke's temptation.	Avon T-171	57	.35
BATES, H. E.			
The darling buds of May.	Sig S1649	59	.35
Love for Lydia.	Pop 550	54	.25
_____.	Pop SP37	59	.50
The nature of love.	Pop 654	55	.25
The purple plain.	Ban 820	50	.25
The scarlet sword.	Pop G127	53	.35
The sleepless moon.	Pop G192	57	.35
Summer in Salandar.	Sig S1602	58	.35
The valley of love.	Pop 683	55	.25
BAUER, W. W.			
The official American Medical Association book of health.	DelF B101	57	.35

Author/Title	Pub./Stock No.	Yr.	Price
BAUM, VICKI			
Back stage.	Avon 64	45	.25
Grand hotel.	Bart 28	46	.25
_____.	Prmb P208	53	.35
_____.	Dell D239	58	.35
Mortgage on life.	Avon 265	50	.25
The mustard seed.	Pyr G328	58	.35
Once in Vienna.	Dell 524	51	.25
One tropical night.	Prmb P109	51	.35
Theme for ballet.	Dell F83	59	.50
BAUME, ERIC			
Yankee woman.	Prmb P235	53	.35
BAX, ROGER			
Disposing of Henry.	PB 606	49	.25
The trouble with murder.	PB 716	50	.25
Two if by sea.	Dell 634	52	.25
BAXTER, GEORGE OWEN			
Horseback hellion.	Sig 785	50	.25
BAXTER, JOHN			
A foreign affair.	Avon T-78	54	.35
Unfaithful.	Avon 647	55	.25
_____.	Avon 836	58	.25
BAXTER, WALTER			
The image and the search.	Pop G151	55	.35
Look down in mercy.	Pop G121	53	.35
_____.	Pop SP41	59	.50
BAYLEY, JAMES with Houston Peterson			
Essays in philosophy.	PBL PL518	59	.50
BAYNES, JACK			
Hand of the mafia.	Crst 224	58	.25
Meet Morocco Jones.	Crst 195	57	.25
_____.	Crst 344	59	.25
Morocco Jones in the case of the golden angel.	Crst 325	59	.25
The Peeping Tom murders.	Crst 234	58	.25
BEACH, EDWARD L.			
Run silent, run deep.	Perm 4061	56	.35
Submarine!	Sig S1043	53	.35
_____.	Sig S1459	57	.35
BEARD, JAMES A.			
with Sam Aaron			
How to eat better for less money.	Perm M-4065	57	.35
with Isabel E. Callvert			
The James Beard cookbook.	Dell X1	59	.75
with Patrick Gavin Duffy			
The standard bartender's guide.	Perm M-4030	55	.35
BEASLEY, NORMAN			
Main Street merchant.	Ban A-3	50	.25

Author/Title	Pub./Stock No.	Yr.	Price
BEATER, JACK with MacLennan Roberts			
Sea avenger.	DelF B113	58	.35
BEATTY, JEROME JR.			
Sex rears its lovely head.	Ban 1523	56	.25
BEATY, DAVID			
The four winds.	Pop G168	56	.35
The proving flight.	Perm M-4093	58	.35
BEAUMONT, CHARLES			
The hunger and other stories.	Ban A1917	59	.35
The intruder.	Dell F94	59	.50
Yonder.	Ban A1759	58	.35
BECHDOLT, FREDERICK R.			
Bold raiders of the West.	Pnnt P30	54	.25
Horse thief trail.	Pnnt P57	54	.25
BECKER, BELLE with Robert N. Linscott			
Bedside book of famous French stories.	Dell F57	56	.50
BECKER, BERIL			
The spitfires.	Pyr G86	53	.35
BECKER, EDWIN			
Earth woman.	Lion unk	52	.25
BECKHARDT, ISRAEL with Wenzell Brown			
The violators.	Pop 734	56	.25
BEEDING, FRANCIS			
Coffin for one.	Avon (37)	43	.25
Heads off at midnight.	Pop 381	51	.25
Hell let loose.	Pop 71	46	.25
Murdered: one by one.	Pop 42	44	.25
The nine waxed faces.	Pop 268	50	.25
Ten holy horrors.	Pen 544	44	.25
The twelve disguises.	Pop 57	45	.25
BEKKER, C. D.			
Defeat at sea.	Ball 183	56	.35
BELBENOIT, RENÉ			
I escaped from Devil's Island.	Ban 728	49	.25
BELL, VEREEN			
Swamp water.	Ban 97	47	.25
————.	Ban 1225	54	.25
Trial by marriage.	Dell 582	52	.25
BELLAH, JAMES WARNER			
The Apache.	GM 155	51	.25
Divorce.	Pop 404	52	.25
Massacre.	Lion 43	50	.25
Ordeal at Blood River.	Ball 352K	59	.35

Author/Title	Pub./Stock No.	Yr.	Price
Rear guard.	Pop 380	51	.25
The valiant Virginians.	Ball 44	53	.35
Ward 20.	Pop 195	49	.25
————.	Eag EB3	53	.25
————.	Pop G350	59	.35
BELLAMANN, HENRY			
Kings Row.	Card C-2	51	.35
————.	Card GC-55	58	.50
BELLAMY, FRANCIS RUFUS			
Atta.	Ace D-79	54	.35
BELLE Bradley, her story.	GM 342	53	.25
BELLEM, ROBERT LESLIE			
The window with the sleeping nude.	Han 118	50	.25
BELLER, WILLIAM with Erik Bergaust			
Satellite!	Ban A1765	57	.35
BELLOW, SAUL			
The adventures of Augie March.	Pop SP2	55	.50
Seize the day.	Pop G289	58	.35
BELLUS, JEAN			
Clementine chérie.	Crst 266	59	.25
BELMONTE Y GARCÍA, JUAN with Manuel Chaves Nogales			
Juan Belmonte: killer of bulls.	Ban A1160	53	.35
BEMELMANS, LUDWIG			
Dirty Eddie.	Sig 858	51	.25
————.	Sig 1278	56	.25
Hotel Splendide.	Pen 637	47	.25
I love you, I love you, I love you.	Sig 693	48	.25
Now I lay me down to sleep.	Sig 776	50	.25
Small beer.	PB 306	45	.25
BENCHLEY, NATHANIEL			
One to grow on.	Pyr G431	59	.35
BENCHLEY, ROBERT			
My ten years in a quandary.	PB 449	47	.25
BENDER, JAMES with Lee Graham			
Your way to popularity and personal power.	Sig 889	51	.25
————.	SigK K313	54	.25
BENDER, WILLIAM JR.			
Tokyo intrigue.	Ace S-198	57	.25

Author/Title	Pub./Stock No.	Yr.	Price
BENEDICT, RUTH			
Patterns of culture.	Pel P2	46	.25
———.	Ment M89	53	.35
BENEFIELD, BARRY			
Valiant is the word for			
Carrie.	Ban 24	46	.25
BENÉT, JAMES			
A private killing.	Ban 825	50	.25
BENÉT, STEPHEN VINCENT			
O'Halloran's luck.	Pen 546	44	.25
The Stephen Vincent Benét			
Pocket book.	PB 360	46	.25
BENGTSSON, FRANS G.			
The long ships.	Sig D1391	57	.50
BENNETT, DWIGHT			
The avenger.	Perm M-3045	56	.25
Border graze.	Pnnt P21	53	.25
Lost Wolf River.	Ban 1141	53	.25
Stormy range.	Ban 1001	52	.25
Top hand.	Perm M-3023	55	.25
BENNETT, EDNA			
The best cartoons from			
France.	Lion LL 17	55	.35
with Brant House			
Love from France.	Pop 777	56	.25
BENNETT, GEORGE			
Great tales of action			
and adventure.	DelL LB126	59	.35
BENNETT, HAL			
Blonde mistress.	Pyr 14	49	.25
BENNETT, HARRY with Paul Marcus			
We never called him			
Henry.	GM 185	51	.25
BENNETT, JAMES O'DONNELL			
Much loved books, volume			
I.	Prem d81	59	.50
BENNETT, MARGOT			
Someone from the past.	Crst s332	59	.35
BENNEY, MARK			
Low company.	Avon 470	52	.25
BENSON, BEN			
The affair of the			
exotic dancer.	Ban 2001	59	.25
Alibi at dusk.	Ban 1014	52	.25
Beware the pale horse.	Ban 1070	53	.25
The black mirror.	Ban 1909	58	.25
The blonde in black.	Ban 1974	59	.25

Author/Title	Pub./Stock No.	Yr.	Price
Broken shield.	Ban 1552	57	.25
The burning fuse.	Ban 1421	56	.25
The girl in the cage.	Ban 1359	55	.25
Lily in her coffin.	Pnnt P16	53	.25
The ninth hour.	Ban A1698	57	.35
The running man.	Ban 1910	59	.25
The silver cobweb.	Ban 1468	56	.25
Stamped for murder.	Pnnt P4	53	.25
Target in taffeta.	Ban 1323	55	.25
The Venus death.	Ban 1271	54	.25
with Howard D. Tawney			
Hypnosis and you.	GM s583	56	.35
BENSON, SALLY			
Junior miss.	PB 332	45	.25
Meet me in St. Louis.	Ban 15	45	.25
———.	Ban A1891	58	.35
BENTLEY, E. C.			
The chill.	Dell 704	53	.25
Trent's last case.	PB 269	44	.25
with H. Warner Allen			
Trent's own case.	Pen 510	42	.25
BERCKMAN, EVELYN			
The evil of time.	Dell 841	55	.25
The strange bedfellow.	Dell D268	58	.35
Worse than murder.	Dell 936	57	.25
BERENSTAIN, JANICE with Stanley Berenstain			
Berenstains' baby book.	Ban 1074	53	.25
Lover boy.	Dell 998	59	.25
Marital blitz.	DelF 50	55	.25
———.	DelF B143	59	.35
BERENSTAIN, STANLEY with Janice Berenstain			
Berenstains' baby book.	Ban 1074	53	.25
Lover boy.	Dell 998	59	.25
Marital blitz.	DelF 50	55	.25
———.	DelF B143	59	.35
BERESFORD-HOWE, CONSTANCE			
My Lady Greensleeves.	Ball 112	55	.35
BERG, LOUIS			
Prison nurse.	Ban 427	49	.25
———.	Ban A2008	59	.35
BERGAUST, ERIK with William Beller			
Satellite!	Ban A1765	57	.35
BERGMAN, LEE			
Dark violence.	Pyr G443	59	.35
BERGQUIST, LILLIAN with Irving Moore			
Your shot, darling.	Graf 84	54	.25
BERKELEY, ANTHONY			
The poisoned chocolates			
case.	PB 814	51	.25
Trial and error.	PB 307	45	.25

Author/Title	Pub./Stock No.	Yr.	Price
BERLE, MILTON			
Out of my trunk.	Ban 550	48	.25
BERLIN, ISAIAH			
The age of enlightenment.	Ment MD172	56	.50
The hedgehog and the fox.	Ment M198	57	.35
BERMAN, HAROLD			
The Pocket book of dog stories.	PB 187	42	.25
BERNARD, WILLIAM			
Jailbait.	Pop 392	51	.25
_____.	Pop 743	56	.25
_____.	Pop G321	59	.35
BERNHARD, HUBERT J. et al.			
New handbook of the heavens.	Ment M52	50	.35
_____.	Ment Ms114	54	.50
BERNSTEIN, ABRAHAM			
Taxi.	Chek 8	49	.15
BERNSTEIN, MOREY			
The search for Bridey Murphy.	Card GC-37	56	.50
BERRILL, N. J.			
The living tide.	Prem s26	56	.35
Man's emerging mind.	Prem d50	57	.50
Sex and the nature of things.	Card C-169	55	.35
You and the universe.	Prem d80	59	.50
BERSON, FRED			
After the big house.	Pop G122	53	.35
BERTO, GIUSEPPE			
The brigand.	Sig 1053	53	.25
The sky is red.	Sig S971	52	.35
BERZEN, A. H.			
Washington bachelor.	Ace S-126	55	.25
BEST, HERBERT			
Diane.	Card C-184	55	.35
The BEST cartoons from Argosy.	Zen ZB-5	58	.35
BEST cartoons from True.	Crst 114	55	.25
The BEST from True.	GM 99	49	.25
BESTER, ALFRED			
The demolished man.	Sig 1105	54	.25
_____.	Sig S1593	59	.35
The rat race.	Berk G-19	56	.35
Starburst.	Sig S1524	58	.35

Author/Title	Pub./Stock No.	Yr.	Price
The stars, my destination.	Sig S1389	57	.35
BEST-SELLER digest no. 1.	Card C-193	55	.35
BEVAN, A. J.			
Zarak.	Avon T-150	56	.35
BEVERIDGE, ELIZABETH			
The Pocket book of home canning.	PB 217	43	.25
BEVERLEY-GIDDINGS, A. R.			
River of rogues.	PB 946	53	.25
BEYER, WILLIAM			
Murder secretary.	Bart 24	46	.25
BEZZERIDES, A. I.			
They drive by night.	Dell 416	50	.25
Thieves' market.	Ban 750	50	.25
_____.	Ban A1768	58	.35
Tough guy.	Lion 153	53	.25
BICKHAM, JACK M.			
Feud fury.	Ace D-384	59	.35
Gunman's gamble.	Ace D-308	58	.35
BIDDLE, LIVINGSTON JR.			
Main line.	Pop 402	52	.25
BIERCE, AMBROSE			
The monk and The hangman's daughter.	Avon 628	55	.25
BIERSTADT, EDWARD HALE			
Satan was a man.	Eag EB16	54	.25
BIG league baseball.	Avon 307	51	.25
BIGGERS, EARL DERR			
The agony column.	Avon (17)	42	.25
_____.	Avon 337	51	.25
Behind that curtain.	PB 191	43	.25
The black camel.	PB 133	41	.25
Charlie Chan carries on.	PB 207	43	.25
_____.	Avon 350	51	.25
The Chinese parrot.	PB 168	42	.25
_____.	Avon 344	51	.25
The house without a key.	PB 50	40	.25
Keeper of the keys.	Dell 47	44	.25
Seven keys to Baldpate.	Pop 132	48	.25
BILLINGS, BUCK			
The Owlhoot trail.	Pyr 182	56	.25
BINGHAM, JOHN			
Murder is a witch.	Dell 941	57	.25
My name is Michael Sibley.	Dell 813	54	.25

Author/Title	Pub./Stock No.	Yr.	Price
BINGHAM, JOHN (cont.)			
The tender poisoner.	Dell 873	55	.25
BIRD, BRANDON			
Dead and gone.	Dell 857	55	.25
Death in four colors.	Dell 531	51	.25
BIRD, HORACE V. with Walter Karig			
Don't tread on me.	Ban A1340	55	.35
BIRKENFELD, GÜNTHER			
A room in Berlin.	Avon 675	55	.25
BIRKLEY, DOLAN			
The blue geranium.	Bart 8	44	.25
BIRMINGHAM, FREDERIC A.			
The art of mixing drinks.	Ban F1688	57	.50
BIRMINGHAM, STEPHEN			
Young Mr. Keefe.	Card C-342	59	.35
BIRNEY, HOFFMAN			
Ann Carmeny.	Ban A1017	53	.35
The dice of God.	Perm M-4073	57	.35
BIRREN, FABER			
Make mine love.	Pyr G423	59	.35
BISCH, LOUIS E.			
Be glad you're neurotic.	Perm M-4013	55	.35
Cure your nerves			
yourself.	Prem d57	57	.50
BISHOP, CURTIS			
Quick draw.	Ban 108	47	.25
Reach for your guns.	Pyr 230	56	.25
BISHOP, JIM			
The day Christ died.	Card GC-73	59	.50
The day Lincoln was shot.	Ban F1428	56	.50
	Ban F2035	59	.50
with Richard H. Hoffmann			
The girl in Poison			
Cottage.	GM 351	53	.25
BISHOP, LEONARD			
The butchers.	Pop SP11	57	.50
Creep into thy narrow			
bed.	Pyr G206	56	.35
Days of my love.	Sig D1107	54	.50
Down all your streets.	Sig D1009	53	.50
BISHOP, MALDEN GRANGE			
Scylla.	Ace D-40	54	.35
BISSELL, BETTY			
The Betty Bissell book			
of home cleaning.	Ban A1897	59	.35

Author/Title	Pub./Stock No.	Yr.	Price
BISSELL, RICHARD			
High water.	Sig 1230	55	.25
Pajama.	Sig 1129	54	.25
_____.	Sig S1425	57	.35
River in my blood.	Sig 1193	55	.25
Say, darling.	Ban F1740	58	.50
A stretch on the river.	Sig 876	51	.25
_____.	Sig S1731	59	.35
BLACK, HILLEL with Sam Kolman			
The royal vultures.	Perm M-4103	58	.35
BLACK, IAN STUART			
The passionate city.	Crst s322	59	.35
BLACK, THOMAS			
Million dollar murder.	Ban 1448	56	.25
BLACKBURN, THOMAS W.			
Broken Arrow range.	DelT 20	51	.10
Buckskin man.	DelF A171	58	.25
Navajo Canyon.	Pnnt P1	53	.25
Raton Pass.	Ban 958	52	.25
Short grass.	Ban 207	48	.25
_____.	Ban 1164	53	.25
Sierra baron.	Ban A1798	58	.35
BLACKMORE, R. D.			
Lorna Doone.	PBL PL508	56	.50
BLACKSTOCK, LEE			
The woman in the woods.	Dell D301	59	.35
BLAIR, CLAY JR.			
Beyond courage.	Ball 134	56	.35
with William R. Anderson			
Nautilus 90 north.	Sig D1692	59	.50
BLAKE, ELEANOR			
Death down East.	Pen 571	45	.25
BLAKE, FORRESTER			
Johnny Christmas.	Ban 989	52	.25
_____.	Ban A1809	58	.35
Wilderness passage.	Ban A1808	58	.35
BLAKE, NICHOLAS			
The beast must die.	Dell D227	58	.35
The corpse in the			
snowman.	Pop 60	45	.25
Head of a traveler.	PB 742	50	.25
Malice in Wonderland.	Pen 592	46	.25
Minute for murder.	PB 548	49	.25
A question of proof.	Pop 123	47	.25
Shell of death.	Pen 543	44	.25
The smiler with the			
knife.	Pop 41	44	.25
There's trouble brewing.	Pop 30	44	.25

Author/Title	Pub./Stock No.	Yr.	Price
BLAND, MARGOT			
Julia.	Eag EB9	54	.25
_____.	Pop G368	59	.35
BLANKFORT, MICHAEL			
The juggler.	Dell 686	53	.25
BLASCO IBÁÑEZ, VINCENTE			
Blood and sand.	Dell 500	51	.25
BLASSINGAME, WYATT			
John Smith hears death walking.	Bart 5	44	.25
BLAYNE, SEBASTIAN			
Gay ghastly holiday.	GM 175	51	.25
Terror in the night.	GM 325	53	.25
BLEILER, EVERETT F. with T. E. Dikty			
Frontiers in space.	Ban 1328	55	.25
Imagination unlimited.	Berk G233	59	.35
BLISH, JAMES			
A case of conscience.	Ball 256	58	.35
ESPer.	Avon T-268	58	.35
Earthman, come home.	Avon T-225	58	.35
The frozen year.	Ball 197	57	.35
Galactic cluster.	Sig S1719	59	.35
The seedling stars.	Sig S1622	59	.35
The triumph of time.	Avon T-279	58	.35
VOR.	Avon T-238	58	.35
Year 2018!	Avon T-193	57	.35
BLISS, TIP			
The Broadway butterfly murders.	Chek 2	49	.15
BLIZARD, MARIE			
The late lamented lady.	GD unk	47	.25
BLOCH, ROBERT			
The kidnaper.	Lion 185	54	.25
The scarf.	Avon 494	53	.25
Scarf of passion.	Avon 211	49	.25
Shooting star.	Ace D-265	58	.35
Spiderweb.	Ace D-59	54	.35
Terror in the night.	Ace D-265	58	.35
The will to kill.	Ace S-67	54	.25
BLOCHMAN, LAWRENCE G.			
Bengal fire.	Dell 311	49	.25
Blow-down.	Dell 156	47	.25
_____.	Dell 740	53	.25
Bombay mail.	Dell 488	51	.25
Death walks in marble halls.	DelT unk	51	.10
Diagnosis: homicide.	PB 793	51	.25
Here's how! A round-the-world bar guide.	SigK Ks350	57	.35
Midnight sailing.	Dell 43	44	.25
Pursuit.	Han 128	51	.25
Recipe for homicide.	Dell 833	55	.25
See you at the morgue.	Dell (7)	43	.25
_____.	Dell 638	52	.25
Wives to burn.	Dell 134	46	.25
BLOCK, ANITA ROWE			
Love is a four-letter word.	Pop G298	59	.35
BLOCK, LIBBIE			
Bedeviled.	Dell 344	49	.25
BLOND, GEORGES			
The death of Hitler's Germany.	Pyr R318	58	.35
BLOOD, MATTHEW			
The avenger.	GM 235	52	.25
_____.	GM 924	59	.25
Death is a lovely dame.	GM 423	54	.25
BLOOM, ROLFE with Allan Ullman			
The naked spur.	Pnnt P29	54	.25
BLOOMFIELD, ROBERT			
When strangers meet.	PB 1171	57	.25
BLUNDEN, GODFREY			
A room on the route.	Ban 947	51	.25
BOCCACCIO, GIOVANNI			
Tales from the Decameron.	PB 477	48	.25
_____.	Card C-106	53	.35
_____.	PBL PL43	56	.35
BODENHEIM, MAXWELL			
Duke Herring.	Chek 6	49	.15
Georgie May.	Avon 152	48	.25
_____.	Avon 427	52	.25
Naked on roller skates.	NL 46	50	.25
Ninth Avenue.	Avon 352	51	.25
Replenishing Jessica.	Avon 191	49	.25
Sixty seconds.	NL 38	50	.25
Virtuous girl.	Avon 168	48	.25
BODIN, PAUL			
All women's flesh.	Berk G-93	57	.35
_____.	Berk G-226	59	.35
The sign of Eros.	Berk G-13	55	.35
_____.	Berk G-54	57	.35
_____.	Berk G216	59	.35
BOGAR, JEFF			
My gun, her body.	Lion unk	52	.25
The tigress.	Lion unk	52	.25
BOILEAU, PIERRE with Thomas Narcejac			
Vertigo.	Dell 977	58	.25

Author/Title	Pub./Stock No.	Yr.	Price
BOLES, PAUL DARCY			
All that love allows.	Pop 691	55	.25
The streak.	Ban A1276	54	.35
BOLLES, BLAIR			
How to get rich in Washington.	Dell 611	52	.25
BOLTAR, RUSSELL			
By appointment only.	DelF B111	57	.35
The two lives of Dr. Stratton.	DelF B124	59	.35
Woman's doctor.	Ace D-163	56	.35
BOLTE, CHARLES G.			
The new veteran.	Pen 602	46	.25
BOLTINOFF, HENRY			
Bed and broad.	Pyr G343	58	.35
The howls of ivy.	Ban 1389	55	.25
Sex is better in college.	Pyr G240	57	.35
BONAR, D. L.			
Lawman without a badge.	Ace D-106	55	.35
BOND, J. HARVEY			
Bye-bye, baby!	Ace D-279	58	.35
Kill me with kindness.	Ace D-349	59	.35
Murder isn't funny.	Ace D-301	58	.35
BOND, NELSON			
No time like the future.	Avon T-80	54	.35
BONETT, EMERY with John Bonett			
Dead lion.	PB 738	50	.25
BONETT, JOHN with Emery Bonett			
Dead lion.	PB 738	50	.25
BONHAM, FRANK			
Blood on the land.	Ball 7	52	.35
	Ball 254	58	.35
_____.			
Bold passage.	PB 859	52	.25
Defiance mountain.	Eag EB77	56	.25
The feud at Spanish Ford.	Ball 85	54	.35
Hardrock.	Ball 269K	58	.35
Last stage West.	DelF A186	59	.25
Lost Stage Valley.	PB 604	49	.25
Night raid.	Ball 64	54	.35
Rawhide guns.	Pop 707	55	.25
Snaketrack.	PB 967	53	.25
Sound of gunfire.	DelF A177	59	.25
Tough country.	DelF A150	58	.25
The wild breed.	Lion LL 54	55	.35
BONNAMY, FRANCIS			
Dead reckoning.	Pen 584	46	.25
The king is dead on Queen Street.	Pen 629	47	.25

Author/Title	Pub./Stock No.	Yr.	Price
Murder as a fine art.	Sig 713	49	.25
A rope of sand.	Pen 606	46	.25
BONNELL, JAMES FRANCIS			
Death over Sunday.	Dell 19	43	.25
BONNER, PARKER			
Outlaw brand.	Pop 603	54	.25
Superstition range.	Pop 480	53	.25
BONNER, PAUL HYDE			
Hotel Talleyrand.	Ban A1405	55	.35
The other side of paradise.	Pop G172	56	.35
Summer in Rome.	Prmb P224	53	.35
BONNET, THEODORE			
The mudlark.	Prmb P114	51	.35
BOONE, JACK			
Backwoods woman.	Dell 557	51	.25
BOOTH, CHARLES G.			
The general died at dawn.	PB 100	41	.25
Mr. Angel comes aboard.	Sup M651	45	.25
Murder strikes thrice.	Bond 4	46	.25
BOOTH, EDWIN			
Jinx rider.	Ace D-236	57	.35
The man who killed Tex.	Ace D-284	58	.35
Showdown at Warbird.	Ace D-226	57	.35
The trail to Tomahawk.	Ace D-288	58	.35
Wyoming welcome.	Ace D-408	59	.35
BOOTH, ERNEST			
With sirens screaming.	Pyr 121	54	.25
BORDAGES, ASA			
The glass lady.	Lion 56	51	.25
BORDEN, LEE			
The secret of Sylvia.	GM 744	58	.25
BOROS, EVA			
The doll's smile.	Sig 1582	58	.25
BOSQUET, JEAN			
The flesh agents.	Avon T-195	57	.35
BOSWELL, CHARLES			
They all died young.	Han 94	49	.25
with Lewis Thompson			
The girl in lover's lane.	GM 334	53	.25
The girl in the stateroom.	GM 180	51	.25
The girl with the scarlet brand.	GM 384	54	.25
The girls in Nightmare House.	GM 480	55	.25
Surrender to love.	Pop 688	55	.25

Author/Title	Pub./Stock No.	Yr.	Price
BOSWELL, JAMES			
Boswell's Johnson sampler.	Prem s47	57	.35
Boswell's London journal.	Sig D1305	56	.50
BOSWORTH, ALLAN R.			
Border roundup.	Ban 86	47	.25
Bury me not.	Dell 858	55	.25
Double deal.	Ban 119	47	.25
The drifters.	Pop 736	56	.25
Only the brave.	Pop 684	55	.25
Steel to the sunset.	Ban 929	51	.25
BOSWORTH, JIM			
Speed demon.	Ace D-267	58	.35
BOTEIN, BERNARD			
The prosecuter.	Card C-279	58	.35
BOTKIN, B. A.			
The Pocket treasury of American folklore.	PB 684	50	.25
BOTTOME, PHYLLIS			
The mortal storm.	Pop 94	46	.25
Under the skin.	PB 798	51	.25
BOTTUME, CARL			
The runaways.	Sig 805	50	.25
Sailor's choice.	Sig 990	52	.25
BOUCHER, ANTHONY			
The case of the crumpled knave.	Pop 154	48	.25
The case of the seven sneezes.	Dell 334	49	.25
The case of the solid key.	Pop 59	45	.25
Far and away.	Ball 109	55	.35
The Pocket book of true crime stories.	PB 213	43	.25
Rocket to the morgue.	Dell 591	52	.25
BOULLE, PIERRE			
The bridge over the River Kwai.	Ban A1677	57	.35
BOUMA, J. L.			
The avenging gun.	Pop 835	58	.25
Border vengeance.	Eag EB61	56	.25
Burning valley.	Eag EB87	57	.25
Danger trail.	Eag EB29	54	.25
Texas spurs.	Eag EB41	55	.25
_____.	Pop G387	59	.35
BOURGET, PAUL			
Crime d'amour.	Ace D-16	53	.35
BOURJAILY, VANCE			
discovery no. 2.	Card C-115	53	.35

Author/Title	Pub./Stock No.	Yr.	Price
discovery no. 3.	Card C-130	54	.35
discovery no. 4.	Card C-143	54	.35
discovery no. 5.	Card C-159	55	.35
discovery no. 6.	Card C-185	55	.35
The end of my life.	Ban 1047	52	.25
The hound of earth.	Perm M-4052	56	.35
The violated.	Ban F1955	59	.50
with John W. Aldridge			
discovery no. 1.	Card C-80	53	.35
BOURNE, PETER			
Drums of destiny.	Pop 237	50	.25
_____.	Pop SP28	58	.50
The golden road.	Pop G107	52	.35
BOUTELL, ANITA			
Death has a past.	Ban 897	51	.25
BOWEN, CATHERINE DRINKER			
Yankee from Olympus.	BanB FB411	57	.50
BOWEN, CROSWELL			
They went wrong.	Ban A1375	55	.35
BOWEN, JOHN			
After the rain.	Ball 284K	59	.35
BOWEN, ROBERT O.			
Bamboo.	Sig 1201	55	.25
The weight of the cross.	Ban A1183	53	.35
BOWEN, ROBERT SIDNEY			
Make mine murder.	BK unk	47	.25
_____.	Chek 3	49	.15
BOWER, B. M.			
The Flying U strikes.	Pop 157	48	.25
The Flying U's last stand.	Pop 118	47	.25
Gun fight at Horsethief range.	Avon 374	51	.25
_____.	Avon 505	53	.25
The haunted hills.	Pop 306	51	.25
Pirates of the range.	Dell 466	50	.25
Trigger vengeance.	Sig 1045	53	.25
The Whoop-up trail.	PB 310	46	.25
BOWIE, SAM			
Thunderhead range.	Mon 113	59	.35
BOWLES, CYNTHIA			
At home in India.	PyrR PG26	59	.35
BOWLES, PAUL			
The delicate prey.	Sig 919	52	.25
_____.	Sig 1296	56	.25
Let it come down.	Sig 1002	53	.25
The sheltering sky.	Sig 840	51	.25
_____.	Sig S1249	55	.35

Author/Title	Pub./Stock No.	Yr.	Price
BOWMAN, JOHN CLARKE			
Isle of demons.	Pop 571	54	.25
BOWRA, C. M.			
The Greek experience.	Ment MD275	59	.50
BOX, EDGAR			
Death before bedtime.	Sig 1093	54	.25
	Sig 1526	58	.25
Death in the fifth			
position.	Sig 1036	53	.25
	Sig 1475	57	.25
Death likes it hot.	Sig 1217	55	.25
	Sig 1484	58	.25
BOYD, EUNICE MAYS			
Murder wears mukluks.	Dell 259	48	.25
BOYD, FRANK			
The flesh peddlers.	Mon 133	59	.35
BOYD, JAMES			
Bitter creek.	Ban F1579	57	.50
Long hunt.	Ban 836	50	.25
BOYINGTON, PAPPY			
Baa baa black sheep.	Dell F88	59	.50
BOYLAN, EDWARD J. JR.			
Terry and the Pirates in			
the adventures of the			
jewels of jade.	Chek 1	49	.15
BOYLSTON, HELEN DORE			
Sue Barton, senior nurse.	PBJr J-53	50	.25
Sue Barton, student			
nurse.	Com 9	48	.25
BRACCO, EDGAR JEAN			
Boots and saddles.	Berk G-180	58	.35
Chattels of Eldorado.	Avon T-98	55	.35
	Avon T-248	58	.35
China doll.	Berk G-136	58	.35
Flight.	Berk G291	59	.35
BRACKEEN, STEVE			
Baby Moll.	Crst 206	58	.25
Danger in my blood.	Crst 316	59	.25
BRACKETT, LEIGH			
The big jump.	Ace D-103	55	.35
The galactic breed.	Ace D-99	55	.35
No good from a corpse.	Han 32	44	.15
Rio Bravo.	Ban 1893	59	.25
The sword of Rhiannon.	Ace D-36	53	.35
BRADBURY, RAY			
The circus of Dr. Lao and			
other improbable			
stories.	Ban A1519	56	.35
Dandelion wine.	Ban A1922	59	.35
Fahrenheit 451.	Ball 41	53	.35
The golden apples of the			
sun.	Ban A1241	54	.35
The illustrated man.	Ban 991	52	.25
	Ban 1282	54	.25
The Martian chronicles.	Ban 886	51	.25
	Ban 1261	54	.25
	Ban A1885	59	.35
The October country.	Ball F139	56	.50
Timeless stories for			
today and tomorrow.	Ban A944	52	.35
BRADFORD, ROARK			
Ol' man Adam an' his			
chillun.	Sup M638	44	.25
BRADLEY, DAVID			
No place to hide.	Ban 421	49	.25
BRADY, LEO			
The edge of doom.	Pop 260	50	.25
BRADY, MATT			
Take your last look.	GM 376	54	.25
	GM 811	58	.25
BRAHAM, HAL			
Call me deadly.	Graf 152	57	.25
BRAINE, JOHN			
Room at the top.	Sig S1569	58	.35
BRANCH, HOUSTON with Frank Waters			
Diamond Head.	Dell D127	53	.35
BRAND, CHRISTIANNA			
Cat and mouse.	Avon 385	52	.25
Fog of doubt.	Dell 881	56	.25
BRAND, MAX			
The bandit of the Black			
Hills.	PB 717	50	.25
Blood on the trail.	PB 1228	59	.25
Border guns.	PB 991	54	.25
The border kid.	PB 491	48	.25
Brother of the Cheyennes.	Sig 757	49	.25
	Sig 1046	53	.25
Brothers on the trail.	Pop 721	56	.25
Danger trail.	PB 848	52	.25
Dead or alive.	Pop G270	58	.35
Desert showdown.	Pop 693	55	.25
Destry rides again.	PB 250	44	.25
The false rider.	PB 1122	56	.25
Fightin' fool.	PB 316	46	.25
The fighting four.	PB 423	47	.25
Fire brain.	PB 1244	59	.25
Flaming irons.	PB 687	50	.25
Galloping broncos.	PB 1133	56	.25
The gambler.	PB 1149	57	.25

Author/Title	Pub./Stock No.	Yr.	Price
BRAND, MAX (cont.)			
The gun tamer.	PB 1018	54	.25
Gunman's gold.	PB 877	52	.25
The hair-trigger kid.	PB 930	53	.25
The happy valley.	Pop G230	58	.35
Hired guns.	PB 705	50	.25
Hunted riders.	PB 744	50	.25
The invisible outlaw.	PB 1180	57	.25
The Jackson Trail.	Pop 801	57	.25
King of the range.	PB 584	49	.25
Law of the gun.	Mon 126	59	.35
The longhorn feud.	PB 523	48	.25
Lucky Larribee.	Card C-368	59	.35
Mystery ranch.	PB 895	52	.25
The night horseman.	PB 1033	54	.25
The outlaw.	PB 797	51	.25
Outlaw breed.	PB 1190	58	.25
Rancher's revenge.	Pop 152	48	.25
_____.	Pop 475	53	.25
_____.	Pop G369	59	.35
Rustlers of Beacon Creek.	PB 781	51	.25
Seven trails.	PB 1056	55	.25
Silvertip.	PB 369	46	.25
Silvertip's chase.	PB 634	49	.25
Silvertip's strike.	PB 547	48	.25
Singing guns.	PB 144	42	.25
Single Jack.	PB 950	53	.25
Six-gun ambush.	Pop 637	55	.25
_____.	Pop G398	59	.35
Smiling desperado.	PB 1168	57	.25
South of Rio Grande.	PB 390	46	.25
Speedy.	PB 1221	58	.25
The stolen stallion.	PB 509	48	.25
The streak.	PB 910	53	.25
The tenderfoot.	PB 1065	55	.25
Timbal Gulch trail.	Pop 78	46	.25
_____.	Pop 445	52	.25
_____.	Pop G327	59	.35
Tragedy trail.	PB 1097	56	.25
Trail partners.	PB 1203	58	.25
The untamed.	PB 1084	55	.25
Valley of vanishing men.	PB 609	49	.25
Valley thieves.	PB 668	50	.25
Valley vultures.	Pop 822	57	.25
Vengeance trail.	PB 979	54	.25
Young Doctor Kildare.	Dell 329	49	.25
BRAND, MILLEN			
The outward room.	Lion 26	50	.25
_____.	Lion LL 49	55	.35
BRANDE, DOROTHEA			
Wake up and live.	PB 2	39	.25
BRANDEL, MARC			
Maniac rendezvous.	Avon 387	51	.25
The moron.	Avon 393	51	.25
The time of the fire.	Ban A1332	55	.35
BRANDON, CURT			
Bugle's wake.	Sig 1037	53	.25
High, wide and handsome.	Sig 903	51	.25
BRANDON, MICHAEL			
Nonce.	Avon 506	53	.25
BRANDON, WILLIAM			
The dangerous dead.	Han 50	46	.15
BRANDT, FRANK			
Cartoons for fighters.	PenS S231	45	.25
BRANDT, TOM			
Kiss me hard.	Pop 539	53	.25
Run, brother, run!	Pop 584	54	.25
BRANNER, H. C.			
The mistress.	Sig 1056	53	.25
BRANNON, WILLIAM T.			
The lady killers.	Han 139	51	.25
with "Yellow Kid" Weil			
Yellow Kid Weil.	Pyr G280	57	.35
BRANSON, H. C.			
I'll eat you last.	Bond unk	46	.25
BRANTÔME, ABBÉ de			
Tales of fair and gallant			
ladies.	Ban F1804	58	.50
BRATTES, LEO			
Forbidden.	Avon 576	54	.25
BREAN, HERBERT			
The clock strikes 13.	Dell 758	54	.25
The darker the night.	PB 698	50	.25
Dead sure.	Dell D221	58	.35
Hardly a man is now			
alive.	Dell 675	53	.25
How to stop smoking.	PB 1025	54	.25
Wilders walk away.	PB 582	49	.25
BREBNER, WINSTON			
Dream of Eden.	Sig 1011	53	.25
BREGER, DAVE			
But that's unprintable!	Ban 1330	55	.25
BREIT, HARVEY with Marc Slonim			
This thing called love.	Sig 1234	55	.25
BRELIS, DEAN			
The mission.	PB 1246	59	.25
BRENNAN, DAN			
The naked night.	Lion 197	54	.25
_____.	Lion LB 147	57	.25

Author/Title	Pub./Stock No.	Yr.	Price
BRENNAN, FREDERICK HAZLITT			
Memo to a firing squad.	Dell 30	43	.25
One of our H-bombs is missing.	GM 498	55	.25
BRENNAN, LOUIS A.			
An affair of dishonor.	Dell D174	56	.35
Death at flood tide.	DelF A149	58	.25
More than flesh.	DelF B108	57	.35
These items of desire.	Pop G141	54	.35
_____.	Pop SP45	59	.50
BRENNECKE, H. J. with Theodor Krancke			
Pocket battleship.	Berk BG-177	58	.50
BRESLIN, HOWARD			
Bad day at Black Rock.	GM 451	55	.25
Shad run.	Perm M-4058	56	.35
The silver oar.	Perm M-4043	56	.35
BRETT, MARTIN			
Blondes are my trouble.	Pop 695	55	.25
Flee from terror.	Pop 811	57	.25
Hot freeze.	Pop 612	54	.25
BRETT, MIKE			
The guilty bystander.	Ace D-349	59	.35
Scream street.	Ace D-333	59	.35
BREUER, BESSIE			
Memory of love.	Avon 196	49	.25
_____.	Prmb 245	53	.25
BREUER, GUSTAV			
The spell.	Pop 412	52	.25
BREWER, GIL			
And the girl screamed.	Crst 147	56	.25
The bitch.	Avon 830	58	.25
The brat.	GM 708	57	.25
Flight to darkness.	GM 277	53	.25
The girl from Hateville.	Zen ZB-7	58	.35
Hell's our destination.	GM 345	53	.25
A killer is loose.	GM 380	54	.25
Little tramp.	Crst 173	57	.25
The red scarf.	Crst 310	59	.25
Satan is a woman.	GM 169	51	.25
77 Rue Paradis.	GM 448	55	.25
So rich, so dead.	GM 196	51	.25
Some must die.	GM 409	54	.25
The squeeze.	Ace D-123	55	.35
Sugar.	Avon T-335	59	.35
13 French Street.	GM 211	52	.25
_____.	GM 418	54	.25
_____.	GM 858	59	.25
The vengeful virgin.	Crst 238	58	.25
Wild.	Crst 229	58	.25
Wild to possess.	Mon 107	59	.35
BRICK, JOHN			
Homer Crist.	PB 1001	54	.25
Jubilee.	Pop G210	58	.35
The raid.	PB 867	52	.25
The rifleman.	Prmb P283	54	.35
Troubled spring.	Pop 405	52	.25
BRICKELL, HERSCHEL			
The Pocket book of O. Henry prize stories.	PB 446	47	.25
BRICKHILL, PAUL			
The dam busters.	Ball 101	55	.35
_____.	Ball 245	57	.35
BRICKMAN, MORRIS			
Do it yourself.	Perm M-3029	56	.25
Don't do it yourself.	Perm M-3090	57	.25
BRIER, HOWARD M.			
Skycruiser.	Com 11	48	.25
BRIFFAULT, ROBERT			
Carlotta.	Avon 250	50	.25
Europa.	Avon 272	50	.25
BRIGHT, ROBERT			
The intruders.	Prmb 278	54	.25
BRINCOURT, ANDRÉ			
The paradise below the stairs.	Ban 1169	53	.25
BRINIG, MYRON			
No marriage in paradise.	Ban 767	50	.25
BRINKLEY, WILLIAM			
Don't go near the water.	Sig D1458	57	.50
Quicksand.	Sig S1362	56	.35
with Sister Cecilia The deliverance of Sister Cecilia.	Sig S1420	57	.35
BRINTON, CRANE			
The shaping of the modern mind.	Ment M98	53	.35
_____.	Ment MD173	56	.50
BRISTER, RICHARD			
The Kansan.	Avon 606	54	.25
_____.	Avon 732	56	.25
Law killer.	Avon T-373	59	.35
Renegade brand.	GM 527	55	.25
The shoot-out at Sentinel Peak.	Ace D-86	54	.35
The wolf streak.	Avon 833	58	.25
BRISTOW, BOB			
Sin street.	DelF B139	59	.35
BRISTOW, GWEN			
Deep summer.	PB 482	47	.25

Author/Title	Pub./Stock No.	Yr.	Price
BRISTOW, GWEN (cont.)			
The handsome road.	PB 589	49	.25
Jubilee trail.	Card C-49	52	.35
BRITTON, FLORENCE			
Best TV plays: 1957.	Ball 238	57	.35
BROADLEY, CHARLES V. with Margaret E. Broadley			
Know your real abilities.	Prmb P65	53	.35
BROADLEY, MARGARET E. with Charles V. Broadley			
Know your real abilities.	Prmb P65	53	.35
BROCK, LILYAN			
Queer patterns.	Eton E121	53	.25
BROCK, STUART			
Bring back her body.	Ace D-23	53	.35
Double-Cross Ranch.	Pyr 255	57	.25
Just around the corner.	Dell 337	49	.25
Killer's choice.	Graf 136	56	.25
Railtown sheriff.	Pyr 333	58	.25
Whispering Canyon.	Ace D-166	56	.35
BRODERICK, GERRY P. with Erwin N. Nistler			
Roadside night.	Pyr 33	51	.25
_____.	Pyr 148	55	.25
BROME, VINCENT			
The spy.	Pyr G379	59	.35
BROMFIELD, LOUIS			
Colorado.	Ban 957	52	.25
The farm.	Sig D1260	55	.50
The green bay tree.	PB 56	40	.25
	Sig S1025	53	.35
The man who had everything.	Avon 52	44	.25
Mister Smith.	Sig S954	52	.35
Mrs. Parkington.	Pyr R305	58	.50
Night in Bombay.	Ban 28	46	.25
	Ban A869	51	.35
_____.	Card C-138	54	.35
Pleasant Valley.	Sig S979	52	.35
Possession.			
The rains came.	Sig 904AB	51	.50
	Sig D1263	56	.50
The strange case of Miss Annie Spragg.	Pen 512	42	.25
	Berk G-36	56	.35
What became of Anna Bolton?	Ban 462	48	.25
The wild country.	Pop G179	57	.35
Wild is the river.	Ban A910	51	.35
BRONTË, CHARLOTTE			
Jane Eyre.	Card C-88	53	.35
_____.	PBL PL44	56	.35
_____.	PBL PL544	59	.50
BRONTË, EMILY			
Wuthering Heights.	PB 7	39	.25
Wuthering Heights.	Card C-33	52	.35
_____.	PBL PL10	54	.35
_____.	SigC CD10	59	.50
BROOKER, CLARK			
Fight at Sun Mountain.	Ball 198	57	.35
Lone gun.	Ball 121	55	.35
BROOKS, JOHN			
The big wheel.	PB 767	51	.25
_____.	Berk G-187	58	.35
The man who broke things.	Card C-340	59	.35
BROOKS, RICHARD			
The producer.	Card C-84	53	.35
BROOKS, WIN			
The shining tides.	PB 984	54	.25
BROSSARD, CHANDLER			
All passion spent.	Pop 626	54	.25
The bold sabateurs.	Dell D137	54	.35
The first time.	Pyr G260	57	.35
Who walk in darkness.	Sig 974	54	.25
BROTHERS, JOYCE with Edward P. F. Eagan			
10 days to a successful memory.	Perm M-4125	59	.35
BROTHERS, WILLIAM			
Morocco episode.	Hill 111	59	.35
Portrait of Lisa.	GM S403	54	.35
BROWER, MILLICENT			
Ingenue.	Ball 286K	59	.35
BROWN, BETH			
Wedding ring.	Avon 97	46	.25
BROWN, CARTER			
The blonde.	Sig 1565	58	.25
The body.	Sig 1527	58	.25
The corpse.	Sig 1606	58	.25
The dame.	Sig 1738	59	.25
The lover.	Sig 1620	59	.25
The loving and the dead.	Sig 1654	59	.25
The mistress.	Sig 1594	59	.25
None but the lethal heart.	Sig 1694	59	.25
The passionate.	Sig 1674	59	.25
Suddenly by violence.	Sig 1722	59	.25
Terror comes creeping.	Sig 1750	59	.25
The victim.	Sig 1633	59	.25
Walk softly, witch.	Sig 1663	59	.25
The wanton.	Sig 1713	59	.25
BROWN, DEE			
Cavalry scout.	Perm M-3101	58	.25
Yellowhorse.	Ball 202	57	.35

Author/Title	Pub./Stock No.	Yr.	Price
BROWN, EUGENE			
Beyond the call of duty.	PB 1212	58	.25
Trespass.	PB 964	53	.25
BROWN, FRANCIS			
Highlights of modern literature.	Ment M104	54	.35
BROWN, FREDRIC			
The bloody moonlight.	Ban 783	50	.25
The case of the dancing sandwiches.	DelT unk	51	.10
Compliments of a fiend.	Ban 876	51	.25
The dead ringer.	Ban 361	49	.25
	Ban 1216	54	.25
Death has many doors.	Ban 1040	52	.25
_____.	Ban 1567	57	.25
The deep end.	Ban 1215	54	.25
The fabulous clipjoint.	Ban 302	48	.25
_____.	Ban 1134	53	.25
_____.	Ban 1566	57	.25
The far cry.	Ban 1133	53	.25
Here comes a candle.	Ban 943	51	.25
His name was Death.	Ban 1436	56	.25
Honeymoon in hell.	Ban A1812	58	.35
The lenient beast.	Ban 1712	58	.25
The lights in the sky are stars.	Ban 1285	55	.25
Madball.	DelF 2E	53	.25
Martians, go home.	Ban A1546	56	.35
Mostly murder.	Pnnt P59	54	.25
Night of the Jabberwock.	Ban 990	52	.25
One for the road.	Ban 1990	59	.25
A plot for murder.	Ban 735	49	.25
Rogue in space.	Ban A1701	57	.35
The Screaming Mimi.	Ban 831	50	.25
_____.	Ban 1312	55	.25
_____.	Ban 1757	58	.25
Space on my hands.	Ban 1077	53	.25
Star shine.	Ban 1423	56	.25
We all killed Grandma.	Ban 1176	53	.25
The wench is dead.	Ban 1565	57	.25
What mad universe.	Ban 835	50	.25
_____.	Ban 1253	54	.25
with Mack Reynolds			
Science fiction carnival.	Ban A1615	57	.35
BROWN, HARRY			
A walk in the sun.	Lion unk	52	.25
_____.	Sig S1467	57	.35
BROWN, JOE DAVID			
Combat mission.	PB 1162	57	.25
The freeholder.	PB 810	51	.25
Kings go forth.	Card C-315	58	.35
Stars in my crown.	PB 645	49	.25
BROWN, LYLE			
Lyle Brown's sports quiz.	PB 996	54	.25

Author/Title	Pub./Stock No.	Yr.	Price
BROWN, MARION			
The southern cook book.	Card C-85	53	.35
BROWN, PETE			
Guns and hunting.	Dell D155	55	.35
BROWN, WENZELL			
The big rumble.	Pop 685	55	.25
Cry kill.	GM s897	59	.35
Dark drums.	Pop 374	51	.25
_____.	Pop 581	54	.25
_____.	Pop G317	59	.35
Devil's spawn.	Prmb P186	52	.35
Gang girl.	Avon 560	54	.25
_____.	Avon 722	56	.25
_____.	Avon T-235	58	.35
The hoods ride in.	Pyr G439	59	.35
The lonely hearts murders.	Sig 981	52	.35
Monkey on my back.	Pop 549	54	.25
The naked hours.	Pop 732	56	.25
Prison girl.	Pyr G345	58	.35
Run, Chico, run.	GM 292	53	.25
_____.	GM s522	55	.35
Teen-age mafia.	GM s917	59	.35
Teen-age terror.	GM s734	58	.35
They died in the chair.	Pop G228	58	.35
The wicked streets.	GM 640	57	.25
with Israel Beckhardt			
The violators.	Pop 734	56	.25
BROWN, WILL C.			
The border jumpers.	Dell 878	55	.25
Guns along the Chisholm.	Pop 715	55	.25
Laredo Road.	DelF A183	59	.25
Man of the West.	Dell 986	58	.25
Trouble on the Brazos.	Eag EB91	57	.25
BROWN, WILLIAM F.			
Beat, beat, beat.	Sig S1652	59	.35
The girl in the Freudian slip.	Sig S1743	59	.35
BROWN-BURNHAM, CREIGHTON			
Born innocent.	Pyr G414	59	.35
BROWNE, ELEANORE			
The immodest maidens.	NL 26	49	.25
Innocent madame.	Lion unk	52	.25
BROWNE, HOWARD			
Thin air.	Dell 894	56	.25
BROWNE, LEWIS			
See what I mean?	Avon 54	44	.25
BROWNING, ELIZABETH BARRETT			
Sonnets from the Portuguese.	Avon 251	50	.25

Author/Title	Pub./Stock No.	Yr.	Price
BRUCE, ROBERT			
Tina.	Lion 226	54	.25
BRUFF, NANCY			
The manatee.	Pyr 24	50	.25
BRUNINI, JOHN GILLAND			
Gold Medal treasury of			
American verse.	GM S312	53	.35
BRUNNER, JOHN			
Echo in the skull.	Ace D-385	59	.35
The 100th millenium.	Ace D-362	59	.35
Threshold of eternity.	Ace D-335	59	.35
The world swappers.	Ace D-391	59	.35
BRUSH, KATHARINE			
Bad girl from Maine.	Avon 239	50	.25
Free woman.	DelT unk	51	.10
Red-headed woman.	Avon (22)	42	.25
When she was bad.	Avon 154	48	.25
Young man of Manhattan.	Avon 192	49	.25
BRYAN, JOSEPH III			
Aircraft carrier.	Ball 67	54	.35
_____.	Ball 228	57	.35
BRYAN, MICHAEL			
Intent to kill.	DelF 88	56	.25
Murder in Majorca.	DelF A145	57	.25
BRYANT, ARTHUR HERBERT			
Roadside motel.	Berk 317	55	.25
BRYANT, MATT			
Cue for murder.	Berk 333	55	.25
BRYANT, PETER			
Red alert.	Ace D-350	59	.35
BRYSON, LEIGH			
The gloved hand.	Han 61	47	.20
BUCHAN, JOHN			
Greenmantle.	PB 94	41	.25
Mountain meadow.	Ban 71	46	.25
_____.	Ban 1143	53	.25
The thirty-nine steps.	PB 69	40	.25
Three hostages.	Ban 31	46	.25
BUCHWALD, ART			
Art Buchwald's Paris.	Lion LL 80	56	.35
A gift from the boys.	Card C-350	59	.35
BUCK, FRANK with Edward Anthony			
Bring 'em back alive.	PB 47	40	.25
BUCK, PEARL S.			
The angry wife.	Card C-334	59	.35
Come, my beloved.	Card C-108	54	.35

Author/Title	Pub./Stock No.	Yr.	Price
Dragon seed.	PB 359	46	.25
God's men.	Card C-114	53	.35
The good earth.	PB 11	39	.25
_____.	Card C-111	53	.35
The hidden flower.	PB 993	54	.25
Imperial woman.	Card GC-41	58	.50
Journey for life.	DelT 8	51	.10
Kinfolk.	Card C-46	52	.35
Letter from Peking.	Card C-308	58	.35
The long love.	Card C-372	59	.35
The mother.	Pen 505	42	.25
My several worlds.	Card GC-35	56	.50
Pavilion of women.	PB 642	49	.25
_____.	Card C-105	53	.35
Peony.	PB 679	50	.25
Portrait of a marriage.	PB 951	53	.25
The promise.	Bart 21	46	.25
The townsman.	Card GC-46	58	.50
BUCKLER, ERNEST			
The mountain and the			
valley.	Sig S1090	54	.35
BUCKLEY, DAVID			
Pride of innocence.	Pop G227	58	.35
BUCKNER, ROBERT			
Sigrid and the sergeant.	Sig S1597	59	.35
BUDD, LILLIAN			
April snow.	PB 994	54	.25
BUDRYS, ALGIS			
The falling torch.	Pyr G416	59	.35
False night.	Lion 230	54	.25
Man of earth.	Ball 243	58	.35
Who?	Pyr G339	58	.35
BUGBEE, EMMA			
Peggy covers the news.	Com 6	48	.25
BULFINCH, THOMAS			
Bulfinch's mythology.	DelL LX111	59	.75
BULL, LOIS			
Broadway virgin.	NL 23	49	.25
Gold diggers.	NL 14	49	.25
BULLOCK, ALAN			
Hitler, a study in			
tyranny.	Ban F1896	58	.50
BULMER, KENNETH			
The changeling worlds.	Ace D-369	59	.35
City under the sea.	Ace D-255	57	.35
The secret of ZI.	Ace D-331	58	.35
BULOSAN, CARLOS			
The laughter of my			
father.	Ban 48	46	.25

Author/Title	Pub./Stock No.	Yr.	Price
BUNCE, FRANK			
So young a body.	PB 777	51	.25
BUNKER, ROBERT with Raymond Thorp			
Crow killer.	Sig S1691	59	.35
BUNYAN, JOHN			
The pilgrim's progress.	PBL PL53	57	.35
BURCH, GUY I. with Elmer Pendell			
Human breeding and survival.	Pel P17	47	.35
BURDICK, EUGENE			
The ninth wave.	Dell F60	57	.50
BURGAN, JOHN			
Cry attack!	Avon T-265	58	.35
BURGESS, ALAN			
The Inn of the Sixth Happiness.	Ban A1800	58	.35
BURGESS, JOHN H.			
Blue Earth.	Sig S1141	54	.35
BURKE, JACK			
The natural way to better golf.	Ban 1311	55	.25
BURKE, JAMES WAKEFIELD			
The big rape.	Pop G126	53	.35
	Lion LL 135	56	.35
_____.	Pop 766	56	.25
Fraulein Lili Marlene.	Pop 766	56	.25
Of a strange woman.	Pyr 164	55	.25
Taboo.	Pyr G263	57	.35
with Edward Grace			
Three day pass--to kill.	Berk 106	55	.25
_____.	Berk G-164	58	.35
BURKE, NOEL			
The shivering bough.	Bart 7	44	.25
BURKE, RICHARD			
Chinese Red.	Dell 260	48	.25
The fourth star.	Han 64	47	.20
The frightened pigeon.	Dell 204	47	.25
Here lies the body.	Pop 310	51	.25
BURLINGAME, ROGER			
Benjamin Franklin.	SigK K321	55	.25
General Billy Mitchell.	Sig S1280	56	.35
Henry Ford.	SigK K337	56	.25
Machines that built America.	SigK Ks327	55	.35
BURMAN, BEN LUCIEN			
The four lives of Mundy Tolliver.	Ban A1439	56	.35
Steamboat round the bend.	PB 363	46	.25

Author/Title	Pub./Stock No.	Yr.	Price
BURNETT, HALLIE (SOUTHGATE)			
The brain pickers.	Dell D237	58	.35
This heart, this hunter.	Pop 541	53	.25
with Whit Burnett			
19 tales of terror.	Ban A1550	57	.35
The tough ones.	Eag EB28	54	.25
_____.	Pop G352	59	.35
BURNETT, W. R.			
Adobe walls.	Ban 1547	56	.25
The asphalt jungle.	PB 714	50	.25
Bitter ground.	Ban 1973	59	.25
Captain Lightfoot.	Ban A1331	55	.35
Dark hazard.	Hill 20	49	.25
High Sierra.	Ban 826	50	.25
Iron man.	Avon 212	49	.25
Little Caesar.	Avon 66	45	.25
_____.	Avon 329	51	.25
_____.	Ban A1871	59	.35
Little men, big world.	Ban 1124	53	.25
Nobody lives forever.	Ban 888	51	.25
Romelle.	Ban 942	51	.25
Stretch Dawson.	GM 106	50	.25
Tomorrow's another day.	Ban 998	52	.25
Underdog.	Ban A1819	58	.35
Vanity Row.	Pnnt P7	53	.25
BURNETT, WHIT			
The scarlet treasury of great confessions.	Pyr R361	58	.50
The story Pocket book.	PB 276	44	.25
This is my funniest.	Perm M-3094	57	.25
with Hallie Burnett			
19 tales of terror.	Ban A1550	57	.35
The tough ones.	Eag EB28	54	.25
_____.	Pop G352	59	.35
BURNS, ELIZABETH			
The late Liz.	Pop SP35	59	.50
BURNS, EUGENE			
Fresh and salt water spinning.	Dell D148	55	.35
The sex life of wild animals.	Prem d23	56	.50
BURNS, JOHN HORNE			
A cry of children.	Ban 1147	53	.25
	Pop G194	57	.35
The gallery.	Ban A807	50	.35
_____.	Ban A1146	53	.35
BURNS, ROBERT E.			
I am a fugitive from a chain gang!	Pyr 45	52	.25
BURNS, VINCENT G.			
Female convict.	Pyr 58	52	.25
_____.	Pyr 191	56	.25
_____.	Pyr G377	58	.35

Author/Title	Pub./Stock No.	Yr.	Price
BURNS, WALTER NOBLE			
The saga of Billy the Kid.	Pen 520	43	.25
_____.	Sig 1085	53	.25
Tombstone.	Pen 514	42	.25
_____.	Sig S1205	55	.35
BURROUGHS, EDGAR RICE			
The cave girl.	Dell 320	49	.25
Tarzan and the lost empire.	Dell 536	51	.25
Tarzan in the forbidden city.	BPLA 23	40	.10
BURT, KATHARINE NEWLIN			
The lady in the tower.	Dell 191	47	.25
BURT, KENDAL with James Leasor			
The one that got away.	Ball F262	58	.50
BURTON, CARL D.			
Satan's Rock.	Ban 1517	56	.25
BURTT, EDWIN A.			
The teachings of the compassionate Buddha.	Ment MD131	55	.50
BUSBEE, JAMES JR.			
Son of Egypt.	Avon AT-64	53	.35
Yankee mariner.	Avon T-73	54	.35
BUSCH, FRITZ-OTTO			
Holocaust at sea; the drama of the Scharnhorst.	Berk G-115	58	.35
BUSCH, HARALD			
U-boats at war.	Ball 120	55	.35
BUSCH, NIVEN			
The actor.	Pop 770	56	.25
Duel in the sun.	Pop 102	46	.25
_____.	Pop 489	53	.25
_____.	Eag EB94	57	.25
The furies.	Ban 777	50	.25
The hate merchant.	Ban A1204	54	.35
BUSH, RAYMOND with George Kimble			
The weather.	Pel P9	46	.25
BUTCHER, MARGARET JUST			
The Negro in American culture.	Ment MD206	57	.50
BUTLER, GERALD			
Blow hot, blow cold.	Dell 726	53	.25
Kiss the blood off my hands.	Dell 197	47	.25
The lurking man.	Lion 81	52	.25
Slippery hitch.	Dell 511	51	.25

Author/Title	Pub./Stock No.	Yr.	Price
The unafraid.	Dell 242	48	.25
BUTLER, SAMUEL			
The way of all flesh.	PB 8	39	.25
_____.	WSP W561	59	.50
BYRAM, GEORGE			
Stronger than passion.	Mon 117	59	.35
BYRNE, BRENDAN			
3 weeks to a better memory.	Ban A1414	56	.35
BYRNE, DONN			
Messer Marco Polo.	Pen 611	46	.25
BYRNE, JACK			
Gunswift.	Pop 449	52	.25
BYRON, JAMES			
TNT for two.	Ace D-197	57	.35

Author/Title	Pub./Stock No.	Yr.	Price
C			
CABELL, JAMES BRANCH			
Jurgen.	Pen 601	46	.25
CADELL, ELIZABETH			
The singing heart.	Berk G-209	59	.35
CAEN, HERB			
Baghdad-by-the-Bay.	Prmb P261	53	.35
CAESAR, GENE			
Mark of the hunter.	Pop 614	54	.25
CAIDIN, MARTIN			
Boeing 707.	Ball F322K	59	.50
Zero.	Ball F201	57	.50
with Robert S. Johnson			
Thunderbolt!	Ball F323K	59	.50
with others			
Samurai!	Ball F248	58	.50
CAIN, JAMES M.			
The butterfly.	Sig 720	49	.25
.	Sig 1195	55	.25
Career in C major.	Avon 141	47	.25
Double indemnity.	Avon 60	45	.25
.	Avon 137	47	.25
.	Sig 784	50	.25
.	Sig 1427	57	.25
The embezzler.	Avon 99	46	.25
Everybody does it and			
The embezzler.	Sig 759	49	.25
Galatea.	Sig 1152	54	.25
Jealous woman.	Avon 348	51	.25
.	Avon 479	52	.25
Love's lovely			
counterfeit.	Avon 161	48	.25
.	Avon 421	52	.25
.	Avon 581	54	.25
.	Sig 1445	57	.25
Mildred Pierce.	Pen 591	46	.25
The moth.	Sig 811	50	.25
Past all dishonor.	Sig 680	48	.25
The postman always rings			
twice.	PB 443	47	.25
The root of his evil.	Avon 455	52	.25
Serenade.	Pen 621	47	.25
.	Sig 1153	54	.25
Shameless.	Avon T-285	58	.35
Sinful woman.	Avon 174	48	.25
.	Avon 599	54	.25
.	Avon 768	57	.25
CAIN, PAUL			
Fast one.	Avon 178	48	.25
.	Avon 496	53	.25
Seven slayers.	Avon 268	50	.25
CALAHAN, H. A.			
Back to Treasure Island.	PBJr J-69	51	.35

Author/Title	Pub./Stock No.	Yr.	Price
CALDER, RITCHIE			
Medicine and man.	Ment MD217	58	.50
Science in our lives.	SigK Ks320	55	.35
CALDWELL, ERSKINE			
The bastard.	Nov 51	55	.25
Call it experience.	SigK Ks344	56	.35
Certain women.	Sig S1568	58	.35
The complete stories of			
Erskine Caldwell.	Sig D1199	55	.50
The courting of Susie			
Brown.	Sig 1016	53	.25
.	Sig S1621	58	.35
Episode in Palmetto.	Sig 983	53	.25
.	Sig S1598	58	.35
Georgia boy.	Avon 134	47	.25
.	Sig 760	50	.25
.	Sig S1666	59	.35
God's little acre.	Pen 581	46	.25
Gretta.	Sig 1342	56	.25
Gulf coast stories.	Sig S1430	57	.35
A house in the uplands.	Sig 686	48	.25
.	Sig 1456	57	.25
The humorous side of			
Erskine Caldwell.	Sig 899	51	.25
Journeyman.	Pen 646	47	.25
.	Sig S1592	58	.35
Kneel to the rising sun.	Sig 869	51	.25
.	Sig S1733	59	.35
A lamp for nightfall.	Sig 1091	54	.25
.	Sig S1672	59	.35
Love and money.	Sig 1272	56	.25
Midsummer passion.	Avon 177	48	.25
.	Avon 309	50	.25
.	Avon 340	51	.25
A place called			
Estherville.	Sig 918	52	.25
.	Sig 1479	57	.25
.	Sig S1623	59	.35
The Pocket book of			
Erskine Caldwell			
stories.	PB 392	47	.25
.	Card C-270	57	.35
The sacrilege of Alan			
Kent.	Sig S1497	58	.35
Southways.	Sig 933	52	.25
.	Sig S1734	59	.35
The sure hand of God.	Sig 732	49	.25
.	Sig S1589	58	.35
A swell-looking girl.	Sig 818	50	.25
.	Sig S1739	59	.35
This very earth.	Sig 838	51	.25
.	Sig 1417	57	.25
.	Sig S1564	58	.35
Tobacco road.	Pen 627	47	.25
Tragic ground.	PenN 661	48	.25
.	Sig S1611	59	.35
Trouble in July.	Pen 567	45	.25
.	Sig S1608	58	.35
We are the living.	Sig 1136	54	.25
.	Sig S1735	59	.35

Author/Title	Pub./Stock No.	Yr.	Price
CALDWELL, ERSKINE (cont.)			
Where the girls were different.	Avon 151	48	.25
A woman in the house.	Sig 705	49	.25
CALDWELL, JAY THOMAS			
Me an' you.	Lion 220	54	.25
CALDWELL, TAYLOR			
Dynasty of death.	Card C-252	57	.35
The earth is the Lord's.	Ban A956	52	.35
_____.	Ban F1702	57	.50
The final hour.	Card C-311	58	.35
Maggie--her marriage.	GM 288	53	.25
Melissa.	Ban A1139	53	.35
Never victorious, never defeated.	Card C-202	56	.35
The sound of thunder.	Ban S1879	59	.75
The strong city.	Card C-274	58	.35
Tender victory.	Card C-245	57	.35
This side of innocence.	Ban A760	50	.35
Your sins and mine.	GM 525	55	.25
CALET, HENRI			
Paris, my love.	Berk G-20	56	.35
Young man of Paris.	Berk G-28	56	.35
CALITRI, CHARLES			
Rickey.	Pop 503	53	.25
Strike heaven on the face.	Sig D1746	59	.50
CALLAGHAN, MORLEY			
The loved and the lost.	Sig 944	52	.25
_____.	Sig S1689	59	.35
CALLAHAN, JOHN			
Bad blood at Black Range.	Ace D-192	56	.35
Land beyond the law.	Ace D-288	58	.35
The rawhide breed.	Ace D-252	57	.35
The sidewinders.	Ace D-24	53	.35
Texas fury.	Dell 677	53	.25
_____.	Crst 205	58	.25
CALLVERT, ISABEL E. with James Beard			
The James Beard cookbook.	Dell X1	59	.75
CALMER, NED			
The strange land.	Sig S851	51	.35
_____.	Sig D1355	56	.50
CAMERER, DAVID			
The damned wear wings.	Crst s280	59	.35
CAMERON, BRUCE			
The sins of Maria.	Pop G373	59	.35
CAMERON, DON			
Dig another grave.	Han 86	49	.25
White for a shroud.	BH unk	48	.25
CAMERON, OWEN			
The butcher's wife.	Dell 896	56	.25
Catch a tiger.	Ban 1195	54	.25
The demon stirs.	Dell 983	58	.25
The mountains have no shadow.	Ban 1101	53	.25
CAMPBELL, E. SIMMS			
Chorus of cuties.	Avon 499	53	.25
CAMPBELL, GEORGE			
Cry for happy.	Ban A1899	59	.35
CAMPBELL, JOHN W. JR.			
Astounding science fiction anthology.	Berk G-41	56	.35
Astounding tales of space and time.	Berk G-47	57	.35
Who goes there?	Dell D150	55	.35
CAMPBELL, THORA with Beth Bailey McLean			
Martha Logan's meat cook book.	PB 852	52	.25
CAMPBELL, WILLIAM T.			
Big beverage.	Prmb P249	53	.35
CANBY, COURTLANDT			
Lincoln and the Civil War.	DelL LC108	58	.50
with Nancy E. Gross			
The world of history.	Ment M109	54	.35
CANIZIO, FRANK with Robert Markel			
A man against fate.	Perm M-4133	59	.35
CANNAN, JOANNA			
A taste of murder.	Dell 596	52	.25
CANNAVALE, RENATO			
Desire in the streets.	Pop 658	55	.25
CANNING, VICTOR			
Bird of prey.	Ban 1177	54	.25
The captives of Mora Island.	Perm M-4139	59	.35
The chasm.	Ban 313	49	.25
The forbidden road.	Perm M-4121	59	.35
A forest of eyes.	Ban 948	51	.25
The golden salamander.	Ban 834	50	.25
Panther's moon.	Ban 734	50	.25
Twist of the knife.	Berk 377	57	.25
CANNON, CORNELIA JAMES			
Red rust.	PB 623	49	.25
CANNON, CURT			
I like 'em tough.	GM 743	58	.25
I'm Cannon--for hire.	GM 814	58	.25

Author/Title	Pub./Stock No.	Yr.	Price
CANNON, LE GRAND JR.			
Look to the mountain.	Ban A933	51	.35
CANT, GILBERT			
This is the navy.	PenS S227	44	.25
————.	PenS S239	44	.25
CANTRELL, WADE B.			
Brand of Cain.	Pyr 173	55	.25
CANTUS, HOLLY			
The Pocket book of household hints.	Perm M-4131	59	.35
ČAPEK, KAREL			
War with the newts.	Ban A1292	55	.35
————.	BanC FC46	59	.50
CAPOTE, TRUMAN			
Breakfast at Tiffany's.	Sig D1727	59	.50
The glass harp.	Sig 1020	53	.25
The glass harp and A tree of night.	Sig S1333	56	.35
Other voices, other rooms.	Sig 700	49	.25
A tree of night.	Sig 878	51	.25
CAPP, AL			
The life and times of the Shmoo.	PB 621	49	.25
The world of Li'l Abner.	Ball 8	53	.35
————.	Ball 172	56	.35
————.	Ball 350K	59	.35
CAPRIO, FRANK S.			
Unfaithful.	Prem s38	56	.35
Why we behave as we do.	Pop 595	54	.25
CARCO, FRANCIS			
Depravity.	Berk G-81	57	.35
Infamy.	Berk G-140	58	.35
Only a woman.	Berk 337	55	.25
————.	Berk 369	57	.25
————.	Berk G-174	58	.35
Perversity.	Avon 302	51	.25
————.	Avon 401	52	.25
————.	Berk G-33	56	.35
————.	Berk G-155	58	.35
Rue Pigalle.	Avon 555	54	.25
CARDER, MICHAEL			
Action at War Bow Valley.	Pnnt P14	53	.25
Cimarron crossing.	Ban 1057	52	.25
Decision at sundown.	Ace D-160	56	.35
Return of the outlaw.	Ban 1639	57	.25
CARDOZO, PETER			
A wonderful world for children.	Ban A1464	56	.35
with Lilli Taylor			
A wonderful world for children, no. 2.	Ban A1790	58	.35
CAREN, ELLEN			
Mirabelle: woman of passion.	NL 22	49	.25
CAREY, ERNESTINE with Frank B. Gilbreth Jr.			
Cheaper by the dozen.	Ban 960	51	.25
————.	Ban A2073	59	.35
CAREY, MICHAEL			
The vice net.	Avon 809	58	.25
Vice squad cop.	Avon 763	57	.25
CARGOE, RICHARD			
Brave harvest.	Ball 95	55	.35
Girl in the red dress.	Graf 103	55	.25
Maharaja.	Pop 451	52	.25
CARHART, ARTHUR			
Fresh water fishing.	Dell D134	54	.35
CARLAW, BOGART			
The wild place.	Lion LL 22	55	.35
CARLETON, MARJORIE			
Cry wolf.	Ban 98	47	.25
CARLEY, CLYDE			
Cartoon laffs from True.	GM 249	52	.25
CARLOVA, JOHN			
Adam and evil.	Berk G-167	58	.35
CARMICHAEL, JOHN			
My greatest day in baseball.	Ban 500	48	.25
CARNEGIE, DALE			
How to develop self-confidence.	Card C-237	56	.35
How to stop worrying and start living.	Card C-112	53	.35
How to win friends and influence people.	PB 68	40	.25
————.	Card C-303	58	.35
Little known facts about well known people.	Pop 182	49	.25
The unknown Lincoln.	PB 891	52	.25
CARNEGIE, MRS. DALE			
How to help your husband get ahead.	Pyr R237	57	.35
CARNEY, OTIS			
The country club set.	Perm M-4105	58	.35
CARPENTER, JOHN JO			
Signal guns at Sunup.	PB 834	51	.25

Author/Title	Pub./Stock No.	Yr.	Price
CARPENTER, MARGARET			
Experiment perilous.	PB 278	45	.25
CARR, HARRIETT H.			
Sharon.	Berk G276	59	.35
CARR, JOHN DICKSON			
The Arabian nights murder.	Hill 1	43	.25
Below suspicion.	Ban 1119	53	.25
The blind barber.	Pen 528	43	.25
	Berk G-80	57	.35
The bride of Newgate.	Avon 476	52	.25
The burning court.	Pop 28	44	.25
	Ban 1207	54	.25
Captain Cut-throat.	Ban A1472	56	.35
The case of the constant suicides.	Dell 91	45	.25
	Berk G-60	57	.35
Castle Skull.	PB 448	47	.25
The corpse in the waxworks.	Avon (33)	43	.25
	Dell 775	54	.25
	Berk G-143	58	.35
The crooked hinge.	Pop 19	43	.25
	Dell 859	55	.25
	Berk G-157	58	.35
Death turns the tables.	PB 350	46	.25
	Berk G281	59	.35
Death-watch.	Dell 564	52	.25
	Berk G-101	58	.35
The Devil in velvet.	Ban A1009	52	.35
The eight of swords.	Berk G-48	57	.35
The emperor's snuff-box.	PB 372	46	.25
	Berk G287	59	.35
Fire, burn!	Ban A1847	59	.35
The four false weapons.	Pop 282	50	.25
	Berk G-91	57	.35
Hag's nook.	Pen 532	44	.25
	Dell 537	51	.25
	Berk G-129	58	.35
He who whispers.	Ban 896	51	.25
	Ban 1684	57	.25
It walks by night.	PB 101	41	.25
	Avon 621	55	.25
The lost gallows.	PB 436	47	.25
The mad hatter mystery.	Pop 61	45	.25
	Dell 706	53	.25
	Berk G-117	58	.35
The man who could not shudder.	Ban 365	49	.25
	Ban 1504	56	.25
The nine wrong answers.	Ban 1325	55	.25
Patrick Butler for the defense.	Ban 1682	57	.25
Poison in jest.	Pop 349	51	.25
	Berk G-72	57	.35
The problem of the green capsule.	Ban 101	47	.25
	Ban 1505	56	.25
The problem of the wire cage.	Ban 304	48	.25
	Ban 1503	56	.25
The sleeping sphinx.	Ban 996	52	.25
	Ban A1849	58	.35
The third bullet.	Ban 1447	56	.25
The three coffins.	Pop 174	49	.25
Till death do us part.	Ban 793	50	.25
	Ban 1683	57	.25
To wake the dead.	Pop 10	43	.25
	Dell 635	52	.25
	Berk G-42	56	.35
with Adrian Conan Doyle			
The exploits of Sherlock Holmes.	Ace D-181	56	.35
CARR, ROBERT SPENCER			
Beyond infinity.	Dell 781	54	.25
CARRIER, WARREN			
A hell of a murder.	Avon T-283	58	.35
The lost and the damned.	Berk 375	57	.25
CARROLL, CURT			
The golden herd.	PB 837	52	.25
CARROLL, LEWIS			
Alice in Wonderland and other favorites.	PB 835	51	.25
CARROLL, RICHARD with Gregory Mason			
Border woman.	Lion 59	51	.25
CARSE, ROBERT			
The Devil's spawn.	DelF 95	56	.25
Drums of empire.	Pop G357	59	.35
End to innocence.	Mon 129	59	.35
The fabulous buccaneer.	DelF B109	57	.35
From the sea and the jungle.	Pop G102	52	.35
	Pop G244	58	.35
Great circle.	Ban A1820	58	.35
The wicked blade.	Pop G284	58	.35
Woman of the night.	Berk G257	59	.35
CARSON, RACHEL L.			
The edge of the sea.	Ment MD242	59	.50
The sea around us.	Ment M100	54	.35
	Ment MD272	59	.50
Under the sea wind.	Ment M128	55	.35
CARSON, ROBERT			
The bride saw red.	Ban 307	48	.25
The celluloid jungle.	Prmb P269S	54	.50
I take all.	Pop 562	54	.25
Love affair.	Pop SP49	59	.50
Stranger in our midst.	Pop 496	53	.25
You got to stay happy.	PB 538	49	.25
CARTER, HODDING			
The winds of fear.	Pop 300	50	.25

Author/Title	Pub./Stock No.	Yr.	Price
CARTER, MAX			
Call me killer.	Avon 542	53	.25
CARTER, ROSS			
Those devils in baggy			
pants.	Sig 972	52	.25
_____.	Sig S1466	57	.35
CARTMELL, VAN H. with Charles Grayson			
The golden Argosy.	Ban F1441	56	.50
CARTOON fun from True.	GM 383	54	.25
_____.	GM 904	59	.25
CARUSO, JOSEPH			
The priest.	Pop G234	58	.35
CARY, JOYCE			
Herself surprised.	Dell D153	55	.35
CASANOVA, GIACOMO			
The affairs of Casanova.	Pyr R316	58	.50
Casanova's memoirs.	Hill 3	48	.25
The memoirs of Casanova.	BanB FB415	57	.50
CASPARY, VERA			
Bedelia.	Pop 111	47	.25
The husband.	Pyr G400	59	.35
Laura.	Pop 284	50	.25
_____.	Dell D188	57	.35
The weeping and the			
laughter.	Pop 373	51	.25
CASSIDAY, BRUCE			
The brass shroud.	Ace D-285	58	.35
The buried motive.	Ace D-253	57	.35
While murder waits.	Graf 145	57	.25
CASSILL, R. V.			
The buccaneer.	Avon T-293	59	.35
Dormitory women.	Lion 216	54	.25
	Sig 1646	59	.25
_____.			
The hungering shame.	Avon 686	56	.25
Lustful summer.	Avon T-281	58	.35
Naked morning.	Avon T-173	57	.35
A taste of sin.	Ace S-136	55	.25
Tempest.	GM d852	59	.50
The wife next door.	GM 921	59	.25
The wound of love.	Avon 710	56	.25
with Eric Protter			
Left bank of desire.	Ace S-104	55	.25
CASSON, MEL with Alfred Andriola			
Ever since Adam and Eve.	Sig 1361	57	.25
CASTILLO, CARLOS et al.			
The University of Chicago			
Spanish-English, English-			
Spanish dictionary.	PB 715	50	.35
_____.	Card C-122	<u>53</u>	.35

Author/Title	Pub./Stock No.	Yr.	Price
CASTLE, FRANK			
Border buccaneers.	Ace D-112	55	.35
Dakota boomtown.	GM 752	58	.25
Dead and kicking.	GM 605	56	.25
Fort Desperation.	GM 816	58	.25
Gun talk at Yuma.	GM 679	57	.25
Lovely--and lethal.	GM 695	57	.25
Move along, stranger.	GM 275	53	.25
Murder in red.	GM 709	57	.25
Vengeance under law.	GM 636	57	.25
The violent hours.	GM 554	56	.25
CASTLE, JEFFERY LLOYD			
Satellite E One.	Ban A1766	58	.35
CASTLE, JOHN			
The password is courage.	Ball 221	57	.35
CASTLE, MARIAN			
The golden fury.	PB 785	51	.25
Roxana.	Card C-227	56	.35
CATANZARO, ANGELA			
The home book of Italian			
cooking.	Prem s41	57	.35
_____.	Crst s183	57	.35
CATER, DOUGLASS with Marquis W. Childs			
Ethics in a business			
society.	Ment M107	54	.35
CATHARINE II, EMPRESS OF RUSSIA			
The memoirs of Catherine			
the Great.	BanB FB410	57	.50
CATLIN, RALPH			
Good-by to gunsmoke.	Dell 913	56	.25
CATTO, MAX			
All or nothing.	Eag EB66	56	.25
Gold in the sky.	Pop G299	59	.35
CATTON, BRUCE			
A stillness at			
Appomattox.	Card GC-48	58	.50
CAULFIELD, M. F.			
The black city.	Sig 1164	54	.25
CAUSEY, JAMES O.			
The baby doll murders.	GM 698	57	.25
Killer, take all!	Graf 147	57	.25
CAVANAH, FRANCES with Ruth Weir			
Dell book of jokes.	Dell 89	45	.25
Liberty laughs.	Dell 38	44	.25
CAVANAUGH, JAMES			
The big gun.	Pyr 208	56	.25

Author/Title	Pub./Stock No.	Yr.	Price
CAVANNA, BETTY			
Black spaniel mystery.	PBJr J-61	51	.25
Puppy stakes.	Com 32	49	.25
CECILIA, SISTER with William Brinkley			
The deliverance of Sister Cecilia.	Sig S1420	57	.35
CELA, CAMILO JOSÉ			
The hive.	Sig S1157	54	.35
CÉLINE, LOUIS-FERDINAND			
Death on the installment plan.	Avon G-1022	55	.50
Journey to the end of the night.	Avon G-1014	54	.50
CELLINI, BENVENUTO			
Autobiography of Benvenuto Cellini.	PB 42	40	.25
_____.	BanB FB404	56	.50
Cellini.	Pyr 100	53	.25
CERF, BENNETT			
Anything for a laugh.	Ban 57	46	.25
Good for a laugh.	Ban A1231	54	.35
Laughter, incorporated.	Ban 1010	52	.25
_____.	Ban 1166	53	.25
_____.	Ban A1342	55	.35
The life of the party.	Ban A1732	58	.35
The Pocket book of cartoons.	PB 233	43	.25
The Pocket book of jokes.	PB 294	45	.25
The Pocket book of modern American plays.	PB 145	42	.25
The Pocket book of war humor.	PB 197	43	.25
Shake well before using.	Ban 901	51	.25
Try and stop me.	PB 596	49	.25
The unexpected.	Ban 502	48	.25
CERVANTES, MIGUEL de			
Don Quixote.	Ment MD207	57	.50
_____.	PBL PL517	57	.50
CHABER, M. E.			
All the way down.	Pop 530	53	.25
Don't get caught.	Pop 482	53	.25
A hearse of another color.	PB 1259	59	.25
The lady came to kill.	PB 1240	59	.25
A lonely walk.	Ace D-225	57	.35
The man inside.	Pop G282	58	.35
Now it's my turn.	Pop 632	54	.25
The splintered man.	Perm M-3080	57	.25
CHADWICK, JOSEPH			
Come out shooting.	GM 374	54	.25
Devil's legacy.	GM 261	52	.25
Double cross.	GM 245	52	.25

Author/Title	Pub./Stock No.	Yr.	Price
The golden frame.	GM 493	55	.25
Gunsmoke reckoning.	GM 149	51	.25
_____.	GM 314	53	.25
Rebel raider.	GM 442	54	.25
Renegade gun.	GM 390	54	.25
Rider from nowhere.	GM 174	51	.25
_____.	GM 338	53	.25
Savage breed.	GM 857	59	.25
A town to tame.	GM 722	58	.25
Whip hand.	GM 284	53	.25
CHAFFIN, JAMES B.			
Guns of Abilene.	Pop G314	59	.35
CHAMALES, TOM T.			
Never so few.	Sig T1645	59	.75
CHAMBERLAIN, ANNE			
Possessed.	Pyr G454	59	.35
The tall dark man.	Dell 925	56	.25
CHAMBERLAIN, ELINOR			
The far command.	Ball 32	53	.35
CHAMBERLAIN, GEORGE AGNEW			
The phantom filly.	PB 347	46	.25
The red house.	Pop 116	47	.25
CHAMBERLAIN, WILLIAM			
Trumpets of Company K.	Ball 76	54	.35
CHAMBERS, DANA			
The blonde died first.	Han 22	44	.15
Darling, this is death.	Han 51	46	.15
Death against Venus.	Han 57	46	.20
The frightened man.	Han 28	44	.15
The last secret.	Han 34	45	.15
She'll be dead by morning.	Pop 238	50	.25
_____.	Eag EB5	53	.25
Some day I'll kill you.	Pop 177	49	.25
_____.	Pop 554	54	.25
CHAMBERS, WHITMAN			
The come-on.	Pyr 74	53	.25
In savage surrender.	Mon 139	59	.35
Season for love.	Mon 122	59	.35
CHAMBLISS, WILLIAM C.			
Boomerang!	Inf J101	45	.25
_____.	Ban 156	48	.25
The silent service.	Sig S1658	59	.35
CHAMPION, D. L.			
Run the wild river.	Lion 117	53	.25
CHAMPION, SELWYN GURNEY with Dorothy Short			
Readings from world religions.	Prem d85	59	.50

Author/Title	Pub./Stock No.	Yr.	Price
CHANCE, JOHN NEWTON			
Up to her neck.	Pop 646	55	.25
CHANDLER, RAYMOND			
The big sleep.	Avon (38)	43	.25
	PB 696	50	.25
Farewell, my lovely.	PB 212	43	.25
Finger man.	Avon 219	50	.25
Five murderers.	Avon 63	45	.25
Five sinister characters.	Avon 88	46	.25
The high window.	PB 320	45	.25
The lady in the lake.	PB 389	46	.25
	Card C-344	59	.35
The little sister.	PB 750	51	.25
The long goodbye.	PB 1044	55	.25
	Card C-213	56	.35
Pick-up on Noon Street.	PB 846	52	.25
The simple art of murder.	PB 916	53	.25
Trouble is my business.	PB 823	51	.25
CHANDOHA, WALTER with Rhar Dee			
Catnips at love and			
marriage.	GM 160	51	.25
CHANSLOR, ROY			
Hazard.	Ban 474	49	.25
Johnny Guitar.	PB 1017	54	.25
The naked I.	Pop 641	55	.25
CHAPIN, VICTOR			
Career.	DelF B148	59	.35
CHAPLIN, J. P.			
Rumor, fear and the			
madness of crowds.	Ball 347K	59	.35
CHAPMAN, MARION			
Loves of Goya.	Pyr 82	53	.25
CHAPMAN, MARISTAN			
Rogue's march.	Avon T-231	58	.35
CHARBONNEAU, LOUIS			
Night of violence.	Crst 303	59	.25
No place on earth.	Crst s342	59	.35
CHARLSON, DAVID			
Frenchie.	Zen ZB-34	59	.35
CHARNWOOD, LORD			
Abraham Lincoln.	PB 19	39	.25
	Card C-51	52	.35
CHARTERIS, LESLIE			
The ace of knaves.	Avon 663	55	.25
Alias the Saint.	Avon 818	58	.25
Arrest the Saint!	Prmb P124	51	.35
	Avon 708	56	.25
The avenging Saint.	Avon 147	48	.25
	Avon 518	53	.25

Author/Title	Pub./Stock No.	Yr.	Price
Call for the Saint.	Avon 526	53	.25
Concerning the Saint.	Avon 834	58	.25
Death stops at a			
tourist's camp.	SML 124	59	.35
Enter the Saint.	PB 257	44	.25
	Avon 718	56	.25
Featuring the Saint.	Avon 803	58	.25
Follow the Saint.	Avon 533	53	.25
The frightened			
millionaire.	SML 121	59	.35
The happy highwayman.	PB 272	45	.25
Murder in the family.	SML 123	59	.35
Murder made in Moscow.	SML 122	59	.35
Red snow at Darjeeling.	SML 125	59	.35
The Saint and Mr. Teal.	Avon 629	55	.25
The Saint and the last			
hero.	Avon 544	53	.25
The Saint and the			
sizzling saboteur.	Avon 744	56	.25
The Saint around the			
world.	Perm M-3103	58	.25
The Saint at the			
thieves' picnic.	Avon 347	51	.25
	Avon 440	52	.25
The Saint cleans up.	Avon 848	59	.25
Saint errant.	Avon 588	54	.25
The Saint goes on.	Avon (34)	43	.25
	Avon 653	55	.25
The Saint goes West.	Avon 130	48	.25
	Avon 420	52	.25
	Avon 635	54	.25
The Saint in action.	Avon 118	47	.25
	Avon 463	52	.25
The Saint in England.	Avon T-250	58	.35
The Saint in Europe.	Avon 611	54	.25
The Saint in Miami.	Avon T-234	58	.35
The Saint in New York.	Avon 44	44	.25
	Avon 321	51	.25
	Avon T-317	59	.35
The Saint intervenes.	Avon 71	45	.25
The Saint meets his			
match.	Avon 489	53	.25
The Saint meets the			
Tiger.	Avon 477	52	.25
The Saint on guard.	Avon 827	58	.25
The Saint on the Spanish			
Main.	Avon 771	57	.25
Saint overboard.	Pop (1)	43	.25
	Avon 432	52	.25
The Saint sees it			
through.	Avon 341	51	.25
	Avon 619	54	.25
The Saint steps in.	Avon 610	54	.25
The Saint—the brighter			
buccaneer.	Avon 756	57	.25
The Saint—the happy			
highwayman.	Avon 680	55	.25
The Saint vs. Scotland			
Yard.	Avon T-199	57	.35
The Saint—wanted for			
murder.	Avon 694	56	.25

Author/Title	Pub./Stock No.	Yr.	Price
CHARTERIS, LESLIE (cont.)			
Saint's getaway.	Avon 473	52	.25
Stairway to murder.	SML 118	59	.35
Thanks to the Saint.	PB 1233	59	.25
Witness to death.	SML 119	59	.35
CHASE, ALLAN			
Shadow of a hero.	Pop 335	51	.25
CHASE, BORDEN			
Lone star.	GM 236	52	.25
Red River.	Ban 205	48	.25
_____.	Ban 1725	58	.25
CHASE, ILKA			
In bed we cry.	Avon 140	47	.25
New York 22.	PB 879	52	.25
Past imperfect.	PB 404	46	.25
CHASE, JAMES HADLEY			
The case of the strangled starlet.	Sig 1586	58	.25
Dead ringer.	Ace D-135	55	.35
The double shuffle.	Sig 1112	54	.25
The guilty are afraid.	Sig 1749	59	.25
I'll bury my dead.	Sig 1187	55	.25
Kiss my fist!	Eton E112	52	.25
The marijuana mob.	Eton E116	52	.25
No orchids for Miss Blandish.	Avon 355	51	.25
Shock treatment.	Sig 1696	59	.25
Too dangerous to be free.	Avon A436	52	.25
12 Chinamen and a woman.	NL 37	50	.25
12 Chinks and a woman.	Avon 485	52	.25
The villain and the virgin.	NL 11	49	.25
You're lonely when you're dead.	Pop 378	51	.25
CHASE, MARY ELLEN			
A goodly heritage.	Avon 73	45	.25
CHASE, RICHARD			
American folk tales and songs.	SigK KD340	56	.50
CHATTERTON, RUTH			
Homeward borne.	PB 830	51	.25
CHAUCER, GEOFFREY			
Canterbury tales.	BanC FC24	59	.50
CHAVES NOGALES, MANUEL			
with Juan Belmonte y García			
Juan Belmonte: killer of bulls.	Ban A1160	53	.35
CHAVIS, ROBERT			
The terror package.	Ace D-221	57	.35
CHAYEFSKY, PADDY			
The bachelor party.	Sig S1385	57	.35
Middle of the night.	Ban A1966	59	.35
CHAZE, ELLIOTT			
Black wings has my angel.	GM 296	53	.25
Love on the rocks.	Berk G-26	56	.35
_____.	Berk G-217	59	.35
The stainless steel kimono.	Perm M-3011	55	.25
CHEEVER, JOHN			
The enormous radio and other stories.	Berk G-119	58	.35
The Wapshot chronicle.	Ban F1833	58	.50
CHEKHOV, ANTON			
Four great plays.	BanC FC5	58	.50
Great stories by Chekhov.	DelL LC126	59	.50
The kiss <u>and</u> The duel.	Avon T-120	56	.35
CHELTON, JOHN			
My deadly angel.	GM 524	55	.25
CHENEY, L. J.			
A history of the Western World.	Ment MD274	59	.50
CHESHIRE, GIFF			
Starlight Basin.	Ban 1612	57	.25
Year of the gun.	DelF A147	57	.25
CHESSER, EUSTACE			
How to make a success of your marriage.	SigK K301	54	.25
Love without fear.	Sig 751	49	.25
CHESSMAN, CARYL			
Cell 2455, Death Row.	Perm M-4063	56	.35
CHESTERTON, G. K.			
The amazing adventures of Father Brown.	Dell 819	55	.25
_____.	Dell D230	58	.35
The Pocket book of Father Brown.	PB 236	43	.25
The scandal of Father Brown.	PB 60	40	.25
The secret of Father Brown.	Pop 153	48	.25
CHEVALLIER, GABRIEL			
The affairs of Flavie.	Ban A1044	52	.35
Scandals of Clochemerle.	Ban 141	48	.25
_____.	Ban 1377	55	.25
The wicked village.	Dell D195	57	.35
CHEYNEY, PETER			
The case of the dark hero.	Avon 123	47	.25

Author/Title	Pub./Stock No.	Yr.	Price
CHEYNEY, PETER (cont.)			
The case of the dark hero.	Avon 734	56	.25
Case of the dark wanton.	Avon T-212	58	.35
Cocktails and the killer.	Avon 797	57	.25
Counterspy murders.	Avon 699	56	.25
Dark interlude.	Ban 730	49	.25
The dark street murders.	Avon 93	46	.25
_____.	Avon 764	57	.25
I'll bring her back.	Eton E115	52	.25
The London spy murders.	Avon 49	44	.25
The man nobody saw.	Avon 712	56	.25
Mistress murder.	Avon 349	51	.25
Set-up for murder.	Pyr 16	50	.25
Sinister errand.	Avon 114	47	.25
Sinister murders.	Avon 776	57	.25
The terrible night.	Avon T-365	59	.35
Undressed to kill.	Avon T-314	59	.35
The unscrupulous Mr. Callaghan.	Han 18	43	.15
You can't keep the change.	Avon 80	46	.25
CHIDSEY, DONALD BARR			
Buccaneer's blade.	Ace D-410	59	.35
Captain Adam.	Avon T-81	54	.35
_____.	Avon T-134	56	.35
Captain Bashful.	Graf G214	56	.35
Captain Crossbones.	Ace D-318	58	.35
The flaming island.	Ace D-394	59	.35
His Majesty's highwayman.	Perm M-4129	59	.35
Lord of the Isles.	Avon T-96	55	.35
_____.	Avon T-318	59	.35
The naked sword.	Avon T-305	59	.35
Nobody heard the shot.	BPLA 25	41	.10
Panama passage.	Prmb P248	53	.35
The pipes are calling.	Ace D-364	59	.35
Singapore passage.	DelF 107	56	.25
Stronghold.	Prmb P174	52	.35
This bright sword.	Ace D-278	58	.35
CHILDE, V. GORDON			
Man makes himself.	Ment M64	51	.35
_____.	Ment MD154	55	.50
What happened in history.	Pel P6	46	.25
CHILDERS, ERSKINE			
The riddle of the sands.	PB 84	40	.25
CHILDERS, JAMES with James Street			
Tomorrow we reap.	Card C-74	53	.35
CHILDS, MARQUIS W.			
Sweden: the middle way.	Pel P24	48	.35
with Douglass Cater			
Ethics in a business society.	Ment M107	54	.35
CHIN KEE ONN			
Silent army.	Ball 37	53	.35

Author/Title	Pub./Stock No.	Yr.	Price
CHOJNOWSKA, WLDYSLAWA			
Polish nights.	Mon K51	59	.50
CHOUINARD, J. JEROD			
Conducted to a grave.	Ban A1928	59	.35
The hangman's overture.	Pnnt P78	55	.25
Rhapsody in death.	Ban 1202	54	.25
Sonata with bullets.	Ban 1829	58	.25
A very silent symphony.	Ban 1501	56	.25
CHRISTENSEN, ERWIN O.			
The history of Western art.	Ment MT262	59	.75
CHRISTIAN, PAULA			
Edge of twilight.	Crst s267	59	.35
CHRISTIE, AGATHA			
The ABC murders.	PB 88	41	.25
And then there were none.	PB 261	44	.25
_____.	Card C-360	59	.35
Appointment with death.	Dell 105	46	.25
_____.	Dell D236	58	.35
The big four.	Avon (3)	41	.25
_____.	Avon 245	50	.25
_____.	Avon 690	56	.25
The blue geranium.	BPLA 26	41	.10
The body in the library.	PB 341	46	.25
The boomerang clue.	Dell 46	44	.25
_____.	Dell 664	53	.25
Cards on the table.	Dell 293	49	.25
_____.	Dell 912	56	.25
Crooked house.	PB 753	50	.25
Dead man's folly.	PB 1174	57	.25
Dead man's mirror.	Dell D235	58	.35
Death comes as the end.	PB 465	47	.25
_____.	Card C-335	59	.35
Death in the air.	Avon 89	46	.25
_____.	Avon 379	51	.25
_____.	Avon 658	55	.25
Death on the Nile.	Avon 46	44	.25
_____.	Avon 317	51	.25
_____.	Avon T-149	56	.35
Easy to kill.	PB 319	45	.25
Evil under the sun.	PB 285	45	.25
Funerals are fatal.	PB 1003	54	.25
Hickory dickory death.	PB 1151	57	.25
A holiday for murder.	Avon 124	47	.25
_____.	Avon 443	52	.25
_____.	Avon 616	54	.25
_____.	Avon T-176	57	.35
The hollow.	PB 485	48	.25
The labors of Hercules.	Dell 491	51	.25
_____.	Dell D305	59	.35
The man in the brown suit.	Dell 319	49	.25
_____.	Dell D249	58	.35
Mr. Parker Pyne, detective.	Dell 550	51	.25
_____.	Dell 961	57	.25

Author/Title	Pub./Stock No.	Yr.	Price
CHRISTIE, AGATHA (cont.)			
The moving finger.	Avon 164	48	.25
.	Avon 636	54	.25
.	Avon 793	57	.25
Mrs. McGinty's dead.	PB 956	53	.25
Murder after hours.	Dell 753	54	.25
Murder at Hazelmoor.	Dell 391	50	.25
.	Dell 937	57	.25
Murder at the Vicarage.	Dell 226	48	.25
.	Dell 888	56	.25
Murder in Mesopotamia.	Dell 145	47	.25
.	Dell 805	54	.25
Murder in retrospect.	Dell 257	48	.25
.	Dell 871	55	.25
Murder in the Calais coach.	PB 79	40	.25
Murder in three acts.	Avon 61	45	.25
.	Avon 316	51	.25
.	Avon 648	55	.25
.	Avon T-243	58	.35
A murder is announced.	PB 820	51	.25
.	Card C-362	59	.35
The murder of Roger Ackroyd.	PB 5	39	.25
Murder on the links.	Dell 454	50	.25
.	Dell D288	59	.35
Murder with mirrors.	PB 1021	54	.25
The mysterious affair at Styles.	Avon 75	45	.25
.	Avon 312	51	.25
.	Avon T-204	57	.35
The mysterious Mr. Quin.	Dell 570	52	.25
.	Dell D326	59	.35
The mystery of the Baghdad chest.	BPLA unk	43	.10
The mystery of the blue train.	PB 38	40	.25
The mystery of the crime in Cabin 66.	BPLA unk	43	.10
N or M?	Dell 187	47	.25
An overdose of death.	Dell 683	53	.25
The patriotic murders.	PB 249	44	.25
Peril at End house.	PB 167	42	.25
.	Card C-349	59	.35
A pocket full of rye.	PB 1036	55	.25
Poirot investigates.	Avon 716	56	.25
Poirot loses a client.	Avon 70	45	.25
.	Avon 353	51	.25
.	Avon T-192	57	.35
The regatta mystery.	Avon 85	46	.25
.	Avon 371	51	.25
.	Avon T-220	58	.35
Remembered death.	PB 451	47	.25
.	Card C-312	58	.35
Sad cypress.	Dell 172	47	.25
.	Dell 529	51	.25
.	Dell D217	58	.35
The secret adversary.	Avon 100	46	.25
.	Avon 410	52	.25
.	Avon T-210	58	.35
The secret of chimneys.	Dell 199	47	.25
.	Dell D262	59	.35
Seven dials mystery.	Avon T-167	57	.35
So many steps to death.	PB 1114	56	.25
There is a tide.	PB 617	49	.25
.	Dell 830	55	.25
They came to Baghdad.	PB 897	52	.25
Thirteen at dinner.	Dell 60	44	.25
.	Dell 770	54	.25
Three blind mice.	Dell 633	52	.25
Towards zero.	PB 398	47	.25
.	Card C-361	59	.35
The Tuesday Club murders.	Dell 8	43	.25
.	Avon T-245	58	.35
The under dog and other mysteries.	PB 1085	55	.25
What Mrs. McGillicuddy saw!	Card C-318	58	.35
The witness for the prosecution.	Dell 855	55	.25
.	Dell D218	58	.35
CHRISTIE, ROBERT			
Inherit the night.	Pyr R279	57	.50
CHRISTOPHER, JOHN			
The caves of night.	Crst s273	59	.35
No blade of grass.	PB 1183	58	.25
Planet in peril.	Avon T371	59	.35
CHRISTY, HELEN			
Mr. Ace.	Bart 101	46	.25
CHURCHILL, EDWARD			
Steel horizon.	Ace D-186	56	.35
CHURCHILL, WINSTON			
The eloquence of Winston Churchill.	SigK Ks348	57	.35
CHUTE, MARCHETTE			
Stories from Shakespeare.	Ment MD247	59	.75
.	Ment MT257	59	.75
CHUTE, VERNE			
Flight of an angel.	Dell 470	51	.25
Sweet and deadly.	Pop 443	52	.25
Wayward angel.	Ban 755	50	.25
CIRACI, NORMA			
Detour.	Prmb P192	52	.35
CLAD, NOEL			
The savage.	Perm M-4152	59	.35
White barrier.	Avon 676	55	.25
CLAGETT, JOHN			
Captain Whitecap.	Pop G169	56	.35
Cradle of the sun.	Pop 566	54	.25
.	Pop G341	59	.35

Author/Title	Pub./Stock No.	Yr.	Price
CLAGETT, JOHN (cont.)			
Run the river gauntlet.	Ace D-296	58	.35
The slot.	Sig S1682	59	.35
Wilderness virgin.	Pop 739	56	.25
CLAIRE, MARVIN			
The drowning wire.	Ace D-37	53	.35
CLAPESATTLE, HELEN			
The Doctors Mayo.	Card GC-30	56	.50
CLARK, CHRISTOPHER			
Good is for angels.	Sig 901	52	.25
The unleashed will.	Lion LL 15	55	.35
CLARK, DALE			
Mambo to murder.	Ace D-109	55	.35
The narrow cell.	Pony 48	45	.25
A run for the money.	Ace D-149	56	.35
CLARK, DORENE			
Scarlet angel.	Berk G-186	58	.35
CLARK, G. GLENWOOD			
Thomas Alva Edison.	Berk G270	59	.35
CLARK, GEORGE			
The neighbors' kids.	GM 532	55	.25
CLARK, GORDON			
Naked sin.	Avon T-244	58	.35
CLARK, J. BIGELOW			
The dreamers.	Perm M-3020	55	.25
The long run.	Prmb P211	53	.35
CLARK, LeMON			
The enjoyment of love in marriage.	Prem s14	55	.35
———.	Crst s318	59	.35
CLARK, WALTER VAN TILBURG			
The Ox-Bow incident.	Pen 521	43	.25
———.	Sig 745	49	.25
———.	Sig 1160	54	.25
———.	Sig S1470	57	.35
The track of the cat.	Sig 801	50	.25
CLARKE, ARTHUR C.			
Against the fall of night.	Prmb 310	54	.25
Childhood's end.	Ball 33	53	.35
The city and the stars.	Sig S1464	57	.35
The deep range.	Sig S1583	58	.35
Earthlight.	Ball 97	55	.35
———.	Ball 249	58	.35
Expedition to earth.	Ball 52	53	.35
The exploration of space.	Card C-135	54	.35
The other side of the sky.	Sig S1729	59	.35

Author/Title	Pub./Stock No.	Yr.	Price
Prelude to space.	Ball 68	54	.35
Reach for tomorrow.	Ball 135	56	.35
Sands of Mars.	PB 989	54	.25
———.	Perm M-4149	59	.35
Tales from the White Hart.	Ball 186	57	.35
CLARKE, DONALD HENDERSON			
Alabam'.	Avon 120	47	.25
———.	Avon 232	49	.25
———.	Berk G-34	56	.35
The chastity of Gloria Boyd.	Avon 270	50	.25
———.	Avon 456	52	.25
———.	Berk G-76	57	.35
Confidential.	Avon 253	50	.25
———.	Avon 438	52	.25
———.	Avon 650	55	.25
———.	Avon T-300	59	.35
The headstrong young man.	Avon 472	52	.25
The housekeeper's daughter.	Avon 336	51	.25
———.	Avon 503	53	.25
Impatient virgin.	Avon 193	49	.25
———.	Avon 365	51	.25
———.	Avon 530	53	.25
———.	Avon 656	55	.25
———.	Avon T-233	58	.35
Joe and Jennie.	Berk 331	55	.25
———.	Berk G-124	58	.35
John Bartel, Jr.	Avon 149	48	.25
Kelly.	Avon 116	46	.25
Lady Ann.	Avon 105	46	.25
A lady named Lou.	Avon 483	52	.25
———.	Avon 671	55	.25
Louis Beretti.	NL 19	49	.25
———.	Avon 384	51	.25
———.	Avon 575	54	.25
Millie.	Avon 480	52	.25
Millie's daughter.	Avon 351	51	.25
———.	Avon 543	53	.25
Murderer's holiday.	Avon 394	51	.25
———.	Avon 631	55	.25
Nina.	Avon 213	49	.25
———.	Avon 397	52	.25
———.	Avon 593	54	.25
The regenerate lover.	NL 8	48	.25
Tawny.	Avon 237	50	.25
———.	Avon 408	51	.25
———.	Avon 615	54	.25
———.	Avon 747	56	.25
That Mrs. Renney.	Avon 431	52	.25
CLASON, CLYDE B.			
Green shiver.	Pop 50	45	.25
CLAUSSEN, W. EDMUNDS			
El Paso.	Lion 55	51	.25
Gun devil!	Lion 28	50	.25
Rebel's roundup.	Avon 495	53	.25

Author/Title	Pub./Stock No.	Yr.	Price
CLAUSSEN, W. EDMUNDS (cont.)			
Ride the dark hills.	PB 1048	55	.25
CLAWSON, AUGUSTA H.			
Shipyard diary of a woman welder.	PenS S218	44	.25
CLAY, LEWIS			
The wanton hour.	Pyr 174	55	.25
CLAY, WESTON			
Boot Hill.	Han 133	51	.25
CLAYTON, JOHN BELL			
And come back a man.	Crst s194	57	.35
Six angels at my back.	Pop 521	53	.25
_____.	Pop G235	58	.35
Wait, son, October is near.	Ban A1236	54	.35
CLEARY, JON			
Dust in the sun.	Pop G204	57	.35
Naked in the night.	Pop 634	55	.25
The sundowners.	PB 939	53	.25
You can't see around corners.	Pop 497	53	.25
CLEEVE, BRIAN TALBOT			
The night winds.	Ball 62	54	.35
CLEMENT, HAL			
Cycle of fire.	Ball 200	57	.35
From outer space.	Avon T-175	57	.35
Mission of gravity.	Gal 33	58	.35
CLEMENTS, CALVIN			
Barge girl.	GM 303	53	.25
Dark night of love.	Pop 752	56	.25
Hell ship to Kuma.	GM 412	54	.25
Satan takes the helm.	GM 252	52	.25
CLENDENING, LOGAN			
The human body.	PB 198	43	.25
CLEWES, HOWARD			
The long memory.	Dell 787	54	.25
CLIFT, CHARMIAN with George Henry Johnston			
High valley.	PB 818	51	.25
CLIFTON, BUD			
The bad girls.	Pyr G364	58	.35
D for delinquent.	Ace D-270	58	.35
The murder specialist.	Ace D-383	59	.35
Muscle boy.	Ace D-330	58	.35
The power gods.	Pyr G410	59	.35
CLIFTON, MARK with Frank Riley			
The forever machine.	Gal 35	58	.35

Author/Title	Pub./Stock No.	Yr.	Price
CLIPPINGER, FRANCES			
Cassandra.	Hill 117	59	.35
Don't get in my way.	Eag EB50	55	.25
Elinda.	Sig 951	52	.25
CLOETE, STUART			
Congo song.	Pop 110	47	.25
_____.	Pop G110	52	.35
_____.	Mon K50	58	.50
The curve and the tusk.	Sig S1078	54	.35
Mamba.	Pop G205	57	.35
The mask.	Perm M-4102	58	.35
The turning wheels.	Pen 573	46	.25
_____.	Prmb P147	52	.35
Watch for the dawn.	Pop G132	53	.35
CLOSE, ROBERT S.			
Love me sailor.	Pop 396	52	.25
CLOSTERMANN, PIERRE			
The big show.	Ball F261	58	.50
CLOU, JOHN			
The golden blade.	Graf G209	55	.35
_____.	Graf G220	57	.35
CLUGSTON, KATE			
Twist the knife slowly.	Ace D-3	52	.35
CLUNE, HENRY W.			
Big fella.	Pop SP12	58	.50
COATES, JOHN			
The widow's tale.	Perm M-4145	59	.35
COATES, ROBERT M.			
The night before dying.	Lion LL 45	55	.35
The night is so dark.	Pop G173	56	.35
The outlaw years.	Pnnt P31	54	.25
Wisteria Cottage.	Dell 371	50	.25
COBB, HUMPHREY			
Paths of glory.	Dell D209	57	.35
COBEAN, SAMUEL E.			
Cobean's naked eye.	PB 899	52	.25
COBLENTZ, STANTON A.			
Into Plutonian depths.	Avon 281	50	.25
COBURN, WALT			
Barb wire.	Pop 191	49	.25
Beyond the wild Missouri.	Ace D-294	58	.35
Branded.	Avon 858	59	.25
Drift fence.	Dmnd D2013	59	.35
Fast gun.	Avon 852	59	.25
Guns blaze on Spiderweb range.	Avon 821	58	.25
Law rides the range.	Pop 135	47	.25

Author/Title	Pub./Stock No.	Yr.	Price
COBURN, WALT (cont.)			
Mavericks.	Pop 250	50	.25
The night-branders.	Ace D-196	57	.35
One step ahead of the posse.	Ace D-180	56	.35
Pardners of the dim trails.	Pop 415	52	.25
The ringtailed rannyhans.	Pop 290	50	.25
Sky-pilot cowboy.	Pop 166	48	.25
Violent maverick.	Avon 749	56	.25
COCHRAN, HAMILTON			
Captain Ebony.	Dell D125	53	.35
Rogue's holiday.	Dell D144	54	.35
Windward passage.	Ace D-251	57	.35
COCHRAN, JEFF			
Guns of Circle 8.	Avon 556	54	.25
COCHRAN, LOUIS			
Son of Haman.	Ban 1191	54	.25
COCHRELL, BOYD			
Rage in the wind.	Pop 509	53	.25
COCKRELL, MARIAN			
Yesterday's madness.	Ban 401	48	.25
CODY, AL			
The big corral.	Pop 353	51	.25
Bitter Creek.	PB 769	51	.25
Bloody Wyoming.	Avon 812	58	.25
Brand of iron.	Berk 378	57	.25
Disaster Trail.	PB 648	50	.25
_____.	Avon 832	58	.25
Empty saddles.	Han 81	48	.25
_____.	Avon 724	56	.25
Forbidden river.	Berk 353	56	.25
Guns blaze at sundown.	Avon 426	52	.25
_____.	Avon 525	53	.25
Marshal of Deer Creek.	Avon 378	51	.25
_____.	Avon 511	53	.25
Montana helltown.	Avon 810	58	.25
Outlaw justice at Hangman's Coulee.	Avon 460	52	.25
Powder burns.	Berk 335	55	.25
Red man's range.	Berk 374	57	.25
West of the law.	PB 610	49	.25
_____.	Avon T-274	58	.35
Whiplash war.	Avon 704	56	.25
Wyoming ambush.	Avon 842	59	.25
CODY, C. S.			
Lie like a lady.	Ace S-108	55	.25
The witching night.	Dell 670	53	.25
COE, CHARLES FRANCIS			
Ashes.	Sig 1058	53	.25
Pressure.	Sig 942	52	.25
COEN, FRANKLIN			
Night of the quarter moon.	Ban A1942	59	.35
COGGINS, CAROLYN			
Cookbook of fabulous foods for people you love.	Pyr R459	59	.50
COHEN, LESTER			
Stella and Joe.	Pyr G77	53	.35
Sweepings.	Crst s190	57	.35
COHEN, LOUIS H.			
Murder, madness and the law.	Sig 1119	54	.25
COHEN, OCTAVUS ROY			
A bullet for my love.	Pop 462	52	.25
The corpse that walked.	GM 138	51	.25
_____.	GM 650	57	.25
Danger in paradise.	Pop 144	48	.25
Dangerous lady.	Pop 264	50	.25
Don't ever love me.	Pop 332	51	.25
The golden hussy.	Crst s124	56	.35
The intruder.	Graf 125	56	.25
Lost lady.	GM 172	51	.25
Love has no alibi.	Pop 162	48	.25
More beautiful than murder.	Pop 427	52	.25
Murder in season.	Pop 74	46	.25
My love wears black.	Pop 369	51	.25
Romance in the first degree.	Pop 88	47	.25
Sound of revelry.	Pop 46	45	.25
There's always time to die.	Pop 196	49	.25
COHN, ART			
The joker is wild.	Ban F1647	57	.50
The nine lives of Michael Todd.	Card C-353	59	.35
COKER, ELIZABETH BOATWRIGHT			
Daughter of strangers.	Dell D138	54	.35
COLBY, ROBERT			
The captain must die.	GM 835	59	.25
The deadly desire.	GM 940	59	.25
Make mine vengeance.	Avon 854	59	.25
Murder mistress.	Ace D-361	59	.35
The quaking widow.	Ace D-195	56	.35
Secret of the second door.	GM 855	59	.25
These lonely, these dead.	Pyr G380	59	.35
COLE, JACKSON			
Border hell.	Pyr 51	52	.25
Bullets high.	Pyr 124	54	.25

Author/Title	Pub./Stock No.	Yr.	Price
COLE, JACKSON (cont.)			
The death riders.	Pyr 56	52	.25
Gun town.	Pyr 111	54	.25
Gun-blaze.	Pyr 162	55	.25
Gun-runners.	Pyr 87	53	.25
Guns of Mist River.	Pop 298	50	.25
Gunsmoke trail.	Pyr 153	55	.25
Killer country.	Pyr 73	53	.25
Land grab.	Pyr 91	53	.25
Massacre canyon.	Pyr 70	53	.25
Outlawed.	Pyr 117	54	.25
Texas fists.	Pyr 81	53	.25
Texas fury.	Pyr 40	51	.25
_____.	Pyr 167	55	.25
Texas manhunt.	Pyr 144	55	.25
Texas tornado.	Pyr 108	54	.25
Thunder range.	Pyr 47	52	.25
Trigger law.	Pyr 66	52	.25
Trouble shooter.	Pyr 155	55	.25
Two-gun devil.	Pyr 171	55	.25
COLE, WILLIAM with Douglas McKee			
French cartoons.	DelF 21	54	.25
More French cartoons.	DelF 64	55	.25
COLEMAN, JAMES A.			
Relativity for the layman.	Ment MD234	58	.50
COLEMAN, LONNIE			
Clara.	Ban 1109	53	.25
Escape the thunder.	Prmb 295	54	.25
Hot spell.	Avon T-214	58	.35
The sea is a woman.	Dell 615	52	.25
Ship's company.	Dell D185	57	.35
COLEMAN, RICHARD			
Don't you weep, don't you moan.	Lion LL 28	55	.35
COLERIDGE, SAMUEL TAYLOR			
Coleridge.	DelL LB122	59	.35
COLES, MANNING			
Drink to yesterday.	Ban 76	47	.25
No entry.	Ace D-389	59	.35
A toast to tomorrow.	Ban 118	47	.25
COLETTE, SIDONIE			
Chéri and The last of Chéri.	Sig S1189	55	.35
Claudine.	Avon T-301	59	.35
Diary of a 16-year old French girl.	Avon T-200	57	.35
Gigi and Julie de Carneilhan.	Sig 1096	54	.25
_____.	Sig S1525	58	.35
Mitsou.	Avon T-269	58	.35
The ripening seed.	Sig 1402	57	.25
COLLANS, DEV with Stewart Sterling			
I was a house detective.	Pyr 139	55	.25
_____.	Pyr G261	57	.35
COLLIER, JOHN, 1884-			
Indians of the Americas.	Ment M33	48	.35
_____.	Ment MD171	56	.50
COLLIER, JOHN, 1901-			
Fancies and goodnights.	Ban A1106	53	.35
_____.	Ban F1703	57	.50
COLLIER, RICHARD			
10,000 eyes.	Pyr R433	59	.50
COLLIERS, LYON			
The heart beats once.	Pyr 13	49	.25
COLLINS, HUNT			
The proposition.	Pyr 151	55	.25
Tomorrow and tomorrow.	Pyr G214	56	.35
COLLINS, MARY			
Dead center.	Ban 62	46	.25
Death warmed over.	Ban 718	49	.25
Dog eat dog.	Ban 877	51	.25
The fog comes.	Ban 23	46	.25
Only the good.	Ban 147	48	.25
The sister of Cain.	Ban 787	50	.25
COLLINS, NORMAN			
Black ivory.	PB 632	49	.25
The blazing land.	Ban 790	50	.25
COLLINS, WILKIE			
The moonstone.	Pyr 19	50	.25
_____.	Pyr G88	53	.35
_____.	PyrR PR11	58	.35
COLLISON, WILSON			
Diary of death.	NL 30	49	.25
Dishonorable darling.	NL 32	49	.25
One night with Nancy.	NL 20	49	.25
COLLODI, CARLO			
Pinocchio.	PB 18	39	.25
COLT, CLEM			
Quick-trigger country.	Sig 1403	57	.25
Six-gun buckaroo.	Eag EB31	54	.25
Smoke wagon kid.	Berk G-201	59	.35
Strawberry roan.	Dell 828	55	.25
Tough company.	PB 973	53	.25
COLTER, ELI			
Blood on the range.	Graf 80	54	.25
_____.	Graf 137	56	.25
The outcast of Lazy S.	Han 95	49	.25

Author/Title	Pub./Stock No.	Yr.	Price
COLTER, LILLIAN			
The awakening of Jenny.	GM 109	50	.25
_____.	GM s829	58	.35
COLTON, MEL			
The big fix.	Ace D-3	52	.35
Double take.	Ace D-27	53	.35
Never kill a cop!	Ace D-19	53	.35
Point of no escape.	Ace D-101	55	.35
COLWELL, MIRIAM			
Young.	Ball 100	55	.35
COLYTON, HENRY JOHN			
Sir Pagan.	Prmb P168	52	.35
COMFORT, WILL LEVINGTON			
Apache.	Ban 922	52	.25
COMING, Aphrodite!	Avon 683	55	.25
COMMAGER, HENRY STEELE			
America in perspective.	Ment M30	48	.35
_____.	Ment MD169	56	.50
The Pocket history of			
the second world war.	PB 338	45	.25
with Allan Nevins			
The Pocket history of			
the United States.	PB 195	43	.25
_____.	PBL PL512	56	.50
COMMINS, SAXE with Robert N. Linscott			
Man and man: the social			
philosophers.	PBL PL2	54	.50
Man and spirit: the			
speculative			
philosophers.	PBL PL4	54	.50
Man and the state: the			
political philosophers.	PBL PL1	54	.50
Man and the universe:			
the philosophers of			
science.	PBL PL3	54	.50
The COMPACT Bible.	PyrR PR10	56	.95
COMSTOCK, HARRIET T.			
Terry.	Bart 18	45	.25
CONANT, JAMES B.			
On understanding science.	Ment M68	51	.35
CONANT, PAUL			
Dr. Gatskill's blue			
shoes.	Dell 741	53	.25
CONFUCIUS			
The living thoughts of			
Confucius.	Prem d74	59	.50
The sayings of Confucius.	Ment M151	55	.35

Author/Title	Pub./Stock No.	Yr.	Price
CONGDON, DON			
Combat: European Theater--			
World War II.	DelF C107	59	.50
Combat: Pacific Theater--			
World War II.	DelF C108	59	.50
Sensual love.	Ball 305K	59	.35
Stories for the dead			
of night.	DelF B107	57	.35
The wild sweet wine.	Ball 239	58	.35
CONKLIN, GROFF			
The big book of science			
fiction.	Berk G-53	57	.35
Br-r-r-!	Avon T-289	59	.35
Crossroads in time.	Prmb P254	53	.35
Four for the future.	Pyr G434	59	.35
The graveyard reader.	Ball 257	58	.35
In the grip of terror.	Prmb P117	51	.35
Invaders of earth.	PB 1074	55	.25
Operation future.	Perm M-4022	55	.35
Possible worlds of			
science fiction.	Berk G-3	55	.35
Science fiction omnibus.	Berk G-31	56	.35
Science fiction terror			
tales.	PB 1045	55	.25
Science-fiction thinking			
machines.	Ban 1352	55	.25
6 great short novels of			
science fiction.	DelF D9	54	.35
A treasury of science			
fiction.	Berk G-63	57	.35
CONNELL, VIVIAN			
Bachelors anonymous.	Lion LL 140	57	.35
The Chinese room.	Ban 454	48	.25
_____.	Ban A1268	54	.35
_____.	Ban A1621	57	.35
The dream and the flesh.	Lion 173	53	.25
_____.	Lion LL 112	56	.35
_____.	Pyr G387	59	.35
The golden sleep.	Sig 724	49	.25
_____.	Sig 1250	55	.25
A man of parts.	GM 130	50	.25
_____.	GM 711	57	.25
Monte Carlo mission.	GM 365	54	.25
The naked rich.	Pop G115	53	.35
_____.	Pop G280	58	.35
CONNER, REARDEN			
Shake hands with the			
devil.	Crst s301	59	.35
CONNOLLY, PAUL			
Get out of town.	GM 188	51	.25
So fair, so evil.	GM 500	55	.25
Tears are for angels.	GM 224	52	.25
CONRAD, BARNABY			
The innocent villa.	Avon 537	52	.25
Matador.	Dell 714	53	.25

Author/Title	Pub./Stock No.	Yr.	Price
CONRAD, EARL			
Rock bottom.	Ban 1135	53	.25
with Haywood Patterson			
Scottsboro boy.	Ban 920	51	.25
CONRAD, HAROLD			
The battle at Apache			
Pass.	Avon 437	52	.25
————.	Avon 729	56	.25
CONRAD, JOSEPH			
Almayer's folly.	Pen 619	47	.25
Heart of darkness <u>and</u>			
The secret sharer.	Sig 834	50	.25
————.	Sig S1254	55	.35
————.	Sig D1410	57	.50
————.	SigC CD4	59	.50
Lord Jim.	Ban F1597	57	.50
	BanC FC7	58	.50
An outcast of the			
islands.	Pyr G378	59	.35
CONROY, ALBERT			
The chiselers.	GM 289	53	.25
	GM 608	56	.25
The mob says murder.	GM 780	58	.25
Murder in Room 13.	GM 806	58	.25
Nice guys finish dead.	GM 676	57	.25
The road's end.	GM 231	52	.25
————.	GM 579	56	.25
CONROY, JIM			
Destination revenge.	Prmb 288	54	.25
CONSIDINE, BOB with Babe Ruth			
The Babe Ruth story.	PB 562	49	.25
CONSTANT, BENJAMIN			
Adolphe <u>and</u> The red			
notebook.	SigC CD1	59	.50
CONSTINER, MERLE			
The fourth gunman.	Ace D-328	58	.35
Last stand at Anvil			
Pass.	Crst 161	57	.25
CONTENT, NIKKI			
Hideaway.	GM 308	53	.25
CONWAY, JOHN			
Hell is my destination.	Mon 128	59	.35
Madigan's women.	Mon 115	59	.35
COOK, FRED J.			
The girl in the death			
cell.	GM 306	53	.25
The girl on the lonely			
beach.	GM 431	54	.25

Author/Title	Pub./Stock No.	Yr.	Price
COOK, WHITFIELD			
A night with Mr.			
Primrose.	Avon 497	53	.25
COOK, WILL			
Apache ambush.	Pop 773	56	.25
Badman's holiday.	GM 748	58	.25
Bullet range.	Pop 687	55	.25
The fighting Texan.	Pop 722	56	.25
Frontier feud.	Pop 596	54	.25
Fury at Painted Rock.	Pop 652	55	.25
————.	Pop G276	58	.35
Guns of North Texas.	GM 798	58	.25
Lone hand from Texas.	Pop 827	57	.25
Outcast of Cripple Creek.	GM 837	59	.25
Prairie guns.	Pop 631	54	.25
Sabrina Kane.	Pop 799	57	.25
Trumpets to the West.	Pop 748	56	.25
We burn like fire.	Mon 130	59	.35
The Wind River kid.	Crst 242	58	.25
COOKE, DAVID C.			
Fighting Indians of			
the West.	Eag EB53	55	.25
COOLEY, DONALD G.			
The new way to eat and			
get slim.	GM 465	55	.25
The science book of			
wonder drugs.	Card C-132	54	.35
COOLIDGE, DANE			
Bear Paw.	Hill unk	50	.25
Comanche chaser.	Ban 99	47	.25
Fighting men of the West.	Ban A1043	52	.35
COON, HORACE			
43,000 years later.	Sig S1534	58	.35
Hobbies for pleasure			
and profit.	SigK Ks318	55	.35
How to be a better			
member.	SigK Ks341	56	.35
How to spell and increase			
your word power.	SigK Ks370	59	.35
Speak better--write			
better--English.	SigK K302	54	.25
————.	SigK Ks354	57	.35
COOPER, COURTNEY RYLEY			
The pioneers.	Dell 290	49	.25
Teen-age vice!	Pyr G43	52	.35
————.	Pyr G127	54	.35
————.	Pyr G252	57	.35
COOPER, EDMUND			
Deadly image.	Ball 260	58	.35
Seed of light.	Ball 327K	59	.35
Tomorrow's gift.	Ball 279K	58	.35

Author/Title	Pub./Stock No.	Yr.	Price
COOPER, JAMES FENIMORE			
The last of the Mohicans.	PBL PL62	57	.35
COOPER, JEFFERSON			
Arrow in the hill.	PB 1071	55	.25
The bloody sevens.	Perm M-3064	57	.25
Captain Seadog.	PB 1237	59	.25
The questing sword.	Perm M-4113	58	.35
The swordsman.	Card C-262	57	.35
Veronica's veil.	Perm M-4117	59	.35
COOPER, JOHN C.			
The haunted strangler.	Ace D-359	59	.35
COOPER, MAE			
Lily Henry.	Sig 790	50	.25
COOPER, MORTON			
Anything for kicks.	Avon T-311	59	.35
Come feed on me.	GM 317	53	.25
Delinquent!	Avon T-247	58	.35
The flesh and Mr. Rawlie.	GM 538	56	.25
Ginny.	Avon T-316	59	.35
High school confidential.	Avon T-257	58	.35
The innocent and willing.	GM s588	56	.35
The ungilded lily.	GM s812	58	.35
Young and wild.	Avon T-229	58	.35
COOPER, PAGE			
The big book of horse stories.	Berk G-222	59	.35
COOPER, SAUL			
The Jayhawkers.	Hill 118	59	.35
COPLAND, AARON			
Music and imagination.	Ment MD261	59	.50
What to listen for in music.	Ment M81	53	.35
COPPEL, ALFRED			
Hero driver.	PB 1059	55	.25
Night of fire and snow.	Crst s212	58	.35
CORBETT, JIM			
Maneaters of Kumaon.	Pnnt P23	53	.25
CORBIN, GLENN			
Trouble on Big Cat.	DelF 25	54	.25
CORD, BARRY			
Boss of barbed wire.	Ace D-230	57	.35
Cain Basin.	Ace D-264	58	.35
Concho Valley.	Ace D-380	59	.35
The guns of Hammer.	Ace D-284	58	.35
The gunsmoke trail.	Ace D-276	58	.35
Last chance at Devil's Canyon.	Ace D-400	59	.35
Maverick gun.	Hill 127	59	.35
Mesquite Johnny.	Ace D-316	58	.35

Author/Title	Pub./Stock No.	Yr.	Price
The prodigal gun.	Ace D-208	57	.35
Savage valley.	Ace D-216	57	.35
Sheriff of Big Hat.	Ace D-346	59	.35
Six bullets left.	Avon 861	59	.25
War in Peaceful Valley.	Ace D-360	59	.35
CORES, LUCY			
Painted for the kill.	Dell 87	45	.25
Woman in love.	Prmb P161	52	.35
CORLE, EDWIN			
Apache devil.	Pyr 63	52	.25
Billy the Kid.	Ban A1246	54	.35
Burro alley.	Pnnt P27	53	.25
In winter light.	Pnnt P65	54	.25
Mojave.	Pnnt P6	53	.25
CORLISS, ALLENE			
Illusion.	Ban 420	49	.25
Summer lightning.	Ban 711	49	.25
CORNE, M. E.			
Death is no lady.	BK 26	46	.25
CORNELL, BETTY			
Betty Cornell's glamour guide for teens.	PB 1210	58	.25
CORRELL, A. BOYD with Philip MacDonald			
Sweet and deadly.	Zen ZB-29	59	.35
CORREY, LEE			
Contraband rocket.	Ace D-146	56	.35
CORT, DAVID			
The calm man.	DelF 34	54	.25
COSTAIN, THOMAS B.			
The black rose.	Ban A818	50	.35
For my great folly.	Ban A951	51	.35
——————.	Ban F1444	56	.50
High towers.	Ban A1027	52	.35
The moneyman.	Ban F1186	54	.50
Ride with me.	Ban A984	52	.35
The silver chalice.	Prmb P284S	54	.50
——————.	Perm M-5003	56	.50
Son of a hundred kings.	Perm M-5000	55	.50
COSTIGAN, LEE			
Never kill a cop.	PB 1256	59	.25
COTLOW, LEWIS			
Amazon head-hunters.	Sig S1094	54	.35
COTTON, WILL			
The night was made for murder.	Avon T-306	59	.35
COTTRELL, LEONARD			
The anvil of civilization.	Ment MD197	57	.50

Author/Title	Pub./Stock No.	Yr.	Price	Author/Title	Pub./Stock No.	Yr.	Price
COUNSEL, FIRTH				Mrs. Murdock takes a			
Juvenile jungle.	Avon T-219	58	.35	case.	Dell 202	47	.25
				Murder for the asking.	Dell 58	44	.25
COURTIER, SIDNEY H.				Murder for two.	Dell 276	49	.25
Gold for my fair lady.	Dell D111	52	.35	Murder in Havana.	Dell 423	50	.25
				Murder on their minds.	Dell D271	59	.35
COUSTEAU, JACQUES-YVES with Frédéric Dumas				Murder with pictures.	Dell 101	46	.25
The silent world.	Card C-163	55	.35	_____.	Dell 441	50	.25
				Murdock's acid test.	Dell 169	47	.25
COVINGTON, FORREST				Never bet your life.	Dell 931	57	.25
The sheriff.	Pyr 287	57	.25	No time to kill.	Dell 182	47	.25
				Silent are the dead.	Dell 225	48	.25
COWAN, JOHN with Arthur Rose Guérard				Venturous lady.	Dell 745	53	.25
Love, health and							
marriage.	Avon 148	48	.25	COYLE, DAVID CUSHMAN			
				The United Nations and			
COWARD, NOEL				how it works.	SigK Ks324	55	.35
Short stories, short				_____.	Ment MD220	58	.50
plays and songs by				The United States			
Noel Coward.	DelF D80	55	.35	political system and			
To step aside.	Avon 78	46	.25	how it works.	SigK K303	54	.25
Tonight at 8:30.	Avon (28)	43	.25				
				COZZENS, JAMES GOULD			
COWELL, ROBERTA				By love possessed.	Crst t326	59	.75
Roberta Cowell's story.	Lion LL 50	55	.35	Castaway.	Ban 1007	52	.25
				Guard of honor.	Prmb P148	52	.35
COWLES, VIRGINIA				S.S. San Pedro.	Berk 103	55	.25
Who dares, wins.	Ball F313K	59	.50	_____.	Berk G-106	58	.35
COX, WILLIAM R.				CRABB, ALFRED LELAND			
Hell to pay.	Sig 1555	58	.25	Dinner at Belmont.	Card C-81	53	.35
The lusty men.	Pyr G254	57	.35				
Make my coffin strong.	GM 447	55	.25	CRAIG, JONATHAN			
The tycoon and the				Alley girl.	Lion 206	54	.25
tigress.	GM s762	58	.35	The case of the			
				beautiful body.	GM 702	57	.25
COXE, GEORGE HARMON				Case of the cold			
Alias the dead.	Dell 377	50	.25	coquette.	GM 645	57	.25
Assignment in Guiana.	Dell 321	49	.25	Case of the nervous nude.	GM 872	59	.25
The camera clue.	Dell 27	<u>43</u>	.25	Case of the petticoat			
_____.	Dell 453	50	.25	murder.	GM 784	58	.25
The charred witness.	Dell 240	48	.25	Case of the village			
The crimson clue.	Perm M-3010	55	.25	tramp.	GM 930	59	.25
Dangerous legacy.	Dell 586	52	.25	Come night, come evil.	GM 716	57	.25
Eye witness.	Dell 902	56	.25	The dead darling.	GM 531	55	.25
Fashioned for murder.	Dell 678	53	.25	Morgue for Venus.	GM 582	56	.25
The fifth key.	Dell 644	52	.25	Renegade cop.	Dmnd D2015	59	.35
Flash Casey, detective.	Avon 143	48	.25	So young, so wicked.	GM 669	57	.25
Focus on murder.	Dell 970	58	.25				
Four frightened women.	Dell 5	43	.25	CRAIG, MARGARET MAZE			
The frightened fiancée.	Dell 838	55	.25	Marsha.	Berk G-109	58	.35
The glass triangle.	Dell 81	45	.25	Trish.	Berk G-88	57	.35
_____.	Dell 522	51	.25				
The groom lay dead.	Dell 502	51	.25	CRAIG, PAUL			
The hollow needle.	Dell 757	54	.25	Gunfighter.	Eton E125	53	.25
Inland passage.	Dell 799	54	.25				
The jade Venus.	Dell 549	51	.25	CRAIGE, JOHN HOUSTON			
The lady is afraid.	Dell 147	47	.25	Your life in the atom			
_____.	Dell 734	53	.25	world.	Pony 45	46	.25
Man on a rope.	Dell 984	58	.25				

Author/Title	Pub./Stock No.	Yr.	Price
CRAIGIN, ELISABETH			
Either is love.	Lion unk	52	.25
_____.	Lion LB 122	56	.25
CRAMPTON, GERTRUDE			
Your own joke book.	Com 8	48	.25
Your own party book.	Com 23	49	.25
CRANE, AIMÉE			
G.I. sketch book.	PenS S225	44	.25
CRANE, CLARKSON			
Frisco gal.	NL 17	49	.25
Naomi Martin.	Berk G-126	58	.35
CRANE, FRANCES			
The amethyst spectacles.	Ban 49	46	.25
The applegreen cat.	Pop 344	51	.25
The cinnamon murder.	Ban 130	47	.25
The golden box.	Pop 80	46	.25
The indigo necklace			
murders.	Ban 312	49	.25
Murder on the purple			
water.	Ban 874	51	.25
The pink umbrella murder.	Pop 218	50	.25
The turquoise shop.	Pop 58	45	.25
The yellow violet.	Pop 108	47	.25
CRANE, MILTON			
Fifty great short			
stories.	Ban A950	52	.35
_____.	Ban F1302	55	.50
_____.	BanC FC29	59	.50
Sins of New York.	Ban 786	50	.25
CRANE, ROBERT			
Hero's walk.	Ball 71	54	.35
CRANE, STEPHEN			
The bride comes to			
Yellow Sky.	Avon T-137	56	.35
The red badge of courage.	PB 154	42	.25
_____.	PBL PL20	54	.35
CRANKSHAW, EDWARD			
Gestapo.	Pyr R281	57	.35
_____.	Pyr G467	59	.35
CRANSTON, RUTH			
The miracle of Lourdes.	Pop G199	57	.35
CRAVEN, THOMAS			
Famous artists and			
their models.	PB 579	49	.25
The Pocket book of			
Greek art.	PB 677	50	.25
CRAWFORD, MARION			
The little princesses.	Ban 969	52	.25

Author/Title	Pub./Stock No.	Yr.	Price
CRAWFORD, OLIVER			
Blood on the branches.	Ace S-141	56	.25
CREASEY, JOHN			
The case of the acid			
throwers.	Avon 641	55	.25
The creepers.	Avon 563	54	.25
Death of a postman.	Ban 1883	59	.25
The figure in the dusk.	Avon 590	54	.25
_____.	Avon T366	59	.35
The gelignite gang.	Ban 1884	59	.25
Give a man a gun.	Avon 720	56	.25
So young, so cold,			
so fair.	Dell 985	58	.25
CREEKMORE, HUBERT			
The chain in the heart.	Sig D1156	54	.50
Cotton country.	Ban 812	50	.25
CREIGHTON, JOHN			
Destroying angel.	Ace D-167	56	.35
Evil is the night.	Ace D-393	59	.35
Not so evil as Eve.	Ace D-247	57	.35
Stranglehold.	Ace D-333	59	.35
Trial by perjury.	Ace D-321	58	.35
The wayward blonde.	Ace D-317	58	.35
CRICHTON, KYLE			
The Marx brothers.	Pop 410	52	.25
CRITTENDEN, LOUISE with Rosejeanne Slifer			
The new Pocket quiz book.	PB 255	44	.25
The Pocket quiz book.	PB 132	41	.25
CROCKETT, DAVY			
Life of Davy Crockett.	Sig S1214	55	.35
CROCKETT, LUCY HERNDON			
The magnificent bastards.	Dell D145	55	.35
_____.	Dell F95	59	.50
CROCKETT, VIVIAN			
Messalina.	Berk G-14	55	.35
_____.	Dmnd D2012	59	.35
CROFTS, FREEMAN WILLS			
The cask.	Pen 575	46	.25
Cold-blooded murder.	Avon 126	47	.25
A losing game.	Pop 121	47	.25
The purple sickle			
murders.	Pen 533	44	.25
Sir John Magill's last			
journey.	PB 105	41	.25
Tragedy in the hollow.	Pop 18	43	.25
Wilful and premeditated.	Avon (9)	41	.25
CROMPTON, JOHN			
The life of the spider.	Ment M105	54	.35

Author/Title	Pub./Stock No.	Yr.	Price
CRONIN, A. J.			
Beyond this place.	Ban F1321	55	.50
The citadel.	Ban A930	51	.35
———.	Ban F1429	56	.50
Grand canary.	Ban A1050	52	.35
The green years.	Ban F1536	56	.50
The keys of the kingdom.	Ban 782	50	.25
———.	Ban A1060	52	.35
———.	Ban F1474	56	.50
The northern light.	Ban F1947	59	.50
Shannon's way.	Ban F1537	56	.50
The Spanish gardener.	Ban A1719	57	.35
The stars look down.	Ban F1042	53	.50
A thing of beauty.	Ban F1624	57	.50
CROSBY, BING			
Call me lucky.	Card C-146	54	.35
CROSS, BEVERLEY			
The nightwalkers.	Sig 1528	58	.25
CROSS, CHRISTOPHER			
A minute of prayer.	Card C-155	54	.35
CROSS, JAMES			
Root of evil.	Crst 225	58	.25
CROSS, MILTON			
Stories of the great operas.	Perm M-5004	56	.50
CROSSEN, KENDELL FOSTER			
The tortured path.	Perm M-4099	58	.35
Year of consent.	DelF 32	54	.25
CROSSMAN, RICHARD			
The God that failed.	Ban 963	52	.35
———.	Ban A1229	54	.35
———.	Ban F2011	59	.50
CROSSWORD puzzles.	Pop 107	46	.25
———.	Pop SP3	56	.25
CROSSWORD puzzles, book two.	Pop 150	48	.25
CROUSE, RUSSEL			
Murder won't out.	Pnnt P24	53	.25
CROUSE, WILLIAM H.			
Home guide to repair, upkeep and remodeling.	Pop 323	51	.25
CROW, CARL			
Four hundred million customers.	PB 323	45	.25
CROY, HOMER			
Family honeymoon.	Ban 413	50	.25
He hanged them high.	Prmb P313	54	.35

Author/Title	Pub./Stock No.	Yr.	Price
Last of the great outlaws.	Sig S1495	58	.35
CROYDON, HOLBORN G.			
Return postage guaranteed.	Avon T-1	54	.35
CRUICKSHANK, ALLAN D.			
The Pocket guide to birds.	Card GC-18	54	.50
CULBERTSON, ELY			
Contract bridge for everyone.	Sig 681	48	.25
CULLEN, CARTER			
The deadly chase.	GM 629	57	.25
Don't get caught.	GM 210	52	.25
———.	GM 610	56	.25
CUMMINGS, RAY			
Beyond the vanishing point.	Ace D-331	58	.35
Brigands of the moon.	Ace D-324	58	.35
The man who mastered time.	Ace D-173	56	.35
Princess of the atom.	AvnF 1	50	.25
CUNNINGHAM, A. B.			
The affair at the boat landing.	Dell 410	50	.25
Death haunts the dark lane.	Dell 465	50	.25
Death of a bullionaire.	Dell 313	49	.25
The death of a worldly woman.	Dell 365	49	.25
CUNNINGHAM, EUGENE			
Border guns.	Dell 935	57	.25
Bravo trail.	Pyr 265	57	.25
Buckaroo.	Pop 77	46	.25
———.	Pop G294	58	.35
Diamond River range.	Pop 176	49	.25
Gun bulldogger.	Dell 776	54	.25
Mesquite maverick.	Eag EB55	55	.25
Pistol passport.	Ban 77	47	.25
Quick triggers.	Pop 234	50	.25
———.	Pop 624	54	.25
The ranger way.	Pop 148	48	.25
———.	Pop 542	53	.25
Red range.	PB 791	51	.25
———.	Pop 834	58	.25
Riders of the night.	Ban 113	47	.25
Riding gun.	Dell 956	57	.25
Spiderweb trail.	PB 345	46	.25
———.	Pop G272	58	.35
Texas sheriff.	Pop 375	51	.25
———.	Pop G332	59	.35
Texas triggers.	PB 554	48	.25
———.	Pop G238	58	.35

Author/Title	Pub./Stock No.	Yr.	Price
CUNNINGHAM, EUGENE (cont.)			
Trail of the Macaw.	Pop 289	50	.25
Whistling lead.	Sig 740	49	.25
_____.	Sig 1269	56	.25
CUNNINGHAM, JOHN			
Warhorse.	Dell D177	56	.35
CUNNINGHAM, SHIRLEY			
The Pocket entertainer.	PB 165	42	.25
CUPPY, WILL			
The decline and fall of			
practically everybody.	Dell D257	59	.35
CURIE, ENID with Donald Porter Geddes			
About the Kinsey report.	Sig 675	48	.25
CURIE, EVE			
Madame Curie.	PB 400	46	.25
_____.	Card GC-57	59	.50
CURRAN, DALE			
Dupree blues.	Berk 348	56	.25
CURRIER, JAY L.			
Cargo of fear.	Han 76	48	.25
CURRY, PEGGY SIMSON			
So far from spring.	Pop G213	58	.35
CURTIN, ARTHUR			
Love off-limits.	Pyr 176	56	.25
CURTIS, CAROL			
Carol Curtis' complete			
book of knitting and			
crocheting.	Card C-125	54	.35
CURTIS, JEAN-LOUIS			
Dark streets of Paris.	Pop 587	54	.25
CURTISS, URSULA			
Catch a killer.	PB 940	53	.25
The deadly climate.	PB 1077	55	.25
Voice out of darkness.	PB 659	50	.25
Widow's web.	PB 1157	57	.25
CURWOOD, JAMES OLIVER			
Steele of the Royal			
Mounted.	PB 362	46	.25
CUSHMAN, CLARISSA FAIRCHILD			
Young widow.	PB 339	46	.25
CUSHMAN, DAN			
Badlands justice.	Dell 656	53	.25
The fabulous Finn.	GM 392	54	.25
The fastest gun.	DelF 67	55	.25
The forbidden land.	GM 785	58	.25

Author/Title	Pub./Stock No.	Yr.	Price
Jewel of the Java Sea.	GM 142	51	.25
_____.	GM s840	59	.35
Jungle she.	GM 290	53	.25
Montana, here I be!	Dell 575	52	.25
Naked ebony.	GM 158	51	.25
_____.	GM s828	58	.35
The old copper collar.	Ball 281K	58	.35
Port Orient.	GM 535	55	.25
The ripper from Rawhide.	Dell 720	53	.25
Savage interlude.	GM 241	52	.25
The silver mountain.	Crst d264	59	.50
Stay away, Joe.	Pop 548	54	.25
_____.	Eag EB102	58	.25
Tall Wyoming.	DelF A140	57	.25
Timberjack.	GM 332	53	.25
Tongking!	Ace D-49	54	.35
CUTHBERT, CLIFTON			
Art colony.	Lion 58	51	.25
	Lion LL 98	56	.35
Joy street.	Lion 54	51	.25
_____.	Lion 101	52	.25
_____.	Lion LL 75	56	.35
The robbed heart.	Dell 512	51	.25
The shame of Mary Quinn.	Pyr 28	51	.25
_____.	Pyr 179	56	.25
_____.	Pyr G413	59	.35
CUTOLO, S. R. et al.			
Bellevue is my home.	Perm M-4083	57	.35

Author/Title	Pub./Stock No.	Yr.	Price

D

D'AGOSTINO, GUIDO
My enemy, the world.   Pop 540 53 .25

DAHNKE, MARYE
Marye Dahnke's salad
  book.   Card C-129 54 .35

d'ALESSIO, GREGORY
These women.   Pop 719 56 .25

DALRYMPLE, BYRON
All you need to know
  about fishing, hunting
  and camping.   PB 674 50 .25
The fundamentals of
  fishing and hunting.   Perm M-4136 59 .35

DALY, ELIZABETH
Any shape or form.   Ban 811 50 .25
The book of the dead.   Ban 353 48 .25
Deadly nightshade.   Ban 78 47 .25
Evidence of things seen. Ban 4 45 .25
The house without the
  door.   Sup M653 45 .25
Murder listens in.   Ban 713 49 .25
Murders in volume II.   Pen 549 44 .25
Nothing can rescue me.   Ban 53 46 .25
Unexpected night.   Sup M639 44 .25

DALY, MAUREEN
The perfect hostess.   PB 751 51 .25

DANA, RICHARD HENRY
Two years before the
  mast.   Pyr 76 53 .25
  _____.   PyrR PR12 58 .35
  _____.   BanC FC20 59 .50

DANFORTH, HAROLD R. with James D. Horan
The D.A.'s man.   Perm M-4118 59 .35

DANGEROUS game.   Pyr 156 55 .25

DANIELS, ANNA K.
It's never too late to
  love.   Pyr R188 56 .35
  _____.   PyrR PR19 59 .35

DANIELS, FRANK
The mating cry.   GM 449 55 .25
  _____.   GM 885 59 .25

DANIELS, HAROLD R.
The accused.   DelF B116 58 .35
The girl in 304.   DelF A112 56 .25
In his blood.   DelF 73 55 .25
The snatch.   DelF A170 58 .25

DANIELS, JOHN S.
Gunflame.   Ban 1189 54 .25
The land grabbers.   Ban 1769 58 .25
The man from yesterday.   Sig 1435 57 .25
The nester.   Pnnt P69 54 .25
Smoke of the gun.   Sig 1505 58 .25
Ute country.   Sig 1605 59 .25

DANIELS, NORMAN
The captive.   Avon T-370 59 .35
The deadly game.   Avon 864 59 .25

DANIELSSON, BENGT
Love in the South Seas.   Dell D199 57 .35

DANOËN, ÉMILE
Tides of time.   Ball 6 53 .35

DANTE ALIGHIERI
The Inferno.   Ment Ms113 54 .50

DARIEN, KIM
Dark rapture.   Ace S-117 55 .25
Golden girl.   Ace S-158 56 .25

DARLING, ESTHER BIRDSALL
Baldy of Nome.   PBJr J-38 50 .25

DARNTON, CHRISTIAN
You and music.   Pel P3 46 .25

DARRELL, R. D.
Good listening.   Ment MD122 55 .50

DARROW, WHITNEY JR.
Hold it, Florence.   Dell 786 54 .25

DARWIN, CHARLES
The living thoughts of
  Darwin.   Prem d82 59 .50
The origin of the
  species.   Ment MD222 58 .50
The voyage of the Beagle. BanC FC11 58 .50

DAUDET, ALPHONSE
Sappho.   Avon 294 50 .25
  _____.   Avon 691 56 .25

DAUGHERTY, KERMIT
Out of the Red Brush.   Sig 1202 55 .25

DAUGHTERS of Eve.   Berk G-40 56 .35

DAVENPORT, BASIL
Deals with the Devil.   Ball 326K 59 .35
Great escapes.   Card C-118 53 .35

DAVENPORT, GWEN
Belvedere.   Ban 729 49 .25

Author/Title	Pub./Stock No.	Yr.	Price
DAVENPORT, MARCIA			
My brother's keeper.	Card C-224	56	.35
DAVES, DELMER			
Stage door canteen.	Avon (32)	43	.25
DAVIDOFF, HENRY			
The Pocket book of			
quotations.	PB 176	42	.25
_____.	Card C-16	51	.35
DAVIDSON, DAVID			
The hour of truth.	Ban 754	50	.25
The night is mine.	Pop 510	53	.25
The steeper cliff.	Ban 801	50	.25
DAVIDSON, LOUIS B. with Eddie Doherty			
Captain Marooner.	Card C-117	53	.35
DAVIES, A. POWELL			
The first Christian.	Ment MD252	59	.50
The meaning of the Dead			
Sea scrolls.	SigK Ks339	56	.35
_____.	Ment MD219	58	.50
The Ten commandments.	SigK Ks343	56	.35
DAVIES, JOSEPH E.			
Mission to Moscow.	PB 203	43	.25
DAVIES, RHYS			
Marianne.	Pop G113	52	.35
DAVIES, VALENTINE			
It happens every spring.	Avon 249	50	.25
Miracle on 34th Street.	PB 903	52	.25
DAVIS, BURKE			
The ragged ones.	Card C-89	53	.35
Yorktown.	Card C-123	54	.35
DAVIS, CHRISTOPHER			
Lost summer.	Crst d319	59	.50
DAVIS, CLYDE BRION			
The rebellion of Leo			
McGuire.	Ban 838	50	.25
DAVIS, DEXTER			
The 7-day system for			
gaining self-confidence,			
popularity and			
financial success.	Ace D-88	55	.35
DAVIS, DON			
Death on treasure trail.	PB 853	52	.25
Return of the Rio Kid.	PB 660	50	.25
Rio Kid justice.	PB 921	53	.25
Two-gun Rio Kid.	PB 1023	54	.25

Author/Title	Pub./Stock No.	Yr.	Price
DAVIS, DORIS			
The women of Champion			
City.	PB 905	52	.25
DAVIS, DOROTHY SALISBURY			
The clay hand.	Ban 1013	52	.25
A gentle murderer.	Ban 1083	53	.25
_____.	Dell D286	59	.35
The Judas cat.	Ban 927	51	.25
A town of masks.	Dell 823	55	.25
DAVIS, EDDIE			
Campus joke book.	Ace S-171	56	.25
Gag writer's private			
joke book.	Ace S-161	56	.25
Laugh yourself well.	Pop 812	57	.25
Playgirls, U.S.A.	Pyr 205	56	.25
Stories for stags.	Lion LL 95	56	.35
DAVIS, ELMER			
But we were born free.	Perm M-4040	56	.35
DAVIS, FRANKLIN M. JR.			
The naked and the lost.	Lion 221	54	.25
Spearhead.	Perm M-3118	58	.25
DAVIS, FREDERICK C.			
The deadly Miss Ashley.	PB 804	51	.25
Drag the dark.	Ace D-63	54	.35
DAVIS, GARTH			
Gallows trail.	Pyr 389	59	.25
DAVIS, GORDON			
I came to kill.	GM 349	53	.25
DAVIS, H. L.			
Beulah Land.	PB 889	52	.25
Honey in the horn.	Card C-18	51	.35
Winds of morning.	PB 944	53	.25
DAVIS, HARRY			
My brother's wife.	Pop 809	57	.25
Portrait of Rene.	Eag EB100	57	.25
DAVIS, HELEN MILES			
The chemical elements.	Ball BSF320	59	.50
DAVIS, JADA M.			
One for hell.	RS 24	53	.35
The outraged sect.	Avon 713	56	.25
DAVIS, JULIA			
No other white men.	Com 30	49	.25
DAVIS, KENNETH S.			
Soldier of democracy.	Ban F1021	52	.50
DAVIS, LAVINIA R.			
Hobby Horse hill.	Com 22	49	.25

Author/Title	Pub./Stock No.		Yr.	Price
DAVIS, MAC				
Great American sports				
humor.	PB	718	50	.25
Sports shorts.	Ban	A1981	59	.35
DAVIS, MAXINE				
The sexual responsibility				
of woman.	Perm	M-5009	59	.50
Woman's medical problems.	PB	957	53	.25
DAVIS, MILDRED				
The room upstairs.	PB	638	49	.25
DAVIS, NORBERT				
Dead little rich girl.	Han	40	45	.15
Oh, murderer mine.	Han	54	46	.20
DAVIS, ROBERT				
Partners of Powder Hole.	PBJr	J-77	51	.35
DAVIS, WESLEY FORD				
The time of the panther.	Pop	G315	59	.35
DAWSON, PETER				
The big outfit.	Ban	1361	55	.25
Canyon hell.	Lion	10	49	.25
The crimson horseshoe.	Ban	94	47	.25
———.	Ban	1113	53	.25
———.	Ban	A1999	59	.35
Dead Man Pass.	Ban	1396	55	.25
Guns on the Santa Fe.	Lion	37	50	.25
Gunsmoke graze.	Dell	352	49	.25
———.	Dell	716	53	.25
High country.	Pnnt	P77	55	.25
The killers.	Ban	1363	55	.25
Leashed guns.	Lion	LB 61	55	.25
Long ride.	Pnnt	P22	53	.25
Man on the buckskin.	Ban	1642	57	.25
The outlaw of Longbow.	Ban	974	52	.25
———.	Ban	1856	58	.25
Renegade canyon.	Dell	559	51	.25
———.	Dell	938	57	.25
Royal Gorge.	Ban	1206	54	.25
Ruler of the range.	Pnnt	P9	53	.25
The savages.	Ban	1984	59	.25
The Stagline feud.	Ban	250	48	.25
———.	Ban	1277	54	.25
The stirrup boss.	Dell	490	51	.25
———.	Dell	832	55	.25
Trail boss.	Ban	36	46	.25
———.	Ban	1064	52	.25
———.	Ban	1695	57	.25
Treachery at Rock Point.	DelF	A148	57	.25
The wild bunch.	Lion	143	53	.25
DAY, A. GROVE with James A. Michener				
Rascals in paradise.	Ban	F1844	58	.50
DAY, BETH				
No hiding place.	Perm	M-4112	58	.35

Author/Title	Pub./Stock No.		Yr.	Price
DAY, CHON				
Brother Sebastian.	PB	1224	59	.25
DAY, CLARENCE				
Life with father.	PB	280	44	.25
DAY, JOHN I. with Rowland Barber				
1953 racing almanac.	Dell	671	53	.25
DEAD on arrival.	Hill	27	49	.25
DEAL, BORDEN				
Killer in the house.	Sig	1383	57	.25
Search for surrender.	GM	s632	57	.35
Walk through the valley.	Pop	G222	58	.35
DEAN, ABNER				
What am I doing here?	Sig	1382	57	.25
DEAN, AMBER				
The devil threw dice.	PB	1090	56	.25
DEAN, DUDLEY				
Ambush at Rincon.	GM	318	53	.25
Border renegade.	Crst	177	57	.25
The broken spur.	GM	511	55	.25
The diehards.	GM	584	56	.25
Gun in the valley.	GM	655	57	.25
Lawless guns.	GM	882	59	.25
The man from Riondo.	GM	436	54	.25
Six-gun vengeance.	Crst	154	56	.25
Song of the gun.	GM	471	55	.25
———.	GM	925	59	.25
Tough hombre.	GM	601	56	.25
with Les Savage Jr.				
Gun shy.	GM	912	59	.25
DEAN, GRAHAM				
Riders of the Gabilans.	PBJr	J-74	51	.35
DEAN, ROBERT GEORGE				
A murder by marriage.	Ban	6	45	.25
Murder in mink.	Sup	M645	45	.25
On ice.	Sup	M654	45	.25
———.	Ban	148	48	.25
DEAN, SPENCER				
Dishonor among thieves.	PB	1248	59	.25
The frightened fingers.	Dell	893	56	.25
Marked down for murder.	Ace	D-253	57	.35
Murder on delivery.	PB	1220	58	.25
DEAN, VERA MICHELES				
The nature of the non-				
western world.	Ment	MD190	57	.50
de BOUT, JACQUES				
Pierre's woman.	Pyr	133	54	.25
de CAMP, L. SPRAGUE				
Cosmic manhunt.	Ace	D-61	54	.35

Author/Title	Pub./Stock No.	Yr.	Price
de CAMP, L. SPRAGUE (cont.)			
Rogue queen.	Dell 600	52	.25
DEE, RHAR with Walter Chandoha			
Catnips at love and marriage.	GM 160	51	.25
DEE, ROGER			
An earth gone mad.	Ace D-84	54	.35
Let the sky fall.	Pop 819	57	.25
DEFOE, DANIEL			
Moll Flanders.	Card C-44	52	.35
Robinson Crusoe.	PBL PL510	57	.50
Tales of piracy, crime and ghosts.	Pen 554	45	.25
DEISS, JAY			
The blue chips.	Ban A1845	58	.35
DEKOBRA, MAURICE			
The bachelor's widow.	Ace S-85	54	.25
Bedroom eyes.	NL 18	49	.25
The love clinic.	NL 28	49	.25
Madonna of the sleeping cars.	Dell 256	48	.25
Street of painted lips.	NL 9	48	.25
Venus on wheels.	NL 25	49	.25
deKRUIF, PAUL			
Hunger fighters.	PB 155	42	.25
Microbe hunters.	PB 49	40	.25
_____.	Card GC-76	59	.50
DELANO, FRED			
Hellgate Canyon.	Pop 455	52	.25
de la ROCHE, MAZO			
Jalna.	PB 290	45	.25
_____.	Ban A1864	58	.35
Whiteoaks of Jalna.	PB 375	46	.25
DE LA TORRE, LILLIAN			
The truth about Belle Gunness.	GM 487	55	.25
DEL CASTILLO, MICHEL			
Child of our time.	Dell D319	59	.35
DE LEEUW, HENDRIK			
Sinful cities of the western world.	Pyr 27	51	.25
de LIMA, SIGRID			
A mask of guilt.	Lion LL 27	55	.35
DELMAN, DAVID			
The hard sell.	Ban A1921	59	.35
DELMAR, VIÑA			
About Mrs. Leslie.	PB 838	52	.25
Bad girl.	Avon 81	46	.25
_____.	Avon AT51	53	.35
Beloved.	Dell F69	58	.50
Kept woman.	Avon 121	47	.25
_____.	Avon 286	50	.25
Loose ladies.	Avon 92	46	.25
The love trap.	Avon 187	49	.25
The marriage racket.	Avon 107	46	.25
New Orleans lady.	Avon 209	49	.25
The restless passion.	Avon 145	47	.25
Ruby.	PB 915	53	.25
Strangers in love.	DelT 9	51	.10
del REY, LESTER			
Nerves.	Ball 151	56	.35
Robots and changelings.	Ball 246	58	.35
deMARE, GEORGE			
The empire--and Martin Brill.	Crst s163	57	.35
The ruling passion.	Crst s343	59	.35
DEMARIS, OVID			
The hoods take over.	GM 680	57	.25
The long night.	Avon T-372	59	.35
The lusting drive.	GM 750	58	.25
Ride the gold mare.	GM 644	57	.25
The slasher.	GM s910	59	.35
DE MEYER, JOHN			
Bailey's daughters.	Lion 102	52	.25
_____.	Berk 358	56	.25
_____.	Berk G-147	58	.35
de MILLE, AGNES			
Dance to the piper.	Ban A1185	54	.35
DEMING, RICHARD			
Dragnet: the case of the courteous killer.	PB 1198	58	.25
Dragnet: the case of the crime king.	PB 1214	59	.25
Fall girl.	Zen ZB-20	59	.35
The gallows in my garden.	Dell 682	53	.25
DE MOTTE, WARREN			
The long playing record guide.	DelF FE75	55	.50
DEMPSEY, DAVID			
Flood.	Ball 143	56	.35
DEMPSTER, DEREK D. with Kenneth W. Gatland			
The inhabited universe.	Prem d83	59	.50
DENBY, WILLIAM			
Act of outrage.	Lion LL 20	55	.35
DENKER, HENRY			
I'll be right home, Ma.	Pop 355	51	.25

Author/Title	Pub./Stock No.	Yr.	Price
DENKER, HENRY (cont.)			
Salome, the princess of Galilee.	Prmb P237	53	.35
DENNIS, PATRICK			
Around the world with Auntie Mame.	Sig D1709	59	.50
Auntie Mame.	Pop SP6	56	.50
with Dorothy Erskine			
The pink hotel.	Crst s227	58	.35
with Barbara Hooton			
Guestward ho!	Pop SP16	58	.50
DENT, LESTER			
Cry at dusk.	GM 247	52	.25
High stakes.	Ace D-21	53	.35
Lady in peril.	Ace D-357	59	.35
DENZER, PETER W.			
Episode.	Pop 621	54	.25
I'm no good.	Pop 744	56	.25
The last hero.	Pop G308	59	.35
Lust to live.	Mon 127	59	.35
de ONÍS, HARRIET			
Spanish stories and tales.	PBL PL-40	56	.35
DE PEREDA, PRUDENCIO			
All the girls we loved.	Sig 691	48	.25
————.	Berk 110	55	.25
DEPEW, WALLY			
Breakaway.	Perm M-4080	57	.35
DERBY, MARK			
Afraid in the dark.	Pop G124	53	.35
The bad step.	Perm M-3028	56	.25
The big water.	Perm M-3017	55	.25
Echo of a bomb.	Ban A1824	58	.35
Element of risk.	Prmb 265	54	.25
Sun in the hunter's eyes.	Crst s306	59	.35
The sunlit ambush.	Dell D320	59	.35
DERLETH, AUGUST			
Beachheads in space.	Berk G-77	57	.35
Beyond time and space.	Berk G-104	58	.35
The other side of the moon.	Berk G249	59	.35
The outer reaches.	Berk G-116	58	.35
Strange ports of call.	Berk G-131	58	.35
Time to come.	Berk G-189	58	.35
Worlds of tomorrow.	Berk G-163	58	.35
DE ROO, EDWARD			
The fires of youth.	Ace S-105	55	.25
————.	Ace D-338	59	.35
Go, man, go!	Ace D-406	59	.35
The young wolves.	Ace D-343	59	.35
de ROPP, ROBERT S.			
If I forget thee.	Pop SP22	58	.50
DeROSSO, H. A.			
End of the gun.	Perm M-3014	55	.25
.44.	Lion 129	53	.25
————.	Lion LB 145	56	.25
The gun trail.	Lion 175	53	.25
The man from Texas.	Lion LB 154	57	.25
DERVAL, PAUL			
Folies-Bergère.	Pop G170	56	.35
de SANTILLANA, GIORGIO			
The age of adventure.	Ment MD184	56	.50
des CARS, GUY			
The brute.	Pyr G69	53	.35
The damned one.	Pyr G224	56	.35
Woman of Paris.	Pop 711	55	.25
DESMOND, WARREN			
Night of flame.	Sig 721	49	.25
de STEIGUER, WALTER			
Jewels for a shroud.	Dell 614	52	.25
DEVEREUX, JAMES P. S.			
The story of Wake Island.	Ace D-280	58	.35
DEVIGNY, ANDRÉ			
A man escaped.	Berk BG254	59	.50
DEVLIN, B.			
Forbidden pleasures.	Berk G-205	59	.35
DE VRIES, MARVIN			
Frontier.	Ball 164	56	.35
DE VRIES, PETER			
Comfort me with apples.	Sig S1451	57	.35
The Mackerel Plaza.	Sig S1648	59	.35
No but I saw the movie.	Sig S1698	59	.35
The tunnel of love.	Lion LL 34	55	.35
————.	Sig S1507	58	.35
DE VRIES, ROBERT			
Of sin and the flesh.	Crst s140	56	.35
DEWELL, MICHAEL			
Hell and high water.	Pyr 198	56	.25
DEWEY, JOHN			
Reconstruction in philosophy.	Ment M53	50	.35
DEWEY, THOMAS B.			
And where she stops.	Pop 816	57	.25
As good as dead.	PenN 663	48	.25
The brave, bad girls.	Perm M-3089	57	.25

Author/Title	Pub./Stock No.	Yr.	Price
DEWEY, THOMAS B. (cont.)			
The case of the murdered model.	Avon 626	55	.25
.	Avon 787	57	.25
Dame in danger.	Sig 1538	58	.25
Draw the curtain close.	Sig 736	49	.25
Every bet's a sure thing.	Avon 564	54	.25
Go to sleep, Jeannie.	Pop G302	59	.35
Handle with fear.	Graf 73	54	.25
The mean streets.	Perm M-3032	56	.25
Mourning after.	Ace D-41	54	.35
My love is violent.	Pop 730	56	.25
Room for murder.	Sig 814	50	.25
You've got him cold.	Crst 323	59	.25
DEWLEN, AL			
The golden touch.	Pop SP52	59	.50
de WOHL, LOUIS			
The living wood.	Pop G392	59	.35
The spear.	Pop SP10	57	.50
DIAMOND, FRANK			
Love me to death.	Ace D-123	55	.35
DIAMOND, I. A. L. with Billy Wilder			
Some like it hot.	Sig S1656	59	.35
DIBNER, MARTIN			
The deep six.	Prmb P311	54	.35
.	Perm M-4028	55	.35
Journey to nowhere.	Prmb P185	52	.35
Showcase.	Crst d312	59	.50
DICK, PHILIP K.			
The cosmic puppets.	Ace D-249	57	.35
Eye in the sky.	Ace D-211	57	.35
The man who japed.	Ace D-193	56	.35
Solar lottery.	Ace D-103	55	.35
.	Ace D-340	59	.35
The variable man and other stories.	Ace D-261	57	.35
The world Jones made.	Ace D-150	56	.35
DICKENS, CHARLES			
A Christmas carol.	PB 29	39	.25
.	PBL PL68	58	.35
David Copperfield.	Dell F70	58	.50
.	PBL PL751	58	.75
Great expectations.	PBL PL50	56	.35
Oliver Twist.	PB 519	48	.25
.	PBL PL514	57	.50
A tale of two cities.	PB 14	39	.25
.	Card C-35	52	.35
.	PBL PL22	54	.35
.	PBL PL522	58	.50
DICKSON, CARTER			
And so to murder.	Dell 175	47	.25
Behind the crimson blind.	Dell 690	53	.25

Author/Title	Pub./Stock No.	Yr.	Price
The bowstring murders.	PB 46	40	.25
.	Berk G-214	59	.35
The curse of the bronze lamp.	PB 568	49	.25
Death--and the gilded man.	PB 478	47	.25
Death in five boxes.	Dell 108	46	.25
Fear is the same.	Ban A2000	59	.35
A graveyard to let.	Dell 543	51	.25
He wouldn't kill Patience.	Dell 370	50	.25
The Judas window.	PB 231	43	.25
My late wives.	PB 633	49	.25
Night at the Mocking Widow.	Dell 650	53	.25
Nine--and death makes ten.	PB 335	46	.25
The peacock feather murders.	PB 180	42	.25
The Plague court murders.	Avon (7)	41	.25
.	Berk G267	59	.35
The Punch and Judy murders.	PB 219	43	.25
The reader is warned.	PB 303	45	.25
The red widow murders.	PB 86	40	.25
Scotland Yard.	Dell 65	44	.25
Seeing is believing.	PB 386	46	.25
She died a lady.	PB 507	48	.25
The skeleton in the clock.	Dell 481	51	.25
The unicorn murders.	Dell 16	43	.25
The White priory murders.	PB 156	42	.25
with John Rhode			
Fatal descent.	Pop 87	47	.25
DICKSON, GORDON R.			
Alien from Arcturus.	Ace D-139	56	.35
Mankind on the run.	Ace D-164	56	.35
di DONATO, PIETRO			
Christ in concrete.	Lion 18	50	.25
This woman.	Ball F277K	58	.50
DIETRICH, ROBERT			
Be my victim.	DelF 106	56	.25
The cheat.	Pyr 135	54	.25
The house on Q Street.	DelF A175	59	.25
Murder on the rocks.	DelF A141	57	.25
One for the road.	Pyr 128	54	.25
.	Pyr 235	57	.25
DIETZ, DAVID			
Atomic energy in the coming era.	Avon 76	45	.25
DIKTY, T. E.			
Five tales from tomorrow.	Crst s197	57	.35
Six from worlds beyond.	Crst s258	58	.35
with Everett F. Bleiler			
Frontiers in space.	Ban 1328	55	.25

Author/Title	Pub./Stock No.	Yr.	Price
DIKTY, T. E. (cont.)			
with Everett F. Bleiler			
Imagination unlimited.	Berk G233	59	.35
DILLON, JOHN			
The spotted horse.	Ball 194	57	.35
DI MAGGIO, JOE			
Baseball for everyone.	Sig 719	49	.25
Lucky to be a Yankee.	Ban 506	49	.25
DIMNET, ERNEST			
The art of thinking.	PB 160	42	.25
————.	Prem s16	55	.35
DINESEN, ISAK			
Winter's tales.	Dell D191	57	.35
DINGWALL, ERIC J.			
The American woman.	Sig D1591	58	.50
with John Langdon-Davies			
The unknown--is it			
nearer?	SigK Ks336	56	.35
DINNEEN, JOSEPH F.			
The anatomy of a crime.	Avon 701	56	.25
Underworld U.S.A.	Perm M-4085	57	.35
DIRKSEN, JOAN			
I'll find my love.	Berk G-221	59	.35
DISNEY, DORIS MILES			
Dead stop.	Dell 929	56	.25
Straw man.	Dell 885	56	.25
Too innocent to kill.	Avon T-319	59	.35
DISNEY, DOROTHY CAMERON			
The balcony.	PB 152	42	.25
Crimson Friday.	Dell 137	46	.25
Death in the back seat.	Dell 76	45	.25
Explosion.	Ban 761	50	.25
The golden swan murder.	Dell 15	43	.25
The hangman's tree.	Ban 863	51	.25
The seventeenth letter.	Ban 91	47	.25
The strawstack murders.	Dell 62	44	.25
DIVINE, DAVID			
Boy on a dolphin.	Avon T-165	57	.35
DIX, BEULAH MARIE with Bertram Millhauser			
Hot leather.	Ban 554	48	.25
DIXON, H. VERNOR			
Cry blood.	GM s564	56	.35
Deep is the pit.	GM G212	52	.35
The hunger and the hate.	GM S454	55	.35
Killer in silk.	GM s616	56	.35
A lover for Cindy.	GM 370	54	.25
The marriage bed.	RS 18	52	.35
Something for nothing.	Ban 875	51	.25

Author/Title	Pub./Stock No.	Yr.	Price
To hell together.	GM 198	51	.35
————.	GM s922	59	.35
Too rich to die.	GM 285	53	.25
Up a winding stair.	GM 316	53	.25
DJEBAR, ASSIA			
Nadia.	Avon T-338	59	.35
DOBBIN, JOHN			
The flesh and the sea.	Avon T-100	55	.35
DOBIE, J. FRANK			
Apache gold and Yaqui			
silver.	Ban 940	51	.25
Coronado's children.	Ban A1089	53	.35
The mustangs.	Ban A1212	54	.35
————.	Ban F1778	58	.50
A vaquero of the brush			
country.	Pnnt P51	54	.25
DOBZHANSKY, TH. with L. C. Dunn			
Heredity, race and			
society.	Pel P11	46	.25
————.	Pel P23	47	.35
————.	Ment M74	52	.35
DODGE, DAVID			
Angel's ransom.	Dell D304	59	.35
Bullets for the			
bridegroom.	Pop 252	50	.25
Death and taxes.	Pop 168	48	.25
It ain't hay.	Dell 270	49	.25
————.	Dell 350	49	.25
The long escape.	Dell 405	50	.25
Plunder of the sun.	Dell 478	51	.25
The red tassel.	Dell 565	52	.25
Shear the black sheep.	Pop 202	49	.25
To catch a thief.	Dell 658	53	.25
DODGE, GIL			
Flint.	Sig 1414	57	.25
DODGE, STEVE			
Shanghai incident.	GM 456	55	.25
DODSON, KENNETH			
Away all boats.	Ban F1415	56	.50
DOHERTY, EDDIE			
The corpse who wouldn't			
die.	Han 49	46	.15
with Louis B. Davidson			
Captain Marooner.	Card C-117	53	.35
DOLAN, MARY			
Hannibal.	Avon T-151	57	.35
DOLINSKY, MEYER			
Hot rod gang rumble.	Avon 783	57	.25

Author/Title	Pub./Stock No.	Yr.	Price
d'OLIVE, GENE			
Chiara.	Sig D1680	59	.50
DOLPH, JACK			
Murder is mutuel.	Dell 419	50	.25
DOLSON, HILDEGARDE			
The husband who ran away.	Ban 887	51	.25
DONALDS, GORDON			
The desperate Donigans.	Ace D-204	57	.35
Top gun.	Crst 185	57	.25
DONISTHORPE, G. SHEILA			
Loveliest of friends.	Berk 102	55	.25
———.	Berk 359	56	.25
———.	Berk G-172	58	.35
DONLEAVY, J. P.			
The ginger man.	Berk BG264	59	.50
DONNER, JAMES			
Women in trouble.	MonB MB501	59	.35
DOOLEY, THOMAS A.			
Deliver us from evil.	Berk G271	59	.35
The edge of tomorrow.	Berk G272	59	.35
DORIAN, EDITH			
Mystery on Graveyard Head.	Berk G-176	58	.35
DORIEN, RAY			
Lyn Darling, M.D.	Crst 339	59	.25
DORNBERGER, WALTER			
V-2: the Nazi rocket.	Ball F273K	58	.50
DORTORT, DAVID			
Burial of the fruit.	Avon 183	48	.25
———.	Avon 326	51	.25
———.	Avon 541	53	.25
———.	Avon T-143	56	.35
DOS PASSOS, JOHN			
Adventures of a young man.	Lion LL 42	55	.35
The big money.	Card GC-26	55	.50
The 42nd parallel.	Card C-72	52	.35
The great days.	Pop SP53	59	.50
Manhattan transfer.	Pen 577	46	.25
———.	BanC FC28	59	.50
1919.	Card C-131	54	.35
Number one.	Lion LL 1	54	.35
DOSTOYEVSKY, FYODOR			
The brothers Karamazov.	Dell F55	56	.50
———.	Sig T1488	58	.75
Crime and punishment.	Sig 733	49	.25
———.	Avon G-1024	56	.50

Author/Title	Pub./Stock No.	Yr.	Price
Crime and punishment.	Ban F1735	58	.50
———.	BanC FC30	59	.50
———.	DelL LX106	59	.75
The house of the dead.	DelL LC131	59	.50
The idiot.	BanC SC4	58	.75
DOUGALL, BERNARD			
The singing corpse.	Pony 46	45	.25
DOUGLAS, DEAN			
Man divided.	GM 407	54	.25
DOUGLAS, LLOYD C.			
The Big Fisherman.	Card GC-59	59	.50
Disputed passage.	PB 352	46	.25
———.	Card C-176	55	.35
Doctor Hudson's secret journal.	Dell 304	49	.25
———.	PB 1096	56	.25
Forgive us our trespasses.	PB 405	47	.25
———.	Card C-240	57	.35
Green light.	PB 175	42	.25
———.	Card C-269	57	.35
Invitation to live.	Dell 380	50	.25
Magnificent obsession.	PB 215	43	.25
———.	Card C-257	57	.35
The robe.	Card GC-53	58	.50
White banners.	PB 387	46	.25
———.	Card C-336	59	.35
DOUGLAS, MALCOLM			
The deadly dames.	GM 614	56	.25
Murder comes calling.	GM 776	58	.25
Prey by night.	GM 477	55	.25
Pure sweet hell.	GM 654	57	.25
Rain of terror.	GM 539	56	.25
DOUGLAS, NORMAN			
South wind.	Ban 65	46	.25
———.	Ban F1777	58	.50
DOUGLASS, DONALD McNUTT			
Rebecca's pride.	PB 1178	57	.25
DOW, JOHN			
The blonde is dead.	Han 45	45	.15
DOWD, HARRISON			
The night air.	Avon AT52	53	.35
DOWDEY, CLIFFORD			
Bugles blow no more.	Prmb P159	52	.35
Jasmine Street.	Pop G119	53	.35
The proud retreat.	Prmb P282	54	.35
Tidewater.	Prmb P143	52	.35
DOWNEY, FAIRFAX			
Indian-fighting army.	Ban F1661	57	.50

Author/Title	Pub./Stock No.	Yr.	Price
DOWNING, TODD			
The cat screams.	Pop 68	45	.25
DOWNS, ROBERT B.			
Books that changed the world.	Ment M168	56	.35
————.	Ment MD229	58	.50
DOWST, ROBERT			
Win, place and show.	PB 458	48	.25
DOYLE, ADRIAN CONAN with John Dickson Carr			
The exploits of Sherlock Holmes.	Ace D-181	56	.35
DOYLE, ARTHUR CONAN			
The case book of Sherlock Holmes.	PB 670	50	.25
The hound of the Baskervilles.	Ban 366	49	.25
————.	Dell D302	59	.35
The lost world.	Prmb 279	54	.25
————.	PyrR PR15	58	.35
The memoirs of Sherlock Holmes.	Ban 704	49	.25
The Sherlock Holmes Pocket book.	PB 95	41	.25
The valley of fear.	Ban 733	50	.25
DOYLE, WILLIAM with Scott O'Dell			
Man alone.	Ban 1247	54	.25
DRACHMAN, THEODORE S.			
Cry plague!	Ace D-13	53	.35
DRAGO, HARRY SINCLAIR			
Buckskin empire.	Dell 660	53	.25
Decision at Broken Butte.	Perm M-3068	57	.25
The desert hawk.	Pop 305	51	.25
Love toy.	NL 21	49	.25
Montana road.	Pop 406	52	.25
————.	Eag EB71	56	.25
Pay-off at Black Hawk.	Perm M-3038	56	.25
Rebel basin.	PB 1257	59	.25
Showdown at sunset.	Perm M-3115	58	.25
Stagecoach kingdom.	Dell 789	54	.25
Their guns were fast.	Dell 919	56	.25
Top hand with a gun.	Crst 116	55	.25
Trigger gospel.	Ace D-112	55	.35
Wild grass.	Perm M-3085	57	.25
Women to love.	NL 16	49	.25
DRAKE, ALFRED			
Anyone can win at gin rummy and canasta.	Avon 218	49	.25
DRAKE, ARNOLD			
The steel noose.	Ace S-83	54	.25
DRATLER, JAY J.			
All for a woman.	Pop G269	58	.35
Doctor Paradise.	Pop 818	57	.25
Dream of a woman.	Pop G242	58	.35
The Judas kiss.	Pop 704	55	.25
The pitfall.	Ban 710	49	.25
————.	Pop 745	56	.25
DRECH, WOLFGANG von			
Cleaning house.	Ban A1521	56	.35
DREISER, THEODORE			
An American tragedy.	Sig 755	49	.25
————.	DelL LY101	59	.95
Sister Carrie.	PB 644	49	.25
————.	BanC FC6	58	.50
The titan.	DelL LX109	59	.75
DRESSER, DAVIS			
Death rides the Pecos.	PB 706	50	.25
Gunsmoke on the mesa.	Crst 131	56	.25
The hangman of Sleepy Valley.	PB 871	52	.25
Lynch-rope law.	PB 906	52	.25
DRESSLER, DAVID			
Parole chief.	Ban 1092	53	.25
DREW, ELIZABETH			
Poetry: a modern guide to its understanding and enjoyment.	DelL LC130	59	.50
DREW, LINCOLN			
Die in the saddle.	Perm M-3063	56	.25
Rifle ranch.	Perm M-3120	58	.25
Yellow rope.	Perm M-3107	58	.25
DRISCOLL, CHARLES B.			
Doubloons.	Pnnt P40	54	.25
DRUON, MAURICE			
The Iron King.	Ace D-302	58	.35
DRYER, BERNARD (VICTOR)			
The image makers.	Ban F1946	59	.50
Murder in Port Afrique.	Avon T-142	56	.35
Port Afrique.	Avon 224	50	.25
DuBOIS, THEODORA			
Seeing red.	Dell 860	55	.25
DUDLEY, ERNEST			
Picaroon.	Ban A1220	54	.35
DUDLEY, OWEN			
The deep end.	Ace D-195	56	.35
Murder for charity.	Ace D-231	57	.35
DUFF, JAMES			
Dangerous to know.	Ace D-361	59	.35
Some die young.	Graf 139	56	.25
Who dies there?	Graf 134	56	.25

Author/Title	Pub./Stock No.	Yr.	Price
DUFFY, CLINTON T. with Dean Jennings			
The San Quentin story.	PB 831	51	.25
DUFFY, PATRICK GAVIN			
The standard bartender's guide.	Prmb P5	51	.35
with James A. Beard			
The standard bartender's guide.	Perm M-4030	55	.35
DUFTY, WILLIAM			
with Billy Holiday			
Lady sings the blues.	Pop G208	58	.35
with Edward G. Robinson Jr.			
My father--my son.	Pop SP32	58	.50
DUHART, WILLIAM H.			
The deadly pay-off.	GM 805	58	.25
DUKE, WILL			
Fair prey.	Graf 142	56	.25
DUMAS, ALEXANDRE			
The Count of Monte Cristo.	Ban F1520	56	.50
The three musketeers, volume 1.	PB 36	40	.25
The three musketeers, volume 2.	PB 37	40	.25
DUMAS, ALEXANDRE, fils			
Camille.	Ban 745	49	.25
DUMAS, FRÉDÉRIC with Jacques-Yves Cousteau			
The silent world.	Card C-163	55	.35
du MAURIER, DAPHNE			
Frenchman's Creek.	PB 415	47	.25
Hungry hill.	Card C-6	51	.35
Jamaica Inn.	PB 403	46	.25
———.	Card C-326	59	.35
The king's general.	PB 483	48	.25
———.	Card C-99	53	.35
Kiss me again, stranger.	Card C-168	55	.35
Mary Anne.	Card C-216	56	.35
My cousin Rachel.	Card C-153	54	.35
The parasites.	Card C-68	52	.35
Rebecca.	PB 205	43	.25
———.	Card C-53	52	.35
The scapegoat.	Card C-276	58	.35
DUNCAN, DAVID			
Beyond Eden.	Ball 102	55	.35
Dark dominion.	Ball 56	54	.35
Occam's razor.	Ball 230	57	.35
Wives and husbands.	Sig 1047	53	.25
Worse than murder.	PB 985	54	.25
DUNCAN, ELEANOR S.			
Parents' magazine book of baby care.	Lion LL 39	55	.35
DUNCAN, PETER			
Sweet cheat.	DelF A182	59	.25
DUNCAN, THOMAS W.			
Gus the Great.	Dell F50	53	.50
DUNLAP, KATHARINE			
Encore for love.	Ban 412	48	.25
DUNN, BOB			
Hospital happy.	Avon 411	52	.25
DUNN, DOROTHY			
Murder's web.	PB 806	51	.25
DUNN, ELIZABETH			
Moonlit voyage.	Ban 450	48	.25
DUNN, L. C. with Th. Dobzhansky			
Heredity, race and society.	Pel P11	46	.25
———.	Pel P23	47	.35
———.	Ment M74	52	.35
DURAFOUR, MICHEL			
The girl from Rome.	Pop G150	55	.35
DURAND, G. FORBES			
Be silent forever.	PB 1258	59	.25
C.O.D. death.	Sig 1125	54	.25
A cold bier.	Sig 1406	57	.25
What hath God rot.	Eton E126	53	.25
X marks the shot.	Hill unk	49	.25
DURANT, WILL			
The story of philosophy.	Card GC-4	53	.50
———.	PBL PL11	54	.50
———.	PBL PL500	57	.50
DURAS, MARGUERITE			
The whispers of love.	Sig S1309	56	.35
DURRANT, THEO			
The big fear.	Pop 507	53	.25
DÜRRENMATT, FRIEDRICH			
The judge and his hangman.	Berk G-190	58	.35
DURST, PAUL			
Bloody river.	Lion 178	53	.25
———.	Lion LB 139	56	.25
Die, damn you!	Lion 75	52	.25
John Law, keep out!	Ace D-204	57	.35
Kansas guns.	Ace D-356	59	.35
Prairie reckoning.	GM 619	56	.25
DU SOE, ROBERT			
The devil thumbs a ride.	Avon 208	49	.25

Author/Title	Pub./Stock No.	Yr.	Price	Author/Title	Pub./Stock No.	Yr.	Price
DUTOURD, JEAN							
A dog's head.	Lion 196	54	.25				
DUVALL, EVELYN MILLIS							
Facts of life and love							
for teen-agers.	Pop 523	53	.25				
_____.	Pop G203	57	.35				
DYER, GEORGE							
The Catalyst club.	Pen 513	42	.25				

Author/Title	Pub./Stock No.	Yr.	Price

E

EAGAN, EDWARD P. F. with Joyce Brothers
| 10 days to a successful memory. | Perm M-4125 | 59 | .35 |

EAGLE, JOHN
| The hoodlums. | Avon 546 | 53 | .25 |

EARL, LAWRENCE
| The frozen jungle. | Ban A1670 | 57 | .35 |
| River of eyes. | Eag EB48 | 55 | .25 |

EAST, MICHAEL
| The concubine. | DelF A169 | 58 | .25 |

EASTERN shame girl and
| other stories. | Avon 127 | 47 | .25 |

EASTMAN, ELIZABETH
| His dead wife. | Lion 44 | 50 | .25 |

EASTON, LAWRENCE
| The driven flesh. | Ace S-119 | 55 | .25 |

EATON, EVELYN
| Quietly my captain waits. | Prmb P136 | 51 | .35 |
| Restless are the sails. | Prmb P188 | 52 | .35 |

EATON, FRANK
| Pistol Pete. | Sig 1050 | 53 | .25 |

EBERHART, MIGNON G.
Another man's murder.	Dell D259	59	.35
Another woman's house.	Ban 849	50	.25
Danger in the dark.	Pop (2)	43	.25
Dead man's plans.	Dell 767	54	.25
Deadly is the diamond.	DelT 7	51	.10
Escape the night.	Ban 46	46	.25
From this dark stairway.	Pop 27	44	.25
The hangman's whip.	Pop 293	50	.25
Hasty wedding.	Pop 73	46	.25
House of storm.	Ban 885	51	.25
The house on the roof.	Pop 17	43	.25
Hunt with the hounds.	Dell 546	51	.25
Man missing.	Dell 877	55	.25
The man next door.	Dell 161	47	.25
Murder by an aristocrat.	Pen 501	42	.25
The mystery of Hunting's end.	Pop 35	44	.25
Never look back.	Dell 669	53	.25
Pattern of murder.	Pop 167	48	.25
Postmark murder.	Dell 955	57	.25
Speak no evil.	Dell 25	43	.25
_____.	Dell 628	52	.25
Stranger in flight.	BPLA 28	41	.10
Unidentified woman.	Dell 213	48	.25
The unknown quantity.	Dell 811	54	.25
While the patient slept.	PB 64	40	.25
The white dress.	Ban 739	49	.25
Wings of fear.	Ban 137	48	.25

| With this ring. | Dell 83 | 45 | .25 |
| Wolf in man's clothing. | Dell 136 | 46 | .25 |

EBY, LOIS with John Fleming
| The velvet fleece. | Dell 272 | 49 | .25 |

ECHARD, MARGARET
| A man without friends. | Ban 967 | 52 | .25 |

ECHOLS, ALLAN K.
Double-cross brand.	Ace D-20	53	.35
The renegade hills.	Eton E113	52	.25
Terror rides the range.	Ace D-8	53	.35
Vengeance valley.	Eton E131	53	.25

ECKERT, RALPH G.
| Sex attitudes in the home. | Pop G224 | 58 | .35 |

EDDY, ROGER
| The bulls and the bees. | PB 1164 | 57 | .25 |
| A family affair. | Perm M-4126 | 59 | .35 |

EDELMAN, MAURICE
| How Russia prepared. | PenS S206 | 42 | .25 |

EDGLEY, LESLIE
False face.	Han 114	50	.25
Fear no more.	Ace D-19	53	.35
The Judas goat.	Ace D-13	53	.35
Tracked down.	Ace D-45	54	.35

EDMAN, IRWIN
| Arts and the man. | Ment M40 | 49 | .35 |
| Philosopher's holiday. | Pen 517 | 43 | .25 |

EDMONDS, WALTER D.
The Boyds of Black River.	Ban A1254	54	.35
The captive women.	Ban 708	49	.25
Chad Hanna.	Prmb P132	51	.35
Drums along the Mohawk.	Ban A804	50	.35
_____.	Ban F1648	57	.50
Rome haul.	Ban A1099	53	.35
The wedding journey.	DelT 6	51	.10
Young Ames.	Card C-121	53	.35

EDMONDSON, PAUL
| A little revolution. | Crst s335 | 59 | .35 |

EDWARDS, FRANK
| My first 10,000,000 sponsers. | Ball 138 | 56 | .35 |

EDWARDS, MORTON
| Your child from 2 to 5. | Perm M-4035 | 55 | .35 |

EDWARDS, SAMUEL
Devil's prize.	Crst s259	58	.35
The naked maja.	Ban A1941	59	.35
The scimitar.	Ban A1657	57	.35
That Randall girl.	Pop G333	59	.35

Author/Title	Pub./Stock No.	Yr.	Price
EHLE, JOHN			
The survivor.	Pyr G385	59	.35
EHRENWALD, JAN			
From medicine man to Freud.	DelF C103	56	.50
EHRLICH, JACK			
Court martial.	Pyr G463	59	.35
Revenge.	DelF A168	58	.25
EHRLICH, LEONARD			
God's angry man.	Card C-128	54	.35
EHRLICH, MAX			
The big eye.	Pop 273	50	.25
.	Ban A1860	58	.35
First train to Babylon.	Ban A1859	59	.35
Spin the glass web.	Ban 1096	53	.25
.	Pop 798	57	.25
EICHLER, ALFRED			
Death of an ad man.	Berk 105	55	.25
EIDELBERG, LUDWIG			
Take off your mask.	Pyr R273	57	.35
.	Pyr G404	59	.35
EIKER, KARL V.			
Star of Macedon.	Perm M-4094	58	.35
EIMERL, SAREL			
The cautious bachelor.	Crst 287	59	.25
EINSTEIN, CHARLES			
The bloody spur.	DelF 5	53	.25
The last laugh.	DelF A121	56	.25
No time at all.	Dell D224	58	.35
The only game in town.	DelF 47	55	.25
While the city sleeps.	DelF D86	56	.35
Wiretap!	DelF 76	55	.25
EISENHOWER, DWIGHT D.			
Crusade in Europe.	Prmb P158S	52	.50
EISINGER, JO			
The walls came tumbling down.	Han 36	45	.15
EISNER, SIMON			
The naked storm.	Lion 109	52	.25
.	Lion LL 125	56	.35
EKERT-ROTHOLZ, ALICE			
The time of the dragons.	Sig T1668	59	.75
ELBOGEN, PAUL			
The jealous mistress.	Pyr G222	56	.35

Author/Title	Pub./Stock No.	Yr.	Price
ELDRIDGE, PAUL with George Sylvester Viereck			
My first two thousand years.	Crst s148	56	.35
Salome.	Ace D-43	54	.35
ELIAT, HÉLÈNE			
Arena of love.	Lion 53	51	.25
ELIOT, ALEXANDER			
Proud youth.	Sig 1177	55	.25
.	Berk G-144	58	.35
ELIOT, GEORGE			
Adam Bede.	PBL PL507	56	.50
The mill on the Floss.	PBL PL509	56	.50
Silas Marner.	PB 552	48	.25
.	PBL PL27	55	.35
ELLIN, STANLEY			
The big night.	Lion 41	50	.25
The eighth circle.	Dell D311	59	.35
The key to Nicholas Street.	Dell 763	54	.25
Quiet horror.	Dell D325	59	.35
ELLINGTON, RICHARD			
Exit for a dame.	PB 941	53	.25
It's a crime.	PB 756	51	.25
Shakedown.	Ban 1286	55	.25
Shoot the works.	PB 624	49	.25
Stone cold dead.	PB 813	51	.25
ELLIOTT, BRUCE			
One is a lonely number.	Lion 100	52	.25
ELLIOTT, CHARLES			
Trial by fire.	Pop G254	58	.35
ELLIS, ALBERT			
Sex without guilt.	Hill 106	59	.50
ELLIS, HAVELOCK			
On life and sex.	Ment MD191	57	.50
Psychology of sex.	Ment Ms119	54	.50
Sex and marriage.	Pyr R246	57	.35
ELLIS, WILLIAM			
The bounty lands.	Dell F71	58	.50
ELLISON, HARLAN			
The deadly streets.	Ace D-312	58	.35
Rumble.	Pyr G352	58	.35
ELLISON, JAMES WHITFIELD			
I'm Owen Harrison Harding.	Sig S1452	57	.35
ELLISON, JEROME			
The prisoner ate a hardy breakfast.	Avon 521	53	.25

Author/Title	Pub./Stock No.	Yr.	Price
ELLISON, RALPH			
Invisible man.	Sig D1030	53	.50
ELLSON, HAL			
Duke.	Pop 219	50	.25
———.	Pop 757	56	.25
———.	Pop G358	59	.35
The golden spike.	Ball 2	52	.35
I'll fix you.	Pop 725	56	.25
Jailbait street.	Mon 137	59	.35
A killer's kiss.	Hill 119	59	.35
Rock.	Ball 103	55	.35
Stairway to nowhere.	Ball 319K	59	.35
Summer street.	Ball 27	53	.35
Tell them nothing.	Ball 129	56	.35
This is it.	Pop 776	56	.25
Tomboy.	Ban 945	51	.25
———.	Ban 1561	57	.25
ELMO, HORACE T.			
Hollywood humor.	Ace S-212	57	.25
Honeymoon humor.	Ace S-140	56	.25
Modern Casanova's			
handbook.	Ace S-93	55	.25
ELSTON, ALLAN VAUGHAN			
Colorado showdown.	Dell 742	53	.25
Deadline at Durango.	Dell 643	52	.25
Forbidden Valley.	PB 1116	56	.25
Gold brick range.	Dell 707	53	.25
Grand Mesa.	PB 1211	58	.25
Guns on the Cimarron.	PB 530	48	.25
Hit the saddle.	PB 585	49	.25
Last stage to Aspen.	PB 1191	58	.25
The marked men.	PB 1181	57	.25
Rio Grande deadline.	PB 1254	59	.25
Roundup on the			
Picketwire.	Dell 810	54	.25
Saddle up for sunlight.	Dell 861	55	.25
The sheriff of San			
Miguel.	Dell 545	51	.25
Showdown.	PB 1103	56	.25
Stage road to Denver.	PB 1064	55	.25
Wagon Wheel Gap.	PB 1086	55	.25
The Wyoming bubble.	PB 1163	57	.25
ELWOOD, MURIEL			
Heritage of the river.	Ban 774	50	.25
Web of destiny.	Ban A1002	52	.35
EMERICK, LUCILLE			
The city beyond.	Pop G120	53	.35
The web of evil.	Dell 479	51	.25
EMERSON, RALPH WALDO			
Basic selections from			
Emerson.	Ment M102	54	.35
Emerson.	DelL LC116	58	.50
Emerson: the basic			
writings of America's			
sage.	Pel P15	47	.25

Author/Title	Pub./Stock No.	Yr.	Price
The living thoughts of			
Ralph Waldo Emerson.	Prem d67	58	.50
EMERY, GUY			
Front for murder.	Avon 288	51	.25
High, inside!	PBJr J-66	51	.25
ENDERS, ROBERT K. with C. Brooke Worth			
The nature of living			
things.	SigK Ks326	55	.35
ENDORE, GUY			
The furies in her body.	Avon 323	51	.25
King of Paris.	Card GC-42	58	.50
Nightmare.	Dell D183	56	.35
The werewolf of Paris.	PB 97	41	.25
———.	Avon 354	51	.25
ENGEL, LEONARD			
New worlds of modern			
science.	DelF B102	56	.35
ENGEL, LOUIS			
How to buy stocks.	Ban A1296	55	.35
———.	Ban A1651	57	.35
ENGLE, WILLIAM			
Enter the G-men.	BPLA unk	40	.10
ENGSTRAND, STUART			
Beyond the forest.	Sig 739	49	.25
A husband in the house.	Sig 1024	53	.25
The invaders.	Sig 890	51	.25
More deaths than one.	Sig S1408	57	.35
The scattered seed.	Sig 1159	54	.25
The sling and the arrow.	Sig 786	50	.25
———.	Sig 1176	55	.25
Son of the giant.	Sig 826	50	.25
———.	Crst s129	56	.35
They sought for paradise.	Sig 867	51	.25
EPSTEIN, SAMUEL with Beryl Williams			
The great Houdini.	PBJr J-63	51	.25
ERICSON, WALTER			
The darkness within.	Ace D-17	53	.35
ERMINE, WILL			
Apache Crossing.	Pop 368	51	.25
———.	Eag EB63	56	.25
Avenger from Texas.	Crst 120	55	.25
Boss of the plains.	PB 1040	55	.25
Brave in the saddle.	Sig 737	49	.25
———.	Sig 1360	56	.25
Buckskin marshal.	Sig 885	51	.25
———.	Sig 1323	56	.25
Busted range.	PB 1031	54	.25
Cowboy, say your prayers!	PB 1124	56	.25
Frenchman's River.	Perm M-3024	55	.25
The iron bronc.	PB 1134	57	.25
Laramie rides again.	PenN 679	48	.25

Author/Title	Pub./Stock No.	Yr.	Price
ERMINE, WILL (cont.)			
Laramie rides alone.	Sig 1251	55	.25
Last of the longhorns.	Dell 378	50	.25
———.	Dell 916	56	.25
Lobo law.	Sig 685	48	.25
———.	Sig 1287	56	.25
Longhorn empire.	Pnnt P37	54	.25
My gun is my law.	PB 911	53	.25
Outlaw on horseback.	Dell 284	49	.25
———.	Dell 653	53	.25
Rider of the midnight range.	PB 1091	56	.25
Rustlers' Bend.	Dell 592	52	.25
———.	Dell 932	57	.25
Rustlers' moon.	PB 761	51	.25
The silver star.	Dell 684	53	.25
Singing lariat.	PB 719	50	.25
War on the Saddle Rock.	PB 1169	57	.25
Watchdog of Thunder River.	PB 986	54	.25
ERNENWEIN, LESLIE			
Boss of Panamint.	Han 75	48	.25
Bullet barricade.	GM 464	55	.25
———.	GM 916	59	.25
Bullet breed.	Han 69	47	.20
———.	Ban 740	49	.25
The Faro Kid.	Han 83	49	.25
Give a man a gun.	GM 220	52	.25
Gun hawk.	Graf 44	52	.25
———.	Graf 62	53	.25
———.	Graf 112	55	.25
The gun-hung men.	Lion LB 155	57	.25
Gunfighter's return.	GM 140	51	.25
———.	GM 329	53	.25
Gunhawk harvest.	Sig 982	52	.25
Gunsmoke.	Sig 828	50	.25
Hell for leather.	Sig 874	51	.25
Hell-town in Texas.	Avon 659	55	.25
High gun.	GM 620	56	.25
Kinkaid of Red Butte.	Berk 368	57	.25
Mystery raider.	GM 293	53	.25
Rampage.	GM 361	54	.25
Ramrod from hell.	Pop G292	58	.35
Rebel yell.	Han 93	49	.25
Renegade ramrod.	Han 111	50	.25
Rio renegade.	HanW 2	47	.20
The Texas gun.	GM 156	51	.25
Texas guns.	Graf 120	56	.25
Trigger justice.	Sig 727	49	.25
———.	Sig 1340	56	.25
ERNO, RICHARD B.			
My old man.	Lion LL 120	56	.35
ERNST, MORRIS L. with David Loth			
American sexual behavior and the Kinsey report.	Ban 227	48	.25
ERNST, PAUL			
The bronze mermaid.	Pnnt P41	54	.25
Hangman's hat.	PB 923	53	.25
ERSKINE, ALBERT with Robert Penn Warren			
A new southern harvest.	Ban F1556	57	.50
Short story masterpieces.	DelF F16	54	.50
———.	DelL LX102	58	.75
Six centuries of great poetry.	DelF FE69	55	.50
———.	DelL LC109	58	.50
———.	DelL LX110	59	.75
ERSKINE, DOROTHY with Patrick Dennis			
The pink hotel.	Crst s227	58	.35
ERSKINE, JOHN			
The private life of Helen of Troy.	Pop 147	48	.25
———.	Graf G216	56	.35
ERTZ, SUSAN			
Mary Hallam.	Ban 789	50	.25
ESCHER, FRANKLIN JR.			
A brief history of the United States.	SigK K304	54	.25
———.	SigK Ks367	59	.35
ESKELUND, KARL			
My Chinese wife.	Dell 489	51	.25
ESPY, WILLARD R.			
Bold new program.	Ban 840	50	.25
ESTEVEN, JOHN			
While murder waits.	Pop 343	51	.25
ESTEY, NORBERT			
All my sins.	Crst s133	56	.35
ESTIN, MERLYN			
Blind entry.	Pnnt P62	54	.25
When in doubt, kill.	Berk 357	56	.25
EUNSON, ROBERT			
Mig alley.	Ace D-365	59	.35
EURIPIDES			
Three great plays of Euripides.	Ment MT241	58	.75
EUSTIS, HELEN			
The fool killer.	PB 1079	55	.25
The horizontal man.	PB 557	48	.25
EVAN, PAUL			
Gunsmoke kingdom.	Ace D-28	53	.35
Gunsmoke over Sabado.	Ace D-138	56	.35
Lynch law.	Pyr 203	56	.25
Thunder Creek Range.	Ace D-298	58	.35
West of the Pecos.	Pyr G376	58	.35

Author/Title	Pub./Stock No.	Yr.	Price
EVANS, DEAN			
This kill is mine.	Graf 131	56	.25
EVANS, E. EVERETT			
Man of many minds.	Pyr G458	59	.35
EVANS, EVAN			
The border bandit.	Ban 254	48	.25
Gunman's legacy.	Ban 784	50	.25
Lone hand.	Ban 882	51	.25
Montana rides!	Pen 600	46	.25
_____.	Sig 836	51	.25
_____.	Sig 1398	57	.25
Montana rides again.	Pen 620	47	.25
_____.	Sig 935	52	.25
_____.	Sig 1436	57	.25
Outlaw valley.	Pnnt P38	54	.25
_____.	Ban 1837	58	.25
Outlaw's code.	Ban 1709	58	.25
The rescue of Broken			
Arrow.	Ban 211	49	.25
Sawdust and sixguns.	Ban 966	52	.25
Song of the whip.	Pen 645	47	.25
_____.	Sig 1015	53	.25
Strange courage.	Ban 1102	53	.25
EVANS, JACK			
Lona.	Lion 94	52	.25
EVANS, JOHN			
Andrews' harvest.	Berk 314	55	.25
	Berk G-61	57	.35
Halo for Satan.	Ban 800	50	.25
	Ban 1729	58	.25
Halo in blood.	Ban 74	46	.25
_____.	Ban 1728	58	.25
Halo in brass.	PB 709	50	.25
_____.	Ban 1727	58	.25
If you have tears.	Han 74	48	.25
Love in the shadows.	Avon T-104	55	.35
_____.	Avon T-263	58	.35
EVANS, LESLEY			
Strange are the ways			
of love.	Crst s336	59	.35
EVARTS, HAL G.			
Ambush rider.	Pop 741	56	.25
Apache agent.	Pop 651	55	.25
_____.	Pop G263	58	.35
Bullet brand.	Pop 329	51	.25
Fugitive's canyon.	Eag EB47	55	.25
Highgrader.	Pop 582	54	.25
The long rope.	DelF A172	59	.25
The man from Yuma.	Pop G232	58	.35
Man without a gun.	Eag EB85	57	.25
The night raiders.	Pop 778	56	.25
Renegade of Rainbow			
Basin.	Pop 511	53	.25
The settling of the sage.	Perm M-3021	55	.25

Author/Title	Pub./Stock No.	Yr.	Price
Shortgrass.	Pop 279	50	.25
_____.	Pop 568	54	.25
EVENS, OWEN			
Chain link.	Ball 240	57	.35
EVERARD, KATHERINE			
Cry shame!	Pyr 23	50	.25
EVEREST, FRANK K. JR. with John Guenther			
The fastest man alive.	Pyr G373	58	.35
EVERETT, MILLARD S.			
The hygiene of marriage.	Eton 103	51	.25
EVERETT, WADE			
First command.	Ball 344K	59	.35
Fort Starke.	Ball 309K	59	.35
EVERETT COOPER, C.			
The Mycenaid.	Pen 556	45	.25
EVERYBODY'S dream book.	BPLA unk	40	.10
EWEN, DAVID			
Music for the millions.	Ment M47	50	.35
EWING, FREDERICK R.			
I, libertine.	Ball 165	56	.35
EXNER, M. J.			
The sexual side of			
marriage.	PB 500	48	.25
EYSTER, WARREN			
Far from customary skies.	Ban A1304	55	.35

Author/Title	Pub./Stock No.	Yr.	Price
F			
FADIMAN, EDWIN JR.			
An act of violence.	Sig 1374	57	.25
The glass playpen.	Sig 1316	56	.25
FAGALY, AL with Harry Shorten			
More there oughta be			
a law!	Graf 85	54	.25
_____.	Graf 109	55	.25
There oughta be a law!	Graf 52	52	.25
FAGAN, NORBERT			
The crooked mile.	GM 319	53	.25
One against the odds.	GM 382	54	.25
FAGERTY, SHIRLEY JAMES			
Having a gay old time.	Ban F1889	59	.50
FAHERTY, ROBERT			
Big old sun.	Prmb P179	52	.35
Swamp babe.	Crst 210	58	.25
FAIN, WILLIAM			
In search of love.	Eag EB92	57	.25
FAIR, A. A.			
Bats fly at dusk.	Dell 254	48	.25
_____.	Dell 691	53	.25
Bedrooms have windows.	Dell 603	52	.25
_____.	Dell D212	58	.35
The bigger they come.	PB 228	43	.25
Cats prowl at night.	Dell 315	49	.25
_____.	Dell 899	56	.25
Crows can't count.	Dell 472	51	.25
_____.	Dell 778	54	.25
Double or quits.	Dell 160	47	.25
_____.	Dell 718	53	.25
Fools die on Friday.	Dell 542	51	.25
_____.	Dell 939	57	.25
Give 'em the ax.	Dell 389	50	.25
_____.	Dell 460	50	.25
_____.	Dell D213	58	.35
Gold comes in bricks.	Dell 84	45	.25
_____.	Dell 836	55	.25
Owls don't blink.	Dell 211	48	.25
_____.	Dell 243	48	.25
_____.	Dell D210	57	.35
Some women won't wait.	Dell 809	54	.25
Spill the jackpot.	Dell 109	46	.25
_____.	Dell 619	52	.25
_____.	Dell D211	58	.35
Top of the heap.	Dell 772	54	.25
_____.	Dell D309	59	.35
Turn on the heat.	Dell 59	44	.25
_____.	Dell 620	52	.25
_____.	Dell D253	58	.35
FAIRBAIRN, DOUGLAS			
Money, marbles and chalk.	Berk G269	59	.35
FAIRBANK, WALTON			
Houseboy.	Pyr 93	53	.25
_____.	Pyr 215	56	.25
FAIRCHILD, JOHNSON E.			
The way of woman.	Prem s19	56	.35
FAIRMAN, PAUL W.			
The glass ladder.	Han 110	50	.25
The heiress of Copper			
Butte.	Han 129	51	.25
The joy wheel.	Lion 190	54	.25
The Montana vixen.	Lion 113	52	.25
FAIRSERVIS, WALTER A. JR.			
The origins of oriental			
civilization.	Ment MD251	59	.50
FAISON, S. LANE JR.			
Manet.	PBA A13	54	.50
FALCARO, JOE with Murray Goodman			
The Dell bowling			
handbook.	Dell 728	53	.25
FALL, THOMAS			
Prettiest girl in town.	Sig 861	51	.25
_____.	Berk BG-212	59	.50
FALLADA, HANS			
The drinker.	Dell D162	56	.35
FALSTEIN, LOUIS			
Face of a hero.	PB 826	51	.25
_____.	Pop G316	59	.35
Slaughter street.	Lion 151	53	.25
_____.	Lion LB 172	57	.25
_____.	Pyr G437	59	.35
Sole survivor.	DelF 29	54	.25
Spring of desire.	Mon 112	59	.35
FANGER, HORST			
A life for a life.	Ball 92	54	.35
FANTE, JOHN			
Ask the dust.	Ban 1194	54	.25
Full of life.	Ban 1108	53	.25
_____.	Ban 1574	57	.25
FARJEON, JEFFERSON			
Greenmask.	Dell 111	46	.25
FARLEY, RALPH MILNE			
An earth man on Venus.	Avon 285	50	.25
FARMER, FANNIE			
The Boston Cooking-School			
cook book.	Ban S1581	57	.75
Fannie Farmer's handy			
cook book.	Sig 800	50	.25

Author/Title	Pub./Stock No.	Yr.	Price
FARMER, PHILIP JOSÉ			
The green odyssey.	Ball 210	57	.35
FARR, JOHN			
The deadly combo.	Ace D-301	58	.35
The lady and the snake.	Ace D-235	57	.35
She shark.	Ace S-159	56	.25
FARRAR, LARSTON			
The sins of Sandra Shaw.	Sig 1480	58	.25
Washington lowdown.	Sig 1300	56	.25
FARRAR, MARGARET PETHERBRIDGE			
The 4th Pocket book of crossword puzzles.	PB 966	53	.25
The 5th Pocket book of crossword puzzles.	PB 1072	55	.25
The 6th Pocket book of crossword puzzles.	PB 1129	56	.25
The 7th Pocket book of crossword puzzles.	PB 1154	57	.25
The 8th Pocket book of crossword puzzles.	PB 1175	57	.25
The 9th Pocket book of crossword puzzles.	PB 1182	58	.25
The 10th Pocket book of crossword puzzles.	PB 1227	59	.25
FARRELL, CLIFF			
California passage.	Eag EB98	57	.25
Follow the new grass.	Ban 1502	57	.25
Gun hand.	Pop G240	58	.35
Rawhide river.	Pop 742	56	.25
FARRELL, JAMES T.			
An American dream girl.	Sig 1031	53	.25
Bernard Carr.	Sig S893	51	.35
A dangerous woman.	Sig S1457	57	.35
Ellen Rogers.	Sig 779	50	.25
The face of time.	Sig 1275	56	.25
Father and son.	Sig D1066	53	.50
French girls are vicious.	Sig 1349	56	.25
Gas-house McGinty.	Avon 290	50	.25
———.	Avon 466	52	.25
	Crst s200	58	.35
Hell of a good time.	Avon 252	50	.25
———.	Avon 468	52	.25
Judgment day.	Sig S875	51	.35
My days of anger.	Sig S1118	54	.35
No star is lost.	Sig D946	52	.50
Saturday night.	Sig 831	50	.25
	Sig S1624	59	.35
Short stories of James T. Farrell.	Pen 603	46	.25
Studs Lonigan.	Sig T1518	58	.75
This man and this woman.	Sig 1158	54	.25
When boyhood dreams come true.	Sig 994	53	.25
A world I never made.	Sig D926	52	.50
Yesterday's love.	Avon 157	48	.25
Yesterday's love.	Avon 260	50	.25
———.	Avon 475	52	.25
Young Lonigan.	Pen 643	47	.25
The young manhood of Studs Lonigan.	Sig 810	50	.25
FARREN, JULIAN			
So sweet, so cruel.	Crst 125	56	.25
The train from Pittsburgh.	Pop 428	52	.25
FARRÈRE, CLAUDE			
Black opium.	Berk G-120	58	.35
FARRIS, JOHN			
The corpse next door.	Graf 138	56	.25
Harrison High.	Dell F90	59	.50
FAST, HOWARD			
Citizen Tom Paine.	Ban 30	46	.25
———.	BanC FC44	59	.50
Conceived in liberty.	Pen 569	45	.25
Freedom road.	PB 382	46	.25
The last frontier.	PB 322	45	.25
———.	Avon 205	49	.25
The unvanquished.	Pen 588	46	.25
FAST, JULIUS			
And then murder.	Hill 126	59	.35
Down through the night.	Crst 136	56	.25
Out of this world.	Pen 537	44	.25
FAULKNER, JOHN			
Ain't gonna rain no more.	GM 927	59	.25
Cabin Road.	GM 178	51	.25
———.	GM 439	54	.25
———.	GM 730	58	.25
Dollar cotton.	Ban 972	52	.25
Men working.	Ban 1023	52	.25
The sin shouter of Cabin Road.	GM 455	55	.25
———.	GM 633	57	.25
Uncle Good's girls.	GM 238	52	.25
———.	GM 410	54	.25
———.	GM 729	58	.25
FAULKNER, WILLIAM			
Intruder in the dust.	Sig 743	49	.25
———.	Sig S1253	55	.35
———.	Sig S1511	58	.35
Knight's gambit.	Sig 825	50	.25
———.	Sig 1315	56	.25
The long hot summer.	Sig S1501	58	.35
Mosquitoes.	Avon (12)	41	.25
———.	Dell 708	53	.25
———.	Dell D168	56	.35
The old man.	Sig 692	48	.25
Pylon.	Sig 863	51	.25
———.	Sig S1485	58	.35
Sanctuary.	Pen 632	47	.25

Author/Title	Pub./Stock No.	Yr.	Price
FAULKNER, WILLIAM (cont.)			
Sanctuary and Requiem			
for a nun.	Sig S1079	54	.35
_____.	Sig D1486	58	.50
Sartoris.	Sig S1032	53	.35
_____.	Sig D1614	58	.50
Soldiers' pay.	Sig 887	51	.25
_____.	Sig D1629	59	.50
The sound and the fury.	Sig D1628	59	.50
The unvanquished.	Sig 977	52	.25
_____.	Sig S1616	58	.35
_____.	SigC CD9	59	.50
The wild palms.	Pen 659	48	.25
The wild palms and			
The old man.	Sig S1148	54	.35
_____.	Sig D1643	59	.50
FAURE, RAOUL C.			
Lady Godiva and Master			
Tom.	Ban 469	49	.25
FAVIELL, FRANCES			
A house on the Rhine.	Pop G221	58	.35
FEARING, KENNETH			
The big clock.	Ban 738	49	.25
Cry killer!	Avon 823	58	.25
Dagger of the mind.	Ban 93	47	.25
FEDER, SID			
with Joachim Joesten			
The Luciano story.	Pop G155	56	.35
with Burton B. Turkus			
Murder, inc.	Prmb P187S	52	.50
FELDMAN, GENE with Max Gartenberg			
The beat generation and			
the angry young men.	Dell F84	59	.50
FELDT, ERIC D.			
The coast watchers.	Ball F318K	59	.50
FELLER, BOB			
Strikeout story.	Ban 501	48	.25
FELSEN, HENRY GREGOR			
Hot rod.	Ban 923	51	.25
_____.	Ban A1892	58	.35
Medic mirth.	Ace S-152	56	.25
Rag top.	Ban 1538	56	.25
Street rod.	Ban 1437	56	.25
Two and the town.	Pnnt P20	53	.25
FENISONG, RUTH			
Deadlock.	Dell 808	54	.25
Death is a gold coin.	Pop 245	50	.25
Death is a lovely lady.	Pop 173	49	.25
Murder needs a name.	Bond unk	46	.25
FENTON, CHARLES			
Conduct unbecoming.	DelF 19	54	.25

Author/Title	Pub./Stock No.	Yr.	Price
FENWICK, E. P.			
The inconvenient corpse.	Pony 62	46	.25
FERBER, EDNA			
American beauty.	Pen 650	47	.25
Cimarron.	Pen 605	46	.25
_____.	Ban A1754	58	.35
Giant.	Card C-120	54	.35
Great son.	Pen 633	47	.25
Ice Palace.	Ban F1912	59	.50
Nobody's in town.	Avon 51	44	.25
One basket.	Ban S1843	58	.75
Saratoga trunk.	Pen 617	47	.25
Show boat.	PB 13	39	.25
_____.	Pen 653	47	.25
So big.	Pen 639	47	.25
Trees die at the top.	DelT 10	51	.10
FERBER, RICHARD			
The hostiles.	DelF A162	58	.25
The outcast.	DelF A143	57	.25
The raiders.	DelF A174	59	.25
FEREVA, ANTON			
Come desire me.	Crst s144	56	.35
FERGUSON, JAMES HENRY			
Why can't we have a baby?	Pyr R256	57	.35
FERGUSON, MARGARET			
The sign of the ram.	Ban 158	48	.25
FERGUSSON, HARVEY			
The conquest of Don			
Pedro.	PB 1066	55	.25
Grant of kingdom.	PB 861	52	.25
In those days.	Pnnt P5	53	.25
What a man wants.	Ban 961	52	.25
Wolf song.	Ban 891	51	.25
FERNÁNDEZ-FLÓREZ, DARÍO			
Lola.	Sig D1678	59	.50
FERRARS, E. X.			
The March Hare murders.	PB 735	50	.25
FERSEN, NICHOLAS			
Tombolo.	Eag EB36	55	.25
FESSIER, MICHAEL			
Fully dressed and in his			
right mind.	Lion 214	54	.25
FEUCHTWANGER, LION			
Jew Süss.	Avon 1001	51	.50
Raquel.	Sig D1477	57	.50
The ugly duchess.	Avon 313	51	.25
FEUILLE, FRANK			
The Cotton Road.	Perm M-4037	55	.35

Author/Title	Pub./Stock No.	Yr.	Price
FICKLING, G. G.			
Girl on the loose.	Pyr G366	58	.35
Girl on the prowl.	Pyr G453	59	.35
A gun for Honey.	Pyr G344	58	.35
Honey in the flesh.	Pyr G411	59	.35
This girl for hire.	Pyr G274	57	.35
FIELD, ALEXANDER			
The Perma X-word puzzle book.	Perm M-3057	56	.25
FIELD, HOPE			
Stormy present.	Dell 661	53	.25
FIELD, MEDORA			
Blood on her shoe.	Pop 201	49	.25
Who killed Aunt Maggie?	Pop 72	46	.25
FIELD, PETER			
Blacksnake Trail.	PB 1213	59	.25
The boss of the Lazy 9.	PB 683	50	.25
Canyon of death.	PB 962	53	.25
Coyote gulch.	PB 990	54	.25
Death rides the night.	PB 882	52	.25
Doctor Two-Guns.	PB 982	54	.25
The end of the trail.	PB 902	52	.25
Gambler's gold.	PB 1054	55	.25
Gringo guns.	PB 348	46	.25
Guns from Powder Valley.	Ban 68	46	.25
Guns in the saddle.	PB 1088	56	.25
Hell's corner.	Ban 775	50	.25
The land grabber.	Ban 210	49	.25
Law badge.	PB 1027	54	.25
The man from Thief River.	PB 914	53	.25
Maverick's return.	PB 1161	57	.25
Midnight round-up.	PB 711	50	.25
Mustang Mesa.	PB 1068	55	.25
The outlaw of Eagle's Nest.	PB 1035	55	.25
Outlaw valley.	PB 1241	59	.25
Outlaws three.	PB 567	49	.25
Powder Valley pay-off.	Ban 104	47	.25
Powder Valley showdown.	PB 1187	58	.25
Ravaged range.	PB 1081	55	.25
Return to Powder Valley.	PB 1205	58	.25
The road to Laramie.	PB 1123	56	.25
Sheriff on the spot.	PB 937	53	.25
Sheriff wanted!	PB 1173	57	.25
Sheriff's revenge.	Ban 731	49	.25
The smoking iron.	PB 847	52	.25
The tenderfoot kid.	PB 759	51	.25
Trail from Needle Rock.	PB 1260	59	.25
Trail South from Powder Valley.	Ban 201	48	.25
FIELDING, HENRY			
Tom Jones.	Crst d176	57	.50
.	Crst d330	59	.50
FIELDING, WILLIAM H.			
Beautiful humbug.	GM 430	54	.25

Author/Title	Pub./Stock No.	Yr.	Price
Take me as I am.	GM 272	52	.25
The unpossessed.	GM 202	51	.25
FIELDING, WILLIAM J.			
Self-mastery through psycho-analysis.	Eton E109	52	.25
Sex and the love-life.	Perm M-4019	55	.35
Strange customs of courtship and marriage.	Eag EB62	56	.25
FIGEN, MILTON			
The Pocket aviation quiz book.	PB 230	43	.25
FINCH, PERCY with Holland M. Smith			
Coral and brass.	Ace D-287	58	.35
FINDLEY, FERGUSON			
Counterfeit corpse.	Ace D-197	57	.35
Killer cop.	Mon 114	59	.35
Murder makes me mad.	Pop 780	56	.25
My old man's badge.	Pop 324	51	.25
Waterfront.	Pop 408	52	.25
FINE, BENJAMIN			
1,000,000 delinquents.	Sig D1368	57	.50
FINKELHOR, DOROTHY C.			
How to make your emotions work for you.	Berk G-210	59	.35
FINLAY, LUCILE			
Grant of land.	Ban A954	51	.35
FINNEGAN, ROBERT			
The bandaged nude.	Sig 807	50	.25
.	Sig 1379	57	.25
The lying ladies.	Ban 351	48	.25
Many a monster.	Ban 363	49	.25
FINNEY, JACK			
The body snatchers.	DelF 42	55	.25
Five against the house.	PB 1078	55	.25
The house of numbers.	DelF A139	57	.25
The third level.	Dell D274	59	.35
FIRTH, RAYMOND			
Human types.	Ment MD227	58	.50
FISCHER, BRUNO			
The bleeding scissors.	Sig 1256	55	.25
The dead men grin.	Pyr 22	50	.25
The fast buck.	GM 270	52	.25
.	GM s783	58	.35
The fingered man.	Ace D-27	53	.35
The flesh was cold.	Sig 833	50	.25
.	Sig 1474	57	.25
Fools walk in.	GM 209	52	.25
.	GM 600	56	.25
The hornets' nest.	Dell 79	45	.25

Author/Title	Pub./Stock No.	Yr.	Price
FISCHER, BRUNO (cont.)			
House of flesh.	GM 123	50	.25
———.	GM 537	55	.25
———.	GM 886	59	.25
Knee-deep in death.	GM 591	56	.25
The lady kills.	GM 148	51	.25
———.	GM 755	58	.25
The lustful ape.	GM 901	59	.25
More deaths than one.	PB 521	48	.25
Murder in the raw.	GM 694	57	.25
The pigskin bag.	Dell 817	55	.25
The restless hands.	Sig 780	50	.25
———.	Dell 910	56	.25
Run for your life.	GM 343	53	.25
Second-hand nude.	GM 928	59	.25
The silent dust.	Sig 892	51	.25
So wicked my love.	GM 437	54	.25
———.	GM 753	58	.25
The spider lily.	Dell 752	54	.25
Stairway to death.	Pyr 29	51	.25
———.	Pyr G270	57	.35
Stripped for murder.	Sig 988	53	.25
FISCHER, LOUIS			
Gandhi: his life and message for the world.	SigK K300	54	.25
FISCHER, MARJORIE			
Embarrassment of riches.	Sup M644	45	.25
FISCHER, MARKOOSHA			
The right to love.	Crst 165	57	.25
FISHBEIN, MORRIS			
The handy home medical adviser.	Prmb P242	53	.35
FISHER, CLAY			
The big pasture.	PB 1137	56	.25
The blue mustang.	PB 1159	57	.25
The brass command.	PB 1108	56	.25
The crossing.	Card C-373	59	.35
Red blizzard.	PB 927	53	.25
Santa Fe passage.	Pnnt P26	53	.25
———.	PB 1186	57	.25
The tall men.	Ball 59	54	.35
War bonnet.	Ball 11	53	.35
Yellow Hair.	Ball 40	53	.35
Yellowstone Kelly.	PB 1209	58	.25
FISHER, JOHN with Mario Pei			
Getting along in French.	Ban A1801	58	.35
FISHER, LAINE			
Fare prey.	Ace D-387	59	.35
FISHER, ROBERT MOORE			
How to know and predict the weather.	Ment M84	53	.35
———.	SigK KD353	57	.50

Author/Title	Pub./Stock No.	Yr.	Price
FISHER, STEVE			
Be still my heart.	RS 21	52	.35
Giveaway.	Ban 1376	55	.25
Homicide Johnny.	Pop 229	50	.25
I wake up screaming.	Han 27	44	.15
———.	Pop 129	48	.25
The night before murder.	Pop 317	51	.25
The sheltering night.	GM 219	52	.25
Take all you can get.	Pop 781	56	.25
Winter kill.	Pop 361	51	.25
FISHER, VARDIS			
The divine passion.	Pyr R419	59	.50
In tragic life.	Card C-3	51	.35
No villain need be.	Card C-177	55	.35
Passions spin the plot.	Card C-73	52	.35
Pemmican.	Card C-253	57	.35
We are betrayed.	Card C-119	53	.35
The wild ones.	Pyr G57	52	.35
———.	Pyr G141	55	.35
———.	Pyr G310	58	.35
FISHER, WILLIAM			
The waiters.	Sig 1097	54	.25
FISHMAN, E. A.			
The one I love.	Ball 81	54	.35
The whirligig of love.	Ball 330K	59	.35
FITZGERALD, ED			
Kick-off!	Ban 504	48	.25
The story of the Brooklyn Dodgers.	Ban 556	49	.25
FITZGERALD, F. SCOTT			
The beautiful and the damned.	Prmb P123	51	.35
The great Gatsby.	Ban 8	45	.25
———.	Ban A1228	54	.35
Tender is the night.	Ban A867	51	.35
This side of paradise.	Dell D140	54	.35
FITZGERALD, JOHN D.			
Mamma's boarding house.	Pyr G422	59	.35
FITZGIBBON, CONSTANTINE			
Officers' plot to kill Hitler.	Avon T-222	58	.35
Room for a stranger.	Lion 232	55	.25
FLAGG, JOHN			
Dear, deadly beloved.	GM 391	54	.25
Death and the naked lady.	GM 151	51	.25
Death's lovely mask.	GM 787	58	.25
The lady and the cheetah.	GM 197	51	.25
Murder in Monaco.	GM 628	57	.25
The Persian cat.	GM 103	50	.25
Woman of Cairo.	GM 282	53	.25
FLAIANO, ENNIO			
The short cut.	Sig 846	51	.25

Author/Title	Pub./Stock No.	Yr.	Price
FLAIANO, ENNIO (cont.)			
The short cut.	Sig S1370	57	.35
FLAIR, TERRANCE			
Halfway to heaven.	Ball 191	57	.35
FLANNAGAN, ROY			
The forest cavalier.	Pop G118	53	.35
.	Pop SP20	58	.50
Luther.	Lion 114	52	.25
.	Lion LB 94	56	.25
The whipping.	Ban 817	50	.25
FLAUBERT, GUSTAVE			
Madame Bovary.	PB 240	43	.25
.	Card C-59	52	.35
.	PBL PL69	58	.35
.	BanC AC35	59	.35
.	DelL LC118	59	.50
Salambô.	Berk G-5	55	.35
.	Berk BG-73	57	.50
FLAVIN, MARTIN			
Mr. Littlejohn.	Pen 551	44	.25
FLECK, HENRIETTA with Elizabeth Munves			
Everybody's book of modern diet and nutrition.	DelF D53	55	.35
.	DelL LC124	59	.50
FLEISCHER, NAT			
Jack Dempsey.	Ban 557	49	.25
FLEISCHMAN, A. S.			
Blood Alley.	GM 499	55	.25
Counterspy express.	Ace D-57	54	.35
Danger in paradise.	GM 295	53	.25
Look behind you, lady.	GM 223	52	.25
.	GM 572	56	.25
Malay woman.	GM 368	54	.25
Shanghai Flame.	GM 181	51	.25
.	GM 514	55	.25
FLEISHER, SIEGEL			
Down the dark street.	Pop 649	55	.25
FLEMING, IAN			
Diamonds are forever.	Perm M-3084	57	.25
Doctor No.	Sig S1670	59	.35
From Russia, with love.	Sig S1563	58	.35
Live and let die.	Perm M-3048	56	.25
.	Sig S1723	59	.35
Too hot to handle.	Perm M-3070	57	.25
You asked for it.	Pop 660	55	.25
FLEMING, JOHN with Lois Eby			
The velvet fleece.	Dell 272	49	.25
FLENDER, HAROLD			
Paris blues.	Ball 203	57	.35
FLES, BARTHOLD			
The Saturday evening post fantasy stories.	Avon 389	51	.25
The Saturday evening post western stories.	Avon 311	51	.25
Seven short novels from the Woman's home companion.	PB 607	49	.25
FLESCH, RUDOLF			
Why Johnny can't read.	Pop 764	56	.25
FLETCHER, H. L. V.			
Miss Agatha doubles for death.	Ban 352	48	.25
FLETCHER, INGLIS			
Bennett's welcome.	Prmb P171	52	.35
Lusty wind for Carolina.	Prmb P137	51	.35
Man of Ablemarle.	Prmb P189	52	.35
Queen's gift.	Prmb P268	54	.35
Raleigh's Eden.	Prmb P207	53	.35
Roanoke hundred.	Prmb P151	52	.35
Toil of the brave.	Prmb P216	53	.35
FLETCHER, J. S.			
The middle temple murder.	Pen 518	43	.25
FLETCHER, LUCILLE with Allan Ullman			
Night man.	Ban 1140	53	.25
.	Pyr G354	58	.35
Sorry, wrong number.	Ban 356	48	.25
.	Ban 1771	58	.25
FLEXNER, JAMES THOMAS			
The Pocket history of American painting.	PB 708	50	.25
.	PBL PL-515	57	.50
FLOOD, CHARLES BRACELEN			
Love is a bridge.	Sig D1198	55	.50
FLORA, FLETCHER			
The brass bed.	Lion LB 87	56	.25
Desperate asylum.	Lion LL 44	55	.35
The hotshot.	Avon 693	56	.25
Leave her to hell!	Avon 839	58	.25
Let me kill you, sweetheart.	Avon 811	58	.25
Park Avenue tramp.	GM 761	58	.25
Strange sisters.	Lion 215	54	.25
Take me home.	Mon 120	59	.35
Wake up with a stranger.	Sig 1688	59	.25
Whisper of love.	Pyr G384	59	.35
Whispers of the flesh.	Sig D1542	58	.50
FLOREN, LEE			
Burn 'em out.	Ace D-230	57	.35
Deadly draw.	Avon 844	59	.25
Four Texans North.	Ace D-106	55	.35
Guns along the Arrowhead.	Dmnd D2002	59	.35

Author/Title	Pub./Stock No.	Yr.	Price
FLOREN, LEE (cont.)			
Guns along the Pecos.	Dmnd D2017	59	.35
The gunslammer.	Lion 169	53	.25
Hangman's range.	Berk G255	59	.35
Riders in the night.	Ace D-272	58	.35
Rifle law.	Dmnd D2009	59	.35
The saddle wolves.	Ace D-260	57	.35
Thruway west.	Ace D-156	56	.35
FLOWERS, DON			
Glamor girls.	Avon 453	52	.25
————.	Avon 557	54	.25
FLYNN, ERROL			
Beam ends.	Dell 195	47	.25
Showdown.	Dell 351	49	.25
FLYNN, J. M.			
The deadly boodle.	Ace D-313	58	.35
Drink with the dead.	Ace D-379	59	.35
Terror tournament.	Ace D-409	59	.35
FLYNN, JAY			
McHugh.	Avon T-377	59	.35
FLYNN, T. T.			
The angry man.	DelF 103	56	.25
The man from Laramie.	DelF 14	54	.25
Man from nowhere.	DelF A166	58	.25
Two faces West.	DelF 33	54	.25
FOLDES, YOLANDA			
Golden earrings.	Dell 216	48	.25
FOLEY, CHARLES			
Commando extraordinary.	Ball 209	57	.35
FOLEY, MARTHA			
The best American short stories 1956.	Ball F204	57	.50
The best short stories of 1955.	Ball F133	56	.50
with Joyce F. Hartman			
The best short stories of 1953.	Ball 34	53	.50
FOLEY, RAE			
The girl from nowhere.	PB 707	50	.25
FONTAINE, ROBERT			
The happy time.	Dell 566	52	.25
Young awakening.	Avon T-364	59	.35
FONTENAY, CHARLES L.			
Twice upon a time.	Ace D-266	58	.35
FOOTE, SHELBY			
Follow me down.	Sig 860	51	.25
————.	Sig S1685	59	.35
Love in a dry season.	Sig 970	52	.25
The night before Chancellorsville.	Sig S1415	57	.35
Shiloh.	Sig 1104	54	.25
FOOTNER, HULBERT			
The dark ships.	Pop 38	44	.25
Death of a saboteur.	Pen 559	45	.25
The murder that had everything.	Dell 74	45	.25
FOR a night of love.	Avon 259	50	.25
FORBES, ESTHER			
Paradise.	Ban A1151	53	.35
FORBES, GORDON			
Too near the sun.	DelF D56	55	.35
FORBES, KATHRYN			
Mama's bank account.	Ban 135	48	.25
————.	Ban 1513	56	.25
FORBES, MURRAY			
The big fake.	Pyr 97	53	.25
FORD, COREY with Klondy Nelson			
Daughter of the Gold Rush.	PyrR PG24	59	.35
FORD, ED et al.			
Can you top this?	Bart 39	47	.25
Cream of the crop.	Dell 328	49	.25
FORD, LESLIE			
All for the love of a lady.	Ban 359	49	.25
The Bahamas murder case.	Dell 689	53	.25
The clue of the Judas tree.	Dell 61	44	.25
Date with death.	Dell 547	51	.25
Devil's stronghold.	Dell 395	50	.25
False to any man.	Ban 80	47	.25
Ill met by moonlight.	Dell 6	43	.25
Murder is the pay-off.	Dell 788	54	.25
Murder with Southern hospitality.	Dell 505	51	.25
Old lover's ghost.	Ban 114	47	.25
The Philadelphia murder story.	Dell 354	49	.25
Reno rendezvous.	Pop 24	44	.25
Road to folly.	Ban 42	46	.25
The simple way of poison.	PB 122	41	.25
Siren in the night.	Ban 303	48	.25
The strangled witness.	Pop 158	48	.25
Three bright pebbles.	Pop 6	43	.25
The town cried murder.	Ban 16	45	.25
Washington whispers murder.	Dell 908	56	.25
The watchman's clock.	PB 33	39	.25
The woman in black.	Dell 447	50	.25

Author/Title	Pub./Stock No.		Yr.	Price
FORD, LEWIS				
Gunfighter from Montana.	Eag	EB49	55	.25
Gunmen's grass.	Eag	EB14	54	.25
Maverick empire.	Pop	810	57	.25
FORD, TERENCE				
The drunk, the damned and				
the bedevilled.	Avon	395	52	.25
Easy living.	Berk	G-229	59	.35
FOREMAN, L. L.				
Arrow in the dust.	DelF	11	54	.25
Desperado's gold.	PB	702	50	.25
Gunfire men.	Dell	825	55	.25
Gunning for trouble.	Pop	560	54	.25
Gunsmoke men.	Sig	1607	58	.25
Lone hand.	DelF	A127	57	.25
The renegade.	PB	627	49	.25
Return of the Texan.	Ball	259	58	.35
The road to San Jacinto.	PB	824	51	.25
Woman of the Avalon.	DelF	57	55	.25
FOREMAN, ROBERT L.				
The hot half hour.	Avon	T-295	59	.35
FOREMAN, RUSSELL				
Long pig.	Ace	G-390	59	.50
FORESTER, C. S.				
The African queen.	Ban	712	49	.25
Beat to quarters.	PB	174	42	.25
_____.	Ban	A1816	58	.35
Captain from Connecticut.	Ban	40	46	.25
Captain Horatio				
Hornblower.	Ban	A912	51	.35
Flying colours.	Ban	772	50	.25
The general.	Ban	1170	53	.25
The good shepherd.	Ban	A1587	57	.35
The gun.	Ban	993	52	.25
_____.	Ban	1610	57	.25
Lieutenant Hornblower.	Ban	A1811	58	.35
Mr. Midshipman				
Hornblower.	Ban	A1305	55	.35
	Ban	A1815	58	.35
Payment deferred.	Ban	816	51	.25
Plain murder.	DelF	30	54	.25
Randall and the river				
of time.	Ban	A1611	57	.35
Rifleman Dodd.	Ban	1011	52	.25
The ship.	Ban	A1196	54	.35
	Ban	A1619	57	.35
_____.				
Single-handed.	Ban	1080	53	.25
Sink the Bismarck!	Ban	A2060	59	.35
To the Indies.	Ban	917	51	.25
_____.	Ban	A1314	55	.35
FORREST, WILLIAMS				
The great debauch.	GM	s725	58	.35
Seed of violence.	Crst	s182	57	.35
Stigma for valor.	Crst	s236	58	.35

Author/Title	Pub./Stock No.		Yr.	Price
The woman with claws.	GM	s597	56	.35
FORSTER, E. M.				
A passage to India.	Pen	574	46	.25
FORSTER, LOGAN				
Proud land.	Ban	A1857	58	.35
FOSBURGH, HUGH				
The hunter.	Ban	865	51	.25
The sound of white water.	Ban	1590	57	.25
View from the air.	Ban	A1355	55	.35
FOSDICK, HARRY EMERSON				
A great time to be alive.	PB	980	54	.25
The man from Nazareth.	PB	959	53	.25
FOSTER, BENNETT				
Badlands.	Ban	255	48	.25
.	Ban	1112	53	.25
Barbed wire.	Ban	252	48	.25
Blackleg range.	Ban	725	49	.25
Bullets for a badman.	PB	807	51	.25
The cow thief trail.	Ban	873	51	.25
Dust of the trail.	Lion	17	50	.25
The kid from Dodge City.	Lion	LL 43	55	.35
Lone wolf.	PB	1166	57	.25
Man tracks.	Lion	35	50	.25
The owl hoot trail.	Ban	808	50	.25
Pay-off at Ladron.	Ban	260	49	.25
Rider of the Rifle Rock.	Ban	841	50	.25
Seven slash range.	Ban	762	50	.25
Trigger kid.	Ban	88	47	.25
_____.	Ban	1116	53	.25
FOSTER, JOHN				
Dark heritage.	GM	486	55	.25
FOSTER, JOSEPH				
A cow is too much trouble				
in Los Angeles.	Sig	1072	53	.25
Stephana.	Mon	138	59	.35
Street of the barefoot				
lovers.	Sig	S1197	55	.35
Time to embrace.	Eag	EB52	55	.25
FOSTER, RICHARD				
Bier for a chaser.	GM	899	59	.25
Blonde and beautiful.	Pop	667	55	.25
The girl from Easy				
Street.	Eag	EB32	55	.25
The rest must die.	GM	s853	59	.35
FOUR fallen women.	Dell	667	53	.25
FOUR great comedies of the				
Restoration and eighteenth				
century.	BanC	FC2	58	.50
FOUR great Russian short				
novels.	DelL	LC133	59	.50

Author/Title	Pub./Stock No.	Yr.	Price
FOWLER, GENE			
Beau James.	Ban A1626	57	.35
Good night, sweet prince.	PB 430	47	.25
The great mouthpiece.	Ban 32	46	.25
_____.	Ban A904	51	.35
Schnozzola.	Prmb P210	53	.35
Shoe the wild mare.	Avon 47	44	.25
_____.	RCL 7	50	.25
Trumpet in the dust.	Avon (25)	43	.25
FOWLER, HELEN			
The intruder.	PB 1026	54	.25
FOWLER, KENNETH			
Outcast of murder mesa.	GM 452	55	.25
The range bum.	Avon 667	55	.25
Summons to Silverhorn.	GM 713	57	.25
FOX, GARDNER F.			
The Borgia blade.	GM 300	53	.25
_____.	GM 609	56	.25
The conquering prince.	Crst 166	57	.25
Creole woman.	Crst 304	59	.25
The gentleman rogue.	GM 394	54	.25
Iron lover.	Avon T-341	59	.35
Madame Buccaneer.	GM 328	53	.25
One sword for love.	GM 360	54	.25
Queen of Sheba.	GM s549	56	.35
Rebel wench.	GM 484	55	.25
Terror over London.	GM 648	57	.25
Witness this woman.	GM 942	59	.25
Woman of Kali.	GM 438	54	.25
FOX, GILL			
Wilbert.	Perm M-3065	56	.25
FOX, H. MUNRO			
The personality of animals.	Pel P16	47	.25
FOX, JAMES M.			
Code three.	Pnnt P79	55	.25
Death commits bigamy.	Graf 14	49	.25
_____.	Dell 845	55	.25
Fatal in furs.	Dell 623	52	.25
Free ride.	Eag EB82	57	.25
The gentle hangman.	Dell 526	51	.25
The inconvenient bride.	Dell 463	50	.25
The iron virgin.	Dell 719	53	.25
The lady regrets.	Dell 338	49	.25
Save them for violence.	Mon 132	59	.35
The scarlet slippers.	Dell 685	53	.25
The wheel is fixed.	Dell 573	52	.25
FOX, MILTON S.			
Renoir.	PBA A11	53	.50
FOX, NORMAN A.			
The Badlands beyond.	Dell 1002	59	.25
Broken wagon.	Ball 70	54	.35
Cactus cavalier.	Dell 406	50	.25
The devil's saddle.	Ace D-72	54	.35
Ghostly hoofbeats.	Dell 737	53	.25
Long lightning.	Dell 783	54	.25
The longhorn legion.	DelT 12	51	.10
Night passage.	Dell 950	57	.25
The rawhide years.	Dell 831	55	.25
The rider from yonder.	Han 105	50	.25
Roughshod.	Dell 694	53	.25
Shadow on the range.	Dell 539	51	.25
_____.	Dell 907	56	.25
Silent in the saddle.	Dell 362	49	.25
The six-gun syndicate.	Pyr 195	56	.25
Stormy in the West.	Dell 569	52	.25
_____.	Dell 927	56	.25
Stranger from Arizona.	Dell 969	58	.25
Tall man riding.	Dell 642	52	.25
_____.	Dell 980	58	.25
The thirsty land.	Dell 480	51	.25
_____.	Dell 864	55	.25
The thundering trail.	Crst 128	56	.25
War on the range.	Crst 137	56	.25
FOX, PAUL			
Sailor town.	Ban 813	50	.25
_____.	Ban 1283	54	.25
FOX, TED			
That girl on the river.	Eag EB38	55	.25
FRAME, BART			
Georgia girl.	Zen ZB-22	59	.35
Sinful.	Avon T-277	58	.35
The strange co-ed.	Avon T-336	59	.35
FRANCE, ANATOLE			
Penguin Island.	BanC FC13	58	.50
The red lily.	Lion LL 170	57	.35
_____.	Pyr G417	59	.35
FRANCE, HECTOR			
Musk, hashish and blood.	Avon 308	51	.25
_____.	Avon 415	52	.25
FRANCIS, DALE			
A Catholic prayer book.	DelL LC112	58	.50
FRANCIS, WILLIAM			
The corrupters.	Lion 174	53	.25
Don't dig deeper.	Lion 123	53	.25
I.O.U.--murder.	Sig 865	51	.25
Kill or cure.	Sig 742	49	.25
FRANK, ANNE			
The diary of a young girl.	PB 970	53	.25
_____.	Card C-317	58	.35
FRANK, GEROLD			
with Diana Barrymore			
Too much, too soon.	Sig D1490	58	.50

Author/Title	Pub./Stock No.	Yr.	Price
FRANK, GEROLD (cont.)			
with Sheilah Graham			
Beloved infidel.	Ban F2033	59	.50
FRANK, JEANNETTE			
The modern meat cookbook.	DelL LC106	58	.50
FRANK, LAWRENCE K. with Mary Frank			
How to help your child			
in school.	SigK Ks314	54	.35
Your adolescent at home			
and in school.	SigK KD372	59	.50
FRANK, LEONHARD			
Desire me.	PenN 657	48	.25
_____.	Sig 1359	57	.25
FRANK, MARY with Lawrence K. Frank			
How to help your child			
in school.	SigK Ks314	54	.35
Your adolescent at home			
and in school.	SigK KD372	59	.50
FRANK, Pat			
An affair of state.	Ban 829	50	.25
Forbidden area.	Ban A1553	57	.35
Hold back the night.	Ban 1078	53	.25
_____.	Ban 1511	56	.25
Mr. Adam.	PB 498	48	.25
FRANK, WOLFGANG			
The sea wolves.	Ball F258	58	.50
with Bernhard Rogge			
The German raider			
Atlantis.	Ball 184	57	.35
FRANKEN, ROSE			
Another Claudia.	PB 499	48	.25
Claudia.	PB 218	43	.25
Claudia and David.	PB 296	45	.25
Young Claudia.	Dell 528	51	.25
FRANKLAND, EDWARD			
The long swords.	Ban A1425	56	.35
FRANKLIN, BENJAMIN			
The autobiography of			
Benjamin Franklin.	PB 23	39	.25
	PBL PL18	54	.35
_____.			
The Benjamin Franklin			
sampler.	Prem s31	56	.35
FRANKLIN, FRIEDA K.			
Combat nurse.	PB 1147	57	.25
To hate and to love.	Pop 753	56	.25
FRASER, PHYLLIS with Edith Young			
Puzzles, quizzes and			
games.	Ban 81	47	.25
FRAY, AL			
And kill once more.	Graf 118	55	.25
Built for trouble.	DelF A167	58	.25
Come back for more.	DelF A161	58	.25
The dice spelled murder.	DelF A146	57	.25
FRAZEE, STEVE			
Cry, coyote.	PB 1101	56	.25
Desert guns.	DelF A135	57	.25
Gold at Kansas Gulch.	Crst 261	58	.25
The gunthrowers.	Lion 217	54	.25
_____.	Lion LB 173	57	.25
He rode alone.	GM 613	56	.25
High hell.	Crst 211	58	.25
Lawman's feud.	Lion 150	53	.25
_____.	Lion LB 108	56	.25
Many rivers to cross.	GM 457	55	.25
_____.	GM 935	59	.25
Pistolman.	Lion unk	52	.25
_____.	Lion LB 78	56	.25
Rendezvous.	Crst 315	59	.25
Running target.	GM 637	57	.25
Sharp the bugle calls.	Lion 130	53	.25
The sky block.	Lion LL 3	54	.35
_____.	PyrR PG13	58	.35
Smoke in the valley.	GM s836	59	.35
Spur to the smoke.	Perm M-3003	55	.25
Tumbling Range woman.	Perm M-3049	56	.25
Utah hell guns.	Lion 96	52	.25
_____.	Lion LB 69	56	.25
FRAZER, ANDREW			
Find Eileen Hardin--			
alive!	Avon T-343	59	.35
FRAZER, ROBERT CAINE			
Mark Kilby solves a			
murder.	PB 1261	59	.25
FRAZIER, ROBERT			
Malenkov.	Lion 145	53	.25
FREDE, RICHARD			
Entry E.	Sig S1712	59	.35
FREDERICKS, DIANA			
Diana.	Berk G-11	55	.35
_____.	Berk G-50	57	.35
FREDERICKS, ERNEST JASON			
Cry flood!	Ace D-370	59	.35
Shakedown hotel.	Ace D-273	58	.35
FREDERICKS, VIC			
Crackers in bed.	PB 1053	55	.25
FREE, MONTAGUE			
A complete guide to			
gardening.	Perm M-5006	57	.50

Author/Title	Pub./Stock No.	Yr.	Price
FREE, MONTAGUE (cont.)			
Gardening.	Prmb P285S	54	.50
The Pocket book of			
flower gardening.	PB 200	43	.25
FREEDMAN, BENEDICT with Nancy Freedman			
Mrs. Mike.	Ban 152	49	.25
_____.	Ban A1904	59	.35
FREEDMAN, NANCY with Benedict Freedman			
Mrs. Mike.	Ban 152	49	.25
_____.	Ban A1904	59	.35
FREEMAN, EUGENE with David Appel			
The wisdom and ideas of			
Plato.	Prem s28	56	.35
_____.	Prem d84	59	.50
FREEMAN, JAMES			
The new Crest crossword			
puzzle book.	Crst 196	57	.25
FREEMAN, LUCY			
"Before I kill more..."	Card C-221	56	.35
Fight against fears.	Card C-82	53	.35
Hope for the troubled.	Card C-147	54	.35
FREEMAN, R. AUSTIN			
The adventures of Dr.			
Thorndyke.	Pop 122	47	.25
Dr. Thorndyke's			
discovery.	Avon (10)	41	.25
Mr. Polton explains.	Pop 70	46	.25
A silent witness.	PB 184	42	.25
The stoneware monkey.	Pop 11	43	.25
The unconscious witness.	Avon 122	47	.25
FREEMAN, WALTER			
All the way home.	Sig 1186	55	.25
The last blitzkrieg.	Sig 1634	59	.25
FREIDIN, SEYMOUR with William Richardson			
The fatal decisions.	Berk BG-121	58	.50
FREMANTLE, ANNE			
The age of belief.	Ment Ms126	55	.50
The papal encyclicals in			
their historical			
context.	Ment MD177	56	.50
_____.	Ment MT256	59	.75
FRENCH, E. T.			
Never smile at children.	Pyr G388	59	.35
FRENCH, PETER			
The Southern Cross.	Perm M-4135	59	.35
FRENCH postcards.	Avon 609	54	.25
_____.	Avon 853	59	.25

Author/Title	Pub./Stock No.	Yr.	Price
FREUCHEN, PETER			
The sea tyrant.	Pyr 98	53	.25
FREUD, SIGMUND			
Beyond the pleasure			
principle.	BanC FC49	59	.50
A general introduction			
to psychoanalysis.	Prmb P202S	53	.50
_____.	Perm M-5001	55	.50
Psychopathology of			
everyday life.	Ment M67	51	.35
FREY, RICHARD			
According to Hoyle.	Prem s37	56	.35
_____.	Crst d180	57	.50
How to play canasta.	NL 43	49	.25
How to play samba.	Avon 287	51	.25
FREYER, FREDERIC			
Case of the black			
black hearse.	Avon 677	55	.25
FRIEDMAN, BRUCE JAY			
The rascal's guide.	Zen ZB-12	59	.35
FRIEDMAN, STUART			
The bedside corpse.	Lion LL 148	57	.35
Ex-con.	Pyr 131	54	.25
Nikki.	Mon 125	59	.35
The woman and the			
prowler.	Avon 773	57	.25
FRIEND, OSCAR J.			
Barricade.	Han 113	50	.25
Gun harvest.	Han 79	48	.25
The long noose.	HanW 3	47	.20
The range doctor.	Han 101	50	.25
The range maverick.	Han 71	48	.25
The round-up.	Avon 299	51	.25
with Leo Margulies			
My best science fiction			
story.	PB 1007	54	.25
Race to the stars.	Crst s245	58	.35
FRIENDLICH, DICK			
Pivot man.	PBJr J-59	50	.25
FRISON-ROCHE, R.			
First on the rope.	Ace D-222	57	.35
FRITCH, CHARLES E.			
Negative of a nude.	Ace D-367	59	.35
FRIZELL, BERNARD			
Ten days in August.	Pop G202	57	.35
FROME, DAVID			
The Eel Pie murders.	Pop 9	43	.25
The Hammersmith murders.	Dell 36	44	.25

Author/Title	Pub./Stock No.	Yr.	Price
FROME, DAVID (cont.)			
The man from Scotland Yard.	PB 153	42	.25
Mr. Pinkerton at the Old Angel.	Pop 34	44	.25
Mr. Pinkerton finds a body.	PB 111	41	.25
Mr. Pinkerton goes to Scotland Yard.	PB 124	41	.25
Mr. Pinkerton grows a beard.	Pen 541	44	.25
Mr. Pinkerton has the clue.	Pop 26	44	.25
FROST, ROBERT			
The Pocket book of Robert Frost's poems.	PB 374	46	.25
————.	Card C-94	53	.35
————.	PBL PL47	56	.35
FRY, MONROE			
Sex, vice and business.	Ball 311K	59	.35
FUCHIDA, MITSUO with Masatake Okumiya			
Midway.	Ball F224	58	.50
FULLER, BLAIR			
Forbid me not.	Berk G-103	58	.35
FULLER, LESTER with Edwin Rolfe			
The glass room.	Ban 310	48	.25
FULLER, ROGER			
Sign of the pagan.	Card C-182	55	.35
FULLER, TIMOTHY			
Harvard has a homicide.	Dell 54	44	.25
Keep cool, Mr. Jones.	Dell 594	52	.25
Reunion with murder.	Pop 207	49	.25
This is murder, Mr. Jones.	Pop 117	48	.25
Three thirds of a ghost.	Pop 81	46	.25
FULLER, WILLIAM			
Back country.	DelF 8	54	.25
Brad Dolan's blonde cargo.	DelF A153	57	.25
Brad Dolan's Miami manhunt.	DelF A158	58	.25
The girl in the frame.	DelF A133	57	.25
Goat Island.	DelF 28	54	.25
The pace that kills.	DelF 105	56	.25
Tight squeeze.	DelF A189	59	.25
FUNK, WILFRED			
Six weeks to words of power.	Card C-166	55	.35
with Norman Lewis			
30 days to a more powerful vocabulary.	PB 569	49	.25

Author/Title	Pub./Stock No.	Yr.	Price
FUNNY side up.	Dell 607	52	.25
FURCOLOWE, CHARLES			
Search for the sun.	Sig S1171	54	.35
FURMAN, A. L.			
The mystery companion.	Pop 130	48	.25
FURST, BRUNO			
The practical way to a better memory.	Prem d59	57	.50

Author/Title	Pub./Stock No.	Yr.	Price
G			
GABY, ALEX			
To end the night.	Sig 1035	53	.25
GADDIS, PEGGY			
Love to burn.	Han 90	49	.25
GADDIS, THOMAS E.			
Birdman of Alcatraz.	Sig D1550	58	.50
GAER, JOSEPH			
How the great religions began.	SigK K308	54	.25
_____.	SigK KD359	58	.50
GAGE, JOSEPH			
Hard rock town.	Eag EB69	56	.25
A score to settle.	Ace D-368	59	.35
GAILLARD, ROBERT			
Marie of the Isles.	Pop G139	54	.35
_____.	Pop SP33	58	.50
GAINES, AUDREY			
While the wind howled.	Dell 51	44	.25
GAINES, DIANA			
Tasker Martin.	Ban 880	51	.25
GAINES, WILLIAM M.			
The bedside Mad.	Sig S1647	59	.35
The brothers Mad.	Ball 267K	58	.35
Son of Mad.	Sig S1701	59	.35
Utterly Mad.	Ball 178	56	.35
_____.	Ball 266K	58	.35
GALE, GLORIA			
Calendar model.	Pop G260	58	.35
GALLAGHER, THOMAS			
The double life.	Pop 733	56	.25
The gathering darkness.	Pop G131	53	.35
GALLAND, ADOLF			
The first and the last.	Ball F193	57	.50
GALLI de BIBIENA, JEAN			
Amorous Philandre.	Avon 171	48	.25
GALLICO, PAUL			
Farewell to sport.	PB 318	45	.25
The lonely.	Sig 819	50	.25
	Sig 1295	56	.25
_____.	Avon 760	57	.25
Love of seven dolls.	Avon 760	57	.25
Thief is an ugly word.	DelT unk	51	.10
Trial by terror.	Dell 717	53	.25
GALLUN, RAYMOND Z.			
People minus X.	Ace D-291	58	.35

Author/Title	Pub./Stock No.	Yr.	Price
GALLUP, GEORGE			
The 1954 Pocket almanac.	Card nn	53	.50
The 1955 Pocket almanac.	Card GC1955	54	.50
The 1956 Pocket almanac of facts.	Card GC1956	55	.50
GAMOW, GEORGE			
Biography of the earth.	PelM M27	48	.35
_____.	Ment MD138	55	.50
The birth and death of the sun.	Pel P4	46	.25
_____.	Ment M77	52	.35
_____.	Ment Ms120	54	.50
The creation of the universe.	Ment MD214	57	.50
One two three...infinity.	Ment Ms97	53	.50
GANN, ERNEST K.			
The high and the mighty.	Prmb P301	54	.35
_____.	Perm M-4002	55	.35
Island in the sky.	Pop 516	53	.25
The raging tide.	Prmb P134	51	.35
Soldier of fortune.	Perm M-4034	55	.35
Twilight for the gods.	Perm M-4091	58	.35
GANNETT, LEWIS			
I saw it happen.	PB 178	42	.25
GANT, JONATHAN			
Never say no to a killer.	Ace D-157	56	.35
GANT, MATTHEW			
The manhunter.	Sig 1423	57	.25
Valley of angry men.	GM 335	53	.25
GARDNER, CURTISS T.			
The fatal cast.	Graf 83	54	.25
GARDNER, ERLE STANLEY			
The case of the angry mourner.	PB 1092	56	.25
The case of the backward mule.	PB 855	51	.25
The case of the baited hook.	PB 414	47	.25
The case of the black-eyed blonde.	PB 792	51	.25
The case of the borrowed brunette.	PB 856	52	.25
The case of the buried clock.	PB 678	50	.25
The case of the careless kitten.	PB 724	50	.25
_____.	Card C-299	58	.35
The case of the caretaker's cat.	PB 138	42	.25
The case of the cautious coquette.	PB 1009	54	.25
_____.	Card C-332	59	.35

Author/Title	Pub./Stock No.		Yr.	Price
GARDNER, ERLE STANLEY (cont.)				
The case of the counterfeit eye.	PB	157	42	.25
The case of the crooked candle.	PB	758	51	.25
_____.	Card	C-302	58	.35
The case of the curious bride.	PB	177	42	.25
_____.	Card	C-324	59	.35
The case of the dangerous dowager.	PB	252	44	.25
The case of the demure defendant.	Card	C-323	59	.35
The case of the drowning duck.	PB	643	49	.25
The case of the drowsy mosquito.	PB	689	50	.25
The case of the dubious bridegroom.	PB	976	54	.25
_____.	Card	C-376	59	.35
The case of the empty tin.	PB	619	49	.25
_____.	Card	C-284	58	.35
The case of the fan-dancer's horse.	PB	886	52	.25
The case of the fiery fingers.	PB	1089	56	.25
The case of the forgotten murder.	Card	C-307	58	.35
The case of the fugitive nurse.	PB	1138	57	.25
The case of the gilded lily.	Card	C-337	59	.35
The case of the glamorous ghost.	Card	C-282	58	.35
The case of the golddigger's purse.	PB	812	51	.25
The case of the green-eyed sister.	PB	1155	57	.25
The case of the grinning gorilla.	PB	1121	56	.25
The case of the half-wakened wife.	PB	832	51	.25
_____.	Card	C-283	58	.35
The case of the haunted husband.	PB	590	49	.25
_____.	Card	C-325	59	.35
The case of the hesitant hostess.	PB	1127	56	.25
The case of the howling dog.	PB	116	41	.25
The case of the lame canary.	PB	223	43	.25
The case of the lazy lover.	PB	909	52	.25
_____.	Card	C-285	58	.35
The case of the lonely heiress.	PB	922	53	.25
The case of the lucky legs.	PB	106	41	.25

Author/Title	Pub./Stock No.		Yr.	Price
The case of the lucky legs.	Card	C-329	59	.35
The case of the lucky loser.	Card	C-341	59	.35
The case of the moth-eaten mink.	PB	1107	56	.25
The case of the musical cow.	PB	1063	55	.25
The case of the negligent nymph.	PB	1029	54	.25
The case of the nervous accomplice.	Card	C-297	58	.35
The case of the one-eyed witness.	PB	1041	55	.25
_____.	Card	C-320	59	.35
The case of the perjured parrot.	PB	378	47	.25
The case of the restless redhead.	PB	1170	57	.25
The case of the rolling bones.	PB	464	47	.25
The case of the runaway corpse.	Card	C-281	57	.35
The case of the shoplifter's shoe.	PB	312	45	.25
The case of the silent partner.	PB	468	48	.25
The case of the sleepwalker's niece.	PB	277	44	.25
The case of the smoking chimney.	PB	667	50	.25
The case of the stuttering bishop.	PB	201	43	.25
The case of the substitute face.	PB	242	43	.25
The case of the sulky girl.	PB	90	41	.25
_____.	Card	C-309	58	.35
The case of the sun bather's diary.	Card	C-268	58	.35
The case of the terrified typist.	Card	C-275	58	.35
The case of the turning tide.	PB	544	48	.25
The case of the vagabond virgin.	PB	965	53	.25
_____.	Card	C-355	59	.35
The case of the velvet claws.	PB	73	40	.25
The clue of the forgotten murder.	PB	438	47	.25
The court of last resort.	Card	C-126	54	.35
The D.A. breaks a seal.	PB	869	52	.25
_____.	Card	C-292	58	.35
The D.A. breaks an egg.	PB	1052	55	.25
_____.	Card	C-294	58	.35
The D.A. calls a turn.	PB	595	49	.25
_____.	Card	C-291	58	.35
The D.A. calls it murder.	PB	263	44	.25
_____.	Card	C-295	58	.35

Author/Title	Pub./Stock No.	Yr.	Price
GARDNER, ERLE STANLEY (cont.)			
The D.A. cooks a goose.	PB 561	49	.25
⎯⎯⎯⎯⎯.	Card C-345	59	.35
The D.A. draws a circle.	PB 334	46	.25
⎯⎯⎯⎯⎯.	Card C-346	59	.35
The D.A. goes to trial.	PB 407	46	.25
⎯⎯⎯⎯⎯.	Card C-347	59	.35
The D.A. holds a candle.	PB 287	45	.25
⎯⎯⎯⎯⎯.	Card C-348	59	.35
The D.A. takes a chance.	PB 1010	54	.25
⎯⎯⎯⎯⎯.	Card C-293	58	.35
Murder up my sleeve.	PB 368	46	.25
This is murder.	PB 512	48	.25
Two clues.	PB 949	53	.25
GARDNER, HY			
Tales out of (night) school.	Perm M-4151	59	.35
GARDNER, MARTIN			
Great essays in science.	PBL PL-58	57	.35
GARLAND, GEORGE			
Apache warpath.	Sig 1714	59	.25
The big dry.	Sig 1101	54	.25
Doubtful Valley.	Sig 996	53	.25
⎯⎯⎯⎯⎯.	Sig 1418	58	.25
GARLAND, RODNEY			
The heart in exile.	Lion LL 76	56	.35
The troubled midnight.	Lion LL 128	56	.35
GARNER, CLAUD			
Cornbread aristocrat.	Sig 894	51	.25
GARNETT, DAVID			
Aspects of love.	Dell D193	57	.35
Lady into fox and A man in the zoo.	Pen 615	46	.25
GARNIER, CHRISTINE			
Fetish.	Dell 731	53	.25
GARREAU, GARTH			
Bat boy of the Giants.	Com 17	49	.25
GARRETT, JAMES			
And save them for pallbearers.	Ban F1920	59	.50
GARRITY, DEVIN A.			
Irish stories and tales.	PBL PL48	56	.35
GARSIDE, E. B.			
A lust to live.	Berk G-15	56	.35
The man from Brazil.	Ban A1205	54	.35
GARST, SHANNON			
Buffalo Bill.	PBJr J-48	50	.25

Author/Title	Pub./Stock No.	Yr.	Price
GARTENBERG, MAX with Gene Feldman			
The beat generation and the angry young men.	Dell F84	59	.50
GARTH, DAVID			
Appointment with danger.	Pop 136	48	.25
Challenge for three.	Pop 84	46	.25
Tiger milk.	Pop 49	45	.25
GARTH, JOHN			
Hill man.	Pyr 112	54	.25
GARVE, ANDREW			
By-line for murder.	Dell 765	54	.25
The end of the track.	Berk G-114	58	.35
A hole in the ground.	Dell D275	59	.35
The Megstone plot.	Pyr G360	58	.35
Murder through the looking glass.	Dell 827	55	.25
No mask for murder.	Dell 571	52	.25
No tears for Hilda.	Dell 655	53	.25
GARVIN, FERNANDE SILVE			
The art of French cooking.	Ban A1827	58	.35
GARY, ROMAIN			
The colors of the day.	PB 1032	54	.25
The roots of heaven.	Card GC-61	58	.50
GASSER, HENRY			
How to draw and paint.	DelF FE54	55	.50
⎯⎯⎯⎯⎯.	DelL LC125	59	.50
GATLAND, KENNETH W. with Derek D. Dempster			
The inhabited universe.	Prem d83	59	.50
GAULDEN, RAY			
Shadow of the rope.	Perm M-3095	57	.25
The vengeful men.	Perm M-3110	58	.25
GAULT, WILLIAM CAMPBELL			
Blood on the boards.	Dell 835	55	.25
The bloody Bokhara.	Dell 746	53	.25
The canvas coffin.	Dell 795	54	.25
The convertible hearse.	Ban 1927	59	.25
Day of the ram.	Ban 1638	57	.25
Don't cry for me.	Dell 672	53	.25
End of a call girl.	Crst 248	58	.25
Murder in the raw.	Dell 926	56	.25
Night lady.	Crst 260	58	.25
Run, killer, run.	Dell 868	55	.25
Square in the middle.	Ban 1602	57	.25
The sweet blonde trap.	Zen ZB-25	59	.35
Sweet wild wench.	Crst 309	59	.25
The wayward widow.	Crst 281	59	.25
GAUNTIER, GENE			
Sporting lady.	Pyr 113	54	.25

Author/Title	Pub./Stock No.	Yr.	Price
GAUTIER, THÉOPHILE			
Mademoiselle de Maupin.	Prem s17	55	.35
_____.	Pyr G161	55	.35
GAZEL, STEFAN			
To live and kill.	Ball F339K	59	.50
GAZZO, MICHAEL VINCENTE			
A hatful of rain.	Sig S1412	57	.35
GEARON, JOHN			
The velvet well.	Pen 624	47	.25
GEBLER, ERNEST			
The Plymouth adventure.	Prmb P166	52	.35
GEDDES, DONALD PORTER			
An analysis of the Kinsey reports on sexual behavior in the human male and female.	Ment Ms108	54	.50
The atomic age opens.	PB 340	45	.25
Franklin Delano Roosevelt: a memorial.	PB 300	45	.25
with Enid Curie			
About the Kinsey report.	Sig 675	48	.25
GEER, ANDREW			
Canton barrier.	Card C-271	57	.35
The sea chase.	PB 652	50	.25
GEHMAN, RICHARD			
Driven.	GM D387	54	.50
Each life to live.	RS 8	52	.35
Murder in Paradise.	Sig S1307	56	.35
The slander of witches.	Sig 1353	56	.25
GEIST, STANLEY			
French stories and tales.	PBL PL-37	56	.35
GELLHORN, MARTHA			
Liana.	Pop 529	53	.25
_____.	Pop G253	58	.35
The wine of astonishment.	Ban 736	49	.25
GÉRARD, FRANCIS			
The mark of the moon.	Pop 544	53	.25
GERHARDI, WILLIAM with Leopold Loewenstein			
Analyze yourself.	Ban A1493	56	.35
GERNSBACK, HUGO			
Ralph 124C41+.	Crst s226	58	.35
GEROULD, CHRISTOPHER			
Sexual practices of American women.	Lion 160	53	.25
GERSON, NOEL B.			
The Cumberland rifles.	Dell 736	53	.25
The forest lord.	Ban A2010	59	.35
The golden eagle.	Prmb P298	54	.35
The highwayman.	Perm M-4070	57	.35
Port Royal.	Ban A1370	55	.35
Savage cavalier.	Pop G104	52	.35
_____.	Pop G191	57	.35
The silver lion.	Pop G217	58	.35
Sword of fortune.	Pop G116	53	.35
GERSTELL, RICHARD			
How to survive an atomic bomb.	Ban 845	50	.25
GERSTINE, JACK			
Play it cool.	Ace D-337	59	.35
GHISELIN, BREWSTER			
The creative process.	Ment MD132	55	.50
GIANT mystery reader.	Avon G1004	51	.50
GIBB, H. A. R.			
Mohammedanism.	Ment M136	55	.35
GIBBONS, FLOYD			
The Red knight of Germany.	Ban A1919	59	.35
GIBBS, WILLA			
Fruit of desire.	Lion LL 37	55	.35
Seed of mischief.	Prmb P280	54	.35
GIBSON, CHRISTINE with I. A. Richards			
English through pictures, book 1.	Card C-75	53	.35
_____.	WSP W1	59	.35
English through pictures, book 2.	Card C-258	57	.35
_____.	WSP W4	59	.35
First steps in reading English.	Card C-256	57	.35
_____.	WSP W2	59	.35
A first workbook of French.	WSP W10	59	.35
GIBSON, JEWEL			
Black gold.	Sig 853	51	.25
GIBSON, WALTER			
The boat.	Eag EB20	54	.25
GIBSON, WILLIAM			
The cobweb.	Ban F1337	55	.50
GIDDINGS, HARRY			
Loser by a head.	Ace D-225	57	.35
GIES, JOSEPH			
A matter of morals.	Pop 421	52	.25
_____.	Pop G386	59	.35

Author/Title	Pub./Stock No.	Yr.	Price
GIFFORD, ARNOLD			
Hotel fever.	Pop 751	56	.25
GILBERT, ANTHONY			
Death at the door.	Ban 85	47	.25
Death in the blackout.	Ban 51	46	.25
Death lifts the latch.	Ban 768	50	.25
The innocent bottle.	Ban 851	51	.25
Murder cheats the bride.	Ban 138	48	.25
Murder is cheap.	Ban 317	49	.25
Riddle of a lady.	Ban 1758	58	.25
The woman in red.	Han 29	44	.15
GILBERT, EDWIN			
Hard to get.	Pop 469	52	.25
The hot and the cool.	Pop G142	54	.35
Native stone.	Ban F1580	57	.50
See how they burn.	Pop G340	59	.35
Silver spoon.	Ban F1767	58	.50
The squirrel cage.	Pop G250	58	.35
GILBERT, ELLIOTT			
Don't push me around.	Pop 681	55	.25
The vice trap.	Avon T-266	58	.35
GILBERT, MICHAEL			
The danger within.	Dell 870	55	.25
Death has deep roots.	Dell 744	53	.25
GILBERT, WILLIAM SCHWENCK with Arthur Sullivan			
Gilbert and Sullivan operas.	Avon 228	50	.25
GILBRETH, FRANK B. JR. with Ernestine Gilbreth Carey			
Cheaper by the dozen.	Ban 960	51	.25
_____.	Ban A2073	59	.35
GILES, HASCAL			
Kansas trail.	Ball 176	56	.35
GILES, HENRY			
Harbin's Ridge.	Ban 1081	53	.25
GILES, JANICE HOLT			
The Kentuckians.	Ban A1336	55	.35
GILES, RAY			
How to retire and enjoy it.	Crst s275	59	.35
GILL, BRENDAN			
The day the money stopped.	PB 1199	58	.25
GILL, ELISABETH			
Young sinner.	Zen ZB-21	59	.35
GILL, TOM			
Border feud.	Pop 397	52	.25

Author/Title	Pub./Stock No.	Yr.	Price
Firebrand.	Pop 119	47	.25
The gay bandit of the border.	Pop 190	49	.25
Gentlemen of the jungle.	Dell 456	50	.25
Guardians of the desert.	Pop 142	48	.25
Starlight pass.	Pop 338	51	.25
GILLIAN, MICHAEL			
Warrant for a wanton.	Pnnt P12	53	.25
GILLIGAN, EDMUND			
The gaunt woman.	Dell 312	49	.25
GILLON, PHILIP			
Frail barrier.	Sig 1026	53	.25
GILMAN, LaSELLE			
The red gate.	Ball 9	53	.35
Wine of desire.	Pop 747	56	.25
GILMAN, WILLIAM			
The spy trap.	Bart 3	44	.25
GILMORE, JOHN with S. A. Lewin			
Sex after forty.	Dell 761	54	.25
GILPATRIC, GUY			
French summer.	Avon 180	48	.25
Mister Glencannon.	PB 87	40	.25
GINGRICH, ARNOLD			
Best of the bedside Esquire.	Ban F1274	54	.50
GINIGER, KENNETH S.			
The compact treasury of inspiration.	Card C-196	55	.35
GIOVANNITTI, LEN			
The prisoners of Combine D.	Ban F1870	59	.50
GIPSON, FRED			
Cowhand: the story of a working cowboy.	Ban F1749	58	.50
Hound-dog man.	PB 713	50	.25
_____.	Perm M-4168	59	.35
Old Yeller.	PB 1177	57	.25
The **GIRL** with the hungry eyes.	Avon 184	49	.25
GIRVAN, HELEN			
Blue treasure.	PBJr J-49	50	.25
GIVENS, CHARLES			
Big Mike.	Pyr 104	53	.25
GLASGOW, ELLEN			
Vein of iron.	Pen 583	46	.25

Author/Title	Pub./Stock No.	Yr.	Price
GLAY, GEORGE ALBERT			
Gina.	Dell D131	53	.35
Oath of seven.	Ace S-102	55	.25
GLEESON, JAMES with T. J. Waldron			
The frogmen.	Berk G246	59	.35
GLEMSER, BERNARD			
Gallery of women.	Sig D1519	58	.50
GLENDINNING, RICHARD			
Carnival girl.	Pop 718	56	.25
Mission to murder.	GM 444	54	.25
Passion road.	Pop 656	55	.25
Retreat into night.	GM 389	54	.25
Terror in the sun.	GM 237	52	.25
Too fast we live.	Pop 607	54	.25
Who evil thinks.	GM 262	52	.25
GODDEN, JON			
The seven islands.	PB 1172	57	.25
GOETHALS, THOMAS			
Panzer ghost division.	Avon T-197	57	.35
GOETHE, JOHANN WOLFGANG von			
Great writings of Goethe.	Ment MT235	58	.75
GOLD, HERBERT			
Room clerk.	Sig 1185	55	.25
The wild life.	Perm M-3073	57	.25
GOLDBERG, HYMAN			
How I became a girl reporter.	Pop 357	51	.25
GOLDEN, FRANCIS LEO			
For doctors only.	PB 796	51	.25
Jest what the doctor ordered.	PB 872	52	.25
Laughter is legal.	PB 948	53	.25
Tales for salesmen.	PB 1013	54	.25
GOLDEN, HARRY			
Only in America.	Perm M-5011	59	.50
GOLDMAN, LAWRENCE			
Black fire.	Ace D-170	56	.35
GOLDMAN, WILLIAM			
The temple of gold.	Ban A1834	58	.35
GOLDSMITH, OLIVER			
The vicar of Wakefield.	PBL PL54	57	.35
GOLDTHWAITE, EATON K.			
The body next door.	Han 48	46	.15
Date with death.	Ban 132	47	.25
Root of evil.	Dell 442	50	.25
Scarecrow.	Dell 193	47	.25

Author/Title	Pub./Stock No.	Yr.	Price
The scarlet spade.	Ace D-5	52	.35
The Sixpenny dame.	Pnnt P49	54	.25
GOLDWATER, ROBERT			
Van Gogh.	PBA A6	53	.50
GOLIGHTLY, BONNIE			
Beat girl.	Avon T-310	59	.35
High cost of loving.	Avon T-237	58	.35
Legend of the lost.	Berk G-92	57	.35
The wild one.	Avon T-194	57	.35
GONCOURT, EDMOND de			
Elisa.	Hill 128	59	.35
with Jules de Goncourt			
Germinie.	Ace D-16	53	.35
GONCOURT, JULES de with Edmond de Goncourt			
Germinie.	Ace D-16	53	.35
GONZALES, JOHN			
Death for Mr. Big.	GM 204	51	.25
The magnificent Moll.	RS 23	52	.35
GOOD housekeeping's the better way.	Pop G364	59	.35
GOOD reading.	Pel P19	47	.35
————.	Ment M76	52	.35
————.	Ment Ms124	54	.50
————.	Ment MD178	56	.50
GOODEN, ARTHUR HENRY			
Call of the range.	Avon 562	54	.25
Guns on the high mesa.	Hill unk	48	.25
The shadowed trail.	Hill unk	49	.25
Trouble in the saddle.	Avon 532	53	.25
The valley of dry bones.	PB 353	46	.25
GOODIN, PEGGY			
The lie.	Sig 1179	55	.25
Mickey.	Ban 406	48	.25
GOODIS, DAVID			
Behold this woman.	Ban 407	48	.25
	Pop 775	56	.25
Black Friday.	Lion 224	54	.25
The blonde on the street corner.	Lion 186	54	.25
The burglar.	Lion 124	53	.25
Cassidy's girl.	GM 189	51	.25
	GM 544	56	.25
The dark chase.	Lion 133	53	.25
Dark passage.	Dell 221	48	.25
Down there.	GM 623	56	.25
Fire in the flesh.	GM 691	57	.25
The moon in the gutter.	GM 348	53	.25
Nightfall.	Lion LB 131	56	.25
Of missing persons.	PB 833	51	.25
Of tender sin.	GM 226	52	.25

Author/Title	Pub./Stock No.	Yr.	Price
GOODIS, DAVID (cont.)			
Of tender sin.	GM 626	56	.25
Street of no return.	GM 428	54	.25
Street of the lost.	GM 256	52	.25
	GM 652	57	.25
The wounded and the			
slain.	GM 530	55	.25
GOODMAN, MURRAY			
with Joe Falcaro			
The Dell bowling			
handbook.	Dell 728	53	.25
with Leonard Lewin			
My greatest day in			
football.	Ban 715	49	.25
GOODMAN, ROGER B. with David Lewin			
New ways to greater			
word power.	DelF 43	55	.25
	DelL LB110	57	.35
GOODPASTURE, W. W.			
The complete book of			
gardening.	DelF F48	55	.50
GOODRICH, MARCUS			
Delilah.	Ban A1088	53	.35
GOODWIN, HAROLD LELAND			
The science book of			
space travel.	Card C-207	56	.35
GORDIMER, NADINE			
The lying days.	Sig D1237	55	.50
The soft voice of the			
serpent.	Sig S1266	56	.35
GORDON, AD			
The flesh painter.	Lion LL 46	55	.35
Slade.	Lion LL 79	56	.35
GORDON, ARTHUR			
Reprisal.	PB 801	51	.25
GORDON, CAROLINE			
Green centuries.	Ban F1130	53	.50
GORDON, DAN with Richard Wormser			
The longhorn trail.	Ace D-92	55	.35
GORDON, GERALD			
Dark brother.	Pyr G129	54	.35
GORDON, IAN			
After innocence.	DelF 58	55	.25
The big success.	DelF A111	56	.25
The burden of guilt.	Dell 727	53	.25
Deep is my desire.	Pop 662	55	.25
Harlem is my heaven.	Berk G-78	57	.35
	Berk G259	59	.35

Author/Title	Pub./Stock No.	Yr.	Price
The night thorn.	Pop 474	53	.25
GORDON, JAMES			
Collision.	Lion LL 41	55	.35
The lust of Private			
Cooper.	Lion unk	52	.25
GORDON, NOAH			
Night ward.	Sig 1660	59	.25
GORDON, REX			
First on Mars.	Ace D-233	57	.35
First to the stars.	Ace D-405	59	.35
GORDON, RUSSELL			
She posed for death.	Avon 283	50	.25
GORDON, STEWART			
Gunswift.	Crst 164	57	.25
GORDONS, the (Gordon and Mildred Gordon)			
The big frame.	Ban 1782	58	.25
Campaign train.	Ban 1475	56	.25
Case file: FBI.	Ban 1273	54	.25
The case of the talking			
bug.	Ban 1455	56	.25
F.B.I. story.	Ban 1348	55	.25
GOREN, CHARLES H.			
The fundamentals of			
contract bridge.	Prmb P184	52	.35
	Perm M-4016	55	.35
Goren presents the			
Italian bridge system.	Ban A1953	59	.35
GORHAM, CHARLES			
The future Mr. Dolan.	Sig 752	49	.25
	Pyr G197	56	.35
	Pyr G449	59	.35
The gilded hearse.	Sig 714	49	.25
	Pop 593	54	.25
The gold of their bodies.	Sig D1244	55	.50
Make me an offer.	Berk G-199	59	.35
Martha Crane.	Pop 555	54	.25
	Berk G-83	57	.35
Trial by darkness.	Sig D1130	54	.50
Wine of life.	Crst d285	59	.50
GORHAM, NICHOLAS			
Queen's blade.	Ace D-342	59	.35
GORKY, MAXIM			
26 men and a girl.	Avon T-154	57	.35
GORN, LESTER			
The greater glory.	Pop SP51	59	.50
GOSCINNY, RENÉ			
Cartoons the French way.	Lion LL 38	55	.35
French and frisky.	Lion LB 99	56	.25

Author/Title	Pub./Stock No.	Yr.	Price
GOTSHALL, JACK			
Pappy and the promised land.	GM 358	54	.25
Pappy's women.	Crst s257	58	.35
GOTTSCHO, SAMUEL			
The Pocket guide to the wildflowers.	PB 788	51	.35
GOUDGE, ELIZABETH			
A city of bells.	PB 564	49	.25
Green Dolphin street.	Prmb P178S	52	.50
Pilgrim's inn.	PB 672	50	.25
GOULD, CHESTER			
Dick Tracy and the Woo Woo sisters.	Dell nn	47	.25
GOULD, JOHN			
Farmer takes a wife.	PB 496	48	.25
GOULD, LAWRENCE			
Your most intimate problems.	Avon 200	49	.25
GOULD, R. E.			
Yankee storekeeper.	Ban 456	48	.25
GOURMONT, RÉMY de			
The physiology of love.	Hill unk	<u>49</u>	.25
GOWEN, EMMETT			
Dark moon of March.	Dell 572	52	.25
GRABACH, JOHN R.			
How to draw the human figure.	DelL LC115	58	.50
_____.	DelL LX120	59	.75
GRACE, EDWARD with James Wakefield Burke			
Three day pass--to kill.	Berk 106	55	.25
_____.	Berk G-164	58	.35
GRADY, LESTER			
The best from Captain Billy's whizbang.	Crst 118	55	.25
Drink and be merry.	Crst s331	59	.35
GRADY, TEX			
High mesa.	Pop 493	53	.25
GRAFTON, C. W.			
Beyond a reasonable doubt.	PB 752	51	.25
The rat began to gnaw the rope.	Dell 180	47	.25
The rope began to hang the butcher.	Dell 232	48	.25
GRAFTON, SAMUEL			
A most contagious game.	PB 1102	56	.25

Author/Title	Pub./Stock No.	Yr.	Price
GRAHAM, ALICE WALWORTH			
The Natchez woman.	Dell D105	52	.35
GRAHAM, BILLY			
Peace with God.	Perm M-4003	55	.35
GRAHAM, CARROLL			
Border town.	Dell 625	52	.25
GRAHAM, GWETHALYN			
Earth and high heaven.	Ban 460	48	.25
GRAHAM, LEE			
If you are a woman.	Pop 692	55	.25
with James Bender			
Your way to popularity and personal power.	Sig 889	51	.25
_____.	SigK K313	54	.25
GRAHAM, LEWIS			
The great I am.	Han 85	49	.25
GRAHAM, SHEILAH with Gerold Frank			
Beloved infidel.	Ban F2033	59	.50
GRAHAM, WINSTON			
Night without stars.	Prmb P128	51	.35
GRANBERRY, EDWIN			
Strangers and lovers.	Sig 864	51	.25
GRANGE, RED			
My favorite football stories.	Dell 862	55	.25
GRANGER, K. R. G.			
Tejanos!	Perm M-3018	55	.25
Ten against Caesar.	Pop 505	53	.25
GRANT, MAXWELL			
The Shadow and the voice of murder.	BPLA 21	<u>40</u>	.10
GRANT, OZRO			
Bad 'un.	Ace D-50	54	.35
GRANTLAND, KEITH			
Run from the hunter.	GM 701	57	.25
GRAU, SHIRLEY ANN			
The black prince and other stories.	Sig S1318	56	.35
The hard blue sky.	Sig T1726	59	.75
GRAVES, RALPH			
The lost eagles.	Card C-225	56	.35
GRAVES, ROBERT			
I, Claudius.	Avon AT-68	53	.35
They hanged my saintly Billy.	Avon G-1037	59	.50

Author/Title	Pub./Stock No.	Yr.	Price
GRAY, HARRIET			
Bride of violence.	Avon T-156	57	.35
Gold for the gay masters.	Avon T-126	56	.35
GRAY, RUSSELL			
The lustful ape.	Lion 38	50	.25
GRAYSON, CHARLES			
The golden temptress.	Ace D-49	54	.35
Hollywood doctor.	Ace D-207	57	.35
New stories for men.	Prmb P122	51	.35
with Van H. Cartmell			
The golden Argosy.	Ban F1441	56	.50
GRAZIANO, ROCKY with Rowland Barber			
Somebody up there likes me.	Card C-210	56	.35
GREAT murder stories.	Pen 655	48	.25
GREAT tales of the deep South.	Lion LL 30	55	.35
GREEN, ABEL with Joe Laurie Jr.			
Show biz.	Prmb P217S	53	.50
GREEN, ALAN			
They died laughing.	Dell 701	53	.25
What a body!	Dell 483	51	.25
GREEN, CHALMERS			
The scarlet Venus.	GM 246	52	.25
GREEN, F. L.			
Odd man out.	PB 472	47	.25
GREEN, GERALD			
The last angry man.	Card GC-757	59	.75
GREEN, JULIAN			
The dark journey.	Avon T-91	54	.35
Moira.	Sig 998	53	.25
GREENBERG, CLEMENT			
Matisse.	PBA A10	53	.50
GREENBERG, MARTIN			
Men against the stars.	Pyr G234	57	.35
GREENE, GRAHAM			
Brighton Rock.	Ban 315	49	.25
The confidential agent.	Pen 515	43	.25
_____.	Ban 971	52	.25
_____.	Ban A1773	58	.35
The end of the affair.	Ban A1306	55	.35
_____.	Ban F2004	59	.50
The heart of the matter.	Ban A1424	56	.35
The man within.	Ban 355	48	.25
_____.	Berk G-146	58	.35
The ministry of fear.	Pen 530	44	.25

Author/Title	Pub./Stock No.	Yr.	Price
Nineteen stories.	Lion LL 31	55	.35
Orient express.	Ban 1333	55	.25
The power and the glory.	Ban A1217	54	.35
The quiet American.	Ban A1669	57	.35
The shipwrecked.	Ban A1480	56	.35
The third man.	Ban 797	50	.25
This gun for hire.	Sup M652	45	.25
_____.	Ban 1316	55	.25
GREENE, JOSEPH I. with Elizabeth Abell			
First love.	Ban 503	48	.25
Husbands and lovers.	Ban 742	49	.25
Stories for here and now.	Ban A914	51	.35
Stories of sudden truth.	Ball 19	53	.35
GREENE, JOSIAH E.			
The man with one talent.	Prmb P150	52	.35
GREENE, LAURENCE			
O'Mara.	Lion 182	53	.25
GREENE, WARD			
Cora Potts.	Lion 115	<u>52</u>	.25
_____.	Lion LL 55	<u>55</u>	.35
Death in the deep South.	Avon 266	50	.25
Desire in the deep South.	Avon 664	55	.25
The life and loves of a modern Mr. Bluebeard.	Avon 190	49	.25
Route 28.	Lion 89	52	.25
GREENHOOD, DAVID			
Love in dishevelment.	Sig 711	49	.25
_____.	Crst 119	55	.25
GREENWALD, HAROLD			
The call girl.	Ball F280K	58	.50
Great cases in psychoanalysis.	Ball F333K	59	.50
GREGG, ALAN			
The mystery of Batty Ridge.	PBJr J-47	50	.25
Winged mystery.	Com 7	48	.25
GREGORY, DAN			
Three must die!	Graf 143	56	.25
GREGORY, FRANKLIN			
The cipher of death.	HH unk	46	.25
GREGORY, HORACE with Marya Zaturenska			
The Mentor book of religious verse.	Ment MD189	57	.50
GREGORY, JACKSON			
Ace in the hole.	Pop 337	51	.25
The far call.	Pop 313	51	.25
Guardians of the trail.	Pop 430	52	.25
Hardcase range.	Eag EB103	58	.25
The lone rider.	Pop 255	50	.25

Author/Title	Pub./Stock No.	Yr.	Price
GREGORY, JACKSON (cont.)			
The man from Texas.	Pop 383	51	.25
.	Pop G396	59	.35
Marshal of Sundown.	Pop 184	49	.25
.	Pop 597	54	.25
.	Pop G380	59	.35
Mystery at Spanish			
hacienda.	Avon (13)	42	.25
Powder smoke.	Pop 789	56	.25
The red law.	Pop 95	46	.25
.	Eag EB10	54	.25
Secret valley.	Pop 140	48	.25
.	Eag EB17	54	.25
The silver star.	Pop 160	48	.25
.	Pop 545	53	.25
.	Pop G257	58	.35
Sudden Bill Dorn.	Pop 226	50	.25
GREIG, MAYSIE			
Candidate for love.	Dell 239	48	.25
Doctor's wife.	PB 463	47	.25
Professional lover.	PB 541	48	.25
Reluctant millionaire.	Dell 170	47	.25
Romance for sale.	Ban 110	47	.25
Satin straps.	Dell 309	49	.25
Unmarried couple.	PB 574	49	.25
Whispers in the sun.	Dell 496	51	.25
Yours ever.	Dell 446	50	.25
GRESHAM, WILLIAM LINDSAY			
Limbo Tower.	Sig 839	51	.25
Nightmare alley.	Sig 738	49	.25
.	Sig 1326	56	.25
GREW, DAVID			
Beyond rope and fence.	PBJr J-72	51	.35
GREW, WILLIAM			
Doubles in death.	Perm M-3019	55	.25
Murder has many faces.	Graf 105	55	.25
GREY, HARRY			
Call me Duke.	Graf G215	56	.35
The hoods.	Sig S999	53	.35
.	Sig D1211	55	.50
.	Sig D1575	59	.50
Portrait of a mobster.	Sig S1572	58	.35
GREY, ROBIN			
Puzzle in porcelain.	Bart 29	46	.25
GREY, ZANE			
The border legion.	Card C-239	57	.35
The drift fence.	Card C-264	57	.35
The last of the			
plainsmen.	Ban 73	46	.25
.	Pnnt P2	53	.25
.	Ban A1718	58	.35
The last trail.	PB 371	46	.25
Nevada.	Ban 3	45	.25

Author/Title	Pub./Stock No.	Yr.	Price
Nevada.	Ban 1067	52	.25
.	Ban 1298	55	.25
.	Ban A1717	58	.35
The spirit of the border.	PB 161	42	.25
The trail driver.	Card C-333	59	.35
The U.P. trail.	Card C-231	56	.35
Valley of wild horses.	Card C-351	59	.35
GRIDER, GEORGE with Lydel Sims			
War fish.	Pyr G406	59	.35
GRIERSON, EDWARD			
Royalist.	Ban A1525	56	.35
GRIFFIN, JOHN HOWARD			
The devil rides outside.	Card GC-14	54	.50
GRIFFITH, BEATRICE			
American me.	Pnnt P39	54	.25
GRIFFITH, MAXWELL			
The gadget maker.	Card C-215	56	.35
Port of call.	Prmb P197	53	.35
GRINIOFF, VLADIMIR B.			
The banker's daughter.	Pyr G424	59	.35
GRINNELL, DAVID			
Across time.	Ace D-286	58	.35
Edge of time.	Ace D-362	59	.35
GRINSTEAD, J. E.			
Hell range in Texas.	Avon 829	58	.25
Maverick guns.	Han 103	50	.25
Range king.	Han 115	50	.25
When Texans ride.	Han 123	50	.25
GRISMAN, ARNOLD E.			
Early to rise.	Berk G-198	59	.35
GROMBACH, JOHN V.			
Olympic cavalcade of			
sports.	Ball 161	56	.35
GROSS, FRED			
How to work with tools			
and wood.	PB 1057	55	.25
.	Card C-260	57	.35
GROSS, NANCY E. with Courtlandt Canby			
The world of history.	Ment M109	54	.35
GROSSER, MAURICE			
The painter's eye.	Ment M159	56	.35
GROTE, WILLIAM			
Cain's girl friend.	Ace D-203	57	.35
GROVE, FRED			
Flame of the Osage.	Pyr G313	58	.35

Author/Title	Pub./Stock No.	Yr.	Price
GROVE, FRED (cont.)			
No bugles, no glory.	Ball 324K	59	.35
Sun dance.	Ball 251	58	.35
GROVE, WALT			
Down.	DelF 1E	53	.25
	DelF D81	55	.35
Hell-bent for danger.	GM 134	50	.25
	GM 545	56	.25
The joy boys.	DelF B136	59	.35
The man who said no.	GM 120	50	.25
	GM s801	58	.35
The wings of eagles.	GM s649	57	.35
GRUBB, DAVIS			
A dream of kings.	Crst d160	57	.50
The night of the hunter.	Dell D149	55	.35
GRUBER, FRANK			
The big land.	Ban A1598	57	.35
Bitter Sage.	Ban 1287	55	.25
	Ban 1527	56	.25
Broken lance.	Ban 1198	54	.25
The buffalo box.	Ban 50	46	.25
Bugles west.	Ban 1666	57	.25
Fighting man.	Ban 212	49	.25
	Ban 1743	58	.25
Fort Starvation.	Pnnt P43	54	.25
The fourth letter.	Sig 799	50	.25
French key mystery.	Avon 91	46	.25
The gamecock murders.	Sig 753	49	.25
The gift horse.	Ban 2	45	.25
Gunsight.	Lion 163	53	.25
	Lion LB 93	56	.25
The highwayman.	Ace D-196	57	.35
The honest dealer.	Sig 707	49	.25
A job of murder.	Sig 827	50	.25
Johnny Vengeance.	Ban 1347	55	.25
The laughing fox.	Pen 538	44	.25
The limping goose.	Ban 1488	56	.25
The lone gunhawk.	Lion 157	53	.25
	Lion LB 117	56	.25
Lonesome river.	Ban 1742	58	.25
The man from Missouri.	Pop 761	56	.25
Market for murder.	Pen 651	47	.25
The marshal.	Ban A2021	59	.35
The mighty blockhead.	Sup M655	45	.25
	Ban 144	48	.25
Mood for murder.	Graf 119	56	.25
The Navy Colt.	Sup M649	45	.25
	Ban 151	48	.25
Outlaw.	Ban 1934	59	.25
Peace marshal.	Ban 1741	58	.25
Quantrill's raiders.	Ace D-39	54	.35
Rebel road.	Ace D-39	54	.35
Run, thief, run.	Crst 115	55	.25
The silver jackass.	Pen 623	47	.25
The Silver Tombstone.	Sig 689	48	.25
The Silver Tombstone mystery.	Sig 1677	59	.25
Simon Lash, private detective.	Pen 562	45	.25
Tales of Wells Fargo.	Ban 1726	58	.25
The talking clock.	Pen 545	44	.25
Town tamer.	Ban A1998	59	.35
The whispering master.	Sig 726	49	.25
	Sig 1636	59	.25
The yellow overcoat.	Pop 188	49	.25
GRUENBERG, SIDONIE			
Your child and you.	GM 112	50	.25
GUARESCHI, GIOVANNI			
Don Camillo and his flock.	PB 1067	55	.25
The little world of Don Camillo.	PB 1000	54	.25
GUDERIAN, HEINZ			
Panzer leader.	Ball F225	57	.50
GUENTHER, JOHN with Frank K. Everest Jr.			
The fastest man alive.	Pyr G373	58	.35
GUÉRARD, ALBERT			
The bystander.	Crst s328	59	.35
GUÉRARD, ARTHUR ROSE with John Cowan			
Love, health and marriage.	Avon 148	48	.25
GUILD, LEO			
Bachelor's joke book.	Avon 513	53	.25
	Avon T-346	59	.35
The loves of Liberace.	Avon T-118	56	.35
What are the odds?	PB 636	49	.25
GUINN, WILLIAM			
Death lies deep.	GM 503	55	.25
GULICK, BILL			
Bend of the Snake.	Ban 906	51	.25
A drum calls west.	Ban 1094	53	.25
The mountain men.	Pop 755	56	.25
Showdown in the sun.	Pop G247	58	.35
Trail drive.	Pop 701	55	.25
GUNFIGHT at the O.K. Corral.	Avon 774	57	.25
GUNMAN'S land.	Lion LL 72	56	.35
GUNN, JAMES E.			
Deadlier than the male.	Sig 709	49	.25
	Sig 1084	53	.25
	Berk G232	59	.35
Station in space.	Ban A1825	58	.35
This fortress world.	Ace D-223	57	.35
with Jack Williamson			
Star bridge.	Ace D-169	56	.35

Author/Title	Pub./Stock No.	Yr.	Price
GUNN, TOM			
Painted Post gunplay.	PB 1002	54	.25
Painted Post law.	PB 841	52	.25
Painted Post range.	PB 942	53	.25
The sheriff of Painted Post.	PB 808	51	.25
GUNTHER, JOHN			
D-Day.	Avon T-239	58	.35
Death be not proud.	Pyr R243	57	.35
Inside U.S.A., volume 1.	Ban A1033	52	.35
Inside U.S.A., volume 2.	Ban A1034	52	.35
GURALNIK, DAVID B.			
Webster's new world dictionary of the American language.	Pop SP15	58	.50
GUTHEIL, EMIL A.			
What your dreams mean.	Prem s46	57	.35
GUTHRIE, A. B. JR.			
The big sky.	PB 600	49	.25
_____.	Card C-52	52	.35
These thousand hills.	Card C-267	57	.35
Trouble at Moon Dance.	Pop 376	51	.25
_____.	Pop G274	58	.35
The way west.	PB 780	51	.25
_____.	Card C-30	52	.35
_____.	PBL PL17	54	.50
_____.	PBL PL513	57	.50
GUTTMACHER, ALAN F.			
Having a baby.	Sig 788	50	.25
_____.	SigK Ks332	55	.35
Pregnancy and birth.	SigK KD358	58	.50
The story of human birth.	Pel P12	47	.25
GUTWILLIG, ROBERT			
After long silence.	Pop G330	59	.35
GWALTNEY, FRANCIS IRBY			
Between heaven and hell.	Pop SP5	56	.50
A moment of warmth.	Pop SP27	58	.50
The whole town knew.	Pop 699	55	.25
GWINN, WILLIAM			
Jazz bum.	Lion 225	54	.25
A way with women.	Lion 209	54	.25

Author/Title	Pub./Stock No.	Yr.	Price
H			
H.R.H.			
Confessions of a princess.	Avon T-106	55	.35
HAASE, JOHN			
The young who sin.	Avon T-251	58	.35
HABAS, RALPH A.			
How to live without liquor.	SigK K335	56	.25
HABE, HANS			
The devil's agent.	Crst s270	59	.35
Off limits.	Crst s207	58	.35
HABER, HEINZ			
The Walt Disney story of our friend the atom.	DelF B104	56	.35
HACHIYA, MICHIHIKO			
Hiroshima diary.	Avon T-259	58	.35
HACKETT, FRANCIS			
Henry the Eighth.	BanB FB401	56	.50
——————.	BanC FC9	58	.50
HADEN, ALLEN			
My enemy, my wife.	Dell 595	52	.25
HADLEY, HAROLD			
Come see them die.	Pyr G242	57	.35
HAGGARD, H. RIDER with Don Ward			
She.	Dell 339	49	.25
with Jean Francis Webb			
King Solomon's mines.	Dell 433	50	.25
HAGGARD, HOWARD W.			
Devils, drugs and doctors.	PB 379	46	.25
——————.	Card C-101	53	.35
——————.	Card GC-70	59	.50
HAHN, EMILY			
Affair.	Lion 57	51	.25
——————.	Crst 121	55	.25
Francie comes home.	Berk G274	59	.35
House in Shanghai.	Crst s203	58	.35
Miss Jill from Shanghai.	Avon 217	50	.25
With naked foot.	Ban 858	51	.25
——————.	Ban 1479	56	.25
HAIG-BROWN, RODERICK L.			
Starbuck valley winter.	Com 21	49	.25
HAINES, DONAL HAMILTON			
Southpaw.	Com 16	49	.25

Author/Title	Pub./Stock No.	Yr.	Price
HAINES, WILLIAM WISTER			
Command decision.	PB 571	49	.25
——————.	Ban A1964	59	.35
High tension.	PB 502	48	.25
The Hon. Rocky Slade.	Ban A1901	59	.35
Slim.	PB 412	47	.25
——————.	Ban F1902	59	.50
HALE, CHRISTOPHER			
Hangman's tie.	Bart 32	46	.25
Midsummer nightmare.	Dell 150	47	.25
HALE, NANCY			
The prodigal women.	Prmb P199S	53	.50
HALECKI, OSCAR with James F. Murray Jr.			
Pius XII: Eugenio Pacelli, Pope of peace.	Lion LL 67	56	.50
HALES, CAROL			
Such is my beloved.	Berk G-95	58	.35
HALES, NORMAN			
The spider in the cup.	Sig 1173	55	.25
HALEVY, JULIAN			
The young lovers.	Dell D170	56	.35
HALL, CALVIN S.			
The meaning of dreams.	Dell D287	59	.35
A primer of Freudian psychology.	Ment M147	55	.35
——————.	Ment MD271	59	.50
HALL, DESMOND			
A woman of forty.	Pop 413	52	.25
HALL, EVAN			
Logan.	Lion LB 132	56	.25
HALL, GEOFFREY HOLIDAY			
The end is known.	PB 776	51	.25
HALL, JAMES NORMAN with Charles Nordhoff			
Botany Bay.	Perm M-4001	55	.35
Falcons of France.	Mon 141	59	.35
The hurricane.	PB 188	43	.25
Men against the sea.	PB 358	46	.25
Mutiny on the Bounty.	PB 216	43	.25
——————.	Card C-34	52	.35
Pitcairn's Island.	PB 457	47	.25
HALL, OAKLEY			
Corpus of Joe Bailey.	Perm M-4006	55	.35
Mardios Beach.	Perm M-4042	56	.35
Murder city.	PB 828	51	.25
So many doors.	Ban 908	51	.25
——————.	Ban A1898	59	.35
Warlock.	Ban F1980	59	.50

Author/Title	Pub./Stock No.	Yr.	Price
HALL, RADCLYFFE			
The well of loneliness.	Prmb P112	51	.35
_____.	Perm M-4024	55	.35
_____.	Perm M-5010	59	.50
HALL, WARNER			
Untamed.	DelF B122	58	.35
HALLAS, RICHARD			
You play the black and the red comes up.	Dell 510	51	.25
HALLERAN, E. E.			
Blazing border.	Ball 153	56	.35
Colorado Creek.	Lion 134	53	.25
Devil's Canyon.	Ball 142	56	.35
Double cross trail.	PB 876	52	.25
High prairie.	Ban 1004	52	.25
The hostile hills.	Ball 205	57	.35
No range is free.	Dell 616	52	.25
Outlaw guns.	Avon 367	51	.25
	Avon 522	53	.25
Outlaw trail.	PB 783	51	.25
Rustlers' canyon.	PB 703	50	.25
Smoky Range.	Dell 755	54	.25
Spanish Ridge.	Ball 219	57	.35
Straw boss.	Avon 507	53	.25
Wagon captain.	Ball 170	56	.35
Winter ambush.	Ban 1385	55	.25
HALLIBURTON, RICHARD			
The royal road to romance.	PB 147	42	.25
HALLIDAY, BRETT			
Before I wake.	Dell 829	55	.25
The blonde cried murder.	Dell 946	57	.25
Blood on Biscayne Bay.	Dell 268	49	.25
	Dell 459	50	.25
Blood on the black market.	Dell 64	44	.25
Blood on the stars.	Dell 385	50	.25
	Dell 891	56	.25
Bodies are where you find them.	Pop 192	49	.25
	Dell 668	53	.25
	Dell D327	59	.35
Call for Michael Shayne.	Dell 428	50	.25
	Dell D269	59	.35
The case of the walking corpse.	Han 15	43	.15
The corpse came calling.	Dell 168	47	.25
	Dell 324	49	.25
	Dell 842	55	.25
Counterfeit wife.	Dell 280	49	.25
	Dell 590	52	.25
Dead man's diary and A taste for cognac.	Dell D292	59	.35
Dead man's diary and Dinner at Dupre's.	Dell 427	50	.25
Death has three lives.	Dell 865	55	.25
Dividend on death.	Pop 98	46	.25
	Dell 617	52	.25
_____.	Dell D293	59	.35
Fit to kill.	Dell D314	59	.35
Framed in blood.	Dell 578	52	.25
_____.	Dell 958	57	.25
Heads you lose.	Dell 987	58	.25
In a deadly vein.	Dell 905	56	.25
Marked for murder.	Dell 222	48	.25
_____.	Dell 503	51	.25
_____.	Dell D291	59	.35
Michael Shayne's long chance.	Dell 112	46	.25
_____.	Dell 325	49	.25
_____.	Dell 866	55	.25
Mum's the word for murder.	Dell 743	53	.25
Murder and the married virgin.	Dell 128	46	.25
_____.	Dell 323	49	.25
_____.	Dell 960	57	.25
Murder and the wanton bride.	Dell D283	59	.35
Murder in Miami.	Dell D331	59	.35
Murder is my business.	Dell 184	47	.25
_____.	Dell 326	49	.25
_____.	Dell 965	58	.25
Murder wears a mummer's mask.	Dell 78	45	.25
_____.	Dell 388	50	.25
One night with Nora.	Dell 803	54	.25
The private practice of Michael Shayne.	Dell 23	43	.25
_____.	Dell 429	50	.25
_____.	Dell D248	58	.35
She woke to darkness.	Dell 867	55	.25
Shoot the works.	Dell 988	58	.25
Stranger in town.	Dell 914	56	.25
A taste for cognac.	DelT 15	51	.10
A taste for violence.	Dell 426	50	.25
_____.	Dell 458	50	.25
_____.	Dell 934	57	.25
This is it, Michael Shayne.	Dell 533	51	.25
_____.	Dell 957	57	.25
Tickets for death.	Dell 387	50	.25
_____.	Dell 989	58	.25
The uncomplaining corpses.	Dell 386	50	.25
	Dell 981	58	.25
Weep for a blonde.	Dell 978	58	.25
What really happened.	Dell 768	54	.25
When Dorinda dances.	Dell 723	53	.25
HALLOCK, GRACE T. with Donald B. Armstrong			
What to do till the doctor comes.	PB 220	43	.25
HALPER, ALBERT			
Atlantic Avenue.	DelF 94	56	.25

Author/Title	Pub./Stock No.	Yr.	Price
HAM, ROSWELL G. JR.			
The gifted.	Avon 512	53	.25
The gifted sinners.	Avon T-139	56	.35
Till the rafters ring.	Perm M-4098	58	.35
HAMILL, ETHEL			
A nurse for Galleon Key.	Ban 1841	58	.25
HAMILTON, ALEXANDER			
The basic ideas of			
Alexander Hamilton.	PBL PL33	57	.35
HAMILTON, BRUCE			
Hanging judge.	Hill 15	49	.25
HAMILTON, DONALD			
Assignment: murder.	DelF A123	56	.25
The big country.	DelF B115	58	.35
Date with darkness.	Dell 375	50	.25
Line of fire.	DelF 46	55	.25
Mad River.	DelF 91	56	.25
Murder twice told.	Dell 577	52	.25
Night walker.	DelF 27	54	.25
Smoky Valley.	DelF 18	54	.25
The steel mirror.	Dell 473	51	.25
HAMILTON, EDITH			
The Greek way to			
western civilization.	Ment M32	48	.35
Mythology.	Ment Ms86	53	.50
The Roman way to			
western civilization.	Ment MD213	57	.50
HAMILTON, EDMOND			
Beyond the moon.	Sig 812	50	.25
City at world's end.	Crst s184	57	.35
The star of life.	Crst s329	59	.35
The sun smasher.	Ace D-351	59	.35
HAMILTON, HARRY			
Thunder in the			
wilderness.	Prmb P260	53	.35
HAMILTON, WADE			
The longhorn brand.	Pyr 396	59	.25
Rimrock renegade.	Pyr 403	59	.25
HAMMETT, CATHERINE T.			
Your own book of			
campcraft.	PBJr J-46	50	.25
	PB 893	52	.35
———.	Card C-180	55	.35
HAMMETT, DASHIELL			
Blood money.	Dell 53	44	.25
	Dell 486	51	.25
The Continental Op.	Dell 129	46	.25
The creeping Siamese.	Dell 538	51	.25
The Dain curse.	PB 295	45	.25
Dead yellow women.	Dell 308	49	.25

Author/Title	Pub./Stock No.	Yr.	Price
Dead yellow women.	Dell 421	50	.25
The glass key.	PB 211	43	.25
Hammett homicides.	Dell 223	48	.25
The Maltese falcon.	PB 268	44	.25
———.	Perm M-3074	57	.25
A man called Spade.	Dell 90	45	.25
———.	Dell 411	50	.25
	Dell 452	50	.25
Nightmare town.	Dell 379	50	.25
Red Harvest.	PB 241	43	.25
———.	Perm M-3043	56	.25
Return of the			
Continental Op.	Dell 154	47	.25
The thin man.	PB 196	43	.25
HAMNER, EARL JR.			
Fifty roads to town.	Sig S1271	56	.35
HAMPSHIRE, STUART			
The age of reason.	Ment MD158	56	.50
HAN SUYIN			
A many-splendored thing.	Sig D1183	55	.50
The mountain is young.	Sig T1717	59	.75
HANCOCK, LUCY AGNES			
Doctor Kim.	Ban 408	48	.25
Graduate nurse.	Ban 1433	56	.25
Special nurse.	PB 692	50	.25
Student nurse.	PB 520	48	.25
HANCOCK, W. K.			
Empire in the changing			
world.	PenS S213	43	.25
HANDLEY, ALAN			
Terror in Times Square.	Pyr 20	50	.25
HANKINS, R. M.			
Ace-in-the-Hole Haggarty.	Ban 757	50	.25
The man from Wyoming.	Ban 259	49	.25
Rio Grande Kid.	Ban 214	49	.25
HANLEY, GERALD			
The consul at sunset.	Pyr G120	54	.35
Drinkers of darkness.	Pyr R211	56	.35
HANLEY, JACK			
The guy from Coney			
Island.	Avon 580	54	.25
Immoral woman.	Berk G252	59	.35
Let's make Mary.	Hill nn	48	.25
	Hill nn	52	.25
———.	Hill 120	59	.35
Stag stripper.	Berk G-171	58	.35
Star lust.	Avon 417	52	.25
Strip street.	Berk G261	59	.35
HANLIN, TOM			
Mima.	Ban 978	52	.25

Author/Title	Pub./Stock No.	Yr.	Price
HANO, ARNOLD			
Western roundup!	Ban 256	48	.25
Western triggers.	Ban 200	48	.25
HANSEN, ALVIN H.			
America's role in the world economy.	Pel P10	46	.25
HANSEN, EVA HEMMER			
Scandal in Troy.	Pop 825	57	.25
HANSEN, ROBERT P.			
Dead pigeon.	Ban 1188	54	.25
Murder is where you find it.	Perm M-3066	57	.25
Trouble comes double.	Ban 1469	56	.25
Walk a wicked mile.	Pop 774	56	.25
HARDIN, CLEMENT			
Cross me in gunsmoke.	Ace D-248	57	.35
Hellbent for a hangrope.	Ace D-56	54	.35
HARDIN, DAVE			
Brandon's empire.	Ball 57	54	.35
HARDIN, PETER			
The frightened dove.	Ban 1030	52	.25
The hidden grave.	Dell 922	56	.25
HARDY, LINDSAY			
The Nightshade Ring.	Sig 1283	56	.25
Requiem for a redhead.	Sig 1154	54	.25
Show no mercy.	Pop 709	55	.25
HARDY, RENÉ			
Bitter victory.	Sig S1462	57	.35
HARDY, RONALD			
The place of jackals.	Berk G-23	56	.35
HARDY, THOMAS			
Jude the obscure.	DelL LX108	59	.75
The mayor of Casterbridge.	PBL PL52	56	.35
The return of the native.	PB 20	39	.25
———.	Card C-42	52	.35
———.	PBL PL23	54	.35
———.	SigC CD7	59	.50
Tess of the D'Urbervilles.	Card C-47	52	.35
———.	PBL PL25	54	.35
———.	PBL PL525	58	.50
HARDY, W. G.			
All the trumpets sounded.	Pop G189	57	.35
The city of libertines.	Pop SP31	58	.50
Turn back the river.	Avon AT-70	53	.35
The unfulfilled.	Pop 464	52	.25
HARDY, WILLIAM M.			
Lady killer.	Dell 995	58	.25
HARGROVE, MARION			
The girl he left behind.	Sig S1364	56	.35
See here, Private Hargrove.	PB 206	43	.25
Something's got to give.	Pop 222	49	.25
HARKEY, DEE			
Mean as hell.	Sig 856	51	.25
———.	Sig 1196	55	.25
HARKINS, PHILIP			
Lightning on ice.	Com 29	49	.25
Touchdown twins.	PBJr J-55	50	.25
HARMAN, CARTER			
A popular history of music.	DelF C102	56	.50
HARMON, BOB with Hank Ketcham			
Baby sitter's guide, by Dennis the menace.	PB 1080	55	.25
HARNESS, CHARLES L.			
The paradox men.	Ace D-118	55	.35
HARPER, DANIEL			
Paris escort.	Eton E122	53	.25
The wrong turn.	Avon 591	54	.25
HARPER'S magazine reader.	Ban A1037	53	.35
HARRÉ, EVERETT			
The heavenly sinner.	Pyr G64	52	.35
———.	Pyr G146	55	.35
HARRIMAN, JOHN			
The magnate.	Ace D-246	57	.35
HARRIS, ELEANOR			
The real story of Lucille Ball.	Ball 78	54	.35
HARRIS, H. E.			
The Pocket stamp album.	PB 892	52	.25
HARRIS, JOHN, 1911- with Margaret Harris			
Arrow in the moon.	PB 1061	55	.25
The medicine whip.	PB 995	54	.25
HARRIS, JOHN, 1916 or 17-			
The undaunted.	Ban A1289	55	.35
HARRIS, MARGARET with John Harris, 1911-			
Arrow in the moon.	PB 1061	55	.25
The medicine whip.	PB 995	54	.25
HARRIS, MARK			
Something about a soldier.	Sig S1659	59	.35
The southpaw.	Prmb P299	54	.35

Author/Title	Pub./Stock No.	Yr.	Price
HARRIS, MEL with Weegee			
Naked Hollywood.	Berk G-9	55	.35
HARRIS, SARA			
Father Divine: holy			
husband.	Prmb P300	54	.35
Nobody cares for me.	Sig S1613	59	.35
The wayward ones.	Sig 1146	54	.25
_____.	Sig 1341	56	.25
with John M. Murtagh			
Cast the first stone.	Card C-286	58	.35
HARRIS, WILLIAM HOWARD			
The golden jungle.	Berk G-151	58	.35
HARRISON, C. WILLIAM			
Barbed wire kingdom.	Ban 1926	59	.25
Border fever.	Perm M-3030	56	.25
Eat dog or die!	Lion 103	52	.25
The guns of Fort			
Petticoat.	GM 560	56	.25
The Missouri maiden.	Lion unk	52	.25
The Oxbow kill.	Lion 181	53	.25
_____.	Lion LB 123	56	.25
Unarmed killer.	Perm M-3093	57	.25
HARRISON, G. B.			
Introducing Shakespeare.	Pel P14	47	.25
HART, CONSTANCE			
The handbook of beauty.	DelF D40	55	.35
_____.	DelF C106	58	.50
HART, FRANCES NOYES			
The Bellamy trial.	PB 264	45	.25
_____.	Dell D233	58	.35
HART, HENRY			
Venetian adventurer:			
Marco Polo.	BanB FB403	56	.50
HART, MOSS			
Winged victory--the Army			
Air Force play.	Avon 58	44	.25
with George S. Kaufman			
The man who came to			
dinner.	PB 143	42	.25
HARTE, BRET			
The outcasts of Poker			
Flat.	Avon 446	52	.25
HARTLEY, WILLIAM B.			
The cruel tower.	Pop 765	56	.25
HARTMAN, JOYCE F. with Martha Foley			
The best short stories			
of 1953.	Ball 34	53	.50
HARTOG, JAN de			
The little ark.	PB 1042	55	.25

Author/Title	Pub./Stock No.	Yr.	Price
The sea.	PB 953	53	.25
The spiral road.	Ban F1846	58	.50
Stella.	PB 952	53	.25
HARTT, FREDERICK			
Botticelli.	PBA A9	53	.50
HARVEY, FRANK			
Air Force!	Ball 329K	59	.35
Jet.	Ball 116	55	.35
HARVEY, GENE			
Leg artist.	RC 3	49	.25
HARVIN, EMILY			
Madwoman?	Avon 276	50	.25
HARWIN, BRIAN			
Home is upriver.	Sig 1063	53	.25
Touch me not.	Mon 110	59	.35
HAŠEK, JAROSLAV			
The good soldier Schweik.	PenS S211	42	.25
_____.	Pen 572	46	.25
HASHIMOTO, MOCHITSURA			
Sunk!	Avon T-246	58	.35
HASSEL, SVEN			
The legion of the damned.	Crst s217	58	.35
HASTINGS, PHYLLIS			
Her French husband.	Pop G177	57	.35
The innocent and the			
wicked.	Pop 762	56	.25
A time for pleasure.	Pop 672	55	.25
HASTINGS, RODERIC			
Naked tide.	Avon T-267	58	.35
HASTY, JOHN EUGENE			
The man without a face.	Zen ZB-9	58	.35
HATCH, ALDEN			
Red carpet for Mamie			
Eisenhower.	Pop G164	56	.35
HATCH, ERIC			
Crockett's woman.	GM 176	51	.25
_____.	GM 690	57	.25
The delinquent ghost.	Bart (2)	44	.25
Five nights.	Ban 453	48	.25
The golden woman.	GM 213	52	.25
My man Godfrey.	Ban 121	47	.25
_____.	Ban 1694	57	.25
Road show.	Ban 476	49	.25
Spendthrift.	Ban 414	48	.25
HATCH, RICHARD WARREN			
Go down to glory.	Dell D114	52	.35

Author/Title	Pub./Stock No.	Yr.	Price
HATLO, JIMMY			
Another new Jimmy Hatlo book.	Avon 826	58	.25
Cartoons by Jimmy Hatlo.	Avon 639	55	.25
Hatlo cartoons--1956.	Avon 707	56	.25
Hatlo's inferno.	Avon 652	55	.25
Little Iodine.	DelF 78	55	.25
More they'll do it every time.	Avon 789	57	.25
The new Jimmy Hatlo book.	Avon 524	53	.25
	Avon 612	54	.25
_____.			
The newest Jimmy Hatlo cartoon book.	Avon 857	59	.25
They'll do it every time.	PB 298	45	.25
	Avon 366	51	.25
_____.			
HATTEN, HOMER			
Bride of the sword.	RS 15	52	.35
Conquest.	GM 215	52	.25
Eagle on his wrist.	GM 352	53	.25
Horsemen from hell.	GM 541	56	.25
Jezebel in crinoline.	GM 416	54	.25
Plunder range.	GM 492	55	.25
Westport Landing.	GM 157	51	.25
The **HAUNTED** hotel and 25 other ghost stories.	Avon (6)	41	.25
HAUSER, GAYELORD			
Be happier, be healthier.	Pop 559	54	.25
Look younger, live longer.	Prem s18	56	.35
HAWES, GENE R.			
The New American guide to colleges.	SigK KD373	59	.50
HAWKINS, JOHN with Ward Hawkins			
A girl, a man and a river.	Pop 824	57	.25
If I kill him.	Han 41	45	.15
Violent city.	Ace D-289	58	.35
HAWKINS, WARD with John Hawkins			
A girl, a man and a river.	Pop 824	57	.25
If I kill him.	Han 41	45	.15
Violent city.	Ace D-289	58	.35
HAWLEY, CAMERON			
Cash McCall.	Card GC-751	56	.75
	Card C-313	58	.35
_____.			
Executive suite.	Ball 1	52	.35
HAWTHORNE, NATHANIEL			
The house of the seven gables.	PB 52	40	.25
	PBL PL15	54	.35
_____.			
The marble fawn.	PBL PL59	58	.35
The scarlet letter.	PB 551	48	.25

Author/Title	Pub./Stock No.	Yr.	Price
The scarlet letter.	Card C-65	52	.35
_____.	PBL PL26	55	.35
_____.	SigC CD8	59	.50
HAWTON, HECTOR			
Philosophy for pleasure.	Prem s20	56	.35
_____.	Prem d75	59	.50
HAYCOX, ERNEST			
Action by night.	PB 608	49	.25
_____.	Card C-370	59	.35
The adventurers.	Card C-204	56	.35
Alder Gulch.	Dell 317	49	.25
_____.	Dell 450	50	.25
_____.	Dell 945	57	.25
The border trumpet.	PB 301	45	.25
Brand fires on the ridge.	Mon 108	59	.35
Bugles in the afternoon.	Ban 25	46	.25
_____.	Ban A980	52	.35
By rope and lead.	PB 864	52	.25
Canyon passage.	PB 640	49	.25
Chaffee of Roaring Horse.	Pop 171	49	.25
_____.	Pop 486	53	.25
_____.	Pop G237	58	.35
Dead man range.	Pop 831	57	.25
Deep West.	PB 594	49	.25
The earthbreakers.	Card C-97	53	.35
_____.	Ban F1872	59	.50
Free grass.	Pop 143	48	.25
_____.	Pop 517	53	.25
_____.	Pop G261	58	.35
The grim canyon.	Pop 537	53	.25
Gun talk.	Pop 728	56	.25
Guns of the Tom Dee and The valley of the Rogue.	Pop G347	59	.35
Guns up.	Pop 589	54	.25
Head of the mountain.	Pop 442	52	.25
_____.	Pop G351	59	.35
The last rodeo.	PB 1148	57	.25
Lone rider.	Pop G300	59	.35
Long storm.	Ban 788	50	.25
_____.	Ban A1627	57	.35
Man in the saddle.	Dell 120	46	.25
_____.	Dell 618	52	.25
_____.	Dell 952	57	.25
Murder on the frontier.	PB 1011	54	.25
On the prod.	Pop 804	57	.25
Outlaw.	PB 1028	54	.25
Pioneer loves.	PB 983	54	.25
Prairie guns.	PB 1069	55	.25
Rawhide Range.	Pop 460	52	.25
_____.	Pop G367	59	.35
Return of a fighter.	Dell 598	52	.25
_____.	Dell 975	58	.25
A rider of the high mesa.	Pop 767	56	.25
Riders West.	Pop 271	50	.25
_____.	Pop 616	54	.25
_____.	Pop G318	59	.35
Rim of the desert.	PB 466	47	.25
Rough justice.	PB 790	51	.25

Author/Title	Pub./Stock No.	Yr.	Price
HAYCOX, ERNEST (cont.)			
Saddle and ride.	PB 531	48	.25
Secret river.	Pop 700	55	.25
The silver desert.	Pop 360	51	.25
_____.	Pop 796	57	.25
Starlight rider.	Pop 235	50	.25
_____.	Pop 567	54	.25
_____.	Pop G326	59	.35
Sundown Jim.	PB 573	49	.25
Trail smoke.	Pop 398	52	.25
_____.	Pop G283	58	.35
Trail town.	Dell 227	48	.25
_____.	Dell 347	49	.25
_____.	Dell 748	54	.25
_____.	Dell D290	59	.35
Trouble shooter.	Pop 85	47	.25
_____.	Pop 450	52	.25
_____.	Pop G218	58	.35
Vengeance trail.	Pop 644	55	.25
Whispering range.	Pop 199	49	.25
_____.	Eag EB4	53	.25
The wild bunch.	Ban 261	49	.25
_____.	Ban 1115	53	.25
_____.	Ban 1628	57	.25
HAYDN, HIRAM			
The time is noon.	Perm M-4007	55	.35
HAYES, ALFRED			
All thy conquests.	Lion 40	50	.25
_____.	Lion LL 68	56	.35
_____.	Pyr G365	58	.35
The girl on the Via Flaminia.	PB 666	50	.25
In love.	PB 1019	54	.25
My face for the world to see.	Ban A1880	59	.35
HAYES, JOSEPH			
The desperate hours.	Perm M-3007	55	.25
The hours after midnight.	Ban 1948	59	.25
with Marrijane Hayes			
Bon voyage!	Sig D1546	58	.50
HAYES, MARRIJANE with Joseph Hayes			
Bon voyage!	Sig D1546	58	.50
HAYWARD, RICHARD			
The soft arms of death.	GM 479	55	.25
Trapped.	GM 242	52	.25
_____.	GM 558	56	.25
HAZEL, ROBERT			
The farmer's bride.	Sig 1231	55	.25
The lost year.	Sig 1115	54	.25
HAZLITT, HENRY			
Economics in one lesson.	PB 553	48	.25
HEAD, MATTHEW			
The accomplice.	Dell 346	49	.25
The Cabinda affair.	Dell 390	50	.25
The Congo Venus.	Dell 605	52	.25
The devil in the bush.	Dell 158	47	.25
The smell of money.	Dell 219	48	.25
HEAL, EDITH			
The teen-age manual.	PBJr J-68	51	.35
HEALY, RAYMOND J.			
New tales of space and time.	PB 908	52	.25
_____.	Card C-319	58	.35
with J. Francis McComas			
Adventures in time and space.	Pnnt P44	54	.25
More adventures in time and space.	Ban 1310	55	.25
HEARD, H. F. or GERALD			
Is another world watching?	Ban 1079	53	.25
Reply paid.	Dell 44	44	.25
A taste for honey.	Avon 108	46	.25
A taste for murder.	Avon 625	55	.25
_____.	Avon 808	58	.25
HEARNE, L. A.			
Westward the drums.	GM 656	57	.25
HEATH, WILLIAM L.			
Temptation in a southern town.	Hill 114	59	.35
Violent Saturday.	Ban 1438	56	.25
HEATTER, BASIL			
Act of violence.	Lion 228	54	.25
The captain's lady.	Pop 266	50	.25
_____.	Eag EB1	53	.25
The dim view.	PenN 668	48	.25
_____.	Pop 602	54	.25
A night out.	Pop 771	56	.25
Sailor's luck.	Lion 170	53	.25
HEBER, WILLIAM E.			
Some die slow.	Ban 1476	56	.25
HEBERDEN, M. V.			
They can't all be guilty.	Dell 401	50	.25
HEBSON, ANN			
A fine and private place.	Zen ZB-23	59	.35
HECHLER, KEN			
The bridge at Remagen.	Ball F234	57	.50
HECHT, BEN			
A child of the century.	Sig T1212	55	.75
_____.	Sig Q1742	59	.95
Count Bruga.	Avon (11)	41	.25
The Florentine dagger.	Chek 9	49	.15
Hollywood mystery.	Bart 25	46	.25

Author/Title	Pub./Stock No.	Yr.	Price
HECHT, BEN (cont.)			
The sensualists.	Dell D294	59	.35
HECKELMANN, CHARLES N.			
Bullet law.	Sig 1373	57	.25
Deputy marshal.	Ban 206	48	.25
Fighting ramrod.	Sig 965	52	.25
Guns of Arizona.	Lion 34	50	.25
Hard man with a gun.	Sig 1232	55	.25
Hell in his holsters.	Sig 1108	54	.25
Lawless range.	Sig 694	48	.25
Let the guns roar!	Sig 910	51	.25
River queen.	Graf G202	53	.35
_____.	Graf G-221	57	.35
Six-gun outcast.	Ban 128	47	.25
Two-bit rancher.	Sig 842	51	.25
Vengeance trail.	Sig 775	50	.25
HEDDEN, WORTH TUTTLE			
The other room.	Ban 463	49	.25
_____.	Ban A1192	54	.35
HEFFNER, RICHARD D.			
A documentary history of the United States.	Ment M78	52	.35
HEGGEN, THOMAS			
Mister Roberts.	PB 550	48	.25
HEIMER, MEL			
The girl in Murder Flat.	GM 458	55	.25
HEINLEIN, ROBERT A.			
Assignment in eternity.	Sig 1161	54	.25
The day after tomorrow.	Sig 882	51	.25
_____.	Sig S1577	58	.35
The door into summer.	Sig S1639	59	.35
Double star.	Sig S1444	57	.35
The green hills of earth.	Sig 943	52	.25
_____.	Sig S1537	58	.35
The man who sold the moon.	Sig 847	51	.25
_____.	Sig S1644	59	.35
The puppet masters.	Sig 980	52	.35
_____.	Sig S1544	58	.35
Revolt in 2100.	Sig 1194	55	.25
_____.	Sig S1699	59	.35
Tomorrow, the stars.	Sig 1044	53	.25
Universe.	DelT 36	51	.10
Waldo: genius in orbit.	Avon T-261	58	.35
HEINRICH, WILLI			
Crack of doom.	Ban F1913	59	.50
The cross of iron.	Ban F1599	57	.50
HEINZ, W. C.			
The professional.	Berk BG-197	59	.50
HEISS, GÜNTHER			
One plus one.	Prmb P104	51	.35

Author/Title	Pub./Stock No.	Yr.	Price
HELBRANT, MAURICE			
Narcotic agent.	Ace D-15	53	.35
HELD, JOHN JR.			
Crosstown.	Dell 477	51	.25
HELD, JULIUS S.			
Rubens.	PBA A17	54	.50
HELD, PETER			
Take my face.	Pyr G327	58	.35
HELLER, LARRY			
I get what I want.	Pop 760	56	.25
HELLER, MIKE			
So I'm a heel.	GM 664	57	.25
HELSETH, HENRY EDWARD			
The chair for Martin Rome.	PB 484	48	.25
HEMINGWAY, ERNEST			
Across the river and into the trees.	Dell D117	53	.35
A farewell to arms.	Ban 467	49	.25
_____.	Ban A1240	54	.35
For whom the bell tolls.	Ban A883	51	.35
Green hills of Africa.	Prmb P296	54	.35
_____.	Perm M-3056	56	.25
Men at war.	Avon G1006	52	.50
_____.	Berk S-127	58	.75
The sun also rises.	Ban 717	49	.25
_____.	Ban A1249	54	.35
To have and have not.	Prmb 253	53	.25
_____.	Perm M-3041	56	.25
HENDERSON, GEORGE WYLIE			
Jule.	Berk G-218	59	.35
Jule: Alabama boy in Harlem.	Avon 400	52	.25
_____.	Avon 577	54	.25
HENDERSON, J. Y. with Richard Taplinger			
Circus doctor.	Ban 992	52	.25
HENDERSON, JAMES LEAL			
Whirlpool.	Pop 399	52	.25
HENDERSON, JOHN			
The complete book of first aid.	Ban F1365	55	.50
A parent's guide to children's illnesses.	Ban F1665	57	.50
HENDRYX, JAMES B.			
Edge of beyond.	Pop 314	51	.25
The long chase.	Dell 876	55	.25
The stampeders.	Dell 587	52	.25

Author/Title	Pub./Stock No.	Yr.	Price
HENKIN, LEO J.			
New standard book of model letters for all occasions.	Prmb P98	51	.35
_____.	Perm M-4018	55	.35
HENNING, WILLIAM E.			
The heller.	Ban 724	49	.25
_____.	Ban A1708	58	.35
HENRI, FLORETTE			
Kings Mountain.	Avon AT-60	53	.35
HENRY, ALAN			
Wagon train woman.	GM 344	53	.25
HENRY, JOAN			
Women in prison.	Prmb 239	53	.25
HENRY, LEWIS C.			
Best quotations for all occasions.	Prem s15	55	.35
HENRY, O.			
Cabbages and kings.	Pen 595	46	.25
The four million.	PB 65	40	.25
The Pocket book of O. Henry stories.	PB 510	48	.25
_____.	PBL PL38	56	.35
HENRY, WILL			
The fourth horseman.	Ban A1482	56	.35
No survivors.	Ban 946	51	.25
_____.	Ban 1168	53	.25
The North Star.	Ban 1855	58	.25
Pillars of the sky.	Ban A1483	56	.35
The raiders.	Ban A1481	56	.35
Reckoning at Yankee Flat.	Ban A1935	59	.35
Who rides with Wyatt.	Ban A1411	56	.35
HEPPENSTALL, RAYNER			
The blaze of noon.	Berk G-27	56	.35
_____.	Berk G-204	59	.35
HERBER, WILLIAM E.			
Live bait for murder.	Ban 1589	57	.25
HERBERT, ARTHUR			
Bugles in the night.	Sig 916	52	.25
HERBERT, F. HUGH			
A lover would be nice.	Han 97	49	.25
HERBERT, FRANK			
21st century sub.	Avon T-146	56	.35
HÉRIAT, PHILIPPE			
The spoiled children.	Eag EB86	57	.25
HERLIHY, JAMES LEO with William Noble			
Blue denim.	Ban A1957	59	.35
HERLING, GUSTAW			
A world apart.	Ment M75	52	.35
HERMAN, WILLIAM			
Captain McRae.	Ban 1584	57	.25
HERMANN, WALTER			
Operation intrigue.	Avon 706	56	.25
HERRIES, NORMAN			
Death has two faces.	Ace S-97	55	.25
My private hangman.	Ace D-147	56	.35
HERRINGTON, LEE			
Carry my coffin slowly.	Dell 641	52	.25
HERSEY, JOHN			
A bell for Adano.	PB 279	44	.25
_____.	Ban 45	46	.25
Hiroshima.	Ban 404	48	.25
_____.	Ban 1219	54	.25
_____.	Ban 1529	56	.25
	BanC AC26	59	.35
Into the valley.	PB 225	43	.25
_____.	Dell D263	59	.35
South of Cancer.	DelT 25	51	.10
The wall.	Card GC-12	54	.50
HERSHFIELD, HARRY			
Now I'll tell one.	Avon 65	45	.25
_____.	Avon 158	48	.25
The sin of Harold Diddlebock.	Bart 102	47	.25
HERTZLER, ARTHUR E.			
The horse and buggy doctor.	PB 356	46	.25
HERVEY, HARRY			
She-devil.	Pyr 89	53	.25
_____.	Pyr G301	57	.35
HERZBERG, MAX			
This is America.	PB 730	51	.25
HETH, EDWARD HARRIS			
The big bet.	Ban 553	48	.25
HEUMAN, WILLIAM			
The girl from Frisco.	PB 1112	56	.25
Gunhand from Texas.	Avon 569	54	.25
Guns at Broken Bow.	GM 131	50	.25
_____.	GM 322	53	.25
Heller from Texas.	GM 681	57	.25
Hunt the man down.	GM 187	51	.25
Keelboats North.	GM 310	53	.25
My brother the gunman.	Ace D-380	59	.35
On to Santa Fe.	GM 287	53	.25
The range buster.	GM 429	54	.25
_____.	GM 944	59	.25

Author/Title	Pub./Stock No.	Yr.	Price
HEUMAN, WILLIAM (cont.)			
Red runs the river.	GM 216	52	.25
Ride for Texas.	GM 414	54	.25
Rimrock town.	Hill 104	57	.25
Roll the wagons.	GM 146	51	.25
_____.	GM 330	53	.25
Secret of Death Valley.	GM 267	52	.25
Stagecoach West.	GM 705	57	.25
Then came Mulvane.	Avon 855	59	.25
Violence valley.	GM 631	57	.25
Wagon train West.	GM 842	59	.25
HEYER, GEORGETTE			
A blunt instrument.	Pen 519	43	.25
HEYERDAHL, THOR			
Kon-Tiki.	Prmb P243	53	.35
_____.	Perm M-4062	56	.35
HEYES, DOUGLAS			
The kiss-off.	Sig 949	52	.25
_____.	Sig 1329	56	.25
HEYN, ERNEST			
The Pocket book of true stories.	PB 545	48	.25
HEYWARD, DU BOSE			
Porgy.	Pen 558	45	.25
_____.	Ban A1689	57	.35
HIBBS, BEN			
Great stories from the Saturday evening post.	Ban 116	47	.25
Great stories from the Saturday evening post, 1947.	Ban 555	48	.25
HICKOK, WILL			
The restless gun.	Sig 1541	58	.25
Trail of the restless gun.	Sig 1675	59	.25
Web of gunsmoke.	Sig 1242	55	.25
HIGGINS, MARGUERITE			
War in Korea.	Lion unk	52	.25
HIGHSMITH, PATRICIA			
Lament for a lover.	Eag EB58	56	.25
Strangers on a train.	Ban 905	51	.25
The talented Mr. Ripley.	Dell D282	59	.35
HIKEN, NAT			
Sergeant Bilko.	Ball 229	57	.35
HILL, ERNESTINE			
My love must wait.	Prmb P247	53	.35
HILL, JANET McKENZIE			
Cooking for two.	Dell 798	54	.25

Author/Title	Pub./Stock No.	Yr.	Price
HILL, WELDON			
Onionhead.	Pop SP13	58	.50
HILLARY, RICHARD			
Falling through space.	Dell D244	58	.35
HILLS, TYNETTE with Floyd H. Ross			
The great religions by which men live.	Prem s39	56	.35
_____.	Crst s269	59	.35
HILTON, CONRAD			
Be my guest.	Pop PC400	59	.50
HILTON, FRANCIS W.			
Blazing trails.	Dell 509	51	.25
The long rope.	Dell 451	50	.25
Skyline riders.	Dell 250	48	.25
HILTON, JAMES			
And now good-bye.	PB 89	41	.25
Catherine herself.	Avon 79	46	.25
Goodbye, Mr. Chips.	PB 93	41	.25
_____.	Ban A1636	57	.35
Ill wind.	Avon (4)	41	.25
_____.	Avon 325	51	.25
Lost horizon.	PB 1	39	.25
Morning journey.	Card C-70	52	.35
Nothing so strange.	Avon 381	51	.25
The passionate year.	Avon 42	44	.25
Rage in heaven.	Avon (39)	43	.25
Random harvest.	PB 275	44	.25
So well remembered.	PB 630	49	.25
Three loves had Margaret.	Avon 223	49	.25
Time and time again.	PB 1046	55	.25
Was it murder?	Ban 29	46	.25
We are not alone.	PB 118	41	.25
_____.	Avon 301	51	.25
Without armor.	PB 136	41	.25
HILTON, JOSEPH			
Angels in the gutter.	GM 475	55	.25
_____.	GM s913	59	.35
Beyond Mombasa.	Avon T-178	57	.35
Cry baby killer.	Avon T-230	58	.35
That French girl.	GM 278	53	.25
HIMES, CHESTER			
The crazy kill.	Avon T-357	59	.35
For love of Imabelle.	GM 717	57	.25
If he hollers let him go.	Sig 756	49	.25
_____.	Berk G-6	55	.35
_____.	Berk G-139	58	.35
The primitive.	Sig 1264	56	.25
The real cool killers.	Avon T-328	59	.35
The third generation.	Sig D1299	56	.50
HIMMEL, RICHARD			
Beyond desire.	GM 274	53	.25
_____.	GM s859	59	.35

Author/Title	Pub./Stock No.	Yr.	Price
HIMMEL, RICHARD (cont.)			
The Chinese keyhole.	GM 143	51	.25
————.	GM 543	56	.25
Cry of the flesh.	GM 488	55	.25
I have Gloria Kirby.	GM 179	51	.25
————.	GM 566	56	.25
I'll find you.	GM 104	50	.25
————.	GM 460	55	.25
The rich and the damned.	GM s735	58	.35
The shame.	Avon T-329	59	.35
The sharp edge.	GM 234	52	.25
Two deaths must die.	GM 373	54	.25
————.	GM 800	59	.25
HINDS, ARTHUR			
The complete sayings of Jesus.	PB 291	45	.25
HINE, AL			
An unfound door.	Ban A1073	53	.35
HINES, DUNCAN			
The Duncan Hines dessert book.	Card C-188	55	.35
HINES, JACK			
Wolf dogs of the north.	PBJr J-75	51	.35
HINKLE, THOMAS C.			
Black storm.	PBJr J-41	50	.25
Mustang.	PBJr J-58	50	.25
Shag.	PBJr J-70	51	.35
Silver: the story of a wild horse.	Com 14	49	.25
Tawny.	Com 4	48	.25
HINSDALE, HARRIET			
Be my love.	Prmb P170	52	.35
HIRSCH, EDWIN			
Modern sex life.	Sig S1463	57	.35
HIRSHBERG, AL with Robert Pfau			
Prodigal shepherd.	Pop G342	59	.35
with Jim Piersall			
Fear strikes out.	Ban A1582	57	.35
HITCHCOCK, ALFRED			
Bar the doors!	Dell 143	46	.25
Fear and trembling.	Dell 264	48	.25
Hold your breath.	Dell 206	47	.25
Rope.	Dell 262	48	.25
Suspense stories.	Dell 92	45	.25
————.	Dell 367	50	.25
13 more stories they wouldn't let me do on TV.	Dell D281	59	.35
12 stories they wouldn't let me do on TV.	Dell D231	58	.35
HITCHENS, BERT with Dolores Hitchens			
End of the line.	PB 1230	59	.25
F.O.B. murder.	Perm M-3051	56	.25
One-way ticket.	Perm M-3100	58	.25
HITCHENS, DOLORES			
Fool's gold.	PB 1239	59	.25
Sleep with strangers.	Perm M-3040	56	.25
Stairway to an empty room.	Dell 659	53	.25
Widows won't wait.	Dell 779	54	.25
with Bert Hitchens			
End of the line.	PB 1230	59	.25
F.O.B. murder.	Perm M-3051	56	.25
One-way ticket.	Perm M-3100	58	.25
HITREC, JOSEPH			
Angel of gaiety.	Ban 1029	52	.25
HITT, ORRIE			
I'll call every Monday.	Avon 554	54	.25
HIX, ELSIE			
Strange as it seems.	Ban 1334	55	.25
HŁASKO, MAREK			
The eighth day of the week.	Sig S1706	59	.35
HOAGLAND, EDWARD			
Cat man.	Sig S1392	57	.35
————.	Sig S1499	58	.35
HOBART, ALICE TISDALE			
Oil for the lamps of China.	Ban 20	45	.25
This earth is mine.	Dell F80	59	.50
HOBSON, LAURA Z.			
The celebrity.	Prmb P190	52	.35
Gentleman's agreement.	Prmb P154	52	.35
HODAPP, WILLIAM			
Crazy mixed-up kids.	Berk G-12	55	.35
The pleasures of the jazz age.	Berk 101	55	.25
HODGES, CARL G.			
Murder by the pack.	Ace D-33	53	.35
HODGINS, ERIC			
Mr. Blandings builds his dream house.	PB 505	48	.25
HOEHLING, A. A. with Mary Hoehling			
The last voyage of the Lusitania.	Pop G184	57	.35
HOEHLING, MARY with A. A. Hoehling			
The last voyage of the Lusitania.	Pop G184	57	.35

Author/Title	Pub./Stock No.	Yr.	Price
HOFF, SYD			
Oops! Wrong party!	Pop 698	55	.25
HOFFER, ERIC			
The true believer.	Ment MD228	58	.50
HOFFMAN, WILLIAM			
Days in the yellow leaf.	Crst d278	59	.50
The trumpet unblown.	Crst s156	57	.35
HOFFMANN, RICHARD H. with Jim Bishop			
The girl in Poison			
Cottage.	GM 351	53	.25
HOGAN, BEN			
Power golf.	PB 928	53	.25
_____.	Card C-358	59	.35
HOGAN, RAY			
Ex-marshal.	Ace D-186	56	.35
The friendless one.	Ace D-220	57	.35
Hangman's valley.	Ace D-368	59	.35
Land of the strangers.	Ace D-260	57	.35
Longhorn law.	Ace D-248	57	.35
Marshal without a badge.	GM 892	59	.25
Outlaw marshal.	GM 843	59	.25
Walk a lonely trail.	Ace D-236	57	.35
Wanted: alive!	Ace D-346	59	.35
HOGAN, ROBERT J.			
The challenge of Smoke			
Wade.	Avon 454	52	.25
_____.	Avon 674	55	.25
Renegade guns.	Avon 550	53	.25
Roaring guns at Apache			
Landing.	Avon 469	52	.25
Stampede Canyon.	Avon 820	58	.25
HOGARTH, EMMETT			
The goose is cooked.	Bond unk	46	.25
HOKE, HELEN			
1000 ways to make $1000.	Ban F1854	59	.50
HOKE, NEWTON WILSON			
Double entendre.	PB 1160	57	.25
HOLDEN, CURRY			
Episode in the sun.	Pop G188	57	.35
HOLDEN, LARRY			
Crime cop.	Pyr G429	59	.35
Dead wrong.	Pyr G306	57	.35
Hide-out.	Eton E132	53	.25
HOLDEN, RICHARD			
Snow fury.	Perm M-3034	56	.25
HOLDER, WILLIAM			
The case of the dead			
divorcée.	Sig 1539	58	.25

Author/Title	Pub./Stock No.	Yr.	Price
HOLDING, ELISABETH SANXAY			
The blank wall.	PB 662	50	.25
The death wish.	Pop 189	49	.25
The innocent Mrs. Duff.	Dell 194	47	.25
Murder is a kill-joy.	Dell 103	46	.25
Net of cobwebs.	Ban 26	46	.25
The old battle ax.	Pop 302	50	.25
Who's afraid?	Bond 14	47	.25
HOLIDAY, BILLY with William Dufty			
Lady sings the blues.	Pop G208	58	.35
HOLK, AGNETE			
Strange friends.	Pyr G170	55	.35
HOLLAND, MARTY			
Blonde baggage.	NL 45	50	.25
Her private passions.	Avon 181	48	.25
HOLLANDS, D. J.			
Able Company.	Sig D1506	58	.50
HOLLIS, JIM			
The case of the			
bludgeoned teacher.	Avon 725	56	.25
HOLLOWAY, ELIZABETH			
Cobweb house.	Dell 133	46	.25
HOLLYWOOD bedside reader.	Avon 338	51	.25
HOLMAN, HUGH			
Another man's poison.	Sig 718	49	.25
Slay the murderer.	Sig 684	48	.25
HOLMES, CLELLON			
Go.	Ace D-238	57	.35
The horn.	Crst s307	59	.35
HOLMES, DAVID C.			
The velvet ape.	Perm M-3122	58	.25
HOLMES, H. H.			
Nine times nine.	Pen 553	45	.25
Rocket to the morgue.	Phan nn	45	.25
HOLMES, L. P.			
Apache desert.	Pnnt P13	53	.25
Black sage.	Ban 898	51	.25
	Ban 1103	52	.25
Dead man's saddle.	Ban 988	52	.25
Delta deputy.	Ban 1384	55	.25
Desert rails.	PB 675	50	.25
Flame of sunset.	PB 514	48	.25
Gunman's creed.	Graf 77	54	.25
_____.	Graf 144	57	.25
High starlight.	Pnnt P25	53	.25
Hill smoke.	Ban 2031	59	.25
Modoc, the last sundown.	Ban 1873	59	.25
The plunderers.	Ban 1822	58	.25
Range pirate.	Ban 823	50	.25

Author/Title	Pub./Stock No.	Yr.	Price
HOLMES, L. P. (cont.)			
Somewhere they die.	Ban 1514	56	.25
Summer range.	Ban 1048	52	.25
HOLT, FELIX			
The Gabriel horn.	Dell 750	54	.25
Mountain boy.	Dell D202	58	.35
HOLT, L. EMMETT JR.			
The Good housekeeping book of baby and child care.	Pop SP42	59	.50
HOLT, TEX			
Dark Canyon.	Han 136	51	.25
Thunder of hoofs.	Han 117	50	.25
HOMER, DALE			
The trail from Texas.	Ban 1838	58	.25
HOMERUS			
The Iliad.	Ment M46	50	.35
_____.	Ment Ms110	54	.50
The Odyssey.	Pen 613	46	.25
_____.	Pel P21	47	.35
_____.	Ment M92	53	.35
HOMES, GEOFFREY			
Build my gallows high.	Ace D-185	56	.35
The case of the Mexican knife.	Ban 309	48	.25
The case of the unhappy angels.	Ban 779	50	.25
Dead as a dummy.	Ban 701	49	.25
The doctor died at dusk.	Dell 14	43	.25
Finders keepers.	Ban 89	47	.25
The man who didn't exist.	Dell 41	44	.25
The man who murdered Goliath.	Dell 86	45	.25
The man who murdered himself.	Avon (18)	42	.25
No hands on the clock.	Ban 52	46	.25
Stiffs don't vote.	Ban 117	47	.25
Then there were three.	Ban 12	45	.25
HONIG, DONALD			
Sidewalk Caesar.	Pyr G359	58	.35
HOOD, MARGARET PAGE			
The silent women.	Dell 880	55	.25
Tequila.	Dell 602	52	.25
HOOF trails and wagon tracks.	Ban F1972	59	.50
HOOPES, ROY JR.			
Wit from overseas.	Eton E129	53	.25
HOOTON, BARBARA with Patrick Dennis			
Guestward ho!	Pop SP16	58	.50

Author/Title	Pub./Stock No.	Yr.	Price
HOOVER, J. EDGAR			
Masters of deceit.	Card GC-39	59	.50
HOOVER, P. A.			
Backwater woman.	Ace S-219	57	.25
Riverboat girl.	Ace S-168	56	.25
A woman called Trouble.	Ace D-290	58	.35
HOPE, ANTHONY			
The prisoner of Zenda.	Ban 33	46	.25
HOPE, BOB			
Have tux, will travel.	Card C-205	56	.35
HOPE, EDWARD			
She loves me not.	Ban 66	46	.25
HOPKINS, TOM J.			
Buzzard tracks.	Hill 30	50	.25
Dead man's range.	Ban 208	48	.25
Drumfire.	Avon 474	52	.25
Horsethief Crossing.	Perm M-3008	55	.25
Range war.	Prmb 271	54	.25
Trail end.	Prmb 238	53	.25
Trails by night.	Pop 390	51	.25
Trouble in Tombstone.	Sig 989	53	.25
HOPLEY, GEORGE			
Fright.	Pop 424	52	.25
HOPPER, MILLARD			
How to play winning checkers.	PB 239	43	.25
HOPSON, WILLIAM			
Apache greed.	Lion 195	54	.25
Backlash at Cajon Pass.	Ace D-272	58	.35
Border raider.	Berk 107	55	.25
Bullet-brand empire.	Ace D-68	54	.35
Cowpoke justice.	Berk 324	55	.25
Cry viva!	Ban 1461	56	.25
The gringo bandit.	Avon 414	52	.25
_____.	Avon 516	53	.25
Gunfighters pay.	Ban 1180	53	.25
Gunfire at Salt Fork.	GM 569	56	.25
A gunman rode north.	Pyr 225	56	.25
Gunthrower.	Berk G-87	57	.35
Hangtree range.	Lion LB 156	57	.25
High saddle.	Ace D-128	55	.35
Killers five.	Lion unk	51	.25
The last Apaches.	Ban 1117	53	.25
The last shoot-out.	Ace D-320	58	.35
Long ride to Abilene.	Avon 837	58	.25
Montana gunslinger.	Avon 709	56	.25
Notched guns.	Avon 824	58	.25
Outlaw of hidden valley.	Berk 341	55	.25
Rambling top hand.	Berk G-230	59	.35
Ramrod vengeance.	Berk 366	57	.25
Ranch cat.	Lion unk	51	.25
Tombstone stage.	Berk 347	56	.25

Author/Title	Pub./Stock No.	Yr.	Price
HOPSON, WILLIAM (cont.)			
Trouble rides tall.	GM 501	55	.25
Twin mavericks.	Dmnd D2014	59	.35
Vegas, gunman marshal.	Avon 687	56	.25
Yucca City outlaw.	Han 137	51	.25
———.	Avon 723	56	.25
HORAN, JAMES D.			
Desperate men.	Avon 330	51	.25
King's rebel.	Ban A1402	55	.35
Seek out and destroy.	Pop G381	59	.35
The wild bunch.	Sig S1557	58	.35
with Harold R. Danforth			
The D.A.'s man.	Perm M-4118	59	.35
HORGAN, PAUL			
Give me possession.	Perm M-4108	58	.35
HORNBLOW, LEONORA			
The love-seekers.	Sig D1548	58	.50
Memory and desire.	Sig 854	51	.25
HORNSTEIN, LILLIAN HERLANDS et al.			
The reader's companion			
to world literature.	Ment MD179	56	.50
———.	Ment MT232	58	.75
HORROR and homicide.	Chek 5	49	.15
HOSTOVSKÝ, EGON			
Missing.	Ban 1161	53	.25
HOTCHNER, A. E.			
The dangerous American.	Sig S1671	59	.35
HOUGH, EMERSON			
The covered wagon.	PB 410	46	.25
———.	PB 1014	54	.25
North of 36.	PB 429	47	.25
HOUGHTON, NORRIS			
Great Russian short			
stories.	DelL LC110	58	.50
HOUGRON, JEAN			
Blaze of the sun.	Dell D190	57	.35
Reap the whirlwind.	Dell D135	54	.35
Trapped!	Dell 1006	59	.25
HOUSE, BRANT			
Cartoon annual no. 2.	Ace S-132	55	.25
Cartoon annual no. 3.	Ace S-275	58	.25
From Eve on.	Ace D-307	58	.35
Lincoln's wit.	Ace D-268	58	.35
The little monsters.	Ace S-145	56	.25
Love and hisses.	Ace S-165	56	.25
Squelches.	Ace S-179	56	.25
They goofed!	Ace S-188	56	.25
The violent ones.	Ace D-323	58	.35
Words fail me!	Ace S-116	55	.25

Author/Title	Pub./Stock No.	Yr.	Price
with Edna Bennett			
Love from France.	Pop 777	56	.25
HOUSEHOLD, GEOFFREY			
Delilah of the back			
stairs.	DelT 29	51	.10
Rogue male.	Ban 9	45	.25
A rough shoot.	Ban 1019	53	.25
The Spanish cave.	Com 12	48	.25
A time to kill.	Pnnt P11	53	.25
HOUSEPIAN, MARJORIE			
A houseful of love.	Dell D229	58	.35
HOUSMAN, A. E.			
A Shropshire lad.	Avon 246	50	.25
HOUSTON, JACK			
Open all night.	Ace D-35	53	.35
Waiting for Willy.	Avon 412	52	.25
———.	Avon 492	53	.25
———.	Avon T-294	59	.35
HOW the Jap army fights.	PenS S204	42	.25
HOW to use premiums in			
your business to increase			
your sales and profits.	Ban A-4	50	.25
HOWARD, ELIZABETH METZGER			
Before the sun goes down.	Prmb P153	52	.35
HOWARD, JAMES			
Blow out my torch.	Eag EB70	56	.25
Die on easy street.	Eag EB90	57	.25
I like it tough.	Eag EB46	55	.25
I'll get you yet.	Eag EB30	54	.25
———.	Pop G346	59	.35
Murder takes a wife.	PB 1255	59	.25
HOWARD, JOHN TASKER with James Lyons			
Modern music.	Ment MD212	58	.50
HOWARD, ROBERT E.			
Conan the conqueror.	Ace D-36	53	.35
HOWARD, ROBERT WEST			
This is the West.	Sig S1424	57	.35
HOWARD, TONI			
Shriek with pleasure.	Sig 820	50	.25
———.	Pyr G157	55	.35
Three sinners in Paris.	Sig 1207	55	.25
HOWARD, VECHEL			
Murder on her mind.	GM 878	59	.25
Murder with love.	GM 854	59	.25
Stage to Painted Creek.	GM 943	59	.25
Sundown at Crazy Horse.	GM 685	57	.25
Tall in the West.	GM 789	58	.25

Author/Title	Pub./Stock No.	Yr.	Price
HOWARTH, DAVID			
The sledge patrol.	Ball 283K	58	.35
We die alone.	Ace D-228	57	.35
HOWE, CLIFF			
Lovers and libertines.	Ace D-271	58	.35
Scoundrels, fiends, and			
human monsters.	Ace D-282	58	.35
HOWE, GEORGE			
Call it treason.	PB 748	50	.25
HOWE, HELEN			
The circle of the day.	Dell D115	52	.35
The success.	Perm M-4104	58	.35
HOWE, MARGARET			
Debutante nurse.	Ban 2002	59	.25
Special nurse.	Ban 1711	58	.25
Visiting nurse.	PB 1236	59	.25
HOWE, QUINCY			
The Pocket book of the			
war.	PB 127	41	.25
HOWELLS, J. HARVEY			
The big company look.	Ace G-376	59	.50
HOYER, NIELS			
Man into woman.	Pop SP100	53	.25
HOYLE, FRED			
The black cloud.	Sig S1673	59	.35
The frontiers of			
astronomy.	Ment MD200	57	.50
The nature of the			
universe.	Ment M125	55	.35
HUBBARD, L. RON			
Return to tomorrow.	Ace S-66	54	.25
HUBLER, RICHARD G.			
The brass god.	Pop 594	54	.25
Chase.	Avon 504	53	.25
HUDIBURG, EDWARD			
Killers' game.	Lion LB 137	56	.25
HUDSON, W. H.			
Green mansions.	PB 16	39	.25
———.	Ban 63	46	.25
———.	Ban F1878	59	.50
HUESTON, ETHEL			
Calamity Jane of			
Deadwood Gulch.	Avon 362	51	.25
HUFFAKER, CLAIR			
Badge for a gunfighter.	Crst 158	57	.25
Badman.	Crst 167	57	.25
Cowboy.	GM 736	58	.25

Author/Title	Pub./Stock No.	Yr.	Price
Guns of Rio Conchos.	GM 733	58	.25
Posse from hell.	Crst 222	58	.25
Rider from Thunder			
Mountain.	Crst 193	57	.25
HUGGINS, ROY			
The double take.	PB 524	48	.25
Lovely lady, pity me.	Avon 282	51	.25
77 Sunset Strip.	DelF A176	59	.25
Too late for tears.	PB 602	49	.25
HUGHES, DOROTHY B.			
The bamboo blonde.	PB 394	46	.25
The blackbirder.	Dell 149	47	.25
The body on the bench.	Dell 853	55	.25
The candy kid.	PB 845	52	.25
The cross-eyed bear			
murders.	Dell 48	44	.25
The delicate ape.	PB 422	47	.25
Dread journey.	PB 454	47	.25
The fallen sparrow.	Dell 31	43	.25
In a lonely place.	PB 587	49	.25
Johnnie.	Bond 11	46	.25
Ride the pink horse.	Dell 210	48	.25
———.	Dell D225	58	.35
The so blue marble.	Dell 100	46	.25
HUGHES, RICHARD			
In hazard.	Pen 536	44	.25
The innocent voyage.	Pen 628	47	.25
HUGHES, THOMAS			
Tom Brown's school days.	PB 58	40	.25
HUGO, VICTOR			
The hunchback of Notre			
Dame.	Ban F1526	56	.50
———.	Avon T-190	57	.35
———.	Ban F1678	57	.50
The hunchback of Notre			
Dame, volume 1.	PB 31	39	.25
The hunchback of Notre			
Dame, volume 2.	PB 32	39	.25
HUIE, WILLIAM BRADFORD			
The execution of Private			
Slovik.	Sig 1113	54	.25
Mud on the stars.	Sig S1162	55	.35
The revolt of Mamie			
Stover.	Sig 959	52	.25
Ruby McCollum.	Sig S1439	57	.35
Wolf whistle and other			
stories.	Sig S1651	59	.35
HULBURD, DAVID			
H is for heroin.	Pop 495	53	.25
HULL, E. M.			
The captive of the			
Sahara.	Dell 402	50	.25
The sheik.	Dell 174	47	.25

Author/Title	Pub./Stock No.	Yr.	Price
HULL, E. M. (cont.)			
Sons of the sheik.	Dell 279	49	.25
	Dell 342	49	.25
HULL, RICHARD			
The murder of my aunt.	PB 381	47	.25
My own murderer.	Pen 526	43	.25
HULME, KATHRYN			
The nun's story.	Card GC-54	58	.50
HUMOROUS stories and			
anecdotes.	BPLA 24	40	.10
HUMPHREY, WILLIAM			
Home from the hill.	Perm M-4128	59	.35
HUMPHREYS, JOHN R.			
The dirty shame.	DelF 61	55	.25
HUMPHRIES, ADELAIDE			
Flight nurse.	Berk G288	59	.35
Nurse Landon's challenge.	Ban 1496	56	.25
Office nurse.	Ban 422	49	.25
HUMPHRIES, ROLFE			
New poems by American			
poets.	Ball 39	53	.35
New poems by American			
poets no. 2.	Ball 226	57	.35
HUNEKER, JAMES			
Painted veils.	Avon T-71	53	.35
	Avon T-260	58	.35
HUNGER, ANNA with R. DeWitt Miller			
The man who lived			
forever.	Ace D-162	56	.35
HUNT, GEORGE P.			
Coral comes high.	Sig 1440	57	.25
HUNT, HOWARD			
Bimini run.	Avon 457	52	.25
Cruel is the night.	Berk 345	55	.25
	Dmnd D2001	59	.35
Dark encounter.	Sig 768	50	.25
The Judas hour.	GM 167	51	.25
	GM s869	59	.35
Lovers are losers.	GM 297	53	.25
Stranger in town.	Sig 729	49	.25
The violent ones.	GM 113	50	.25
	GM 738	58	.25
Whisper her name.	GM 268	52	.25
HUNT, KYLE			
Kill a wicked man.	Sig 1573	58	.25
Kill my love.	Crst 334	59	.25
Kill once, kill twice.	Sig 1472	57	.25

Author/Title	Pub./Stock No.	Yr.	Price
HUNT, PETER			
Murders at Scandal house.	Dell 42	44	.25
HUNTER, EDWARD			
Brainwashing.	Pyr R340	58	.35
HUNTER, EVAN			
The blackboard jungle.	Card C-187	55	.35
Don't crowd me.	Pop 478	53	.25
	Pop G277	58	.35
The jungle kids.	PB 1126	56	.25
Quartet in "H".	Card C-236	57	.35
Strangers when we meet.	Card GC-56	59	.50
HUNTER, GEORGIANA			
The girl on the couch.	Pyr 200	56	.25
	Pyr G334	58	.35
HUNTER, HALL			
The Bengal tiger.	Prmb P223	53	.35
HUNTER, J. A.			
Hunter.	Ban A1391	55	.35
HUNTER, JOHN			
Badlands buccaneer.	PB 1249	59	.25
The marshal from			
Deadwood.	Perm M-3123	58	.25
Ride the wind south.	Perm M-3092	57	.25
West of justice.	Ball 65	54	.35
HUNTER, SAMUEL			
Modern American painting			
and sculpture.	DelL LY102	59	.95
Modern French painting,			
1855-1956.	DelF FE98	56	.50
Toulouse-Lautrec.	PBA A3	53	.50
HUNTINGTON, ELLSWORTH			
Mainsprings of			
civilization.	Ment MT248	59	.75
HURST, FANNIE			
Back street.	Pen 589	46	.25
	Sig S961	52	.35
Imitation of life.	Perm M-4124	59	.35
Lummox.	Pop 101	46	.25
The name is Mary.	DelT 14	51	.10
HUSTON, H. C.			
With murder for some.	Prmb 277	54	.25
HUTCHINS, MAUDE			
A diary of love.	Pyr 49	52	.25
	Pyr 130	54	.25
	Pyr G436	59	.35
The memoirs of Maisie.	Crst 138	56	.25
HUTCHINSON, A. S. M.			
If winter comes.	PB 486	48	.25

Author/Title	Pub./Stock No.	Yr.	Price
HUTCHINSON, LORING			
Secret of Hidden Valley.	Sig 1447	57	.25
HUTSCHNECKER, ARNOLD A.			
The will to live.	Prmb P276	54	.35
_____.	Perm M-4059	56	.35
HUTTER, CATHERINE			
The alien heart.	Sig S1337	56	.35
This dear encounter.	Sig S1041	54	.35
HUTTON, BRETT			
The green death.	BPLA 22	40	.10
HUTTON, J. F.			
Dead man Friday.	Ace D-29	53	.35
HUXLEY, ALDOUS			
After many a summer dies the swan.	Avon 388	51	.35
_____.	Avon AT435	52	.35
_____.	Avon T-75	54	.35
_____.	Avon G-2001	59	.50
After the fireworks.	Avon T-160	57	.35
Antic hay.	Ban 1142	53	.25
_____.	Ban A1560	57	.35
Ape and essence.	Ban A1793	58	.35
Brave new world.	Ban A1071	53	.35
_____.	Ban A1369	55	.35
_____.	BanC AC1	58	.35
Crome yellow.	Ban A1260	55	.35
_____.	BanC AC22	59	.35
Eyeless in Gaza.	Ban F1233	54	.50
_____.	Ban F1622	56	.50
The genius and the goddess.	Ban A1490	56	.35
Point counter point.	Avon G-1020	55	.50
_____.	Avon G-1031	57	.50
_____.	Avon V-2031	59	.75
Those barren leaves.	Avon G-1027	56	.50
Time must have a stop.	Berk BG-66	57	.50
HUXLEY, ELSPETH			
The African poison murders.	Pop 100	47	.25
HUXLEY, JULIAN			
Evolution in action.	Ment MD204	57	.50
Man in the modern world.	Ment M31	48	.35
	Ment MD148	55	.50
Religion without revelation.	Ment MD244	58	.50
HYMAN, MAC			
No time for sergeants.	Sig S1285	56	.35
_____.	Sig D1530	58	.50
HYND, ALAN			
The case of the attic lover.	Pyr G304	57	.35

Author/Title	Pub./Stock No.	Yr.	Price
The case of the burning bride.	Avon 604	54	.25
The case of the lady who took a bath.	Berk G-75	57	.35
Murder! Great true crime cases.	Pen 641	47	.25
The Pinkerton case book.	PenN 667	48	.25
Violence in the night.	GM 473	55	.25
We are the public enemies.	GM 101	50	.25

Author/Title	Pub./Stock No.	Yr.	Price
I			
I am a marked woman.	Avon T-272	58	.35
I, mobster.	GM 171	51	.25
_____.	GM 739	58	.25
I worked for Lucky Luciano.	Avon 568	54	.25
IAMS, JACK			
The body missed the boat.	Dell 274	49	.25
Death draws the line.	Dell 457	50	.25
Do not murder before			
Christmas.	Dell 514	51	.25
The French touch.	Lion 22	50	.25
Girl meets body.	Dell 384	50	.25
Love--and the countess			
to boot.	Dell 139	46	.25
A shot of murder.	Dell 722	53	.25
A slight case of scandal.	Lion 46	50	.25
What rhymes with murder?	Dell 631	52	.25
IBSEN, HENRIK			
Four great plays by			
Ibsen.	BanC FC23	59	.50
Three plays by Ibsen.	DelL LC123	59	.50
IDELL, ALBERT			
This woman.	RS 9	52	.35
ILES, FRANCIS			
Before the fact.	PB 419	47	.25
_____.	Dell D215	58	.35
Malice aforethought.	PB 432	47	.25
ILG, FRANCES L. with Louise Bates Ames			
Child behavior: Gesell			
Institute.	Dell D180	56	.35
_____.	DelL LC120	59	.50
ILTON, PAUL			
The last days of Sodom			
and Gomorrah.	Sig 1399	57	.25
The secret of Mary			
Magdalene.	Sig 1301	56	.25
with MacLennan Roberts			
Moses and the Ten			
commandments.	DelF B105	56	.35
INCHARDI, J.			
Good night, sailor.	Sig 1344	56	.25
The INDISCREET confessions			
of a nice girl.	Lion 30	50	.25
INGE, WILLIAM			
Bus stop.	Ban 1518	56	.25
Picnic.	Ban 1457	56	.25

Author/Title	Pub./Stock No.	Yr.	Price
INGERSOLL, RALPH			
The battle is the			
pay-off.	PenS S226	44	.25
The great ones.	Pop 248	50	.25
The naked and the guilty.	Lion LL 48	55	.35
Wine of violence.	Pop 401	52	.25
INGLES, JAMES WESLEY			
A woman of Samaria.	Pop 299	50	.25
INNES, HAMMOND			
Air bridge.	Ban 1125	53	.25
The angry mountain.	Ban 1058	52	.25
Campbell's kingdom.	Ban 1516	56	.25
Fire in the snow.	Ban 364	49	.25
Gale warning.	Ban 741	49	.25
Run by night.	Ban 890	51	.25
The survivors.	Ban 1024	52	.25
The wreck of the Mary			
Deare.	Perm M-4079	57	.35
INNES, MICHAEL			
The case of the			
journeying boy.	PB 741	50	.25
Death by moonlight.	Avon 752	57	.25
Murder is an art.	Avon T-351	59	.35
IRISH, WILLIAM			
Bluebeard's seventh wife.	Pop 473	52	.25
The dancing detective.	Pop 309	51	.25
Deadline at dawn.	Graf 16	49	.25
Deadly night call.	Graf 31	51	.25
_____.	Graf 81	54	.25
Dilemma of the dead lady.	Graf 20	50	.25
I married a dead man.	Avon 220	49	.25
If I should die before			
I wake.	Avon 104	46	.25
Marihuana.	DelT 11	51	.10
Night has a thousand			
eyes.	Dell 679	53	.25
Nightmare.	RCL 12	50	.25
Phantom lady.	PB 253	44	.25
_____.	Graf 108	55	.25
_____.	Dell D207	57	.35
Six nights of mystery.	Pop 258	50	.25
Six times death.	Pop 137	48	.25
Strangler's serenade.	Pop 431	52	.25
Waltz into darkness.	Ace D-40	54	.35
You'll never see me			
again.	DelT unk	51	.10
IRVING, ALEXANDER			
Bitter ending.	Dell 289	49	.25
IRVING, CLIFFORD			
The losers.	Pop G311	59	.35
The quick and the loving.	Pop G187	57	.35
IRWIN, THEODORE D.			
Collusion.	Hill unk	49	.25

Author/Title	Pub./Stock No.	Yr.	Price	Author/Title	Pub./Stock No.	Yr.	Price
ISHERWOOD, CHRISTOPHER							
Goodbye to Berlin.	Sig 937	52	.25				
_____.	Sig S1252	55	.35				
Great English short stories.	DelL LC102	57	.50				
The last of Mr. Norris.	Avon 448	52	.25				
_____.	Berk G-153	58	.35				
The world in the evening.	Pop 710	55	.25				
ISRAEL, CHARLES							
The mark.	Crst s313	59	.35				
IVES, BURL							
The Burl Ives song book.	Ball 48	53	.50				
_____.	Ball F295K	59	.50				
Sea songs of sailing, whaling and fishing.	Ball 146	56	.35				

Author/Title	Pub./Stock No.	Yr.	Price

J

JACKSON, CHARLES
Earthly creatures.	Ball 36	53	.35
The fall of valor.	Sig 715	49	.25
_____.	Lion LL 35	55	.35
The lost weekend.	Sig 683	48	.25
_____.	Berk G-1	55	.35
The outer edges.	Sig 781	50	.25
The sisters.	Zen ZB-1	58	.35
The sunnier side.	Dell 504	51	.25
Thread of evil.	Lion LL 143	57	.35

JACKSON, DELMAR
| The cut of the ax. | Pop G279 | 58 | .35 |
| The night is my undoing. | Pop 599 | 54 | .25 |

JACKSON, FELIX
| So help me God. | Ban A1462 | 56 | .35 |
| A strange affair. | Pop G281 | 58 | .35 |

JACKSON, GILES
| The court of shadows. | Han 25 | 44 | .15 |
| Witch's moon. | Han 82 | 49 | .25 |

JACKSON, JOSEPH HENRY
| San Francisco murders. | Ban 354 | 48 | .25 |
with Lenore Glen Offord
| The girl in the belfry. | GM s688 | 57 | .35 |

JACKSON, RALPH
| Violent night. | Ace S-137 | 55 | .25 |

JACKSON, SHIRLEY
Life among the savages.	Perm M-3004	55	.25
_____.	Ball 337K	59	.35
Lizzie.	Sig S1400	57	.35
The lottery.	Lion 14	50	.25
The other side of the street.	Pyr G212	56	.35
Raising demons.	Ball 342K	59	.35
The road through the wall.	Lion 36	50	.25

JACOBS, BRUCE
Baseball stars of 1950.	Lion 23	50	.25
Baseball stars of 1953.	Lion 125	53	.25
Baseball stars of '54.	Lion 194	54	.25
Baseball stars of 1955.	Lion LL 12	55	.35
Baseball stars of 1956.	Lion LL 74	56	.35
Baseball stars of 1957.	Lion LL 150	57	.35
Korea's heroes.	Lion 172	53	.25

JACOBSON, EDMUND
| You must relax. | PB 330 | 46 | .25 |

JAEDIKER, KERMIT
| Hero's lust. | Lion 156 | 53 | .25 |
| Tall, dark and dead. | Lion 51 | 51 | .25 |

JAFFE, BERNARD
| Crucibles: the story of chemistry. | Prem s49 | 57 | .35 |

JAFFE, RONA
| The best of everything. | Card GC-68 | 59 | .50 |

JAKES, JOHN
| A night for treason. | Ace D-209 | 57 | .35 |
| Wear a fast gun. | Ace D-220 | 57 | .35 |

JAMES, DAN
| Gunsmoke mesa. | Pyr 269 | 57 | .25 |

JAMES, DON
| Dark hunger. | Mon 101 | 58 | .35 |
| The sexual side of love. | MonB MB502 | 59 | .35 |

JAMES, HENRY
The Aspern papers and The spoils of Poynton.	DelL LC121	59	.50
Daisy Miller and An international episode.	Pen 625	47	.25
Daisy Miller and The turn of the screw.	Dell 800	54	.25
_____.	Dell D181	56	.35
Washington Square.	BanC AC38	59	.35
Washington Square and The Europeans.	DelL LC136	59	.50
The wings of the dove.	DelL LC117	59	.50

JAMES, M. E. CLIFTON
| The counterfeit General Montgomery. | Avon 692 | 56 | .25 |

JAMES, VINCENT
| Island of the pit. | Pop 800 | 57 | .25 |

JAMES, WILL
| Home ranch. | Ban 47 | 46 | .25 |

JAMES, WILLIAM
| The varieties of religious experience. | Ment MD221 | 58 | .50 |

JAMIESON, LELAND
| Attack! | Ace S-262 | 57 | .25 |

JANEWAY, ELIZABETH
| Daisy Kenyon. | PB 442 | 47 | .25 |
| The Walsh girls. | PB 393 | 46 | .25 |

JANNEY, RUSSELL
| The miracle of the bells. | Dell 474 | 51 | .25 |

JANSON, HANK
| Lady, mind that corpse. | Chek 10 | 49 | .15 |

JANUARY, STEVE
| Rusty Desmond. | Avon 553 | 54 | .25 |

Author/Title	Pub./Stock No.	Yr.	Price
JANUARY, STEVE (cont.)			
Rusty Desmond.	Avon T-359	59	.35
JASPER, BOB			
Feud at Sundown.	Avon 487	53	.25
JASTROW, JOSEPH			
Freud: his dream and			
sex theories.	PB 522	48	.25
_____.	Card C-150	54	.35
_____.	Perm M-4134	59	.35
JAVELLANA, STEVAN			
The lost ones.	Pop 435	52	.25
JAY, CHARLOTTE			
Beat not the bones.	Avon 623	55	.25
_____.	Avon T-376	59	.35
The fugitive eye.	Avon 670	55	.25
The yellow turban.	Avon 736	56	.25
JEANS, JAMES			
The growth of physical			
science.	Prem d70	58	.50
JEFFERSON, THOMAS			
The living thoughts of			
Thomas Jefferson.	Prem d61	57	.50
Thomas Jefferson on			
democracy.	Pel P13	47	.25
JENKINS, DOROTHY H.			
The complete book of			
roses.	Ban A1418	56	.35
JENKINS, ELIZABETH			
Harriet.	Ban 64	46	.25
JENKINS, WILL F.			
Dallas.	GM 126	50	.25
The murder of the U.S.A.	Han 62	47	.20
Son of the Flying Y.	GM 161	51	.25
_____.	GM 346	53	.25
JENNINGS, DEAN with Clinton T. Duffy			
The San Quentin story.	PB 831	51	.25
JENNINGS, JOHN			
Chronicle of the Calypso			
clipper.	Perm M-3071	57	.25
Gentleman ranker.	Prmb P293	54	.35
The golden eagle.	Dell D267	59	.35
Land of vengeance.	Prmb P141	51	.35
The pepper tree.	Card C-22	52	.35
River to the West.	Prmb P157	52	.35
Rogue's yarn.	PB 1047	55	.25
The Salem frigate.	Prmb P125	51	.35
The sea eagles.	Prmb P133	51	.35
The shadow and the glory.	Prmb P256	53	.35
The strange brigade.	Card C-137	54	.35

Author/Title	Pub./Stock No.	Yr.	Price
The wind in his fists.	Pop SP19	58	.50
JEPSON, SELWYN			
Killer by proxy.	Ban 803	50	.25
JEROME, OWEN FOX			
The corpse awaits.	Han 58	47	.20
JESSUP, M. K.			
The case for the UFO.	Ban A1374	55	.35
JESSUP, RICHARD			
Cheyenne Saturday.	GM 647	57	.25
Comanche vengeance.	GM 699	57	.25
Cry passion.	DelF 109	56	.25
The cunning and the			
haunted.	GM S440	54	.35
Long ride West.	GM 672	57	.25
Lowdown.	DelF B118	58	.35
Night boat to Paris.	DelF 92	56	.25
A rage to die.	GM s515	55	.35
Texas outlaw.	GM 771	58	.25
The young don't cry.	GM s660	57	.35
JOESTEN, JOACHIM			
Dope, inc.	Avon 538	53	.25
Vice, inc.	Ace S-58	54	.25
with Sid Feder			
The Luciano story.	Pop G155	56	.35
JOHNEN, WILHELM			
Battling the bombers.	Ace D-326	58	.35
JOHNS, RALPHA			
A date with Dr.			
Guillotine.	Ban 318	49	.25
_____.	Pnnt P58	54	.25
The grave gentlemen.	Perm M-3121	58	.25
Kill me if you can.	Berk 352	56	.25
Never kill on Sundays.	Ban 1218	54	.25
JOHNSON, ANNABEL			
The hungry years.	Crst s201	58	.35
JOHNSON, CROCKETT			
Barnaby.	PB 366	46	.25
JOHNSON, DOROTHY M.			
The hanging tree.	Ball 274K	58	.35
Indian country.	Ball 29	53	.35
_____.	Ball 241	57	.35
JOHNSON, GERALD			
Andrew Jackson.	BanB FB408	56	.50
JOHNSON, GRADY			
The five pennies.	DelF B128	59	.35
JOHNSON, J. E.			
Wing leader.	Ball F195	57	.50

Author/Title	Pub./Stock No.	Yr.	Price
JOHNSON, JAMES WELDON			
The autobiography of an ex-coloured man.	PelM M29	48	.35
JOHNSON, LUCY BLACK with Pyke Johnson Jr.			
Cartoon treasury.	Ban F1558	57	.50
JOHNSON, PYKE JR. with Lucy Black Johnson			
Cartoon treasury.	Ban F1558	57	.50
JOHNSON, ROBERT S. with Martin Caidin			
Thunderbolt!	Ball F323K	59	.50
JOHNSON, RYERSON			
Lady in dread.	GM 459	55	.25
Mississippi flame.	RS 28	53	.35
Naked in the streets.	RS 10	52	.35
JOHNSON, VICTOR H.			
Bold moment.	Pyr 125	54	.25
_____.	Pyr 229	56	.25
Cry torment.	Graf 101	55	.25
JOHNSTON, GEORGE HENRY with Charmian Clift			
High valley.	PB 818	51	.25
JOHNSTON, MARY			
To have and to hold.	PB 354	46	.25
_____.	Card C-322	59	.35
JOHNSTON, STANLEY			
Queen of the flat-tops.	Dell 37	44	.25
_____.	Ace D-334	59	.35
JOHNSTONE, LANE			
The Dr. Lewis affair.	Pop G383	59	.35
JOKES and wisecracks.	BPLA unk	40	.10
JONAS, CARL			
Jefferson Selleck.	Dell D124	53	.35
Snowslide.	Dell D120	53	.35
JONES, ARTHUR FREDERICK			
Care and training of dogs.	PB 629	50	.25
_____.	Card C-304	58	.35
JONES, CONSTANCE with Guy Pearce Jones			
Peabody's mermaid.	PB 503	48	.25
JONES, DENYS			
Look not upon me.	Sig S1387	57	.35
JONES, EVAN			
High gear.	Ban 1313	55	.25
JONES, GEORGE E.			
Trap.	Graf 106	55	.25
JONES, GREGORY			
Prowl cop.	Ace D-147	56	.35

Author/Title	Pub./Stock No.	Yr.	Price
JONES, GUY PEARCE			
Two survived.	Pen 506	42	.25
with Constance Jones			
Peabody's mermaid.	PB 503	48	.25
JONES, H. SPENCER			
Life on other worlds.	Ment M39	49	.35
_____.	Ment MD144	55	.50
JONES, JACK			
Journey into death.	GM 517	55	.25
JONES, JAMES			
From here to eternity.	Sig T1075	53	.75
Some came running.	Sig T1637	59	.75
JONES, JENNIFER			
Murder-on-Hudson.	Dell 3	43	.25
JONES, KEN			
Etched in murder.	Zen ZB-15	59	.35
The FBI in action.	Sig S1476	57	.35
"I was there".	Lion 142	53	.25
JONES, NARD			
I'll take what's mine.	GM 388	54	.25
Ride the dark storm.	GM 512	55	.25
The scarlet petticoat.	Avon T-79	54	.35
_____.	Avon T-164	57	.35
JONES, NATHANIEL			
Saturday mountain.	Ace D-201	57	.35
JORDAN, DAVID with Charles O'Brien Kennedy			
American ballads.	RS 22	52	.35
_____.	Prem s32	56	.35
JORDAN, GAIL			
Palm Beach apartment.	Pyr 15	49	.25
JORGENSON, IVAR			
Starhaven.	Ace D-351	59	.35
JOSCELYN, ARCHIE			
Cheyenne kid.	Avon 819	58	.25
Fighting kid from Texas.	Avon 813	58	.25
Gunhand's pay.	Pyr 259	57	.25
Hired gun.	Avon 739	56	.25
The king of Thunder Valley.	Han 89	49	.25
The man from Salt Creek.	Ace D-392	59	.35
Outlaw.	Avon 798	58	.25
River to the sunset.	Ace D-304	58	.35
Shannahan's feud.	Han 109	50	.25
Six-gun sawbones.	Avon 788	57	.25
Texas revenge.	Avon 791	57	.25
JOSEPH, GEORGE			
Leave it to me.	Eag EB44	55	.25
This is for keeps.	Pop G265	58	.35

Author/Title	Pub./Stock No.	Yr.	Price
JOYCE, JAMES			
Portrait of the artist as a young man.	PenN 664	48	.25
———.	Sig S1150	55	.35
JOYEUX, ODETTE			
The bride is much too beautiful.	Pyr G415	59	.35
JUDAH, CHARLES B.			
Christopher Humble.	Perm M-4075	57	.35
Tom Bone.	Prmb P146	52	.35
JUDD, CYRIL			
Gunner Cade.	Ace D-227	57	.35
Outpost Mars.	Dell 760	54	.25
JUDSON, JEANNE			
Carol Trent, air stewardess.	Ban 1667	57	.25
Nancy Ross, private secretary.	Ban 1751	58	.25
Visiting nurse.	Ban 1614	57	.25
JULIAN, PETER			
The seventh trumpet.	Lion LL 174	57	.35
JUNG, C. G.			
The undiscovered self.	Ment MD259	59	.50
JUST married.	Pyr 152	55	.25
JUVENILE jungle.	Berk G-86	57	.35

Author/Title	Pub./Stock No.	Yr.	Price
K			
KADES, HANS			
The doctor's secret.	Dell D265	59	.35
KAHN, LAWRENCE H.			
The tank destroyers.	PB 1202	58	.25
KAINS, M. G.			
Five acres and			
independence.	PB 543	48	.25
KALMAN, VICTOR			
AMF guide to natural			
bowling.	Perm M-4147	59	.35
KAMAL, AHMAD			
High pressure.	Ban 716	49	.25
KANE, FRANK			
About face.	Ace D-33	53	.35
Bare trap.	Dell 749	54	.25
Bullet proof.	Dell 785	54	.25
Dead weight.	Dell 665	53	.25
Death about face.	Han 72	48	.25
The fatal foursome.	Dell 973	58	.25
Grave danger.	Dell 886	56	.25
Green light for death.	RCL 8	50	.25
_____.	Dell 918	56	.25
Johnny Liddell's morgue.	DelF A117	56	.25
Juke box king.	DelF B137	59	.35
Key witness.	DelF A126	57	.25
The lineup.	DelF B125	59	.35
The living end.	DelF A142	57	.25
Poisons unknown.	Dell 822	55	.25
A real gone guy.	Dell D226	58	.35
Red hot ice.	Dell 901	56	.25
Slay ride.	Pop 400	52	.25
_____.	Dell D264	59	.35
Syndicate girl.	DelF B123	59	.35
Trigger mortis.	Dell D280	59	.35
KANE, HARNETT T.			
The smiling rebel.	Perm M-4071	57	.35
KANE, HENRY			
Armchair in hell.	Dell 316	49	.25
_____.	Avon 703	56	.25
The case of the			
murdered madame.	Avon 646	55	.25
A corpse for Christmas.	Dell 735	53	.25
The deadly doll.	Zen ZB-19	59	.35
The deadly finger.	Pop 806	57	.25
Death for sale.	DelF A144	57	.25
Death is the last lover.	Avon T-291	59	.35
Death on the double.	Avon 761	57	.25
Edge of panic.	Dell 535	51	.25
_____.	Sig 1523	58	.25
Fistful of death.	Avon T-276	58	.35
A halo for nobody.	Dell 231	48	.25
_____.	Dell 348	49	.25

Author/Title	Pub./Stock No.	Yr.	Price
Hang by your neck.	Dell 455	50	.25
_____.	Sig 1515	58	.25
Laughter came screaming.	Avon 572	54	.25
Martinis and murder.	Avon 745	56	.25
A mask for murder.	Avon 796	57	.25
Murder of the Park			
Avenue playgirl.	Avon 751	57	.25
My business is murder.	Avon 602	54	.25
_____.	Avon 790	57	.25
The name is Chambers.	Pyr G284	57	.35
Private eyeful.	Pyr G432	59	.35
Report for a corpse.	Dell 330	49	.25
Too French and too			
deadly.	Avon 672	55	.25
Trinity in violence.	Avon 618	54	.25
_____.	Avon T-264	58	.35
Until you are dead.	Dell 580	52	.25
Who killed sweet Sue?	Avon 733	56	.25
KANE, IRENE with Mary McGee Williams			
On becoming a woman.	DelF A179	59	.25
KANE, JOSEPH NATHAN			
The Perma quiz book.	Perm M-3039	56	.25
The second Perma quiz			
book.	Perm M-4101	58	.35
KANIN, FAY with Michael Kanin			
Teacher's pet.	Ban 1780	58	.25
KANIN, MICHAEL with Fay Kanin			
Teacher's pet.	Ban 1780	58	.25
KANTOR, MacKINLAY			
Andersonville.	Sig T1388	57	.75
Arouse and beware.	Ban 900	51	.25
_____.	Ban A1625	57	.35
The daughter of Bugle			
Ann.	Ban 1237	54	.25
Diversey.	Pop G161	56	.35
Don't touch me.	Ban 1038	52	.25
_____.	Pop G241	58	.35
Frontier.	Sig S1703	59	.35
Gentle Annie.	Pop 183	49	.25
_____.	Eag EB13	54	.25
_____.	Pop G379	59	.35
God and my country.	Ban 1351	55	.25
Long remember.	PB 135	42	.25
_____.	Ban A1008	52	.35
Midnight lace.	Ban 753	50	.25
One wild oat.	GM 122	50	.25
_____.	GM 675	57	.25
Signal thirty-two.	Ban A965	52	.35
Silent grow the guns.	Sig S1543	58	.35
The voice of Bugle Ann			
and The romance of			
Rosy Ridge.	Pen 636	47	.25
Warwhoop.	Ban 1175	53	.25
Wicked water.	Ban 809	50	.25
_____.	Ban 1238	54	.25

Author/Title	Pub./Stock No.	Yr.	Price
KAPELNER, ALLAN			
Lonely boy blues.	Lion LB 92	56	.25
KAPLAN, EDGAR			
The complete Italian system of winning bridge.	SigK KD368	59	.50
KAPPAN, P. D.			
Something for nothing.	Prmb P103	51	.35
KARELITZ, SAMUEL			
When your child is ill.	Perm M-5008	59	.50
KARIG, WALTER			
Caroline Hicks.	Card C-56	52	.35
Lower than angels.	Pop 419	52	.25
	Pop SP24	58	.50
with Horace V. Bird			
Don't tread on me.	Ban A1340	55	.35
KARLOVA, IRINA			
Dreadful hollow.	Dell 126	46	.25
KARNEY, JACK			
Cop.	PB 898	52	.25
Cry, brother, cry.	Pop G304	59	.35
Cut me in.	Pyr G444	59	.35
The knave of diamonds.	Ace D-373	59	.35
Knock 'em dead.	Ace D-101	55	.35
Some like it tough.	Mon 116	59	.35
There goes Shorty Higgins.	Pyr 99	53	.25
Tough town.	Pyr 31	51	.25
Work of darkness.	Pop G212	58	.35
KARP, DANIEL			
The big feeling.	Lion 93	52	.25
KARP, DAVID			
The brotherhood of velvet.	Lion 105	52	.25
Cry, flesh.	Lion 132	53	.25
Escape to nowhere.	Lion LL 10	55	.35
The girl on Crown Street.	Lion LL 86	56	.35
Hardman.	Lion 119	53	.25
KARR, DAVID			
Fight for control.	Ball 157	56	.35
KARR, MADELINE with Dale Kramer			
Teen-age gangs.	Pop 592	54	.25
	Pop 820	57	.25
KASTLE, HERBERT D.			
Bachelor summer.	Avon T-355	59	.35
One thing on my mind.	Pop 823	57	.25
Seven keys to Koptic Court.	Crst d271	59	.50

Author/Title	Pub./Stock No.	Yr.	Price
KATCHER, LEO			
Hard man.	PB 1197	58	.25
KATKOV, NORMAN			
Eagle at my eyes.	Pop 251	50	.25
KA-TZETNIK 135633			
House of dolls.	Lion LL 106	56	.35
	Pyr G326	58	.35
KAUFFMANN, LANE			
Kill the beloved.	Lion LL 64	56	.35
KAUFFMANN, STANLEY			
Great dog stories.	Ball 118	55	.35
Man of the world.	Pop G183	57	.35
A new desire.	Pop 705	55	.25
The philanderer.	Pop SP30	58	.50
The tightrope.	Pop 520	53	.25
KAUFMAN, GEORGE S. with Moss Hart			
The man who came to dinner.	PB 143	42	.25
KAUFMAN, LENARD			
The color of green.	Ace D-202	57	.35
Jubel's children.	Sig 896	51	.25
Juvenile delinquents.	Avon 433	52	.25
	Avon T-105	55	.35
	Avon T-217	58	.35
Tender mercy.	Dell 444	50	.25
KAUFMAN, MAXINE			
I am Adam.	Pyr R289	57	.35
KAUFMANN, MYRON S.			
Remember me to God.	Sig T1578	58	.75
KAUFMANN, RICHARD			
Heaven pays no dividends.	Sig S1052	53	.35
KAVINOKY, BERNICE			
Honey from a dark hive.	Pop G185	57	.35
So strong a flame.	Pop G375	59	.35
We burn like candles.	Pop 580	54	.25
	Pop G297	59	.35
KAY, CAMERON			
Thieves fall out.	GM 311	53	.25
KAYE, M. M.			
Shadow of the moon.	Pop SP18	58	.50
KAYE, PHILIP B.			
Taffy.	Avon 377	51	.25
KAZ			
Nellie the nurse.	DelF A173	58	.25
Taking a turn for the nurse.	Pyr 193	56	.25

Author/Title	Pub./Stock No.	Yr.	Price
KEARNEY, PAUL			
I drive the turnpikes--			
and survive.	Ball 177	56	.35
KEATING, E. P.			
A good time man.	NL 13	49	.25
KEATS, CHARLES			
The body of love.	Berk G-51	57	.35
KEATS, JOHN, 1795-1821			
Keats.	DelL LB131	59	.35
KEATS, JOHN, 1920-			
The crack in the picture			
window.	Ball 233	57	.35
The insolent chariots.	Crst s317	59	.35
KEELEY, JOSEPH C.			
How to take better			
pictures.	Dell F62	57	.50
KEENE, DAY			
About Doctor Ferrel.	GM 254	52	.25
	GM 617	56	.25
_____. The big kiss-off.	Graf 75	54	.25
	Dmnd D2003	59	.35
Bring him back dead.	GM 603	56	.25
The dangling carrot.	Ace D-129	55	.35
Dead dolls don't talk.	Crst 286	59	.25
Dead in bed.	Pyr G448	59	.35
Death house doll.	Ace D-41	54	.35
Flight by night.	Ace D-170	56	.35
Framed in guilt.	Graf 51	52	.25
His father's wife.	Pyr 138	54	.25
	Pyr G266	57	.35
_____. Home is the sailor.	GM 225	52	.25
Homicidal lady.	Graf 87	54	.25
Hunt the killer.	Avon 705	56	.25
If the coffin fits.	Graf 43	52	.25
It's a sin to kill.	Avon 814	58	.25
Joy house.	Lion 210	54	.25
Moran's woman.	Zen ZB-24	59	.35
Mrs. Homicide.	Ace D-11	53	.35
Murder on the side.	GM 622	56	.25
My flesh is sweet.	Lion unk	51	.25
Naked fury.	Dmnd D2020	59	.35
Notorious.	GM 372	54	.25
Passage to Samoa.	GM 823	58	.25
The passion murders.	Avon 684	55	.25
Sleep with the devil.	Lion 204	54	.25
So dead, my lovely.	Pyr G395	59	.35
Strange witness.	Graf 58	53	.25
Take a step to murder.	GM 874	59	.25
There was a crooked man.	GM 405	54	.25
This is murder, Mr.			
Herbert.	Avon 159	48	.25
To kiss or kill.	GM 206	52	.25
Too hot to hold.	GM 931	59	.25
Wake up to murder.	Avon 660	55	.25

Author/Title	Pub./Stock No.	Yr.	Price
Wake up to murder.	Berk G258	59	.35
Who has Wilma Lathrop?	GM 494	55	.25
KEENE, JAMES			
The brass and the blue.	Dell 959	57	.25
Justice, my brother!	Dell 1000	59	.25
McCracken in command.	DelF A190	59	.25
The Texas pistol.	Dell 930	57	.25
KEITH, AGNES NEWTON			
Land below the wind.	PB 267	45	.25
KEITH, CARLETON			
A gem of a murder.	Dell 1007	59	.25
KELLAND, CLARENCE BUDINGTON			
Arizona.	Ban 257	48	.25
	Ban 1061	52	.25
_____. The case of the			
nameless corpse.	Pyr G355	58	.35
Desert law.	Ban 726	49	.25
Double treasure.	Dell 335	49	.25
Gold.	Hill 16	49	.25
The great mail robbery.	Pop 432	52	.25
Sugarfoot!	Ban 203	48	.25
Tombstone.	Pnnt P47	54	.25
KELLEAM, JOSEPH E.			
Blackjack.	Ban 700	49	.25
Overlords from space.	Ace D-173	56	.35
KELLER, ALLAN			
Thunder at Harper's			
Ferry.	Ace D-395	59	.35
KELLER, DAN			
Flee the night in anger.	Pop 625	54	.25
KELLER, JAMES			
Government is your			
business.	Prmb P172	52	.35
Make each day count.	Dell F65	58	.50
Three minutes a day.	Prmb P105	51	.35
You can change the world.	Sig 762	50	.25
_____.	Prmb P131	51	.35
KELLER, REAMER			
Mating manual.	Ban 1623	57	.25
Why the long puss?	Ban 1460	56	.25
KELLEY, FRANK with Cornelius Ryan			
MacArthur--man of action.	Lion 67	51	.25
KELLEY, THOMAS P.			
The black Donnellys.	Sig 1221	55	.25
with Herbert Emerson Wilson			
I stole $16,000,000.	Sig 1293	56	.25
KELLEY, WELBOURN			
Alabama empire.	Ban F1783	58	.50

Author/Title	Pub./Stock No.	Yr.	Price
KELLOGG, LOIS S.			
The quick cook book.	Card C-243	57	.35
KELLY, FRED C.			
The Wright brothers.	Ball 155	56	.35
KELLY, G. LOMBARD			
Sexual feeling in married men and women.	PB 825	51	.25
KELLY, JAMES			
The insider.	Pop SP48	59	.50
KELSTON, ROBERT			
Kill one, kill two.	Ace D-297	58	.35
Murder's end.	Graf 126	56	.25
KELTON, ELMER			
Barbed wire.	Ball 247	58	.35
Buffalo wagons.	Ball 187	57	.35
Hot iron.	Ball 128	56	.35
Shadow of a star.	Ball 304K	59	.35
KENDRICK, BAYNARD			
Blind man's bluff.	Dell 230	48	.25
Blood on Lake Louisa.	Pen 635	47	.25
Bright victory.	Ban 937	51	.25
Death knell.	Dell 273	49	.25
Eleven of diamonds.	Pen 616	46	.25
The flames of time.	Ban A902	51	.35
The iron spiders.	Dell 50	44	.25
The last express.	Dell 95	45	.25
The murderer who wanted more.	DelT 32	51	.10
Odor of violets.	Dell 162	47	.25
Out of control.	Dell 376	50	.25
The whistling hangman.	Dell 113	46	.25
KENDRICKS, JAMES			
Beyond our pleasure.	Mon 123	59	.35
Sword of Casanova.	Mon 111	59	.35
KENNAN, GEORGE F.			
American diplomacy: 1900-1950.	Ment M80	52	.35
KENNEDY, BURT			
Seven men from now.	Berk 361	56	.25
KENNEDY, CHARLES O'BRIEN with David Jordan			
American ballads.	RS 22	52	.35
————.	Prem s32	56	.35
KENNEDY, JAY RICHARD			
Prince Bart.	Pop G136	54	.35
KENNEDY, JOHN F.			
Profiles in courage.	Card C-238	57	.35
KENNEDY, MARGARET			
The constant nymph.	PB 41	40	.25

Author/Title	Pub./Stock No.	Yr.	Price
KENNEDY, MARK			
Boy gang.	Perm M-3006	55	.25
KENNEDY, STETSON			
Passage to violence.	Lion LL 9	54	.35
KENNERLEY, JUBA			
The terror of the leopard men.	Avon 339	51	.25
KENT, DAVID			
A knife is silent.	Lion LL 91	56	.35
KENT, MADELEINE FABIOLA			
The corsair.	Perm M-4076	57	.35
KENT, MONA			
Mirror, mirror on the wall.	Pop 269	50	.25
KENT, NIAL			
The divided path.	Pyr 32	51	.25
————.	Pyr G452	59	.35
KENT, RICHARD			
The householder's manual.	SigK K312	54	.25
KENT, SIMON			
The doctor on Bean Street.	Dell D143	54	.35
Fire down below.	Pop W500	57	.35
Tonight and forever.	Eag EB40	55	.25
KENT, W. H. B.			
Range rider.	Ban 102	47	.25
The tenderfoot.	Ban 202	48	.25
KENYON, F. W.			
Emma: my Lord Admiral's mistress.	Avon T-128	56	.35
KENYON, JOSEPHINE H. with Ruth K. Russell			
Healthy babies are happy babies.	Sig 795	50	.25
KEOGH, THEODORA			
The double door.	Sig 958	52	.25
The fascinator.	Sig 1209	55	.25
Meg.	Sig 857	51	.25
————.	Sig 1284	56	.25
The mistress.	Avon T-358	59	.35
My name is Rose.	Sig S1560	58	.35
Street music.	Sig 1049	53	.25
The tattooed heart.	Sig 1100	54	.25
KEON, MICHAEL			
The tiger in summer.	Pop 558	54	.25
KER, W. P.			
The Dark Ages.	Ment MD225	58	.50

Author/Title	Pub./Stock No.		Yr.	Price

KERNAN, W. F.
  Defense will not win
    the war. · PB · 170 · 42 · .25

KERNER, BEN with Tom Van Dycke
  Not with my neck. · Han · 80 · 48 · .25

KERNER, FRED
  Love is a man's affair. · Pop · G360 · 59 · .35

KEROUAC, JACK
  The Dharma bums. · Sig · D1718 · 59 · .50
  Maggie Cassidy. · Avon · G-1035 · 59 · .50
  On the road. · Sig · D1619 · 58 · .50
  The subterraneans. · Avon · T-302 · 59 · .35
  _____. · Avon · T-340 · 59 · .35

KERR, BEN
  The blonde and Johnny
    Malloy. · Eag · EB104 · 58 · .25
  Club 17. · Pop · 803 · 57 · .25
  Damned if he does. · Pop · 785 · 56 · .25
  Down I go. · Pop · 653 · 55 · .25
  I fear you not. · Pop · 763 · 56 · .25
  Shakedown. · Pop · 467 · 52 · .25

KERR, JEAN
  Please don't eat the
    daisies. · Crst · s263 · 59 · .35

KERSH, GERALD
  Dishonor. · Avon · T-111 · 55 · .35
  Night and the city. · Dell · 374 · 50 · .25
  On an odd note. · Ball · 268 · 58 · .35
  Prelude to a certain
    midnight. · Lion · 98 · 52 · .25
  The secret masters. · Ball · 28 · 53 · .35

KESSEL, JOSEPH
  Cry of violence. · Sig · 877 · 51 · .25

KESSELRING, JOSEPH
  Arsenic and old lace. · PB · 199 · 43 · .25

KETCHAM, HANK
  Dennis the menace. · Avon · 519 · 53 · .25
  _____. · Avon · 665 · 55 · .25
  _____. · Avon · 735 · 56 · .25
  Dennis the menace:
    household hurricane. · PB · 1217 · 58 · .25
  Dennis the menace rides
    again. · PB · 1125 · 56 · .25
  Dennis the menace vs.
    everybody. · PB · 1179 · 57 · .25
  In this corner...
    Dennis the menace. · Crst · 298 · 59 · .25
  More Dennis the menace. · Avon · 600 · 54 · .25
  Wanted: Dennis the
    menace. · PB · 1153 · 57 · .25

with Bob Harmon
  Baby sitter's guide, by
    Dennis the menace. · PB · 1080 · 55 · .25

KETCHUM, PHILIP
  The big gun. · Eag · EB75 · 56 · .25
  Dead man's trail. · Pop · 813 · 57 · .25
  The dead-shot kid. · Sig · 1744 · 59 · .25
  Death in the library. · Dell · 1 · 43 · .25
  Decision at Piute Wells. · Pop · G337 · 59 · .35
  Desperation Valley. · Pop · 645 · 55 · .25
  The Elkhorn feud. · Eag · EB65 · 56 · .25
  Feud at Forked River. · GM · 772 · 58 · .25
  Gun code. · Sig · 1686 · 59 · .25
  Gun law. · Pop · 604 · 54 · .25
  _____. · Pop · G355 · 59 · .35
  Gunfire man. · Pop · G389 · 59 · .35
  Guns of the Barricade
    bunch. · Pop · 499 · 53 · .25
  The hard man. · Avon · T-322 · 59 · .35
  Longhorn stampede. · Eag · EB57 · 56 · .25
  The night of the coyotes. · Ball · 158 · 56 · .35
  Rider from Texas. · Pop · 673 · 55 · .25
  The saddle bum. · Pop · 532 · 53 · .25
  Six-gun maverick. · Pop · 797 · 57 · .25
  Texan on the prod. · Pop · 472 · 52 · .25
  The Texas gun. · Pop · 575 · 54 · .25

KEVESON, PETER
  Tubie's monument. · Ban · A1836 · 58 · .35

KEY, ALEXANDER
  The wrath and the wind. · Pop · 291 · 50 · .25
  _____. · Pop · 608 · 54 · .25

KEY, TED
  Hazel. · Ban · 1404 · 55 · .25
  Here's Hazel. · Ban · 1477 · 56 · .25
  If you like Hazel. · Ban · 1813 · 58 · .25
  Phyllis. · Berk · 386 · 59 · .25

KEYES, FRANCES PARKINSON
  Blue camellia. · Crst · d232 · 58 · .50
  Crescent carnival. · Dell · 561 · 52 · .25
  Dinner at Antoine's. · Dell · 443 · 50 · .25
  Fielding's Folly. · PB · 349 · 45 · .25
  Joy Street. · Crst · d314 · 59 · .50
  The river road. · Dell · 692 · 53 · .25
  The royal box. · Sig · D1291 · 56 · .50
  Steamboat Gothic. · Crst · d293 · 59 · .50
  Victorine. · Crst · d333 · 59 · .50

KEYHOE, DONALD
  The flying saucers are
    real. · GM · 107 · 50 · .25
  Flying saucers from
    outer space. · Prmb · 297 · 54 · .25

KIELY, BENEDICT
  The evil men do. · Dell · 792 · 54 · .25

Author/Title	Pub./Stock No.	Yr.	Price
KIERAN, JAMES			
Come murder me.	GM 150	51	.25
_____.	GM 419	54	.25
KIKI			
The education of a French model.	Crst 127	56	.25
KILLENS, JOHN O.			
Youngblood.	Card GC-28	55	.50
KILRAIN, GEORGE			
Maverick with a star.	Ace D-14	53	.35
South to Santa Fé.	Ace D-30	53	.35
KIMBLE, GEORGE with Raymond Bush			
The weather.	Pel P9	46	.25
KIMBROUGH, EDWARD			
Night fire.	Ace D-65	54	.35
KIMBROUGH, EMILY with Cornelia Otis Skinner			
Our hearts were young and gay.	Ban 105	47	.25
_____.	Ban A1894	58	.35
KING, LOUIS			
Cornered.	Ace D-305	58	.35
KING, RUFUS			
The case of the constant god.	Pop 193	49	.25
Crime of violence.	Pop (3)	43	.25
The deadly dove.	Pop 318	51	.25
Design in evil.	Pop 124	47	.25
The fatal kiss mystery.	Pop 43	45	.25
Homicide holiday.	Dell 22	43	.25
Murder by latitude.	Pop 246	50	.25
Murder by the clock.	Pop 31	44	.25
Murder challenges Valcour.	Dell 39	44	.25
Murder in the Willett family.	Pop 55	45	.25
Murder masks Miami.	Pop 22	44	.25
Murder on the yacht.	Pop 67	45	.25
Never walk alone.	Pop 362	51	.25
Secret beyond the door.	Ban 120	47	.25
Somewhere in this house.	Pop 276	50	.25
Valcour meets murder.	Pop 13	43	.25
A variety of weapons.	Pop 97	46	.25
KING, SHERWOOD			
If I die before I wake.	Ace D-9	53	.35
KING-HALL, MAGDALEN			
The life and death of the wicked Lady Skelton.	Dell 640	52	.25
KINGERY, DON			
Death must wait.	GM 561	56	.25

Author/Title	Pub./Stock No.	Yr.	Price
Paula.	DelF B132	59	.35
Swamp fire.	Pop 815	57	.25
KINKAID, MATT			
Hardcase.	Avon 539	53	.25
The race of giants.	DelF A118	56	.25
KINNAIRD, CLARK			
Avon complete crosswords and cryptograms.	Avon 162	48	.25
KIPLING, RUDYARD			
"Captains courageous".	Ban 58	46	.25
_____.	Ban A1509	56	.35
Kim.	PB 616	49	.25
_____.	DelL LB128	59	.35
The Kipling sampler.	Prem d53	57	.50
The light that failed.	PB 45	40	.25
A treasury of short stories.	Ban S1609	57	.75
KIRBY, DAN			
Cimarron territory.	Ace D-372	59	.35
KIRK, JEREMY			
The build-up boys.	PB 849	52	.25
KIRKLAND, JACK			
Tobacco Road.	Sig 978	52	.25
KITCHIN, C. H. B.			
Death of my aunt.	Pen 547	44	.25
KJELGAARD, JIM			
Big Red.	Com 18	49	.25
Buckskin brigade.	PBJr J-60	51	.25
Forest patrol.	Com 27	49	.25
KLAAS, JOE			
Maybe I'm dead.	Dell F66	58	.50
KLEIN, ALEXANDER			
The counterfeit traitor.	Perm M-4122	59	.35
KLEIN, ERNST			
The blackmailer.	Avon 404	52	.25
KLEMPNER, JOHN			
Letter to five wives.	Dell 554	51	.25
KLING, KEN			
How I pick winners.	Pop 181	49	.25
KLING, SAMUEL G.			
Handy legal advisor for home and business.	Prmb P25	51	.35
How to win and hold a mate.	Perm M-4074	57	.35
The legal encyclopedia for home and business.	Perm M-5012	59	.50

Author/Title	Pub./Stock No.	Yr.	Price
KLING, SAMUEL G. (cont.)			
Your legal advisor.	Perm M-4023	55	.35
KLUCKHOHN, CLYDE			
Mirror for man.	Prem d58	57	.50
KNIBBS, HENRY HERBERT			
The ridin' kid from			
Powder River.	Dell 399	50	.25
The Tonto kid.	Ban 56	46	.25
	Ban 1062	52	.25
KNICKERBOCKER, CHARLES H.			
The boy came back.	Pop 457	52	.25
_____.	Pop G307	59	.35
KNIGHT, ADAM			
Girl running.	Sig 1347	56	.25
I'll kill you next!	Sig 1276	56	.25
Kiss and kill.	Sig 1139	54	.25
Knife at my back.	Sig 1022	53	.25
Murder for madame.	Sig 920	52	.25
_____.	Sig 1395	57	.25
Stone cold blonde.	Sig 883	51	.25
_____.	Sig 1322	56	.25
The sunburned corpse.	Sig 1103	54	.25
Triple slay.	Sig 1724	59	.25
KNIGHT, ARTHUR			
The liveliest art.	Ment MD263	59	.50
KNIGHT, CLIFFORD			
The affair of the			
scarlet crab.	Dell 75	45	.25
KNIGHT, DAMON			
Hell's pavement.	Lion LL 13	55	.35
Masters of evolution.	Ace D-375	59	.35
The people maker.	Zen ZB-14	59	.35
KNIGHT, DAVID			
Dragnet, case no. 561.	PB 1120	56	.25
Pattern for murder.	Graf 48	52	.25
KNIGHT, ERIC			
The flying Yorkshireman.	PB 493	48	.25
KNIGHT, JOHN			
The story of my			
psychoanalysis.	PB 866	52	.25
KNIGHT, KATHLEEN MOORE			
Death blew out the match.	Bond 7	46	.25
KNIGHT, RUTH ADAMS			
Women must weep.	Dell 482	51	.25
KNOKE, HEINZ			
I flew for the Führer.	Berk G-224	59	.35

Author/Title	Pub./Stock No.	Yr.	Price
KNOX, CALVIN M.			
Lest we forget thee,			
earth.	Ace D-291	58	.35
The plot against earth.	Ace D-358	59	.35
KOBER, ARTHUR			
My dear Bella.	Ban 35	46	.25
The KODAK camera guide.	Card GC-58	59	.50
KOEHLER, ROBERT PORTNER			
Here come the dead.	HH unk	47	.25
The road house murders.	HH 17	47	.25
KOEHLER, WILHELM			
Rembrandt.	PBA A8	53	.50
KOENIG, H. P.			
And sin no more.	Avon T-308	59	.35
The doctor's woman.	Avon 657	55	.25
_____.	Avon 817	58	.25
KOESTLER, ARTHUR			
The age of longing.	Sig S985	53	.35
Darkness at noon.	PenN 671	48	.25
_____.	Sig S1220	55	.35
_____.	Sig D1638	58	.50
The gladiators.	Graf G206	54	.35
_____.	Graf G213	56	.35
KOGON, EUGEN			
The theory and practice			
of hell.	Berk BG-110	58	.50
KÖHLER, WOLFGANG			
Gestalt psychology.	Ment MD279	59	.50
KOHNER, FREDERICK			
Gidget.	Ban 1806	58	.25
KOLB, JOHN with Sylvia Kolb			
A treasury of folk songs.	Ban 123	48	.25
_____.	Ban A1227	54	.35
KOLB, SYLVIA with John Kolb			
A treasury of folk songs.	Ban 123	48	.25
_____.	Ban A1227	54	.35
KOLMAN, SAM with Hillel Black			
The royal vultures.	Perm M-4103	58	.35
KOMROFF, MANUEL			
Echo of evil.	Pop 394	52	.25
Every man's Bible.	Lion 167	53	.25
Gods and demons.	Lion LL 8	54	.35
His great journey.	Lion 128	53	.25
_____.	Lion LL 110	56	.35
In the years of Our Lord.	Ban A1275	54	.35
The life, the loves, the			
adventures of Omar			
Khayyam.	Sig 1377	57	.25

Author/Title	Pub./Stock No.	Yr.	Price	Author/Title	Pub./Stock No.	Yr.	Price
KOMROFF, MANUEL (cont.)				KRANCKE, THEODOR with H. J. Brennecke			
Two thieves.	Lion LL 65	56	.35	Pocket battleship.	Berk BG-177	58	.50
KONINGSBERGER, HANS				KRASNER, WILLIAM			
The affair.	Pyr G407	59	.35	The gambler.	Ban 976	52	.25
				The stag party.	Ban 1823	58	.25
KOPPLIN, DOROTHEA S.				Walk the dark streets.	Ban 780	50	.25
Something to live by.	Prmb P183	52	.35	KRASNEY, SAMUEL A.			
KORMENDI, FERENC				Death cries in the			
The forsaken.	Pop G111	52	.35	street.	Pop 749	56	.25
				Design for dying.	Ace D-313	58	.35
KORNBLUTH, C. M.				Morals squad.	Ace D-336	59	.35
The explorers.	Ball 86	54	.35	The rapist.	Ace D-363	59	.35
The marching morons.	Ball 303K	59	.35				
Not this August.	Ban A1492	56	.35	KRAVCHENKO, VICTOR			
The Syndic.	Ban 1317	55	.25	I chose freedom.	Hill unk	48	.25
Takeoff.	Pnnt P15	53	.25				
with Frederik Pohl				KREPPS, ROBERT W.			
Gladiator-at-law.	Ball 107	55	.35	The courts of the Lion.	Ban A894	51	.35
Presidential year.	Ball 144	56	.35	_____.	Ban A1410	56	.35
Search the sky.	Ball 61	54	.35	Earthshaker.	Dell D284	59	.35
The space merchants.	Ball 21	53	.35	Tell it on the drums.	Dell D156	55	.35
A town is drowning.	Ball 123	55	.35				
Wolfbane.	Ball 335K	59	.35	KRICH, A. M.			
				Men.	DelF D15	54	.35
KOSLOW, JULES				The ribald reader.	DelF F10	54	.50
The Bohemian.	Pyr 83	53	.25	The second ribald reader.	DelF C104	56	.50
				Women.	DelF D3	53	.35
KOUSOULAS, D. G.							
Key to economic progress.	Ball 269	58	.35	KRIM, SEYMOUR			
				Manhattan.	Ban A1201	54	.35
KOVACS, ERNIE							
Zoomar.	Ban F1869	59	.50	KROLL, HARRY HARRISON			
				The cabin in the cotton.	Dell 589	52	.25
KOZLENKO, WILLIAM				The smoldering fire.	Ace S-111	55	.25
Acts of violence.	Pyr G425	59	.35	Their ancient grudge.	Dell 435	50	.25
Men and women.	Lion 177	53	.25				
				KRONENBERGER, LOUIS			
KOZOL, JONATHAN				Company manners.	Ment M156	55	.35
The fume of poppies.	Ban A1986	59	.35				
				KRONHAUSEN, EBERHARD with Phyllis Kronhausen			
KRAMER, DALE				Pornography and the law.	Ball S346K	59	.75
Violent streets.	Sig 1226	55	.25				
	Sig 1687	59	.25	KRONHAUSEN, PHYLLIS with Eberhard Kronhausen			
with Madeline Karr				Pornography and the law.	Ball S346K	59	.75
Teen-age gangs.	Pop 592	54	.25				
_____.	Pop 820	57	.25	KRUGER, PAUL			
				A bullet for a blonde.	DelF A160	58	.25
KRAMER, KARL							
Action along the				KUBECK, JAMES			
Humboldt.	Ace D-160	56	.35	The calendar epic.	Perm M-4090	58	.35
Fair game.	Pop 650	55	.25				
Kiss me quick.	Mon 121	59	.35	KUMMER, FREDERIC ARNOLD			
Not for a curse.	Mon 136	59	.35	Ladies in Hades.	Dell 415	50	.25
KRAMER, N. MARTIN				KUPRIN, ALEXANDRE			
The hearth and the				Yama, the hell-hole.	Pyr G50	52	.35
strangeness.	Pyr R236	57	.50	_____.	Pyr R207	56	.35

Author/Title	Pub./Stock No.	Yr.	Price		Author/Title	Pub./Stock No.	Yr.	Price
KURNITZ, HARRY								
Invasion of privacy.	Perm M-3053	56	.25					
KURTZMAN, HARVEY								
Harvey Kurtzman's jungle								
book.	Ball 338K	59	.35					
The humbug digest.	Ball 242	57	.35					
Inside Mad.	Ball 124	55	.35					
_____.	Ball 265K	58	.35					
The Mad reader.	Ball 93	54	.35					
_____.	Ball 263	58	.35					
_____.	Ball 296K	59	.35					
Mad strikes back.	Ball 106	55	.35					
_____.	Ball 264	58	.35					
_____.	Ball 297K	59	.35					
KUTAK, ROSEMARY								
Darkness of slumber.	PB 402	46	.25					
KUTTNER, HENRY								
Ahead of time.	Ball 30	53	.35					
Destination: infinity.	Avon T-275	58	.35					
Man drowning.	Ban 1154	53	.25					
Murder of a mistress.	Perm M-4082	57	.35					
Murder of a wife.	Perm M-4096	58	.35					
The murder of Ann Avery.	Perm M-3058	56	.25					
The murder of Eleanor								
Pope.	Perm M-3046	56	.25					
with C. L. Moore								
No boundaries.	Ball 122	55	.35					
KUWAHARA, YASUO with Gordon T. Allred								
Kamikaze.	Ball 244	58	.35					
_____.	Ball 317K	59	.35					
KYLE, ROBERT								
Blackmail, inc.	DelF A155	58	.25					
The crooked city.	DelF 17	54	.25					
The golden urge.	DelF 36	54	.25					
Model for murder.	DelF A192	59	.25					
Nice guys finish last.	DelF 51	55	.25					
A tiger in the night.	DelF 66	55	.25					
KYNE, PETER B.								
Jim the conqueror.	Dell 294	49	.25					
Money to burn.	Dell 467	50	.25					

Author/Title	Pub./Stock No.	Yr.	Price

L

LaCAPRIA, RAFFAELE
First affair. — Sig 1223 — 55 — .25

LACKNER, STEPHEN
Discover your self! — Prem s43 — 57 — .35
_____. — Prem d86 — 59 — .50

LACY, ED
Blonde bait. — Zen ZB-18 — 59 — .35
Breathe no more, my lady. — Avon T-253 — 58 — .35
Enter without desire. — Avon 561 — 54 — .25
Go for the body. — Avon 566 — 54 — .25
Lead with your left. — Perm M-3106 — 58 — .25
The men from the boys. — PB 1152 — 57 — .25
Room to swing. — Pyr G353 — 58 — .35
Shakedown for murder. — Avon T-288 — 58 — .35
Sin in their blood. — Eton E111 — 52 — .25
Strip for violence. — Eton E123 — 53 — .25
Visa to death. — Perm M-3036 — 56 — .25
The woman aroused. — Avon 342 — 51 — .25

LA DUE, RUSSELL
Hell-bent with Jake. — Avon 467 — 52 — .25

LA FARGE, OLIVER
Laughing Boy. — Pen 539 — 44 — .25
_____. — PB 764 — 51 — .25
_____. — PBL PL71 — 59 — .35

LA FOUCHARDIÈRE, GEORGES de
Sensualité. — Avon 669 — 55 — .25

LA FRANCE, MARSTON
Miami murder-go-round. — PB 896 — 52 — .25

LAGARD, GARALD
Scarlet Cockerel. — Prmb P144 — 52 — .35

LAING, ALEXANDER
Jonathan Eagle. — Ban F1643 — 57 — .50

LAING, PATRICK
If I should murder. — BH unk — 47 — .25
Stone dead. — BK unk — 46 — .25

LAIRD, CHARLTON
The miracle of language. — Prem d51 — 57 — .50
Thunder on the river. — Ban 827 — 50 — .25
West of the river. — Ban A1603 — 57 — .35

LAIRD, EMMA
Of former love. — Ban A1123 — 53 — .35

LAIT, JACK with Lee Mortimer
Big city after dark. — Dell 400 — 50 — .25
Chicago confidential. — Dell D101 — 52 — .35
New York confidential. — Dell 440 — 50 — .25
_____. — Dell 534 — 51 — .25

Washington confidential. — Dell D108 — 52 — .35

LAKE, ALEXANDER
Killers in Africa. — Prmb P281 — 54 — .35

LAKE, STUART N.
Wyatt Earp, frontier marshal. — Ban A986 — 52 — .35
_____. — Ban F2015 — 59 — .50

LAMB, HAROLD
Alexander of Macedon. — Ban A1353 — 55 — .35
Charlemagne. — BanB FB416 — 58 — .50
Genghis Khan. — Pen 516 — 43 — .25
_____. — Ban 1127 — 53 — .25
_____. — Ban A1382 — 55 — .35
_____. — BanB FB412 — 57 — .50
Omar Khayyam. — Ban A1545 — 56 — .35
Suleiman the Magnificent. — Ban A1234 — 54 — .35
Tamerlane. — Ban A1291 — 55 — .35

LAMBERT, ALICE ELINOR
Hospital nocturne. — Dell 220 — 48 — .25
Women are like that. — Dell 117 — 46 — .25

LAMBERT, JANET
Star spangled summer. — Com 3 — 48 — .25

LAMKIN, SPEED
Fast and loose. — Pop 663 — 55 — .25
Tiger in the garden. — Sig 845 — 51 — .25

LAMONT, NEDDA
The beauty makers. — Pyr G399 — 59 — .35

LA MORLIÈRE, JACQUES ROCHETTE de
The palace of pleasure. — Avon 206 — 49 — .25

LAMOTT, KENNETH
The stockade. — Dell 703 — 53 — .25

L'AMOUR, LOUIS
The burning hills. — Ban 1486 — 56 — .25
Crossfire trail. — Ace D-52 — 54 — .35
The first fast draw. — Ban 1905 — 59 — .25
Guns of the timberlands. — Ban 1390 — 55 — .25
Heller with a gun. — GM 478 — 55 — .25
_____. — GM 728 — 58 — .25
Hondo. — GM 347 — 53 — .25
_____. — GM 905 — 59 — .25
Kilkenny. — Ace S-82 — 54 — .25
Last stand at Papago Wells. — GM 686 — 57 — .25
Radigan. — Ban 1853 — 58 — .25
Silver Canyon. — Ban 1681 — 57 — .25
Sitka. — Ban A1713 — 58 — .35
Taggart. — Ban 1977 — 59 — .25
The tall stranger. — GM 700 — 57 — .25
To tame a land. — GM 516 — 55 — .25
_____. — GM 893 — 59 — .25

Author/Title	Pub./Stock No.	Yr.	Price
LAMPELL, MILLARD			
The hero.	Pop 278	50	.25
LaMURE, PIERRE			
Beyond desire.	Sig D1407	57	.50
Moulin Rouge.	Sig 921AB	52	.50
_____.	Sig D1574	58	.50
LANCASTER, BRUCE			
Bright to the wanderer.	Prmb P266	54	.35
No bugles tonight.	Prmb P234	53	.35
Phantom fortress.	Prmb P149	52	.35
The scarlet patch.	Prmb P196	53	.35
The secret road.	Perm M-3016	55	.25
Trumpet to arms.	Prmb P176	52	.35
Venture in the East.	Prmb P219	53	.35
LAND, MYRICK			
The search.	Dell D315	59	.35
LANDOLF, CHARLES A. with Browning Norton			
I prefer murder.	Graf 132	56	.25
LANDON, JOSEPH			
Angle of attack.	Pop G117	53	.35
Bomber crew.	Avon T-191	57	.35
LANDON, MARGARET			
Anna and the King of			
Siam.	PB 576	49	.25
_____.	Card C-222	56	.35
LANDSBOROUGH, GORDON			
Desert fury.	Ace D-344	59	.35
Tobruk commando.	Avon T-215	58	.35
LANE, FRANK			
Animal wonder world.	Prem s44	57	.35
LANE, JEREMY			
Kill him tonight.	BK unk	47	.25
Murder menagerie.	BH unk	47	.25
LANGDON, JOHN			
Night in Manila.	Pyr 136	54	.25
LANGDON-DAVIES, JOHN			
Seeds of life.	SigK Ks345	57	.35
with Eric J. Dingwall			
The unknown--is it			
nearer?	SigK Ks336	56	.35
LANGENSCHEIDT'S German-			
English, English-German			
dictionary.	Card GC-7	53	.50
LANGER, SUSANNE K.			
Philosophy in a new key.	PelM P25	48	.35
_____.	Ment MD101	55	.50

Author/Title	Pub./Stock No.	Yr.	Price
LANGHAM, JAMES R.			
Sing a song of homicide.	Pop 63	45	.25
LANGLEY, ADRIA LOCKE			
A lion is in the streets.	Ban A815	50	.35
LANGLEY, NOEL			
Cage me a peacock.	Lion unk	51	.25
_____.	Lion LL 71	56	.35
The innocent at large.	Pop 565	54	.25
LANHAM, EDWIN			
Death in the wind.	Perm M-3072	57	.25
Headlined for murder.	Ban 301	48	.25
The iron maiden.	Pop G157	56	.35
Politics is murder.	Ban 746	50	.25
LAO-TZU			
The way of life.	Ment M129	55	.35
LARDNER, RING			
The big town.	Ban 466	49	.25
The love nest.	Sup M646	45	.25
_____.	Ban 145	48	.25
LAREDO, JOHNNY			
Come and get me.	Pop 720	56	.25
LARIAR, LAWRENCE			
The day I died.	Sig 1083	53	.25
Death is confidential.	Hill 125	59	.35
Friday for death.	Avon 289	51	.25
The girl with the			
frightened eyes.	Han 92	49	.25
_____.	Avon 746	56	.25
How green was my sex			
life.	Sig 1261	55	.25
The man with the lumpy			
nose.	Han 38	45	.15
Win, place and die!	Sig 1203	55	.25
You can't catch me.	Pop 448	52	.25
You've got me in			
stitches.	Pop 740	56	.25
LaROCHE, C. J. with J. H. Plenn			
The fastest gun in Texas.	Sig 1312	56	.25
_____.	Sig 1635	59	.25
LaROE, ELSE K.			
Woman surgeon.	Pop SP26	58	.50
LAROM, HENRY V.			
Mountain pony.	PBJr J-40	50	.25
Mountain pony and the			
pinto calf.	PBJr J-65	51	.25
LAROUSSE'S French-English,			
English-French dictionary.	Card GC-24	55	.50

Author/Title	Pub./Stock No.	Yr.	Price
LARRICK, NANCY			
A parent's guide to children's reading.	Card C-314	58	.35
LARRIMORE, LIDA			
Robin Hill.	Dell 119	46	.25
Stars still shine.	Dell 249	48	.25
LASHER, M. H.			
Logging chance.	PBJr J-54	50	.25
LASKY, JESSE L. JR.			
Cry the lonely flesh.	Pop 628	54	.25
LASLY, WALT			
Turn the tigers loose.	Ball 173	56	.35
LATHAM, JOHN H.			
Bad bunch of the Brasada.	Ace D-294	58	.35
Johnny Sixgun.	Ace D-360	59	.35
LATIMER, JONATHAN			
Dark memory.	Prmb P194	53	.35
The dead don't care.	Pop 16	43	.25
The fifth grave.	Pop 301	50	.25
Headed for a hearse.	Dell D196	57	.35
The lady in the morgue.	PB 246	44	.25
Murder in the madhouse.	Pop (4)	43	.25
Sinners and shrouds.	PB 1136	56	.25
LATTIMORE, OWEN			
Ordeal by slander.	Ban 843	51	.25
LAUFERTY, LILIAN			
The hungry house.	Bond 3	46	.25
LAUGHS around the world.	Berk G292	59	.35
LAURENCE, ROSS			
The fast buck.	Ace D-29	53	.35
LAURENCE, SCOTT			
Georgia hotel.	Pyr 68	53	.25
_____.	Pyr G272	57	.35
LAURIE, JOE JR. with Abel Green			
Show biz.	Prmb P217S	53	.50
LAURITZEN, JONREED			
Blade of conquest.	Avon T-76	54	.35
The rose and the flame.	Avon AT-59	53	.35
Suzanne, savage vixen.	Avon T-116	56	.35
LA VANWAY, ED			
Lazy H feud.	Dell 911	56	.25
LAW, M. L.			
Aimée.	Pop G382	59	.35

Author/Title	Pub./Stock No.	Yr.	Price
LAWLER, RAY			
Summer of the seventeenth doll.	Sig S1711	59	.35
LAWRENCE, D. H.			
Aaron's rod.	Avon T-2	54	.35
_____.	Avon G-1025	56	.50
_____.	Avon G-1039	59	.50
The captain's doll.	Berk G-43	56	.35
The first Lady Chatterley.	Avon 238	50	.25
_____.	Avon T-114	55	.35
_____.	Berk BG-150	58	.50
Lady Chatterley's lover.	Pen 610	46	.25
_____.	Sig S1086	53	.35
_____.	Sig D1428	57	.50
_____.	Card C-363	59	.35
_____.	PyrR PR25	59	.50
_____.	Sig D1736	59	.50
Love among the haystacks.	Avon 248	50	.25
_____.	Avon 423	52	.25
_____.	Avon T-163	57	.35
The lovely lady.	Pen 576	46	.25
_____.	Sig S1747	59	.35
A modern lover.	Avon 296	50	.25
_____.	Avon T-218	58	.35
The rainbow.	Avon G-1028	56	.50
_____.	Avon G-1038	59	.50
Sons and lovers.	Sig S1039	53	.35
_____.	Sig D1509	57	.50
The thorn in the flesh.	Berk G-17	56	.35
_____.	Berk G290	59	.35
The virgin and the gypsy.	Avon 98	46	.25
_____.	Avon 449	52	.25
_____.	Avon 587	54	.25
_____.	Berk G-52	57	.35
The woman who rode away.	Berk G-59	57	.35
Women in love.	Avon G-1021	55	.50
LAWRENCE, GIL			
Fury with legs.	Pyr G311	58	.35
The woman racket.	Pyr G468	59	.35
LAWRENCE, HILDA			
Blood upon the snow.	PB 336	46	.25
The deadly pavilion.	PB 492	48	.25
Death of a doll.	PB 540	48	.25
A time to die.	PB 439	47	.25
LAWRENCE, MICHAEL			
Naked and alone.	Pop 488	53	.25
_____.	Pop G354	59	.35
LAWRENCE, STEVEN C.			
Brand of a Texan.	GM 788	58	.25
The naked range.	Ace D-156	56	.35
Saddle justice.	GM 667	57	.25
LAWSON, LARRY			
Blood brand.	Pyr 245	57	.25

Author/Title	Pub./Stock No.	Yr.	Price
LAWSON, LARRY (cont.)			
Naked spurs.	Pyr 325	58	.25
LAWSON, TED W.			
Thirty seconds over Tokyo.	PenS S221	44	.25
LAWTON, S. U. with Jules Archer			
Sexual conduct of the teen-ager.	Berk G-2	55	.35
———.	Berk G-200	59	.35
LAY, BEIRNE JR. with Sy Bartlett			
Twelve o'clock high.	Ban 743	49	.25
LAY, MARGARET REBECCA			
Ceylun.	Lion 32	50	.25
Georgia girl.	Dell 597	52	.25
LEA, FANNY HEASLIP			
Half angel.	Dell 118	46	.25
LEA, TOM			
The brave bulls.	PB 771	51	.25
The wonderful country.	Ban A1190	54	.35
———.	Ban F1956	59	.50
LEACOCK, STEPHEN			
Laugh with Leacock.	PB 396	47	.25
LEARY, FRANCIS			
Fire and morning.	Ace G-352	59	.50
LEASOR, JAMES with Kendal Burt			
The one that got away.	Ball F262	58	.50
LEBHERZ, RICHARD			
Altars of the heart.	Berk G279	59	.35
LEBLANC, MAURICE			
Wanton Venus.	NL 5	48	.25
LECKIE, ROBERT			
Helmet for my pillow.	Ban A1826	58	.35
LECOMTE du NOÜY, PIERRE			
Human destiny.	Sig 746	49	.25
———.	Ment MD165	55	.50
LEDERER, WILLIAM J.			
All the ship's at sea.	PB 763	51	.25
Ensign O'Toole and me.	PB 1218	59	.25
LEE, C. Y.			
The flower drum song.	Dell D241	58	.35
Lover's point.	Dell D285	59	.35
LEE, CAROLINA			
Satan's gal.	Han 102	50	.25
Yaller gal.	Han 84	49	.25

Author/Title	Pub./Stock No.	Yr.	Price
Yaller gal.	Pyr G309	58	.35
LEE, EDNA			
The queen bee.	Ban 848	50	.25
The web of days.	Ban 709	49	.25
LEE, GYPSY ROSE			
The G-string murders.	PB 425	47	.25
———.	Eag EB15	54	.25
———.	Avon T-258	58	.35
Gypsy.	Dell D307	59	.35
Mother finds a body.	Pop 37	44	.25
———.	Pop 547	53	.25
LEE, WAYNE C.			
Broken Wheel Ranch.	Ace D-240	57	.35
LEE, WILLIAM			
Junkie.	Ace D-15	53	.35
LEEMING, JOSEPH			
Fun with puzzles.	Com 34	49	.25
LEEMING, PHIL with Brad Anderson			
Marmaduke.	Pop 795	57	.25
Marmaduke rides again.	Mon 109	59	.35
LEES, HANNAH			
The dark device.	Dell 302	49	.25
Prescription for murder.	Dell 80	45	.25
Woman doctor.	Ban 1432	56	.25
Women will be doctors.	Ban 115	47	.25
with Lawrence Bachmann			
Death in the doll's house.	Dell 122	46	.25
———.	Dell 356	49	.25
LE FANU, JOSEPH S.			
The room in the Dragon Inn.	Avon 702	56	.25
LEHMAN, ERNEST			
The comedian and other stories.	Sig 1446	57	.25
Sweet smell of success.	Sig S1413	57	.35
LEHMAN, PAUL EVAN			
Bandit in black.	Avon 806	58	.25
Blood of the West.	Sig 682	48	.25
———.	Sig 1352	56	.25
Brother of the Kid.	Sig 849	51	.25
Bullets don't bluff.	Ace D-64	54	.35
Calamity range.	Han 77	48	.25
The cold trail.	Han 99	49	.25
Cow kingdom.	HanW 1	47	.20
Faces in the dust.	Graf 47	52	.25
———.	Graf 100	55	.25
Fighting buckaroo.	Avon 759	57	.25
The fighting Texan.	Avon 642	55	.25
Gun-whipped!	Avon 825	58	.25

Author/Title	Pub./Stock No.	Yr.	Price
LEHMAN, PAUL EVAN (cont.)			
The gunhand.	Pyr 194	56	.25
Gunsmoke at Buffalo Basin.	Avon 843	59	.25
Idaho.	Han 87	49	.25
The man from the Badlands.	Avon 845	59	.25
The manhunter.	Avon 850	59	.25
Montana man.	Sig 731	49	.25
_____.	Sig 1258	55	.25
Only the brave.	Han 73	48	.25
Outlaw loot.	Avon 741	56	.25
Outlaws of Lost River.	Berk 356	56	.25
Passion in the dust.	RC 6	49	.25
Pistol law.	Berk 364	56	.25
Pistols on the Pecos.	Avon 540	53	.25
Renegade marshal.	Avon 831	58	.25
Rustlers of the Rio Grande.	Berk 372	57	.25
The siren of Silver Valley.	Han 107	50	.25
Stagecoach to Hellfire Pass.	Eton E128	53	.25
Texas men.	Graf 34	51	.25
_____.	Graf 56	52	.25
Texas vengeance.	Berk 370	57	.25
Thunderbolt range.	Avon 816	58	.25
The tough Texan.	Avon 805	58	.25
The twisted trail.	Berk 332	55	.25
The valley of hunted men.	PenN 666	48	.25
_____.	Sig 1297	56	.25
The vengeance trail.	Avon 715	56	.25
Vengeance Valley.	Han 119	50	.25
Vultures of Paradise Valley.	Graf 39	51	.25
_____.	Graf 66	53	.25
Vultures on horseback.	Ace D-14	53	.35
West of the Wolverine.	HanW 4	47	.20
The young Texan.	Pyr 347	58	.25
LEHMANN, ROSAMOND			
The ballad and the source.	PB 536	48	.25
Invitation to the waltz.	PenN 662	48	.25
LEIBER, FRITZ			
Conjure wife.	Lion 179	53	.25
The green millenium.	Lion LL 7	54	.35
LEIGH, MICHAEL			
Rogue errant.	Prmb P200	53	.35
LEIGHTON, LEE			
Beyond the pass.	Ball 148	56	.35
Law man.	Ball 51	53	.35
Tomahawk.	Ball 255	58	.35
with Chad Merriman Colorado gold.	Ball 282K	58	.35
LEIGHTON, MARGARET			
Comanche of the 7th.	Berk G275	59	.35

Author/Title	Pub./Stock No.	Yr.	Price
LEINSTER, MURRAY			
The brain-stealers.	Ace D-79	54	.35
City on the moon.	Ace D-277	58	.35
The forgotten planet.	Ace D-146	56	.35
Four from Planet 5.	GM s937	59	.35
Gateway to elsewhere.	Ace D-53	54	.35
The monster from world's end.	GM s832	59	.35
Monsters and such.	Avon T-345	59	.35
The mutant weapon.	Ace D-403	59	.35
Operation: outer space.	Sig S1346	57	.35
The other side of here.	Ace D-94	55	.35
The pirates of Zan.	Ace D-403	59	.35
The planet explorer.	Avon T-202	57	.35
Space platform.	PB 920	53	.25
Space tug.	PB 1037	55	.25
War with the Gizmos.	GM s751	58	.35
LEITFRED, ROBERT H.			
The corpse that spoke.	GC unk	46	.25
LEITHEAD, J. EDWARD			
Bloody hoofs.	Ace D-2	52	.35
Bronc buckaroo.	Avon 170	48	.25
_____.	Avon 486	52	.25
The lead-slingers.	Ace D-18	53	.35
LeMAY, ALAN			
Cattle kingdom.	Sig 672	48	.25
_____.	Sig 1219	55	.25
Gunsight trail.	Pop 209	49	.25
_____.	Pop 561	54	.25
_____.	Pop G363	59	.35
Hell for breakfast.	Ban 134	47	.25
Painted ponies.	Pop 261	50	.25
_____.	Pop G267	58	.35
The searchers.	Pop 731	56	.25
Thunder in the dust.	Pop 161	48	.25
_____.	Pop 535	53	.25
_____.	Pop G345	59	.35
The unforgiven.	Crst s244	58	.35
Wild justice.	Ban 253	48	.25
Winter range.	Pop 141	48	.25
_____.	Mon 102	58	.35
LENGYEL, OLGA			
I survived Hitler's ovens.	Avon T-213	58	.35
LENORMAND, H.-R.			
Renée.	Sig 927	52	.25
_____.	Berk G-22	56	.35
_____.	Berk G-168	58	.35
LEOKUM, ARKADY			
Please send me absolutely free!	Pop 366	51	.25
LEONARD, BURGESS			
The thoroughbred and the tramp.	Ace D-374	59	.35

Author/Title	Pub./Stock No.	Yr.	Price
LEONARD, CHARLES			
The stolen squadron.	Pony 57	46	.25
Treachery in Trieste.	Ace D-57	54	.35
LEONARD, ELMORE			
The bounty hunters.	Ball 54	54	.35
Escape from Five Shadows.	Dell 940	57	.25
Last stand at Saber River.	DelF A184	59	.25
The law at Randado.	Dell 863	55	.25
LEONARD, JONATHAN N.			
Flight into space.	SigK Ks317	54	.35
LEONARDO da VINCI with Robert Payne			
The deluge.	Lion 233	55	.25
LEOPOLD, JULES			
Check your wits.	Pop 315	51	.25
LERNER, ALAN JAY			
My fair lady.	Sig S1551	58	.35
LEROUX, GASTON			
The phantom of the opera.	Dell 24	43	.25
LESKE, GOTTFRIED			
I was a Nazi flier.	Dell 21	43	.25
LESLIE, (A.) SCOTT			
Arizona ranger.	Pyr 26	51	.25
The stranger in boots.	Pyr 44	52	.25
	Pyr 204	56	.25
The Texan.	Pyr 61	52	.25
	Pyr 149	55	.25
Tombstone trail.	Pyr 36	51	.25
LESLIE, JEAN			
The man who held five aces.	PB 739	50	.25
LESLIE, WARREN			
The best thing that ever happened.	Sig S1070	53	.35
LESSER, MILTON			
Recruit for Andromeda.	Ace D-358	59	.35
LESSING, DORIS			
The grass is singing.	Ban 1045	52	.25
LESSING, LAWRENCE P.			
Understanding chemistry.	Ment MD276	59	.50
LETERMAN, ELMER G.			
The new art of selling.	Ban F1814	58	.50
LEVANT, OSCAR			
A smattering of ignorance.	Bart 33	46	.25
LEVERIDGE, RALPH			
The last combat.	Pyr G349	58	.35
Walk on the water.	Sig 940	52	.25
LEVEY, ROBERT A.			
Dictators die hard.	Ace D-393	59	.35
Murder in Lima.	Avon 792	57	.25
LEVI, CARLO			
Christ stopped at Eboli.	Pen 656	48	.25
LEVIN, BRAD			
The curse of the Fen.	Ban 157	48	.25
LEVIN, DAN			
Mask of glory.	Pop G103	52	.35
LEVIN, IRA			
A kiss before dying.	Sig 1147	54	.25
LEVIN, MEYER			
Compulsion.	Card GC-756	58	.75
The young lovers.	Sig 911	52	.25
LEVIN, ROBERT			
Five who vanished.	Lion LL 175	57	.35
_____.	Pyr G401	59	.35
LEVINREW, WILL			
The wheelchair corpse.	Bart 14	45	.25
LEVINSON, LEN			
Impossible greeting cards.	Pyr G268	57	.35
LEVINSON, SAUL			
Murder is dangerous.	Han 134	51	.25
LEVY, BERT "YANK"			
Guerrilla warfare.	PenS S203	42	.25
LEWIN, DAVID with Roger B. Goodman			
New ways to greater word power.	DelF 43	55	.25
_____.	DelL LB110	57	.35
LEWIN, LEONARD with Murray Goodman			
My greatest day in football.	Ban 715	49	.25
LEWIN, S. A. with John Gilmore			
Sex after forty.	Dell 761	54	.25
LEWIS, ADA COOK			
Jenny.	Card C-266	57	.35
LEWIS, C. S.			
Out of the silent planet.	Avon 195	49	.25
	Avon T-127	56	.35
Perelandra.	Avon 277	50	.25

Author/Title	Pub./Stock No.	Yr.	Price
LEWIS, C. S. (cont.)			
Perelandra.	Avon T-157	57	.35
The tortured planet.	Avon T-211	58	.35
LEWIS, GITA with Henriette Martin			
The naked eye.	PB 770	51	.25
LEWIS, HERBERT CLYDE			
The silver dark.	Pyr G383	59	.35
LEWIS, HILDA			
The case of the little			
doctor.	Prmb P120	51	.35
LEWIS, KEN			
Look out behind you.	Ace D-247	57	.35
LEWIS, LANGE			
The birthday murder.	Dell 214	48	.25
Juliet dies twice.	Dell 68	44	.25
Meat for murder.	Dell 135	46	.25
Murder among friends.	Bart 36	46	.25
LEWIS, NORMAN			
Word power made easy.	Prmb P209	53	.35
_____.	Perm M-4020	55	.35
with Wilfred Funk			
30 days to a more			
powerful vocabulary.	PB 569	49	.25
LEWIS, SINCLAIR			
Arrowsmith.	PB 162	42	.25
Babbitt.	Ban 22	46	.25
Cass Timberlane.	Ban A893	51	.35
	Ban F1572	57	.50
Dodsworth.	PB 115	41	.25
_____.	Dell F63	57	.50
Elmer Gantry.	Avon (1)	41	.25
_____.	DelL LC119	58	.50
The ghost patrol and			
other stories.	Avon 74	46	.25
Kingsblood royal.	Ban 705	49	.25
_____.	Pop SP50	59	.50
World so wide.	Lion LL 113	56	.35
LEWISOHN, LUDWIG			
Anniversary.	Lion 9	49	.25
Don Juan.	Avon 221	50	.25
For ever wilt thou love.	Sig 749	49	.25
In a summer season.	Sig 1397	57	.25
The sins of Joy Munson.	Lion LL 60	55	.35
The tyranny of sex.	Pen 649	47	.25
_____.	Sig S1363	56	.35
The vehement flame.	Sig 702	49	.25
LEWTON, VAL			
No bed of her own.	NL 39	50	.25
LEY, WILLY			
Satellites, rockets and			
outer space.	SigK Ks360	58	.35

Author/Title	Pub./Stock No.	Yr.	Price
LICHTY, GEORGE			
Grin and bear it.	Dell 872	55	.25
LIDDELL HART, B. H.			
The German generals talk.	Berk BG-135	58	.50
LIEBERMAN, JERRY			
The laff parade.	PB 1144	57	.25
Off the cuff.	PB 1100	56	.25
with Powers Moulton			
Best jokes for all			
occasions.	Perm M-3060	56	.25
LIEBERMAN, WILLIAM S.			
Picasso (blue and rose			
periods).	PBA A20	54	.50
LIEBLING, A. J.			
The telephone booth			
Indian.	Pen 527	44	.25
LIEBMAN, JOSHUA LOTH			
Peace of mind.	Ban A1320	55	.35
LIEF, MAX			
Wild parties.	NL 40	50	.25
with Georges Pichard			
Bachelor's guide to the			
opposite sex.	Avon 815	58	.25
LIEFERANT, HENRY with Sylvia Lieferant			
Dr. Anders' dilemma.	Crst 219	58	.25
Doctor's temptation.	Crst 297	59	.25
LIEFERANT, SYLVIA with Henry Lieferant			
Dr. Anders' dilemma.	Crst 219	58	.25
Doctor's temptation.	Crst 297	59	.25
LILIENTHAL, DAVID E.			
Big business: a new era.	Card C-217	56	.35
TVA: democracy on the			
march.	PB 288	45	.25
LIN YUNG			
A single step.	Ban F1882	59	.50
LIN YUTANG			
Famous Chinese short			
stories.	Card C-36	52	.35
_____.	PBL PL8	54	.35
LINCOLN, ABRAHAM			
The Lincoln reader.	Card GC-23	55	.50
LINCOLN, VICTORIA			
February hill.	Ban 125	47	.25
Out from Eden.	PB 935	53	.25
LINDBERGH, ANNE MORROW			
Gift from the sea.	Sig S1367	57	.35
Listen! The wind.	Dell D182	56	.35

Author/Title	Pub./Stock No.	Yr.	Price
LINDBERGH, ANNE MORROW (cont.)			
The steep ascent.	Dell D171	56	.35
LINDEMAN, EDUARD C. with T. V. Smith			
The democratic way of life.	Ment M59	51	.35
LINDGREN, HENRY CLAY			
How to live with yourself and like it.	Prem d71	58	.50
LINDLAHR, VICTOR H.			
Eat and reduce.	Prmb P7	52	.35
————.	Perm M-4015	55	.35
LINDNER, ROBERT			
The fifty-minute hour.	Ban A1413	56	.35
LINDOP, AUDREY ERSKINE			
The bandit and the priest.	Card C-149	54	.35
Soldiers' daughters never cry.	Pop 328	51	.25
The tormented.	Pop G160	56	.35
LINDSAY, NORMAN			
Age of consent.	PB 539	48	.25
The cautious amorist.	Ban 100	47	.25
————.	Ban 1288	55	.25
LINDSAY, PERRY			
Passionate virgin.	Pyr 11	49	.25
LINDSAY, PHILIP			
An artist in love.	Avon T-112	55	.35
The merry mistress.	Avon T-89	54	.35
————.	Avon T-286	58	.35
The rake's progress.	Avon AT55	53	.35
Royal scandal.	Avon T-110	55	.35
Sir Naked Blade.	Avon T-136	56	.35
To love by candlelight.	Avon T-122	56	.35
LINFORD, DEE			
Man without a star.	Ban A1307	55	.35
LINK, HENRY C.			
The return to religion.	PB 183	42	.25
LINKLATER, JOSEPH			
Odd woman out.	Ace D-285	58	.35
LINKLETTER, ART			
Kids say the darndest things!	Card C-330	59	.35
LINKS, MARTY			
Bobby sox.	Pop 678	55	.25
More Bobby sox.	Eag EB97	57	.25
LINNA, VÄINÖ			
The unknown soldier.	Ace D-293	58	.50
LINSCOTT, ROBERT N.			
Omnibus of American humor.	Pop 170	49	.25
with Belle Becker			
Bedside book of famous French stories.	Dell F57	56	.50
with Saxe Commins			
Man and man: the social philosophers.	PBL PL2	54	.50
Man and spirit: the speculative philosophers.	PBL PL4	54	.50
Man and the state: the political philosophers.	PBL PL1	54	.50
Man and the universe: the philosophers of science.	PBL PL3	54	.50
LIPCHITZ, JACQUES			
Modigliani.	PBA A16	54	.50
LIPMAN, CLAYRE with Michel Lipman			
House of evil.	Lion 231	54	.25
LIPMAN, MICHEL with Clayre Lipman			
House of evil.	Lion 231	54	.25
LIPPMANN, WALTER			
Public opinion.	Pel P1	46	.25
The public philosophy.	Ment M174	56	.35
U.S. foreign policy.	PB 244	43	.25
LIPS, JULIUS E.			
The origin of things.	Prem s33	56	.35
LIPSKY, ELEAZAR			
The hoodlum.	Lion 161	53	.25
The kiss of death.	Pen 642	47	.25
Lincoln McKeever.	Card C-110	54	.35
Murder one.	PB 737	50	.25
The people against O'Hara.	PB 863	52	.25
LITTEN, FREDERIC NELSON			
Kingdom of flying men.	PBJr J-51	50	.25
LITTLE, CONSTANCE with Gwenyth Little			
The black-headed pins.	Pop 83	46	.25
The black shrouds.	Pop 112	47	.25
Great black Kanba.	Dell 181	47	.25
LITTLE, GWENYTH with Constance Little			
The black-headed pins.	Pop 83	46	.25
The black shrouds.	Pop 112	47	.25
Great black Kanba.	Dell 181	47	.25
The LIVING Talmud: the wisdom of the fathers.	Ment MD199	57	.50
LIVINGSTON, HAROLD			
The coasts of the earth.	Ball 66	54	.35

Author/Title	Pub./Stock No.	Yr.	Price
LIVINGSTON, HAROLD (cont.)			
The Detroiters.	Ban F1987	59	.50
LLEWELLYN, RICHARD			
How green was my valley.	PB 462	47	.25
LOCKE, CHARLES O.			
The hell bent kid.	Pop G225	58	.35
The last princess.	Pop 622	54	.25
_____.	Pop G312	59	.35
LOCKE, ROBERT DONALD			
A taste of brass.	DelF A136	57	.25
LOCKRIDGE, FRANCES with Richard Lockridge			
Case of the murdered			
redhead.	Avon 800	57	.25
Curtain for a jester.	Avon 608	54	.25
Dead as a dinosaur.	Avon 535	53	.25
Death has a small voice.	Avon 583	54	.25
Death of a tall man.	Dell 322	49	.25
Death on the aisle.	PB 411	46	.25
Death takes a bow.	Avon 131	48	.25
The dishonest murderer.	Avon 369	51	.25
Hanged for a sheep.	Ban 305	48	.25
A key to death.	Avon 666	55	.25
Killing the goose.	Avon 142	48	.25
Mr. and Mrs. North and			
a pinch of poison.	Avon 502	53	.25
Mr. and Mrs. North and			
the poisoned playboy.	Avon 766	57	.25
Mr. and Mrs. North meet			
murder.	Avon 471	52	.25
Murder comes first.	Avon 434	52	.25
Murder in a hurry.	Avon 484	52	.25
Murder is served.	Avon 363	51	.25
Murder out of turn.	PB 376	47	.25
_____.	Avon 515	53	.25
Murder within murder.	Dell 229	48	.25
The Norths meet murder.	PB 166	42	.25
Payoff for the banker.	PB 501	48	.25
A pinch of poison.	PB 346	46	.25
Stand up and die.	Graf 82	54	.25
Untidy murder.	Avon 242	50	.25
LOCKRIDGE, NORMAN with Virgil Partch			
Sex without tears.	Crst 141	56	.25
LOCKRIDGE, RICHARD with Frances Lockridge			
Case of the murdered			
redhead.	Avon 800	57	.25
Curtain for a jester.	Avon 608	54	.25
Dead as a dinosaur.	Avon 535	53	.25
Death has a small voice.	Avon 583	54	.25
Death of a tall man.	Dell 322	49	.25
Death on the aisle.	PB 411	46	.25
Death takes a bow.	Avon 131	48	.25
The dishonest murderer.	Avon 369	51	.25
Hanged for a sheep.	Ban 305	48	.25
A key to death.	Avon 666	55	.25
Killing the goose.	Avon 142	48	.25
Mr. and Mrs. North and			
a pinch of poison.	Avon 502	53	.25
Mr. and Mrs. North and			
the poisoned playboy.	Avon 766	57	.25
Mr. and Mrs. North meet			
murder.	Avon 471	52	.25
Murder comes first.	Avon 434	52	.25
Murder in a hurry.	Avon 484	52	.25
Murder is served.	Avon 363	51	.25
Murder out of turn.	PB 376	47	.25
_____.	Avon 515	53	.25
Murder within murder.	Dell 229	48	.25
The Norths meet murder.	PB 166	42	.25
Payoff for the banker.	PB 501	48	.25
A pinch of poison.	PB 346	46	.25
Stand up and die.	Graf 82	54	.25
Untidy murder.	Avon 242	50	.25
LOCKRIDGE, ROSS JR.			
Raintree County.	Dell F58	57	.50
LOCKWOOD, SARAH			
The man from Mesabi.	Card C-218	56	.35
LODWICK, JOHN			
Brother Death.	Dell 609	52	.25
LOEWENSTEIN, LEOPOLD with William Gerhardi			
Analyze yourself.	Ban A1493	56	.35
LOFTS, NORAH			
Bless this house.	Card C-214	56	.35
Jassy.	Ban 766	50	.25
The lute player.	Ban A1137	53	.35
Scent of cloves.	Perm M-4127	59	.35
Silver nutmeg.	Prmb P193	53	.35
Winter harvest.	Perm M-4068	57	.35
LOGAN, CAROLYNNE with Malcolm Logan			
One of these seven.	Han 59	47	.20
LOGAN, FORD			
Fire in the desert.	Ball 87	54	.35
LOGAN, MALCOLM with Carolynne Logan			
One of these seven.	Han 59	47	.20
LOMAX, BLISS			
Ambush at Coffin Canyon.	Ace D-56	54	.35
Colt comrades.	PB 809	51	.25
The fight for the			
Sweetwater.	PB 768	51	.25
Guns along the			
Yellowstone.	Dell 724	53	.25
Gunsmoke and trail dust.	Dell 271	49	.25
_____.	Dell 418	50	.25
Honky-tonk woman.	Perm M-3009	55	.25
It happened at Thunder			
River.	Avon 849	59	.25
The law bringers.	Pyr G277	57	.35
The law busters.	Dell 666	53	.25

Author/Title	Pub./Stock No.	Yr.	Price	Author/Title	Pub./Stock No.	Yr.	Price
LOMAX, BLISS (cont.)				**LOOMIS, FREDERIC**			
The loner.	DelF 87	56	.25	Consultation room.	PB 654	50	.25
The Lost Buckaroo.	Dell 581	52	.25				
Mavericks of the plains.	Ace D-22	53	.35	**LOOMIS, NOEL M.**			
Outlaw river.	Ace D-38	53	.35	Above the Palo Duro.	GM 865	59	.25
Pardners of the Badlands.	Avon 156	48	.25	The buscadero.	Ban 1515	56	.25
	Avon 462	52	.25	Cheyenne war cry.	Avon T-368	59	.35
Riders of the buffalo				Johnny Concho.	GM s587	56	.35
grass.	Dell 801	54	.25	The Maricopa trail.	GM s661	57	.35
Rusty guns.	Hill unk	50	.25	North to Texas.	Ball 125	56	.35
Saddle hawks.	Berk 313	55	.25	Rim of the Caprock.	Ban 1132	53	.25
The sagebrush bandit.	Dell 517	51	.25	The twilighters.	Dell 897	56	.25
	Dell 942	57	.25	West to the sun.	GM 485	55	.25
Secret of the wastelands.	Dell 967	58	.25	Wild country.	Pyr G218	56	.35
Stranger with a gun.	Dell 1005	59	.25	with Paul Leslie Peil			
				Hang the men high.	GM 692	57	.25
LONDON, JACK							
Adventures of Captain				**LOOMIS, RAE**			
David Grief.	Pop PC300	57	.25	House of deceit.	Ace S-124	55	.25
The call of the wild.	PB 593	49	.25	Luisita.	Ace S-70	54	.25
Martin Eden.	Pen 587	46	.25		Ace D-396	59	.35
	DelL LC114	58	.50	The Marina Street girls.	Ace D-35	53	.35
The sea-wolf.	PB 325	46	.25		Ace D-341	59	.35
The seed of McCoy.	Pyr G180	56	.35				
Smoke Bellew.	Sig 1120	54	.25	**LOOS, ANITA**			
South sea tales.	Lion 92	52	.25	Gentlemen prefer blondes.	Pop 221	49	.25
				A mouse is born.	Avon 441	52	.25
LONG, AMELIA REYNOLDS							
4 feet in the grave.	Bart 13	45	.25	**LO PINTO, MARIA** with Milo Miloradovich			
Murder by magic.	GD unk	47	.25	The art of Italian			
				cooking.	Ban A1378	55	.35
LONG, FRANK BELKNAP							
Space Station No. 1.	Ace D-242	57	.35	**LORAC, E. C. R.**			
				Checkmate to murder.	Bart 22	46	.25
LONG, MANNING							
Bury the hatchet.	Bart 26	46	.25	**LORAINE, PHILIP**			
				...And to my beloved			
LONG, MARGARET				husband.	PB 912	53	.25
Louisville Saturday.	Ban 931	51	.25	Outside the law.	PB 958	53	.25
	Ban A1848	58	.35				
				LORANT, STEFAN			
LONGFELLOW, HENRY WADSWORTH				The life of Abraham			
Longfellow.	DelL LB132	59	.35	Lincoln.	SigK KD319	55	.50
LONGSTREET, ETHEL with Stephen Longstreet				**LORD, JAMES**			
Man of Montmartre.	Sig D1617	59	.50	The loving and the lost.	Crst s175	57	.35
LONGSTREET, STEPHEN				**LORD, STERLING**			
The beach house.	Pop G125	53	.35	Men and the sea.	Pop 636	55	.25
	Pop G206	57	.35				
The crystal girl.	NL 34	49	.25	**LORD, WALTER**			
The lion at morning.	Ace D-210	57	.35	Day of infamy.	Ban F1715	58	.50
The Pedlocks.	Card C-98	53	.35	A night to remember.	Ban 1539	56	.25
The promoters.	Card C-290	58	.35		Ban 1945	58	.25
Two beds for Roxane.	Avon 406	52	.25				
with Ethel Longstreet				**LORENZ, FREDERICK**			
Man of Montmartre.	Sig D1617	59	.50	Hot.	Lion LB 144	56	.25
				Night never ends.	Lion 193	54	.25
LOOMIS, EDWARD				A party every night.	Lion LL 63	56	.35
End of a war.	Ball 300K	59	.35	A rage at sea.	Lion 152	53	.25

Author/Title	Pub./Stock No.	Yr.	Price
LORENZ, FREDERICK (cont.)			
A rage at sea.	Lion LB 165	57	.25
Ruby.	Lion LL 104	56	.35
The savage chase.	Lion 223	54	.25
LORING, EMILIE			
For all your life.	Ban 1618	57	.25
I take this man.	Ban 1911	58	.25
My dearest love.	Ban 1938	59	.25
What, then, is love.	Ban 1787	58	.25
LOTH, DAVID			
Gold Brick Cassie.	GM 364	54	.25
with Morris L. Ernst			
American sexual behavior			
and the Kinsey report.	Ban 227	48	.25
with Leroy Street			
I was a drug addict.	Pyr 122	54	.25
LOTT, MILTON			
The last hunt.	Card C-203	56	.35
LOUGHLIN, DAVID			
A private stair.	Sig 1172	55	.25
LOUŸS, PIERRE			
Aphrodite.	Avon 113	46	.25
———.	Avon 257	50	.25
———.	Berk G-46	57	.35
———.	Berk G283	59	.35
The collected works of			
Pierre Louÿs.	Avon G1003	51	.50
———.	Avon G-1018	55	.50
Psyche.	Avon 166	48	.25
Woman and the puppet.	Avon 135	47	.25
———.	Avon 358	51	.25
———.	Avon 668	55	.25
LOVE, EDMUND			
Subways are for sleeping.	Sig S1580	58	.35
LOVE around the world.	Berk G-203	59	.35
LOVE in a junk and other			
exotic tales.	Ace D-26	53	.35
LOVECRAFT, H. P.			
Cry horror!	Avon T-284	58	.35
The Dunwich horror.	Bart 12	45	.25
The lurking fear and			
other stories.	Avon 136	47	.25
Weird shadow over			
Innsmouth.	Bart 4	44	.25
LOVELL, B. E.			
A rage to kill.	Ace D-217	57	.35
LOWELL, JULIET			
Dear doctor.	Dell 976	58	.25
Dear Hollywood.	Dell 1001	59	.25
Dear sir.	Avon 318	51	.25
To whom it may concern.	Berk G-123	58	.35
LOWENBERG, MIRIAM E. with Benjamin Spock			
Feeding your baby and			
child.	PB 1106	56	.25
LOWNDES, MARIE BELLOC			
The lodger.	PB 43	40	.25
LOWREY, WALTER			
Summer boy.	Pyr G369	58	.35
LOWRY, ROBERT			
The big cage.	Pop G105	52	.35
———.	Pop SP46	59	.50
Casualty.	Pop 387	51	.25
Find me in fire.	Pop 244	50	.25
———.	Pop G114	54	.35
———.	Pop G395	59	.35
The last party.	Pop 758	56	.25
New York call girl.	Pop G329	59	.35
That kind of woman.	Pyr G430	59	.35
This is my night.	Pop 676	55	.25
The violent wedding.	Pop 570	54	.25
———.	Pop G259	58	.35
What's left of April.	Pop G220	58	.35
The wolf that fed us.	Pop 295	50	.25
LUCAS, CARY			
Unfinished business.	Dell 366	50	.25
LUCAS, CURTIS			
Angel.	Lion 162	53	.25
Lila.	Lion LL 14	55	.35
So low, so lovely.	Lion 91	52	.25
Third ward, Newark.	Lion unk	52	.25
LUCAS, RICK			
Dreamboat.	Berk G-228	59	.35
LUCAS-DUBRETON, J.			
The Borgias.	BanB FB407	56	.50
LUDWIG, EMIL			
Abraham Lincoln.	Prem d34	56	.50
Cleopatra.	BanB FB400	56	.50
———.	BanC FC27	59	.50
Napoleon.	Card GC-11	54	.50
The Son of man.	Prem d55	57	.50
LUMBARD, C. G.			
Kiss the night away.	Pop 640	55	.25
LUND, ROBERT			
The Alaskan.	Ban F1393	55	.50
Hour of glory.	Card C-39	52	.35
LUPTON, LEONARD			
Murder without tears.	Graf 149	57	.25

Author/Title	Pub./Stock No.	Yr.	Price	Author/Title	Pub./Stock No.	Yr.	Price
LURTON, DOUGLAS							
The power of positive living.	Prem s12	55	.35				
———.	Crst s241	58	.35				
LUSTGARTEN, EDGAR							
Blondie Iscariot.	Avon 179	48	.25				
One more unfortunate.	Ban 360	49	.25				
———.	Dell D299	59	.35				
Verdict in dispute.	Ban 861	51	.25				
LUTZ, GILES A.							
Fight or run.	Eag EB12	54	.25				
Fury trail.	Crst 170	57	.25				
The golden bawd.	GM 567	56	.25				
Gun the man down.	Crst 181	57	.25				
The homing bullet.	GM 877	59	.25				
Law of the trigger.	Ace D-408	59	.35				
Outcast gun.	GM 741	58	.25				
Relentless gun.	GM 804	58	.25				
To hell--and Texas.	GM 548	56	.25				
LUZZATTO, JACK							
Pyramid crossword book.	Pyr 221	56	.25				
LYNCH, JAMES C. with Todhunter Ballard							
Showdown.	Pop 476	53	.25				
———.	Pop G335	59	.35				
LYNCH, WILLIAM							
The intimate stranger.	Lion 25	50	.25				
LYNDON, BARRE with Jimmy Sangster							
The man who could cheat death.	Avon T-362	59	.35				
LYON, DANA							
The lost one.	Pyr G393	59	.35				
LYONS, HERBERT							
Front office.	Prmb P229	53	.35				
LYONS, JAMES with John Tasker Howard							
Modern music.	Ment MD212	58	.50				

Author/Title	Pub./Stock No.	Yr.	Price
M			
MAAS, CARL			
How to know and enjoy New York.	PenG G2	49	.35
The Penguin guide to California.	PenG G1	47	.25
MACARDLE, DOROTHY			
The unforeseen.	Ban 915	51	.25
The uninvited.	Ban 90	47	.25
MACAULEY, ROBIE			
The disguises of love.	Sig 1081	53	.25
MacCORMAC, JOHN			
This time for keeps.	Dell 32	43	.25
MacDONALD, BETTY			
The egg and I.	PB 566	49	.25
Onions in the stew.	PB 1119	56	.25
The plague and I.	Ball F356K	59	.50
MacDONALD, JOHN D.			
All these condemned.	GM 420	54	.25
	GM 894	59	.25
April evil.	DelF 85	56	.25
Area of suspicion.	DelF 12	54	.25
The beach girls.	GM s907	59	.35
Border town girl.	Pop 750	56	.25
The brass cupcake.	GM 124	50	.25
	GM 482	55	.25
	GM 792	58	.25
A bullet for Cinderella.	DelF 62	55	.25
Cancel all our vows.	Sig S1131	55	.35
	Sig S1665	59	.35
Clemmie.	GM s777	58	.35
Contrary pleasure.	Pop 697	55	.25
Cry hard, cry fast.	Pop 675	55	.25
	Pop G271	58	.35
The damned.	GM 240	52	.25
	GM 481	55	.25
	GM 724	58	.25
Dead low tide.	GM 298	53	.25
	GM 737	58	.25
Deadly welcome.	DelF B127	59	.35
Death trap.	DelF A130	57	.25
The deceivers.	DelF B117	58	.35
The empty trap.	Pop 830	57	.25
The executioners.	Crst s295	59	.35
Judge me not.	GM 186	51	.25
	GM 782	58	.25
The lethal sex.	DelF B141	59	.35
A man of affairs.	DelF B112	58	.35
Murder for the bride.	GM 164	51	.25
	GM 767	58	.25
Murder in the wind.	DelF A113	56	.25
The neon jungle.	GM 323	53	.25
	GM s790	58	.35
Planet of the dreamers.	PB 943	53	.25
The price of murder.	DelF A152	57	.25
Soft touch.	DelF B121	58	.35
Weep for me.	GM 200	51	.25
	GM 884	59	.25
You live once.	Pop 737	56	.25
MACDONALD, (JOHN) ROSS			
The barbarous coast.	Ban 1613	57	.25
Blue city.	Ban 1839	58	.25
The doomsters.	Ban A2024	59	.35
The drowning pool.	PB 821	51	.25
Find a victim.	Ban 1360	55	.25
Marked for murder.	PB 971	53	.25
Meet me at the morgue.	PB 1020	54	.25
The moving target.	PB 680	50	.25
The name is Archer.	Ban 1295	55	.25
The way some people die.	PB 907	52	.25
MacDONALD, PHILIP			
Harbour.	Bond 13	47	.25
The mystery of the dead police.	PB 70	40	.25
	Dell D247	58	.35
The rasp.	Pen 586	46	.25
The Rynox murder mystery.	Sup M642	44	.25
	Ban 146	48	.25
Warrant for X.	PB 328	45	.25
	Dell D194	57	.35
with A. Boyd Correll			
Sweet and deadly.	Zen ZB-29	59	.35
MacDONALD, WILLIAM COLT			
Ambush at Scorpion Valley.	Avon T-369	59	.35
Bad man's return.	Ace D-2	52	.35
Black sombrero.	Sig 698	48	.25
	Sig 1331	56	.25
Blind cartridges.	Sig 1005	53	.25
Boomtown buccaneers.	Ace D-52	54	.35
California gunman.	Avon 765	57	.25
The Comanche scalp.	Crst 149	56	.25
Cow thief.	Pyr 101	53	.25
The crimson quirt.	Sig 723	49	.25
	Sig 1588	58	.25
Dead man's gold.	Sig 835	50	.25
The deputy of Carabina.	Hill 25	49	.25
Destination, danger.	Crst 134	56	.25
The fighting kid from Eldorado.	Avon 678	55	.25
Flaming lead.	Pyr 231	56	.25
Guns between suns.	Pyr G451	59	.35
Gunsight Range.	Sig 880	51	.25
The killer brand.	Sig 925	52	.25
	Sig 1416	57	.25
King of Crazy River.	Hill unk	50	.25
Law and order, unlimited.	Sig 1168	54	.25
The mad marshal.	Pyr G363	58	.35
Mesquiteer mavericks.	Avon 491	53	.25
The Phantom Pass.	Avon 592	54	.25
	Avon 769	57	.25

Author/Title	Pub./Stock No.	Yr.	Price
MacDONALD, WILLIAM COLT (cont.)			
Powdersmoke range.	Avon 799	57	.25
The range kid.	Pyr 172	55	.25
_____.	Pyr 294	57	.25
Ranger man.	Sig 1059	53	.25
Rebel ranger.	Avon 579	54	.25
The red rider of Smoky Range.	Hill unk	49	.25
The riddle of Ramrod Ridge.	Avon 586	54	.25
Riders of the whistling skull.	Avon 689	56	.25
Ridin' through.	Ace D-216	57	.35
The shadow rider.	Sig 792	50	.25
Showdown trail.	Pyr 95	53	.25
The Singing Scorpion.	Graf 25	50	.25
_____.	Graf 50	52	.25
Six-gun Melody.	Avon 343	51	.25
_____.	Avon 498	53	.25
Six-shooter showdown.	Sig 764	50	.25
_____.	Sig 1181	55	.25
Stir up the dust.	Eton E127	53	.25
Three-Notch Cameron.	Avon 536	53	.25
Thunderbird trail.	Pyr G276	57	.35
The town that God forgot.	Avon T-353	59	.35
Two-gun deputy.	Pyr 115	54	.25
_____.	Pyr 286	57	.25
The vanishing gunslinger.	Avon 514	53	.25
Wheels in the dust.	Hill 31	50	.25
MacDONALD, ZILLAH K.			
Nurse Fairchild's decision.	Ban 1562	57	.25
Marcia, private secretary.	Berk G-159	58	.35
MACDONNELL, J. E.			
Enemy in sight.	Pyr G450	59	.35
MacFADYEN, RALPH			
See without glasses.	Prem d68	58	.50
MacGOWAN, KENNETH			
Famous American plays of the 20's.	DelL LX116	59	.75
MacHARG, WILLIAM			
Smart guy.	Pop 340	51	.25
MACHIAVELLI, NICCOLÒ			
The living thoughts of Machiavelli.	Prem d72	58	.50
The prince.	Ment M69	52	.35
MacINNES, HELEN			
Above suspicion.	PB 186	42	.25
Assignment in Brittany.	PB 235	43	.25
Neither five nor three.	Pop 453	52	.25
North from Rome.	Crst d300	59	.50
MACINTYRE, DONALD			
U-boat killer.	Avon T-205	57	.35
MacISAAC, FRED			
Love on the run.	BPLA 18	40	.10
MacKENZIE, DONALD			
Manhunt.	Pop G245	58	.35
Moment of danger.	Dell D328	59	.35
MACKERSEY, IAN			
Position unknown.	Perm M-4081	57	.35
MacKINNON, ALLAN			
House of darkness.	Dell 237	48	.25
MACKLIN, MACK			
The thin edge of mania.	Ace D-149	56	.35
MacLEAN, ALISTAIR			
The guns of Navarone.	Perm M-4089	58	.35
H.M.S. Ulysses.	Perm M-4067	57	.35
South by Java Head.	Perm M-4116	59	.35
MacLEAN, ROBINSON			
The baited blonde.	Dell 508	51	.25
MacLIESH, FLEMING			
A breed apart.	Sig 1106	54	.25
MacNEIL, NEIL			
Death takes an option.	GM 807	58	.25
Third on a seesaw.	GM s844	59	.35
Two guns for hire.	GM s898	59	.35
MacROSS, ROSS			
The beautiful and dead.	GM 386	54	.25
MacVEIGH, SUE			
Murder under construction.	Hill unk	48	.25
MADELEINE.	Pyr 30	51	.25
_____.	Pyr 175	55	.25
MAETERLINCK, MAURICE			
The life of the bee.	Ment M111	54	.35
MAGER, N. H. with S. K. Mager			
The complete letter writer.	Perm M-4066	57	.35
A guide to better living.	Perm M-4148	59	.35
The office encyclopedia.	Card GC-13	55	.50
The Pocket household encyclopedia.	Card C-90	53	.35
_____.	Card GC-19	54	.50

Author/Title	Pub./Stock No.	Yr.	Price
MAGER, S(YLVIA) K.			
A complete guide to home sewing.	PB 890	52	.35
_____ .	Card C-232	56	.35
with N. H. Mager			
The complete letter writer.	Perm M-4066	57	.35
A guide to better living.	Perm M-4148	59	.35
The office encyclopedia.	Card GC-13	55	.50
The Pocket household encyclopedia.	Card C-90	53	.35
_____ .	Card GC-19	54	.50
MAHANNAH, FLOYD			
The broken angel.	PB 1231	59	.25
The broken body.	Sig 957	52	.25
The golden widow.	Perm M-3087	57	.25
No luck for a lady.	Sig 879	51	.25
_____ .	Sig 1540	58	.25
Stopover for murder.	Sig 1268	56	.25
MAHLER, HELEN A.			
Empress of Byzantium.	Ban A1157	53	.35
MAIER, WILLIAM			
Pleasure Island.	Ban 785	50	.25
MAILER, NORMAN			
Barbary shore.	Sig 1019	53	.25
The deer park.	Sig D1375	57	.50
The naked and the dead.	Sig 837AB	51	.50
_____ .	Sig T1549	58	.75
MAINE, CHARLES ERIC			
High vacuum.	Ball 218	57	.35
The tide went out.	Ball 290K	59	.35
Timeliner.	Ban A1470	56	.35
World without men.	Ace D-274	58	.35
MAINE, CONRAD			
Good-time girl.	Pop 679	55	.25
MAINE, HAROLD			
If a man be mad.	Prmb P156	52	.35
MAJDALANY, FRED			
The Battle of Cassino.	Ball F252	58	.50
Patrol.	Ball 23	53	.35
_____ .	Ball 253	58	.35
MAKRIS, JOHN N.			
Nightshade.	Ace D-21	53	.35
MALACHY, FRANK			
Hot town.	Perm M-3059	56	.25
MALAMUD, BERNARD			
The assistant.	Sig S1514	58	.35
The natural.	Dell 712	53	.25

Author/Title	Pub./Stock No.	Yr.	Price
MALAPARTE, CURZIO			
The skin.	Sig S1098	54	.35
MALCOLM-SMITH, GEORGE			
The grass is always greener.	Ban 410	48	.25
Mugs, molls and Dr. Harvey.	Graf 104	55	.25
The trouble with fidelity.	Dell 999	59	.25
MALLET, FRANCOISE			
The loving and the daring.	Pop 508	53	.25
_____ .	Eag EB84	57	.25
The red room.	Pop G215	58	.35
MALLETTE, GERTRUDE E.			
Mystery in blue.	Berk G-208	58	.35
MALLEY, LOUIS			
Horns for the Devil.	PB 894	52	.25
Shadow of the mafia.	Mon 105	58	.35
Stool pigeon.	Avon 551	53	.25
Tiger in the streets.	Ace D-257	57	.35
MALLOY, FRED			
Devil's holiday.	Berk G-170	58	.35
Wicked woman.	Berk G-185	58	.35
MALO, VINCENT GASPARD			
Murder on the mistral.	Crst s327	59	.35
MALONE, DOROTHY			
Cookbook for beginners.	Ace D-32	53	.35
MALONE, TED			
The Pocket book of modern verse.	PB 308	45	.25
MALTZ, MAXWELL			
Doctor Pygmalion.	Perm M-4107	58	.35
MAN story.	GM 102	50	.25
MANCHESTER, WILLIAM			
Cairo intrigue.	PB 1252	59	.25
The city of anger.	Ball 26	53	.50
MANDEL, GEORGE			
Flee the angry strangers.	Ban F1165	53	.50
MANFRED, FREDERICK			
Lord Grizzly.	Card C-192	55	.35
Riders of judgment.	Card C-301	58	.35
MANKIEWICZ, DON M.			
See how they run.	Sig 947	52	.25
Trial.	Dell D160	56	.35

Author/Title	Pub./Stock No.	Yr.	Price
MANKOWITZ, WOLF			
Old soldiers never die.	Sig 1471	58	.25
MANN, E. B.			
Dead man's gorge.	Lion 27	50	.25
Killer's Range.	PB 694	50	.25
Shootin' Melody.	PB 1194	58	.25
Stampede.	Dell 333	49	.25
Troubled range.	PB 1022	54	.25
The Whistler.	PB 987	54	.25
MANN, HEINRICH			
The blue angel.	Sig S1720	59	.35
MANN, PEGGY			
A room in Paris.	Pop G167	56	.35
MANN, THOMAS			
Buddenbrooks.	Card C-60	52	.50
	Card GC-3	53	.50
Confessions of Felix			
Krull, confidence man.	Sig D1411	57	.50
MANNERS, DAVID X.			
Memory of a scream.	HH unk	47	.25
MANNERS, DORINE			
Sin street.	Pyr 21	50	.25
	Pyr G249	57	.35
MANNERS, MARTIN			
The night it happened.	Pyr G241	57	.35
Town quarry.	Pyr 165	55	.25
MANNERS, WILLIAM			
The big lure.	Lion 165	53	.25
The do-it-yourself gadget			
hunter's guide.	Ban A1392	55	.35
Wharf girl.	Lion 219	54	.25
MANNES, MARYA			
Message from a stranger.	Dell 515	51	.25
MANNIN, ETHEL			
At sundown the tiger.	Pop 438	52	.25
MANNING, LEE			
Season for passion.	Pop 341	51	.25
MANNING, ROY			
Beware of this			
tenderfoot.	Ace D-192	56	.35
The desperado code.	Ace D-20	53	.35
Draw and die!	Ace D-308	58	.35
Renegade ranch.	PB 663	50	.25
Tangled trail.	Ace D-86	54	.35
Vengeance valley.	Ace D-46	54	.35
MANNIX, DANIEL P.			
The beast.	Ball 302K	59	.35
The Hell Fire Club.	Ball 354K	59	.35
Kiboko.	Ace G-402	59	.50
Step right up!	Ban 1006	52	.25
Those about to die.	Ball 275K	58	.35
_____.	Ball 355K	59	.35
MANNIX, JULE			
Eagle in the bathtub.	Ball 348K	59	.35
MANOR, JASON			
The girl in the red			
jaguar.	Eag EB42	55	.25
_____.	Pop G362	59	.35
No halo for me.	Eag EB56	56	.25
Too dead to run.	Perm M-3002	55	.25
The tramplers.	Pop 794	57	.25
MANSON, JOHN			
A fool there was.	Crst s218	58	.35
MANTLEY, JOHN			
The 27th day.	Crst s209	58	.35
Woman obsessed.	Perm M-4146	59	.35
MANUS, WILLARD			
The fixers.	Ace D-232	57	.35
MARA, BERNARD			
A bullet for my lady.	GM 472	55	.25
French for murder.	GM 402	54	.25
This gun for Gloria.	GM 562	56	.25
MARAIS, CLAUDE			
Saskia.	Lion 116	52	.25
MARBLE, M. S.			
Die by night.	Graf 102	55	.25
MARCH, WILLIAM			
The bad seed.	Dell 847	55	.25
Company K.	Lion 111	52	.25
_____.	Lion LB 62	55	.25
_____.	Sig S1522	58	.35
Desire and damnation.	Lion LL 121	56	.50
The looking glass.	Ban A1084	53	.35
My brother's bride.	Pyr R367	58	.50
MARCHAL, LUCIE			
The mesh.	Ban 862	51	.25
_____.	Ban A1923	59	.35
MARCUS, A. A.			
Make way for murder.	Graf 115	55	.25
Post-mark homicide.	Graf 67	53	.25
Walk the bloody			
boulevard.	Graf 35	51	.25
_____.	Graf 64	53	.25
The widow gay.	Graf 21	50	.25
MARCUS, ALAN			
The vanquished.	Pop 422	52	.25

Author/Title	Pub./Stock No.	Yr.	Price
MARCUS, MARGARET FAIRBANKS			
Flower painting by the great masters.	PBA A24	55	.50
MARCUS, PAUL with Harry Bennett			
We never called him Henry.	GM 185	51	.25
MARESCA, JAMES			
Mr. Taxicab.	Ban 1756	58	.25
My flag is down.	Ban 419	49	.25
_____.	Ban 1471	56	.25
MARGE			
This is little Lulu.	DelF A125	56	.25
MARGOLIUS, SIDNEY			
The consumer's guide to better buying.	Sig 859	51	.25
_____.	Sig S1055	53	.35
It's your money--come and get it.	GM 191	51	.25
Your guide to financial security.	SigK Ks325	55	.35
MARGULIES, LEO			
Bad girls.	Crst s254	58	.35
Gone to Texas.	Pyr G244	57	.35
Popular book of western stories.	Pop 156	48	.25
Selected western stories.	Pop 187	49	.25
Three from out there.	Crst s282	59	.35
Three times infinity.	GM s726	58	.35
Young and deadly.	Crst s272	59	.35
The young punks.	Pyr G271	57	.35
_____.	Pyr G386	59	.35
with Oscar J. Friend			
My best science fiction story.	PB 1007	54	.25
Race to the stars.	Crst s245	58	.35
MARINO, NICK			
City limits.	Pyr G315	58	.35
One way street.	Pyr 65	52	.25
_____.	Pyr 159	55	.25
MARIO, QUEENA			
Murder meets Mephisto.	Bart 11	45	.25
MARITAIN, JACQUES			
Rouault.	PBA A14	54	.50
MARK, DAVID			
Long shot.	Dell D300	59	.35
MARK, EDWINA			
My sister, my beloved.	Berk G-44	57	.35
_____.	Berk G-141	58	.35
The odd ones.	Berk G245	59	.35
The sinful one.	Hill 121	59	.35
MARKANDAYA, KAMALA			
Nectar in a sieve.	Sig S1336	56	.35
Some inner fury.	Sig S1532	58	.35
MARKEL, ROBERT with Frank Canizio			
A man against fate.	Perm M-4133	59	.35
MARKEY, GENE			
Kentucky pride.	Perm M-4078	57	.35
Kingdom of the spur.	Ball 18	53	.35
MARKEY, MORRIS			
Unhurrying chase.	Pony 53	46	.25
MARKHAM, VIRGIL			
The devil drives.	Bart 10	44	.25
MARKOWITZ, ARTHUR			
The daughter.	Sig 886	51	.25
_____.	Pyr G295	57	.35
MARKSON, DAVID			
Epitaph for a tramp.	DelF A193	59	.25
MARLOWE, CHRISTOPHER			
Doctor Faustus.	WSP W100	59	.35
MARLOWE, DAN			
Doorway to death.	Avon T-307	59	.35
Killer with a key.	Avon T-349	59	.35
MARLOWE, STEPHEN			
Blonde bait.	Avon T-330	59	.35
Catch the brass ring.	Ace D-77	54	.35
Dead on arrival.	Ace D-189	56	.35
Homicide is my game.	GM 880	59	.25
Killers are my meat.	GM 693	57	.25
Mecca for murder.	GM 575	56	.25
Model for murder.	Graf 94	55	.25
Murder is my dish.	GM 658	57	.25
Passport to peril.	Crst 296	59	.25
The second longest night.	GM 523	55	.25
Terror is my trade.	GM 813	58	.25
Trouble is my name.	GM 627	57	.25
_____.	GM 914	59	.25
Turn left for murder.	Ace D-89	55	.35
Violence is my business.	GM 769	58	.25
with Richard S. Prather			
Double in trouble.	GM d926	59	.50
MARQUAND, JOHN P.			
B.F.'s daughter.	Ban A919	51	.35
H. M. Pulham, Esq.	Ban A805	50	.35
_____.	Ban F1675	57	.50
The late George Apley.	PB 258	44	.25
Life at Happy Knoll.	Ban A1781	58	.35
Melville Goodwin, USA.	Ban F1200	54	.50
Point of no return.	Ban A987	52	.35
_____.	Ban F1454	56	.50
Repent in haste.	Ban 881	51	.25

Author/Title	Pub./Stock No.	Yr.	Price	Author/Title	Pub./Stock No.	Yr.	Price
MARQUAND, JOHN P. (cont.)				Forlorn island.	Dell 364	49	.25
Sincerely, Willis Wayde.	Ban F1453	56	.50	The gentleman.	Card C-233	57	.35
So little time.	Ban F1087	53	.50	The great Smith.	Dell D102	52	.35
Stopover: Tokyo.	Ban A1690	57	.35	Gypsy sixpence.	Dell D103	52	.35
Sun, sea and sand.	DelT 13	51	.10	The infinite woman.	Dell D122	53	.35
Thank you, Mr. Moto.	Ban A1691	57	.35	Jungle hunting thrills.	Dell 468	50	.25
Think fast, Mr. Moto.	PB 59	40	.25	Love stories of India.	Dell 530	51	.25
_____.	Ban 1810	58	.25	Riders of the smoky land.	Pop 242	50	.25
Women and Thomas Harrow.	Ban S2013	59	.75	Splendid quest.	Dell 188	47	.25
				Trail's end.	Pop 272	50	.25
MARR, REED				The upstart.	Dell 233	48	.25
Catch a falling star.	GM 576	56	.25	_____.	Dell 341	49	.25
Women without men.	GM 638	57	.25	_____.	Dell F72	59	.50
				The viking.	Dell D139	54	.35
MARRIC, J. J.				_____.	Dell F67	58	.50
Gideon of Scotland Yard.	Berk G-122	58	.35	The voice of the pack.	Pop 128	47	.25
Gideon's month.	Berk G278	59	.35	The white brigand.	Dell 144	47	.25
Gideon's night.	Pyr G335	58	.35	Yankee pasha.	Dell 353	49	.25
Seven days to death.	Pyr G323	58	.35	_____.	Dell 422	50	.25
				_____.	Dell F87	59	.50
MARSH, NGAIO							
Colour scheme.	PB 351	46	.25	MARSHALL, MARGUERITE MOOERS			
Death and the dancing				Her soul to keep.	Ban 1645	57	.25
footman.	PB 437	47	.25	Nurse into woman.	Ban 464	48	.25
Death at the bar.	PB 297	45	.25	Nurse with wings.	Ban 1575	57	.25
Death in a white tie.	PB 137	42	.25	Ward nurse.	Ban 1434	56	.25
Death of a fool.	Avon T-254	58	.35	Wilderness nurse.	PB 746	50	.25
Death of a peer.	PB 475	47	.25				
Died in the wool.	PB 626	49	.25	MARSHALL, ROSAMOND			
Enter a murderer.	PB 113	41	.25	The Bixby girls.	Perm M-4114	59	.35
Final curtain.	PB 527	48	.25	Bond of the flesh.	Pop 527	53	.25
Night at the Vulcan.	Sig 995	53	.25	_____.	Pop G219	58	.35
Overture to death.	PB 221	43	.25	Captain Ironhand.	Ban A1724	58	.35
Swing, brother, swing.	PB 762	51	.25	Celeste.	Dell 382	50	.25
				_____.	Pyr G201	56	.35
MARSH, PETER				_____.	Pyr G428	59	.35
The devil's daughter.	Lion 16	50	.25	Duchess Hotspur.	Egle E3	47	.25
				_____.	Sig S1517	58	.35
MARSH, RONALD				The general's wench.	Sig 1163	55	.25
Irene.	Ban 778	50	.25	Kitty.	PB 469	47	.25
_____.	Ban A2009	59	.35	_____.	Sig 1190	55	.25
				Laird's choice.	Sig 923	52	.25
MARSHACK, ALEXANDER				Mistress of rogues.	Pop 717	56	.25
The world in space.	DelL LB111	58	.35	The rib of the Hawk.	Pop G258	58	.35
				Rogue Cavalier.	Pop G176	57	.35
MARSHALL, BRUCE				The temptress.	Sig 976	52	.25
Father Malachy's miracle.	PB 435	47	.25				
The white rabbit.	Prmb P275	54	.35	MARSHALL, S. L. A.			
The world, the flesh and				Island victory.	PenS S240	44	.25
Father Smith.	Ban 84	47	.25	Pork Chop Hill.	Perm M-4115	59	.35
MARSHALL, EDISON				MARSHE, RICHARD			
American captain.	Card C-194	55	.35	Passion in Panama.	Berk G-196	58	.35
Benjamin Blake.	Dell 431	50	.25	A woman called desire.	Berk G236	59	.35
_____.	Dell D173	56	.35				
Bullets at Clearwater.	Pop 345	51	.25	MARSTEN, RICHARD			
Caravan to Xanadu.	Dell D157	55	.35	Big man.	PB 1235	59	.25
Castle in the swamp.	Dell 487	51	.25	Even the wicked.	Perm M-3117	58	.25
_____.	Dell D119	53	.35	Murder in the Navy.	GM 507	55	.25
The deputy at Snow				Runaway black.	GM 415	54	.25
Mountain.	Pop 208	49	.25	So nude, so dead.	Crst 139	56	.25

Author/Title	Pub./Stock No.	Yr.	Price
MARSTEN, RICHARD (cont.)			
The spiked heel.	Crst s178	57	.35
Vanishing ladies.	Perm M-3097	57	.25
MARTIN, A. E.			
The bridal bed murders.	Dell 840	55	.25
MARTIN, AYLWIN LEE			
The crimson frame.	GM 253	52	.25
Death for a hussy.	Graf 45	52	.25
Death on a ferris wheel.	GM 170	51	.25
Fear comes calling.	GM 214	52	.25
MARTIN, CHARLES M. or CHUCK			
Bloody Kansas.	Avon 654	55	.25
———.	Avon 863	59	.25
Box star buckaroo.	Berk G247	59	.35
Day of vengeance.	Avon 841	59	.25
Law for Tombstone.	Ace D-42	54	.35
Law from back beyond.	Ace D-46	54	.35
Lost river buckaroos.	Chek 4	49	.15
Montana dead-shot.	Avon 822	58	.25
Sixgun helltown.	Hill 122	59	.35
Tall in the saddle.	Avon 828	58	.25
Texas pride.	Graf 86	54	.25
Two-gun fury.	Graf 74	54	.25
———.	Graf 128	56	.25
Vengeance trail.	Dmnd D2011	59	.35
MARTIN, DON			
Blonde menace.	RC 4	49	.25
MARTIN, GEORGE VICTOR			
The bells of St. Mary's.	Ban 103	47	.25
———.	Ban 1595	57	.25
The evil that men do.	Berk G-162	58	.35
The lady said yes.	NL 35	49	.25
Mark it with a stone.	Eton E120	53	.25
MARTIN, HANSFORD			
Send them summer.	Avon T-88	54	.35
Soldier's weekend.	Avon T-206	57	.35
MARTIN, HENRIETTE with Gita Lewis			
The naked eye.	PB 770	51	.25
MARTIN, JOHN BARTLOW			
Break down the walls.	Ball F77	54	.50
Butcher's dozen.	Sig 909	52	.25
The Deep South says never.	Ball 220	57	.35
Jimmy Hoffa's hot.	Crst 340	59	.25
My life in crime.	Sig 1033	53	.25
Why did they kill?	Ball 14	53	.35
MARTIN, PETE			
Hollywood without makeup.	Ban 721	49	.25
Will acting spoil Marilyn Monroe?	Card C-248	57	.35
with Diane Disney Miller			
The story of Walt Disney.	Dell D266	59	.35

Author/Title	Pub./Stock No.	Yr.	Price
with Eleanor "Bumpy" Stevenson			
I knew your soldier.	PenS S230	45	.25
MARTIN, ROBERT			
Dark dream.	PB 913	53	.25
Sleep, my love.	Dell 794	54	.25
Tears for the bride.	Ban 1372	55	.25
The tough die hard.	Ban 1577	57	.25
The widow and the web.	Ban 1397	55	.25
MARTIN du GARD, ROGER			
The postman.	Berk 342	55	.25
	Berk G-194	58	.35
MARVIN, H. M.			
You and your heart.	Sig 1008	53	.25
———.	SigK KD356	57	.50
MASIN, HERMAN L.			
Curve ball laughs.	Lion LL 29	55	.35
———.	Pyr G331	58	.35
Great sports stories.	Berk G-89	57	.35
Sports laughs.	Lion LL 103	56	.35
———.	PyrR PG18	58	.35
MASON, AGNES LECKIE with Phyllis Brown Ohanian			
God's wonderful world.	SigK KD315	54	.50
MASON, (F.) van WYCK			
The barbarians.	PB 1024	54	.25
Blue hurricane.	Card C-211	56	.35
Captain Judas.	PB 1076	55	.25
Captain Nemesis.	PB 1176	57	.25
The China Sea murders.	PB 1219	59	.25
Cutlass empire.	Card C-4	51	.35
Dardanelles derelict.	PB 799	51	.25
Eagle in the sky.	Card GC-9	53	.50
Golden Admiral.	Card C-165	55	.35
The Gracious Lily affair.	PB 1223	58	.25
Himalayan assignment.	PB 929	53	.25
Lysander.	PB 1143	57	.25
Our valiant few.	Ban F1744	58	.50
Proud new flags.	Card GC-17	54	.50
Return of the eagles.	Card C-365	59	.35
Rivers of glory.	Card C-23	52	.35
Saigon singer.	Ban 311	48	.25
Silver leopard.	Card C-242	57	.35
The Singapore exile murders.	PB 129	41	.25
Spider house.	Han 98	49	.25
Stars on the sea.	Card GC-6	53	.50
The Sulu Sea murders.	PB 1201	58	.25
Three harbours.	Card C-57	52	.50
———.	Card GC-2	53	.50
Two tickets for Tangier.	PB 1115	56	.25
Wild drums beat.	PB 977	54	.25
MASON, GREGORY with Richard Carroll			
Border woman.	Lion 59	51	.25

Author/Title	Pub./Stock No.	Yr.	Price
MASON, RAYMOND			
And two shall meet.	GM 395	54	.25
Forever is today.	GM 468	55	.25
Love after five.	GM 589	56	.25
Far from home.	Ban A1003	52	.35
The shadow and the peak.	Sig D1641	59	.50
The wind cannot read.	Ban A1779	58	.35
The world of Suzie Wong.	Sig D1552	58	.50
MASON, SARA ELIZABETH			
The crimson feather.	Dell 207	48	.25
The whip.	Ban 770	50	.25
MASSIE, CHRIS			
The incredible truth.	Berk G256	59	.35
The love letters.	Ban 54	46	.25
MASSON, RENÉ			
Cage of darkness.	Ban 1054	52	.25
MASTERS, JOHN			
Bhowani Junction.	Ban F1381	55	.50
Bugles and a tiger.	Ban F1714	58	.50
Coromandel!	Ban F1416	56	.50
The deceivers.	Ban 1187	54	.25
Far, far the mountain peak.	Ban F1805	58	.50
The lotus and the wind.	Ban A1335	55	.35
Nightrunners of Bengal.	Ban A1072	53	.35
MASTERSON, WHIT			
A cry in the night.	Ban 1487	56	.25
Dead, she was beautiful.	Ban 1543	56	.25
Touch of evil.	Ban A1699	58	.35
MASUR, HAROLD Q.			
The big money.	Dell 874	55	.25
Bury me deep.	PB 558	48	.25
_____.	Dell 944	57	.25
Dolls are murder.	Lion LB 152	57	.25
Murder on Broadway.	Dell D298	59	.35
So rich, so lovely, and so dead.	PB 998	54	.25
Suddenly a corpse.	PB 704	50	.25
_____.	Dell D250	58	.35
Tall, dark and deadly.	Dell D232	58	.35
You can't live forever.	PB 860	52	.25
_____.	Dell D329	59	.35
MATCHA, JACK			
Prowler in the night.	GM 873	59	.25
MATHERS, EDWARD POWYS			
Chinese love tales.	Avon 682	55	.25
Eastern love.	Crst d199	58	.50
MATHESON, RICHARD			
Fury on Sunday.	Lion 180	53	.25
I am legend.	GM 417	54	.25
_____.	GM 643	57	.25
Ride the nightmare.	Ball 301K	59	.35
The shores of space.	Ban A1571	57	.35
The shrinking man.	GM s577	56	.35
Someone is bleeding.	Lion 137	53	.25
A stir of echoes.	Crst s308	59	.35
Third from the sun.	Ban 1294	55	.25
MATSON, NORMAN			
Bats in the belfry.	Pop 200	49	.25
MATTERSDORF, LEO			
A key to the heavens.	Prem s27	56	.35
MATTHEWS, ALLEN R.			
The assault.	Prmb 258	53	.25
_____.	PB 1207	58	.25
MATTHEWS, JOHN D. with Jeffrey Roche			
My name is violence.	Avon 847	59	.25
MATTHEWS, JOHN F.			
El Greco.	PBA A2	53	.50
MATTHEWS, KEVIN			
Barbary slave.	Eag EB54	55	.25
Tory mistress.	Eag EB78	56	.25
Woman of Egypt.	Pop G293	58	.35
MATTHEWS, T. S.			
Darling, I hate you.	Pop 514	53	.25
MATTHIESSEN, PETER			
The passionate seekers.	Avon 753	57	.25
The year of the tempest.	Ban A1578	57	.35
MAUGHAM, ROBIN			
The jungle of love.	Avon 695	56	.25
Line on Ginger.	Avon 333	51	.25
The rough and the smooth.	Avon 464	52	.25
The servant.	Avon 233	50	.25
_____.	Avon 428	52	.25
MAUGHAM, W. SOMERSET			
Ah king.	Berk BG-149	58	.50
Ashenden, or the British agent.	Avon (24)	43	.25
_____.	Avon T-119	56	.35
The Avon book of W. Somerset Maugham.	Avon 115	46	.25
The beachcomber.	DelT 16	51	.10
Cakes and ale.	Avon 50	44	.25
_____.	PB 1158	57	.25
Cakes and ale and other favorites.	Card C-19	51	.35
Catalina.	Ban 852	51	.25
Cosmopolitans.	Berk G268	59	.35
Favorite stories.	Bard 4	55	.35
First person singular.	Berk BG-213	59	.50
Fools and their folly.	Avon 188	49	.25
The gentleman in the parlour.	Avon 129	47	.25

Author/Title	Pub./Stock No.	Yr.	Price
MAUGHAM, W. SOMERSET (cont.)			
Liza of Lambeth.	Avon 139	47	.25
The magician.	Card C-273	58	.35
The moon and sixpence.	Ban 810	50	.25
———.	Ban A1339	55	.35
	BanC AC25	59	.35
Mrs. Craddock.	Dell D106	52	.35
	Dell D176	56	.35
The narrow corner.	Avon 41	44	.25
	Ban 909	51	.25
———.	Ban A1931	59	.35
Of human bondage.	PB 700	50	.25
	Card C-63	52	.35
The painted veil.	PB 581	49	.25
	Card C-261	57	.35
The point of honour.	Avon 364	51	.25
Quartet.	Avon 203	49	.25
Rain.	DelT 2	51	.10
The razor's edge.	PB 418	46	.25
———.	Card C-161	55	.35
The Somerset Maugham Pocket book.	PB 262	44	.25
South sea stories.	Perm M-4056	56	.35
Stranger in Paris.	Ban 423	49	.25
	Ban A1399	55	.35
The summing up.	Pen 597	46	.25
———.	Ment M60	51	.35
	Ment MD203	57	.50
Theatre.	Avon 56	44	.25
———.	Ban A1930	59	.35
Trio.	Avon 331	51	.25
Up at the villa.	Ban 136	47	.25
	Ban 1489	56	.25
———.	Ban 949	51	.25
Woman of the world.	Ban 949	51	.25
The world's ten greatest novels.	Prem s30	56	.35
———.	Crst d276	59	.50
MAUGHAN, A. M.			
Harry of Monmouth.	Ban F1604	57	.50
MAULDIN, BILL			
Back home.	Ban 461	48	.25
A sort of a saga.	Ban 855	51	.25
Up front.	Ban 83	47	.25
MAULE, HARRY E.			
The Pocket book of western stories.	PB 293	45	.25
MAUND, ALFRED			
The big boxcar.	Ball 250	58	.35
MAUPASSANT, GUY de			
Great short stories.	PB 12	39	.25
	PBL PL29	55	.35
The house of Madame Tellier.	Pyr 41	51	.25
	Pyr R202	56	.35
Mademoiselle Fifi and other stories.	Avon 459	52	.25
Maupassant.	DelL LC135	59	.50
The private affairs of Bel Ami.	Avon 87	46	.25
A woman's heart.	Avon 175	48	.25
A woman's life.	Lion LL 2	54	.35
Yvette and other stories.	Avon 198	49	.25
MAURER, DAVID W.			
The big con.	PB 618	49	.25
MAURETTE, MARCELLE			
Anastasia.	Sig S1356	56	.35
MAURIAC, FRANCOIS			
The desert of love.	Ban 1039	52	.25
MAUROIS, ANDRÉ			
Woman without love.	Pyr R232	56	.35
MAWSON, CHRISTOPHER with Katharine Whiting			
Roget's Pocket thesaurus.	PB 383	46	.25
———.	Card C-13	51	.35
MAXFIELD, HENRY S.			
Legacy of a spy.	Crst s288	59	.35
MAXON, P. B.			
The waltz of death.	Bart 9	44	.25
MAY, DANIEL			
Armande.	GM 875	59	.25
MAYER, MARTIN			
Governor's choice.	PB 1110	56	.25
Madison Avenue, U.S.A.	Card GC-66	59	.50
MAYFIELD, JULIAN			
The hit.	PB 1229	59	.25
The long night.	Pyr G461	59	.35
MAYO, JIM			
Showdown at Yellow Butte.	Ace D-38	53	.35
Utah Blaine.	Ace D-48	54	.35
MAYSE, ARTHUR			
Perilous passage.	PB 727	50	.25
McALLISTER, ROBERT with Floyd Miller			
The kind of guy I am.	Pop G252	58	.35
McBAIN, ED			
The con man.	Perm M-3055	57	.25
Cop hater.	Perm M-3037	56	.25
Killer's choice.	Perm M-3108	58	.25
Killer's payoff.	Perm M-3113	58	.25
Killer's wedge.	Perm M-4150	59	.35
Lady killer.	Perm M-3119	58	.25
The mugger.	Perm M-3061	56	.25
The pusher.	Perm M-3062	56	.25
with Craig Rice			
The April robin murders.	Dell D306	59	.35

Author/Title	Pub./Stock No.	Yr.	Price
McCAGUE, JAMES			
The Big Ivy.	Ace D-184	56	.35
McCAIG, ROBERT			
Danger West!	Dell 884	56	.25
Haywire town.	Ban 1435	56	.25
The rangemaster.	Ace D-320	58	.35
Toll mountain.	Pnnt P53	54	.25
McCALL, JEFFERSON			
Brother Buffalo.	Ball 156	56	.35
An Indian's tale.	Ball 79	54	.35
McCARTHY, JUSTIN			
Brother Juniper.	PB 1242	59	.25
McCARTHY, MARY			
A charmed life.	Dell D214	58	.35
The company she keeps.	Dell 824	55	.25
_____.	Dell D184	56	.35
McCARY, REED			
Kiss and kill.	Avon 777	57	.25
McCAULEY, ELFRIEDA with Leon McCauley			
The book of prayers.	DelF 38	54	.25
McCAULEY, LEON			
A treasury of faith.	DelF B106	57	.35
with Elfrieda McCauley			
The book of prayers.	DelF 38	54	.25
McCLARY, THOMAS CALVERT			
Rebirth.	Bart 6	44	.25
3,000 years.	Ace D-176	56	.35
McCLINTOCK, MARSHALL			
How to build and operate a model railroad.	DelF D72	55	.35
Women on the wall.	Pyr 118	54	.25
McCLOY, HELEN			
Better off dead.	DelT unk	51	.10
Cue for murder.	Dell 212	48	.25
Dance of death.	Dell 33	44	.25
The deadly truth.	Dell 107	46	.25
Do not disturb.	Dell 261	48	.25
The goblin market.	Dell 295	49	.25
The man in the moonlight.	Dell 72	45	.25
The one that got away.	Dell 355	49	.25
Panic.	Dell 369	50	.25
She walks alone.	Dell 430	50	.25
Through a glass, darkly.	Dell 519	51	.25
Two-thirds of a ghost.	Dell D228	58	.35
Unfinished crime.	Graf 113	55	.25
Who's calling?	Dell 151	47	.25
McCOMAS, J. FRANCIS with Raymond J. Healy			
Adventures in time and space.	Pnnt P44	54	.25
More adventures in time and space.	Ban 1310	55	.25
McCONNAUGHEY, JAMES			
Three for the money.	PB 1050	55	.25
McCONNAUGHEY, SUSANNE			
Pagan in paradise.	Ban 1398	55	.25
Point Venus.	Pop G112	52	.35
McCORD, DAVID			
The Pocket book of humorous verse.	PB 388	46	.25
McCORMICK, CHARLES P.			
The power of people.	Ban A-5	52	.25
McCOY, HORACE			
Corruption city.	DelF A188	59	.25
I should have stayed home.	Sig 884	51	.25
_____.	Berk 328	55	.25
_____.	Berk G-134	58	.35
Kiss tomorrow good-bye.	Sig 754	49	.25
No pockets in a shroud.	Sig 690	48	.25
Scalpel.	Sig S1017	53	.35
They shoot horses, don't they?	PenN 670	48	.25
_____.	Berk 108	55	.25
McCOY, JOHN PLEASANT			
Big as life.	PB 802	51	.25
Love for a stranger.	Avon 601	54	.25
_____.	Avon T-350	59	.35
Swing the big-eyed rabbit.	Prmb P227	53	.35
McCULLERS, CARSON			
Ballad of the sad café.	Ban F1764	58	.50
The heart is a lonely hunter.	Pen 596	46	.25
_____.	Ban A1091	53	.35
_____.	Ban F1762	58	.50
The member of the wedding.	Ban 822	50	.25
_____.	Ban F1761	58	.50
Reflections in a golden eye.	Ban 821	50	.25
_____.	Ban A1156	53	.35
_____.	Ban F1763	58	.50
Seven.	Ban A1235	54	.35
McCULLEY, JOHNSTON			
Blood on the saddle.	Avon 795	57	.25
Bullet law.	Avon 856	59	.25
The caballero.	Sig 669	48	.25
_____.	Sig 1632	59	.25
Gold of Smoky Mesa.	Sig 704	49	.25
Gunman's gold.	Pyr 187	56	.25
Gunsight showdown.	Avon 748	56	.25

Author/Title	Pub./Stock No.	Yr.	Price
McCULLEY, JOHNSTON (cont.)			
Gunsmoke vengeance.	Avon 779	57	.25
The mark of Zorro.	Dell 553	51	.25
_____.	Dell D204	58	.35
McDERMOTT, C. L.			
A Yank on Piccadilly.	Pop 417	52	.25
McDONALD, N. C.			
Fish the strong waters.	Ball 175	56	.35
Witch doctor.	Ball 312K	59	.35
McDONELL, GORDON			
My sister, goodnight.	Ban 795	50	.25
McDOUGALD, R.			
The deaths of Lora Karen.	Bart 17	45	.25
McDOWELL, EMMETT			
Stamped for death.	Ace D-329	58	.35
Switcheroo.	Ace D-51	54	.35
Three for the gallows.	Ace D-329	58	.35
McELFRESH, ADELINE			
Calling Doctor Jane.	Ban 1776	58	.25
Doctor Jane.	Ban 1498	56	.25
Hill country nurse.	Ban 1951	59	.25
Kay Manion, M.D.	DelF A187	59	.25
Nurse Kathy.	Perm M-3099	58	.25
Young Doctor Randall.	Ban 1929	59	.25
McFEATTERS, DALE			
Strictly business.	Berk 349	56	.25
McFEE, WILLIAM			
Great sea stories of modern times.	Graf G207	54	.35
McGERR, PAT			
Follow, as the night.	Dell 612	52	.25
Pick your victim.	Dell 307	49	.25
Seven deadly sisters.	Dell 412	50	.25
McGIVERN, WILLIAM P.			
The big heat.	PB 981	54	.25
The crooked frame.	PB 961	53	.25
Heaven ran last.	Dell 599	52	.25
Margin of terror.	PB 1062	55	.25
Night extra.	PB 1193	58	.25
Odds against tomorrow.	Card C-316	59	.35
Rogue cop.	PB 1030	54	.25
The 7 file.	PB 1156	57	.25
Shield for murder.	PB 870	52	.25
Very cold for May.	PB 786	51	.25
Waterfront cop.	PB 1105	56	.25
The whispering corpse.	PB 693	50	.25
McGOLDRICK, EDWARD J. JR.			
Tormented women.	MonB MB503	59	.35
McGOVERN, ANN			
Treasure book of fairy tales.	Crst s324	59	.35
McGOVERN, JAMES			
Erika.	Pop G181	57	.35
McGREEVEY, JOHN			
Bounty man.	Ace D-120	55	.35
McGUIRE, ATHA			
Homicide hussy.	GM 502	55	.25
McGUIRE, JOHN J. with H. Beam Piper			
Crisis in 2140.	Ace D-227	57	.35
A planet for Texans.	Ace D-299	58	.35
McGUIRE, PAUL			
A funeral in Eden.	Pen 631	47	.25
McHUGH, VINCENT			
Edge of the world.	Ball 53	54	.35
I am thinking of my darling.	Sig 778	50	.25
McILVAINE, JANE S.			
Blue ribbon romance.	Berk G285	59	.35
McINNES, GRAHAM			
Lost island.	Sig S1215	55	.35
McINTOSH, J. T.			
One in 300.	Ace D-113	55	.35
The rule of the pagbeasts.	Crst 150	56	.25
World out of mind.	Perm M-3027	56	.25
Worlds apart.	Avon T-249	58	.35
McINTYRE, BILL			
Cartoon laffs from True.	Crst 239	58	.25
McINTYRE, MARJORIE			
The River Witch.	PB 1117	56	.25
McKAY, CLAUDE			
Home to Harlem.	Avon 376	51	.25
McKAYE, RICHARD			
Portrait of the damned.	Sig 1110	54	.25
McKEE, DOUGLAS with William Cole			
French cartoons.	DelF 21	54	.25
More French cartoons.	DelF 64	55	.25
McKENNA, GEORGE			
Yanqui's woman.	Crst s221	58	.35
McKENNEY, RUTH			
My sister Eileen.	PB 189	42	.25
_____.	Berk G284	59	.35

Author/Title	Pub./Stock No.	Yr.	Price
McKERNAN, MAUREEN			
The amazing crime and trial of Leopold and Loeb.	Sig D1469	57	.50
McKIE, RONALD			
The survivors.	Pop 609	54	.25
McKIMMEY, JAMES			
The perfect victim.	DelF A159	58	.25
Winner take all.	DelF A185	59	.25
McKNIGHT, BOB			
The bikini bombshell.	Ace D-387	59	.35
Downwind.	Ace D-217	57	.35
Murder mutuel.	Ace D-279	58	.35
Swamp sanctuary.	Ace D-411	59	.35
McLEAN, BETH BAILEY with Thora Campbell			
Martha Logan's meat cook book.	PB 852	52	.25
McLOUGHLIN, E. V.			
Questions and answers from the Book of knowledge.	Card C-61	52	.35
McMILLEN, V. A.			
The fall of Suzanne Swift.	GM 353	53	.25
McMULLEN, MARY			
Strangle hold.	Dell 713	53	.25
McMULLEN, RICHARD			
Awake to darkness.	Pop 212	49	.25
_____.	Pop G229	58	.35
Country girl.	Pop 572	54	.25
_____.	Pop G385	59	.35
McNEILLY, MILDRED MASTERSON			
Each bright river.	PB 844	52	.25
Matthew Steel.	Card C-116	53	.35
McNICHOLS, CHARLES L.			
Crazy weather.	Ban 1272	54	.25
McNULTY, JOHN			
A man gets around.	Ban 1232	54	.25
McPARTLAND, JOHN			
Affair in Tokyo.	GM 406	54	.25
Big Red's daughter.	GM 354	53	.25
Danger for breakfast.	GM 574	56	.25
The face of evil.	GM 393	54	.25
I'll see you in hell.	GM 571	56	.25
The kingdom of Johnny Cool.	GM 881	59	.25
The last night.	GM 909	59	.25
Love me now.	GM 263	52	.25

Author/Title	Pub./Stock No.	Yr.	Price
No down payment.	Card C-298	58	.35
Ripe fruit.	GM 732	58	.25
Sex in our changing world.	Berk BG-128	58	.50
Tokyo doll.	GM 336	53	.25
The wild party.	GM 596	56	.25
MEAD, HAROLD			
Bright phoenix.	Ball 147	56	.35
MEAD, MARGARET			
The coming of age in Samoa.	Ment M44	49	.35
_____.	Ment MD153	55	.50
Cultural patterns and technical change.	Ment MD134	55	.50
Growing up in New Guinea.	Ment M91	53	.35
_____.	Ment MD255	59	.50
Male and female.	Ment MD150	55	.50
Sex and temperament in three primitive societies.	Ment M56	50	.35
_____.	Ment MD133	55	.50
MEAD, SHEPHERD			
The big ball of wax.	Ball 174	56	.35
How to succeed in business without really trying.	Ball 127	56	.35
How to succeed with women without really trying.	Ball 287K	59	.35
The sex machine.	Pop 228	50	.25
MEANY, TOM			
Babe Ruth.	Ban 505	48	.25
Baseball's greatest players.	Dell 839	55	.25
Baseball's greatest teams.	Ban 763	50	.25
MEIER, FRANK			
Men under the sea.	Dell 265	48	.25
MEISSNER, HANS-OTTO			
The man with three faces.	Ace D-319	58	.35
MEJO, OSCAR de			
Diary of a nun.	Pyr 158	55	.25
MELLETT, LOWELL			
Handbook of politics and voter's guide.	Pen 593	46	.25
MELONEY, WILLIAM BROWN			
Farm girl.	Pyr 37	51	.25
_____.	Pyr G154	55	.35
_____.	Pyr G460	59	.35
Many loves have I.	Pop G154	55	.35
Mooney.	Pop 391	51	.25

Author/Title	Pub./Stock No.	Yr.	Price
MELVILLE, HERMAN			
Four short novels.	BanC FC16	59	.50
Moby Dick.	PB 612	49	.25
_____.	PBL PL28	55	.35
_____.	Sig D1229	55	.50
_____.	DelL LX105	59	.75
Typee.	Avon T-117	56	.35
_____.	Ban F1803	58	.50
MENDE, ROBERT			
Tough kid from Brooklyn.	Avon 382	51	.25
_____.	Avon T-99	55	.35
MENEN, AUBREY			
The abode of love.	PB 1188	58	.25
MEONI, ARMANDO			
Strange lovers.	Pop 534	53	.25
MERCER, CHARLES			
The Drummond tradition.	Ban F1818	58	.50
Rachel Cade.	Ban F1723	58	.50
MEREDITH, ANNE			
The unknown path.	Dell 588	52	.25
MEREDITH, SCOTT			
Bar 4 roundup of best western stories.	Perm M-3035	56	.25
Bar 5 roundup of best western stories.	Perm M-3082	57	.25
Bar 6 roundup of best western stories.	Perm M-3116	58	.25
with Sidney Meredith			
The best from Manhunt.	Perm M-3111	58	.25
MEREDITH, SIDNEY with Scott Meredith			
The best from Manhunt.	Perm M-3111	58	.25
MERGENDAHL, CHARLES			
The bramble bush.	Ban F1968	59	.50
The girl cage.	Pop 484	53	.25
_____.	Crst s302	59	.35
Rage of desire.	Dell D240	58	.35
A strange innocence.	Hill 116	59	.35
This spring of love.	Pop 304	51	.25
_____.	Eag EB18	54	.25
_____.	Pop G372	59	.35
Tiger by the tail.	Pop G275	58	.35
Tonight is forever.	Pop 351	51	.25
MÉRIMÉE, PROSPER			
Carmen and other stories.	PB 559	48	.25
MERIWETHER, SAM			
The black riders.	Eton E130	53	.25
The deadly derringer.	Ball 83	54	.35
The last holdup.	PB 1238	59	.25
The monster of the butte.	Ball 271K	58	.35
Nigger John.	Ban 1122	53	.25

Author/Title	Pub./Stock No.	Yr.	Price
Outlaw woman.	Ball 321K	59	.35
MERRIAM, ROBERT E.			
The Battle of the Bulge.	Ball 190	57	.35
The **MERRIAM**-Webster Pocket dictionary.	PB 421	47	.25
_____.	Card C-5	51	.35
MERRICK, GORDON			
Between darkness and day.	Pop G158	56	.35
Lovers in torment.	Pop 703	55	.25
The night and the naked.	Pop 446	52	.25
_____.	Pop G344	59	.35
MERRIL, JUDITH			
Beyond human ken.	Pnnt P56	54	.25
Galaxy of ghouls.	Lion LL 25	55	.35
Human?	Lion 205	54	.25
Off the beaten orbit.	Pyr G397	59	.35
S-F: the year's greatest science-fiction and fantasy.	DelF B103	56	.35
SF: the year's greatest science-fiction and fantasy 2nd annual volume.	DelF B110	57	.35
S-F: the year's greatest science-fiction and fantasy 3rd annual volume.	DelF B119	58	.35
SF: the year's greatest science-fiction and fantasy 4th annual volume.	DelF B129	59	.35
Shot in the dark.	Ban 751	50	.25
MERRILL, MARK			
The love-makers.	Pyr G227	56	.35
Women and vodka.	Pyr R210	56	.35
MERRIMAN, CHAD			
The avengers.	Ball 289K	59	.35
Blood on the sun.	GM 271	52	.25
Bunch quitter.	Ball 315K	59	.35
Fury on the plains.	GM 381	54	.25
Ridge runner.	GM 305	53	.25
Stampede.	Ball 343K	59	.35
with Lee Leighton			
Colorado gold.	Ball 282K	58	.35
MERRITT, A.			
Burn, witch, burn!	Avon 43	44	.25
_____.	Avon 392	51	.25
Creep, shadow, creep.	Avon 117	47	.25
Dwellers in the mirage.	Avon 413	52	.25
Face in the abyss.	Avon 386	51	.25
_____.	Avon T-161	57	.35
The fox woman and other stories.	Avon 214	49	.25

Author/Title	Pub./Stock No.	Yr.	Price	Author/Title	Pub./Stock No.	Yr.	Price
MERRITT, A. (cont.)				Belly laughs annual.	Avon T-227	58	.35
The metal monster.	Avon 315	51	.25	The big fights.	Avon 230	50	.25
_____.	Avon T-172	57	.35	Can can Americana.	Avon 359	51	.25
The moon pool.	Avon 370	51	.25	Caveman cartoons.	Avon 627	55	.25
_____.	Avon T-135	56	.35	_____.	Avon 860	59	.25
Seven footprints to				Honeymoon guide.	Avon T-95	55	.35
Satan.	Avon (26)	43	.25	_____.	Avon T-282	58	.35
_____.	Avon 235	50	.25	Klever kid kartoons.	Avon 633	55	.25
_____.	Avon T-115	56	.35	Naughty 90's joke book.	Avon 133	47	.25
_____.	Avon T-208	57	.35	Nudist cartoons.	Avon 649	55	.25
The ship of Ishtar.	Avon 324	51	.25	Showgirl cartoons,			
_____.	Avon T-152	57	.35	photographs, stories.	Avon 681	55	.25
				Smoking-room jokebook.	Avon 698	56	.25
MERTON, THOMAS				South sea cartoons.	Avon 643	55	.25
The living bread.	Dell D256	59	.35	Teen-age cartoons and			
No man is an island.	Dell D189	57	.35	jokes.	Avon 662	55	.25
Seeds of contemplation.	Dell 725	53	.25				
_____.	Dell D208	58	.35	MEYERS, LESTER			
The seven storey				High-speed math self-			
mountain.	Sig D929	52	.50	taught.	Card GC-67	59	.50
The silent life.	Dell D313	59	.35				
				MEYNIER, GIL			
MERWIN, SAM JR.				Stranger at the door.	Crst 117	55	.25
The big frame.	Han 12	43	.15				
The creeping shadow.	GM 227	52	.25	MEYRICK, GORDON			
Knife in my back.	Han 44	45	.15	Body on the pavement.	Han 43	45	.15
A matter of policy.	GD unk	47	.25				
Three faces of time.	Ace D-121	55	.35	MEZZROW, MEZZ with Bernard Wolfe			
				Really the blues.	Dell D118	53	.35
MESERVEY, RUSS				MICHAEL, D. J.			
Masquerade into madness.	GM 302	53	.25	Win--or else!	Lion 208	54	.25
MESKIL, PAUL				MICHAEL, MARJORIE			
Sin pit.	Lion 198	54	.25	I married a hunter.	PyrR PR14	58	.35
METALIOUS, GRACE				MICHAELS, ROY			
Peyton Place.	Dell F61	57	.50	By any other name.	Sig 1048	53	.25
				More equal than others.	Ball 270K	58	.35
METZELTHIN, PEARL V.				Now you see me, now you			
The Avon improved cook				don't.	Ban 424	49	.25
book.	Avon 101	47	.25	_____.	Ban A1129	53	.35
_____.	Avon 261	50	.25				
				MICHAELSON, JOHN NAIRNE			
MEYER, J. A. with Alan E. Nourse				Morning, winter and			
The invaders are coming!	Ace D-366	59	.35	night.	Sig 1116	54	.25
				_____.	Berk G-166	58	.35
MEYER, JEROME S.							
Fun for the family.	PB 580	49	.25	MICHEL, M. SCOTT			
_____.	Perm M-4138	59	.35	The black key.	Han 60	47	.20
Fun with mathematics.	Prem d56	57	.50	The psychiatric murders.	BK unk	46	.25
_____.	Crst d262	58	.50	Sweet murder.	Han 47	46	.15
				The X-ray murders.	Han 30	44	.15
MEYERS, DAVID with Richard L. Williams							
What, when, where and				MICHELFELDER, WILLIAM			
how to drink.	DelF 55	55	.25	A seed upon the wind.	Berk G-7	55	.35
				_____.	Berk G-65	57	.35
MEYERS, HAROLD							
Animals are funnier				MICHENER, JAMES A.			
than people.	Avon 637	54	.25	The bridge at Andau.	Ban A1650	57	.35
Belly laughs annual.	Avon T-92	54	.35				

Author/Title	Pub./Stock No.	Yr.	Price
MICHENER, JAMES A. (cont.)			
The bridges at Toko-ri.	Ban 1269	55	.25
The fires of spring.	Ban A884	51	.35
_____.	Ban F1350	55	.50
_____.	Ban F1705	57	.50
Return to paradise.	Ban A999	52	.35
_____.	Ban F1674	57	.50
Sayonara.	Ban A1318	55	.35
_____.	Ban A1641	57	.35
Tales of the south Pacific.	PB 516	48	.25
_____.	Card C-226	57	.35
The voice of Asia.	Ban A1000	52	.35
with A. Grove Day			
Rascals in paradise.	Ban F1844	58	.50
MIDDLETON, TED			
Operation Tokyo.	Avon 731	56	.25
MIK			
The adventures of Ferd'nand.	Graf 107	55	.25
MILBURN, GEORGE			
All over town.	Dell 676	53	.25
_____.	Zen ZB-2	58	.35
Hoboes and harlots.	Lion 202	54	.25
_____.	Lion LL 160	57	.35
Julie.	Lion LL 82	56	.35
Sin people.	Lion 159	53	.25
with Émile Zola			
The human beast.	Dell 608	52	.25
MILES, YUKON			
Stampede.	GM 201	51	.25
MILLAR, GEORGE			
A crossbowman's story.	Ban F1591	57	.50
MILLAR, KENNETH			
Blue city.	Dell 363	49	.25
	Dell 408	50	.25
The dark tunnel.	Lion 48	50	.25
I die slowly.	Lion LL 52	55	.35
The three roads.	Dell 497	51	.25
Trouble follows me.	Lion 47	50	.25
_____.	Lion LL 40	55	.35
MILLAR, MARGARET			
Beast in view.	Ban 1542	56	.25
Do evil in return.	Dell 558	51	.25
Fire will freeze.	Dell 157	47	.25
The iron gates.	Dell 209	47	.25
The lively corpse.	Dell 920	56	.25
Vanish in an instant.	Dell 730	53	.25
Wall of eyes.	Dell 110	46	.25
MILLARD, JOSEPH			
Edgar Cayce, mystery man of miracles.	GM s590	56	.35

Author/Title	Pub./Stock No.	Yr.	Price
Mansion of evil.	GM 129	50	.25
The wickedest man.	GM 404	54	.25
MILLAY, EDNA ST. VINCENT			
Collected lyrics.	WSP W550	59	.50
Collected sonnets.	WSP W551	59	.50
MILLEN, GILMORE			
Sweet man.	Pyr G59	52	.35
_____.	Pyr G142	55	.35
MILLER, ARTHUR			
The crucible.	BanC AC31	59	.35
Death of a salesman.	Ban 952	51	.25
_____.	Ban A1322	55	.35
Focus.	Pop 230	50	.25
_____.	Dell D273	59	.35
MILLER, BILL with Bob Wade			
Murder--queen high.	Graf 11	49	.25
_____.	Graf 54	52	.25
MILLER, DIANE DISNEY with Pete Martin			
The story of Walt Disney.	Dell D266	59	.35
MILLER, DOUGLAS			
You can't do business with Hitler.	PB 139	42	.25
MILLER, FLOYD			
The dream peddlers.	Pop 787	56	.25
Just so far.	Eag EB96	57	.25
The savage streets.	Pop 746	56	.25
with Robert McAllister			
The kind of guy I am.	Pop G252	58	.35
MILLER, FRANK			
Tejas country.	Ban 1576	57	.25
MILLER, HARRY			
Common sense book of puppy and dog care.	Ban A1528	56	.35
MILLER, HELEN TOPPING			
Desperate angel.	Dell 462	50	.25
Flame vine.	Avon 254	50	.25
Spotlight.	PB 653	50	.25
Wicked sister.	Avon 210	49	.25
MILLER, HENRY			
A devil in paradise.	Sig 1317	56	.25
The intimate Henry Miller.	Sig D1653	59	.50
Nights of love and laughter.	Sig 1246	55	.25
MILLER, JOHN A.			
Men and volts at war.	Ban A-1	48	.25
MILLER, LEE			
The story of Ernie Pyle.	Ban A1098	53	.35

Author/Title	Pub./Stock No.	Yr.	Price
MILLER, LLEWELLYN			
Prize articles of 1954.	Ball 72	54	.35
MILLER, MERLE			
The sure thing.	Pop 277	50	.25
That winter.	Pop 210	49	.25
MILLER, NOLAN			
New campus writing.	Ban F1367	55	.50
New campus writing, no. 2.	Ban F1649	57	.50
Why I am so beat.	Ace S-87	55	.25
_____.	Ace D-398	59	.35
MILLER, R. DeWITT			
Reincarnation--the whole startling story.	Ban 1507	56	.25
with Anna Hunger			
The man who lived forever.	Ace D-162	56	.35
MILLER, TEVIS			
Gun-play in Killer Canyon.	Eton E118	52	.25
MILLER, WADE			
The big guy.	GM 279	53	.25
_____.	GM s936	59	.35
Branded woman.	GM 257	52	.25
_____.	GM s791	58	.35
Calamity fair.	Sig 843	51	.25
_____.	Sig 1270	56	.25
Deadly weapon.	Pen 648	47	.25
_____.	Sig 928	52	.25
Devil may care.	GM 108	50	.25
_____.	GM 758	58	.25
Fatal step.	Sig 695	48	.25
_____.	Sig 1180	55	.25
Guilty bystander.	Han 65	47	.20
_____.	Sig 677	48	.25
_____.	Sig 1089	54	.25
_____.	Sig 1482	58	.25
The killer.	GM 152	51	.25
_____.	GM 521	55	.25
_____.	GM 810	58	.25
Killer's choice.	Sig 771	50	.25
_____.	Sig 1235	55	.25
Kiss her goodbye.	Lion LL 96	56	.35
_____.	Sig 1662	59	.25
Kitten with a whip.	GM s845	59	.35
Mad Baxter.	GM 469	55	.25
Murder charge.	Sig 908	51	.25
Shoot to kill.	Sig 1013	53	.25
_____.	Sig 1369	57	.25
South of the sun.	GM 331	53	.25
Stolen woman.	GM 139	51	.25
_____.	GM 513	55	.25
The tiger's wife.	GM 173	51	.25
_____.	GM 682	57	.25
_____.	GM 945	59	.25
Uneasy street.	Sig 722	49	.25
_____.	Sig 1257	55	.25
MILLER, WARREN			
The way we live now.	Crst s299	59	.35
MILLER, WILLIAM			
A history of the United States.	Dell LX101	58	.75
MILLHAUSER, BERTRAM with Beulah Marie Dix			
Hot leather.	Ban 554	48	.25
MILLIGAN, HAROLD VINCENT			
Stories of famous operas.	SigK KD331	55	.50
MILLIS, WALTER			
Arms and men.	Ment MD208	58	.50
MILLS, MERVYN			
The long haul.	Avon T-201	57	.35
MILNE, A. A.			
The red house mystery.	PB 81	40	.25
_____.	Dell D321	59	.35
MILORADOVICH, MILO with Maria Lo Pinto			
The art of Italian cooking.	Ban A1378	55	.35
MIRBEAU, OCTAVE			
Diary of a chambermaid.	Avon T-94	55	.35
_____.	Avon T-145	56	.35
Torture garden.	Berk 111	55	.25
_____.	Berk G-39	56	.35
MIRVISH, ROBERT F.			
The eternal voyagers.	Sig S1222	55	.35
A house of her own.	Sig S1137	54	.35
The long watch.	Pop 690	55	.25
Red sky at midnight.	Pop G174	56	.35
Wide-open town.	Pop 647	55	.25
MITCHELL, ALBERT			
Here's the answer.	Pyr G296	57	.35
MITCHELL, ANTHEA			
The naked sword.	Pop 601	54	.25
MITCHELL, FRANCIS			
Naked acre.	Avon T-84	54	.35
_____.	Avon T-132	56	.35
MITCHELL, JOSEPH			
McSorley's wonderful saloon.	Pen 557	45	.25
MITCHELL, MARGARET			
Gone with the wind.	Prmb P294	54	.75

Author/Title	Pub./Stock No.	Yr.	Price
MITCHELL, MARGARET (cont.)			
Gone with the wind.	Perm M-7500	58	.75
MITCHELL, WILL			
The goldfish murders.	GM 118	50	.25
MITFORD, NANCY			
The blessing.	Sig 1012	53	.25
	Sig S1625	59	.35
Madame de Pompadour.	BanB FB409	56	.50
The pursuit of love.	PB 506	49	.25
MITTELHOLZER, EDGAR			
The old blood.	Crst d305	59	.50
Shadows move among			
them.	PB 918	53	.25
Sylvia.	Dell D151	55	.35
MOCK, ELIZABETH B. with J. M. Richards			
An introduction to			
modern architecture.	Pel P20	47	.35
MOCKRIDGE, NORTON with Robert Prall			
This is Costello.	GM 177	51	.25
	GM s704	57	.35
MODEL railroading.	Ban A-2	50	.25
	Ban A979	51	.35
	Ban F1152	53	.50
	Ban F1430	55	.50
	Ban S1663	57	.75
MODELL, MERRIAM			
My sister, my bride.	Ban 425	49	.25
	Pyr G181	56	.35
MODLEY, RUDOLF			
A history of the war.	PenS S216	43	.25
MOLE, WILLIAM			
Shadow of a killer.	Dell D272	59	.35
MOLL, ELICK			
Night without sleep.	Ban 926	51	.25
MONAGHAN, JAY			
The great rascal.	Ban A1145	53	.35
MONAHAN, JOHN			
Big Stan.	GM 355	54	.25
MONASH, PAUL			
Hellbound.	Avon 622	55	.25
How brave we live.	Avon 405	52	.25
	Avon 595	54	.25
The unholy lovers.	Avon T-342	59	.35
MONATH, NORMAN with Jack Bassett			
Play it yourself.	Perm M-3054	56	.25

Author/Title	Pub./Stock No.	Yr.	Price
MONIG, CHRISTOPHER			
Don't count the corpses.	Dell 992	58	.25
MONS, H. M.			
The sword of Satan.	Pop 564	54	.25
MONSARRAT, NICHOLAS			
Castle Garac.	PB 1139	56	.25
The cruel sea.	Card GC-10	53	.50
Depends what you mean			
by love.	Sig 1092	54	.25
Leave cancelled.	Dell 327	49	.25
The story of Esther			
Costello.	PB 1043	55	.25
The tribe that lost			
its head.	Card GC-755	58	.75
MONTAGU, ASHLEY			
The cultured man.	Perm M-4141	59	.35
Man: his first million			
years.	Ment MD239	58	.50
MONTAGUE, EWEN			
The man who never was.	Avon 640	55	.25
MONTAGUE, JOSEPH F.			
How to overcome nervous			
stomach trouble.	Prmb P106	51	.35
MONTAIGNE, MICHEL de			
The selected essays of			
Montaigne.	PBL PL520	59	.50
MONTANA, DUKE			
Nevada killing.	Lion 60	51	.25
MONTGOMERY, L. M.			
Anne of Windy Poplars.	PB 72	40	.25
MONTGOMERY, RUTHERFORD			
Gray wolf.	Com 24	49	.25
Husky: co-pilot of the			
Pilgrim.	Com 20	49	.25
Midnight.	Com 26	49	.25
MONTHERLANT, HENRY de			
Desert love.	Berk G277	59	.35
MOON, BUCKLIN			
Champs and bums.	Lion 229	54	.25
The darker brother.	Ban 737	49	.25
Without magnolias.	PB 697	50	.25
MOONEY, BOOTH			
Here is my body.	GM 218	52	.25
	GM 781	58	.25
The insiders.	Ace D-292	58	.35
MOORE, BRIAN			
The lonely passion of			
Judith Hearne.	Dell D205	57	.35

Author/Title	Pub./Stock No.	Yr.	Price
MOORE, BRIAN (cont.)			
Sailor's leave.	Pyr 94	53	.25
MOORE, C. L.			
Doomsday morning.	Avon T-297	59	.35
with Henry Kuttner			
No boundaries.	Ball 122	55	.35
with Lewis Padgett			
Beyond earth's gates.	Ace D-69	54	.35
MOORE, DAN TYLER			
The terrible game.	Berk G-169	58	.35
MOORE, IRVING with Lillian Bergquist			
Your shot, darling.	Graf 84	54	.25
MOORE, ISABEL			
The other woman.	Ban 706	49	.25
MOORE, LUCIA B.			
The wheel and the hearth.	Ball 15	53	.35
MOORE, MARY FURLONG			
Baby sitter's guide.	Berk 384	59	.25
MOORE, PAMELA			
Chocolates for breakfast.	Ban A1630	57	.35
MOORE, ROBIN			
Pitchman.	Pop G211	58	.35
MOORE, ROSALIND with Kathleen Rafferty			
Dell crossword puzzles.	DelF 60	55	.25
MOORE, RUTH			
Candlemas Bay.	PB 938	53	.25
Deep waters.	PB 508	48	.25
A fair wind home.	PB 1051	55	.25
MOORE, WALTER L.			
Courage and confidence from the Bible.	Sig 862	51	.25
MOORE, WARD			
Bring the jubilee.	Ball 38	53	.35
MOOREHEAD, ALAN			
The Russian revolution.	Ban F2070	59	.50
MORAN, MIKE			
Double cross.	Pop 494	53	.25
MORAVIA, ALBERTO			
Bitter honeymoon.	Sig S1520	58	.35
The conformist.	Sig S1071	53	.35
	Sig D1510	58	.50
Conjugal love.	Sig 922	52	.25
	Sig 1288	56	.25
The fancy dress party.	Sig 1122	54	.25
A ghost at noon.	Sig S1306	56	.35
Roman tales.	Sig S1612	59	.35
The time of indifference.	Sig S1213	55	.35
Two adolescents.	Sig 960	52	.25
	Sig 1372	57	.25
Two women.	Sig D1657	59	.50
The woman of Rome.	Sig S844	51	.35
	Sig D1596	58	.50
MORAY, HELGA			
Dark fury.	Pop SP44	59	.50
This naked love.	Mon K52	59	.50
Tisa.	Pop G130	53	.35
	Pop SP25	58	.50
Untamed.	Dell 484	51	.25
	Dell 630	52	.25
MORE all about girls.	Avon 598	54	.25
	Avon 859	59	.25
MORE stories in the modern manner.	Avon T-77	54	.35
MOREHEAD, ALBERT H.			
The Pocket book of games.	PB 260	44	.25
with James Morehead			
101 best loved songs.	PB 955	54	.25
101 favorite hymns.	PB 925	53	.25
with Loy Morehead			
The New American handy college dictionary.	Sig D1328	56	.50
with Geoffrey Mott-Smith			
Hoyle's rules of games.	SigK K307	54	.25
	SigK KD363	59	.50
The new quiz book.	Pen 652	48	.25
The Penguin Hoyle.	Pen 614	46	.25
The Signet crossword puzzle book.	Sig 678	48	.25
MOREHEAD, JAMES with Albert H. Morehead			
101 best loved songs.	PB 955	54	.25
101 favorite hymns.	PB 925	53	.25
MOREHEAD, LOY with Albert H. Morehead			
The New American handy college dictionary.	Sig D1328	56	.50
MORETTI, UGO			
Rogue Wind.	Pop 585	54	.25
MORGAN, AL			
Cast of characters.	Card C-306	58	.35
The great man.	Card C-223	56	.35
MORGAN, CLAIRE			
The price of salt.	Ban 1148	53	.25
	Ban A1831	58	.35
MORGAN, HENRY			
Henry Morgan's joke book.	Avon 673	55	.25

Author/Title	Pub./Stock No.	Yr.	Price
MORGAN, JOE			
Expense account.	Sig S1610	59	.35
MORGAN, JOHN MEDFORD			
The Roman and the slave girl.	Sig S1690	59	.35
MORGAN, MARK			
Fighting man.	Lion 136	53	.25
	Lion LB 70	56	.25
MORGAN, MICHAEL			
The blonde body.	Lion 11	49	.25
Decoy.	Ace D-9	53	.35
His kind of woman.	Pyr 116	54	.25
MORGAN, NANCY			
City of women.	RS 12	52	.35
_____.	GM S453	55	.35
_____.	GM d839	59	.50
Somebody loves me.	GM 433	54	.25
MORGAN, WILLIAM J.			
The O.S.S. and I.	PB 1204	58	.25
MORISON, SAMUEL ELIOT			
Christopher Columbus, mariner.	Ment M181	56	.35
MORLEY, CHRISTOPHER			
Kitty Foyle.	Pen 529	44	.25
_____.	Sig 793	50	.25
_____.	Sig S1491	58	.35
Thunder on the left.	PB 51	40	.25
_____.	Pen 582	46	.25
MORLEY, SUSAN			
Making of a mistress.	Sig S1279	56	.35
Mistress Glory.	Sig 748	49	.25
MOROSO, JOHN A.			
Passionate fool.	RC 2	49	.25
MORRIS, DONALD R.			
China station.	Sig 939	52	.25
A girl in every port.	Berk G-25	56	.35
Warm bodies.	Perm M-4132	59	.35
MORRIS, ROBERT T.			
Fifty years a surgeon.	SigK Ks329	55	.35
MORRIS, WRIGHT			
The field of vision.	Sig D1455	57	.50
Love among the cannibals.	Sig S1531	58	.35
MORRISON, RAY			
Angels Camp.	Ban 794	50	.25
MORSE, JAMES			
Folk songs of the Caribbean.	Ban F1788	58	.50

Author/Title	Pub./Stock No.	Yr.	Price
MORTIMER, JOHN			
The silver hook.	Ban 977	52	.25
MORTIMER, LEE with Jack Lait			
Big city after dark.	Dell 400	50	.25
Chicago confidential.	Dell D101	52	.35
New York confidential.	Dell 440	50	.25
_____.	Dell 534	51	.25
Washington confidential.	Dell D108	52	.35
MORTON, STANLEY			
Yankee trader.	Pyr G54	52	.35
_____.	Pyr G140	55	.35
MOSELY, DANA			
Dead of summer.	Dell 953	57	.25
The MOST dangerous game.	Berk G-62	57	.35
MOTLEY, WILLARD			
Knock on any door.	Sig 802AB	50	.50
_____.	Sig D1576	58	.50
Let no man write my epitaph.	Sig D1693	59	.50
We fished all night.	Sig D992	53	.50
MOTT, FRANK LUTHER			
A gallery of Americans.	Ment M61	51	.35
MOTT-SMITH, GEOFFREY with Albert H. Morehead			
Hoyle's rules of games.	SigK K307	54	.25
_____.	SigK KD363	59	.50
The new quiz book.	Pen 652	48	.25
The Penguin Hoyle.	Pen 614	46	.25
The Signet crossword puzzle book.	Sig 678	48	.25
MOULTON, POWERS			
Best jokes.	Perm M-4014	55	.35
with Jerry Lieberman			
Best jokes for all occasions.	Perm M-3060	56	.25
MOWAT, FARLEY			
The dog who wouldn't be.	PyrR PR20	59	.35
MOWERY, WILLIAM BYRON			
Guns in the valley.	Pop 214	49	.25
Outlaw breed.	Pop 179	49	.25
Paradise trail.	Pop 127	48	.25
The phantom canoe.	Pop 103	47	.25
MOYZISCH, L. C.			
Operation Cicero.	Ban 982	52	.25
_____.	Pyr G337	58	.35
MULFORD, CLARENCE E.			
Bar-20 days.	Dell 246	48	.25
Hopalong Cassidy returns.	PB 337	46	.25
Hopalong Cassidy takes cards.	Pop 146	48	.25

Author/Title	Pub./Stock No.	Yr.	Price
MULFORD, CLARENCE E. (cont.)			
Hopalong Cassidy's			
saddle mate.	Pop 198	49	.25
The man from Bar 20.	Graf 23	50	.25
Mesquite Jenkins,			
tumbleweed.	Pop 104	47	.25
The orphan outlaw.	Pyr 25	50	.25
Tex.	Graf 15	49	.25
_____.	Graf 28	51	.25
_____.	Graf 53	52	.25
_____.	Graf 91	54	.25
MULHOLLAND, P. J.			
The calypso murders.	Avon 781	57	.25
MULLEN, CLARENCE			
Thereby hangs a corpse.	HH unk	47	.25
MULLER, HERBERT J.			
The uses of the past.	Ment Ms112	54	.50
MULVIHILL, WILLIAM P.			
Fire mission.	Ball 189	57	.35
MUNRO, W. CARROLL			
The lessons of love.	Berk BG238	59	.50
The untamed wife of			
Louis Scott.	Avon 383	51	.25
_____.	Avon 501	53	.25
MUNVES, ELIZABETH with Henrietta Fleck			
Everybody's book of			
modern diet and			
nutrition.	DelF D53	55	.35
_____.	DelL LC124	59	.50
MURGER, HENRI			
Love in the Latin			
Quarter.	Avon 163	48	.25
MURPHY, AUDIE			
To hell and back.	Prmb P119	51	.35
_____.	Prmb P214	53	.35
_____.	Perm M-4029	55	.35
MURPHY, BILL			
The red sands of Santa			
Maria.	Pop G201	57	.35
MURPHY, DENNIS			
The sergeant.	Crst s291	59	.35
MURPHY, JOHN D.			
Secrets of successful			
selling.	Dell D243	58	.35
MURRAY, CHALMERS S.			
Here comes Joe Mungin.	Ban A1193	54	.35

Author/Title	Pub./Stock No.	Yr.	Price
MURRAY, JAMES F. JR. with Oscar Halecki			
Pius XII: Eugenio Pacelli,			
Pope of peace.	Lion LL 67	56	.50
MURRAY, KEN			
Feud in Piney Flats.	Ace D-34	53	.35
Hellion's hole.	Ace D-34	53	.35
Ken Murray's giant joke			
book.	Ace D-62	54	.35
MURRAY, MARRIS			
The color of the blood.	Sig 1165	55	.25
MURRAY, MAX			
Good luck to the corpse.	Dell 639	52	.25
_____.	Pyr G362	58	.35
The neat little corpse.	Dell 560	51	.25
The queen and the corpse.	Dell 485	51	.25
The voice of the corpse.	Ban 358	48	.25
MURRAY, WILLIAM			
Best seller.	Pop G251	58	.35
The fugitive Romans.	Pop 726	56	.25
MURTAGH, JOHN M. with Sara Harris			
Cast the first stone.	Card C-286	58	.35
MYERS, BERNARD			
50 great artists.	Ban F1171	53	.50
_____.	Ban S1692	57	.75
_____.	BanC NC33	59	.95
MYERS, BETH			
The doctor is a lady.	Ban 1936	59	.25
MYERS, JOHN MYERS			
Dead warrior.	Hill 115	59	.35
MYERS, VIRGINIA			
Escape from Morales.	GM 320	53	.25
MYRER, ANTON			
The big war.	Ban F1707	58	.50

Author/Title	Pub./Stock No.	Yr.	Price
N			
NABARRO, DERRICK			
Too hard to handle.	Eag EB34	55	.25
NABLO, JAMES BENSON			
The long November.	Sig 968	52	.25
NABOKOV, VLADIMIR			
Laughter in the dark.	Sig 777	50	.25
_____.	Berk G-156	58	.35
Lolita.	Crst d338	59	.50
Pnin.	Avon T-323	59	.35
Spring in Fialta.	Pop G365	59	.35
NARCEJAC, THOMAS with Pierre Boileau			
Vertigo.	Dell 977	58	.25
NASH, ANNE			
Said with flowers.	Bart 19	45	.25
NASH, ELEANOR			
The women in his life.	NL 33	<u>50</u>	.25
NASH, N. RICHARD			
The rainmaker.	Ban 1559	57	.25
NASH, OGDEN			
The Ogden Nash Pocket			
book.	PB 251	44	.25
The Pocket book of			
Ogden Nash.	Card C-158	55	.35
NATHAN, LEONARD			
Night after night.	Pop 664	55	.25
NATHAN, ROBERT			
One more spring.	Ban 19	45	.25
A portrait of Jennie.	Pen 638	47	.25
So love returns.	Pyr G438	59	.35
NATHAN, SIMON			
How you can take better			
photos.	Crst s223	58	.35
NEBEL, FREDERICK			
Six deadly dames.	Avon 264	50	.25
The NECRONOMICON.	BPLA unk	40	.10
_____.	Ban 1248	54	.25
_____.	BanC AC36	59	.35
NEHER, FRED			
Hi-teens.	Berk 385	59	.25
Will-Yum.	Berk 383	58	.25
NEIDER, CHARLES			
Man against nature.	Ban A1452	56	.35
NELKIN, SANDY			
Cartoons for men only.	Pyr G346	58	.35

Author/Title	Pub./Stock No.	Yr.	Price
College humor.	Lion LL 119	56	.35
with Pat Untermeyer			
For stags only.	Lion LL 24	55	.35
Stag gags.	Lion 213	54	.25
NELSON, HUGH LAWRENCE			
Dead giveaway.	Dell 520	51	.25
NELSON, KLONDY with Corey Ford			
Daughter of the Gold			
Rush.	PyrR PG24	59	.35
NEUMANN, ALFRED			
Strange conquest.	Ball 88	54	.35
NEVILLE, MARGOT			
Murder of a nymph.	PB 829	52	.25
NEVINS, ALLAN with Henry Steele Commager			
The Pocket history of			
the United States.	PB 195	43	.25
_____.	PBL PL512	56	.50
NEW American Roget's			
college thesaurus in			
dictionary form.	Sig D1431	58	.50
The NEW American Webster			
dictionary.	Sig 808	51	.25
NEW Avon bedside companion.	Avon 182	49	.25
The NEW Hammond-Dell world			
atlas.	DelF FE84	56	.50
NEW short novels no. 2.	Ball 140	56	.35
NEW soldier's handbook.	PenS S202	42	.25
The NEW testament.	PB 254	44	.25
NEW world writing no. 1.	Ment Ms73	52	.50
NEW world writing no. 2.	Ment Ms79	52	.50
NEW world writing no. 3.	Ment Ms85	53	.50
NEW world writing no. 4.	Ment Ms96	53	.50
NEW world writing no. 5.	Ment Ms106	54	.50
NEW world writing no. 6.	Ment Ms118	54	.50
NEW world writing no. 7.	Ment MD130	55	.50
NEW world writing no. 8.	Ment MD146	55	.50
NEW world writing no. 9.	Ment MD170	56	.50
NEW world writing no. 10.	Ment MD183	56	.50
NEW world writing no. 11.	Ment MD196	57	.50
NEW world writing no. 12.	Ment MD210	57	.50
NEW world writing no. 13.	Ment MT233	58	.75
NEW world writing no. 14.	Ment MT246	58	.75
NEW world writing no. 15.	Ment MT260	59	.75
NEWBOROUGH, LADY			
Fire in my blood.	Pyr G462	59	.35

Author/Title	Pub./Stock No.	Yr.	Price
NEWHOUSE, EDWARD			
The temptation of Roger Heriott.	Berk 323	55	.25
NEWMAN, FRANK EATON			
The Perma cross word puzzle dictionary.	Prmb P89	51	.35
_____.	Perm M-4021	55	.35
NEWMEYER, SARAH			
Enjoying modern art.	Ment MD211	57	.50
NEWSOM, ED			
Wagons to Tucson.	Ban A1685	57	.35
NEWSOM, JOHN D.			
Wiped out.	Dell 165	47	.25
NEWTON, D. B.			
Guns along the Wickiup.	GM 357	54	.25
The outlaw breed.	GM 534	55	.25
Range boss.	PB 563	49	.25
Shotgun guard.	Pop 367	51	.25
Six-gun gamble.	Pop 437	52	.25
The **NEXT** Germany.	PenS S217	43	.25
NEZELOF, N. P.			
Josephine, the great lover.	Avon T-166	57	.35
NICHOLS, FAN			
Angel face.	Pop 706	55	.25
Ask for Linda.	Pop 483	53	.25
_____.	Pop G325	59	.35
The caged.	GM 251	52	.25
Count me in.	Pop 536	53	.25
_____.	Berk G243	59	.35
Devil take her.	Pop 586	54	.25
_____.	Berk G253	59	.35
He walks by night.	Pop 791	57	.25
Hideaway.	Dmnd D2008	59	.35
I know my love.	Pop G231	58	.35
I'll never let you go.	Pop 642	55	.25
Love me now.	Mon 103	58	.35
One by one.	Pop 409	52	.25
Possess me not.	Avon 346	51	.25
NICHOLSON, MARGARET			
A dictionary of American-English usage.	Sig T1547	58	.75
NICKLES, MARIONE R.			
Honey, I'm home.	Ban 1364	55	.25
NIELSEN, HELEN			
Dead on the level.	Dell 747	54	.25
Detour to death.	Dell 837	55	.25
False witness.	Ball 310K	59	.35
The kind man.	Dell 649	53	.25
Obit delayed.	Dell 806	54	.25
Seven days before dying.	Dell 971	58	.25
The woman on the roof.	Dell 900	56	.25
NIELSEN, LOU			
G.I. jokes.	Dell 77	45	.25
NILES, BLAIR			
Strange brother.	Avon 407	52	.25
_____.	Avon 493	53	.25
NIMIER, ROGER			
The blue hussar.	Sig S1273	56	.35
NIN, ANAÏS			
A spy in the house of love.	Avon 755	57	.25
NISSLEY, CHARLES			
The Pocket book of vegetable gardening.	PB 148	42	.25
NISTLER, ERWIN N. with Gerry P. Broderick			
Roadside night.	Pyr 33	51	.25
_____.	Pyr 148	55	.25
NIXON, HENRY LEWIS			
The caves.	Ace S-100	55	.25
The golden couch.	Ace S-190	56	.25
NOBLE, JOHN WESLEY with Bernard Averbuch			
Never plead guilty.	Ball 141	56	.35
NOBLE, WILLIAM with James Leo Herlihy			
Blue denim.	Ban A1957	59	.35
NOEL, STERLING			
Few die well.	Avon 584	54	.25
_____.	Avon 719	56	.25
I killed Stalin.	Eton E110	52	.25
_____.	Eton E119	52	.25
I see red.	Ace D-109	55	.35
Intrigue in Paris.	Avon T-159	57	.35
Prelude to murder.	Avon T-290	59	.35
Run for your life!	Avon T-270	58	.35
We who survived.	Avon T-360	59	.35
NORDHOFF, CHARLES with James Norman Hall			
Botany Bay.	Perm M-4001	55	.35
Falcons of France.	Mon 141	59	.35
The hurricane.	PB 188	43	.25
Men against the sea.	PB 358	46	.25
Mutiny on the Bounty.	PB 216	43	.25
_____.	Card C-34	52	.35
Pitcairn's Island.	PB 457	47	.25
NORMAN, EARL			
Kill me in Shimbashi.	Dmnd D2010	59	.35
Kill me in Tokyo.	Berk G-192	58	.35
NORMAN, JAMES			
Cimarron trace.	DelF A119	56	.25

Author/Title	Pub./Stock No.	Yr.	Price
NORRIS, FRANK			
The octopus.	BanC FC8	58	.50
NORRIS, KATHLEEN			
An apple for Eve.	PB 710	50	.25
Burned fingers.	PB 605	49	.25
The foolish virgin.	PB 525	48	.25
Mink coat.	PB 625	49	.25
Mother.	PB 44	40	.25
Motionless shadows.	Bart 20	45	.25
Mystery house.	PB 453	47	.25
Passion flower.	PB 480	47	.25
Secret marriage.	PB 599	49	.25
Three men and Diana.	PB 688	50	.25
Walls of gold.	PB 488	48	.25
Wife for sale.	PB 440	47	.25
Younger sister.	PB 549	48	.25
NORTH, ANDREW			
Plague ship.	Ace D-345	59	.35
Sargasso of space.	Ace D-249	57	.35
Voodoo planet.	Ace D-345	59	.35
NORTH, STERLING			
So dear to my heart.	Dell 291	49	.25
NORTON, ANDRE			
The crossroads of time.	Ace D-164	56	.35
Daybreak: 2250 A.D.	Ace D-69	54	.35
The last planet.	Ace D-96	55	.35
Scarface.	Com 28	49	.25
Secret of the lost race.	Ace D-381	59	.35
Star born.	Ace D-299	58	.35
Star guard.	Ace D-199	57	.35
The stars are ours.	Ace D-121	55	.35
NORTON, BROWNING with Charles A. Landolf			
I prefer murder.	Graf 132	56	.25
NOURSE, ALAN E.			
A man obsessed.	Ace D-96	55	.35
Rocket to limbo.	Ace D-385	59	.35
with J. A. Meyer			
The invaders are coming!	Ace D-366	59	.35
NOVAK, ROBERT			
B-girl.	Ace S-174	56	.25
Climb a broken ladder.	Ace S-151	56	.25
NUDE croquet.	Berk G-97	58	.35
NYE, HERMES			
Fortune is a woman.	Sig S1604	58	.35
NYE, NELSON			
Arizona dead-shot.	Avon 758	57	.25
Bandido.	Sig 1473	57	.25
Born to trouble.	Pop 461	52	.25
A bullet for Billy the Kid.	Avon 267	50	.25

Author/Title	Pub./Stock No.	Yr.	Price
A bullet for Billy the Kid.	Avon 478	52	.25
Cartridge-case law.	Berk 330	55	.25
Desert desperadoes.	Dmnd D2018	59	.35
Desert of the damned.	Pop 481	53	.25
———.	Eag EB79	56	.25
G stands for gun.	Berk G-99	58	.35
Gun-quick.	Berk G-79	57	.35
Gunfighter brand.	Berk G-138	58	.35
Gunfighter breed.	Berk 321	55	.25
Guns of Arizona.	Berk G-118	58	.35
Guns of Horse Prairie.	Berk G234	59	.35
Gunshot trail.	Berk 343	55	.25
———.	Berk G-154	58	.35
Hired hand.	PB 1060	55	.25
Horses, women and guns.	Hill 109	59	.35
The lonely grass.	PB 1142	57	.25
Maverick marshal.	Sig 1516	58	.25
The no-gun fighter.	Ace D-180	56	.35
The one-shot kid.	Ace D-78	54	.35
The overlanders.	Sig 1631	59	.25
The parson of Gunbarrel Basin.	PB 1135	56	.25
Plunder valley.	Ace D-6	52	.35
Ranger's revenge.	Berk 363	56	.25
The red sombrero.	Crst 235	58	.25
Riders by night.	PB 754	51	.25
———.	Crst 123	56	.25
Saddle Bow Slim.	Berk 350	56	.25
The Texas tornado.	Ace D-98	55	.35
Thief River.	Pop 441	52	.25
Tornado on horseback.	Ace D-134	55	.35
Wide loop.	Dell 804	54	.25
Wildcats of Tonto Basin.	Dmnd D2006	59	.35

Author/Title	Pub./Stock No.	Yr.	Price
O			
OAKEY, VIRGINIA			
The reckless years.	Pop G162	56	.35
OBETS, BOB			
Blood-moon range.	Pyr 303	57	.25
O'BRIEN, EUGENE			
He swung and he missed.	Avon 508	53	.25
One way ticket.	Pnnt P50	54	.25
O'BRIEN, JOHN A.			
Happy marriage.	Pop G190	57	.35
O'BRIEN, THOMAS L.			
The witch finder.	DelF B135	59	.35
O'CONNOR, EDWIN			
The last hurrah.	Ban F1659	57	.50
The oracle.	Lion LL 102	56	.35
_____.	Pyr G412	59	.35
O'CONNOR, FLANNERY			
A good man is hard to find.	Sig S1345	56	.35
Wise blood.	Sig 1029	53	.25
O'CONNOR, JACK			
Boom town.	Dell D129	53	.35
O'CONNOR, RICHARD			
Bat Masterson.	Ban A1888	58	.35
Down to eternity.	GM s550	56	.35
Guns of Chickamauga.	Ban A1491	56	.35
The Sulu sword.	Ace G-386	59	.50
O'DELL, SCOTT			
Hill of the Hawk.	Ban A1138	53	.35
with William Doyle			
Man alone.	Ban 1247	54	.25
ODLUM, JEROME			
The mirabilis diamond.	Dell 303	49	.25
O'DONNELL, BERNARD			
The world's worst women.	Pyr 183	56	.25
O'FAOLAIN, SEAN			
The finest stories of Sean O'Faolain.	BanC FC47	59	.50
O'FARRELL, WILLIAM			
Brandy for a hero.	Dell 306	49	.25
Causeway to the past.	Dell 555	51	.25
The devil his due.	Berk 373	57	.25
Repeat performance.	Pnnt P55	54	.25
Thin edge of violence.	Ban 1128	53	.25
Walk the dark bridge.	Pnnt P35	54	.25
Wetback.	DelF A120	56	.25

Author/Title	Pub./Stock No.	Yr.	Price
OFFORD, CARL			
The naked fear.	Ace S-54	54	.25
OFFORD, LENORE GLEN			
The glass mask.	Dell 198	47	.25
My true love lies.	Dell 476	51	.25
Skeleton key.	Dell 96	45	.25
with Joseph Henry Jackson			
The girl in the belfry.	GM s688	57	.35
O'FLAHERTY, LIAM			
The informer.	Sup M650	45	.25
_____.	Ban 150	48	.25
_____.	Ban A1357	55	.35
Selected stories.	Sig S1553	58	.35
OGILVIE, ELISABETH			
Honeymoon.	Bart 103	47	.25
OHANIAN, PHYLLIS BROWN with Agnes Leckie Mason			
God's wonderful world.	SigK KD315	54	.50
O'HARA, DENNISON			
The sky tramps.	RS 7	52	.35
O'HARA, DONN			
The fair and the bold.	Graf G222	57	.35
Rogue royal.	Graf G212	56	.35
The wild years.	Pop 635	55	.25
O'HARA, JOHN			
All the girls he wanted.	Avon 368	51	.25
Appointment in Samarra.	PB 27	39	.25
_____.	Pen 563	45	.25
_____.	Sig 766	50	.25
_____.	Sig 1087	53	.25
_____.	Sig S1437	57	.35
Butterfield 8.	Avon 94	46	.25
_____.	Avon 231	49	.25
_____.	Avon 422	52	.25
_____.	Avon T-107	55	.35
_____.	Avon T-183	57	.35
_____.	Avon G-2002	59	.50
The doctor's son.	Avon (31)	43	.25
A family party.	Ban 1640	57	.25
The Farmers Hotel.	Ban 1046	52	.25
_____.	Ban 1594	57	.25
The great short stories of John O'Hara.	Ban A1484	56	.35
Hellbox.	Avon 293	50	.25
_____.	Avon 679	55	.25
Hope of heaven.	Avon 144	47	.25
_____.	Avon 258	50	.25
_____.	Ban 1422	56	.25
Pal Joey.	Pen 580	46	.25
_____.	DelT 24	51	.10
_____.	Ban 1679	57	.25
A rage to live.	Ban F935	51	.50
_____.	Ban F1583	57	.50
Stories of venial sin.	Avon 661	55	.25

Author/Title	Pub./Stock No.	Yr.	Price
O'HARA, JOHN (cont.)			
Ten North Frederick.	Ban F1554	57	.50
OKUMIYA, MASATAKE with Mitsuo Fuchida			
Midway.	Ball F224	58	.50
OLAY, LIONEL			
The heart of a stranger.	Sig 1581	59	.25
OLESKER, HARRY			
Now, will you try for murder?	Dell 996	59	.25
OLIVE, HARRY			
The darkness of love.	Mon 131	59	.35
OLIVER, CHAD			
Another kind.	Ball 113	55	.35
Shadows in the sun.	Ball 91	54	.35
The winds of time.	PB 1222	59	.25
OLIVIA			
Olivia.	Berk G-74	57	.35
⎯⎯⎯⎯.	Berk G-175	58	.35
OLLIVANT, ALFRED			
Bob, son of Battle.	PB 61	40	.25
OLSEN, D. B.			
The cat saw murder.	Dell 35	44	.25
The clue in the clay.	Bart 35	46	.25
Dead babes in the wood.	Dell 784	54	.25
Something about midnight.	PB 817	51	.25
OLSEN, T. V.			
Haven of the hunted.	Ace D-138	56	.35
The man from nowhere.	Ace D-348	59	.35
OLSON, GENE			
The outsiders.	Ace D-134	55	.35
Stampede at Blue Springs.	Dell 974	58	.25
O'MALLEY, BILL			
Blessed event.	Perm M-3047	56	.25
Feeling no pain.	Perm M-3078	57	.25
O'Malley's nuns.	Perm M-3105	58	.25
O'MALLEY, FRANK			
The best go first.	Ban 959	52	.25
OMAR KHAYYĀM			
The Rubáiyát of Omar Khayyām.	Avon (2)	41	.25
⎯⎯⎯⎯.	PB 128	41	.25
⎯⎯⎯⎯.	Avon 262	50	.25
⎯⎯⎯⎯.	Bard 1	55	.35
O'MARA, JIM			
Guns of vengeance.	Pop 465	52	.25
Quick trigger law.	Pop 487	53	.25
Rustler of the owlhorns.	Pop 518	53	.25
Trial by gunsmoke.	Pop 420	52	.25
Wall of guns.	PB 816	51	.25
O'MEARA, WALTER			
The devil's cross.	Perm M-4119	59	.35
The grand portage.	Ban A1036	52	.35
OMURA, KIMIKO with William Vaneer			
Diary of a geisha girl.	Avon T-313	59	.35
100 stories of business success.	Ban A1658	57	.35
1000 facts worth knowing.	BPLA unk	40	.10
O'NEAL, COTHBURN			
Conquests of Tamerlane.	Avon G-1030	57	.50
Master of the world.	Avon G-1011	54	.50
O'NEILL, CHARLES			
Morning time.	Prmb P163	52	.35
O'NEILL, EUGENE			
Desire under the elms.	Sig S1502	58	.35
ONSTOTT, KYLE			
Mandingo.	Crst t202	58	.75
OPITZ, KARLLUDWIG			
The general.	Ace S-256	57	.25
OPPENHEIM, E. PHILLIPS			
The great impersonation.	PB 224	43	.25
The great Prince Shan.	PB 54	40	.25
The lion and the lamb.	Pop 339	51	.25
O'QUINN, ALLEN			
Strangers in my bed.	GM 463	55	.25
⎯⎯⎯⎯.	GM 871	59	.25
Swamp brat.	GM 281	53	.25
⎯⎯⎯⎯.	GM 585	56	.25
A woman for Henry.	GM 399	54	.25
ORCZY, BARONESS			
The Scarlet pimpernel.	PyrR PR16	58	.35
ORDWAY, PETER			
The face in the shadows.	Prmb 252	53	.25
O'ROURKE, FRANK			
Action at Three Peaks.	Ban 720	49	.25
Ambuscade.	Sig 1715	59	.25
Battle royal.	DelF 89	56	.25
The big fifty.	DelF 59	55	.25
Blackwater.	Ban 916	51	.25
The bravados.	DelF A131	57	.25
⎯⎯⎯⎯.	DelF A157	58	.25
Car deal!	Ball 111	55	.35
Concannon.	Ball 10	53	.35

Author/Title	Pub./Stock No.	Yr.	Price
O'ROURKE, FRANK (cont.)			
Dakota rifle.	DelF 41	55	.25
Desperate rider.	Sig 1748	59	.25
The diamond hitch.	Dell 966	58	.25
Gold under Skull Peak.	Ban 1149	53	.25
Gun hand.	Ball 35	53	.35
.	Ball 212	57	.35
Gunsmoke over Big Muddy.	Pnnt P17	53	.25
Hard men.	Ball 149	56	.35
High dive.	Ban 1344	55	.25
High vengeance.	Ball 82	54	.35
.	Ball 214	57	.35
The last chance.	DelF 104	56	.25
The last round.	Perm M-3069	57	.25
Latigo.	Ban 1549	56	.25
Legend in the dust.	Ball 211	57	.35
Ride West.	Ball 49	53	.35
Segundo.	DelF 108	56	.25
A Texan came riding.	Sig 1536	58	.25
Thunder in the sun.	Ball 69	54	.35
Thunder on the Buckhorn.	Ban 799	50	.25
Violence at sundown.	Ball 98	55	.35
.	Ball 213	57	.35
Warbonnet law.	Ban 1005	52	.25
ORR, MARY			
Diamond in the sky.	Perm M-4086	57	.35
ORSBORNE, DOD			
Mission: danger.	Ban 839	50	.25
ORTEGA y GASSET, JOSÉ			
The revolt of the masses.	Ment M49	50	.35
ORWELL, GEORGE			
Animal farm.	Sig 1289	56	.25
.	Sig S1615	58	.35
.	SigC CD3	59	.50
Burmese days.	Pop 459	52	.25
.	Pop G214	58	.35
Coming up for air.	Avon T-144	56	.35
Down and out in Paris and London.	Prmb P267	54	.35
.	Avon T-121	56	.35
.	Berk G262	59	.35
Keep the aspidistra flying.	Pop G193	57	.35
1984.	Sig 798	50	.25
.	Sig D1640	58	.50
OSANN, KATE			
Tizzy.	Berk 382	58	.25
OSBORNE, JOHN			
Look back in anger.	Ban A2034	59	.35
OSBORNE, JUANITA			
Tornado.	Ace D-65	54	.35
OSBORNE, O. O.			
Leave her to God.	GM 301	53	.25

Author/Title	Pub./Stock No.	Yr.	Price
The quest.	RS 17	52	.35
The rise and fall of Dr. Carey.	GM s764	58	.35
O'SULLIVAN, J. B.			
Don't hang me too high.	PB 1109	56	.25
I die possessed.	PB 1055	55	.25
OTIS, G. H.			
Bourbon Street.	Lion 131	53	.25
Hot cargo.	Lion 171	53	.25
OTT, WOLFGANG			
Sharks and little fish.	Dell F73	59	.50
OTTO, MAX			
Science and the moral life.	Ment M43	49	.35
.	Ment MD139	55	.50
OTWAY, HOWARD			
Strangers in paradise.	Crst s171	57	.35
OURSLER, FULTON			
The greatest book ever written.	Prmb P250S	53	.50
.	Perm M-1600	54	.50
.	Perm M-5014	59	.50
The greatest faith ever known.	Perm M-4036	55	.35
The greatest story ever told.	Prmb P135	51	.35
.	Perm M-4046	56	.35
Lights along the shore.	Perm M-4041	56	.35
Modern parables.	Prmb P177	52	.35
.	Perm M-4017	55	.35
The wager and The house at Fernwood.	Pony 50	46	.25
Why I know there is a God.	Prmb 272	54	.25
OURSLER, WILL			
As tough as they come.	Prmb P118	51	.35
Departure delayed.	Ace D-37	53	.35
N.Y., N.Y.	Card C-173	55	.35
with Laurence D. Smith			
Hooked.	Pop 528	53	.25
OVERHOLSER, WAYNE D.			
Buckaroo's code.	Dell 372	50	.25
.	Dell 699	53	.25
Cast a long shadow.	Dell 924	56	.25
Desperate man.	Dell 993	58	.25
Draw or drag.	Dell 556	51	.25
.	Dell 903	56	.25
Fabulous gunman.	Dell 729	53	.25
Gunlock.	Dell 972	58	.25
The lone deputy.	Dell 1008	59	.25
Steel to the south.	Dell 624	52	.25
.	Dell 948	57	.25
Tough hand.	Dell 846	55	.25

Author/Title	Pub./Stock No.	Yr.	Price
OVERHOLSER, WAYNE D. (cont.)			
Valley of guns.	Dell 815	54	.25
The violent land.	Dell 875	55	.25
West of the rimrock.	Dell 499	51	.25
_____.	Dell 796	54	.25
with William MacLeod Raine			
High Grass Valley.	Eag EB81	57	.25
OWEN, DEAN			
Brush rider.	Eag EB33	55	.25
_____.	Pop G388	59	.35
The gunpointer.	Pop 788	56	.25
Last-chance range.	Pop 802	57	.25
The man from Boot Hill.	Ace D-12	53	.35
Point of a gun.	Pop 538	53	.25
Rawhider from Texas.	Mon 104	58	.35
Rifle Pass.	Pop 583	54	.25
_____.	Pop G370	59	.35
This range is mine.	Avon T-348	59	.35
OWEN, MARK			
Trouble at Borrasca Rim.	GM 794	58	.25
OZAKI, MILTON K.			
Case of the cop's wife.	GM 795	58	.25
Case of the deadly kiss.	GM 715	57	.25
The deadly pick-up.	Graf 57	53	.25
_____.	Graf 92	54	.25
Dressed to kill.	Graf 79	54	.25
_____.	Graf 141	56	.25
_____.	Dmnd D2007	59	.35
The dummy murder case.	Graf 33	51	.25
A fiend in need.	Han 116	50	.25
Maid for murder.	Ace D-135	55	.35
Murder doll.	Dmnd D2016	59	.35
Never say die.	Ace D-167	56	.35
Too many women.	Han 100	50	.25
Wake up and scream.	GM 879	59	.25

Author/Title	Pub./Stock No.	Yr.	Price
P			
PACKARD, REYNOLDS			
Dateline: Paris.	Berk BG231	59	.50
Low-down.	Ban 879	51	.25
PACKARD, VANCE			
The hidden persuaders.	Card C-288	58	.35
The human side of			
animals.	PB 755	51	.25
with Clifford R. Adams			
How to pick a mate.	Dell 224	48	.25
PACKER, PETER			
Bitter fruit.	Pop 433	52	.25
	Pop G331	59	.35
Dark surrender.	Pop 468	52	.25
PACKER, VIN			
Come destroy me.	GM 363	54	.25
Dark don't catch me.	GM s624	56	.35
Dark intruder.	GM 250	52	.25
	GM 578	56	.25
The evil friendship.	GM s797	58	.35
5:45 to suburbia.	GM s731	58	.35
Look back to love.	GM 324	53	.25
Spring fire.	GM 222	52	.25
	GM 398	54	.25
	GM s793	58	.35
Three-day terror.	GM 689	57	.25
The thrill kids.	GM 510	55	.25
	GM s903	59	.35
The twisted ones.	GM s861	59	.35
Whisper his sin.	GM 426	54	.25
The young and violent.	GM 581	56	.25
	GM s941	59	.35
PADGETT, LEWIS			
The day he died.	Ban 306	48	.25
Line to tomorrow.	Ban 1251	54	.25
Murder in brass.	Ban 107	47	.25
with C. L. Moore			
Beyond earth's gates.	Ace D-69	54	.35
PADOVER, SAUL K.			
Jefferson.	Ment M70	52	.35
	Ment MD160	55	.50
The living U.S.			
Constitution.	Ment M95	53	.35
PAGANO, JO			
The condemned.	Prmb 286	54	.25
Die screaming.	Zen ZB-4	58	.35
PAGE, MARCO			
Fast company.	PB 222	43	.25
Reclining figure.	PB 931	53	.25
The shadowy third.	PB 537	49	.25
PALEY, FRANK			
Rumble on the docks.	Pop G146	55	.35

Author/Title	Pub./Stock No.	Yr.	Price
PALGRAVE, F. T. with Oscar Williams			
The golden treasury.	Ment Ms90	53	.50
_____.	Ment MT245	58	.75
PALMER, STUART, 1905-			
Before it's too late.	Dell 601	52	.25
Four lost ladies.	Dell 715	53	.25
The puzzle of the			
silver Persian.	Dell 18	43	.25
Unhappy hooligan.	Perm M-3079	57	.25
PALMER, STUART, 1924-			
Understanding other			
people.	Prem s35	56	.35
_____.	Prem d78	59	.50
PANGBORN, EDGAR			
A mirror for observors.	Dell D246	58	.35
PAPASHVILY, GEORGE with Helen Papashvily			
Anything can happen.	PB 556	48	.25
PAPASHVILY, HELEN with George Papashvily			
Anything can happen.	PB 556	48	.25
PAPE, RICHARD			
Boldness be my friend.	Pop 643	55	.25
PAPINI, GIOVANNI			
Life of Christ.	Dell F59	57	.50
PARADISE, JEAN			
The savage city.	Ace D-178	56	.35
PARES, BERNARD			
Russia.	Ment M37	49	.35
_____.	Ment MD230	58	.50
PARISE, GOFFREDO			
Don Gastone and the			
women.	Avon T-209	57	.35
PARK, C. S.			
Showdown at Pistol Flat.	Pop G286	58	.35
Silver bullets.	Pop 814	57	.25
PARK, JORDAN			
Half.	Lion 135	53	.25
The man of cold rages.	Pyr G368	58	.35
Sorority house.	Lion LL 97	56	.35
Valerie.	Lion 176	53	.25
_____.	Lion LB 153	57	.25
PARK, RUTH			
The witch's thorn.	Ball 5	52	.35
PARKER, DAN			
The ABC of horseracing.	Ban 551	48	.25
PARKER, DOROTHY			
After such pleasures.	PB 57	40	.25

Author/Title	Pub./Stock No.	Yr.	Price
PARKER, DOROTHY (cont.)			
Enough rope.	PB 6	39	.25
Sunset gun.	PB 76	40	.25
PARKER, GEORGE			
Guaracha Trail.	Pnnt P46	54	.25
PARKER, GLADYS			
Mopsy.	Berk 336	55	.25
PARKER, ROBERT			
Passport to peril.	Dell 568	52	.25
Ticket to oblivion.	Ban 878	51	.25
PARKES, JAMES			
An enemy of the people:			
anti-semitism.	Pel P5	46	.25
PARKES, LUCAS with John Wyndham			
The outward urge.	Ball 341K	59	.35
PARKHILL, FORBES			
Troopers West.	Eag EB23	54	.25
PARKMAN, FRANCIS			
The Oregon Trail.	Ment M51	50	.35
_____.	Ment MD149	55	.50
PARONE, EDWARD			
Six great modern plays.	DelF FE100	56	.50
_____.	DelL LX103	58	.75
PARROTT, URSULA			
Ex-wife.	Dell 277	49	.25
Strangers may kiss.	Dell 409	50	.25
PARSONS, E. M.			
Texas heller.	DelF A191	59	.25
PARTCH, VIRGIL			
Crazy cartoons by VIP.	Crst 155	56	.25
_____.	Crst 311	59	.25
Funny cartoons by VIP.	GM 445	55	.25
Here we go again and			
Bottle fatigue.	Dell 990	58	.25
Man the beast and The			
wild, wild women.	Dell 843	55	.25
with Norman Lockridge			
Sex without tears.	Crst 141	56	.25
with Ted Shane			
Bar guide.	GM 135	50	.25
_____.	GM 337	53	.25
PARTRIDGE, BELLAMY			
Country lawyer.	PB 327	45	.25
Excuse my dust.	Pop 320	51	.25
PASINETTI, PIER			
Great Italian short			
stories.	DelL LC127	59	.50

Author/Title	Pub./Stock No.	Yr.	Price
PASTERNAK, BORIS			
Last summer.	Avon G-1036	59	.50
Safe conduct.	Sig D1669	59	.50
PATAI, IRENE			
The valley of God.	Pop G195	57	.35
PATER, WALTER			
The Renaissance.	Ment MD265	59	.50
PATERSON, NEIL			
Man on the tightrope.	Avon 552	53	.25
PATMAN, WRIGHT			
Our American government.	Ban A1210	54	.35
PATON, ALAN			
Too late the phalarope.	Sig S1290	56	.35
PATRICK, JOSEPH			
King's arrow.	Prmb P182	52	.35
PATRICK, Q.			
Cottage sinister.	Pop 386	51	.25
Death and the maiden.	Pop 36	44	.25
Death for dear Clara.	Pop 8	43	.25
The girl on the gallows.	GM 397	54	.25
The Grindle nightmare.	Pop 206	49	.25
Murder at Cambridge.	Pop 263	50	.25
Return to the scene.	Pop 47	45	.25
S.S. murder.	Pop 23	44	.25
PATTEN, LEWIS B.			
Fighting rawhide.	Crst 274	59	.25
Five rode West.	GM 723	58	.25
Gun proud.	Graf 151	57	.25
Gunsmoke empire.	GM 526	55	.25
Home is the outlaw.	GM 778	58	.25
The man who rode alone.	Avon T-339	59	.35
The massacre at San			
Pablo.	GM 706	57	.25
Massacre at White River.	Ace D-4	52	.35
Pursuit.	Perm M-3088	57	.25
Rope law.	GM 573	56	.25
The ruthless men.	GM 866	59	.25
Savage star.	Avon T-331	59	.35
Showdown at War Cloud.	GM 815	58	.25
Top man with a gun.	GM 920	59	.25
Valley of violent men.	Crst 174	57	.25
White warrior.	GM 602	56	.25
PATTERSON, HAYWOOD with Earl Conrad			
Scottsboro boy.	Ban 920	51	.25
PATTERSON, ROD			
A killer comes riding.	Ace D-144	56	.35
Prairie terror.	Ace D-252	57	.35
A time for guns.	Ace D-316	58	.35
Whip hand.	Lion 203	54	.25
_____.	Lion LB 164	57	.25

Author/Title	Pub./Stock No.	Yr.	Price
PATTI, ERCOLE			
A Roman affair.	PB 1225	59	.25
PATTINSON, JAMES			
Last in convoy.	Berk BG-202	59	.50
PATTON, FRANCES GRAY			
Good morning, Miss Dove.	PB 1099	56	.25
PATTON, MARTHA with Price A. Patton			
Freedom from money worries.	Prem d62	58	.50
PATTON, PRICE A. with Martha Patton			
Freedom from money worries.	Prem d62	58	.50
PAUL, ELLIOT			
A ghost town on the Yellowstone.	Ban 262	49	.25
Hugger-mugger in the Louvre.	PB 151	42	.25
The last time I saw Paris.	Ban 13	45	.25
Mayhem in B-flat.	Ban 850	50	.25
Murder on the Left Bank.	Ban 1012	52	.25
Mysterious Mickey Finn.	Avon 243	50	.25
PAUL, GENE			
The big make.	Lion LL 158	57	.35
Little killer.	Lion 104	52	.25
Naked in the dark.	Lion 154	53	.25
PAUL, LOUIS			
Breakdown.	Dell 425	50	.25
PAUST, GIL			
Gil Paust's gun book.	Lion LL 126	56	.35
PAVESE, CESARE			
The moon and the bonfires.	Sig 1117	54	.25
PAYNE, ALAN			
This'll slay you.	Ace D-289	58	.35
PAYNE, ROBERT			
Alexander and the camp follower.	Ace D-127	55	.35
The barbarian and the geisha.	Sig S1513	58	.35
Blood royal.	Pop G138	54	.35
	Pop SP40	59	.50
The blue Negro.	Avon 373	51	.25
The chieftain.	Card C-151	54	.35
A house in Peking.	Pop G198	57	.35
Lovers in the sun.	Pyr 143	55	.25
Red Lion Inn.	Pop G108	52	.35
	Pop SP34	58	.50
The tormentors.	Hill 107	59	.35

Author/Title	Pub./Stock No.	Yr.	Price
with Leonardo da Vinci			
The deluge.	Lion 233	55	.25
PAYNE-GAPOSCHKIN, CECILIA			
The stars in the making.	Card GC-69	59	.50
PEACE, FRANK			
The brass brigade.	Perm M-3052	56	.25
Easy money.	Perm M-3026	56	.25
PEACOCK, MAX			
King's rogue.	Graf G205	54	.35
PEALE, NORMAN VINCENT			
The art of living.	Perm M-4009	55	.35
Guideposts.	Ace D-281	58	.35
PEARCE, DICK			
Hell or high water.	Ban 213	49	.25
The impudent rifle.	Pop 418	52	.25
The restless border.	Ban A1239	54	.35
Valley of the tyrant.	Han 125	51	.25
PEARL, CYRIL			
The girl with the swansdown seat.	Sig D1561	58	.50
PEARL, RICHARD M.			
How to know the minerals and rocks.	SigK KD346	57	.50
PEARSON, F. S. II with R. Taylor			
Fractured French.	Perm M-3031	56	.25
PEARSON, MICHAEL with Bill Strutton			
The beachhead spies.	Ace D-355	59	.35
PEARSON, WILLIAM			
The beautiful frame.	PB 1039	55	.25
Hunt the man down.	PB 1141	56	.25
PEASE, HOWARD			
The jinx ship.	PBJr J-71	51	.35
Long wharf.	Com 33	49	.25
Road kid.	Ban 1110	53	.25
The ship without a crew.	PBJr J-76	51	.35
Tattooed man.	Com 10	48	.25
The wind in the rigging.	PBJr J-73	51	.35
PEATTIE, DONALD CULROSS			
Lives of destiny as told for the Reader's digest.	SigK K306	54	.25
PEATTIE, LOUISE REDFIELD			
American acres.	Dell 183	47	.25
PECK, JOSEPH H.			
All about men.	Perm M-4140	59	.35
PEDRICK, JEAN			
The fascination.	Ban 477	49	.25

Author/Title	Pub./Stock No.	Yr.	Price
PEEPLES, SAMUEL A.			
Call of the gun.	Ace D-120	55	.35
Doc Colt.	Ace D-226	57	.35
Gun feud at Stampede Valley.	Avon 596	54	.25
_____.	Avon 782	57	.25
The Lobo horseman.	Ace D-98	55	.35
Outlaw vengeance.	PB 760	51	.25
Terror at Tres Alamos.	Ace D-166	56	.35
PEI, MARIO			
Getting along in Italian.	Ban A1802	58	.35
Language for everybody.	Card GC-44	58	.50
Swords for Charlemagne.	Graf G208	55	.35
_____.	Graf G219	57	.35
with John Fisher			
Getting along in French.	Ban A1801	58	.35
with Robert Politzer			
Getting along in German.	Ban A1944	59	.35
with Eloy Vaquero			
Getting along in Spanish.	Ban A1943	59	.35
PEIL, PAUL LESLIE			
Tucson.	GM 779	58	.25
with Noel Loomis			
Hang the men high.	GM 692	57	.25
PELO, WILLIAM J.			
Pocket self-pronouncing dictionary and vocabulary builder.	PB 126	41	.25
PEMBERTON, LOIS			
The stork didn't bring you.	Lion LL 26	55	.35
PEN, JOHN			
Temptation.	Avon G1008	52	.50
_____.	Avon G-1019	55	.50
_____.	Avon G1033	59	.50
PENDELL, ELMER with Guy I. Burch			
Human breeding and survival.	Pel P17	47	.35
PENDLETON, FORD			
Gun chance.	Graf 155	57	.25
Gunmaster.	Graf 133	56	.25
Hell rider.	Graf 116	55	.25
_____.	Graf 157	57	.25
Outlaw justice.	Graf 88	54	.25
_____.	Graf 154	57	.25
PENNELL, JOSEPH			
Dishonored flesh.	Avon G-1029	56	.50
PENTECOST, HUGH			
The brass chills.	Pop 44	45	.25
Cancelled in red.	Pop 53	45	.25
Chinese nightmare.	DelT 31	51	.10
I'll sing at your funeral.	Pop 109	47	.25
Shadow of madness.	Pop 377	51	.25
The 24th horse.	Pop 82	46	.25
PEPPARD, HAROLD M.			
Sight without glasses.	Perm M-4012	55	.35
_____.	SigK Ks342	56	.35
PERELMAN, S. J.			
Acres and pains.	Pop 240	50	.25
PERKINS, J. R.			
The Emperor's physician.	PB 481	47	.25
PERKINS, KENNETH			
Relentless.	Ban 251	48	.25
PERRETTA, ARMANDO T.			
Take a number.	Pop G262	58	.35
PERRY, GEORGE SESSIONS			
Hold autumn in your hand.	PB 795	51	.25
Walls rise up.	Pnnt P32	54	.25
PERRY, RALPH R.			
Nightrider deputy.	Ace D-72	54	.35
PETERKIN, JULIA			
Scarlet sister Mary.	PB 48	40	.25
PETERS, BILL			
Blondes die young.	Pop 519	53	.25
_____.	Pop G338	59	.35
PETERS, FRITZ			
The descent.	Sig 1064	53	.25
Descent to darkness.	Dmnd D2005	59	.35
Finistère.	Sig 930	52	.25
The world next door.	Sig 813	50	.25
PETERS, MATTHEW			
The joys she chose.	DelF 24	54	.25
PETERS, ROYAL			
Body or soul.	RC 5	49	.25
PETERSEN, HERMAN			
The D.A.'s daughter.	Dell 55	44	.25
Old bones.	Dell 125	46	.25
PETERSON, HOUSTON			
Great essays.	Card C-113	54	.35
with James Bayley			
Essays in philosophy.	PBL PL518	59	.50
PETERSON, ROGER TORY			
How to know the birds.	Ment M36	49	.35
_____.	SigK KD347	57	.50

Author/Title	Pub./Stock No.	Yr.	Price
PETHERBRIDGE, MARGARET			
The Pocket book of crossword puzzles.	PB 210	43	.25
The 2nd Pocket book of crossword puzzles.	PB 450	47	.25
The 3rd Pocket book of crossword puzzles.	PB 731	50	.25
PETRY, ANN			
Country place.	Sig 761	50	.25
_____.	Sig S1426	57	.35
The Narrows.	Sig T1259	55	.75
The street.	Sig 710	49	.25
_____.	Sig S1123	54	.35
PETTIT, CHARLES			
Chinese lover.	Pyr 85	53	.25
The impotent general.	Ace D-26	53	.35
The son of the grand eunuch.	Avon 197	49	.25
The unfaithful lady.	Avon 155	48	.25
PETTIT, WILLIAM E.			
City of chains.	Pyr G402	59	.35
PFAU, RALPH with Albert Hirshberg			
Prodigal shepherd.	Pop G342	59	.35
PFOUTZ, S. E.			
The whipping boy.	Pop 821	57	.25
PHILIPPE, CHARLES-LOUIS			
Bubu of Montparnasse.	Avon 172	48	.25
_____.	Avon 310	51	.25
_____.	Avon 607	54	.25
_____.	Berk 371	57	.25
PHILIPS, JUDSON			
The fourteenth trump.	Han 16	43	.15
Murder in marble.	Han 24	44	.15
PHILLIPS, ARTHUR			
Victory in the dust.	Prmb P175	52	.35
PHILLIPS, JAMES ATLEE			
The case of the shivering chorus girls.	Han 21	43	.15
The deadly mermaid.	DelF 26	54	.25
Pagoda.	Ban 1055	52	.25
Suitable for framing.	PB 725	50	.25
PHILLIPS, JOHN			
The second happiest day.	Ban A1368	55	.35
PHILLIPS, LEON			
Rogue lover.	Mon 106	59	.35
PHILLIPS, THOMAS HAL			
The bitterweed path.	Avon T-83	54	.35
_____.	Avon T-273	58	.35

Author/Title	Pub./Stock No.	Yr.	Price
The loved and the unloved.	Dell D198	57	.35
PHILLIPS, WILLIAM with Philip Rahv			
The Avon book of modern writing.	Avon AT66	53	.35
Avon book of modern writing no. 2.	Avon G-1016	54	.50
Modern writing no. 3.	Berk BG-18	56	.50
PICHARD, GEORGES with Max Lief			
Bachelor's guide to the opposite sex.	Avon 815	58	.25
PICK, ROBERT			
German stories and tales.	PBL PL32	55	.35
PICKTHALL, MOHAMMED MARMADUKE			
The meaning of the glorious Koran.	Ment Ms94	53	.50
_____.	Ment MT223	58	.75
PIERCE, GLENN			
The tyrant of Bagdad.	Ban A1774	58	.35
PIERSALL, JIM with Al Hirshberg			
Fear strikes out.	Ban A1582	57	.35
PIERSON, LOUISE RANDALL			
Roughly speaking.	Bart 23	46	.25
PIEYRE de MANDIARGUES, ANDRÉ			
The girl beneath the lion.	Berk G266	59	.35
PILLSBURY, ANN			
Ann Pillsbury's baking book.	PB 789	51	.25
_____.	Card C-206	56	.35
PINCHOT, ANN			
Rival to my heart.	Ban 1876	59	.25
with Ben Pinchot			
Hear this woman.	Prmb P167	52	.35
PINCHOT, BEN with Ann Pinchot			
Hear this woman.	Prmb P167	52	.35
PINES, NED L.			
Cartoon fun.	Pop 186	48	.25
Popular book of cartoons.	Pop 115	46	.25
PINTO, ORESTE			
Friend or foe?	Pop 629	54	.25
Spy catcher.	Berk G-67	57	.35
PIPER, H. BEAM with John J. McGuire			
Crisis in 2140.	Ace D-227	57	.35
A planet for Texans.	Ace D-299	58	.35

Author/Title	Pub./Stock No.	Yr.	Price
PIRRO, UGO			
The camp followers.	Dell D258	59	.35
PITKIN, WALTER B.			
Life begins at forty.	PB 120	41	.25
What's that plane?	PenS S201	42	.25
PITT, BARRIE			
Zeebrugge.	Ball F332K	59	.50
PITTENGER, TED			
Warrior's return.	Sig 1239	55	.25
PIZER, LAURETTE			
Eve's daughters.	Graf G217	57	.35
PLAGEMANN, BENTZ			
Downfall.	Pyr 55	52	.25
The sin underneath.	Pyr G185	56	.35
This is Goggle.	Sig S1460	58	.35
PLAIDY, JEAN			
Beyond the Blue Mountains.	Prmb P225	53	.35
The king's mistress.	Pyr G42	52	.35
_____.	Pyr G137	54	.35
Madame Serpent.	Avon AT54	53	.35
PLATO			
Dialogues of Plato.	PB 782	51	.25
_____.	Card C-66	52	.35
_____.	PBL PL7	55	.35
Great dialogues of Plato.	Ment MD167	56	.50
PLATT, RUTHERFORD			
A Pocket guide to the trees.	Card C-93	53	.35
PLENN, J. H.			
Texas hellion.	Sig 1174	55	.25
_____.	Sig 1618	58	.25
with C. J. LaRoche			
The fastest gun in Texas.	Sig 1312	56	.25
_____.	Sig 1635	59	.25
PLIEVIER, THEODOR			
Berlin.	Ace G-371	59	.50
Moscow.	Ace D-194	56	.35
Stalingrad.	Berk BG-102	58	.50
PLUTARCHUS			
Life stories of men who shaped history.	Ment M55	50	.35
_____.	Ment MD166	55	.50
Lives of the noble Greeks.	DelL LC138	59	.50
Lives of the noble Romans.	DelL LC139	59	.50
On love, family and the good life.	Ment MD202	57	.50
The POCKET Bible.	PB 92	41	.25
_____.	Card C-9	51	.35
_____.	PBL PL13	54	.50
The POCKET book of boners.	PB 110	41	.25
The POCKET book of Esquire cartoons.	Card C-331	59	.35
PODOLIN, SI			
Bed of hate.	Pyr 163	55	.25
Devil's cargo.	Pyr G150	55	.35
POE, EDGAR ALLAN			
Great tales and poems.	PB 39	40	.25
_____.	Card C-45	52	.35
_____.	PBL PL46	56	.35
Poe.	DelL LB120	59	.35
POHL, FREDERIK			
Alternating currents.	Ball 130	56	.35
Beyond the end of time.	Prmb P145	52	.35
The case against tomorrow.	Ball 206	57	.35
Edge of the city.	Ball 199	57	.35
Shadow of tomorrow.	Prmb P236	53	.35
Slave ship.	Ball 192	57	.35
Star science fiction stories.	Ball 16	53	.35
Star science fiction stories no. 2.	Ball 55	54	.35
Star science fiction stories no. 3.	Ball 96	55	.35
Star science fiction stories no. 4.	Ball 272K	58	.35
Star science fiction stories no. 5.	Ball 308K	59	.35
Star science fiction stories no. 6.	Ball 353K	59	.35
Star short novels.	Ball 89	54	.35
Tomorrow times seven.	Ball 325K	59	.35
with C. M. Kornbluth			
Gladiator-at-law.	Ball 107	55	.35
Presidential year.	Ball 144	56	.35
Search the sky.	Ball 61	54	.35
The space merchants.	Ball 21	53	.35
A town is drowning.	Ball 123	55	.35
Wolfbane.	Ball 335K	59	.35
POKER according to Maverick.	DelF B142	59	.35
POLITZER, ROBERT with Mario Pei			
Getting along in German.	Ban A1944	59	.35
POLLAK, JAMES			
The golden egg.	Prmb P231	53	.35
POLLET, ELIZABETH			
A family romance.	Sig 912	52	.25

Author/Title	Pub./Stock No.	Yr.	Price
POLSKY, THOMAS			
Curtains for the copper.	Dell 29	43	.25
_____.	Dell 700	53	.25
Curtains for the editor.	Dell 82	45	.25
POMERANZ, HERMAN			
Control high blood pressure and live longer.	Eton ET104	52	.35
POOLE, RICHARD			
Desert passage.	Ball 24	53	.35
The peacemaker.	Ball 60	54	.35
West of Devil's Canyon.	Crst 198	58	.25
POPE, DUDLEY			
Graf Spee.	Berk BG-82	57	.50
73 north.	Berk BG-211	59	.50
POPE, EDITH			
Brutally with love.	Dell 705	53	.25
POPKIN, ZELDA			
Dead man's gift.	Dell 190	47	.25
Death wears a white gardenia.	Dell 13	43	.25
The journey home.	PB 364	46	.25
Murder in the mist.	Dell 71	45	.25
No crime for a lady.	Dell 94	45	.25
PORTER, WILLIAM			
The lawbringers.	Ban 1794	58	.25
PORTNOY, LOUIS with Jules Saltman			
Fertility in marriage.	Sig 881	51	.25
POST, MARY BRINKER			
Annie Jordan.	PB 690	50	.25
POSTGATE, RAYMOND			
Verdict of twelve.	PB 331	46	.25
POTTER, CHARLES FRANCIS			
The lost years of Jesus revealed.	GM d768	58	.50
POTTS, JEAN			
The diehard.	Dell 982	58	.25
POWELL, DAWN			
A man's affair.	Crst 135	56	.25
POWELL, MICHAEL			
Death in the South Atlantic.	Ace D-269	58	.35
POWELL, RICHARD			
All over but the shooting.	Pop 92	46	.25
The case of the curious chair.	Han 31	44	.15

Author/Title	Pub./Stock No.	Yr.	Price
Lay that pistol down.	Ban 70	46	.25
Masterpiece in murder.	Dell 915	56	.25
On the hook.	Ace D-47	54	.35
The Philadelphian.	Ban F1817	58	.50
Say it with bullets.	Graf 93	54	.25
_____.	Graf 148	57	.25
Shell game.	Dell 518	51	.25
A shot in the dark.	Graf 55	52	.25
POWELL, TALMAGE			
The killer is mine.	PB 1250	59	.25
POWERS, ANNE			
The ironmaster.	Prmb P162	52	.35
The only sin.	Pop G148	55	.35
Rogue's honor.	Prmb P173	52	.35
POWERS, PAUL S.			
Six-gun doctor.	Ban 832	50	.25
POWERS, TOM			
Virgin with butterflies.	Dell 392	50	.25
PRALL, ROBERT with Norton Mockridge			
This is Costello.	GM 177	51	.25
_____.	GM s704	57	.35
PRASKINS, LEONARD with Barney Slater			
Three violent people.	GM 615	56	.25
PRATHER, RICHARD S.			
Always leave 'em dying.	GM 413	54	.25
	GM 598	56	.25
_____.	GM 849	59	.25
Bodies in bedlam.	GM 147	51	.25
	GM 496	55	.25
_____.	GM 819	58	.25
Case of the vanishing beauty.	GM 127	50	.25
	GM 425	54	.25
_____.	GM 820	58	.25
Dagger of flesh.	Crst 142	56	.25
_____.	Crst 277	59	.25
Darling, it's death.	GM 265	52	.25
	GM 505	55	.25
_____.	GM 838	59	.25
Everybody had a gun.	GM 165	51	.25
	GM 504	55	.25
_____.	GM 818	58	.25
Find this woman.	GM 203	51	.25
	GM 489	55	.25
_____.	GM 821	58	.25
Have gat--will travel.	GM 677	57	.25
	GM 860	59	.25
Lie down, killer.	Lion unk	52	.25
	Crst 132	56	.25
_____.	Crst 255	58	.25
Over her dear body.	GM s887	59	.35
Pattern for panic.	Berk 316	55	.25
_____.	Berk 362	56	.25

Author/Title	Pub./Stock No.	Yr.	Price
PRATHER, RICHARD S. (cont.)			
Pattern for panic.	Berk G-98	58	.35
_____.	Berk G241	59	.35
Ride a high horse.	GM 341	53	.25
The scrambled yeggs.	GM 770	58	.25
Slab happy.	GM s817	58	.35
Strip for murder.	GM 508	55	.25
_____.	GM 848	59	.25
Take a murder, darling.	GM 745	58	.25
Three's a shroud.	GM 665	57	.25
_____.	GM 896	59	.25
Too many crooks.	GM 551	56	.25
_____.	GM 850	59	.25
The wailing frail.	GM 592	56	.25
_____.	GM 712	57	.25
_____.	GM 851	59	.25
Way of a wanton.	GM 233	52	.25
_____.	GM 497	55	.25
_____.	GM 830	58	.25
with Stephen Marlowe			
Double in trouble.	GM d926	59	.50
PRATOLINI, VASCO			
The girls of Sanfrediano.	PB 1015	54	.25
A hero of our time.	Sig 969	53	.25
The naked streets.	Sig 1061	53	.25
A tale of poor lovers.	Sig 797	50	.25
PRATT, FLETCHER			
A short history of the army and navy.	PenS S224	44	.25
A short history of the Civil War.	Card C-7	52	.35
The undying fire.	Ball 25	53	.35
PRATT, REX			
You tell my son.	Sig S1708	59	.35
PRATT, THEODORE			
The big bubble.	Pop 463	52	.25
_____.	Pop G268	58	.35
Cocotte.	GM 153	51	.25
_____.	GM 536	55	.25
Danger trail.	Ban 473	49	.25
Escape to Eden.	GM S339	53	.35
The golden sorrow.	RS 16	52	.35
_____.	GM s641	57	.35
Handsome.	GM G205	52	.35
_____.	GM S432	54	.35
_____.	GM s618	56	.35
Handsome's seven women.	Crst s289	59	.35
Mercy island.	Dell 721	53	.25
Miss Dilly says no.	Ban 416	49	.25
My bride in the storm.	Avon 275	50	.25
Seminole.	GM 369	54	.25
_____.	GM 635	57	.25
Smash-up.	GM 421	54	.25
_____.	GM 867	59	.25
Thunder mountain.	Sig 905	51	.25
The tormented.	GM 119	50	.25
The tormented.	GM s474	55	.35
_____.	GM s933	59	.35
PREEDY, GEORGE			
Queen's caprice.	Avon G-1015	54	.50
PRESCOTT, JOHN			
Guns of Hell Valley.	Graf G218	57	.35
The renegade.	Ban 1467	56	.25
Wagon train.	Ban 1654	57	.25
PRESCOTT, ORVILLE			
Mid-century.	PBL PL65	58	.35
PRESNELL, FRANK G.			
No mourners present.	Dell 646	53	.25
Send another coffin.	Han 39	45	.15
Too hot to handle.	Dell 593	52	.25
PRESNELL, ROBERT JR.			
The witching pool.	Card C-38	52	.35
PRESSER, JACOB			
Breaking point.	Pop G324	59	.35
PRESSON, JAY			
Spring riot.	Lion 42	50	.25
PRESTON, CHARLES			
Battle of the sexes.	Avon 617	54	.25
Bottoms up!	DelF A129	57	.25
Cartoon guide to the battle of the sexes.	Avon 840	59	.25
A cartoon guide to the Kinsey report.	Avon 559	54	.25
Choice cartoons from Sports illustrated.	Perm M-3083	57	.25
Funny business.	GM 462	55	.25
Juvenile delinquency.	DelF 97	56	.25
No money down--36 months to pay!	Berk 365	57	.25
Office laffs.	Crst 159	57	.25
Oh, doctor!	Berk 325	55	.25
Pets--including women.	Perm M-3067	57	.25
The power of negative thinking.	Ball 115	55	.35
The $64,000,000 answer.	Berk 346	55	.25
Too humorous to mention.	PB 1200	58	.25
Zowie! Girl meets boy.	GM 540	56	.25
PRESTON, JOHN HYDE			
Portrait of a woman.	Berk 319	55	.25
A short history of the American Revolution.	Card C-25	52	.35
PRICE, GEORGE			
Cartoons by George Price.	Sup M643	45	.25
Who's in charge here?	Berk 329	55	.25
PRICE, JERAMIE			
Katrina.	Card C-220	56	.35

Author/Title	Pub./Stock No.	Yr.	Price	Author/Title	Pub./Stock No.	Yr.	Price
PRICE, ROGER				**PURDY, KEN W.**			
Droodles.	Perm M-3050	56	.25	The kings of the road.	Ban F1203	54	.50
I'm for me first.	Ball 152	56	.35				
In one head and out				**PURTELL, JOSEPH**			
the other.	Ball 132	56	.35	To a blindfold lady.	Han 20	43	.15
PRIESTLEY, J. B.				**PUTNAM, J. WESLEY**			
Black-out in Gretley.	Pen 548	44	.25	Playthings of desire.	NL 15	49	.25
The old dark house.	Pen 535	43	.25				
				PUZA, MARIO			
PROCHNOW, HERBERT V.				The dark arena.	Dell D164	56	.35
The toastmaster's and							
speaker's handbook.	Card C-199	55	.35	**PUZZA, GIUSEPPE**			
				Henry the Last.	Sig S1571	58	.35
PROCTER, MAURICE				Wind of the western sea.	Prmb P102	51	.35
Hurry the darkness.	Dell 739	53	.25				
Murder, somewhere in				**PYLE, ERNIE**			
this city.	Avon 696	56	.25	Here is your war.	PB 274	44	.25
The Pennycross murders.	Avon 594	54	.25				
The pub crawler.	Berk G-165	58	.35				
The ripper murders.	Avon 794	57	.25				
PROKOSCH, FREDERIC							
Nine days to Mukalla.	Avon T-90	54	.35				
A tale for midnight.	Pop G171	56	.35				
_____.	Pop SP38	59	.50				
PROLÉ, LOZANIA							
The magnificent							
courtesan.	Pop 334	51	.25				
PROSSER, W. H.							
Nine to five.	Prmb 270	54	.25				
PROTTER, ERIC with R. V. Cassill							
Left bank of desire.	Ace S-104	55	.25				
PROUTY, OLIVE HIGGINS							
Fabia.	Dell 648	53	.25				
Now, voyager.	Dell 99	46	.25				
White fawn.	Dell 167	47	.25				
PRUITT, ALAN							
The restless corpse.	Han 104	50	.25				
Typed for a corpse.	Han 135	51	.25				
PSYCHOLOGY for the fighting							
man.	PenS S212	43	.25				
PUGH, JOHN J.							
Captain of the Medici.	Perm M-4032	55	.35				
PUMA, FERNANDO							
7 arts.	Prmb P212S	53	.50				
7 arts no. 2.	Prmb P262S	54	.50				
PUNER, HELEN W.							
Freud: his life and							
his mind.	DelL LC137	59	.50				

Author/Title	Pub./Stock No.	Yr.	Price
Q			
QUARRY, NICK			
The girl with no place to hide.	GM 938	59	.25
The hoods come calling.	GM 747	58	.25
Trail of a tramp.	GM 824	58	.25
QUEEN, ELLERY			
The adventures of Ellery Queen.	PB 99	41	.25
The American gun mystery.	Dell 4	43	.25
————.	Avon 523	53	.25
————.	Avon T-292	59	.35
Calamity town.	PB 283	45	.25
Calendar of crime.	PB 960	53	.25
Cat of many tails.	PB 822	51	.25
————.	Card C-357	59	.35
The Chinese orange mystery.	PB 17	39	.25
The devil to pay.	PB 270	44	.25
The door between.	PB 471	47	.25
Double, double.	PB 874	52	.25
Dragon's teeth.	PB 459	47	.25
Drury Lane's last case.	PB 669	50	.25
————.	Avon 488	53	.25
————.	Avon T-184	57	.35
The Dutch shoe mystery.	PB 202	43	.25
The Egyptian cross mystery.	PB 227	43	.25
Ellery Queen's awards: tenth series.	Perm M-3076	57	.25
The finishing stroke.	Card C-343	59	.35
The four of hearts.	PB 245	44	.25
————.	Avon 509	53	.25
————.	Avon T-242	58	.35
The French powder mystery.	PB 71	40	.25
The glass village.	PB 1082	55	.25
The Greek coffin mystery.	PB 179	42	.25
Halfway house.	PB 259	44	.25
Inspector Queen's own case.	PB 1167	57	.25
The king is dead.	PB 1005	54	.25
The lamp of God.	DelT 23	51	.10
The murderer is a fox.	PB 517	48	.25
The new adventures of Ellery Queen.	PB 134	41	.25
The origin of evil.	PB 926	53	.25
Q.B.I.	PB 1118	56	.25
The Queen's awards: eighth series.	Perm M-3015	55	.25
The Roman hat mystery.	PB 77	40	.25
The scarlet letters.	PB 1049	55	.25
The Siamese twin mystery.	PB 109	41	.25
The Spanish cape mystery.	BPLA unk	40	.10
————.	PB 146	42	.25
Ten days' wonder.	PB 740	50	.25
There was an old woman.	PB 326	46	.25
The tragedy of X.	PB 125	41	.25
The tragedy of X.	Avon 425	52	.25
————.	Avon T-141	56	.35
The tragedy of Y.	PB 313	45	.25
————.	Avon 450	52	.25
————.	Avon T-337	59	.35
The tragedy of Z.	PB 355	46	.25
————.	Avon 465	52	.25
————.	Avon 726	56	.25
QUEEN, ELLERY JR.			
The green turtle mystery.	Com 13	49	.25
QUENTIN, PATRICK			
Black widow.	Dell 759	54	.25
The fate of the immodest blonde.	PB 676	50	.25
The follower.	Dell 710	53	.25
Love is a deadly weapon.	PB 614	49	.25
The man in the net.	Dell D261	59	.35
The man with two wives.	Dell D322	59	.35
My son, the murderer.	Dell 890	56	.25
A puzzle for fools.	PB 83	40	.25
————.	Dell D192	57	.35
A puzzle for players.	PB 164	42	.25
————.	Han 53	46	.15
A puzzle for puppets.	PB 420	47	.25
Run to death.	Dell 851	55	.25
Slay the loose ladies.	PB 460	48	.25
QUIGLEY, MARTIN			
A tent on Corsica.	Lion 144	53	.25
QUINTAVALLE, UBERTO			
The shameless ones.	Berk G-184	58	.35
QUINTET.	Lion LL 114	56	.50

Author/Title	Pub./Stock No.	Yr.	Price

R

RABE, PETER

Author/Title	Pub./Stock No.	Yr.	Price
Agreement to kill.	GM 670	57	.25
Benny muscles in.	GM 520	55	.25
Blood on the desert.	GM s825	58	.35
Bring me another corpse.	GM 864	59	.25
The cut of the whip.	Ace D-297	58	.35
Dig my grave deep.	GM 612	56	.25
A house in Naples.	GM 547	56	.25
It's my funeral.	GM 678	57	.25
_____.	GM 915	59	.25
Journey into terror.	GM 710	57	.25
Kill the boss good-bye.	GM 594	56	.25
Mission for vengeance.	GM s773	58	.35
The out is death.	GM 657	57	.25
A shroud for Jesso.	GM 528	55	.25
Stop this man.	GM 506	55	.25
_____.	GM 763	58	.25
Time enough to die.	GM 939	59	.25

RACE, PHILIP

Author/Title	Pub./Stock No.	Yr.	Price
Killer take all.	GM 888	59	.25
Self-made widow.	GM s796	58	.35

RACKOWE, ALEC

Author/Title	Pub./Stock No.	Yr.	Price
My Lord America.	Prmb P164	52	.35

RADDALL, THOMAS H.

Author/Title	Pub./Stock No.	Yr.	Price
Give and take.	Pop 615	54	.25
The nymph and the lamp.	Pop G101	52	.35
_____.	Pop SP17	58	.50
Roger Sudden.	Ban A1100	53	.35

RADIGUET, RAYMOND

Author/Title	Pub./Stock No.	Yr.	Price
Devil in the flesh.	Sig 750	49	.25
_____.	Sig 1175	55	.25
_____.	Sig S1721	59	.35

RADIN, EDWARD D.

Author/Title	Pub./Stock No.	Yr.	Price
Beyond the law.	Pop 513	53	.25
Crimes of passion.	Pop 605	54	.25
The deadly reasons.	Pop G248	58	.35
Headline crimes of the year.	Pop 470	52	.25
12 against crime.	Ban 921	51	.25
12 against the law.	Ban 997	52	.25
Web of passion.	Pop 674	55	.25

RADIN, MAX

Author/Title	Pub./Stock No.	Yr.	Price
The law and you.	Ment M34	48	.35
_____.	Ment M135	55	.35

RAFFERTY, KATHLEEN

Author/Title	Pub./Stock No.	Yr.	Price
Dell book of crossword puzzles.	Dell 205	47	.25
Dell crossword puzzle dictionary.	Dell 434	50	.25
_____.	Dell D200	57	.35
Dell crossword puzzles.	Dell 654	53	.25
Second Dell book of crossword puzzles.	Dell 278	49	.25
with Rosalind Moore			
Dell crossword puzzles.	DelF 60	55	.25

RAGSDALE, CLYDE

Author/Title	Pub./Stock No.	Yr.	Price
The big fist.	Dell 698	53	.25

RAHV, PHILIP with William Phillips

Author/Title	Pub./Stock No.	Yr.	Price
The Avon book of modern writing.	Avon AT66	53	.35
The Avon book of modern writing no. 2.	Avon G-1016	54	.50
Modern writing no. 3.	Berk BG-18	56	.50

RAINE, NORMAN REILLY

Author/Title	Pub./Stock No.	Yr.	Price
Tugboat Annie.	Dell 192	47	.25

RAINE, WILLIAM MacLEOD

Author/Title	Pub./Stock No.	Yr.	Price
Arizona guns.	Pop 436	52	.25
_____.	Pop 805	57	.25
The bandit trail.	Dell 424	50	.25
_____.	Dell 793	54	.25
Beyond the Rio Grande.	Pop 359	51	.25
_____.	Eag EB51	55	.25
_____.	Pop G394	59	.35
Big-town round-up.	Hill unk	49	.25
Border breed.	PB 721	50	.25
_____.	Eag EB101	58	.25
Bucky follows a cold trail.	Pop 86	47	.25
Bullet ambush.	Pop G278	58	.35
Challenge to danger.	Dell 711	53	.25
Clattering hoofs.	Sig 758	50	.25
_____.	Sig 1396	57	.25
Colorado.	Avon 500	53	.25
Desert feud.	Eag EB67	56	.25
_____.	Pop G390	59	.35
Dry bones in the valley.	Pnnt P67	54	.25
Drygulch trail.	Pop 256	50	.25
_____.	Eag EB35	55	.25
The fighting edge.	PB 691	50	.25
The fighting tenderfoot.	Sig 712	49	.25
Gun showdown.	PB 842	52	.25
Guns of the frontier.	Sig 1140	54	.25
Gunsight Pass.	Dell 238	48	.25
_____.	Dell 629	52	.25
Gunsmoke trail.	Pop 145	48	.25
Hell and high water.	Pop 322	51	.25
Justice comes to Tomahawk.	Sig 1069	53	.25
King of the bush.	Hill unk	50	.25
Man-size.	PB 656	50	.25
_____.	Pop G246	58	.35
Oh, you Tex!	PB 78	40	.25
On the dodge.	PB 743	50	.25
_____.	Pop G197	57	.35
Pistol pardners.	Pop 172	49	.25
_____.	Eag EB27	54	.25
_____.	Pop G374	59	.35

Author/Title	Pub./Stock No.	Yr.	Price
RAINE, WILLIAM MacLEOD (cont.)			
Powdersmoke feud.	Sig 806	50	.25
_____.	Sig 1483	58	.25
Range beyond the law.	Pop 471	52	.25
Ranger's luck.	PB 787	51	.25
Reluctant gunman.	Eag EB43	55	.25
Riders of Buck River.	Hill unk	48	.25
_____.	Dell 821	55	.25
The River Bend feud.	Pop 280	50	.25
_____.	Eag EB21	54	.25
_____.	Pop G305	59	.35
Rustlers' Gap.	Pop 213	49	.25
_____.	Eag EB2	53	.25
Rutledge trails the ace of spades.	Dell 383	50	.25
Saddlebum.	Dell 613	52	.25
The sheriff's son.	PB 815	51	.25
_____.	Pop G223	58	.35
Six-gun feud.	Eag EB59	56	.25
The six-gun kid.	Sig 973	52	.25
_____.	Sig 1303	56	.25
Sons of the saddle.	Sig 673	48	.25
_____.	Sig 1228	55	.25
Square shooter.	PB 611	49	.25
_____.	Pop G264	58	.35
Steve Yeager.	Hill unk	48	.25
Texas breed.	Pop 243	50	.25
_____.	Pop 553	54	.25
_____.	Pop G361	59	.35
The Texas kid.	Pop 414	52	.25
_____.	Eag EB73	56	.25
_____.	Pop G343	59	.35
To ride the river with.	Dell 954	57	.25
The tough tenderfoot.	Pop G295	58	.35
The trail of danger.	Hill unk	49	.25
Trail's end.	Dell 179	47	.25
_____.	Dell 359	49	.25
_____.	Dell 889	56	.25
Under northern stars.	PB 473	47	.25
West of the law.	Pop 531	53	.25
Western stories.	Dell 282	49	.25
Whipsaw.	Lion LL 32	55	.35
The Yukon trail.	PB 487	48	.25
with Wayne D. Overholser			
High Grass Valley.	Eag EB81	57	.25
RAINIER, PETER			
Green fire.	Ban A1086	53	.35
Pipeline to battle.	PenS S237	44	.25
RAND, AYN			
Atlas shrugged.	Sig Q1702	59	.95
The fountainhead.	Sig T934	52	.75
_____.	Sig T1468	57	.75
RAND McNally-Pocket world atlas.	Card C-20	51	.35
RANDALL, CLAY			
Boomer.	Perm M-3077	57	.25
Six-gun boss.	Pnnt P10	53	.25
When oil ran red.	Pnnt P48	54	.25
RANDALL, MARGARET			
The home encyclopedia of moving your family.	Berk G-207	59	.35
RANDAU, CARL with Leane Zugsmith			
The visitor.	Dell 132	46	.25
RANKIN, HUGH F. with George Scheer			
Rebels and redcoats.	Ment MT249	59	.75
RANSOME, STEPHEN			
Hearses don't hurry.	Dell 11	43	.25
I, the executioner.	Ace D-7	53	.35
The men in her death.	Perm M-3091	57	.25
RAPPORT, SAMUEL with Helen Wright			
The crust of the earth.	SigK Ks330	55	.35
_____.	Ment MD264	59	.50
RATCLIFF, J. D.			
Conception, pregnancy and birth.	PB 800	51	.25
RATTIGAN, TERENCE			
The prince and the showgirl.	Sig S1409	57	.35
Separate tables.	Sig S1609	59	.35
RAVETCH, IRVING			
The outriders.	Pop 466	52	.25
RAWICZ, SLAVOMIR			
The long walk.	Ace D-258	57	.35
RAWLINGS, MARJORIE KINNAN			
Gal young 'un.	Ban A1209	54	.35
South moon under.	Ban 10	45	.25
RAWSON, CLAYTON			
Death from a top hat.	Dell 69	45	.25
Footprints on the ceiling.	Dell 121	46	.25
The headless lady.	Dell 176	47	.25
No coffin for the corpse.	Dell 258	48	.25
RAWSON, TABOR			
I want to live!	Sig S1587	58	.35
RAY, WESLEY			
Damaron's gun.	Sig 1566	58	.25
RAYNER, D. A.			
The enemy below.	PB 1192	58	.25
RAYNOLDS, ROBERT			
The sinner of St. Ambrose.	Prmb P273	54	.35

Author/Title	Pub./Stock No.	Yr.	Price
RAYTER, JOE			
Asking for trouble.	PB 1132	56	.25
Stab in the dark.	PB 1145	57	.25
The victim was important.	PB 1070	55	.25
REACH, JAMES			
The innocent one.	Pop 598	54	.25
Late last night.	Graf 70	53	.25
_____.	Graf 130	56	.25
Sunset Strip.	Pop 828	57	.25
REASONER, HARRY			
Tell me about women.	Dell 417	50	.25
REAVEY, GEORGE			
14 great short stories by Soviet authors.	Avon G-1040	59	.50
REDDING, J. SAUNDERS			
Stranger and alone.	Pop 327	51	.25
REDMOND, CATHERINE			
Handbook for army wives and mothers.	PenS S215	43	.25
REED, ELIOT			
The Maras affair.	Perm M-3025	55	.25
Tender to danger.	Perm M-3005	55	.25
REED, HENRY HOPE with Christopher Tunnard			
American skyline.	Ment MD175	56	.50
REEDER, RED			
The Mackenzie raid.	Ball 110	55	.35
REESE, JOHN			
The high passes.	Dell 882	56	.25
REEVES, JAMES			
The Holy Bible in brief.	Ment Ms116	54	.50
REEVES, ROBERT			
Cellini Smith: detective.	Pony 54	46	.25
REID, ED			
Mafia.	Sig 1151	54	.25
_____.	Sig S1500	58	.35
REID, P. R.			
Escape from Colditz.	Berk G-38	56	.35
_____.	Berk G-107	58	.35
REILLY, HELEN			
All concerned notified.	Pen 504	42	.25
The canvas dagger.	Ban 1858	59	.25
The dead can tell.	Dell 17	43	.25
Dead for a ducat.	Pop 56	45	.25
Death demands an audience.	Pop 7	43	.25

Author/Title	Pub./Stock No.	Yr.	Price
The doll's trunk murder.	Pop 211	49	.25
The double man.	Dell 732	53	.25
The farmhouse.	Dell 397	50	.25
Lament for the bride.	Dell 621	52	.25
McKee of Centre Street.	Pop 33	44	.25
Mr. Smith's hat.	Pop 48	45	.25
Mourned on Sunday.	Dell 63	44	.25
Murder at Arroways.	Dell 576	52	.25
Murder in Shinbone Alley.	Pop 20	43	.25
Murder in the mews.	Pop 259	50	.25
Murder on Angler's Island.	Dell 228	48	.25
Name your poison.	Dell 148	47	.25
The opening door.	Dell 200	47	.25
_____.	Dell 917	56	.25
The silver leopard.	Dell 287	49	.25
Staircase 4.	Dell 498	51	.25
Three women in black.	Dell 114	46	.25
_____.	Dell 709	53	.25
REINER, CARL			
Enter laughing.	Crst s279	59	.35
REINHARDT, GUENTHER			
Crime without punishment.	Sig 1067	53	.25
REMARQUE, ERICH MARIA			
All quiet on the western front.	Lion 49	50	.25
_____.	Lion LL 81	56	.35
_____.	Crst s215	58	.35
_____.	Crst s337	59	.35
Arch of Triumph.	Sig S796	50	.35
_____.	Sig D1630	59	.50
The black obelisk.	Crst d249	58	.50
Spark of life.	Sig S1023	53	.35
Three comrades.	Pop G133	53	.35
_____.	Pop SP14	58	.50
A time to love and a time to die.	Pop G153	55	.35
_____.	Pop SP21	58	.50
RENAULT, MARY			
Kind are her answers.	Dell 189	47	.25
_____.	Dell D308	59	.35
Promise of love.	Dell 298	49	.25
Return to night.	Dell 394	50	.25
REPP, ED EARL			
Gun hawk.	Hill unk	48	.25
Hell in the saddle.	Hill unk	48	.25
RESKO, JOHN			
Reprieve.	Ban A1730	58	.35
RESNIK, MURIEL			
Life without father.	Pop G266	58	.35
RESTON, JAMES B.			
Prelude to victory.	PB 192	42	.25

Author/Title	Pub./Stock No.	Yr.	Price
REWALD, JOHN			
Gauguin.	PBA A15	54	.50
Pissarro.	PBA A18	54	.50
REYNOLDS, JACK			
A woman of Bangkok.	Ball F131	56	.50
REYNOLDS, MACK with Fredric Brown			
Science fiction carnival.	Ban A1615	57	.35
REYNOLDS, QUENTIN			
Courtroom.	Pop G106	52	.35
_____.	Pop SP8	57	.50
Headquarters.	Pop G166	56	.35
Raid at Dieppe.	Avon T-226	58	.35
70,000 to 1.	Pyr G351	58	.35
Smooth and deadly.	Pop 533	53	.25
They fought for the sky.	Ban A1785	58	.35
RHOADS, GERDA			
The lonely women.	Ball 196	57	.35
RHODE, JOHN			
The Avon book of crime and detective stories.	Avon (21)	42	.25
Dead of the night.	Pop 99	47	.25
Death sits on the board.	Pop 12	43	.25
Dr. Priestley investigates.	Avon (5)	41	.25
Poison for one.	Avon (35)	43	.25
with Carter Dickson			
Fatal descent.	Pop 87	47	.25
RHODES, EUGENE MANLOVE			
The proud sheriff.	Dell 688	53	.25
Sunset land.	Dell D152	55	.35
RICE, CRAIG			
The big midget murders.	PB 528	48	.25
The corpse steps out.	PB 476	47	.25
45 murderers.	Graf G203	53	.35
The fourth postman.	PB 651	50	.25
Having a wonderful crime.	PB 289	45	.25
Home sweet homicide.	PB 361	46	.25
Innocent bystander.	Dell 461	50	.25
Knocked for a loop.	PB 1215	58	.25
The lucky stiff.	PB 391	47	.25
My kingdom for a hearse.	PB 1189	58	.25
The name is Malone.	Pyr G350	58	.35
The right murder.	Pop 89	46	.25
The Sunday pigeon murders.	PB 434	47	.25
The Thursday turkey murders.	PB 461	48	.25
Trial by fury.	PB 237	43	.25
_____.	Dell D187	57	.35
The wrong murder.	Pop 45	45	.25
Yesterday's murder.	Pop 253	50	.25
with Ed McBain			
The April robin murders.	Dell D306	59	.35
RICE, ELMER			
Imperial city.	Avon 273	50	.25
RICE, GRANTLAND			
The tumult and the shouting.	Dell D161	56	.35
RICE, JOHN ANDREW			
Local color.	DelF 71	55	.25
RICH, DANIEL CATTON			
Degas.	PBA A1	53	.50
RICH, HELEN			
The spring begins.	Ban 744	49	.25
RICH, LOUISE DICKINSON			
We took to the woods.	PB 511	48	.25
RICHARDS, I. A.			
The Pocket book of basic English.	PB 299	45	.25
with Christine Gibson			
English through pictures, book 1.	Card C-75	53	.35
_____.	WSP W1	59	.35
English through pictures, book 2.	Card C-258	57	.35
_____.	WSP W4	59	.35
First steps in reading English.	Card C-256	57	.35
_____.	WSP W2	59	.35
A first workbook of French.	WSP W10	59	.35
with others			
A first workbook of French.	Card C-259	57	.35
French through pictures.	PB 650	50	.35
_____.	Card C-78	53	.35
French through pictures, book 1.	WSP W8	59	.35
German through pictures.	Card C-95	53	.35
German through pictures, book 1.	WSP W15	59	.35
Hebrew reader.	Card C-171	55	.35
_____.	WSP W39	59	.35
Hebrew through pictures.	Card C-170	55	.35
Hebrew through pictures, book 1.	WSP W38	59	.35
Italian through pictures.	Card C-201	55	.35
Italian through pictures, book 1.	WSP W22	59	.35
Spanish through pictures.	PB 720	50	.35
_____.	Card C-83	53	.35
Spanish through pictures, book 1.	WSP W30	59	.35
RICHARDS, J. M. with Elizabeth B. Mock			
An introduction to modern architecture.	Pel P20	47	.35

Author/Title	Pub./Stock No.	Yr.	Price
RICHARDS, LEE			
Hell strip.	GM 495	55	.25
	GM 659	57	.25
Lusty conquest.	GM 671	57	.25
RICHARDS, WILLIAM			
Dead man's tide.	Graf 60	53	.25
RICHARDS, WILLIAM C.			
The last billionaire,			
Henry Ford.	BanB FB405	56	.50
RICHARDSON, WILLIAM with Seymour Freidin			
The fatal decisions.	Berk BG-121	58	.50
RICHLER, MORDECAI			
Wicked we love.	Pop 677	55	.25
RICHMOND, ROE			
Death rides the			
Dondrino.	PB 1094	56	.25
The hard men.	Pyr 307	58	.25
Lash of Idaho.	Perm M-3104	58	.25
Mojave guns.	Lion 126	53	.25
Montana bad man.	Perm M-3086	57	.25
The Utah kid.	Lion 158	53	.25
	Lion LB 101	56	.25
RICHTER, CONRAD			
The fields.	Ban A1850	58	.35
The lady.	Ban A1792	58	.35
The light in the forest.	Ban 1264	54	.25
	Ban 1737	58	.25
The sea of grass.	PB 413	47	.25
	Ban 1208	54	.25
Tacey Cromwell.	Ban 759	50	.25
The town.	Ban F1851	58	.50
The trees.	Ban 962	52	.25
	Ban A1852	58	.35
RICHTER, HANS WERNER			
Beyond defeat.	Crst s188	57	.35
RICHTER, MISCHA			
Keeping women in line.	Avon 585	54	.25
The man on the couch.	PB 1150	57	.25
RICKS, DAVE			
Blood feud.	Pyr 78	53	.25
RIDER, BRETT			
Circle C carries on.	PB 620	49	.25
Circle C moves in.	PB 467	47	.25
Death stalks the range.	PB 542	48	.25
Law of the gun.	PB 766	51	.25
No benefit of law.	PB 699	50	.25
RIDERS West.	DelF A110	56	.25
RIDGWAY, JASON			
West side jungle.	Sig 1504	58	.25

Author/Title	Pub./Stock No.	Yr.	Price
RIESEBERG, HARRY E.			
I dive for treasure.	Pop 551	54	.25
RIFKIN, SHEPARD			
Texas, blood red.	DelF 82	56	.25
RIGHTER, CARROLL			
Astrology and you.	Perm M-4110	58	.35
RIGSBY, HOWARD			
As a man falls.	GM 375	54	.25
Kill and tell.	PB 934	53	.25
The lone gun.	GM 542	56	.25
Lucinda.	GM 400	54	.25
Murder for the holidays.	PB 901	52	.25
Naked to my pride.	Pop G290	58	.35
Rage in Texas.	GM 350	53	.25
The reluctant gun.	GM 646	57	.25
RILEY, FRANK with Mark Clifton			
The forever machine.	Gal 35	58	.35
RILEY, JAMES WHITCOMB			
The best-loved poems and			
ballads of James			
Whitcomb Riley.	PB 367	46	.25
RIMANELLI, GIOSE			
The fall of night.	Pop 713	55	.25
RINEHART, MARY ROBERTS			
The after house.	Pop 21	44	.25
The album.	PB 121	41	.25
Alibi for Isabel.	DelT unk	51	.10
The bat.	Dell 241	48	.25
	Dell 652	53	.25
	Dell D330	59	.35
The case of Jennie Brice.	Dell 40	44	.25
	Dell 404	50	.25
The circular staircase.	PB 98	41	.25
	Dell 585	52	.25
	Dell D197	57	.35
The confession and Sight			
unseen.	Avon 83	46	.25
	Dell D316	59	.35
The door.	PB 140	42	.25
	Dell D220	58	.35
Episode of the wandering			
knife.	Dell 541	51	.25
The frightened wife.	Dell D154	55	.35
The great mistake.	Dell 297	49	.25
	Dell D251	58	.35
Haunted lady.	Dell 361	49	.25
	Dell 814	54	.25
Locked doors.	DelT 4	51	.10
The man in lower ten.	Dell 124	46	.25
	Dell 403	50	.25
	Dell D276	59	.35
Miss Pinkerton.	Pop 5	43	.25
	Dell 494	51	.25
	Dell D242	58	.35

Author/Title	Pub./Stock No.	Yr.	Price
RINEHART, MARY ROBERTS (cont.)			
Murder at the White Cat.	Dell 57	44	.25
The red lamp.	Dell 131	46	.25
_____.	Dell 782	54	.25
The state vs. Elinor Norton.	Dell 203	47	.25
The swimming pool.	Dell D126	53	.35
The wall.	Dell 166	47	.25
_____.	Dell D165	56	.35
The window at the White Cat.	Dell 506	51	.25
The yellow room.	Ban 314	49	.25
_____.	Dell D179	56	.35
RING, ADAM			
Killers play rough.	Han 68	47	.20
RING, DOUGLAS			
The peddler.	Lion 110	52	.25
RIPLEY, AUSTIN			
Minute mysteries.	PB 641	49	.25
RIPLEY, ROBERT			
Believe it or not.	PB 96	41	.25
Ripley's Believe it or not! 4th series.	PB 1165	57	.25
Ripley's Believe it or not! 5th series.	PB 1195	58	.25
Ripley's Believe it or not! 6th series.	PB 1208	58	.25
Ripley's new Believe it or not!	PB 992	54	.25
The second Believe it or not.	PB 426	48	.25
RIPLEY, THOMAS			
They died with their boots on.	PB 646	49	.25
RITCHIE, C. T.			
The willing maid.	Ace G-382	59	.50
RITTWAGEN, MARJORIE			
Sins of their fathers.	Pyr G398	59	.35
RIVETTE, MARC			
The incident.	Sig S1732	59	.35
ROAN, TOM			
Rawhiders.	Zen ZB-10	58	.35
Smoky river.	Hill unk	50	.25
Wyoming gun.	Dell 849	55	.25
ROARK, GARLAND			
Fair wind to Java.	Prmb P127	51	.35
Rainbow in the royals.	Prmb P139	51	.35
Slant of the wild wind.	Prmb P198	53	.35
Wake of the Red Witch.	Dell F52	53	.50

Author/Title	Pub./Stock No.	Yr.	Price
The wreck of the Running Gale.	Prmb P274	54	.35
ROBBINS, HAROLD			
The dream merchants.	Ban A955	52	.35
_____.	Ban F1431	56	.50
Never leave me.	Avon T-74	54	.35
_____.	Avon T-326	59	.35
Never love a stranger.	Ban A814	50	.35
_____.	Ban A1300	55	.35
_____.	Ban A1752	58	.35
79 Park Avenue.	Card C-219	56	.35
A stone for Danny Fisher.	Card C-91	53	.35
ROBERTS, CECIL			
One small candle.	Pony unk	46	.25
ROBERTS, COLETTE			
Millions for love.	NL 31	49	.25
ROBERTS, DOROTHY JAMES			
The enchanted cup.	Ban A1319	55	.35
ROBERTS, EDITH			
The men in her life.	Ban 470	49	.25
ROBERTS, ELIZABETH MADOX			
The time of man.	Sig S1133	54	.35
ROBERTS, HENRY L.			
Russia and America: dangers and prospects.	Ment MD182	56	.50
ROBERTS, KENNETH			
Lydia Bailey.	Prmb P165S	52	.50
ROBERTS, LEE			
Judas journey.	Eag EB80	57	.25
Little sister.	GM 229	52	.25
_____.	GM 565	56	.25
_____.	GM 934	59	.25
Once a widow.	Dell 1003	59	.25
The pale door.	Ban 1535	56	.25
ROBERTS, MacLENNAN			
The great locomotive chase.	DelF 96	56	.25
with Jack Beater Sea avenger.	DelF B113	58	.35
with Paul Ilton Moses and the Ten commandments.	DelF B105	56	.35
ROBERTS, ORAL			
The Oral Roberts reader.	Zen ZB-6	58	.35
ROBERTS, R. M.			
Scout.	Ball 166	56	.35

Author/Title	Pub./Stock No.	Yr.	Price
ROBERTS, RICHARD EMERY			
The Gilded Rooster.	Ban 714	49	.25
Last frontier.	Ban A1426	56	.35
ROBERTS, VIRGINIA			
Nurse Howard's assignment.	Ban 1907	59	.25
Nurse on location.	Ban 1975	59	.25
ROBERTS, WAYNE			
Silent river.	Ban 1925	59	.25
ROBERTSON, CHARLEY			
Hoodlum.	Pop 347	51	.25
ROBERTSON, FRANK C.			
Disaster valley.	Ball 232	57	.35
Lawman's pay.	Ball 208	57	.35
The powder burn.	RCL 4	50	.25
ROBERTSON, TERENCE			
Channel dash.	Berk G235	59	.35
Night raider of the Atlantic.	Ace D-244	57	.35
ROBINSON, DONALD			
The 100 most important people in the world today (1952).	Card C-24	52	.35
The 100 most important people of 1953.	Card C-86	53	.35
ROBINSON, ED			
Raw wind in Eden.	Avon T-271	58	.35
ROBINSON, EDWARD G. JR. with William Dufty			
My father--my son.	Pop SP32	58	.50
ROBINSON, FRANK M.			
The power.	Ban A1593	57	.35
ROBINSON, HENRY MORTON			
The cardinal.	Card C-71	52	.50
	Card GC-1	53	.50
The great snow.	PB 843	52	.25
Tale of two lovers.	PB 1012	54	.25
ROBINSON, MABEL LOUISE			
Bitter forfeit.	Ban 465	49	.25
ROBINSON, RAY			
Baseball stars of 1958.	Pyr G324	58	.35
Baseball stars of 1959.	Pyr G392	59	.35
ROBLES, EMMANUEL			
Dawn on our darkness.	Avon T-87	54	.35
ROCHE, ARTHUR SOMERS			
The case against Mrs. Ames.	Pop 138	48	.25

Author/Title	Pub./Stock No.	Yr.	Price
ROCHE, JEFFREY with John D. Matthews			
My name is violence.	Avon 847	59	.25
RODELL, VIC			
Free-lance murder.	Ace D-305	58	.35
RODEN, H. W.			
One angel less.	Dell 247	48	.25
Too busy to die.	Dell 185	47	.25
.	Dell 349	49	.25
Wake for a lady.	Dell 345	49	.25
You only hang once.	Dell 102	46	.25
RODIN, ARNOLD			
Moment of truth.	GM 326	53	.25
Woman soldier.	GM 232	52	.25
.	GM 559	56	.25
RODMAN, SELDEN			
100 American poems.	PenN 660	48	.25
.	Ment MD186	56	.50
100 modern poems.	Ment M54	51	.35
.	Ment MD187	56	.50
ROE, VINGIE			
Smoke among the plains.	Pyr G288	57	.35
West of Abilene.	Ban 1031	52	.25
ROEBURT, JOHN			
Al Capone.	Pyr G405	59	.35
Case of the hypnotized virgin.	Avon 730	56	.25
Case of the tearless widow.	Han 46	46	.15
Corpse on the town.	Graf 27	50	.25
Did you kill Mona Leeds?	Crst 213	58	.25
The hollow man.	Graf 110	55	.25
The long nightmare.	Crst 246	58	.25
Murder in Manhattan.	Avon 772	57	.25
There are dead men in Manhattan.	Graf 42	51	.25
They who sin.	Avon T-321	59	.35
Tough cop.	Graf 22	50	.25
.	Graf 38	51	.25
.	Graf 63	53	.25
.	Graf 121	56	.25
	Pyr G464	59	.35
The unholy wife.	Avon T-169	57	.35
Wine, women and murder.	Avon 807	58	.25
ROGERS, GARET			
Lancet.	Ban F1738	58	.50
Prisoner in paradise.	Perm M-4039	56	.35
ROGERS, JOEL TOWNSLEY			
Lady with the dice.	Han 56	46	.20
The red right hand.	PB 385	46	.25
.	Dell D203	57	.35

Author/Title	Pub./Stock No.	Yr.	Price
ROGERS, MATILDA			
Flower arrangements anyone can do anywhere.	SigK K305	54	.25
ROGERS, MILTON			
Born reckless.	Avon 846	59	.25
ROGERS, PHILLIPS			
Stag night.	Dell 432	50	.25
ROGERS, SAMUEL			
Don't look behind you.	Pop 287	50	.25
ROGGE, BERNHARD with Wolfgang Frank			
The German raider Atlantis.	Ball 184	57	.35
ROHDE, WILLIAM L.			
Give me a little something.	Pyr G226	56	.35
The gun-crasher.	Pyr 250	57	.25
The heel.	Pyr 79	53	.25
Help wanted--for murder.	GM 115	50	.25
High red for dead.	GM 145	51	.25
Murder on the line.	GM 721	57	.25
Uneasy lies the head.	Ace D-203	57	.35
V.I.P.	Pyr G283	57	.35
ROHMER, SAX			
Daughter of Fu Manchu.	Avon 189	49	.25
Emperor Fu Manchu.	GM s929	59	.35
The fire goddess.	GM 283	53	.25
Hangover House.	Graf 32	51	.25
	Graf 78	54	.25
Nude in mink.	GM 105	50	.25
	GM 321	53	.25
Re-enter Fu Manchu.	GM s684	57	.35
Return of Sumuru.	GM 408	54	.25
	GM 868	59	.25
Sinister madonna.	GM 555	56	.25
Sumuru.	GM 199	51	.25
	GM s757	58	.35
Tales of Chinatown.	Pop 217	50	.25
ROLFE, EDWIN with Lester Fuller			
The glass room.	Ban 310	48	.25
ROLFE, EVANS			
Back issues.	Berk 355	56	.25
Hoops of steel.	Ball 154	56	.35
ROLLAND, ROMAIN			
Jean-Christophe.	PB 631	49	.25
	DelL LC113	58	.50
ROMAINS, JULES			
The lord god of the flesh.	PB 919	53	.25
ROMANO, ROMUALDO			
Scirocco.	PB 900	52	.25
RONALD, JAMES			
The angry woman.	Ban 749	50	.25
They can't hang me.	Pop 64	45	.25
This is temptation.	Pop G147	55	.35
This way out.	Pop 389	51	.25
RONNS, EDWARD			
The art studio murders.	Avon 688	56	.25
The big bedroom.	Pyr G457	59	.35
The black orchid.	Pyr G391	59	.35
But not for me.	Pyr G445	59	.35
Catspaw ordeal.	GM 133	50	.25
	GM 766	58	.25
The cowl of doom.	HH 13	46	.25
Dark destiny.	Graf 59	53	.25
Dark memory.	Han 122	50	.25
The decoy.	GM 194	51	.25
	GM 529	55	.25
Don't cry, beloved.	GM 239	52	.25
Gang rumble.	Avon T-262	58	.35
I can't stop running.	GM 166	51	.25
The lady takes a flyer.	Avon T-228	58	.35
Million dollar murder.	GM 110	50	.25
The net.	Graf 68	53	.25
Passage to terror.	GM 217	52	.25
Pickup alley.	Avon T-181	57	.35
Point of peril.	Ace D-231	57	.35
Say it with murder.	Graf 76	54	.25
State Department murders.	GM 117	50	.25
	GM 634	57	.25
They all ran away.	Graf 114	55	.25
ROOKE, DAPHNE			
A grove of fever trees.	Sig 953	52	.25
Mittee.	Sig 1021	53	.25
Ratoons.	Ball 42	53	.35
ROOS, KELLEY			
Beauty marks the spot.	DelT unk	51	.10
The blonde died dancing.	Dell 968	58	.25
The frightened stiff.	Dell 56	44	.25
	Dell 687	53	.25
Ghost of a chance.	Dell 266	48	.25
Made up to kill.	Dell 106	46	.25
Murder in any language.	Dell 398	50	.25
Sailor, take warning!	Dell 155	47	.25
Scent of mystery.	DelF B152	59	.35
ROOSEVELT, ELEANOR			
On my own.	Dell F86	59	.50
This is my story.	Ban 846	50	.25
ROOT, PAT			
Evil became them.	Dell 773	54	.25
RORICK, ISABEL SCOTT			
Mr. and Mrs. Cugat.	Ban 11	45	.25
ROSCOE, MIKE			
Death is a round black ball.	Sig 966	52	.25

Author/Title	Pub./Stock No.	Yr.	Price
ROSCOE, MIKE			
The midnight eye.	Ace D-273	58	.35
One tear for my grave.	Sig 1358	56	.25
Riddle me this.	Sig 1060	53	.25
Slice of hell.	Sig 1216	55	.25
ROSCOE, THEODORE			
Pigboats.	Ban F1862	58	.50
ROSE, BILLY			
Wine, women and words.	PB 685	50	.25
ROSEN, VICTOR			
Dark plunder.	Lion LL 11	55	.35
A gun in his hand.	GM 154	51	.25
ROSENSON, WILLIAM with Bela Schick			
The care of your child			
from infancy to six.	Dell 340	49	.25
ROSENTHAL, HERBERT C. with Fritz Wittels			
Sex habits of American			
women.	Eton 102	51	.25
_____.	Eton ET51	52	.35
ROSENTHAL, NORMAN C.			
Silenced witnesses.	Ace D-129	55	.35
ROSENTHAL, RAYMOND with Bernard Wolfe			
Hypnotism comes of age.	Berk G-29	56	.35
ROSKE, RALPH J. with Charles Van Doren			
Lincoln's commando.	Pyr G356	58	.35
ROSMANITH, OLGA			
Don't say no.	Eag EB68	56	.25
The long thrill.	Lion 200	54	.25
Unholy flame.	GM 273	52	.25
ROSS, FLOYD H. with Tynette Hills			
The great religions by			
which men live.	Prem s39	56	.35
_____.	Crst s269	59	.35
ROSS, FRED			
Jackson Mahaffey.	Ban 970	52	.25
ROSS, JAMES			
They don't dance much.	Sig 913	52	.25
ROSS, LILLIAN BOS			
The stranger.	Ban 426	49	.25
ROSS, SAM			
He ran all the way.	Lion 19	50	.25
_____.	Lion LL 59	55	.35
The hustlers.	Pop 782	56	.25
Someday, boy.	Ban A1214	54	.35
This, too, is love.	RS 26	53	.35
The tight corner.	Sig 1434	57	.25

Author/Title	Pub./Stock No.	Yr.	Price
You belong to me.	Pop 657	55	.25
ROSS, WALTER			
Diet to suit yourself.	SigK K309	54	.25
The immortal.	Card C-338	59	.35
ROSSI, JEAN-BAPTISTE			
Awakening.	Sig 1155	54	.25
_____.	Berk G-191	58	.35
ROSSITER, CLINTON			
The American presidency.	SigK Ks334	56	.35
_____.	Ment MD267	59	.50
ROSTAND, EDMOND			
Cyrano de Bergerac.	Ban 859	50	.25
_____.	Ban A1230	54	.35
_____.	Ban A1458	56	.35
_____.	BanC AC19	59	.35
ROSTOW, W. W.			
The dynamics of Soviet			
society.	Ment Ms121	54	.50
ROTH, HOLLY			
The crimson in the			
purple.	Pyr G372	58	.35
Mask of glass.	Berk 112	55	.25
The shocking secret.	Dell 850	55	.25
The sleeper.	Lion LB 171	57	.25
_____.	Pyr G338	58	.35
ROTH, LILLIAN			
Beyond my worth.	Pop G323	59	.35
with others			
I'll cry tomorrow.	Pop 696	55	.25
ROTHENBERG, ROBERT E.			
Understanding surgery.	Card GC-27	55	.50
ROTHMAN, NATHAN			
Virgie, goodbye.	Avon 207	49	.25
_____.	Berk G-37	56	.35
_____.	Berk G-183	58	.35
ROUECHÉ, BERTON			
Eleven blue men.	Berk 315	55	.25
The incurable wound.	Berk G-188	58	.35
The last enemy.	DelF D90	56	.35
Rooming house.	Lion 141	53	.25
_____.	Lion LL 133	57	.35
_____.	Pyr G466	59	.35
ROURKE, THOMAS			
Of all my sins.	Avon T-255	58	.35
Thunder below.	Avon 565	54	.25
ROUSE, W. H. D.			
Gods, heroes and men of			
ancient Greece.	SigK KD357	57	.50

Author/Title	Pub./Stock No.	Yr.	Price
ROUSSEAU, JEAN-JACQUES			
The confessions of Jean-Jacques Rousseau.	PBL PL56	57	.35
ROUSSEAU, THEODORE JR.			
Cézanne.	PBA A4	53	.50
ROUTSONG, ALMA			
A gradual joy.	Ball 31	53	.35
ROVERE, RICHARD H.			
The weeper and the blackmailer.	Sig 763	50	.25
ROWANS, VIRGINIA			
House party.	Dell D219	58	.35
The loving couple.	Perm M-4077	57	.35
Oh, what a wonderful wedding.	Perm M-3075	57	.25
ROY, JULES			
The navigator.	Sig 1325	56	.25
The unfaithful wife.	Sig 1429	57	.25
ROYEN, ASTRID van			
Awake Monique.	Crst s231	58	.35
ROYER, LOUIS-CHARLES			
African mistress.	Pyr 102	53	.25
French doctor.	Pyr 35	51	.25
_____.	Pyr 166	55	.25
	Pyr G317	58	.35
The harem.	Dell 567	52	.25
_____.	Pyr 114	54	.25
Love camp.	Pyr 84	53	.25
	Pyr G320	58	.35
The man from Paris.	Pyr G217	56	.35
The redhead from Chicago.	Pyr 110	54	.25
Savage triangle.	Pyr 134	54	.25
Unrepentant sinners.	Pyr G253	57	.35
RUARK, ROBERT			
Something of value.	Card GC-753	57	.75
RUBEL, JAMES			
No business for a lady.	GM 114	50	.25
_____.	GM 765	58	.25
RUBINSTEIN, S. LEONARD			
The battle done.	Eag EB64	56	.25
RUDEL, HANS ULRICH			
Stuka pilot.	Ball F276K	58	.50
RUESCH, HANS			
The racer.	Ball 17	53	.35
Top of the world.	PB 778	51	.25
_____.	Perm M-4142	59	.35

Author/Title	Pub./Stock No.	Yr.	Price
RUNBECK, MARGARET LEE			
Three secrets.	GM 128	50	.25
Time for love.	Sig 870	51	.25
_____.	Sig 1170	54	.25
RUNDELL, E. RALPH			
The color of blood.	Prmb P152	52	.35
RUNYON, DAMON			
The best of Damon Runyon.	PB 53	40	.25
Damon Runyon favorites.	PB 158	42	.25
Guys and dolls.	PB 1098	55	.25
Poems for men.	Prmb P113	51	.35
Runyon à la carte.	PB 406	46	.25
Runyon first and last.	Graf 30	51	.25
_____.	Graf 69	53	.25
Take it easy.	PB 292	45	.25
The three wise guys.	Avon 102	46	.25
RUPPELT, EDWARD J.			
The report on unidentified flying objects.	Ace D-200	57	.35
RUSH, ANN			
Eve Cameron, M.D.	Ban 1799	58	.25
RUSH, WILLIAM MARSHALL			
Yellowstone scout.	PBJr J-62	51	.25
RUSS, MARTIN			
The last parallel.	Sig D1487	58	.50
RUSSELL, ALICE D.			
Strangers in the desert.	Com 15	49	.25
RUSSELL, BERTRAND			
The ABC of relativity.	Ment MD258	59	.50
Bertrand Russell's best.	Ment MD237	58	.50
The conquest of happiness.	Sig 848	51	.25
_____.	SigK Ks322	55	.35
Marriage and morals.	BanC FC32	59	.50
RUSSELL, ERIC FRANK			
Deep space.	Ban 1362	55	.25
Men, Martians and machines.	Berk G-148	58	.35
Sentinels of space.	Ace D-44	54	.35
Six worlds yonder.	Ace D-315	58	.35
The space willies.	Ace D-315	58	.35
Three to conquer.	Ace D-215	57	.35
Wasp.	Perm M-4120	59	.35
RUSSELL, JOHN			
The lost god and other adventure stories.	PB 408	47	.25
RUSSELL, LORD			
The Knights of Bushido.	Berk BG263	59	.50

Author/Title	Pub./Stock No.	Yr.	Price
RUSSELL, LORD (cont.)			
The scourge of the			
Swastika.	Ball F169	56	.50
RUSSELL, RUTH K. with Josephine H. Kenyon			
Healthy babies are			
happy babies.	Sig 795	50	.25
RUSSELL, WILLIAM			
Love affair.	Avon 743	56	.25
A wind is rising.	Sig 900	52	.25
RUTH, BABE with Bob Considine			
The Babe Ruth story.	PB 562	49	.25
RUTLEDGE, NANCY			
Blood on the cat.	Han 55	46	.20
RUTTER, OWEN			
The British navy's Air			
arm.	PenS S222	44	.25
RYAN, CORNELIUS			
One minute to ditch.	Ball 222	57	.35
with Frank Kelley			
MacArthur--man of action.	Lion 67	51	.25
RYAN, DON			
The Devil's brigadier.	Berk G-8	55	.35
RYAN, RILEY			
The Dakota deal.	Lion 187	54	.25
Gun hell.	Lion LB 100	56	.25

Author/Title	Pub./Stock No.	Yr.	Price
S			
SABATIER, ROBERT			
Boulevard.	Dell D310	59	.35
SABATINI, RAFAEL			
Captain Blood.	PB 82	40	.25
Fortunes of Captain Blood.	Pop 241	50	.25
The lion's skin.	Bart 30	46	.25
Master-at-arms.	Chek 7	49	.15
Mistress Wilding.	Avon 84	46	.25
Scaramouche.	Ban 5	45	.25
_____.	Ban A1022	52	.35
The sea-hawk.	Pop 91	46	.25
SABER, ROBERT O.			
The affair of the frigid blonde.	Han 108	50	.25
The black dark murders.	Han 96	49	.25
Chicago woman.	Pyr 90	53	.25
A dame called murder.	Graf 111	55	.25
The dove.	Han 130	51	.25
The scented flesh.	Han 124	51	.25
Sucker bait.	Graf 99	55	.25
_____.	Graf 156	57	.25
A time for murder.	Graf 123	56	.25
Too young to die.	Graf 90	54	.25
_____.	Graf 150	57	.25
SABIN, MARK			
Winchester cut.	GM 144	51	.25
SACHS, PAUL J.			
The Pocket book of great drawings.	PB 765	51	.35
SACHS, RUTH			
For I have sinned.	Pyr 147	55	.25
SACK, JOHN			
From here to Shimbashi.	Perm M-3042	56	.25
SACKETT, BERT			
Sponger's jinx.	PBJr J-39	50	.25
SAFFORD, HENRY B.			
The intimate problems of women.	Pyr R223	56	.35
Tell me, doctor.	Pyr G160	55	.35
SAGAN, FRANCOISE			
Bonjour tristesse.	Dell D166	56	.35
A certain smile.	Dell D206	57	.35
Those without shadows.	Dell D277	59	.35
SAGE, DANA			
The 22 brothers.	PB 775	51	.25
SAHER, LILLA van			
Macamba.	Pop 233	50	.25
Macamba.	Eag EB11	54	.25
ST. CLAIR, MARGARET			
Agent of the unknown.	Ace D-150	56	.35
The green queen.	Ace D-176	56	.35
ST. CLARE, DEXTER			
Saratoga mantrap.	GM 195	51	.25
SAINT EXUPÉRY, ANTOINE de			
Night flight.	Pen 568	45	.25
_____.	Sig 1354	56	.25
Wind, sand and stars.	Ban 14	45	.25
SAINT-LAURENT, CECIL			
The affairs of Caroline chérie.	Dell 852	55	.25
Affairs of Marie-Odette.	Berk G251	59	.35
Caroline chérie.	Dell D121	53	.35
Caroline Coquette.	Dell D133	54	.35
The cautious maiden.	Dell 921	56	.25
The magnificent female.	Pyr G446	59	.35
The secrets of Caroline chérie.	Dell D254	59	.35
ST. LEGER, DAVID			
A treasury of wisdom and inspiration.	SigK Ks310	54	.35
SAKI			
A Saki sampler.	Sup M656	45	.25
The she-wolf.	Ban 143	48	.25
The unbearable Bassington.	Pen 634	47	.25
SALE, RICHARD			
Benefit performance.	Dell 252	48	.25
Death at sea.	Pop 163	48	.25
Home is the hangman.	Pop 205	49	.25
Lazarus murder seven.	Han 13	43	.15
Murder at midnight.	Pop 275	50	.25
Not too narrow...not too deep.	Pop 247	50	.25
Passing strange.	Han 19	43	.15
_____.	Ace D-23	53	.35
SALINGER, J. D.			
The catcher in the rye.	Sig 1001	53	.25
_____.	Sig D1667	59	.50
Nine stories.	Sig 1111	54	.25
_____.	Sig D1498	58	.50
SALINGER, MARGARETTA			
Michelangelo.	PBA A23	55	.50
Velázquez.	PBA A19	54	.50
SALISBURY, HARRISON E.			
The shook-up generation.	Crst s321	59	.35
SALTEN, FELIX			
Bambi.	PB 10	39	.25

Author/Title	Pub./Stock No.	Yr.	Price
SALTER, JAMES			
The hunters.	Ban A1700	58	.35
SALTMAN, JULES with Louis Portnoy			
Fertility in marriage.	Sig 881	51	.25
SALTUS, EDGAR			
The imperial orgy.	Avon 111	47	.25
SAMPLE, GORDON			
Reckless passion.	Pyr 12	49	.25
SAMUELS, CHARLES			
Death was the bridegroom.	GM 466	55	.25
The girl in the red velvet swing.	GM 294	53	.25
with Louise Samuels			
The girl in the house of hate.	GM 359	54	.25
Night fell on Georgia.	DelF 83	56	.25
with Ethel Waters			
His eye is on the sparrow.	Ban A985	52	.35
	Ban F1976	59	.50
SAMUELS, LOUISE with Charles Samuels			
The girl in the house of hate.	GM 359	54	.25
Night fell on Georgia.	DelF 83	56	.25
SANCTON, THOMAS			
The magnificent rascal.	Crst s208	58	.35
SANDBURG, CARL			
Abraham Lincoln: the prairie years.	DelL LX113	59	.75
Abraham Lincoln: the war years, 1861-1864.	DelL LX114	59	.75
Abraham Lincoln: the war years, 1864-1865.	DelL LX115	59	.75
The fiery trial.	Dell F77	59	.50
SANDERS, DAPHNE			
To catch a thief.	Han 26	44	.15
SANDERS, GEORGE			
Stranger at home.	Ace D-77	54	.35
SANDERS, JACQUIN			
The girls from Goldfield.	Pop 807	57	.25
Strip the heart.	Pop 668	55	.25
SANDERSON, DOUGLAS			
Dark passions subdue.	Avon AT-67	53	.35
Mark it for murder.	Avon T-309	59	.35
SANDERSON, IVAN T.			
How to know the American mammals.	Ment M63	51	.35
	SigK KD349	57	.50

Author/Title	Pub./Stock No.	Yr.	Price
SANDERSON, JAMES DEAN			
Boy with a gun.	Pop G301	59	.35
SANDOZ, MARI			
Slogum House.	Dell D116	52	.35
SANDSTRÖM, FLORA			
The midwife of Pont Clery.	Perm M-4097	58	.35
SANFORD, JOHN B.			
The hard guys.	Sig 1432	57	.25
Make my bed in hell.	Avon 574	54	.25
_____.	Avon T-189	57	.35
The old man's place.	Prmb 251	53	.25
SANGSTER, JIMMY with Barre Lyndon			
The man who could cheat death.	Avon T-362	59	.35
SANSOM, WILLIAM			
The face of innocence.	Sig 962	52	.25
SANTEE, ROSS			
Apache land.	Ban F1495	56	.50
Cowboy.	PB 732	50	.25
Lost pony tracks.	Ban F1494	56	.50
SARA, DOROTHY			
Handwriting analysis.	Pyr G228	56	.35
_____.	PyrR PR23	59	.35
SARLAT, NOAH			
America's cities of sin.	Lion unk	51	.25
Combat!	Lion LL 127	56	.35
A handful of hell.	Lion LL 73	56	.35
How I made a million.	Lion LL 21	55	.35
Rogues and lovers.	Lion LL 83	56	.35
Sintown, U.S.A.	Lion 106	52	.25
This is it!	Lion LL 167	57	.35
SAROYAN, WILLIAM			
48 Saroyan stories.	Avon (19)	42	.25
The human comedy.	PB 282	45	.25
Love.	Lion LL 56	55	.35
My name is Aram.	Pen 540	44	.25
_____.	Sig 734	49	.25
Rock Wagram.	Sig 945	52	.25
A secret story.	Pop 563	54	.25
_____.	Pop G334	59	.35
SARTRE, JEAN-PAUL			
The age of reason.	BanC SC43	59	.75
Intimacy.	Avon AT-69	53	.35
_____.	Berk G-30	56	.35
_____.	Berk G-105	58	.35
The SATURDAY review reader.	Ban 913	51	.25
SATURDAY review reader, no. 2.	Ban 1118	53	.25

Author/Title	Pub./Stock No.	Yr.	Price
SATURDAY review reader, no. 3.	Ban A1242	54	.35
SAUNDERS, MACK			
Gun trail.	Graf 140	56	.25
SAVAGE, JAMES			
Girl in a jam.	Avon T-356	59	.35
SAVAGE, JOHN			
A shady place to die.	DelF A137	57	.25
SAVAGE, JUANITA			
Don Lorenzo's bride.	Dell 360	49	.25
SAVAGE, LES JR.			
Beyond Wind River.	PB 1251	59	.25
Black Horse Canyon.	GM 411	54	.25
The doctor at Coffin Gap.	PB 712	50	.25
Hangtown.	Ball 181	57	.35
The hide rustlers.	PB 803	51	.25
Land of the lawless.	PB 978	54	.25
Last of the breed.	DelF 37	54	.25
Once a fighter...	PB 1104	56	.25
Outlaw thickets.	PB 954	53	.25
Return to Warbow.	DelF 65	55	.25
Shadow riders of the Yellowstone.	PB 888	52	.25
Silver Street woman.	Card C-172	55	.35
Teresa.	DelF 23	54	.25
Treasure of the brasada.	Dell 253	48	.25
_____.	Dell 673	53	.25
The wild horse.	GM 111	50	.25
with Dudley Dean			
Gun shy.	GM 912	59	.25
SAVAGE, MILDRED			
Parrish.	Card GC-72	59	.50
SAVAGE, THOMAS			
Lona Hanson.	Sig 728	49	.25
The pass.	Ban A1608	57	.35
SAVOY, WILLARD			
Alien land.	Sig 767	50	.25
SAWYER, MAXINE with Jules Archer			
Sex life and you.	RC 1	49	.25
SAWYER, W. W.			
Mathematician's delight.	Pel P8	46	.25
SAXON, JOHN A.			
Liability limited.	Ace D-81	54	.35
SAYERS, DOROTHY L.			
Busman's honeymoon.	PB 324	46	.25
Clouds of witness.	PB 85	40	.25
Have his carcase.	PB 163	42	.25

Author/Title	Pub./Stock No.	Yr.	Price
In the teeth of the evidence.	Avon (40)	43	.25
_____.	Avon 335	51	.25
Murder must advertise.	PB 21	39	.25
The nine tailors.	PB 185	42	.25
Strong poison.	PB 130	41	.25
_____.	Avon 328	51	.25
Suspicious characters.	Avon (23)	43	.25
The unpleasantness at the Bellona Club.	PB 74	40	.25
Whose body?	Avon 176	48	.25
SCARLETT, WILLIAM			
The Christian demand for social justice.	Sig 744	49	.25
Christianity takes a stand.	Pen 612	46	.25
SCHABELITZ, R. F. with W. A. Barber			
Drawn conclusion.	Pen 531	44	.25
Murder enters the picture.	Pen 542	44	.25
Pencil points to murder.	Pen 524	43	.25
SCHACHT, AL			
Clowning through baseball.	Ban 507	49	.25
SCHAEFER, JACK			
The big range.	Ball 22	53	.35
The canyon.	Ball 45	53	.35
First blood.	Ball 13	53	.35
The pioneers.	Ball 136	56	.35
Shane.	Ban 833	50	.25
_____.	Ban 1297	55	.25
SCHAEFFER, HEINZ			
U-boat 977.	Ball 207	57	.35
SCHAFER, KERMIT			
Pardon my blooper.	Crst 294	59	.25
SCHEER, GEORGE with Hugh F. Rankin			
Rebels and redcoats.	Ment MT249	59	.75
SCHEHEREZADE: tales from The 1001 nights.	Ment M155	55	.35
SCHELLENBERG, WALTER			
Hitler's secret service.	Pyr R330	58	.35
SCHERF, MARGARET			
The case of the hated senator.	Ace D-71	54	.35
SCHEUER, STEVEN H.			
TV movie almanac and ratings, 1958-1959.	Ban F1877	58	.50

Author/Title	Pub./Stock No.	Yr.	Price
SCHICK, BELA with William Rosenson			
The care of your child			
from infancy to six.	Dell 340	49	.25
SCHIDDEL, EDMUND			
Break-up.	Avon 613	54	.25
———.	Avon T-298	59	.35
The girl with the			
golden yo-yo.	Berk 339	55	.25
Love in a hot climate.	Berk G-55	57	.35
The other side of the			
night.	Avon 589	54	.25
———.	Berk G282	59	.35
Safari to dishonor.	Avon 728	56	.25
Scratch the surface.	Avon 520	53	.25
———.	Berk G-45	57	.35
SCHIFF, PEARL			
Scollay Square.	Sig S1051	53	.35
SCHIFFER, DON			
The 1956 baseball			
almanac.	Card C-212	56	.35
The 1959 pro football			
handbook.	Card C-364	59	.35
SCHIFFERES, JUSTUS J.			
Schifferes' family			
medical encyclopedia.	Perm M-5013	59	.50
SCHILLER, CICELY			
Element of shame.	Avon 398	51	.25
No bed of her own.	Berk G-179	58	.35
SCHINDALL, HENRY			
Wilderness rogue.	Pop 556	54	.25
SCHISGALL, OSCAR			
The big store.	PB 1111	56	.25
SCHLESINGER, ARTHUR M. JR.			
The age of Jackson.	Ment M38	49	.35
———.	Ment MD145	55	.50
SCHLEY, STURGES MASON			
Dr. Toby finds murder.	Pen 555	45	.25
SCHLICK, ROBERT			
Tonight it's me.	Pyr G248	57	.35
SCHMITT, GLADYS			
Alexandra.	PB 591	49	.25
Confessors of the Name.	Sig D1068	54	.50
The persistent image.	Pop 738	56	.25
SCHNEIDER, JOHN G.			
The golden kazoo.	Dell D178	56	.35
SCHNEIDER, JOSEF A.			
That's my baby.	Pop 281	50	.25
SCHNITZLER, ARTHUR			
Casanova's homecoming.	Avon 160	48	.25
SCHOENFELD, HOWARD			
Let them eat bullets.	GM 378	54	.25
———.	GM 586	56	.25
———.	GM 870	59	.25
SCHOLZ, JACKSON			
Batter up.	Com 2	48	.25
Fighting coach.	Com 25	49	.25
Gridiron challenge.	PBJr J-52	50	.25
SCHONFIELD, HUGH J.			
The Bible was right.	SigK KD371	59	.50
SCHOONOVER, LAWRENCE			
The burnished blade.	Ban A903	51	.35
———.	Ban F1456	56	.50
The gentle infidel.	Ban A994	52	.35
The golden exile.	Ban A1121	53	.35
The Queen's cross.	Ban F1673	57	.50
The quick brown fox.	Ban 1178	53	.25
The Spider King.	Ban F1366	55	.50
SCHORER, MARK			
Three loves had she.	Avon T-344	59	.35
SCHOYER, PRESTON			
The ringing of the glass.	Pop 364	51	.25
SCHULBERG, BUDD			
Across the Everglades.	Ban A1890	58	.35
The disenchanted.	Ban A1051	52	.35
———.	Ban F1932	58	.50
A face in the crowd.	Ban A1635	57	.35
The harder they fall.	Ban 707	49	.25
———.	Ban A1463	56	.35
Some faces in the crowd.	Ban A1213	54	.35
Waterfront.	Ban F1510	56	.50
What makes Sammy run?	Ban 18	45	.25
———.	Ban A1617	57	.35
SCHULMAN, ARNOLD			
A hole in the head.	GM 891	59	.25
SCHULTZ, ALAN			
Lady for love.	NL 42	50	.25
SCHULTZ, J. W.			
My life as an Indian.	Prem s25	56	.35
SCHURMACHER, EMILE C.			
Adventure in paradise.	Zen ZB-8	58	.35
SCHWARTZ, IRVING			
Fear in the night.	PB 904	52	.25
SCHWEITZER, ALBERT with Everett Skillings			
Out of my life and			
thought.	Ment M83	53	.35

Author/Title	Pub./Stock No.		Yr.	Price
SCHWEITZER, GERTRUDE				
The obsessed.	GM	125	50	.25
————.	GM	754	58	.25
SCOTLAND, JAY				
I, barbarian.	Avon	T-375	59	.35
SCOTT, ANN				
I cried in the dark.	Pyr	G371	58	.35
SCOTT, ANTHONY				
Carnival of love.	RC	13	49	.25
Ladies of chance.	NL	27	49	.25
SCOTT, BRADFORD				
The avenger.	Pyr	219	56	.25
Badlands boss.	Pyr	190	56	.25
The blaze of guns.	Pyr	319	58	.25
Border blood.	Pyr	220	56	.25
Canyon killers.	Pyr	199	56	.25
Curse of Texas gold.	Pyr	264	57	.25
Dead in Texas.	Pyr	409	59	.25
Dead man's trail.	Pyr	238	57	.25
Death canyon.	Pyr	293	57	.25
Gun law.	Pyr	442	59	.25
Gunsmoke over Texas.	Pyr	209	56	.25
Holster law.	Pyr	455	59	.25
Powder burn.	Pyr	258	57	.25
The range terror.	Pyr	426	59	.25
Rustlers' range.	Pyr	34	51	.25
Shootin' man.	Pyr	308	58	.25
Texas badman.	Pyr	420	59	.25
The Texas hawk.	Pyr	282	57	.25
The Texas terror.	Pyr	178	56	.25
Texas vengeance.	Pyr	435	59	.25
Trigger talk.	Pyr	186	56	.25
SCOTT, GLENN				
Farewell, my young lover.	Pop	665	55	.25
SCOTT, J. M.				
Heather Mary.	Dell	854	55	.25
Seawife.	Crst	162	57	.25
SCOTT, L. K.				
Backstairs.	Pyr	103	53	.25
SCOTT, LESLIE				
Badlands masquerader.	Ace	D-22	53	.35
The Brazos firebrand.	Ace	D-10	53	.35
Rimrock raiders.	Pyr	251	57	.25
Tombstone showdown.	Pyr	302	57	.25
SCOTT, MARY SEMPLE				
Crime hound.	Dell	34	44	.25
SCOTT, NATALIE ANDERSON				
Hotel room.	Pop	633	55	.25
The story of Mrs. Murphy.	PB	597	49	.25

Author/Title	Pub./Stock No.		Yr.	Price
SCOTT, PAUL				
Six days in Marapore.	Berk	G-32	56	.35
SCOTT, ROBERT L. JR.				
Between the elephant's				
ears.	Ball	217	57	.35
God is my co-pilot.	Ball	145	56	.35
————.	Ball	314K	59	.35
Look of the eagle.	Ace	D-234	57	.35
Tiger in the sky.	Ball	306K	59	.35
SCOTT, RONEY				
Shakedown.	Ace	D-17	53	.35
SCOTT, TARN				
Don't let her die.	GM	668	57	.25
SCOTT, THURSTON				
I'll get mine.	Pop	452	52	.25
————.	Pop	G287	58	.35
SCOTT, VIRGIL				
The dead tree gives no				
shelter.	Pop	296	50	.25
————.	Pop	576	54	.25
The savage affair.	Pop	G319	59	.35
SCOTT, WALTER				
Ivanhoe.	Card	C-79	52	.35
————.	PBL	PL19	54	.50
————.	PBL	PL-502	56	.50
SCOTT, WARWICK				
Cockpit.	Lion	140	53	.25
Doomsday.	Lion	148	53	.25
Naked canvas.	Pop	648	55	.25
SCOTT, WILLIAM R.				
Hunger Mountain.	DelF	63	55	.25
SCULLY, FRANK				
Behind the flying				
saucers.	Pop	326	51	.25
Fun in bed.	PB	504	48	.25
SEABROOK, WILLIAM				
Asylum.	Ban	106	47	.25
————.	Dell	802	54	.25
SEAGER, ALLAN				
Cage of lust.	Pyr	G48	52	.35
————.	Pyr	G145	55	.35
Hilda Manning.	Card	C-250	57	.35
SEAMAN, AUGUSTA HUIELL				
Mystery of the empty				
room.	Com	19	49	.25
SEATON, GEORGE JOHN				
Isle of the damned.	Pop	444	52	.25

Author/Title	Pub./Stock No.	Yr.	Price
SEATON, GEORGE JOHN (cont.)			
Isle of the damned.	Pyr G291	57	.35
SECONDARI, JOHN H.			
Coins in the fountain.	Prmb P246	53	.35
Hot winds of summer.	Pop G178	57	.35
SECRIST, KELLIHER			
She screamed blue murder.	BK unk	46	.25
SECURITY and the Middle			
East.	Ball 90	54	.35
SEDGWICK, ANNE DOUGLAS			
The little French girl.	PB 30	39	.25
SÉDILLOT, RENÉ			
A history of the world			
in 240 pages.	Ment M88	53	.35
SEELEY, CLINTON			
Storm fear.	Eag EB60	56	.25
SEELEY, MABEL			
The beckoning door.	PB 862	52	.25
The chuckling fingers.	Pop 231	50	.25
The crying sisters.	Pop 370	51	.25
The listening house.	Pop 69	46	.25
The whispering cup.	Pop 51	45	.25
Woman of property.	Ban A806	50	.35
SEIDMAN, T. R. with Marvin H. Albert			
Becoming a mother.	Prem d66	58	.50
SEIFERT, ELIZABETH			
A certain Doctor French.	Ban 122	47	.25
Dr. Woodward's ambition.	Ban 458	48	.25
_____.	Ban 1585	57	.25
The doctor's husband.	Crst s251	58	.35
Substitute doctor.	PB 1245	59	.25
Young Doctor Galahad.	PB 302	46	.25
SELDES, GILBERT			
Previews of			
entertainment.	Ban 936	51	.25
SELIGMAN, SELIG			
The big deal.	PB 1004	54	.25
SELINKO, ANNEMARIE			
Désirée.	Card GC-22	54	.50
SELL, HENRY BLACKMAN with Victor Weybright			
Buffalo Bill and the			
Wild West.	SigK KD362	58	.50
SELTZER, CHARLES ALDEN			
Arizona Jim.	Pop 204	49	.25
Double cross ranch.	Pop 151	48	.25
A son of Arizona.	Sig 717	49	.25

Author/Title	Pub./Stock No.	Yr.	Price
SELTZER, NADINE			
More Sweetie Pie.	Berk 381	57	.25
Sweetie Pie.	Berk 320	55	.25
_____.	Berk 360	56	.25
SERGEANT Bilko joke book.	Ball 298K	59	.35
SERLING, ROD			
Patterns.	Ban F1832	58	.50
SETON, ANYA			
Dragonwyck.	PB 365	46	.25
_____.	Card C-339	59	.35
Foxfire.	PB 850	52	.25
The hearth and the eagle.	PB 723	50	.25
Katherine.	Card GC-752	57	.75
The turquoise.	PB 534	48	.25
_____.	Card C-64	52	.35
The Winthrop woman.	Card GC-77	59	.50
SETON, ERNEST THOMPSON			
Wild animals I have			
known.	Ban 59	46	.25
_____.	Ban A1676	57	.35
SETTEL, IRVING			
Best TV humor of 1957.	Ball 235	57	.35
Best TV humor of the			
year.	Ace D-175	56	.35
SEWELL, ANNA			
Black Beauty.	PBJr J-43	50	.25
SHAFER, ROBERT			
The naked and the damned.	Pop 686	55	.25
SHAKESPEARE, WILLIAM			
As you like it.	DelL LB130	59	.35
The complete sonnets,			
songs and poems of			
Shakespeare.	Card C-55	52	.35
Five great comedies.	PB 114	41	.25
Five great tragedies.	PB 3	39	.25
Four great comedies.	PB 533	48	.25
_____.	Card C-15	51	.35
_____.	PBL PL31	55	.35
Four great historical			
plays.	Card C-1	51	.35
Four great tragedies.	PB 532	48	.25
_____.	Card C-14	51	.35
_____.	PBL PL-30	55	.35
Hamlet.	DelL LB112	58	.35
Henry IV, part 1.	DelL LB134	59	.35
Julius Caesar.	DelL LB119	59	.35
Macbeth.	DelL LB124	59	.35
	WSP W115	59	.35
The merchant of Venice.	PBL PL60	57	.35
_____.	DelL LB118	59	.35
A midsummer's night's			
dream.	PBL PL67	58	.35

Author/Title	Pub./Stock No.	Yr.	Price
SHAKESPEARE, WILLIAM (cont.)			
Othello.	DelL LB129	59	.35
Richard III.	DelL LB115	58	.35
Romeo and Juliet.	DelL LB114	58	.35
_____.	WSP W121	59	.35
The taming of the shrew.	DelL LB113	58	.35
The tragedy of Hamlet, Prince of Denmark.	PBL PL64	58	.35
The tragedy of Julius Caesar.	PBL PL66	58	.35
The tragedy of King Lear.	PBL PL57	57	.35
The tragedy of Macbeth.	PBL PL70	59	.35
The tragedy of Othello, the Moor of Venice.	PBL PL61	57	.35
Twelfth night.	DelL LB125	59	.35
The winter's tale.	DelL LB133	59	.35
SHALLIT, JOSEPH			
The case of the billion dollar body.	Avon 558	54	.25
Juvenile hoods.	Avon T-170	57	.35
Kiss the killer.	Avon 528	53	.25
Lady, don't die on my doorstep.	Avon 461	52	.25
Yell bloody murder.	Avon 490	53	.25
SHANE, TED			
Jokes, gags and wisecracks.	Dell 152	47	.25
with Virgil Partch			
Bar guide.	GM 135	50	.25
_____.	GM 337	53	.25
SHANN, RENÉE			
Student nurse.	Dell 234	48	.25
_____.	Dell D260	59	.35
SHANNON, CARL			
Lady, that's my skull.	HH 21	47	.25
SHANNON, JIMMY			
The devil's passkey.	Sig 1027	53	.25
SHANNON, STEVE			
The hell-fire kid.	Crst 189	57	.25
SHAPIRO, LIONEL			
The sealed verdict.	Ban 357	48	.25
The sixth of June.	Ban F1459	56	.50
Torch for a dark journey.	Ban 932	51	.25
SHAPLEN, ROBERT			
The love-making of Max-Robert.	Sig 789	50	.25
SHAPPIRO, HERBERT			
High pockets.	Sig 688	48	.25
The Texan.	Sig 708	49	.25
SHARP, MARGERY			
Cluny Brown.	PB 395	46	.25

Author/Title	Pub./Stock No.	Yr.	Price
The nutmeg tree.	PB 169	42	.25
The stone of chastity.	Avon 165	48	.25
_____.	Avon 624	55	.25
SHARPE, WILLIAM			
Brain surgeon.	Ball 292K	59	.35
SHATTUCK, RICHARD			
Said the spider to the fly.	Pop 125	47	.25
SHAW, ARNOLD			
The money song.	Sig 1145	54	.25
SHAW, CHARLES			
The flesh and the spirit.	Pop 543	53	.25
Heaven knows, Mr. Allison.	Eag EB88	57	.25
You're wrong, Delaney.	Pyr G292	57	.35
SHAW, CHARLES B.			
American essays.	PelM M26	48	.35
_____.	Ment MD137	55	.50
SHAW, FLOYD			
Devil's daughter.	Avon 570	54	.25
Park Avenue girl.	Avon 740	56	.25
SHAW, GEORGE BERNARD			
Four plays.	DelL LC101	57	.50
Major Barbara.	Pen 608	46	.25
Man and superman.	BanC FC52	59	.50
Pygmalion.	Pen 502	42	.25
_____.	Pen 607	46	.25
Saint Joan.	Pen 609	46	.25
SHAW, IRWIN			
Lucy Crown.	Sig D1438	57	.50
Tip on a dead jockey.	Sig S1453	57	.35
The troubled air.	Sig S931	52	.35
The young lions.	Sig 817AB	50	.50
_____.	Sig T1496	58	.75
SHAW, JOSEPH T.			
The hard-boiled omnibus.	PB 875	52	.25
Spurs west!	Prmb P126	51	.35
SHAW, SAM			
Marilyn Monroe as The Girl.	Ball 108	55	.35
SHAW, WILENE			
The fear and the guilt.	Ace S-80	54	.25
Heat lightning.	Ace S-74	54	.25
The mating call.	Ace D-50	54	.35
Out for kicks.	Ace D-378	59	.35
See how they run.	Ace S-263	57	.25
SHAY, FRANK			
Pirate wench.	Pyr G75	53	.35

Author/Title	Pub./Stock No.	Yr.	Price
SHAYNE, MIKE			
Dangerous dames.	DelF 77	55	.25
SHEA, J. VERNON			
Strange barriers.	Lion LL 47	55	.35
Strange desires.	Lion 191	54	.25
SHEARING, JOSEPH			
The golden violet.	Dell 818	55	.25
So evil my love.	PB 560	48	.25
The strange case of			
Lucile Clery.	PB 592	49	.25
SHECKLEY, ROBERT			
Citizen in space.	Ball 126	56	.35
Immortality, inc.	Ban A1991	59	.35
Pilgrimage to earth.	Ban A1672	57	.35
Untouched by human hands.	Ball 73	54	.35
SHEEAN, VINCENT			
Live for today.	Sig 1208	55	.25
Rage of the soul.	Sig S1038	53	.35
SHEEN, FULTON J.			
The divine romance.	Pop 682	55	.25
The eternal Galilean.	Pop 613	54	.25
Life is worth living.	Pop G209	58	.35
The life of all living.	Pop G273	58	.35
Lift up your heart.	Perm M-4033	55	.35
Moods and truths.	Pop 786	56	.25
Peace of soul.	Perm M-1000	54	.35
Three to get married.	Dell D141	54	.35
Way to happiness.	Crst s168	57	.35
The way to inner peace.	Crst s283	59	.35
SHEFTER, HARRY			
Faster reading self-			
taught.	Card GC-50	58	.50
Short cuts to effective			
English.	Card C-190	55	.35
Six minutes a day to			
perfect spelling.	Card C-145	54	.35
SHELDON, WALT			
The man who paid his way.	Ban A1656	57	.35
Troubling of a star.	Ban A1221	54	.35
SHELLABARGER, SAMUEL			
Captain from Castile.	Ban A860	51	.35
The King's cavalier.	Ban A1131	53	.35
Lord Vanity.	Ban F1284	55	.50
The prince of foxes.	Ban A973	52	.35
Tolbecken.	Ban F1720	58	.50
SHELLEY, JOHN L.			
The avenging gun.	Ace D-348	59	.35
Gunpoint!	Graf 124	56	.25
SHELLEY, MARY WOLLSTONECRAFT			
Frankenstein.	Lion 146	53	.25

Author/Title	Pub./Stock No.	Yr.	Price
Frankenstein.	Pyr R290	57	.35
SHELLEY, PAUL			
Saturday's harvest.	GM 315	53	.25
SHELLEY, PETER			
Soft shoulders.	Lion 15	50	.25
SHELLY, GORDON			
I take the rap.	Pop G239	58	.35
SHEPHERD, ERIC			
Murder in a nunnery.	Dell 951	57	.25
SHEPHERD, JOAN			
The girl on the left			
bank.	Avon 578	54	.25
SHERIDAN, JACK			
Girl from town.	RS 20	52	.35
Mamie Brandon.	Pop 312	51	.25
Paradise Motel.	GM 356	54	.25
Thunderclap.	GM 184	51	.35
_____.	GM s946	59	.35
SHERMAN, HAROLD			
How to use the power			
of prayer.	Prem d73	58	.50
You can live after death.	Crst s145	56	.35
Your key to happiness.	Prem s22	56	.35
_____.	Prem d77	59	.50
SHERMAN, JOAN			
Lulie.	Han 91	49	.25
SHERMAN, RICHARD			
To Mary with love.	Ban 124	47	.25
SHERROD, ROBERT			
Tarawa.	PB 273	44	.25
SHERRY, EDNA			
Murder at nightfall.	Dell 933	57	.25
She asked for murder.	Dell 1004	59	.25
Sudden fear.	Dell 604	52	.25
SHERRY, JOHN OLDEN			
The departure.	Pop 606	54	.25
SHERWOOD, ROBERT E.			
Roosevelt and Hopkins,			
volume 1.	Ban nn	50	.35
Roosevelt and Hopkins,			
volume 2.	Ban nn	50	.35
SHIFFRIN, A. B.			
Glitter.	Pop 485	53	.25
SHIFLET, KENNETH E.			
The strain.	DelF B126	59	.35

Author/Title	Pub./Stock No.	Yr.	Price
SHIKES, RALPH			
Cartoon annual.	Ace S-75	54	.25
SHIP ahoy.	Avon 567	54	.25
————.	Avon 851	59	.25
SHIPMAN, NATALIE			
Love is the winner.	Ban 451	48	.25
SHIR-CLIFF, BERNARD W.			
The wild reader.	Ball 171	56	.35
SHIRAS, WILMAR H.			
Children of the atom.	Avon T-221	58	.35
SHIRER, WILLIAM L.			
The traitor.	Pop 363	51	.25
SHIRREFFS, GORDON D.			
Ambush on the mesa.	GM 714	57	.25
The brave rifles.	GM 876	59	.25
Bugles on the prairie.	GM 639	57	.25
Code of the gun.	Crst 146	56	.25
Fort Suicide.	Avon T-352	59	.35
Fort Vengeance.	Pop 808	57	.25
Last train from Gun Hill.	Sig S1626	59	.35
The lonely gun.	Avon T-312	59	.35
Massacre creek.	Pop 832	58	.25
Range rebel.	Pyr 192	56	.25
Renegade lawman.	Avon 862	59	.25
Rio Bravo.	GM 580	56	.25
Shadow of a gunman.	Ace D-400	59	.35
Shadow valley.	Pop G288	58	.35
SHOLOKHOV, MIKHAIL			
And quiet flows the Don.	Sig T1661	59	.75
SHORE, WILLIAM			
The witch of spring.	PB 811	51	.25
SHORT, DOROTHY with Selwyn Gurney Champion			
Readings from world religions.	Prem d85	59	.50
SHORT, LUKE			
Ambush.	Ban 853	51	.25
	Ban 1104	52	.25
————.	Ban 1710	58	.25
And the wind blows free.	Ban 748	50	.25
————.	Ban 1293	55	.25
————.	Ban 1916	59	.25
Barren land murders.	GM 159	51	.25
Barren land showdown.	GM 720	57	.25
Blood on the moon.	Ban 204	48	.25
Bold rider.	DelF 7	53	.25
	DelF A134	57	.25
Bought with a gun.	DelF 68	55	.25
	DelF A154	58	.25
Bounty guns.	Dell 702	53	.25
————.	Dell 869	55	.25

Author/Title	Pub./Stock No.	Yr.	Price
Brand of empire.	Dell 769	54	.25
	Dell D289	59	.35
The branded man.	DelF A122	56	.25
Bull-whip.	Ban 747	50	.25
Cattle, guns and men.	Ban 1346	55	.25
Colt's law.	Ban 1680	57	.25
Coroner Creek.	Ban 140	48	.25
————.	Ban 1533	56	.25
Dead freight for Piute.	Ban 1564	57	.25
The feud at Single Shot.	Ban 791	50	.25
————.	Ban 1588	57	.25
Fiddlefoot.	Ban 854	51	.25
————.	Ban 1105	52	.25
————.	Ban 1755	58	.25
Frontier: 150 years of the west.	Ban A1401	55	.35
Gunman's chance.	Ban 1532	56	.25
Hands off!	Ban 703	49	.25
Hard money.	Ban 209	49	.25
	Ban A1959	59	.35
Hardcase.	Ban 112	47	.25
————.	Ban 1373	55	.25
High Vermilion.	Ban 1446	56	.25
King colt.	Dell 647	53	.25
	Dell 962	57	.25
The man on the blue.	DelF 31	54	.25
	DelF A151	57	.25
Marauders' moon.	DelF 70	55	.25
	DelF B130	59	.35
Play a lone hand.	Ban 1075	53	.25
	Ban 1821	58	.25
Raiders of the rimrock.	Ban 258	49	.25
————.	Ban 1652	57	.25
Ramrod.	Pop 114	47	.25
————.	Pop 346	51	.25
————.	Pop 792	57	.25
Raw land.	Dell 562	52	.25
————.	Dell 895	56	.25
Rawhide and Bob-wire.	Ban 1865	58	.25
Ride the man down.	Ban 82	47	.25
————.	Ban 1063	52	.25
Rimrock.	Ban 1466	56	.25
The rustlers.	Ban 702	49	.25
Saddle by starlight.	Ball 4	52	.35
————.	Ban A2036	59	.35
Savage range.	Dell 606	52	.25
————.	Dell 826	55	.25
————.	Dell 963	57	.25
Silver rock.	Ball 43	53	.35
————.	Ban A2006	59	.35
Station West.	Ban 139	48	.25
————.	Ban 1356	55	.25
Summer of the smoke.	Ban 1866	58	.25
Sunset graze.	Ban 1531	56	.25
Three complete western novels.	Ban F1417	56	.50
Trumpets West!	DelT 1	51	.10
Vengeance valley.	Ban 911	51	.25
————.	Ban 1485	56	.25
War on the Cimarron.	Ban 792	50	.25

Author/Title	Pub./Stock No.		Yr.	Price
SHORT, LUKE (cont.)				
War on the Cimarron.	Ban	A1989	59	.35
The whip.	Ban	1668	57	.25
SHORTEN, HARRY with Al Fagaly				
More there oughta be a				
law!	Graf	85	54	.25
_____.	Graf	109	55	.25
There oughta be a law!	Graf	52	52	.25
SHRIBER, IONE SANDBERG				
As long as I live.	Ban	320	49	.25
Family affair.	Sup	M641	44	.25
SHUB, DAVID				
Lenin.	Ment	M57	50	.35
_____.	Ment	MD140	55	.50
SHUBIN, SEYMOUR				
Anyone's my name.	Perm	M-4004	55	.35
SHULENBERGER, ARVID				
Roads from the fort.	Dell	D169	56	.35
SHULMAN, IRVING				
The Amboy Dukes.	Avon	169	48	.25
_____.	Avon	300	50	.25
_____.	Avon	T-138	56	.35
_____.	Avon	T-334	59	.35
The big brokers.	Avon	G1009	53	.50
_____.	Avon	G-1023	55	.50
Calibre.	Pop	817	57	.25
Children of the dark.	Pop	G175	57	.35
Cry tough!	Avon	244	50	.25
_____.	Avon	372	51	.25
_____.	Avon	T-124	56	.35
_____.	Avon	T-303	59	.35
The flesh is real.	Pop	G145	55	.35
Good deeds must be				
punished.	Pop	SP29	58	.50
SHULMAN, MAX				
Barefoot boy with cheek.	Ban	A1939	59	.35
The feather merchants.	PB	728	50	.25
_____.	Ban	A1940	59	.35
Rally round the flag,				
boys!	Ban	F1791	58	.50
Sleep till noon.	Ban	A2012	59	.35
The zebra derby.	PB	840	52	.25
SHURTLEFF, BERTRAND				
Long lash.	PBJr	J-36	50	.25
SHUTE, NEVIL				
The chequer board.	Dell	D109	52	.35
The far country.	Dell	D175	56	.35
In the wet.	Perm	M-4095	58	.35
The legacy.	Dell	D123	53	.35
No highway.	Dell	516	51	.25
On the beach.	Sig	D1562	58	.50

Author/Title	Pub./Stock No.		Yr.	Price
Pastoral.	PB	281	46	.25
The rainbow and the rose.	Sig	D1740	59	.50
Round the bend.	Dell	D130	53	.35
SICHEL, PIERRE				
Never say love.	Pop	G149	55	.35
SIEGEL, BENJAMIN				
Witch of Salem.	GM	307	53	.25
SIEMEL, SASHA				
Tigrero!	Ace	D-218	57	.35
SIENKIEWICZ, HENRYK				
Quo vadis?	PB	B70	52	.35
SILLIPHANT, STERLING				
Maracaibo.	Eag	EB74	56	.25
The naked city.	DelF	A180	59	.25
SILONE, IGNAZIO				
Bread and wine.	Pen	578	46	.25
_____.	Sig	D1545	58	.50
SILVERBERG, ROBERT				
Invaders from earth.	Ace	D-286	58	.35
Master of life and death.	Ace	D-237	57	.35
The planet killers.	Ace	D-407	59	.35
Stepsons of Terra.	Ace	D-311	58	.35
The 13th immortal.	Ace	D-223	57	.35
SILVERSTEIN, SHEL				
Grab your socks.	Ball	163	56	.35
SIMAK, CLIFFORD D.				
City.	Prmb	264	54	.25
_____.	Ace	D-283	58	.35
First he died.	Dell	680	53	.25
Ring around the sun.	Ace	D-61	54	.35
_____.	Ace	D-339	59	.35
Strangers in the				
universe.	Berk	G-71	57	.35
SIMENON, GEORGES				
Act of passion.	Sig	993	53	.25
Belle.	Sig	1124	54	.25
The bottom of the bottle.	Sig	1144	54	.25
The brothers Rico.	Sig	1109	54	.25
The burial of Monsieur				
Bouvet.	Berk	379	57	.25
Danger ashore.	Berk	340	55	.25
Danger at sea.	Berk	322	55	.25
Four days in a lifetime.	Sig	1073	53	.25
The fugitive.	Sig	1465	58	.25
The girl in his past.	Sig	948	52	.25
The heart of a man.	Sig	964	51	.25
The hitchhiker.	Sig	1421	57	.25
I take this woman.	Sig	1034	53	.25
In case of emergency.	Dell	D279	59	.35

Author/Title	Pub./Stock No.	Yr.	Price
SIMENON, GEORGES (cont.)			
Inspector Maigret and the burglar's wife.	Dell 964	57	.25
Inspector Maigret and the dead girl.	Avon 757	57	.25
Inspector Maigret and the killers.	Sig 1248	55	.25
Inspector Maigret and the strangled stripper.	Sig 1188	55	.25
Inspector Maigret in New York's underworld.	Sig 1338	56	.25
The magician.	Berk 351	56	.25
Maigret travels south.	Pen 564	45	.25
The man who watched the trains go by.	Berk G-145	58	.35
The matchmaker.	Hill 105	57	.35
The methods of Maigret.	Ban A2063	59	.35
No vacation for Maigret.	Ban 1875	59	.25
Patience of Maigret.	Pen 579	46	.25
The Saint-Fiacre affair.	PB 141	42	.25
The snow was black.	Sig 855	51	.25
———.	Sig 1327	56	.25
Strangers in the house.	Sig 1376	57	.25
Tropic moon.	Berk G-133	58	.35
The widow.	Pop 724	56	.25
SIMMONS, ADDISON			
Dead weight.	BK 31	47	.25
SIMMONS, HERBERT			
Corner boy.	Dell D245	58	.35
SIMON, HENRY with Abraham Veinus			
The Pocket book of great operas.	PB 622	49	.25
———.	PBL PL21	54	.35
SIMPSON, GEORGE GAYLORD			
The meaning of evolution.	Ment M66	51	.35
SIMPSON, SALLY S.			
Popularity plus.	PBJr J-44	50	.25
SIMS, DOROTHY RICE with Valentine Williams			
Fog.	Pop 76	46	.25
SIMS, EDWARD H.			
American aces.	Ball F349K	59	.50
SIMS, LYDEL with George Grider			
War fish.	Pyr G406	59	.35
SINCLAIR, BERTRAND W.			
Gunpowder lightning.	Dell 437	50	.25
Wild West.	Pop 180	49	.25
SINCLAIR, HAROLD			
The horse soldiers.	Dell F76	59	.50
Music out of Dixie.	Prmb P203	53	.35

Author/Title	Pub./Stock No.	Yr.	Price
SINCLAIR, JO			
Sing at my wake.	Prmb P169	52	.35
SINCLAIR, ROBERT B.			
The eleventh hour.	PB 881	52	.25
SINGER, ADAM			
Platoon.	Lion 164	53	.25
———.	Lion LB 109	56	.25
———.	Pyr G375	58	.35
SINGER, BANT			
Blind alley.	Pyr 123	54	.25
SIODMAK, CURT			
Donovan's brain.	Ban 819	50	.25
Riders to the stars.	Ball 58	54	.35
Whomsoever I shall kiss.	Dell 756	54	.25
SIRE, GLEN with Jane Sire			
Something foolish, something gay.	Berk G273	59	.35
SIRE, JANE with Glen Sire			
Something foolish, something gay.	Berk G273	59	.35
SIRINGO, CHARLES A.			
A Texas cowboy.	Sig 898	51	.25
———.	Sig 1192	55	.25
SIX great modern short novels.	DelF F35	54	.50
———.	DelL LC132	59	.50
The $64,000 question quiz book.	DelF 79	55	.25
SKELLY, MIKE			
Halo for a heel.	RS 14	52	.35
SKILLINGS, EVERETT with Albert Schweitzer			
Out of my life and thought.	Ment M83	53	.35
SKINNER, CORNELIA OTIS			
Excuse it, please!	PB 963	53	.25
with Emily Kimbrough			
Our hearts were young and gay.	Ban 105	47	.25
———.	Ban A1894	58	.35
SKLAR, GEORGE			
The housewarming.	Sig S1178	55	.35
The promising young men.	Sig S924	52	.35
The two worlds of Johnny Truro.	Pop 294	50	.25
SLADE, CAROLINE			
Lilly Crackell.	Sig 829	50	.25

Author/Title	Pub./Stock No.	Yr.	Price
SLADE, CAROLINE (cont.)			
Margaret.	Sig 769	50	.25
	Sig 1267	56	.25
_____. The triumph of Willie			
Pond.	Sig 895	51	.25
SLATER, BARNEY with Leonard Praskins			
Three violent people.	GM 615	56	.25
SLATER, ESTELLE			
The strong don't cry.	Pop G144	55	.35
_____.	Pop SP47	59	.50
SLATER, HUMPHREY			
Conspirator.	PB 588	49	.25
Soldiers three.	Sig S1521	58	.35
SLAUGHTER, FRANK G.			
Air surgeon.	Prmb P259	53	.35
	Perm M-4053	56	.35
Apalachee gold.	Ace D-191	56	.35
Battle surgeon.	Prmb P195	52	.35
	Perm M-4048	56	.35
Daybreak.	Perm M-4130	59	.35
Divine mistress.	Prmb P140	51	.35
	Prmb P233	53	.35
_____.	Perm M-4047	56	.35
East side General.	Prmb P218	53	.35
	Perm M-4027	55	.35
Flight from Natchez.	Perm M-4064	56	.35
Fort Everglades.	Prmb P155	52	.35
_____.	Perm M-4054	56	.35
The Galileans.	Prmb P290	54	.35
_____.	Perm M-4049	56	.35
The golden isle.	Prmb P121	51	.35
_____.	Prmb P221	53	.35
_____.	Perm M-4072	57	.35
The healer.	Perm M-4051	56	.35
In a dark garden.	Prmb P107	51	.35
	Prmb P220	53	.35
The mapmaker.	Perm M-4111	58	.35
The road to Bithynia.	Prmb P241	53	.35
_____.	Perm M-4055	57	.35
Sangaree.	Pop G100	52	.35
_____.	Pop G163	56	.35
The scarlet cord.	Perm M-4069	57	.35
Science and surgery.	Perm M-4060	56	.35
The song of Ruth.	Perm M-4031	55	.35
Spencer Brade, M.D.	Prmb P226	53	.35
	Perm M-4025	55	.35
_____.	Perm M-4008	55	.35
Storm haven.	Sig S956	52	.35
The stubborn heart.	Perm M-4092	58	.35
Sword and scalpel.	Prmb P180	52	.35
That none should die.	Perm M-4026	55	.35
_____.	Perm M-4038	56	.35
A touch of glory.	Perm M-4087	58	.35
The warrior.	Sig 986	53	.25
Your body and your mind.	SigK KD365	58	.50
_____.			

Author/Title	Pub./Stock No.	Yr.	Price
SLESAR, HENRY			
The gray flannel shroud.	Zen ZB-33	59	.35
SLIFER, ROSEJEANNE with Louise Crittenden			
The new Pocket quiz book.	PB 255	44	.25
The Pocket quiz book.	PB 132	41	.25
SLIGH, NIGEL			
Copperbelt.	Pop 365	51	.25
SLOANE, ERIC			
How you can forecast the weather.	Prem s42	57	.35
SLOANE, WILLIAM			
To walk the night.	Pen 550	44	.25
	Dell 856	55	.25
The unquiet corpse.	Dell 928	56	.25
SLONIM, MARC			
An outline of Russian literature.	Ment MD268	59	.50
with Harvey Breit			
This thing called love.	Sig 1234	55	.25
SMALL, J. WALTER			
The dance merchants.	Ace D-300	58	.35
SMALL, MARVIN			
How to make more money.	Card C-186	55	.35
The low calorie diet.	PB 968	53	.25
_____.	Card C-359	59	.35
The world's best recipes.	Card C-265	57	.35
SMALL, SIDNEY HERSCHEL			
Sword and candle.	Ban 1243	54	.25
SMITH, ANN T.			
Death in the cards.	Bart 34	46	.25
SMITH, BEN			
Gunfighter's return.	Ban 1949	59	.25
Johnny No-Name.	Ace D-172	56	.35
Stranger in Sundown.	Ace D-332	59	.35
Trouble at Breakdam.	Ace D-304	58	.35
SMITH, BETTY			
Maggie now.	Ban F1900	59	.50
Tomorrow will be better.	Dell D104	52	.35
A tree grows in Brooklyn.	Ban 79	47	.25
_____.	Pop SP7	56	.50
SMITH, CAESAR			
Heat wave.	Ball 293K	59	.35
SMITH, DON			
China coaster.	Pop 522	53	.25
Out of the sea.	RS 11	52	.35
SMITH, E. E.			
The Skylark of space.	Pyr G332	58	.35

Author/Title	Pub./Stock No.	Yr.	Price
SMITH, GEORGE O.			
Fire in the heavens.	Ace D-375	59	.35
The fourth "R".	Ball 316K	59	.35
Hellflower.	Pyr G298	57	.35
The space plague.	Avon T-180	57	.35
SMITH, H. ALLEN			
The age of the tail.	Ban 1541	56	.25
The compleat practical			
joker.	PB 1093	56	.25
Desert island Decameron.	PB 615	49	.25
Life in a putty knife			
factory.	Sig 741	49	.25
Low man on a totem pole.	Ban 409	48	.25
Rhubarb.	PB 695	50	.25
Write me a poem, baby.	Ban 1861	59	.25
SMITH, HOLLAND M. with Percy Finch			
Coral and brass.	Ace D-287	58	.35
SMITH, HUSTON			
The religions of man.	Ment MD253	59	.50
SMITH, JAMES WOODRUFF			
Killer colt.	Pyr G358	58	.35
The loner.	Pyr G465	59	.35
SMITH, LAURENCE D.			
The corpse with the			
listening ear.	GD unk	44	.25
with Will Oursler			
Hooked.	Pop 528	53	.25
SMITH, LILLIAN			
Now is the time.	DelF 44	55	.25
Strange fruit.	PenN 665	48	.25
_____.	Sig S1074	53	.35
SMITH, RED			
The Saturday evening			
post sport stories.	PB 649	50	.25
SMITH, ROBERT M.			
Hits, runs and errors.	Dell 292	49	.25
One winter in Boston.	Pop G128	53	.35
SMITH, ROBERT PAUL			
Because of my love.	Avon 458	52	.25
Circle of desire.	Avon 545	53	.25
A man can love twice.	Avon T-158	57	.35
Plus blood in their			
veins.	Avon 399	52	.25
So it doesn't whistle.	Berk 109	55	.25
_____.	Berk G-125	58	.35
The time and the place.	Avon 534	53	.25
"Where did you go?" "Out"			
"What did you do?"			
"Nothing".	Card C-327	59	.35
SMITH, SHELLEY			
The crooked man.	Prmb 287	54	.25

Author/Title	Pub./Stock No.	Yr.	Price
The shrew is dead.	Dell D318	59	.35
SMITH, STAN			
Soldiers' women.	Hill 113	59	.35
SMITH, T. V.			
Live without fear.	SigK Ks338	56	.35
with Eduard C. Lindeman			
The democratic way of			
life.	Ment M59	51	.35
SMITH, THORNE			
The bishop's jaegers.	PB 314	45	.25
Did she fall?	PB 479	47	.25
The glorious pool.	PB 409	46	.25
The night life of the			
gods.	PB 428	47	.25
The passionate witch.	PB 401	46	.25
Rain in the doorway.	PB 546	49	.25
Skin and bones.	PB 490	48	.25
The stray lamb.	Avon 69	45	.25
_____.	PB 518	48	.25
Topper.	PB 4	39	.25
Topper takes a trip.	PB 209	43	.25
Turnabout.	PB 447	47	.25
SMITH, WALLACE			
Bessie Cotter.	Berk G-21	56	.35
_____.	Berk G-112	58	.35
SMITH, WILFRED CANTWELL			
Islam in modern history.	Ment MD268	59	.50
SMITH, WILLIAM GARDNER			
Anger at innocence.	Sig 907	51	.25
Last of the conquerors.	Sig 706	49	.25
South Street.	Berk G-4	55	.35
_____.	Berk G-193	58	.35
SNEAD, SAM			
Sam Snead's natural golf.	Dell 774	54	.25
SNEIDER, VERN			
The Teahouse of the			
August Moon.	Sig S1348	56	.35
SNYDER, LEONARD			
The velvet whip.	Berk 326	55	.25
SOBOL, LOUIS			
Along the Broadway beat.	Avon 319	51	.25
SOHL, JERRY			
The altered ego.	Pnnt P75	55	.25
Costigan's needle.	Ban 1278	54	.25
The haploids.	Lion 118	53	.25
The Mars monopoly.	Ace D-162	56	.35
One against Herculum.	Ace D-381	59	.35
Point Ultimate.	Ban A1952	59	.35
The time dissolver.	Avon T-186	57	.35
The transcendent man.	Ban A1971	59	.35

Author/Title	Pub./Stock No.	Yr.	Price
SOLDATI, MARIO			
Affair in Capri.	Berk G-69	57	.35
SOLOVIEV, MIKHAIL			
When the gods are silent.	Pop G135	54	.35
SOMETIME, never.	Ball 215	57	.35
The SONG of God: Bhagavad-gita.	Ment M103	54	.35
The SONG of Songs.	Ment MD277	59	.50
SONNICHSEN, C. L.			
Roy Bean: law west of the Pecos.	Hill 108	59	.35
SOPHOCLES			
The Oedipus plays of Sophocles.	Ment MT238	58	.75
Oedipus the King.	WSP W99	59	.35
SORCE, ROSE L.			
The new Italian cook book.	Pyr G381	59	.35
SOUBIRAN, ANDRÉ			
Bedlam.	Pyr G312	58	.35
The doctors.	Pop SP4	56	.50
SOULE, GEORGE			
Ideas of the great economists.	Ment M143	55	.35
Introduction to economic science.	Ment M58	51	.35
Men, wages and employment in the modern U.S. economy.	Ment M115	54	.35
The shape of tomorrow.	SigK Ks352	58	.35
SOURIAN, PETER			
Miri.	Sig S1650	59	.35
SOUTHWORTH, JOHN VAN DUYN			
The story of the world.	Card C-154	54	.35
SPACKMAN, W. M.			
Heyday.	Ball 12	53	.35
SPAFFORD, ROBERT			
Fare thee well.	RS 29	53	.35
My mistress, death.	GM 570	56	.25
SPAIN, JOHN			
Death is like that.	Pop 178	49	.25
Dig me a grave.	Ban 968	52	.25
The evil star.	Pop 239	50	.25
SPAIN, TERRY			
Time to kill.	Pop 500	53	.25

Author/Title	Pub./Stock No.	Yr.	Price
SPARKIA, ROY B.			
Boss man.	Lion 211	54	.25
Build my gallows high.	GM 563	56	.25
The vanishing vixen.	Crst 268	59	.25
SPEARE, DOROTHY			
Desperate choice.	Ban 758	50	.25
SPEARE, M. E.			
The Pocket book of short stories.	PB 91	41	.25
———.	Card C-12	51	.35
———.	PBL PL55	57	.35
The Pocket book of verse.	PB 62	40	.25
———.	Card C-11	51	.35
———.	PBL PL41	56	.35
SPEARMAN, FRANK H.			
Whispering Smith.	Pop 185	49	.25
SPECTORSKY, A. C.			
The exurbanites.	Berk BG-108	58	.50
SPELLMAN, FRANCIS J.			
Action this day.	Avon 67	45	.25
The foundling.	Card C-69	52	.35
The road to victory.	Avon 48	44	.25
SPENCE, HARTZELL			
One foot in heaven.	Sup M648	45	.25
SPENCER, ELIZABETH			
The voice at the back door.	Card C-272	58	.35
SPERLING, ABRAHAM P.			
How to make psychology work for you.	Prem s48	57	.35
SPERRY, ARMSTRONG			
Wagons westward.	Com 1	48	.25
SPEWACK, SAMUEL			
The skyscraper murder.	BH unk	47	.25
SPICER, BART			
Black sheep, run.	Ban 1049	52	.25
Blues for the prince.	Ban 934	51	.25
Day of the dead.	Dell 909	56	.25
The golden door.	Ban 975	52	.25
The long green.	Ban 1126	53	.25
The tall captains.	Ban F1886	59	.50
The taming of Carney Wilde.	Ban 1409	56	.25
The wild Ohio.	Ban A1211	54	.35
SPILLANE, MICKEY			
The big kill.	Sig 915	51	.25
———.	Sig S1700	59	.35
I, the jury.	Sig 699	48	.25
Kiss me, deadly.	Sig 1000	53	.25

Author/Title	Pub./Stock No.	Yr.	Price
SPILLANE, MICKEY (cont.)			
The long wait.	Sig 932	52	.25
_____.	Sig S1705	59	.35
My gun is quick.	Sig 791	50	.25
One lonely night.	Sig 888	51	.25
_____.	Sig S1728	59	.35
Vengeance is mine.	Sig 852	51	.25
_____.	Sig S1710	59	.35
SPILLER, ROBERT E.			
The cycle of American literature.	Ment MD188	57	.50
SPINELLI, MARCOS			
Assignment without glory.	Ban 95	47	.25
The green flames.	Ban 837	50	.25
The lash of desire.	Ace D-254	57	.35
Mocambu.	Ace D-310	58	.35
SPINGARN, ED			
Perfect 36.	Pyr G299	57	.35
SPINOZA, BENEDICTUS de			
The living thoughts of Spinoza.	Prem d76	59	.50
SPOCK, BENJAMIN			
Baby and child care.	Card GC-40	57	.50
The Pocket book of baby and child care.	PB 377	46	.25
_____.	Card C-29	52	.35
with Miriam E. Lowenberg			
Feeding your baby and child.	PB 1106	56	.25
with others			
A baby's first year.	Card GC-33	56	.50
SPOTA, LUIS			
The wounds of hunger.	Sig S1684	59	.35
SPROUL, EDITH E.			
The science book of the human body.	Card C-174	55	.35
SPYRI, JOHANNA			
Heidi.	PB 67	40	.25
STACKELBERG, GENE			
Double agent.	Pop G313	59	.35
STACY, DONALD			
The god of channel 1.	Ball 137	56	.35
STAGG, DELANO			
The glory jumpers.	Mon 140	59	.35
STAGGE, JONATHAN			
The dogs do bark.	Pop 350	51	.25
Murder by prescription.	Pop 52	45	.25
The scarlet circle.	Pop 90	46	.25

Author/Title	Pub./Stock No.	Yr.	Price
The stars spell death.	Pop 40	44	.25
Turn of the table.	Pop 267	50	.25
The yellow taxi.	Pop 62	45	.25
STANDISH, ROBERT			
Lord and master.	Ban 796	50	.25
Storm centre.	Ban A1085	53	.35
A worthy man.	Ban 1153	53	.25
STANFORD, DON			
Bargain in blood.	GM 162	51	.25
The slaughtered lovelies.	GM 116	50	.25
STANLEY, BENNETT			
Sea struck.	Ban A1257	54	.35
STANLEY, FAY GRISSOM			
Murder leaves a ring.	Dell 662	53	.25
STARK, MICHAEL			
Kill-box.	Ace D-55	54	.35
Run for your life.	Han 70	48	.25
STARK, SHELDON			
Too many sinners.	Ace D-81	54	.35
STARNES, RICHARD			
And when she was bad she was murdered.	PB 779	51	.25
Another mug for the bier.	PB 858	52	.25
The other body in Grant's Tomb.	PB 917	53	.25
STARR, JIMMY			
Three short biers.	Bart 15	45	.25
STARRETT, VINCENT			
Best loved books of the twentieth century.	Ban A1403	55	.35
STEARN, JESS			
Sisters of the night.	Pop G196	57	.35
STEARNS, MARSHALL			
The story of jazz.	Ment MD240	58	.50
STECHOW, WOLFGANG			
Bruegel.	PBA A21	55	.50
STEEL, KURT			
Judas, incorporated.	Dell 244	48	.25
STEELE, JACLEN			
The forbidden room.	GM 221	52	.25
STEELE, WILBUR DANIEL			
That girl from Memphis.	Dell 548	51	.25
STEELMAN, ROBERT			
Apache wells.	Ball 294K	59	.35

Author/Title	Pub./Stock No.	Yr.	Price
STEELMAN, ROBERT (cont.)			
Stages South.	Ace D-172	56	.35
Winter of the Sioux.	Ball 334K	59	.35
STEEN, MARGUERITE			
Bell Timson.	Prmb P110	51	.35
STEEVES, HARRISON R.			
Good night, sheriff.	Sup M657	45	.25
———.	Ban 149	48	.25
STEFFERUD, ALFRED			
How to know the wild			
flowers.	Ment M48	50	.35
The wonderful world of			
books.	Ment M82	53	.35
———.	Ment MD157	55	.50
STEGER, SHELBY			
Desire in the Ozarks.	Ace D-224	57	.35
STEGNER, MARY with Wallace Stegner			
Great American short			
stories.	DelL LC103	57	.50
STEGNER, WALLACE			
Remembering laughter.	DelT 17	51	.10
with Mary Stegner			
Great American short			
stories.	DelL LC103	57	.50
STEICHEN, EDWARD			
The family of man.	Card GC-51	58	.50
STEIG, HENRY			
Send me down.	Avon G-1012	54	.50
STEIN, JESS			
The new Dell modern			
American dictionary.	DelL LC104	57	.50
STEINBECK, JOHN			
Burning bright.	Ban 953	51	.25
Cannery Row.	Ban 75	47	.25
———.	Ban 1065	52	.25
———.	Ban 1266	54	.25
———.	BanC AC18	59	.35
Cup of gold.	Pop 216	49	.25
———.	Ban 1184	53	.25
East of Eden.	Ban F1267	55	.50
———.	Ban F1895	59	.50
14 great short stories			
from The long valley.	Avon 132	47	.25
The grapes of wrath.	Ban 7	45	.25
———.	Ban A868	51	.35
———.	Ban F1301	55	.50
The long valley.	Avon 77	45	.25
The moon is down.	PenS S219	43	.25
Of mice and men.	Ban A1329	55	.35
———.	BanC AC12	58	.35

Author/Title	Pub./Stock No.	Yr.	Price
The pastures of heaven.	Pen 509	42	.25
———.	Ban 899	51	.25
———.	Ban 1066	52	.25
———.	Ban A1478	56	.35
The pearl.	Ban 131	48	.25
———.	Ban 1544	56	.25
The red pony.	Ban 402	48	.25
———.	Ban 1406	55	.25
The short reign of			
Pippin IV.	Ban A1753	58	.35
The Steinbeck Pocket			
book.	PB 243	43	.25
Sweet Thursday.	Ban A1412	56	.35
To a god unknown.	Dell 358	49	.25
———.	Dell 407	50	.25
———.	Ban A1324	55	.35
Tortilla Flat.	Pen 599	46	.25
———.	Sig 816	50	.25
———.	Sig 1380	57	.25
———.	Sig S1737	59	.35
The wayward bus.	Ban 752	50	.25
———.	Ban A1555	57	.35
STEINBERG, SAUL			
Cartoons: all in line.	Pen 640	47	.25
STEINCROHN, PETER J.			
How to live with your			
heart.	Graf G204	54	.35
How to stop killing			
yourself.	Ace D-213	57	.35
STEINER, PAUL			
The bedside bachelor.	Lion LL 168	57	.35
Bedtime laughs.	Lion LL 105	56	.35
Women and children first.	Ban A1358	55	.35
STEKEL, WILHELM			
How to understand your			
dreams.	Eton ET105	51	.35
The meaning and			
psychology of dreams.	Bard 2	55	.50
STENDHAL			
The red and the black.	Ban S1734	58	.75
———.	BanC SC40	59	.75
STEPHENS, ANDREW B.			
The secret memoirs of a			
chicken.	Ban 472	49	.25
———.	Ban A1745	58	.35
STEPHENSON, J. L.			
Anyone can have a great			
vocabulary.	Avon 225	50	.25
———.	Bard 3	55	.35
STERLING, STEWART			
Alarm in the night.	Dell 513	51	.25
Alibi baby.	Avon 685	56	.25

Author/Title	Pub./Stock No.	Yr.	Price
STERLING, STEWART (cont.)			
The blonde in suite 14.	Avon T-320	59	.35
Dead of night.	Dell 583	52	.25
Dead sure.	Dell 420	50	.25
Dead wrong.	Dell 314	49	.25
Five alarm funeral.	Han unk	44	.15
_____.	Dell 816	54	.25
The hotel murders.	Avon 762	57	.25
Nightmare at noon.	Dell 693	53	.25
Too hot to kill.	Avon 835	58	.25
Where there's smoke.	Dell 275	49	.25
with Dev Collans			
I was a house detective.	Pyr 139	55	.25
_____.	Pyr G261	57	.35
STERLING, THOMAS			
The house without a door.	PB 774	51	.25
Murder in Venice.	Dell D270	59	.35
STERN, BILL			
Bill Stern's favorite boxing stories.	PB 416	48	.25
Bill Stern's favorite football stories.	PB 555	48	.25
Favorite baseball stories.	PB 572	49	.25
My favorite sports stories.	PB 494	48	.25
STERN, DANIEL			
The girl with the glass heart.	Perm M-4010	55	.35
The guests of fame.	Ball 114	55	.35
STERN, DAVID			
Francis.	Dell 507	51	.25
STERN, JILL			
Nine miles to Reno.	Sig S1570	58	.35
STERN, PHILIP VAN DOREN			
Great tales of fantasy and imagination.	Card C-156	54	.35
Love is the one with wings.	Sig 906	52	.25
The man who killed Lincoln.	Dell D159	55	.35
Manhunt.	Berk 334	55	.25
The Pocket book of adventure stories.	PB 284	45	.25
The Pocket book of America.	PB 182	42	.25
The Pocket book of ghost stories.	PB 384	47	.25
The Pocket book of modern American short stories.	PB 238	43	.25
_____.	PBL PL24	54	.35
The Pocket companion.	PB 142	42	.25
The Pocket reader.	PB 108	41	.25

Author/Title	Pub./Stock No.	Yr.	Price
The Pocket week-end book.	PB 586	49	.25
STERN, RICHARD MARTIN			
The bright road to fear.	Ball 288K	59	.35
Suspense.	Ball 331K	59	.35
STERNE, LAURENCE			
The life and opinions of Tristram Shandy, gentleman.	PBL PL511	57	.50
STETTINIUS, EDWARD R. JR.			
Lend-lease: weapon for victory.	PB 266	44	.25
STEUER, ARTHUR			
Rebel gun.	DelF A124	56	.25
The terrible swift sword.	Ace D-250	57	.35
STEVENS, DAN J.			
Blood money.	Perm M-3033	56	.25
Hangman's mesa.	Mon 135	59	.35
Oregon trunk.	Lion 50	51	.25
_____.	Lion LL 36	55	.35
Wild horse range.	Ace D-12	53	.35
STEVENS, EDMUND			
This is Russia-- uncensored.	Eton ET108	51	.35
STEVENS, WILLIAM OLIVER			
The inspirational reader.	Ban F1442	56	.50
STEVENSON, ELEANOR "BUMPY" with Pete Martin			
I knew your soldier.	PenS S230	45	.25
STEVENSON, ROBERT LOUIS			
The black arrow.	PBJr J-57	51	.25
Dr. Jekyll and Mr. Hyde.	PB 123	41	.25
The great short stories of Robert Louis Stevenson.	Card C-48	52	.35
_____.	PBL PL14	54	.35
Kidnapped.	PBL PL34	58	.35
_____.	SigC CD6	59	.50
Stevenson.	DelL LC140	59	.50
Treasure Island.	PB 25	39	.25
_____.	Ban 142	48	.25
_____.	PBL PL49	57	.35
STEWARD, DAVENPORT			
Caribbean cavalier.	Pop G256	58	.35
Rainbow road.	Pop 578	54	.25
Sail the dark tide.	Pop 669	55	.25
Savage conqueror.	Hill 123	59	.35
They had a glory.	Prmb P181	52	.35
Way of a buccaneer.	Pop G200	57	.35
STEWART, DESMOND			
Leopard in the grass.	Sig 997	53	.25

Author/Title	Pub./Stock No.		Yr.	Price
STEWART, DESMOND (cont.)				
A stranger in Eden.	Sig	1357	56	.25
STEWART, GEORGE R.				
Fire.	Ban	802	50	.25
Storm.	PenS	S238	44	.25
_____.	Ban	155	48	.25
STEWART, LOGAN				
Rails West.	GM	367	54	.25
Savage stronghold.	GM	327	53	.25
The secret rider.	GM	243	52	.25
They died healthy.	GM	182	51	.25
The trail.	GM	193	51	.25
War bonnet pass.	GM	137	51	.25
_____.	GM	313	53	.25
STEWART, RAMONA				
Desert town.	PB	526	48	.25
STEWART, SIDNEY				
Give us this day.	Pop	G233	58	.35
The range grabbers.	GM	377	54	.25
STILES, BERT				
Serenade to the big bird.	Ball	216	57	.35
STILWELL, HART				
Border city.	Ban	765	50	.25
Campus town.	Pop	331	51	.25
STIMPSON, GEORGE				
A book about American				
history.	Prem	s29	56	.35
STINE, G. HARRY				
Earth satellites and the				
race for space				
superiority.	Ace	D-239	57	.35
STINETORF, LOUISE A.				
White witch doctor.	PB	851	52	.25
STOCKTON, J. ROY				
The gashouse gang.	Ban	552	48	.25
STOKER, BRAM				
Dracula.	PB	452	47	.25
_____.	Perm	M-4088	57	.35
STOKES, DONALD				
Appointment with fear.	Sig	873	51	.25
Captive in the night.	Sig	1006	53	.25
_____.	Crst	126	56	.25
STOKES, MANNING LEE				
The crooked circle.	Graf	40	51	.25
Green for a grave.	BK	unk	47	.25
Murder can't wait.	Graf	117	55	.25
Too many murderers.	Graf	98	55	.25
Under cover of night.	DelF	A163	58	.25

Author/Title	Pub./Stock No.		Yr.	Price
STOLBERG, CHARLES				
The Avon book of puzzles.	Avon	(27)	43	.25
STONE, ABRAHAM with Hannah Stone				
A marriage manual.	Card	C-179	55	.35
STONE, ANDREW L.				
Cry terror.	Sig	1508	58	.25
The decks ran red.	Sig	1595	58	.25
Julie.	Sig	1332	56	.25
STONE, GRACE ZARING				
The bitter tea of				
General Yen.	Pop	169	49	.25
The cold journey.	Ban	44	46	.25
STONE, HAMPTON				
The corpse in the				
corner saloon.	Dell	464	50	.25
The corpse that refused				
to stay dead.	Dell	790	54	.25
The girl who kept				
knocking them dead.	Dell	D278	59	.35
The man who had too				
much to lose.	Dell	943	57	.25
The murder that wouldn't				
stay solved.	Dell	883	56	.25
STONE, HANNAH with Abraham Stone				
A marriage manual.	Card	C-179	55	.35
STONE, IRVING				
Clarence Darrow for the				
defense.	BanB	FB418	58	.50
Immortal wife.	Prmb	P228	53	.35
Love is eternal.	Card	GC-32	56	.50
Lust for life.	PB	344	46	.25
_____.	Card	C-10	51	.35
STONE, SCOTT				
Blaze.	Berk	G-227	59	.35
STONE, THOMAS				
Help wanted--male.	NL	41	50	.25
Shameless honeymoon.	Pyr	18	50	.25
STONG, PHIL				
Jessamy John.	Avon	AT57	53	.35
State fair.	Sig	824	50	.25
STORER, JOHN H.				
The web of life.	SigK	Ks333	56	.35
STORIES for tonight.	Avon	644	55	.25
STORIES in the modern				
manner.	Avon	AT-61	53	.35
STORIES of scarlet women.	Avon	T-113	55	.35

Author/Title	Pub./Stock No.	Yr.	Price
STORM, ELLIOT			
Hot date.	RC 7	49	.25
STORME, PETER			
The thing in the brook.	Bond unk	46	.25
STOUT, REX			
Alphabet Hicks.	Dell 146	47	.25
And be a villain.	Ban 824	50	.25
And four to go.	Ban A2016	59	.35
Bad for business.	Dell 299	49	.25
Before midnight.	Ban A1632	57	.35
The black mountain.	Ban 1386	55	.25
Black orchids.	Avon 95	46	.25
The broken vase.	Dell 115	46	.25
.	Dell 674	53	.25
The case of the black			
orchids.	Avon 256	50	.25
.	Avon 714	56	.25
Case of the red box.	Avon T-216	58	.35
Door to death.	DelT 21	51	.10
Double for death.	Dell 9	43	.25
.	Dell 495	51	.25
Fer-de-lance.	PB 112	41	.25
.	Dell D223	58	.35
The golden spiders.	Ban 1387	55	.25
The hand in the glove.	Dell 177	47	.25
How like a god.	Lion LL 23	55	.35
If death ever slept.	Ban A1961	59	.35
In the best families.	Ban 1173	53	.25
Invitation to murder.	Avon 738	56	.25
The league of			
frightened men.	Avon (20)	42	.25
Might as well be dead.	Ban A1795	58	.35
The mountain cat murders.	Dell 28	43	.25
.	Dell D252	58	.35
Murder by the book.	Ban 1252	54	.25
Not quite dead enough.	Dell 267	49	.25
Over my dead body.	Avon 62	45	.25
.	Avon T-296	59	.35
Prisoner's base.	Ban 1326	55	.25
The red box.	Avon 82	46	.25
The red bull.	Dell 70	45	.25
Red threads.	Dell 235	48	.25
The rubber band.	PB 208	43	.25
The second confession.	Ban 1032	52	.25
The silent speaker.	Ban 308	48	.25
.	Ban A1797	58	.35
Three doors to death.	Dell 626	52	.25
Three for the chair.	Ban A1796	58	.35
Three men out.	Ban 1388	55	.25
Three witnesses.	Ban A1633	57	.35
Too many cooks.	Dell 45	44	.25
.	Dell 540	51	.25
Too many women.	Ban 722	49	.25
.	Ban 1395	55	.25
Triple jeopardy.	Ban A1631	57	.35
Trouble in triplicate.	Ban 925	51	.25
.	Ban 1394	55	.25
Where there's a will.	Avon 103	46	.25

Author/Title	Pub./Stock No.	Yr.	Price
Where there's a will.	Avon T-374	59	.35
STOVER, HERBERT E.			
The eagle and the wind.	Eag EB26	54	.25
.	Pop G349	59	.35
Powder mission.	Avon AT-62	53	.35
STOWE, PERRY			
Superstition farm.	DelT unk	51	.10
STRABEL, THELMA			
Reap the wild wind.	Pnnt P19	53	.25
STRACHEY, LYTTON			
Elizabeth and Essex.	PB 26	39	.25
STRANGE, JOHN STEPHEN			
All men are liars.	Dell 438	50	.25
STRANGE but true.	GM 450	55	.25
STRATTON, TED			
Wild breed.	GM 443	54	.25
STRAUSS, THEODORE			
Dark hunger.	Ban 889	51	.25
The haters.	Ban 857	51	.25
STREET, JAMES			
By valour and arms.	Prmb P255	53	.35
Mingo Dabney.	PB 819	51	.25
Oh, promised land.	Card GC-8	53	.50
Tap roots.	Card C-26	52	.35
The velvet doublet.	Perm M-4005	55	.35
with James Childers			
Tomorrow we reap.	Card C-74	53	.35
STREET, LEROY with David Loth			
I was a drug addict.	Pyr 122	54	.25
STREETER, EDWARD			
Father of the bride.	Hill 48	51	.25
STRIKER, FRAN			
The Lone Ranger.	BPLA unk	40	.10
STRUTHER, JAN			
Mrs. Miniver.	PB 159	42	.25
STRUTTON, BILL with Michael Pearson			
The beachhead spies.	Ace D-355	59	.35
STUART, E. B.			
Drag me down.	Pop 671	55	.25
STUART, JEB			
The ordeal of Pvt. Heath.	Pyr 106	53	.25
STUART, JESSE			
Taps for Private Tussie.	PB 357	46	.25

Author/Title	Pub./Stock No.	Yr.	Price
STUART, LYLE			
God wears a bow tie.	Avon 305	50	.25
STUART, MATT			
Bonanza Gulch.	Pop 407	52	.25
Deep hills.	Ban 1419	56	.25
Dusty wagons.	PB 726	50	.25
Gun law at Vermillion.	Ban 1018	52	.25
Gun smoke showdown.	Ban 1696	57	.25
The lonely law.	Perm M-3109	58	.25
Saddle-man.	Ban 924	51	.25
_____.	Pnnt P42	54	.25
The smoky trail.	Ban 1095	53	.25
Sunset rider.	Pnnt P8	53	.25
Wire in the wind.	Pnnt P18	53	.25
STUART, W. J.			
Forbidden planet.	Ban A1443	56	.35
STUART, WILLIAM L.			
Dead ahead.	Ace D-11	53	.35
Night cry.	Avon 186	49	.25
_____.	Avon 597	54	.25
_____.	Avon 801	58	.25
STURGEON, THEODORE			
Aliens 4.	Avon T-304	59	.35
Caviar.	Ball 119	55	.35
The cosmic rape.	DelF B120	58	.35
E pluribus unicorn.	Ball 179	56	.35
The king and four queens.	DelF A128	57	.25
More than human.	Ball 46	53	.35
The synthetic man.	Pyr G247	57	.35
A touch of strange.	Berk G280	59	.35
A way home.	Pyr G184	56	.35
STYRON, WILLIAM			
Lie down in darkness.	Sig D967	52	.50
SUÁREZ CARREÑO, JOSÉ			
The final hours.	Sig 1191	55	.25
SUEHSDORF, ADIE			
What to tell your children about sex.	Perm M-4106	59	.35
SUGRUE, THOMAS			
The story of Edgar Cayce.	Dell F56	56	.50
SULLIVAN, ARTHUR with William Schwenck Gilbert			
Gilbert and Sullivan operas.	Avon 228	50	.25
SULLIVAN, J. W. N.			
Beethoven.	Ment M45	49	.35
The limitations of science.	Ment M35	49	.35
SULLIVAN, KATHERINE			
Girls on parole.	Pop G182	57	.35

Author/Title	Pub./Stock No.	Yr.	Price
SUMMERS, HOLLIS			
City limit.	Ban 727	49	.25
SUMMERS, RICHARD			
Dark madonna.	Ban 1025	52	.25
Vigilante.	Dell 471	51	.25
SUMMERSBY, KAY			
Eisenhower was my boss.	Dell 286	49	.25
SUMNER, CID RICKETTS			
Quality.	Ban 126	47	.25
SUMNER, NICK			
The Border Queen.	Pnnt P52	54	.25
The boss of Broken Spur.	Ban 1551	57	.25
Bullet brand.	Dell 979	58	.25
SUNDGAARD, ARNOLD			
The miracle of growth.	Pyr G213	56	.35
_____.	PyrR PR22	59	.50
SURDEZ, GEORGES			
The demon caravan.	Dell 501	51	.25
SUTTER, LARABIE			
The white squaw.	GM 255	52	.25
_____.	GM 630	57	.25
SUTTON, JEFF			
Bombs in orbit.	Ace D-377	59	.35
First on the moon.	Ace D-327	58	.35
SWADOS, FELICE			
House of fury.	Avon 298	50	.25
_____.	Avon 430	52	.25
_____.	Berk G240	59	.35
SWAIN, DWIGHT V.			
The transposed man.	Ace D-113	55	.35
SWANBERG, W. A.			
Fact detective mysteries.	Dell 332	49	.25
SWANSON, NEIL H.			
The forbidden ground.	Ban A1159	53	.35
The Judas tree.	Ban A1016	52	.35
The phantom emperor.	Dell D113	52	.35
The silent drum.	Ban F1041	52	.50
Unconquered.	Prmb P108	51	.35
SWARTHOUT, GLENDON			
They came to Cordura.	Sig D1679	59	.50
SWENSON, ERIC			
The Pocket book of famous French short stories.	PB 431	47	.25
SWIFT, JONATHAN			
Gulliver's travels.	PB 34	39	.25
_____.	PBL PL51	57	.35

Author/Title	Pub./Stock No.	Yr.	Price
SWIGGETT, HOWARD			
The durable fire.	Crst d228	58	.50
The power and the prize.	Ball F150	56	.50
The strongbox.	Perm M-4045	56	.35
SWITZER, ROBERT			
The living idol.	Sig 1335	56	.25
The tent of the wicked.	Sig 1313	56	.25
SYKES, GERALD			
The center of the stage.	Sig 1099	54	.25
SYLVESTER, ROBERT			
The big boodle.	Perm M-3022	55	.25
Dream street.	Avon 303	50	.25
Indian summer.	Prmb P230	53	.35
The second oldest			
profession.	Avon AT53	53	.35
We were strangers.	Sig 716	49	.25
SYMONS, JULIAN			
The color of murder.	Dell D296	59	.35
The narrowing circle.	Berk 354	56	.25
The 31st of February.	Ban 1059	53	.25
_____.	Berk G-137	58	.35
SYMS			
Small talk.	PB 682	50	.25

Author/Title	Pub./Stock No.	Yr.	Price
T			
TABER, GLADYS			
The heart has April too.	Dell 373	50	.25
TABORI, GEORGE			
The caravan passes.	Sig 963	52	.25
The journey.	Ban A1868	58	.35
TAGGARD, ERNESTINE			
Twenty grand short stories.	Ban 154	48	.25
_____.	Ban A1303	55	.35
TALBOT, DANIEL			
City of love.	Dell 45	55	.25
The damned.	Lion LL 6	54	.35
Thirteen great stories.	DelF D99	56	.35
TALBOT, HAKE			
Rim of the pit.	Dell 173	47	.25
TALES from the Arabian nights.	Card C-17	51	.35
_____.	PBL PL-16	54	.50
_____.	PBL PL506	57	.50
TALES of love and fury.	Avon 549	53	.25
TALES of midsummer passion.	Avon 778	57	.25
The TALL T.	Avon 775	57	.25
TALLANT, ROBERT			
Mrs. Candy and Saturday night.	Pop 358	51	.25
Southern territory.	PB 885	52	.25
TALLMAN, ROBERT			
Adios, O'Shaughnessy.	Pop 348	51	.25
_____.	Berk G-24	56	.35
TANNENBAUM, R. F.			
Panorama: the Laurel reader no. 1.	DelL LC107	58	.50
TAPLINGER, RICHARD with J. Y. Henderson			
Circus doctor.	Ban 992	52	.25
TARG, WILLIAM			
Great western stories.	Pen 654	47	.25
TARKINGTON, BOOTH			
Presenting Lily Mars.	Avon 55	44	.25
Seventeen.	Ban 17	45	.25
_____.	Ban A1586	57	.35
_____.	BanC AC48	59	.35
TATE, SYLVIA			
The fuzzy pink nightgown.	Pyr G275	57	.35

Author/Title	Pub./Stock No.	Yr.	Price
TAUBES, FRANK			
Run...run...run...	Pop 769	56	.25
TAWNEY, HOWARD D. with Ben Benson			
Hypnosis and you.	GM s583	56	.35
TAWNEY, R. H.			
Religion and the rise of capitalism.	Pel P22	47	.35
_____.	Ment MD163	55	.50
TAYLOR, ANGELINE			
Black jade.	PB 635	49	.25
TAYLOR, DANIEL			
All his women.	Pyr G285	57	.35
They move with the sun.	Pop 274	50	.25
TAYLOR, DYSON			
Bitter love.	Pyr G60	52	.35
_____.	Pyr G278	57	.35
TAYLOR, E. B.			
Sex and marriage problems.	Hill 7	48	.25
TAYLOR, EDMOND			
The strategy of terror.	PB 173	42	.25
TAYLOR, GRANT			
"Whip" Ryder's way.	Ban 129	47	.25
TAYLOR, HENRY			
The statesman.	Ment MD250	58	.50
TAYLOR, JOHN			
Shadows of shame.	Pyr G189	56	.35
TAYLOR, LILLI with Peter Cardozo			
A wonderful world for children, no. 2.	Ban A1790	58	.35
TAYLOR, PHOEBE ATWOOD			
Banbury bog.	Dell 251	48	.25
The Cape Cod mystery.	PB 171	42	.25
The criminal C.O.D.	Pop 14	43	.25
The deadly sunshade.	Pop 126	47	.25
Death lights a candle.	PB 204	43	.25
Diplomatic corpse.	Avon 439	52	.25
Octagon House.	Dell 171	47	.25
Out of order.	Pop 25	44	.25
The perennial boarder.	Pen 618	47	.25
Spring harrowing.	Dell 98	46	.25
TAYLOR, RICHARD			
The better Taylors.	Avon 119	47	.25
with F. S. Pearson II			
Fractured French.	Perm M-3031	56	.25

Author/Title	Pub./Stock No.	Yr.	Price
TAYLOR, ROBERT LEWIS			
W. C. Fields: his follies			
and his fortunes.	Ban A938	51	.35
Winston Churchill.	Card C-133	54	.35
TAYLOR, ROBERT SCOTT			
Vera.	Pyr G390	59	.35
TAYLOR, ROBERT W.			
The dark urge.	Pyr G72	53	.35
The glitter and the			
greed.	GM 461	55	.25
The junk pusher.	Pyr 126	54	.25
Mimi.	Pyr 96	53	.25
Scandal.	Pyr 107	53	.25
TAYLOR, ROBERT WILLIAM			
Occasion of sin.	Mon 119	59	.35
TAYLOR, ROSEMARY			
Chicken every Sunday.	PB 321	45	.25
Come clean, my love.	Ban 773	50	.25
TAYLOR, ROSS McLAURY			
Brazos.	Ban 844	50	.25
_____.	Ban 1111	52	.25
TAYLOR, SAM S.			
No head for her pillow.	Sig 1057	53	.25
Sleep no more.	Sig 821	50	.25
So cold, my bed.	Sig 1247	55	.25
TAYLOR, SAMUEL W.			
The grinning gismo.	Ace D-1	52	.35
The man with my face.	PB 639	50	.25
_____.	Berk 338	55	.25
TAYLOR, VALERIE			
The girls in 3-B.	Crst s290	59	.35
Whisper their love.	Crst 187	57	.25
TAYLOR, WARD			
Roll back the sky.	Pop SP9	57	.50
TEAGLE, MIKE			
Murders in silk.	Lion unk	51	.25
TEALE, EDWIN WAY			
The fascinating insect			
world of J. Henri Fabre.	Prem s21	56	.35
TEBBEL, JOHN			
The conqueror.	Card C-41	52	.35
Touched in fire.	Prmb P222	53	.35
TEDESCHI, ALBERTO et al.			
Mondadori's Pocket			
Italian-English,			
English-Italian			
dictionary.	Card GC-47	59	.50
TEILHET, DARWIN L.			
The fear makers.	PB 399	46	.25
The mission of Jeffery			
Tomaly.	Prmb P160	52	.35
Something wonderful			
to happen.	Ban 415	48	.25
TEILHET, HILDEGARDE TOLMAN			
Fear is the hunter.	Prmb P116	51	.35
The rim of terror.	Ban 856	51	.25
TELFAIR, RICHARD			
The bloody medallion.	GM 847	59	.25
The corpse that talked.	GM 890	59	.25
Day of the gun.	GM 827	58	.25
The secret of Apache			
Canyon.	GM 932	59	.25
Wyoming Jones.	GM 759	58	.25
Wyoming Jones for hire.	GM 883	59	.25
TELLIER, ANDRÉ			
Twilight men.	Lion 24	50	.25
.	Pyr G262	57	.35
A woman of Paris.	Pyr 71	53	.25
TEMPLE, DAN			
Bullet lease.	Eag EB99	57	.25
The man from Idaho.	Pop 783	56	.25
Outlaw river.	Eag EB37	55	.25
_____.	Pop G378	59	.35
TEMPLE, WILLIAM			
Christianity and social			
order.	PenS S207	42	.25
TEN nights of love.	Avon 128	47	.25
TENN, WILLIAM			
The human angle.	Ball 159	56	.35
Of all possible worlds.	Ball 99	55	.35
Outsiders: children of			
wonder.	Prmb P291	54	.35
Time in advance.	Ban A1786	58	.35
TENZING NORGAY with James Ramsey Ullman			
Tiger of the snows.	Ban A1465	56	.35
TERHUNE, ALBERT PAYSON			
Lad: a dog.	PB 373	46	.25
TERRALL, ROBERT			
Great scenes from great			
novels.	DelF C105	57	.50
A killer is loose among			
us.	Avon 278	50	.25
Madam is dead.	Avon 284	51	.25
TERRILL, ROGERS			
Argosy book of			
adventure stories.	Ban A1158	53	.35

Author/Title	Pub./Stock No.	Yr.	Price
TERRILL, ROGERS (cont.)			
The Argosy book of sports stories.	Pnnt P61	54	.25
TERROT, CHARLES			
The passionate pilgrim.	Ban 872	51	.25
TERRY, C. V.			
Buccaneer surgeon.	Card C-197	55	.35
Darien venture.	Perm M-4057	56	.35
The golden ones.	Perm M-4100	58	.35
TERRY, J. WILLIAM			
A restless breed.	Sig S1603	58	.35
TERRY, WALTER			
Ballet: a new guide to the liveliest art.	DelL LX112	59	.75
TESCH, GERALD			
Never the same again.	Pyr G342	58	.35
TEY, JOSEPHINE			
Come and kill me.	PB 784	51	.25
The daughter of time.	Berk G265	59	.35
The Franchise affair.	PB 671	50	.25
The man in the queue.	Dell D255	59	.35
THACHER, RUSSELL			
The captain.	PB 883	52	.25
The tender age.	PB 969	53	.25
THACKERAY, WILLIAM MAKEPEACE			
Vanity fair.	PBL PL750	58	.75
THAMES, C. H.			
Violence is golden.	Ace D-177	56	.35
THANE, ELSWYTH			
Dawn's early light.	Card C-43	52	.35
Ever after.	Card C-164	55	.35
Yankee stranger.	Card C-103	53	.35
THAYER, LEE			
Murder is out.	Bart 16	45	.25
THAYER, TIFFANY			
Call her savage.	Avon (14)	42	.25
_____.	Avon 291	50	.25
_____.	Avon 418	52	.25
The illustrious corpse.	Pop 227	50	.25
The old goat.	Avon 234	50	.25
One man show.	Avon 327	51	.25
One woman.	PB 673	50	.25
Three musketeers and a lady.	Sig 772	50	.25
THEY lived by their guns.	Sig 1014	53	.25
THIELEN, BENEDICT			
The lost men.	Lion LL 18	55	.35
THIS is my body.	Berk G-68	57	.35
THOMAS à KEMPIS			
The imitation of Christ.	Card C-104	53	.35
_____.	PBL PL5	54	.35
Of the imitation of Christ.	Ment MD193	57	.50
THOMAS, BOB			
The flesh merchants.	DelF B133	59	.35
THOMAS, DYLAN			
Adventures in the skin trade.	Sig S1281	56	.35
THOMAS, KENNETH			
The devil's mistress.	GM 192	51	.35
_____.	GM s802	58	.35
THOMAS, LOWELL			
Great true adventures.	Dell F89	59	.50
Out of this world to forbidden Tibet.	Avon G1010	54	.50
THOMAS, T. T.			
I, James Dean.	Pop W400	57	.25
THOMAS, W. CRAIG			
House of hate.	Pyr G348	58	.35
THOMAS, WILL			
Love knows no barriers.	Sig 832	50	.25
THOMASON, J. W. JR.			
Gone to Texas.	Avon 306	51	.25
_____.	Avon 451	52	.25
_____.	Avon T-85	54	.35
Lone star preacher.	Berk G-10	55	.35
THOMEY, TEDD			
And dream of evil.	Avon 614	54	.25
_____.	Avon 737	56	.25
I want out.	Ace D-401	59	.35
Jet ace.	Avon T-256	58	.35
Jet pilot.	Avon 632	55	.25
Killer in white.	GM 546	56	.25
THOMPSON, BEN			
Gunman's spawn.	Graf G210	55	.35
_____.	Graf G223	57	.35
THOMPSON, C. HALL			
A gun for Billy Reo.	DelF 49	55	.25
Montana!	DelF B140	59	.35
Under the badge.	DelF A132	57	.25
THOMPSON, CHARLES			
Halfway down the stairs.	Card C-296	58	.35
THOMPSON, GENE			
Six-guns wild.	Graf 146	57	.25

Author/Title	Pub./Stock No.	Yr.	Price
THOMPSON, JIM			
After dark, my sweet.	Pop 716	55	.25
The alcoholics.	Lion 127	53	.25
Bad boy.	Lion 149	53	.25
The criminal.	Lion 184	53	.25
Cropper's cabin.	Lion unk	52	.25
_____.	Pyr G336	58	.35
The getaway.	Sig 1584	59	.25
The golden gizmo.	Lion 192	54	.25
A hell of a woman.	Lion 218	54	.25
_____.	Lion LB 138	56	.25
The kill-off.	Lion LL 142	57	.35
The killer inside me.	Lion 99	52	.25
The nothing man.	DelF 22	54	.25
Nothing more than murder.	Hill unk	50	.25
_____.	Dell 738	53	.25
Recoil.	Lion 120	53	.25
_____.	Lion LB 124	56	.25
Roughneck.	Lion 201	54	.25
Savage night.	Lion 155	53	.25
A swell-looking babe.	Lion 212	54	.25
Wild town.	Sig 1461	57	.25
THOMPSON, JOHN B.			
Sandy.	Berk G-219	59	.35
THOMPSON, LEWIS with Charles Boswell			
The girl in lover's lane.	GM 334	53	.25
The girl in the stateroom.	GM 180	51	.25
The girl with the scarlet brand.	GM 384	54	.25
The girls in nightmare house.	GM 480	55	.25
Surrender to love.	Pop 688	55	.25
THOMPSON, LLOYD S.			
The sin and the flesh.	Lion LL 5	54	.35
THOMPSON, MORTON			
The cry and the covenant.	Sig D1206	55	.50
Not as a stranger.	Sig T1265	56	.75
THOMPSON, OSCAR			
How to understand music.	Prem d64	58	.50
THOMPSON, PAUL W.			
Modern battle.	PenS S210	42	.25
THOMPSON, R. W.			
Battle for the Rhine.	Ball F291K	59	.50
The 85 days.	Ball F231	57	.50
THOMPSON, SYDNEY			
Dr. Parrish, Resident.	Dell 215	48	.25
THOMPSON, THOMAS			
Born to gunsmoke.	Pop 779	56	.25
Brand of a man.	Sig 1695	59	.25
Broken valley.	Ban 864	51	.25

Author/Title	Pub./Stock No.	Yr.	Price
Forbidden valley.	Pop 694	55	.25
Gunman brand.	Ban 1082	53	.25
King of Abilene.	Ball 47	53	.35
Range drifter.	Ban 764	50	.25
Rawhide rider.	Eag EB89	57	.25
Shadow of the butte.	Pnnt P33	54	.25
The steel web.	Ban 1407	56	.25
Sundown riders.	Ban 941	51	.25
They brought their guns.	Ball 84	54	.35
Trouble rider.	Ball 74	54	.35
THOMSON, J. ARTHUR			
Riddles of science.	Prem d65	58	.50
THOREAU, HENRY DAVID			
The living thoughts of Henry David Thoreau.	Prem d63	58	.50
Walden.	Pen 508	42	.25
_____.	Sig 747	49	.25
Walden and Civil disobedience.	Ment M87	53	.35
_____.	Ment MD176	56	.50
THORNE, ANTHONY			
Cabbage holiday.	Ban 452	48	.25
THORNE, EMILY			
Flight hostess.	Perm M-4109	59	.35
THORP, DUNCAN			
Only Akiko.	Dell D303	59	.35
THORP, RAYMOND with Robert Bunker			
Crow killer.	Sig S1691	59	.35
THORWALD, JÜRGEN			
Defeat in the East.	Ball F336K	59	.50
THREE hundred Pillsbury prize recipes.	Dell D112	52	.35
THURBER, JAMES			
Men, women and dogs.	Ban 21	46	.25
My life and hard times.	Ban 92	47	.25
with E. B. White			
Is sex necessary?	Dell 820	55	.25
THURMAN, HARRIETT			
The swift hour.	Dell 141	46	.25
THURMAN, STEVE			
Gun lightning!	Graf 96	55	.25
_____.	Graf 153	57	.25
Night after night.	Mon 142	59	.35
THURSTON, HOWARD			
300 tricks you can do.	Com 5	48	.25
TIEDJENS, VICTOR A. with Albert E. Wilkinson			
The handy book of gardening.	SigK Ks323	55	.35

Author/Title	Pub./Stock No.	Yr.	Price
TIEMPO, E. K.			
Cry slaughter!	Avon T-179	57	.35
TIGER, JOHN			
Death hits the jackpot.	Avon 605	54	.25
TIIRA, ENSIO			
Raft of despair.	Lion LL 134	56	.35
TILLERY, CARLYLE			
Red bone woman.	Avon 334	51	.25
_____.	Avon 452	52	.25
TILSLEY, FRANK			
Rage to love.	Pop G143	54	.35
_____.	Pop SP43	59	.50
TILTON, ALICE			
Cold steal.	Dell 142	46	.25
The left leg.	Dell 164	47	.25
TINA, DOROTHY LES			
Confession.	Ban 417	49	.25
TOCQUEVILLE, ALEXIS de			
Democracy in America.	Ment MD161	56	.50
TODD, LUCAS			
Showdown Creek.	Perm M-3044	56	.25
TOEPFER, RAY			
The scarlet guidon.	Pop G391	59	.35
TOKAY, ELBERT			
The human body and how it works.	SigK KD355	58	.50
TOLBERT, FRANK X.			
The staked plain.	Pop G306	59	.35
TOLSTOY, LEO			
Anna Karenina.	PB 515	48	.25
Polikushka and Two Hussars.	Avon T-133	56	.35
War and peace.	Dell F53	55	.50
_____.	Ban S1497	56	.75
TOMERLIN, JOHN			
Return to Vikki.	GM 900	59	.25
TOMKINSON, CONSTANCE			
Les girls.	Avon T-203	57	.35
TOMPKINS, WALKER A.			
Border ambush.	Dell 632	52	.25
Deadwood.	Ace D-68	54	.35
Flaming Canyon.	Dell 448	50	.25
Gold on the hoof.	Dell 879	55	.25
Manhunt west.	Dell 551	51	.25
One against a bullet horde.	Ace D-42	54	.35

Author/Title	Pub./Stock No.	Yr.	Price
The paintin' pistoleer.	Dell 300	49	.25
Prairie marshal.	Dell 764	54	.25
Rimrock rider.	Ace D-4	52	.35
West of Texas law.	Dell 310	49	.25
_____.	Dell 449	50	.25
TORRES, TERESKA			
The dangerous games.	Crst s243	58	.35
Not yet...	Sig S1579	58	.35
Women's barracks.	GM 132	50	.25
_____.	GM 379	54	.25
_____.	GM s673	57	.35
TORREY, ROGER			
42 days for murder.	Hill 23	49	.25
TOWERS, BENN			
The clock strikes death.	Ban 719	50	.25
_____.	Ban 1224	54	.25
_____.	Ban A1881	59	.35
Cursed be he who moves my bones.	Ban 1573	57	.25
The day the sandman came.	Ban 1114	53	.25
_____.	Ban A1960	59	.35
Death comes to set thee free.	Ban 1512	56	.25
_____.	Ban A1967	59	.35
Friday the fourteenth.	Ban 319	49	.25
_____.	Ban 1223	54	.25
How fares it with the happy dead?	Ban 1686	57	.25
It's lonely being dead.	Ban 1015	52	.25
_____.	Ban 1263	54	.25
_____.	Ban 1863	58	.25
Miles to go before you sleep.	Ban A1830	58	.35
Something's rotten in the State of Texas.	Ban 1222	54	.25
_____.	Ban 1644	57	.25
There was an old killer from Frisco.	Ban 1280	54	.25
_____.	Ban 1652	57	.25
What fools these mortals be.	Ban A1950	59	.35
When the boat sinks.	Ban 153	48	.25
_____.	Pnnt P74	54	.25
_____.	Ban 1530	56	.25
When the bomb ticks.	Bart unk	47	.25
_____.	Pnnt P45	54	.25
_____.	Ban 1522	56	.25
When the bough breaks.	Pony unk	46	.25
_____.	Pnnt P63	54	.25
_____.	Ban 1524	56	.25
Why so pale and wan, fair lover?	Ban 1380	55	.25
TOWNSEND, LEO			
The young life.	Pop G339	59	.35
TOWNSEND, RAY			
Gold town gunman.	Pop 590	54	.25

Author/Title	Pub./Stock No.	Yr.	Price
TOWNSEND, RAY (cont.)			
Gold town gunman.	Pop G353	59	.35
Renegade River.	Pop 623	54	.25
Saddlebow rancher.	Pop 714	55	.25
Stranger from Texas.	Pop 525	53	.25
Sundown Basin.	Pop 666	55	.25
TOYNBEE, ARNOLD J.			
Greek civilization and character.	Ment M99	53	.35
Greek historical thought.	Ment M72	52	.35
_____.	Ment MD164	55	.50
TRACY, CATHERINE			
Cotton moon.	Pop 352	51	.25
TRACY, DON			
The amber fire.	PB 1006	54	.25
Carolina corsair.	Card C-228	57	.35
The cheat.	Lion unk	52	.25
_____.	Lion LL 118	56	.35
Cherokee.	Card C-300	58	.35
Chesapeake cavalier.	PB 729	50	.25
Crimson is the eastern shore.	Card C-127	54	.35
Now sleeps the beast.	Lion 45	50	.25
On the midnight tide.	Card C-321	59	.35
Roanoke renegade.	Card C-189	55	.35
The strumpet sea.	PB 868	52	.25
Too many girls.	Berk G-182	58	.35
White hell.	Berk 318	55	.25
TRAIN, ARTHUR			
Tutt and Mr. Tutt.	Ban 55	46	.25
TRAVEN, B.			
The treasure of the Sierra Madre.	PB 455	48	.25
TRAVER, ROBERT			
Anatomy of a murder.	Dell F75	59	.50
Danny and the boys.	Pop G366	59	.35
Small town D.A.	Crst s233	58	.35
Trouble shooter.	Ban 111	47	.25
TRAVERS, ROBERT			
A funeral for Sabella.	Sig 1065	53	.25
Ten roads to hell.	Pop 618	54	.25
TRAVIS, GERRY			
The big bite.	Ace D-317	58	.35
TREAT, LAWRENCE			
B as in banshee.	Bond unk	46	.25
Big shot.	Ban 1026	52	.25
H as in hunted.	Dell 218	48	.25
Over the edge.	Ace D-51	54	.35
Q as in quicksand.	Dell 301	49	.25
T as in trapped.	Avon 274	50	.25
Weep for a wanton.	Ace D-189	56	.35
TREE, GREGORY			
The case against myself.	Ban 907	51	.25
TREECE, HENRY			
The great captains.	Crst s265	59	.35
The pagan queen.	Avon T-363	59	.35
The savage warriors.	Avon T-325	59	.35
TREGASKIS, RICHARD			
Guadalcanal diary.	PenS S220	43	.25
_____.	Pop G384	59	.35
TRENT, TIMOTHY			
All dames are dynamite.	NL 29	49	.25
TREVOR, ELLESTON			
The killing ground.	Ban A1835	58	.35
Tiger Street.	Lion 207	54	.25
TREVOR-ROPER, H. R.			
The last days of Hitler.	Berk BG-70	57	.50
TREYNOR, BLAIR			
She ate her cake.	Dell 186	47	.25
Silver doll.	Dell 762	54	.25
Widow's pique.	Perm M-3096	57	.25
TRIMBLE, LOUIS			
Blondes are skin deep.	Lion unk	51	.25
Cargo for the Styx.	Ace D-409	59	.35
The corpse without a country.	Ace D-347	59	.35
Crossfire.	Ban 1451	56	.25
Design for dying.	Bart 27	46	.25
Fighting cowman.	Pop 506	53	.25
Gaptown law.	Ban 1120	53	.25
Gunsmoke justice.	Ban 892	51	.25
Mountain ambush.	Ace D-384	59	.35
Nothing to lose but my life.	Ace D-235	57	.35
Obit deferred.	Ace D-401	59	.35
The smell of trouble.	Ace D-321	58	.35
Stab in the dark.	Ace D-157	56	.35
Till death do us part.	Ace D-367	59	.35
Valley of violence.	Ban 769	50	.25
TRIMNELL, ROBERT L.			
The wench and the flame.	Lion 147	53	.25
TROLLOPE, ANTHONY			
Barchester Towers.	BanC FC21	59	.50
TROPICAL passions.	Avon 255	50	.25
_____.	Avon 638	55	.25
TROYAT, HENRI			
The mountain.	Pop 588	54	.25
TRUMBULL, ROBERT			
The raft.	Dell 26	43	.25

Author/Title	Pub./Stock No.	Yr.	Price
TRUMBULL, ROBERT (cont.)			
The raft.	Pyr 38	51	.25
TRUSS, SELDON			
Why slug a postman?	PB 854	52	.25
TRYON, MARK			
The fire that burns.	Berk G-220	59	.35
The sinning lens.	Berk G-206	59	.35
TUBB, E. C.			
The mechanical monarch.	Ace D-266	58	.35
The space-born.	Ace D-193	56	.35
TUCKER, LAEL			
Lament for four virgins.	Ban A1136	53	.35
TUCKER, WILSON			
The Chinese doll.	Dell 343	49	.25
The hired target.	Ace D-241	57	.35
The long loud silence.	Dell 791	54	.25
The man from tomorrow.	Ban 1343	55	.25
The time masters.	Sig 1127	54	.25
Time: X.	Ban 1400	55	.25
To keep or kill.	Lion 21	50	.25
_____.	Lion LL 84	56	.35
Tomorrow plus X.	Avon T-168	57	.35
TULLY, JIM			
The bruiser.	Ban 67	46	.25
_____.	Pyr 53	52	.25
Road show.	Pyr 92	53	.25
TUNIS, JOHN R.			
The kid comes back.	PBJr J-67	51	.25
TUNNARD, CHRISTOPHER with Henry Hope Reed			
American skyline.	Ment MD175	56	.50
TURGENEV, IVAN			
Fathers and sons.	BanC FC41	59	.50
TURKIN, HY			
The 1955 baseball almanac.	Card C-167	55	.35
TURKUS, BURTON B. with Sid Feder			
Murder, inc.	Prmb P187S	52	.50
TURNBULL, AGNES SLIGH			
The bishop's mantle.	PB 657	50	.25
The golden journey.	Card C-241	57	.35
The gown of glory.	Card C-198	56	.35
TURNER, CALVIN			
The sinful love.	Hill 124	59	.35
TURNER, ROBERT			
The girl in the cop's pocket.	Ace D-177	56	.35

Author/Title	Pub./Stock No.	Yr.	Price
The lonely man.	Avon 780	57	.25
The scout.	PB 1216	58	.25
The tobacco auction murders.	Ace D-55	54	.35
Wagonmaster.	PB 1196	58	.25
Wagons West!	PB 1226	59	.25
TURNER, RUSSELL			
The short night.	Hill 103	57	.25
TURNER, WILLIAM O.			
The proud diggers.	Dell 844	55	.25
The settler.	Dell 947	57	.25
TURNEY, CATHERINE			
The other one.	Dell 695	53	.25
TURNGREN, ANNETTE			
Mystery of Hidden Village.	Berk G286	59	.35
Mystery walks the campus.	Berk G-158	58	.35
TUTE, WARREN			
The cruiser.	Ball F162	56	.50
TUTTLE, W. C.			
Bluffer's luck.	Hill unk	48	.25
Gun feud.	Pop 354	51	.25
Hashknife of Stormy River.	Hill unk	50	.25
Hidden blood.	Pop 149	48	.25
The mystery of the red triangle.	Avon 53	44	.25
The redhead from Sun Dog.	Hill unk	49	.25
Shotgun gold.	Pop 297	50	.25
Singing river.	Pop 96	46	.25
Straws in the wind.	Hill unk	49	.25
Thunderbird range.	Pyr 370	58	.25
Trouble at the JHC.	Hill unk	50	.25
The trouble trailer.	Pop 330	51	.25
Twisted trails.	Pop 249	50	.25
Valley of vanishing herds.	Pop 165	48	.25
Wild Horse valley.	Pop 203	49	.25
TWAIN, MARK			
The adventures of Huckleberry Finn.	Card C-139	54	.35
_____.	PBL PL42	55	.35
_____.	SigC CD5	59	.50
The adventures of Tom Sawyer.	PBL PL39	55	.35
_____.	SigC CD2	59	.50
The complete short stories of Mark Twain.	BanC SC3	58	.75
A Connecticut Yankee in King Arthur's court.	PB 497	48	.25
_____.	Card C-107	53	.35
Huckleberry Finn.	PBJr J-42	50	.25
Life on the Mississippi.	Ban 1	45	.25

Author/Title	Pub./Stock No.	Yr.	Price	Author/Title	Pub./Stock No.	Yr.	Price
TWAIN, MARK (cont.)							
Life on the Mississippi.	Ban F1445	56	.50				
_____.	BanC FC39	59	.50				
Mark Twain.	DelL LC111	58	.50				
Pudd'nhead Wilson.	BanC AC50	59	.35				
Tom Sawyer.	PBJr J-37	50	.25				
20 great ghost stories.	Avon 630	55	.25				
25 great ghost stories.	Avon nn	43	.25				
23 women.	Pyr 46	52	.25				
TWERSKY, JACOB							
The face of the deep.	Sig 1132	54	.25				
TWIST, PETER							
The gilded hideaway.	Ace S-107	55	.25				

Author/Title	Pub./Stock No.	Yr.	Price
U			
The U.S. marines on Iwo Jima.	Inf J102	45	.25
UCHARD, MARIO			
The Frenchman in Mohammed's harem.	Avon 416	52	.25
ULLMAN, ALBERT			
The kidnappers.	BK unk	46	.25
ULLMAN, ALLAN			
with Rolfe Bloom			
The naked spur.	Pnnt P29	54	.25
with Lucille Fletcher			
Night man.	Ban 1140	53	.25
	Pyr G354	58	.35
Sorry, wrong number.	Ban 356	48	.25
_____.	Ban 1771	58	.25
ULLMAN, JAMES RAMSEY			
River of the sun.	Card C-58	52	.35
The sands of Karakorum.	Ban 1383	55	.25
Third man on the mountain.	Card C-391	59	.35
The white tower.	Card C-76	53	.35
Windom's way.	PB 1008	54	.25
with Tenzing Norgay			
Tiger of the snows.	Ban A1465	56	.35
UNITED States book of baby and child care.	Eton 101	51	.25
UNTERMEYER, LOUIS			
The concise treasury of great poems.	Prmb P206S	53	.50
	Perm M-5007	58	.50
The Pocket book of American poems.	PB 529	48	.25
_____.	Card C-109	53	.35
The Pocket book of story poems.	PB 342	45	.25
The Pocket treasury.	PB 424	47	.25
Story poems.	PBL PL516	57	.50
A treasury of ribaldry, volume 1.	Pop W600	59	.75
UNTERMEYER, PAT with Sandy Nelkin			
For stags only.	Lion LL 24	55	.35
Stag gags.	Lion 213	54	.25
UNTERMEYER, WALTER JR.			
Dark the summer dies.	Lion 138	53	.25
Evil roots.	Lion 222	54	.25
The UPANISHADS.	Ment MD194	57	.50
UPFIELD, ARTHUR W.			
Death of a swagman.	PenN 658	48	.25
UPSHAW, HELEN			
Day of the harvest.	Prmb P292	54	.35
UPSON, WILLIAM HAZLETT			
Alexander Botts: earthworm tractors.	PB 304	46	.25
UPTON, MONROE			
Electronics for everyone.	SigK KD351	57	.50
URIS, LEON			
The angry hills.	Sig S1365	56	.35
Battle cry.	Ban F1279	54	.50
	Ban F1996	59	.50
_____. Exodus.	Ban S1995	59	.75
USSHER, ARLAND			
Three great Irishmen.	Ment MD205	57	.50

Author/Title	Pub./Stock No.	Yr.	Price

V

VAGTS, ALFRED
Hitler's second army. — PenS S214 — 43 — .25

VAIL, AMANDA
Love me little. — Ban A1914 — 59 — .35

VAIL, JOHN
Blond savage. — GM 476 — 55 — .25
The dark throne. — GM 396 — 54 — .25
Hold back the sun. — GM 556 — 56 — .25
Love isn't for now. — RS 27 — 53 — .35
The sea waifs. — RS 13 — 52 — .35
Sow the wild wind. — GM 441 — 54 — .25
Sword in his hand. — GM 309 — 53 — .25

VALENTINE, JO
And sometimes death. — PB 1083 — 55 — .25

VALTIN, JAN
Wintertime. — Pop 372 — 51 — .25

VAN BUREN, ABIGAIL
Dear Abby. — Card C-356 — 59 — .35

VANCE, ETHEL
Escape. — PB 149 — 42 — .25
Winter meeting. — Ban 400 — 48 — .25

VANCE, JACK
Big planet. — Ace D-295 — 58 — .35
The dying earth. — Hill 41 — 50 — .25
Slaves of the Klau. — Ace D-295 — 58 — .35
To live forever. — Ball 167 — 56 — .35

VANCE, LOUIS JOSEPH
The Lone Wolf. — Dell 10 — 43 — .25

VANCE, WILLIAM E.
Apache war cry. — Eag EB45 — 55 — .25
Avenger from nowhere. — Ace D-28 — 53 — .35
The branded lawman. — Ace D-6 — 52 — .35
Hard rock rancher. — Pop 546 — 53 — .25
Homicide lost. — Graf 122 — 56 — .25
Outlaws welcome! — Ace D-298 — 58 — .35
Way station west. — Ace D-128 — 55 — .35

VANDERBILT, AMY
Amy Vanderbilt's
everyday etiquette. — Ban F1616 — 57 — .50

VANDERCOOK, JOHN W.
Black majesty. — PB 857 — 52 — .25
Murder in Fiji. — Pen 560 — 45 — .25
Murder in Trinidad. — Pen 552 — 44 — .25
Out for a killing. — Avon T-278 — 58 — .35

VAN de WATER, FREDERIC F.
The green cockade. — Ban A1508 — 56 — .35

Hidden ways. — Dell 67 — 44 — .25

VAN de WATER, MARJORIE
Psychology for the
returning serviceman. — PenS S229 — 45 — .25

VAN DINE, S. S.
The Benson murder case. — PB 333 — 45 — .25
The Bishop murder case. — PB 305 — 45 — .25
The canary murder case. — PB 248 — 44 — .25
The dragon murder case. — Ban 362 — 49 — .25
The Greene murder case. — PB 256 — 44 — .25
The kennel murder case. — Ban 60 — 46 — .25
The kidnap murder case. — Ban 300 — 48 — .25
The scarab murder case. — Ban 96 — 47 — .25
_____. — Graf 89 — 54 — .25
The smell of murder. — Ban 756 — 50 — .25

VANDIVERT, RITA with William Vandivert
Common wild animals
and their young. — DelL LC105 — 57 — .50

VANDIVERT, WILLIAM with Rita Vandivert
Common wild animals
and their young. — DelL LC105 — 57 — .50

VAN DOREN, CHARLES with Ralph J. Roske
Lincoln's commando. — Pyr G356 — 58 — .35

van DRUTEN, JOHN
Bell, book and candle. — Ban A1842 — 58 — .35

VAN DYCKE, TOM with Ben Kerner
Not with my neck. — Han 80 — 48 — .25

VANEER, WILLIAM with Kimiko Omura
Diary of a geisha girl. — Avon T-313 — 59 — .35

VAN EVERY, DALE
Bridal journey. — Ban A871 — 51 — .35
The captive witch. — Ban A1090 — 53 — .35
The shining mountains. — Ban A981 — 52 — .35
_____. — Ban F2007 — 59 — .50
The trembling earth. — Ban A1250 — 54 — .35
The voyagers. — Ban F1988 — 59 — .50
Westward the river. — Ban A1144 — 53 — .35

van LOON, HENDRIK WILLEM
The life and times of
Rembrandt. — BanB FB413 — 57 — .50
The story of America. — Dell D142 — 54 — .35
_____. — Prem d79 — 59 — .50
The story of mankind. — PB 15 — 39 — .25
_____. — Card GC-5 — 53 — .50
_____. — PBL PL12 — 54 — .50
_____. — PBL PL501 — 56 — .50
The story of the Bible. — Prmb P201S — 53 — .50
_____. — Perm M-5005 — 56 — .50

Author/Title	Pub./Stock No.	Yr.	Price
VAN PELT, S. J.			
Hypnotism and the			
power within.	Crst s143	56	.35
VAN PRAAG, VAN			
Combat.	PB 747	50	.25
VAN RENSSELAER, ALEXANDER			
Party fun and games.	Prem s36	56	.35
VAN RIPER, ROBERT			
A really sincere guy.	Pyr G427	59	.35
VAN SILLER, HILDA			
Thy name is woman.	RS 25	53	.35
VANSITTART, LORD			
Roots of the trouble			
and The black record			
of Germany.	Avon 45	44	.25
VAN VECHTEN, CARL			
Nigger heaven.	Avon 314	51	.25
van VOGT, A. E.			
Away and beyond.	Avon 548	53	.25
_____.	Berk G-215	59	.35
Destination: universe!	Sig 1007	53	.25
_____.	Sig S1558	58	.35
Empire of the atom.	Ace D-242	57	.35
The mind cage.	Avon T-252	58	.35
Mission: interplanetary.	Sig 914	52	.25
Mission to the stars.	Berk 344	55	.25
One against eternity.	Ace D-94	55	.35
The pawns of null-A.	Ace D-187	56	.35
Siege of the unseen.	Ace D-391	59	.35
Slan.	Dell 696	53	.25
Universe maker.	Ace D-31	53	.35
The weapon shops of			
Isher.	Ace D-53	54	.35
The world of null-A.	Ace D-31	53	.35
VAQUERO, ELOY with Mario Pei			
Getting along in Spanish.	Ban A1943	59	.35
VARIOUS temptations.	Avon T-109	55	.35
VAUGHAN, CARTER A.			
The devil's bride.	Avon T-333	59	.35
VAUGHAN, RICHARD			
Moulded in earth.	Sig 991	53	.25
VEBLEN, THORSTEIN			
The theory of business			
enterprise.	Ment MD218	58	.50
The theory of the			
leisure class.	Ment M93	53	.35
VEILLER, BAYARD with William Almon Wolff			
The trial of Mary Dugan.	PB 647	49	.25

Author/Title	Pub./Stock No.	Yr.	Price
VEINUS, ABRAHAM with Henry Simon			
The Pocket book of			
great operas.	PB 622	49	.25
_____.	PBL PL21	54	.35
VERCORS			
The murder of the			
missing link.	PB 1206	58	.25
You shall know them.	PB 1038	55	.25
VERISSIMO, ERICO			
Evil in the night.	Crst 169	57	.25
VERNE, JULES			
Around the world in 80			
days.	Avon T-148	56	.35
_____.	Lion LL 90	56	.35
From the earth to the			
moon and Round the moon.	Crst s216	58	.35
Journey to the center			
of the earth.	Ace D-155	56	.35
_____.	Ace D-397	59	.35
_____.	Perm M-4161	59	.35
Michael Strogoff.	Pyr R300	57	.35
Off on a comet.	Ace D-245	57	.35
VERNON, ROGER LEE			
The space frontiers.	Sig 1224	55	.25
VERRILL, A. HYATT			
The strange story of our			
earth.	Prem s24	56	.35
VESTAL, STANLEY			
Dodge City: queen of			
cowtowns.	Pnnt P34	54	.25
_____.	Ban F1687	57	.50
The old Santa Fe Trail.	Ban F1662	57	.50
VIALAR, PAUL			
Five soldiers.	Pyr R418	59	.50
VIANDE, CHEVALLIER de			
The Diet of Worms.	Ban A1354	55	.35
The meat cookbook.	Ban A1155	53	.35
_____.	Ban F1750	58	.50
VIAZZI, ALFRED			
The cruel dawn.	Pop 440	52	.25
VICKER, ANGUS			
Fever heat.	DelF 13	54	.25
VIDAL, GORE			
Best television plays.	Ball 160	56	.35
The city and the pillar.	Sig 773	50	.25
_____.	Sig 1218	55	.25
Dangerous voyage.	Sig 1003	53	.25
Messiah.	Ball 94	54	.35
A thirsty evil.	Sig S1535	58	.35

Author/Title	Pub./Stock No.	Yr.	Price
VIERECK, GEORGE SYLVESTER			
Men into beasts.	GM 260	52	.25
_____ .	GM 552	56	.25
with Paul Eldridge			
My first two thousand years.	Crst s148	56	.35
Salome.	Ace D-43	54	.35
VIERTEL, JOSEPH			
The last temptation.	Card C-234	57	.35
VIERTEL, PETER			
White hunter, black heart.	Ban A1281	54	.35
VILLIERS, ALAN			
Great sea stories.	DelL LB127	59	.35
VINCENT, RICHARD			
Red.	Perm M-3098	57	.25
Sing, boy, sing.	Sig 1489	58	.25
VINING, KEITH			
Too hot for hell.	Ace D-1	52	.35
VITTORINI, ELIO			
The red carnation.	Sig 1042	53	.25
VOGUE'S Pocket book of home dressmaking.	PB 234	43	.25
VOLTAIRE			
Candide.	Lion 107	52	.25
_____ .	Lion LB 107	56	.25
_____ .	BanC AC51	59	.35
Voltaire.	DelL LC134	59	.50
VON HAGEN, VICTOR W.			
The Aztec: man and tribe.	Ment MD236	58	.50
Realm of the Incas.	Ment MD192	57	.50
VONNEGUT, KURT JR.			
The sirens of Titan.	DelF B138	59	.35
Utopia 14.	Ban A1262	54	.35
von RHAU, HENRY			
Big Sol.	PB 701	50	.25

Author/Title	Pub./Stock No.	Yr.	Price
W			
WADE, BOB with Bill Miller			
Murder--queen high.	Graf 11	49	.25
_____.	Graf 54	52	.25
WADE, HARRISON			
So lovely to kill.	Graf 127	56	.25
WAER, JACK			
Murder in Las Vegas.	Avon 651	55	.25
_____.	Avon 784	57	.25
Sweet and low-down.	Pop 702	55	.25
WAGER, WALTER			
Death hits the jackpot.	Avon T-280	58	.35
WAGNER, GEOFFREY			
Born of the sun.	Eag EB22	54	.25
Rage on the bar.	Pop G285	58	.35
Sophie.	Dell D297	59	.35
Venables.	Pop 490	53	.25
WAGONER, DAVID			
Money money money.	Avon T-147	56	.35
Rock.	Ban A2020	59	.35
WAHL, LOREN			
If this be sin.	Avon 380	52	.25
Take me as I am.	Berk G-57	57	.35
WAINER, CORD			
Mountain girl.	GM 276	53	.25
_____.	GM 599	56	.25
WAKEMAN, FREDERIC			
Deluxe tour.	Card C-254	57	.35
The hucksters.	Ban 405	48	.25
_____.	Avon 481	52	.25
_____.	Berk BG-178	58	.50
Naked to my past.	Pop 619	54	.25
The Saxon charm.	Sig 783	50	.25
Shore leave.	Sig 687	48	.25
_____.	Sig 1320	56	.25
_____.	Sig 1450	57	.25
The wastrel.	Sig 823	50	.25
_____.	Sig 1390	57	.25
WALDO, MYRA			
Dining out in any language.	Ban A1499	56	.35
The round-the-world cook book.	Ban A1427	56	.35
WALDRON, T. J. with James Gleeson			
The frogmen.	Berk G246	59	.35
WALKER, DAVID			
Harry Black.	Ban A1828	58	.35
The storm and the silence.	Lion LL 33	55	.35

Author/Title	Pub./Stock No.	Yr.	Price
The wire.	Prmb P204	53	.35
WALKER, DOROTHY PIERCE			
Dr. Whitney's secretary.	PB 583	49	.25
Five o'clock surgeon.	PB 686	50	.25
WALKER, GERTRUDE			
So deadly fair.	Pop 434	52	.25
WALKER, KENNETH			
The physiology of sex.	Pen 507	42	.25
_____.	Pel P7	46	.25
WALKER, MILDRED			
Dr. Norton's wife.	Dell 610	52	.25
WALKER, SHEL			
The man I killed.	Lion 112	52	.25
WALKER, TURNLEY			
Dream of innocence.	Sig S1018	53	.35
_____.	Pop 655	55	.25
_____.	Pop SP23	58	.50
WALL, EVANS			
Swamp girl.	Pyr 39	51	.25
_____.	Pyr 168	55	.25
WALLACE, EDGAR			
The door with seven locks.	Avon 125	47	.25
The feathered serpent.	Dell 49	44	.25
On the spot.	Avon 173	48	.25
The squealer.	Avon 112	46	.25
WALLACE, F. L.			
Address: Centauri.	Gal 32	58	.35
Three times a victim.	Ace D-209	57	.35
Wired for scandal.	Ace D-357	59	.35
WALLACE, FRANCIS			
Kid Galahad.	Ban 133	47	.25
WALLACE, LEW			
Ben-Hur.	Ban A1450	56	.35
_____.	Ban F1903	59	.50
_____.	Card GC-75	59	.50
_____.	Dell F79	59	.50
_____.	Sig D1681	59	.50
WALLBANK, T. WALTER			
A short history of India and Pakistan.	Ment MD224	58	.50
WALLENSTEIN, MARCEL			
Red canvas.	Avon AT447	52	.35
Tuck's girl.	Eton E124	53	.25
WALLER, LESLIE			
The bed she made.	Pop 393	52	.25
_____.	Eag EB76	56	.25

Author/Title	Pub./Stock No.	Yr.	Price
WALLING, R. A. J.			
The corpse in the green pajamas.	Avon (8)	41	.25
The corpse with the eerie eye.	Pop 106	47	.25
The corpse with the floating foot.	PB 24	39	.25
The corpse with the grimy glove.	Pop 139	48	.25
The corpse with the red-headed friend.	Pony unk	46	.25
Murder at midnight.	Avon (16)	42	.25
WALLIS, J. H.			
Once off guard.	Pop 385	51	.25
WALLIS, RUTH SAWTELL			
Blood from a stone.	Ban 109	47	.25
No bones about it.	Ban 72	46	.25
Too many bones.	Dell 123	46	.25
WALLOP, DOUGLASS			
The dangerous years.	PB 1146	57	.25
Night light.	Card C-144	54	.35
The year the Yankees lost the pennant.	Card C-328	59	.35
WALN, NORA			
The house of exile.	PB 226	43	.25
WALPOLE, ELLEN WALES			
Andy's everyday encyclopedia.	SigK Ks311	54	.35
WALPOLE, HUGH			
Portrait of a man with red hair.	Avon 204	49	.25
WALSH, MAURICE			
Blackcock's feather.	Pnnt P28	53	.25
WALSH, PAUL			
KKK.	Avon 742	56	.25
Murder in Baracoa.	Avon 802	58	.25
The murder room.	Avon 767	57	.25
WALSH, ROBERT			
Violent hours.	Sig 1492	58	.25
WALSH, THOMAS			
The dark window.	Ban 1840	58	.25
The night watch.	Ban 1150	53	.25
Nightmare in Manhattan.	Ban 895	51	.25
WALTARI, MIKA			
The adventurer.	Card GC-34	56	.50
The dark angel.	Card C-263	57	.35
The Egyptian.	Card GC-31	56	.50
The Etruscan.	Card C-287	58	.35
The wanderer.	Card C-244	57	.35

Author/Title	Pub./Stock No.	Yr.	Price
WALZ, AUDREY with Jay Walz			
The bizarre sisters.	Ban A1182	53	.35
WALZ, JAY with Audrey Walz			
The bizarre sisters.	Ban A1182	53	.35
WARD, BRAD			
The baron of Boot Hill.	Ban 1596	57	.25
Desert showdown.	Ace D-48	54	.35
The hanging hills.	Ace D-18	53	.35
Johnny Sundance.	Ace D-30	53	.35
The man from Andersonville.	Ace S-148	56	.25
The marshal of Medicine Bend.	Ace S-60	54	.25
Six-gun heritage.	Graf 129	56	.25
Thirty notches.	Sig 1481	58	.25
Whiplash.	Pnnt P76	55	.25
WARD, DON			
Branded West.	Sig S1533	58	.35
Gunsmoke.	Ball 236	57	.35
with H. Rider Haggard			
She.	Dell 339	49	.25
WARD, JONAS			
Buchanan gets mad.	GM 803	58	.25
Buchanan says no.	GM 662	57	.25
The name's Buchanan.	GM 604	56	.25
One-man massacre.	GM 742	58	.25
WARD, MARY JANE			
The snake pit.	Sig 696	48	.25
	Sig 1182	55	.25
WARE, HARLAN			
Come fill the cup.	Ban A1097	53	.35
WARNER, REX			
The Greek philosophers.	Ment MD226	58	.50
The young Caesar.	Ment MD254	59	.50
WARREN, CHARLES M.			
Only the valiant.	Ban 776	50	.25
Valley of the shadow.	Ban 732	49	.25
	Ban 1068	52	.25
WARREN, DOUG			
Scarlet starlet.	Ace D-373	59	.35
WARREN, PAUL			
Next time is for life.	DelF 6	53	.25
WARREN, ROBERT PENN			
All the king's men.	Ban A939	51	.35
	Ban F1338	55	.50
	BanC FC34	59	.50
At heaven's gate.	Sig 725	49	.25
Band of angels.	Sig D1330	56	.50
The circus in the attic.	Dell F82	59	.50

Author/Title	Pub./Stock No.	Yr.	Price
WARREN, ROBERT PENN (cont.)			
Night rider.	Sig 804	50	.25
.	Berk BG-35	56	.50
World enough and time.	Sig D975	52	.50
with Albert Erskine			
A new southern harvest.	Ban F1556	57	.50
Short story masterpieces.	DelF F16	54	.50
.	DelL LX102	58	.75
Six centuries of great			
poetry.	DelF FE69	55	.50
.	DelL LC109	58	.50
.	DelL LX110	59	.75
WASHINGTON, BOOKER T.			
Up from slavery.	PB 80	40	.25
.	BanB FB406	56	.50
.	BanC FC37	59	.50
WATERS, ETHEL with Charles Samuels			
His eye is on the			
sparrow.	Ban A985	52	.35
.	Ban F1976	59	.50
WATERS, FRANK			
Fever pitch.	Berk 104	55	.25
with Houston Branch			
Diamond Head.	Dell D127	53	.35
WATERS, HAROLD with Aubrey Wisberg			
The savage soldiers.	Avon T-130	56	.35
WATKIN, LAWRENCE EDWARD			
Darby O'Gill and the			
little people.	DelF A181	59	.25
On borrowed time.	PB 317	45	.25
WATKINS, GLEN			
Tavern girl.	Pyr 17	50	.25
WATSON, JOHN			
The red dress.	PB 734	50	.25
WATSON, LILLIAN E.			
The Bantam book of			
correct letter writing.	Ban F1747	58	.50
WATSON, WILL			
Wolf dog range.	Lion unk	51	.25
WATTS, ALAN W.			
The way of Zen.	Ment MD273	59	.50
WATTS, FRANKLIN			
The Pocket book magazine.	Card C-152	54	.35
The Pocket book magazine			
no. 2.	Card C-160	55	.35
The Pocket book magazine			
no. 3.	Card C-200	55	.35
WAUGH, ALEC			
Island in the sun.	Ban F1568	57	.50

Author/Title	Pub./Stock No.	Yr.	Price
WAUGH, EVELYN			
Brideshead revisited.	Dell D163	56	.35
.	Dell F68	57	.50
.	DelL LX104	58	.75
A handful of dust and			
Decline and fall.	Dell F74	59	.50
The loved one.	Dell 771	54	.25
.	Dell D222	58	.35
Vile bodies.	Dell 807	54	.25
WAUGH, HILLARY			
Case of the brunette			
bombshell.	Crst 172	57	.25
The eighth Mrs.			
Bluebeard.	Crst 292	59	.25
Hope to die.	Han 88	49	.25
If I live to dine.	Graf 12	49	.25
Last seen wearing...	PB 988	54	.25
A rag and a bone.	PB 1075	55	.25
WAYNE, ANDERSON			
Charlie Dell.	Pop G123	53	.35
Time to remember.	Pop G310	59	.35
WAYNE, ARLO			
Hot money girl.	Berk G-195	58	.35
WAYNE, ERNIE			
Ramrod from hell.	Pop 512	53	.25
WAYNE, JOSEPH			
Bunch grass.	Sig 1277	56	.25
By gun and spur.	Sig 1077	54	.25
Gunplay valley.	Sig 891	51	.25
.	Sig 1302	56	.25
The long wind.	Sig 1128	54	.25
The return of the kid.	Sig 1384	57	.25
Showdown at Stony Crest.	DelF A138	57	.25
The snake stomper.	Sig 1028	53	.25
WEATHERLY, MAX			
The long desire.	Zen ZB-11	59	.35
WEAVER, WARD			
End of track.	Pop 342	51	.25
.	Pop G303	59	.35
Hang my wreath.	Pop 388	51	.25
.	Pop G180	57	.35
WEBB, JACK			
The bad blonde.	Sig 1422	57	.25
The badge.	Crst s341	59	.35
The big sin.	Sig 1076	53	.25
The brass halo.	Sig 1556	58	.25
The broken doll.	Sig 1311	56	.25
The damned lovely.	Sig 1233	55	.25
The naked angel.	Sig 1149	54	.25
WEBB, JEAN FRANCIS			
Anna Lucasta.	Dell 331	49	.25

Author/Title	Pub./Stock No.	Yr.	Price
WEBB, JEAN FRANCIS (cont.)			
with Louisa May Alcott			
Little women.	Dell 296	49	.25
with H. Rider Haggard			
King Solomon's mines.	Dell 433	50	.25
WEBB, JON EDGAR			
Four steps to the wall.	Ban 1179	53	.25
WEBB, MARY			
Gone to earth.	Dell 436	50	.25
Precious bane.	PB 535	49	.25
WEBB, NANCY			
Marcia Blake, publicity			
girl.	Perm M-3102	58	.25
WEBB, PAUL			
The mountain boys.	Sig 1441	57	.25
WEBBER, EVERETT			
Louisiana cavalier.	Pop G159	56	.35
with Olga Webber			
Bound girl.	Pop 303	50	.25
Rampart Street.	PB 681	50	.25
WEBBER, GORDON			
The far shore.	Ban 1345	55	.25
WEBBER, OLGA with Everett Webber			
Bound girl.	Pop 303	50	.25
Rampart Street.	PB 681	50	.25
WEBER, LENORA MATTINGLY			
Beany Malone.	Berk G-223	59	.35
Meet the Malones.	Berk G293	59	.35
WEBSTER, JOHN			
The Duchess of Malfi.	WSP W101	59	.35
WEBSTER, MARGARET			
Shakespeare without			
tears.	Prem d54	57	.50
WECHSBERG, JOSEF			
The continental touch.	Lion 33	50	.25
Looking for a bluebird.	Pen 622	46	.25
WECHSLER, HERMAN J.			
The French impressionists			
and their circle.	PBA A7	53	.50
Gods and goddesses in			
art and legend.	PB 661	50	.25
Lives of famous French			
painters.	Card C-28	52	.35
The Pocket book of old			
masters.	PB 578	49	.25
WEEGEE with Mel Harris			
Naked Hollywood.	Berk G-9	55	.35

Author/Title	Pub./Stock No.	Yr.	Price
WEEKLEY, WILLIAM GEORGE			
Castaway island.	Prmb P111	51	.35
WEEKS, EDWARD			
The Pocket Atlantic.	PB 397	46	.25
WEEKS, JACK			
I detest all my sins.	DelF D20	54	.35
WEEKS, JOSEPH			
Never too young.	Pop G165	56	.35
WEEKS, William Rawle			
Knock and wait awhile.	Ban A1706	58	.35
WEENOLSEN, HEBE			
The last Englishman.	Ban A1052	52	.35
WEES, FRANCES SHELLEY			
Someone called Maggie			
Lane.	Ban 418	49	.25
WEIDMAN, JEROME			
A dime a throw.	Berk G-49	57	.35
Give me your love.	Eton E114	52	.25
The hand of the hunter.	Avon AT-63	53	.35
I can get it for you			
wholesale!	Avon 226	49	.25
_____.	Avon 356	51	.25
_____.	Avon T-97	55	.35
_____.	Avon T-240	58	.35
I'll never go there			
any more.	Avon T-82	54	.35
_____.	Avon T-153	57	.35
The price is right.	Avon 279	50	.25
_____.	Avon 429	52	.25
_____.	Avon T-207	57	.35
Slipping beauty.	Avon 322	51	.25
_____.	Avon 442	52	.25
_____.	Avon T-131	56	.35
The third angel.	Avon G-1017	54	.50
_____.	Avon G-1032	58	.50
What's in it for me?	Avon 241	50	.25
_____.	Avon T-103	55	.35
Your daughter Iris.	Avon G-1026	56	.50
WEIGALL, ARTHUR			
Infidelity.	NL 24	49	.25
WEIL, JERRY			
Delay en route.	Sig 1324	56	.25
Escapade.	Sig 1554	58	.25
Nobody dies in Paris.	Sig 1449	57	.25
Office wife.	Sig 1350	57	.25
Paint on their faces.	Sig 1393	57	.25
WEIL, YELLOW KID with W. T. Brannon			
Yellow Kid Weil.	Pyr G280	57	.35
WEINER, ED			
The Damon Runyon story.	Pop 220	49	.25

Author/Title	Pub./Stock No.	Yr.	Price
WEINREB, NATHANIEL NORSEN			
The Babylonians.	Prmb P305	54	.35
The groves of desire.	Pop G356	59	.35
WEIR, RUTH with Frances Cavanah			
Dell book of jokes.	Dell 89	45	.25
Liberty laughs.	Dell 38	44	.25
WEIRAUCH, ANNA ELISABET			
Of love forbidden.	Crst s214	58	.35
The scorpion.	Avon AT58	53	.35
WEISINGER, MORT			
1001 valuable things you can get free.	Ban 1309	55	.25
1001 valuable things you can get free, no. 2.	Ban 1606	57	.25
1001 valuable things you can get free, no. 3.	Ban A2017	59	.35
WEISS, JOE			
How rough can it get?	Avon 582	54	.25
_____.	Avon 717	56	.25
_____.	Avon T-332	59	.35
WEISS, MARTIN			
Death hitches a ride.	Ace D-45	54	.35
Hate alley.	Ace D-214	57	.35
WEISSMAN, SIDNEY			
Backlash.	Ace S-130	55	.25
WELDON, JOHN LEE			
The naked heart.	Sig 1126	54	.25
Thunder in the heart.	Sig 1184	55	.25
WELLARD, JAMES			
Action of the tiger.	Avon T-188	57	.35
Deep is the night.	Dell 812	54	.25
The snake in the grass.	Han 35	45	.15
WELLES, KERMIT			
Blood on Boot Hill.	Ace D-332	59	.35
WELLES, ORSON			
Invasion from Mars.	Dell 305	49	.25
Mr. Arkadin.	Pyr G357	58	.35
WELLMAN, MANLY WADE			
Find my killer.	Sig 703	49	.25
_____.	Sig 1448	57	.25
Fort Sun Dance.	DelF 52	55	.25
Twice in time.	Gal 34	58	.35
WELLMAN, PAUL I.			
Angel with spurs.	Prmb P142	52	.35
The bowl of brass.	Prmb P240	53	.35
Broncho Apache.	PB 794	51	.25
The chain.	Prmb P115	51	.35
The Comancheros.	Prmb 263	54	.25
The female.	Card GC-20	54	.50
The iron mistress.	Card C-96	53	.35
Jericho's daughters.	Card C-278	58	.35
Jubal Troop.	Card C-141	54	.35
Ride the red earth.	Ban F1915	59	.50
The walls of Jericho.	Prmb P129	51	.35
WELLS, ANNA MARY			
Murderer's choice.	Dell 127	46	.25
A talent for murder.	Dell 66	44	.25
WELLS, CHARLES			
The last kill.	Sig 1225	55	.25
Let the night cry.	Sig 1167	54	.25
WELLS, EVELYN			
Jed Blaine's woman.	PB 637	49	.25
WELLS, H. G.			
The first men in the moon.	Dell 201	47	.25
The invisible man.	Dell 269	48	.25
_____.	PB 1140	57	.25
The island of Dr. Moreau.	Ace D-309	58	.35
The Pocket history of the world.	PB 119	41	.25
The time machine.	Berk 380	57	.25
The war of the worlds.	PB 947	53	.25
When the sleeper wakes.	Ace D-388	59	.35
WELLS, LEE E.			
Brother outlaw.	Ace D-264	58	.35
Day of the outlaw.	Dell 906	56	.25
Death in the desert.	Avon 620	54	.25
_____.	Avon T-315	59	.35
Gun for sale.	Avon T-327	59	.35
Gunshot empire.	Avon 529	53	.25
The long noose.	Avon 573	54	.25
_____.	Avon 754	57	.25
The naked land.	Avon T-378	59	.35
Tonto Riley.	PB 865	52	.25
WELLS, MICHAEL			
The roving eye.	Ace D-243	57	.35
WELLS, SUSAN			
Footsteps in the air.	Bond unk	47	.25
WELTY, EUDORA			
The ponder heart.	Dell 887	56	.25
WENDT, GERALD			
You and the atom.	Bard T-06	58	.35
WENDT, STEPHEN			
Pray love, remember.	Pop 458	52	.25
WENTWORTH, PATRICIA			
The blind side.	Pop 66	45	.25
The case is closed.	Pop 105	47	.25

Author/Title	Pub./Stock No.	Yr.	Price
WENTWORTH, PATRICIA (cont.)			
The clock strikes twelve.	Pop 131	48	.25
Dark threat.	Pop 382	51	.25
Dead or alive.	Dell 2	43	.25
In the balance.	Pop 39	44	.25
The key.	Pop 232	50	.25
Lonesome road.	Pop 333	51	.25
Pursuit of a parcel.	Pop 197	49	.25
Rolling stone.	Pop 79	46	.25
Silence in court.	Pop 283	50	.25
Weekend with death.	Pop 29	44	.25
WERFEL, FRANZ			
Embezzled heaven.	Dell F78	59	.50
The song of Bernadette.	PB 433	47	.25
_____.	Card C-67	52	.35
WERNER, ALFRED			
Dufy.	PBA A5	53	.50
Utrillo.	PBA A12	53	.50
WERRY, RICHARD R.			
Hammer me home.	Ban 1506	56	.25
Where town begins.	Sig 938	52	.25
WERSTEIN, IRVING			
July, 1863.	Ace D-325	58	.35
WERTENBAKER, LAEL TUCKER			
Death of a man.	Ban A1693	57	.35
WERTHAM, FREDRIC			
The show of violence.	Eton E106	51	.25
WESCOTT, GLENWAY			
Apartment in Athens.	Ban 87	47	.25
The grandmothers.	Ban 69	46	.25
WESLEY, ELIZABETH			
Nora Meade, M.D.	Ban 1607	57	.25
WEST, ANTHONY			
Heritage.	Card C-235	57	.35
WEST, JESSAMYN			
Cress Delahanty.	PB 1073	55	.25
The witch diggers.	Ban A995	52	.35
WEST, JOHN B.			
An eye for an eye.	Sig 1642	59	.25
WEST, MAE			
Diamond Lil.	Dell 525	51	.25
WEST, MORRIS L.			
Kundu.	DelF A116	56	.25
WEST, NATHANAEL			
The day of the locust.	Ban 1093	53	.25
_____.	Ban A1704	57	.35

Author/Title	Pub./Stock No.	Yr.	Price
The day of the locust.	BanC AC14	59	.35
Miss Lonelyhearts.	Avon 634	54	.25
WEST, RUTH			
Stop dieting! Start losing!	Ban 1592	57	.25
The teen-age diet book.	Ban A1784	58	.35
_____.	Ban A1924	59	.35
WEST, TOKEN			
Showroom girls.	Berk G237	59	.35
Why get married?	RC 12	49	.25
WEST, TOM			
The cactus kid.	Ace D-356	59	.35
Ghost gold.	PB 733	50	.25
Gunsmoke gold.	Ace D-8	53	.35
Lead in his fists.	Ace D-276	58	.35
Lobo legacy.	Ace D-78	54	.35
Outlaw brand.	Pyr 216	56	.25
Slick on the draw.	Ace D-328	58	.35
Torture trail.	Ace D-240	57	.35
Twisted trail.	Ace D-392	59	.35
Vulture Valley.	Ace D-24	53	.35
WEST, WARD			
Halfway to timberline.	PB 972	53	.25
Trouble valley.	Dell 527	51	.25
WESTCOTT, EDWARD NOYES			
David Harum.	Ban 41	46	.25
WESTCOTT, JAN			
The border lord.	Dell 439	50	.25
_____.	Card C-136	54	.35
Captain Barney.	PB 932	53	.25
Captain for Elizabeth.	Graf G101	52	.35
_____.	Graf G201	53	.35
_____.	Graf G211	55	.35
The Hepburn.	PB 827	51	.25
The Walsingham woman.	Card C-157	54	.35
WESTHEIMER, DAVID			
Day into night.	Pop 395	52	.25
Tillie.	Pyr G52	52	.35
_____.	Pyr G233	56	.35
WESTLAND, LYNN			
The dead ride hard.	Avon 838	58	.25
Trail rider.	Han 132	51	.25
WESTLEY, KIRK			
Shanty boat girl.	Berk G260	59	.35
WESTON, CAROLYN			
Tormented.	Berk G-132	58	.35
WESTON, CHRISTINE			
The dark wood.	Ban 723	49	.25
Indigo.	Dell D158	55	.35

Author/Title	Pub./Stock No.	Yr.	Price
WESTON, GEORGE			
His first million women.	Avon 396	52	.25
WESTWOOD, PERRY			
Six-gun code.	GM 299	53	.25
WETHERELL, JUNE			
Free and easy.	Pop G129	53	.35
_____.	Pop G348	59	.35
The glorious three.	Pop G109	52	.35
Possessed.	Pop 557	54	.25
WEXLER, SUSAN STANHOPE			
The story of Sandy.	Sig 1381	57	.25
WEYBRIGHT, VICTOR with Henry Blackman Sell			
Buffalo Bill and the Wild West.	SigK KD362	58	.50
WHAT to wear where.	Ban F1163	53	.50
WHAT today's woman should know about marriage and sex.	GM 100	49	.25
WHATMOUGH, JOSHUA			
Language.	Ment MD209	57	.50
WHEELER, ELMER			
The fat boy's book.	Avon 517	53	.25
WHEELER, KEITH			
The reef.	Pop 403	52	.25
WHELTON, PAUL			
Call the lady indiscreet.	Graf 17	49	.25
_____.	Graf 95	55	.25
Flash--hold for murder.	Graf 13	49	.25
In comes death.	Graf 49	52	.25
Lures of death.	Graf 19	50	.25
Pardon my blood.	Graf 37	51	.25
_____.	Graf 71	54	.25
Uninvited corpse.	Graf 24	50	.25
WHIPPLE, CHANDLER			
Under the mesa rim.	Ace D-64	54	.35
WHITCOMB, CATHARINE			
No narrow path.	Pop 379	51	.25
WHITE, BETTY			
Betty White's teen-age dance book.	Perm M-4123	59	.35
WHITE, DANIEL			
Southern daughter.	Avon 547	53	.25
_____.	Avon 750	56	.25
WHITE, E. B. with James Thurber			
Is sex necessary?	Dell 820	55	.25

Author/Title	Pub./Stock No.	Yr.	Price
with Katherine S. White			
A subtreasury of American humor.	Card C-183	55	.35
WHITE, ETHEL LINA			
Her heart in her throat.	Pop 54	45	.25
Put out the light.	Pen 598	46	.25
She faded into air.	Pop 75	46	.25
The spiral staircase.	Pop 120	47	.25
Step in the dark.	Pen 565	45	.25
The third eye.	Pop 15	43	.25
The wheel spins.	Pop 32	44	.25
WHITE, HARRY			
Shadow at noon.	Pyr 169	55	.25
WHITE, JAMES			
The secret visitors.	Ace D-237	57	.35
WHITE, JOHN			
The sins of skid row.	Hill 112	59	.35
WHITE, JON MANCHIP			
Last race.	PB 1016	54	.25
WHITE, KATHERINE S. with E. B. White			
A subtreasury of American humor.	Card C-183	55	.35
WHITE, LANCELOT LAW			
The next development in man.	Ment M50	50	.35
WHITE, LESLIE TURNER			
The Highland Hawk.	PB 974	53	.25
Look away, look away.	Card C-92	53	.35
Lord Johnnie.	PB 745	50	.25
Magnus the Magnificent.	PB 873	52	.25
Monsieur Yankee.	Card C-305	58	.35
Sir Rogue.	Card C-178	55	.35
The winged sword.	Card C-246	57	.35
WHITE, LIONEL			
The big caper.	GM 470	55	.25
Coffin for a hood.	GM 775	58	.25
Death takes the bus.	GM 663	57	.25
Flight into terror.	Sig 1378	57	.25
Hostage for a hood.	GM 687	57	.25
The house next door.	Sig 1442	57	.25
Invitation to violence.	Sig 1707	59	.25
The killing.	Sig 1310	56	.25
Love trap.	Sig 1204	55	.25
Operation--murder.	GM 606	56	.25
Run, killer, run!	Avon T-361	59	.35
The snatchers.	GM 304	53	.25
To find a killer.	Sig 1241	55	.25
Too young to die.	GM 786	58	.25
WHITE, MAX			
After dark.	Pyr 109	54	.25
Anna Becker.	Ban 830	50	.25

Author/Title	Pub./Stock No.	Yr.	Price
WHITE, MILTON			
Cry down the lonely night.	GM 427	54	.25
WHITE, MORTON			
The age of analysis.	Ment MD142	55	.50
WHITE, NELIA GARDNER			
No trumpet before him.	PB 664	50	.25
WHITE, ROBB			
Jungle fury.	Berk G-16	56	.35
_____.	Berk G-56	57	.35
Secret sea.	PBJr J-64	51	.25
WHITE, STEWART EDWARD			
The long rifle.	Dell D147	55	.35
_____.	Dell D216	58	.35
Ranchero.	Dell F85	59	.50
WHITE, W. L.			
They were expendable.	PenS S223	44	.25
WHITE, WILLIAM CHAPMAN			
The pale blonde of Sands Street.	Pop 254	50	.25
_____.	Eag EB8	54	.25
WHITEHEAD, ALFRED NORTH			
Adventures of ideas.	Ment MD141	55	.50
The aims of education.	Ment M41	49	.35
_____.	Ment MD152	55	.50
Dialogues of Alfred North Whitehead.	Ment MD180	56	.50
Science and the modern world.	PelM M28	48	.35
_____.	Ment MD162	56	.50
WHITEHEAD, DON			
The FBI story.	Card GC-45	58	.50
WHITING, KATHARINE with Christopher Mawson			
Roget's Pocket thesaurus.	PB 383	46	.25
_____.	Card C-13	51	.35
WHITINGER, R. D.			
High trail.	Pyr 314	58	.25
WHITMAN, HOWARD			
Terror in the streets.	Ban A964	52	.35
WHITMAN, ROGER B.			
First aid for the ailing house.	PB 343	46	.25
WHITMAN, S. E.			
Black Rock Valley.	Ball 328K	59	.35
Cavalry raid.	Ball 188	57	.35
Rebel ranger.	Ball 285K	59	.35
Scout commander.	Dell 923	56	.25
WHITMAN, WALT			
Leaves of grass.	Pen 523	43	.25
_____.	Ment Ms117	54	.50
Whitman.	DelL LB121	59	.35
The Whitman reader.	Card GC-25	55	.50
WHITNEY, HALLAM			
The wild seed.	Ace S-153	56	.25
WHITNEY, JOSEPH			
Mirror of your mind.	Avon 700	56	.25
WHITNEY, PHYLLIS A.			
Step to the music.	Berk G294	59	.35
WHITNEY, WALTER			
Take it out in trade.	Ace D-229	57	.35
WHITSON, DENTON			
Fair in love and war.	Pop 759	56	.25
WHITTINGTON, HARRY			
Across that river.	Ace D-201	57	.35
Backwoods tramp.	GM 889	59	.25
The brass monkey.	Han 138	51	.25
Brute in brass.	GM 595	56	.25
Call me killer.	Graf 36	51	.25
Desire in the dust.	GM 611	56	.25
Drawn to evil.	Ace D-5	52	.35
Fires that destroy.	GM 190	51	.25
_____.	GM 831	58	.25
Halfway to hell.	Avon T-299	59	.35
The humming box.	Ace D-185	56	.35
The lady was a tramp.	Han 131	51	.25
Man in the shadow.	Avon T-196	57	.35
Married to murder.	Dmnd D2019	59	.35
Mourn the hangman.	Graf 46	52	.25
Murder is my mistress.	Graf 41	51	.25
The naked jungle.	Ace S-95	55	.25
Native girl.	Berk G250	59	.35
One deadly dawn.	Ace D-241	57	.35
One got away.	Ace D-115	55	.35
Play for keeps.	Ace D-347	59	.35
Saddle the storm.	GM 401	54	.25
Saturday night town.	Crst 151	56	.25
Shack road girl.	Dmnd D2004	59	.35
Slay ride for a lady.	Han 120	50	.25
So dead my love!	Ace D-7	53	.35
Strange bargain.	Avon T-347	59	.35
Strangers on Friday.	Zen ZB-30	59	.35
Teen-age jungle.	Avon T-241	58	.35
Temptations of Valerie.	Avon T-187	57	.35
This woman is mine.	GM 366	54	.25
A ticket to hell.	GM 862	59	.25
Web of murder.	GM 740	58	.25
A woman on the place.	Ace S-143	56	.25
You'll die next!	Ace D-63	54	.35
WIBBERLEY, LEONARD			
The mouse that roared.	Ban A1982	59	.35

Author/Title	Pub./Stock No.	Yr.	Price
WICHELNS, LEE			
Rip tide.	Pop 439	52	.25
WICKER, TOM			
The devil must.	Pop G291	58	.35
The kingpin.	Card C-162	55	.35
WICKWARE, FRANCIS			
Dangerous ground.	Dell 248	48	.25
Tuesday to bed.	Pop 316	51	.25
WIDDEMER, MARGARET			
The golden wildcat.	Pop G152	55	.35
Lani.	PB 601	49	.25
WIDMER, HARRY			
The gunslingers.	Lion LL 89	56	.35
The hardboiled lineup.	Lion LB 130	56	.25
WIEGAND, WILLIAM			
At last, Mr. Tolliver.	Dell 697	53	.25
WIENER, WILLARD			
Four boys, a girl and a gun.	Avon 292	51	.25
_____.	Avon 444	52	.25
The young killers.	Avon T-174	57	.35
WIGGAM, ALBERT EDWARD			
Let's explore your mind.	PB 598	49	.25
WIGHT, FREDERICK S.			
Goya.	PBA A22	55	.50
WILDE, OSCAR			
The picture of Dorian Grey.	Dell 681	53	.25
_____.	Dell D167	56	.35
WILDE, PERCIVAL			
Inquest.	Sup M647	45	.25
WILDER, BILLY with I. A. L. Diamond			
Some like it hot.	Sig S1656	59	.35
WILDER, ROBERT			
And ride a tiger.	Ban A1162	53	.35
Autumn thunder.	Ban A1258	54	.35
Bright feather.	Ban A866	51	.35
_____.	Ban A1172	53	.35
Flamingo Road.	Ban A928	51	.35
_____.	Ban A1664	57	.35
God has a long face.	Ban A983	52	.35
_____.	Ban F1637	57	.50
A stranger in my arms.	Ban A1867	59	.35
Wait for tomorrow.	Ban A1181	53	.35
Walk with evil.	Crst 179	57	.25
The wine of youth.	Ban F1473	56	.50
Written on the wind.	Ban A1028	52	.35
_____.	Ban A1540	56	.35
WILDER, THORNTON			
The bridge of San Luis Rey.	PB 9	39	.25
_____.	PBL PL36	55	.35
Heaven's my destination.	Avon 59	45	.25
Our town.	PB 55	40	.25
Three plays.	Ban F1789	58	.50
WILEY, HUGH			
Murder by the dozen.	Pop 325	51	.25
WILHELM, GALE			
No letters for the dead.	Lion 52	51	.25
No nice girl.	Pyr G440	59	.35
Paula.	Lion LB 115	56	.25
The strange path.	Lion 121	53	.25
_____.	Berk G-111	58	.35
We too are drifting.	Lion unk	51	.25
_____.	Berk 327	55	.25
_____.	Berk 367	57	.25
_____.	Berk G-173	58	.35
WILKINSON, ALBERT E. with Victor A. Tiedjens			
The handy book of gardening.	SigK Ks323	55	.35
WILKINSON, BURKE			
Black Judas.	Prmb P138	51	.35
Proceed at will.	Dell 584	52	.25
WILLARD, JACK			
The wire god.	Pop 577	54	.25
WILLIAMS, BEN AMES			
All the brothers were valiant.	Avon 215	49	.25
Crucible.	Pop 113	47	.25
Death on Scurvy Street.	Pop 194	49	.25
The dreadful night.	Pop 155	48	.25
Evered.	Ban 870	51	.25
It's a free country.	Pop 308	51	.25
A killer among us.	Lion LL 149	57	.35
Lady in peril.	Pop 164	48	.25
Leave her to heaven.	Ban A771	50	.35
_____.	Lion LL 136	56	.50
_____.	Pyr R447	59	.50
The silver forest.	Pop 215	49	.25
The strange woman.	Ban A847	50	.35
_____.	Ban F1660	57	.50
The strumpet sea.	Pop 371	51	.25
The valley vixen.	Avon 153	48	.25
WILLIAMS, BERYL with Samuel Epstein			
The great Houdini.	PBJr J-63	51	.25
WILLIAMS, CHARLES			
All the way.	DelF A165	58	.25
The big bite.	DelF A114	56	.25
Big city girl.	GM 163	51	.25
_____.	GM 651	57	.25

Author/Title	Pub./Stock No.	Yr.	Price
WILLIAMS, CHARLES (cont.)			
The diamond bikini.	GM s607	56	.35
Girl out back.	DelF B114	58	.35
Go home, stranger.	GM 371	54	.25
	GM 625	56	.25
Gulf coast girl.	Dell 898	56	.25
Hell hath no fury.	GM 286	53	.25
Hill girl.	GM 141	51	.25
————.	GM 446	54	.25
————.	GM 697	57	.25
Man on the run.	GM 822	58	.25
Nothing in her way.	GM 340	53	.25
River girl.	GM G207	52	.35
————.	GM s467	55	.35
————.	GM s746	58	.35
Talk of the town.	DelF A164	58	.25
A touch of death.	GM 434	54	.25
Uncle Sagamore and his			
girls.	GM s908	59	.35
WILLIAMS, COE			
Go for your gun.	Eag EB39	55	.25
The plundered land.	Pop 833	58	.25
Trouble trail.	Eag EB25	54	.25
	Pop G397	59	.35
Yellowstone passage.	Eag EB7	54	.25
WILLIAMS, EDGAR with Dave Zinkoff			
Go, man, go.	PyrR PG17	58	.35
WILLIAMS, EDWIN B.			
Diccionario del idioma			
español.	Card GC-60	59	.50
WILLIAMS, ERIC			
The tunnel escape.	Berk G-94	58	.35
The wooden horse.	Ban 842	51	.25
————.	Berk BG239	59	.50
WILLIAMS, GEORGE			
Flesh and the dream.	Card C-100	53	.35
WILLIAMS, HERBERT			
Terror at night.	Avon 110	47	.25
WILLIAMS, IDABEL			
Hell cat.	Dell 521	51	.25
WILLIAMS, J. H.			
Elephant Bill.	Pnnt P36	54	.25
WILLIAMS, JAY			
The rogue from Padua.	Dell D136	54	.35
The siege.	Ban A1557	57	.35
Solomon and Sheba.	Ban A1958	59	.35
The witches.	Ban A1937	59	.35
WILLIAMS, MARY McGEE with Irene Kane			
On becoming a woman.	DelF A179	59	.25

Author/Title	Pub./Stock No.	Yr.	Price
WILLIAMS, MICHAEL			
They walked with God.	Prem d60	57	.50
WILLIAMS, NICK BODDIE			
The atom curtain.	Ace D-139	56	.35
WILLIAMS, OSCAR			
Immortal poems of the			
English language.	Card C-50	52	.35
————.	Card GC-15	54	.50
————.	PBL PL504	57	.50
The new Pocket anthology			
of American verse.	PBL PL35	55	.50
————.	PBL PL503	59	.50
The Pocket book of			
modern verse.	Card GC-16	54	.50
————.	PBL PL505	58	.50
The silver treasury of			
light verse.	Ment MD201	57	.50
with F. T. Palgrave			
The golden treasury.	Ment Ms90	53	.50
————.	Ment MT245	58	.75
WILLIAMS, RICHARD L. with David Meyers			
What, when, where and			
how to drink.	DelF 55	55	.25
WILLIAMS, ROBERT MOORE			
The blue atom.	Ace D-322	58	.35
The chaos fighters.	Ace S-90	55	.25
Conquest of the space			
sea.	Ace D-99	55	.35
Doomsday eve.	Ace D-215	57	.35
The void beyond.	Ace D-322	58	.35
WILLIAMS, ROBERT V.			
The hard way.	Pop 515	53	.25
WILLIAMS, ROSWELL			
Woman without love.	NL 10	49	.25
WILLIAMS, ROY			
The secret world of			
Roy Williams.	Ban 1697	57	.25
WILLIAMS, TENNESSEE			
Baby Doll.	Sig 1334	56	.25
Cat on a hot tin roof.	Sig S1590	58	.35
The Roman spring of			
Mrs. Stone.	Sig 955	52	.25
————.	Sig S1664	59	.35
The rose tattoo.	Sig 1236	55	.25
A streetcar named			
Desire.	Sig 917	51	.25
————.	Sig S1262	55	.35
————.	Sig D1529	58	.50
WILLIAMS, THOMAS			
Ceremony of love.	Perm M-4044	56	.35

Author/Title	Pub./Stock No.	Yr.	Price
WILLIAMS, VALENTINE			
The orange divan.	Pony unk	45	.25
with Dorothy Rice Sims			
Fog.	Pop 76	46	.25
WILLIAMS, WIRT			
The enemy.	Sig S1292	56	.35
Passiontide.	Avon T-224	58	.35
WILLIAMSON, JACK			
Dome around America.	Ace D-118	55	.35
Dragon's island.	Pop 447	52	.25
The green girl.	AvnF 2	50	.25
with James E. Gunn			
Star bridge.	Ace D-169	56	.35
WILLIAMSON, SCOTT GRAHAM			
Torment.	Pop 479	53	.25
WILLIAMSON, THAMES			
The gladiator.	Prmb P215	53	.35
The woods colt.	Ban A1255	54	.35
WILLING, JULES Z.			
How to land the job			
you want.	SigK Ks316	54	.35
WILLINGHAM, CALDER			
End as a man.	Avon 240	50	.25
_____.	Avon AT445	52	.35
_____.	Sig D1386	57	.50
Geraldine Bradshaw.	Avon G1005	51	.50
The girl in the dogwood			
cabin.	Sig S1308	56	.35
Natural child.	Sig S1062	53	.35
Reach to the stars.	Sig 987	53	.25
WILLINGS, THOMAS SKINNER			
Monarch of the vine.	Ban 468	49	.25
_____.	Ban A1199	54	.35
_____.	Ban F1563	57	.50
Persephone.	Dell F54	56	.50
Sir Fool.	Sig D1676	59	.50
WILLKIE, WENDELL L.			
One world.	PB 229	44	.25
WILLS, THOMAS			
Mine to avenge.	GM 490	55	.25
You'll get yours.	Lion 87	52	.25
_____.	Lion LB 129	56	.25
WILMER, DALE			
Dead fall.	Ban 1420	56	.25
Jungle heat.	Pyr 132	54	.25
Memo for murder.	Graf 29	51	.25
WILMOT, ROBERT PATRICK			
Blood in your eye.	PB 975	53	.25
Murder on Monday.	PB 997	54	.25

Author/Title	Pub./Stock No.	Yr.	Price
WILSON, ALEXANDER with Ruth Wilson			
Death watch.	Ace D-89	55	.35
WILSON, CHESLEY			
Live and let live.	Pop 661	55	.25
WILSON, DANA			
Uneasy virtue.	NL 12	49	.25
WILSON, DONALD POWELL			
My six convicts.	Card C-77	53	.35
WILSON, DOROTHY CLARKE			
Prince of Egypt.	Card C-8	51	.35
WILSON, EARL			
I am gazing into my			
8-ball.	PB 489	48	.25
The NBC book of stars.	PB 1184	57	.25
Pikes peek or bust.	Pop 236	50	.25
WILSON, EDMUND			
I thought of Daisy.	Ball 20	53	.35
WILSON, ETHEL			
Lilly's story.	Avon 721	56	.25
WILSON, GUTHRIE			
The feared and the			
fearless.	Pop 600	54	.25
WILSON, HARRY LEON			
Ruggles of Red Gap.	PB 772	51	.25
WILSON, HERBERT EMERSON with Thomas P. Kelley			
I stole $16,000,000.	Sig 1293	56	.25
WILSON, JOHN H.			
Nell Gwyn: royal			
mistress.	Dell 766	54	.25
WILSON, LEE			
This deadly dark.	Han 78	48	.25
WILSON, MARGERY			
The Pocket book of			
etiquette.	PB 107	41	.25
WILSON, MITCHELL			
Footsteps behind her.	Han 17	43	.15
Live with lightning.	Ban A1035	52	.35
The lovers.	Pop 689	55	.25
My brother, my enemy.	Ban A1174	53	.35
The panic-striken.	Dell 263	48	.25
Stalk the hunter.	PB 315	46	.25
WILSON, RICHARD			
The girls from Planet 5.	Ball 117	55	.35
Those idiots from earth.	Ball 237	57	.35

Author/Title	Pub./Stock No.	Yr.	Price
WILSON, RUTH with Alexander Wilson			
Death watch.	Ace D-89	55	.35
WILSON, SLOAN			
The man in the gray flannel suit.	Card C-230	56	.35
A summer place.	Card GC-65	59	.50
Voyage to somewhere.	Ace D-154	56	.35
WILSON, WILLIAM E.			
Crescent City.	Pyr R257	57	.50
The strangers.	Dell 834	55	.25
WINCHESTER, ALICE			
How to know American antiques.	Ment M62	51	.35
_____.	SigK KD328	55	.50
WINDHAM, DONALD			
The dog star.	Sig 871	51	.25
Let me alone.	Pop 754	56	.25
WINDSOR, DUCHESS of			
The heart has its reasons.	Crst t186	57	.75
WINKLER, JOHN K.			
Five and ten.	BanB FB414	57	.50
WINSOR, KATHLEEN			
America, with love.	Sig D1600	58	.50
Forever Amber.	Sig 809AB	50	.50
_____.	Sig D1169	55	.50
_____.	Sig T1567	58	.75
The lovers.	Sig D1227	55	.50
Star money.	Sig 868AB	51	.50
_____.	Sig D1725	59	.50
WINSTON, CLARA			
The closest kin there is.	Pop 501	53	.25
_____.	Pop G296	58	.35
WINTER, J. A.			
Are your troubles psychosomatic?	Pop 579	54	.25
WINTER, RICHARD E.			
Your body and its care.	Zen ZB-28	59	.35
WINTON, JANE			
Passion is the gale.	Eag EB24	54	.25
WINWAR, FRANCES			
Joan of Arc.	Ban 459	48	.25
WIRE, HAROLD CHANNING			
Indian beef.	Dell 637	52	.25
Trail boss of Indian beef.	Dell 97	46	.25
WISBERG, AUBREY with Harold Waters			
The savage soldiers.	Avon T-130	56	.35
WISEMAN, BERNARD			
Cartoon countdown.	Ball 340K	59	.35
WISTER, OWEN			
The Virginian.	Card C-209	56	.35
WITHERS, CARL			
The Penguin book of sonnets.	Pen 525	43	.25
WITHERS, E. L.			
The house on the beach.	Crst s252	58	.35
WITTELS, FRITZ			
Sex habits of American women.	Avon AT-65	53	.35
with Herbert C. Rosenthal			
Sex habits of American women.	Eton 102	51	.25
_____.	Eton ET51	52	.35
WITWER, H. C.			
The leather pushers.	Pop 288	50	.25
WODEHOUSE, P. G.			
The best of Wodehouse.	PB 628	49	.25
Carry on, Jeeves!	PB 495	48	.25
The code of the Woosters.	Dell 393	50	.25
_____.	Ace D-25	53	.35
Jeeves.	PB 28	39	.25
Leave it to Psmith.	Dell 357	49	.25
Meet Mr. Mulliner.	Hill 39	50	.25
Quick service.	Ace D-25	53	.35
Uncle Dynamite.	Dell 469	50	.25
WOLFE, ANNA W. M.			
The parents' manual.	Pop 336	51	.25
WOLFE, BERNARD			
Everything happens at night.	Sig S1238	55	.35
with Mezz Mezzrow			
Really the blues.	Dell D118	53	.35
with Raymond Rosenthal			
Hypnotism comes of age.	Berk G-29	56	.35
WOLFE, DON M.			
New voices: American writing today.	Prmb P213S	53	.50
WOLFE, THOMAS			
The hills beyond.	Avon 57	44	.25
_____.	Lion LL 19	55	.35
_____.	Pyr R321	58	.50
Look homeward, angel, part II.	Sig 697	48	.25

Author/Title	Pub./Stock No.	Yr.	Price
WOLFE, THOMAS (cont.)			
Only the dead know Brooklyn.	Sig 950	52	.25
Short stories of Thomas Wolfe.	Pen 644	47	.25
WOLFE, WINIFRED			
Ask any girl.	Ban A1983	59	.35
WOLFERT, IRA			
An act of love.	Card GC-29	55	.50
American guerrilla in the Philippines.	Ban 828	50	.25
The underworld.	Ban A798	50	.35
WOLFF, LEON			
Low level mission.	Berk G-142	58	.35
WOLFF, MARITTA			
Back of town.	Sig S1010	53	.35
The big nickelodeon.	Ban A1721	58	.35
Night shift.	Sig D1102	54	.50
Whistle stop.	Pop 257	50	.25
_____.	Pop G134	53	.35
_____.	Pop SP39	59	.50
WOLFF, PERRY			
Attack.	PB 836	51	.25
WOLFF, WILLIAM ALMON with Bayard Veiller			
The trial of Mary Dugan.	PB 647	49	.25
WOLFORD, COLBY			
The guns of Witchwater.	PB 1128	56	.25
Stranger in the land.	PB 1234	59	.25
WOLFORD, NELSON with Shirley Wolford			
Dragoon.	Ban A1569	57	.35
WOLFORD, SHIRLEY with Nelson Wolford			
Dragoon.	Ban A1569	57	.35
WOLFSON, P. J.			
Bodies are dust.	Lion 83	52	.25
The flesh baron.	Lion LL 4	54	.35
How sharp the point.	Pyr G394	59	.35
Is my flesh of brass?	Berk G-181	58	.35
This woman is mine.	Pop 356	51	.25
Three of a kind.	Berk G-85	57	.35
_____.	Berk G248	59	.35
WOLFSON, VICTOR			
The passionate season.	Lion LL 16	55	.35
_____.	Pyr G421	59	.35
WOLLHEIM, DONALD A.			
Adventures in the far future.	Ace D-73	54	.35
Adventures on other planets.	Ace S-133	55	.25

Author/Title	Pub./Stock No.	Yr.	Price
The earth in peril.	Ace D-205	57	.35
The end of the world.	Ace S-183	56	.25
The hidden planet.	Ace D-354	59	.35
Let's go naked.	Pyr 62	52	.25
_____.	Pyr 196	56	.25
The macabre reader.	Ace D-353	59	.35
Men on the moon.	Ace D-277	58	.35
The Pocket book of science-fiction.	PB 214	43	.25
Tales of outer space.	Ace D-73	54	.35
The ultimate invader.	Ace D-44	54	.35
WOLPERT, STANLEY			
Aboard the Flying Swan.	Card C-191	56	.35
A WOMAN in Berlin.	Ball 223	57	.35
WOOD, CHARLES ERSKINE SCOTT			
Heavenly discourse.	Pen 594	46	.25
WOOD, CLEMENT			
The corpse in the guest room.	BH unk	47	.25
Desire and other stories.	Berk G-160	58	.35
WOOD, SALLY			
Murder of a novelist.	Bond unk	46	.25
WOODFORD, JACK			
The abortive hussy.	Avon 146	47	.25
Dangerous love.	Avon 280	50	.25
_____.	Avon 402	52	.25
Ecstasy girl.	NL 2	48	.25
Free lovers.	NL 3	48	.25
Grounds for divorce.	NL 7	48	.25
The hard-boiled virgin.	Avon 138	47	.25
Male and female.	NL 36	50	.25
Passionate princess.	NL 4	48	.25
Peeping Tom.	NL 6	48	.25
The rites of love.	Avon 409	52	.25
Teach me to love.	NL 44	50	.25
Three gorgeous hussies.	NL 1	48	.25
Untamed darling.	Avon 297	50	.25
_____.	Avon 403	52	.25
WOODS, WILLIAM			
Manuela.	Sig 1704	59	.25
WOODWARD, C. VANN			
The battle for Leyte Gulf.	Ball 227	57	.35
WOODWARD, DAVID			
The secret raiders.	Avon T-236	58	.35
The Tirpitz.	Berk G-64	57	.35
WOODWARD, W. E.			
George Washington.	Prem d40	56	.50
Meet General Grant.	Prem d45	57	.50

Author/Title	Pub./Stock No.	Yr.	Price
WOODY, ELIZABETH			
The Pocket cook book.	PB 181	42	.25
_____.	Card C-181	56	.35
WOODY, WILLIAM			
Mistress of Horror House.	Ace D-379	59	.35
WOOLF, JAMES			
Song without sermon.	Avon 304	51	.25
WOOLF, VIRGINIA			
Orlando.	Pen 590	46	.25
WOOLFOLK, WILLIAM			
The naked hunter.	Pop 627	54	.25
Run while you can.	Pop 790	56	.25
Way of the wicked.	Mon 118	59	.35
WOOLLCOTT, ALEXANDER			
Long, long ago.	Ban 39	46	.25
While Rome burns.	PB 131	41	.25
WOOLRICH, CORNELL			
Beware the lady.	Pyr 80	53	.25
Beyond the night.	Avon T-354	59	.35
Black alibi.	Han 14	43	.15
Black angel.	Avon 96	46	.25
The black curtain.	Dell 208	47	.25
The black path of fear.	Avon 106	46	.25
The bride wore black.	PB 271	45	.25
_____.	Dell D186	57	.35
Death is my dancing partner.	Pyr G374	58	.35
Rendezvous in black.	PB 570	49	.25
Savage bride.	GM 136	51	.25
_____.	GM 719	57	.25
WORDSWORTH, WILLIAM			
Wordsworth.	DelL LB123	59	.35
WORLEY, DOROTHY			
Dr. John's decision.	Ban A1992	59	.35
WORLEY, WILLIAM			
My dead wife.	PB 773	51	.25
WORMSER, RICHARD			
The body looks familiar.	DelF A156	58	.25
The hanging heiress.	Sig 787	50	.25
The lonesome quarter.	Ban 1056	52	.25
Slattery's range.	Sig 1655	59	.25
The widow wore red.	Crst 230	58	.25
with Dan Gordon			
The longhorn trail.	Ace D-92	55	.35
WORTH, C. BROOKE with Robert K. Enders			
The nature of living things.	SigK Ks326	55	.35
WORTHINGTON, MARJORIE			
The enchanted heart.	Ban 781	50	.25

Author/Title	Pub./Stock No.	Yr.	Price
WORTS, GEORGE F.			
The blue lacquer box.	Pop 93	46	.25
Overboard.	Pop 292	50	.25
WOUK, HERMAN			
Marjorie Morningstar.	Sig T1454	57	.75
Slattery's hurricane.	Perm M-4050	56	.35
WREN, PERCIVAL C.			
Beau Geste.	PB 35	40	.25
_____.	Prmb P191	52	.35
Beau Sabreur.	Prmb P232	53	.35
Stories of the Foreign Legion.	Perm M-4011	55	.35
WRIGHT, FRANCESCA			
The loves of Lucrezia.	Eag EB6	54	.25
_____.	Pop G393	59	.35
WRIGHT, HAROLD BELL			
The shepherd of the hills.	PB 441	47	.25
WRIGHT, HELEN with Samuel Rapport			
The crust of the earth.	SigK Ks330	55	.35
_____.	Ment MD264	59	.50
WRIGHT, LAN			
A man called Destiny.	Ace D-311	58	.35
Who speaks of conquest?	Ace D-205	57	.35
WRIGHT, LEE			
The Pocket book of great detectives.	PB 103	41	.25
The Pocket book of mystery stories.	PB 117	41	.25
The Pocket mystery reader.	PB 172	42	.25
WRIGHT, RICHARD			
Black boy.	Sig 841	51	.25
Native son.	Sig S794	50	.35
The outsider.	Sig S1114	54	.35
Savage holiday.	Avon T-86	54	.35
Uncle Tom's children.	Pen 647	47	.25
_____.	Sig 1095	54	.25
WRIGHT, SEWELL PEASLEE			
Chicago murders.	Ban 127	47	.25
WRIGHT, THEON			
The knife.	Sig S1599	58	.35
WYBLE, EUGENE			
The ripening.	Ace D-131	55	.35
WYLIE, PHILIP			
An April afternoon.	Sup M640	44	.25
As they reveled.	Avon 360	51	.25
_____.	Avon 571	54	.25
Babes and sucklings.	Avon 375	51	.25

Author/Title	Pub./Stock No.	Yr.	Price

WYLIE, PHILIP (cont.)

Author/Title	Pub./Stock No.	Yr.	Price
The best of Crunch and Des.	Crst s240	58	.35
Danger mansion.	BPLA 27	41	.10
The disappearance.	Card C-40	52	.35
Experiment in crime.	Avon 711	56	.25
Finnley Wren.	Sig 701	49	.25
_____.	Berk BG-100	58	.50
Footprint of Cinderella.	Dell 140	46	.25
Generation of vipers.	Card GC-62	59	.50
Gladiator.	Avon 216	49	.25
_____.	Avon T-155	57	.35
The innocent ambassadors.	Card C-280	58	.35
Night unto night.	Sig 830	50	.25
Opus 21.	PB 722	50	.25
The savage gentleman.	Dell 85	45	.25
_____.	Avon 390	52	.25
The smuggled atom bomb.	Avon 727	56	.25
Tomorrow!	Pop G156	56	.35

with Edwin Balmer

Author/Title	Pub./Stock No.	Yr.	Price
When worlds collide.	Dell 627	52	.25

WYLLIE, JOHN

Author/Title	Pub./Stock No.	Yr.	Price
Johnny Purple.	Zen ZB-3	58	.35

WYNDHAM, JOHN

Author/Title	Pub./Stock No.	Yr.	Price
The Midwich cuckoos.	Ball 299K	59	.35
Out of the deeps.	Ball 50	53	.35
Re-birth.	Ball 104	55	.35
Revolt of the triffids.	Pop 411	52	.25
Tales of gooseflesh and laughter.	Ball 182	56	.35

with Lucas Parkes

Author/Title	Pub./Stock No.	Yr.	Price
The outward urge.	Ball 341K	59	.35

WYNNE, BARRY

Author/Title	Pub./Stock No.	Yr.	Price
Count five and die.	Ball 278K	59	.35

WYSS, JOHANN

Author/Title	Pub./Stock No.	Yr.	Price
The Swiss family Robinson.	PB 22	39	.25

Author/Title	Pub./Stock No.	Yr.	Price
X Y Z			
XENOPHON			
The march up country:			
Xenophon's Anabasis.	Ment MD278	59	.50
YAFFE, JAMES			
Nothing but the night.	Ban A1970	59	.35
YARNELL, DUANE			
Mantrap.	Crst 192	57	.25
Murder bait.	Crst 253	58	.25
YATES, BILL			
Forever funny.	DelF 93	56	.25
Laughing on the inside.	Dell 754	54	.25
The other woman.	DelF A178	59	.25
Too funny for words.	DelF 39	54	.25
YATES, DORNFORD			
And Berry came too.	Pen 570	45	.25
YATES, GEORGE WORTHING			
The body that wasn't			
uncle.	Dell 52	44	.25
_____.	Dell 645	52	.25
If a body.	Dell 159	47	.25
YEATS-BROWN, FRANCIS			
The lives of a Bengal			
lancer.	Ban 43	46	.25
_____.	Ban A1748	58	.35
YERBY, FRANK			
Benton's Row.	Card C-208	56	.35
Captain Rebel.	Card C-249	57	.35
The devil's laughter.	Card C-142	54	.35
Fairoaks.	Card C-310	58	.35
Floodtide.	PB 945	53	.25
_____.	Card C-87	53	.35
The Foxes of Harrow.	PB 577	49	.25
_____.	Card C-367	59	.35
The golden hawk.	PB 749	51	.25
_____.	Card C-54	52	.35
Pride's castle.	Card C-21	52	.35
The Saracen blade.	Card C-124	54	.35
The serpent and the			
staff.	Card C-352	59	.35
The treasure of			
Pleasant Valley.	PB 1131	56	.25
The vixens.	PB 655	50	.25
_____.	Card C-175	55	.35
A woman called Fancy.	Card C-102	53	.35
YOHANNAN, JOHN D.			
A treasury of Asian			
literature.	Ment MD243	58	.50
YORDAN, PHILIP			
Man of the West.	PB 1113	56	.25

Author/Title	Pub./Stock No.	Yr.	Price
YORE, CLEM			
Age of consent.	Dell 622	52	.25
YORK, JEREMY			
Hilda, take heed.	Pyr G408	59	.35
Seeds of murder.	Pyr G441	59	.35
So soon to die.	Pyr G382	59	.35
YORKE, SUSAN			
Naked to mine enemies.	Sig 1054	53	.25
YOSELOFF, MARTIN			
The girl in the spike-			
heeled shoes.	Pop 265	50	.25
_____.	Pop 573	54	.25
Lily and the sergeant.	Pop G376	59	.35
YOUNG, CHIC			
Blondie-Dagwood in			
footlight folly.	Dell nn	47	.25
YOUNG, DESMOND			
Rommel, the desert fox.	Berk BG-96	58	.50
YOUNG, EDITH with Phyllis Fraser			
Puzzles, quizzes and			
games.	Ban 81	47	.25
YOUNG, EDWARD			
Hospital doctor.	Pyr G67	52	.35
_____.	Pyr G297	57	.35
YOUNG, GORDON			
Fast on the draw.	Pop 225	50	.25
Fighting blood.	Pop 134	47	.25
_____.	Pop 574	54	.25
Guns of the Arrowhead.	Pop 262	50	.25
Hell on hoofs.	Ace D-10	53	.35
Range boss.	Pop 384	51	.25
Roaring guns.	Pop 175	49	.25
Tall in the saddle.	Dell 780	54	.25
Trouble on the border.	Pop 321	51	.25
Two-gun man.	Pop 429	52	.25
Wanted--dead or alive.	Sig 815	50	.25
YOUNG, I. S.			
Jadie.	Crst 130	56	.25
Jadie Greenway.	Avon 269	50	.25
YOUNG, JEFFERSON			
A good man.	Ban A1245	54	.35
YOUNG, MIRIAM			
Mother wore tights.	Pen 630	47	.25
YOUNG, WASHINGTON			
Ashurbanipal.	BanB FB417	58	.50
YOUR own book of funny			
stories.	PBJr J-45	50	.25

Author/Title	Pub./Stock No.	Yr.	Price
ZAIDENBERG, ARTHUR			
Drawing self-taught.	Card C-148	54	.35
ZANE, LEHI			
Brenda.	GM 264	52	.25
ZANE Grey western award			
stories.	Dell 523	51	.25
ZATTERIN, UGO			
Revolt of the sinners.	Pop 727	56	.25
ZATURENSKA, MARYA with Horace Gregory			
The Mentor book of			
religious verse.	Ment MD189	57	.50
ZEISER, BRUNO			
The road to Stalingrad.	Ball 168	56	.35
ZIFF, WILLIAM B.			
The coming battle of			
Germany.	PB 194	43	.25
ZINBERG, LEN			
Strange desires.	Avon 201	49	.25
Walk hard--talk loud.	Lion 29	50	.25
What d'ya know for sure?	Avon T-93	55	.35
_____.	Berk G-225	59	.35
ZINKOFF, DAVE with Edgar Williams			
Go, man, go.	PyrR PG17	58	.35
ZINSSER, HANS			
Rats, lice and history.	PB 309	45	.25
ZOLA, ÉMILE			
The gin palace.	Avon T-129	56	.35
The human beast.	Avon G-1013	54	.50
The kill.	Ban A1290	55	.35
Lesson in love.	Pyr 105	53	.25
A love episode.	Avon 150	48	.25
Nana.	PB 104	41	.25
_____.	Card C-134	54	.35
_____.	PBL PL63	58	.35
Nana's mother.	Avon 271	50	.25
Piping hot.	Avon 167	48	.25
Restless house.	Ban A1244	54	.35
Shame.	Ace S-76	54	.25
_____.	Ace D-182	56	.35
Theresa.	Ban 1020	52	.25
Thérèse Raquin.	Ace D-182	56	.35
Venus of the counting			
house.	Avon 236	50	.25
with George Milburn			
The human beast.	Dell 608	52	.25
ZOLOTOW, MAURICE			
The great Balsamo.	Pyr 119	54	.25
No people like show			
people.	Ban A1053	52	.35

Author/Title	Pub./Stock No.	Yr.	Price
ZUGSMITH, LEANE with Carl Randau			
The visitor.	Dell 132	46	.25
ZWEIG, STEFAN			
Marie Antoinette.	Card GC-21	54	.50

Title Index

The Amboy Dukes.   Irving Shulman
Ambuscade.   Frank O'Rourke
Ambush.   Luke Short
Ambush at Buffalo Wallow. T. D. Allen
Ambush at Coffin Canyon. Bliss Lomax
Ambush at Rincon.   Dudley Dean
Ambush at Scorpion   William Colt
  Valley.   MacDonald
Ambush hell.   George C. Appell
Ambush on the mesa.   Gordon D. Shirreffs
Ambush range.   Jack Barton
Ambush rider.   Hal G. Evarts
America in perspective.   Henry Steele Commager
America, with love.   Kathleen Winsor
American accent.   Elizabeth Abell
American aces.   Edward H. Sims
American acres.   Louise Redfield
    Peattie
American ballads.   David Jordan
    Charles O'Brien
    Kennedy
American beauty.   Edna Ferber
American captain.   Edison Marshall
American diplomacy:
  1900-1950.   George F. Kennan
An American dream girl.   James T. Farrell
American essays.   Charles B. Shaw
American folk tales
  and songs.   Richard Chase
American guerrilla in
  the Philippines.   Ira Wolfert
The American gun mystery. Ellery Queen
The American heritage
  reader.
American me.   Beatrice Griffith
The American presidency. Clinton Rossiter
American sexual behavior Morris L. Ernst
  and the Kinsey report. David Loth
American skyline.   Henry Hope Reed
    Christopher Tunnard
An American tragedy.   Theodore Dreiser
The American woman.   Eric J. Dingwall
Americans vs. Germans.
America's cities of sin. Noah Sarlat
America's role in the
  world economy.   Alvin H. Hansen
The amethyst spectacles. Frances Crane
Amorous Philandre.   Jean Galli de Bibiena
Amy Vanderbilt's
  everyday etiquette.   Amy Vanderbilt
An analysis of the
  Kinsey reports on
  sexual behavior in the
  human male and female. Donald Porter Geddes
Analyze yourself.   William Gerhardi
    Leopold Loewenstein
Anastasia.   Marcelle Maurette
The anatomy of a crime.   Joseph F. Dinneen
Anatomy of a murder.   Robert Traver
And be a villain.   Rex Stout
...And be my love.   Ledru Baker Jr.

And Berry came too.   Dornford Yates
And come back a man.   John Bell Clayton
And dream of evil.   Tedd Thomey
And four to go.   Rex Stout
And kill once more.   Al Fray
And now good-bye.   James Hilton
And quiet flows the Don. Mikhail Sholokhov
And ride a tiger.   Robert Wilder
And save them for
  pallbearers.   James Garrett
And sin no more.   H. P. Koenig
And so to murder.   Carter Dickson
And sometimes death.   Jo Valentine
And the girl screamed.   Gil Brewer
And the wind blows free. Luke Short
And then murder.   Julius Fast
And then there were none. Agatha Christie
...And to my beloved
  husband.   Philip Loraine
And two shall meet.   Raymond Mason
And when she was bad
  she was murdered.   Richard Starnes
And where she stops.   Thomas B. Dewey
Andersonville.   MacKinlay Kantor
Andrew Jackson.   Gerald Johnson
Andrews' harvest.   John Evans
Andy's everyday
  encyclopedia.   Ellen Wales Walpole
Angel.   Curtis Lucas
Angel face.   Fan Nichols
Angel of gaiety.   Joseph Hitrec
Angel with spurs.   Paul I. Wellman
Angels Camp.   Ray Morrison
Angels in the gutter.   Joseph Hilton
Angel's ransom.   David Dodge
Anger at innocence.   William Gardner Smith
Angle of attack.   Joseph Landon
The angry hills.   Leon Uris
The angry land.   Frank Bass
The angry man.   T. T. Flynn
The angry mountain.   Hammond Innes
The angry wife.   Pearl S. Buck
The angry woman.   James Ronald
Animal farm.   George Orwell
Animal wonder world.   Frank Lane
Animals are funnier
  than people.   Harold Meyers
Ann Carmeny.   Hoffman Birney
Ann Pillsbury's baking
  book.   Ann Pillsbury
Anna and the King of
  Siam.   Margaret Landon
Anna Becker.   Max White
Anna Karenina.   Leo Tolstoy
Anna Lucasta.   Jean Francis Webb
Anne of Windy Poplars.   L. M. Montgomery
Annie Jordan.   Mary Brinker Post
Anniversary.   Ludwig Lewisohn
Another Claudia.   Rose Franken
Another kind.   Chad Oliver
Another man's murder.   Mignon G. Eberhart

Another man's poison.   Hugh Holman
Another mug for the bier. Richard Starnes
Another new Jimmy Hatlo
   book.   Jimmy Hatlo
Another woman's house.   Mignon G. Eberhart
Anthony Adverse in
   Africa.   Hervey Allen
Anthony Adverse in
   America.   Hervey Allen
Anthony Adverse in Italy. Hervey Allen
Antic hay.   Aldous Huxley
The anvil of
   civilization.   Leonard Cottrell
Any shape or form.   Elizabeth Daly
Anyone can have a great
   vocabulary.   J. L. Stephenson
Anyone can win at gin
   rummy and canasta.   Alfred Drake
Anyone's my name.   Seymour Shubin
Anything can happen.   George Papashvily
       Helen Papashvily
Anything for a laugh.   Bennett Cerf
Anything for a quiet
   life.   A. A. Avery
Anything for kicks.   Morton Cooper
The Apache.   James Warner Bellah
Apache.   Will Levington
       Comfort
Apache agent.   Hal G. Evarts
Apache ambush.   Will Cook
Apache Crossing.   Will Ermine
Apache desert.   L. P. Holmes
Apache devil.   Edwin Corle
Apache gold and Yaqui
   silver.   J. Frank Dobie
Apache greed.   William Hopson
Apache land.   Ross Santee
Apache rising.   Marvin H. Albert
Apache war cry.   William E. Vance
Apache warpath.   George Garland
Apache wells.   Robert Steelman
Apalachee gold.   Frank G. Slaughter
Apartment in Athens.   Glenway Wescott
Ape and essence.   Aldous Huxley
Aphrodite.   Pierre Louÿs
The apostle.   Sholem Asch
An apple for Eve.   Kathleen Norris
The applegreen cat.   Frances Crane
Appointment in Paris.   Fay Adams
Appointment in Samarra.   John O'Hara
Appointment with danger. David Garth
Appointment with death.   Agatha Christie
Appointment with fear.   Donald Stokes
An April afternoon.   Philip Wylie
April evil.   John D. MacDonald
The April robin murders. Ed McBain
       Craig Rice
April snow.   Lillian Budd
The Arabian nights
   murder.   John Dickson Carr
Arch of Triumph.   Erich Maria Remarque

Are your troubles
   psychosomatic?   J. A. Winter
Area of suspicion.   John D. MacDonald
Arena of love.   Hélène Eliat
Argosy book of adventure
   stories.   Rogers Terrill
The Argosy book of
   sports stories.   Rogers Terrill
Ariane.   Claude Anet
Arizona.   Clarence Budington
       Kelland
Arizona dead-shot.   Nelson Nye
Arizona feud.   Frank R. Adams
Arizona guns.   William MacLeod
       Raine
Arizona Jim.   Charles Alden Seltzer
Arizona ranger.   A. Scott Leslie
Armande.   Daniel May
Armchair in hell.   Henry Kane
Arms and men.   Walter Millis
The arms of Venus.   John Appleby
Around the world in
   80 days.   Jules Verne
Around the world with
   Auntie Mame.   Patrick Dennis
Arouse and beware.   MacKinlay Kantor
Arrest the Saint!   Leslie Charteris
Arrow in the dust.   L. L. Foreman
Arrow in the hill.   Jefferson Cooper
Arrow in the moon.   John Harris
       Margaret Harris
Arrowsmith.   Sinclair Lewis
Arsenic and old lace.   Joseph Kesselring
Art Buchwald's Paris.   Art Buchwald
Art colony.   Clifton Cuthbert
The art of barbecue and
   outdoor cooking.
The art of French   Fernande Silve
   cooking.   Garvin
The art of Italian   Maria Lo Pinto
   cooking.   Milo Miloradovich
The art of living.   Norman Vincent Peale
The art of mixing drinks. Frederic A.
       Birmingham
The art of thinking.   Ernest Dimnet
The art studio murders.   Edward Ronns
An artist in love.   Philip Lindsay
Arts and the man.   Irwin Edman
As a man falls.   Howard Rigsby
As good as dead.   Thomas B. Dewey
As long as I live.   Ione Sandberg Shriber
As they reveled.   Philip Wylie
As tough as they come.   Will Oursler
As you like it.   William Shakespeare
Ashenden, or, the
   British agent.   W. Somerset Maugham
Ashes.   Charles Francis Coe
Ashurbanipal.   Washington Young
Ask any girl.   Winifred Wolfe
Ask for Linda.   Fan Nichols
Ask the dust.   John Fante

Asking for trouble.   Joe Rayter
Aspects of love.   David Garnett
The Aspern papers and
  The spoils of Poynton.   Henry James
The asphalt jungle.   W. R. Burnett
The assault.   Allen R. Matthews
Assignment--Angelina.   Edward S. Aarons
Assignment--Budapest.   Edward S. Aarons
Assignment--Carlotta
  Cortez.   Edward S. Aarons
Assignment--Helene.   Edward S. Aarons
Assignment in Brittany.   Helen MacInnes
Assignment in eternity.   Robert A. Heinlein
Assignment in Guiana.   George Harmon Coxe
Assignment--Lili Lamaris.   Edward S. Aarons
Assignment--Madeleine.   Edward S. Aarons
Assignment: murder.   Donald Hamilton
Assignment--Stella Marni.   Edward S. Aarons
Assignment--suicide.   Edward S. Aarons
Assignment to disaster.   Edward S. Aarons
Assignment--treason.   Edward S. Aarons
Assignment without glory.   Marcos Spinelli
The assistant.   Bernard Malamud
Astounding science
  fiction anthology.   John W. Campbell Jr.
Astounding tales of
  space and time.   John W. Campbell Jr.
Astrology and you.   Carroll Righter
Asylum.   William Seabrook
At heaven's gate.   Robert Penn Warren
At home in India.   Cynthia Bowles
At last, Mr. Tolliver.   William Wiegand
At sundown the tiger.   Ethel Mannin
Atlantic Avenue.   Albert Halper
Atlas shrugged.   Ayn Rand
The atom curtain.   Nick Boddie Williams
The atomic age opens.   Donald Porter Geddes
Atomic energy in the
  coming era.   David Dietz
Atta.   Francis Rufus Bellamy
Attack!   Leland Jamieson
Attack.   Perry Wolff
Auntie Mame.   Patrick Dennis
Authentic librettos of
  the grand opera.
The authentic New
  testament.
The autobiography of an
  ex-coloured man.   James Weldon Johnson
The autobiography of
  Benjamin Franklin.   Benjamin Franklin
Autobiography of
  Benvenuto Cellini.   Benvenuto Cellini
Autumn thunder.   Robert Wilder
The avenger.   Dwight Bennett
The avenger.   Matthew Blood
The avenger.   Bradford Scott
Avenger from nowhere.   William E. Vance
Avenger from Texas.   Will Ermine
The avengers.   Chad Merriman
The avenging gun.   J. L. Bouma

The avenging gun.   John L. Shelley
The avenging Saint.   Leslie Charteris
The Avon all-American
  fiction reader.
Avon bedside companion.
The Avon book of crime
  and detective stories.   John Rhode
The Avon book of great
  mystery stories.
The Avon book of modern
  short stories.
The Avon book of modern   William Phillips
  writing.   Philip Rahv
Avon book of modern   William Phillips
  writing no. 2.   Philip Rahv
Avon book of new stories
  of the great Wild West.
The Avon book of puzzles.   Charles Stolberg
The Avon book of puzzles
  for everybody.   John Paul Adams
The Avon book of W.
  Somerset Maugham.   W. Somerset Maugham
Avon complete crosswords
  and cryptograms.   Clark Kinnaird
The Avon ghost reader.
The Avon improved cook
  book.   Pearl V. Metzelthin
The Avon mystery
  storyteller.
The Avon story teller.
Avon Webster English
  dictionary.
Awake and die.   Robert Ames
Awake Monique.   Astrid van Royen
Awake to darkness.   Richard McMullen
Awakening.   Jean-Baptiste Rossi
The awakening of Jenny.   Lillian Colter
Away all boats.   Kenneth Dodson
Away and beyond.   A. E. van Vogt
The Aztec: man and tribe.   Victor W. Von Hagen

Beyond the pass.	Lee Leighton
Beyond the pleasure principle.	Sigmund Freud
Beyond the Rio Grande.	William MacLeod Raine
Beyond the vanishing point.	Ray Cummings
Beyond the wild Missouri.	Walt Coburn
Beyond this place.	A. J. Cronin
Beyond time and space.	August Derleth
Beyond Wind River.	Les Savage Jr.
Bhowani Junction.	John Masters
The Bible was right.	Hugh J. Schonfield
Bier for a chaser.	Richard Foster
Big as life.	John Pleasant McCoy
The big ball of wax.	Shepherd Mead
The big bedroom.	Edward Ronns
The big bet.	Edward Harris Heth
Big beverage.	William T. Campbell
The big bite.	Gerry Travis
The big bite.	Charles Williams
The big boodle.	Robert Sylvester
The big book of horse stories.	Page Cooper
The big book of science fiction.	Groff Conklin
The big boxcar.	Alfred Maund
The big brokers.	Irving Shulman
The big bubble.	Theodore Pratt
Big business: a new era.	David E. Lilienthal
The big cage.	Robert Lowry
The big caper.	Lionel White
Big city after dark.	Jack Lait / Lee Mortimer
Big city girl.	Charles Williams
The big clock.	Kenneth Fearing
The big company look.	J. Harvey Howells
The big con.	David W. Maurer
The big corral.	Al Cody
The big country.	Donald Hamilton
The big deal.	Selig Seligman
The big dry.	George Garland
The big eye.	Max Ehrlich
The big fake.	Murray Forbes
The big fear.	Theo Durrant
The big feeling.	Daniel Karp
Big fella.	Henry W. Clune
The big fifty.	Frank O'Rourke
The big fights.	Harold Meyers
The Big Fisherman.	Lloyd C. Douglas
The big fist.	Clyde Ragsdale
The big fix.	Mel Colton
The big four.	Agatha Christie
The big frame.	The Gordons
The big frame.	Sam Merwin Jr.
The big gun.	James Cavanaugh
The big gun.	Philip Ketchum
The big guy.	Wade Miller
The big heat.	William P. McGivern
The Big Ivy.	James McCague
The big jump.	Leigh Brackett
The big kill.	Mickey Spillane
The big kiss-off.	Day Keene
The big land.	Frank Gruber
Big league baseball.	
The big lure.	William Manners
The big make.	Gene Paul
Big man.	Richard Marsten
The big midget murders.	Craig Rice
Big Mike.	Charles Givens
The big money.	John Dos Passos
The big money.	Harold Q. Masur
The big nickelodeon.	Maritta Wolff
The big night.	Stanley Ellin
Big old sun.	Robert Faherty
The big outfit.	Peter Dawson
The big pasture.	Clay Fisher
Big planet.	Jack Vance
The big range.	Jack Schaefer
The big rape.	James Wakefield Burke
Big Red.	Jim Kjelgaard
Big Red's daughter.	John McPartland
The big rumble.	Wenzell Brown
Big shot.	Lawrence Treat
The big show.	Pierre Clostermann
The big sin.	Jack Webb
The big sky.	A. B. Guthrie Jr.
The big sleep.	Raymond Chandler
Big Sol.	Henry von Rhau
Big Stan.	John Monahan
The big steal.	Earle Basinsky
The big store.	Oscar Schisgall
The big success.	Ian Gordon
The big town.	Ring Lardner
Big-town round-up.	William MacLeod Raine
The big war.	Anton Myrer
The big water.	Mark Derby
The big wheel.	John Brooks
The bigger they come.	A. A. Fair
The bikini bombshell.	Bob McKnight
Bill Stern's favorite boxing stories.	Bill Stern
Bill Stern's favorite football stories.	Bill Stern
Billy the Kid.	Edwin Corle
Bimini run.	Howard Hunt
Biography of the earth.	George Gamow
Bird of prey.	Victor Canning
Birdman of Alcatraz.	Thomas E. Gaddis
The birds and the bees.	James Aswell
The birth and death of the sun.	George Gamow
The birthday murder.	Lange Lewis
The Bishop murder case.	S. S. Van Dine
The bishop's crime.	H. C. Bailey
The bishop's jaegers.	Thorne Smith
The bishop's mantle.	Agnes Sligh Turnbull
The bitch.	Gil Brewer
Bitter creek.	James Boyd
Bitter Creek.	Al Cody
Bitter ending.	Alexander Irving
Bitter forfeit.	Mabel Louise Robinson
Bitter fruit.	Peter Packer

Bitter ground.	W. R. Burnett
Bitter honeymoon.	Alberto Moravia
Bitter love.	Dyson Taylor
Bitter Sage.	Frank Gruber
The bitter tea of General Yen.	Grace Zaring Stone
Bitter victory.	René Hardy
The bitterweed path.	Thomas Hal Phillips
The Bixby girls.	Rosamond Marshall
The bizarre sisters.	Audrey Walz / Jay Walz
Black alibi.	Cornell Woolrich
Black angel.	Cornell Woolrich
The black arrow.	Robert Louis Stevenson
Black Beauty.	Anna Sewell
Black boy.	Richard Wright
The black camel.	Earl Derr Biggers
The black city.	M. F. Caulfield
The black cloud.	Fred Hoyle
The black curtain.	Cornell Woolrich
The black dark murders.	Robert O. Saber
The black Donnellys.	Thomas P. Kelley
The black door.	Cleve F. Adams
The black-eyed stranger.	Charlotte Armstrong
Black fire.	Lawrence Goldman
Black Friday.	David Goodis
Black gold.	Jewel Gibson
The black-headed pins.	Constance Little / Gwenyth Little
Black Horse Canyon.	Les Savage Jr.
Black ivory.	Norman Collins
Black jade.	Angeline Taylor
Black Judas.	Burke Wilkinson
The black key.	M. Scott Michel
Black majesty.	John W. Vandercook
The black mirror.	Ben Benson
The black mountain.	Rex Stout
The black obelisk.	Erich Maria Remarque
Black opium.	Claude Farrère
The black orchid.	Edward Ronns
Black orchids.	Rex Stout
The black path of fear.	Cornell Woolrich
Black plumes.	Margery Allingham
The black prince and other stories.	Shirley Ann Grau
The black riders.	Sam Meriwether
Black Rock Valley.	S. E. Whitman
The black rose.	Thomas B. Costain
Black sage.	L. P. Holmes
Black sheep, run.	Bart Spicer
The black shrouds.	Constance Little / Gwenyth Little
Black sombrero.	William Colt MacDonald
Black spaniel mystery.	Betty Cavanna
Black storm.	Thomas C. Hinkle
Black widow.	Patrick Quentin
Black wings has my angel.	Elliott Chaze
The blackbirder.	Dorothy B. Hughes
The blackboard jungle.	Evan Hunter
Blackcock's feather.	Maurice Walsh
Blackjack.	Joseph E. Kelleam
Blackleg range.	Bennett Foster
Blackmail, inc.	Robert Kyle
Blackmailer.	George Axelrod
The blackmailer.	Ernst Klein
Black-out in Gretley.	J. B. Priestley
Blacksnake Trail.	Peter Field
Blackwater.	Frank O'Rourke
Blade of conquest.	Jonreed Lauritzen
The blank wall.	Elisabeth Sanxay Holding
Blaze.	Scott Stone
The blaze of guns.	Bradford Scott
The blaze of noon.	Rayner Heppenstall
Blaze of the sun.	Jean Hougron
Blazing border.	E. E. Halleran
The blazing land.	Norman Collins
Blazing trails.	Francis W. Hilton
The bleeding scissors.	Bruno Fischer
Bless this house.	Norah Lofts
Blessed event.	Bill O'Malley
The blessing.	Nancy Mitford
Blind alley.	Bant Singer
The blind barber.	John Dickson Carr
Blind cartridges.	William Colt MacDonald
Blind entry.	Merlyn Estin
Blind man's bluff.	Baynard Kendrick
Blind man's bullets.	Glenn Balch
The blind side.	Patricia Wentworth
Blizzard range.	Todhunter Ballard
Blond savage.	John Vail
The blonde.	Carter Brown
Blonde and beautiful.	Richard Foster
The blonde and Johnny Malloy.	Ben Kerr
Blonde baggage.	Marty Holland
Blonde bait.	Ed Lacy
Blonde bait.	Stephen Marlowe
The blonde body.	Michael Morgan
The blonde cried murder.	Brett Halliday
The blonde died dancing.	Kelley Roos
The blonde died first.	Dana Chambers
The blonde in black.	Ben Benson
The blonde in suite 14.	Stewart Sterling
The blonde is dead.	John Dow
Blonde menace.	Don Martin
Blonde mistress.	Hal Bennett
The blonde on the street corner.	David Goodis
Blondes are my trouble.	Martin Brett
Blondes are skin deep.	Louis Trimble
Blondes die young.	Bill Peters
Blondie-Dagwood in footlight folly.	Chic Young
Blondie Iscariot.	Edgar Lustgarten
Blood Alley.	A. S. Fleischman
Blood and sand.	Vincente Blasco Ibáñez
Blood brand.	Larry Lawson

Blood brother.	Elliott Arnold
Blood feud.	Dave Ricks
Blood from a stone.	Ruth Sawtell Wallis
Blood in your eye.	Robert Patrick Wilmot
Blood money.	Dashiell Hammett
Blood money.	Dan J. Stevens
Blood-moon range.	Bob Obets
Blood of the lamb.	Charles Baker Jr.
Blood of the West.	Paul Evan Lehman
Blood on Biscayne Bay.	Brett Halliday
Blood on Boot Hill.	Kermit Welles
Blood on her shoe.	Medora Field
Blood on Lake Louisa.	Baynard Kendrick
Blood on the black market.	Brett Halliday
Blood on the boards.	William Campbell Gault
Blood on the branches.	Oliver Crawford
Blood on the cat.	Nancy Rutledge
Blood on the desert.	Peter Rabe
Blood on the forge.	William Attaway
Blood on the land.	Frank Bonham
Blood on the moon.	Luke Short
Blood on the range.	Eli Colter
Blood on the saddle.	Johnston McCulley
Blood on the stars.	Brett Halliday
Blood on the sun.	Chad Merriman
Blood on the trail.	Max Brand
Blood royal.	Robert Payne
Blood upon the snow.	Hilda Lawrence
Blood will tell.	George Bagby
The bloody Bokhara.	William Campbell Gault
Bloody hoofs.	J. Edward Leithead
Bloody Kansas.	Chuck Martin
The bloody medallion.	Richard Telfair
The bloody moonlight.	Fredric Brown
Bloody river.	Paul Durst
The bloody sevens.	Jefferson Cooper
The bloody spur.	Charles Einstein
Bloody Wyoming.	Al Cody
Blow-down.	Lawrence G. Blochman
Blow hot, blow cold.	Gerald Butler
Blow out my torch.	James Howard
The blue angel.	Heinrich Mann
The blue atom.	Robert Moore Williams
Blue camellia.	Frances Parkinson Keyes
The blue chips.	Jay Deiss
Blue city.	Ross Macdonald
Blue city.	Kenneth Millar
The blue cloak.	Temple Bailey
Blue denim.	James Leo Herlihy
	William Noble
Blue Earth.	John H. Burgess
The blue geranium.	Dolan Birkley
The blue geranium.	Agatha Christie
Blue hurricane.	F. van Wyck Mason
The blue hussar.	Roger Nimier
The blue lacquer box.	George F. Worts
The blue mustang.	Clay Fisher

The blue Negro.	Robert Payne
Blue ribbon romance.	Jane S. McIlvaine
Blue treasure.	Helen Girvan
Bluebeard's seventh wife.	William Irish
Blues for the prince.	Bart Spicer
Bluffer's luck.	W. C. Tuttle
A blunt instrument.	Georgette Heyer
The boat.	Walter Gibson
Bob, son of Battle.	Alfred Ollivant
Bobby sox.	Marty Links
Bodies are dust.	P. J. Wolfson
Bodies are where you find them.	Brett Halliday
Bodies in bedlam.	Richard S. Prather
The body.	Carter Brown
The body beautiful.	Bill S. Ballinger
The body in the basket.	George Bagby
The body in the bed.	Bill S. Ballinger
The body in the library.	Agatha Christie
The body looks familiar.	Richard Wormser
The body missed the boat.	Jack Iams
The body next door.	Eaton K. Goldthwaite
The body of love.	Charles Keats
The body on the bench.	Dorothy B. Hughes
Body on the pavement.	Gordon Meyrick
Body or soul.	Royal Peters
The body snatchers.	Jack Finney
The body that wasn't uncle.	George Worthing Yates
Boeing 707.	Martin Caidin
The Bohemian.	Jules Koslow
Bold moment.	Victor H. Johnson
Bold new program.	Willard R. Espy
Bold passage.	Frank Bonham
Bold raiders of the West.	Frederick R. Bechdolt
Bold rider.	Luke Short
The bold sabateurs.	Chandler Brossard
Boldness be my friend.	Richard Pape
Bombay mail.	Lawrence G. Blochman
Bomber crew.	Joseph Landon
Bombs in orbit.	Jeff Sutton
Bon voyage!	Joseph Hayes
	Marrijane Hayes
Bonanza Gulch.	Matt Stuart
Bond of the flesh.	Rosamond Marshall
Bonjour tristesse.	Françoise Sagan
A book about American history.	George Stimpson
The book of prayers.	Elfrieda McCauley
	Leon McCauley
The book of the dead.	Elizabeth Daly
Books that changed the world.	Robert B. Downs
Boom town.	Jack O'Connor
Boomer.	Clay Randall
Boomerang!	William C. Chambliss
The boomerang clue.	Agatha Christie
Boomtown buccaneers.	William Colt MacDonald
Boot Hill.	Weston Clay

Boots and saddles.	Edgar Jean Bracco
Border ambush.	Walker A. Tompkins
The border bandit.	Evan Evans
Border blood.	Bradford Scott
Border breed.	William MacLeod Raine
Border buccaneers.	Frank Castle
Border city.	Hart Stilwell
Border feud.	Tom Gill
Border fever.	C. William Harrison
Border graze.	Dwight Bennett
Border guns.	Max Brand
Border guns.	Eugene Cunningham
Border hell.	Jackson Cole
The border jumpers.	Will C. Brown
The border kid.	Max Brand
The border legion.	Zane Grey
The border lord.	Jan Westcott
The Border Queen.	Nick Sumner
Border raider.	William Hopson
Border renegade.	Dudley Dean
Border roundup.	Allan R. Bosworth
Border town.	Carroll Graham
Border town girl.	John D. MacDonald
The border trumpet.	Ernest Haycox
Border vengeance.	J. L. Bouma
Border woman.	Richard Carroll
	Gregory Mason
The Borgia blade.	Gardner F. Fox
The Borgias.	J. Lucas-Dubreton
Born innocent.	Creighton Brown-Burnham
Born of the sun.	Geoffrey Wagner
Born reckless.	Milton Rogers
Born to gunsmoke.	Thomas Thompson
Born to trouble.	Nelson Nye
Boss man.	Roy B. Sparkia
Boss of barbed wire.	Barry Cord
The boss of Broken Spur.	Nick Sumner
Boss of Panamint.	Leslie Ernenwein
The boss of the Lazy 9.	Peter Field
Boss of the plains.	Will Ermine
The Boston Cooking-School cook book.	Fannie Farmer
Boswell's Johnson sampler.	James Boswell
Boswell's London journal.	James Boswell
Botany Bay.	James Norman Hall
	Charles Nordhoff
Botticelli.	Frederick Hartt
The bottom of the bottle.	Georges Simenon
Bottoms up!	Charles Preston
Bought with a gun.	Luke Short
Boulevard.	Robert Sabatier
Bound girl.	Everett Webber
	Olga Webber
Bounty guns.	Luke Short
The bounty hunters.	Elmore Leonard
The bounty killer.	Marvin H. Albert
The bounty lands.	William Ellis
Bounty man.	John McGreevey
Bourbon Street.	G. H. Otis

The bowl of brass.	Paul I. Wellman
The bowstring murders.	Carter Dickson
Box star buckaroo.	Chuck Martin
The boy came back.	Charles H. Knickerbocker
Boy gang.	Mark Kennedy
Boy on a dolphin.	David Divine
Boy with a gun.	James Dean Sanderson
The Boyds of Black River.	Walter D. Edmonds
Brad Dolan's blonde cargo.	William Fuller
Brad Dolan's Miami manhunt.	William Fuller
Brain guy.	Benjamin Appel
The brain pickers.	Hallie Southgate Burnett
The brain-stealers.	Murray Leinster
Brain surgeon.	William Sharpe
Brain wave.	Poul Anderson
Brainwashing.	Edward Hunter
The bramble bush.	Charles Mergendahl
Brand fires on the ridge.	Ernest Haycox
Brand of a man.	Thomas Thompson
Brand of a Texan.	Steven C. Lawrence
Brand of Cain.	Wade B. Cantrell
Brand of empire.	Luke Short
Brand of fury.	Jack Barton
Brand of iron.	Al Cody
Branded.	A. C. Abbott
Branded.	Walt Coburn
The branded lawman.	William E. Vance
The branded man.	Luke Short
Branded West.	Don Ward
Branded woman.	Wade Miller
Brandon's empire.	Dave Hardin
Brandy for a hero.	William O'Farrell
The brass and the blue.	James Keene
The brass bed.	Fletcher Flora
The brass brigade.	Frank Peace
The brass chills.	Hugh Pentecost
The brass command.	Clay Fisher
The brass cupcake.	John D. MacDonald
The brass god.	Richard G. Hubler
The brass halo.	Jack Webb
The brass monkey.	Harry Whittington
The brass shroud.	Bruce Cassiday
The brat.	Gil Brewer
The bravados.	Frank O'Rourke
The brave, bad girls.	Thomas B. Dewey
The brave bulls.	Tom Lea
The brave cowboy.	Edward Abbey
Brave harvest.	Richard Cargoe
Brave in the saddle.	Will Ermine
Brave new world.	Aldous Huxley
The brave rifles.	Gordon D. Shirreffs
Bravo trail.	Eugene Cunningham
Brazos.	Ross McLaury Taylor
The Brazos firebrand.	Leslie Scott
Bread and wine.	Ignazio Silone
Break down the walls.	John Bartlow Martin
Breakaway.	Wally Depew

Breakdown.	Louis Paul
Breakfast at Tiffany's.	Truman Capote
Breaking point.	Jacob Presser
Break-up.	Edmund Schiddel
Breathe no more, my lady.	Ed Lacy
A breed apart.	Fleming MacLiesh
Brenda.	Lehi Zane
The bridal bed murders.	A. E. Martin
Bridal journey.	Dale Van Every
The bride comes to Yellow Sky.	Stephen Crane
Bride from Broadway.	Faith Baldwin
The bride is much too beautiful.	Odette Joyeux
The bride of Newgate.	John Dickson Carr
Bride of the sword.	Homer Hatten
Bride of violence.	Harriet Gray
The bride saw red.	Robert Carson
The bride wore black.	Cornell Woolrich
Brideshead revisited.	Evelyn Waugh
The bridge at Andau.	James A. Michener
The bridge at Remagen.	Ken Hechler
The bridge of San Luis Rey.	Thornton Wilder
The bridge over the River Kwai.	Pierre Boulle
The bridges at Toko-ri.	James A. Michener
A brief history of the United States.	Franklin Escher Jr.
The brigand.	Giuseppe Berto
Brigands of the moon.	Ray Cummings
Bright feather.	Robert Wilder
Bright phoenix.	Harold Mead
The bright road to fear.	Richard Martin Stern
Bright to the wanderer.	Bruce Lancaster
Bright victory.	Baynard Kendrick
Brighton Rock.	Graham Greene
Bring back her body.	Stuart Brock
Bring 'em back alive.	Edward Anthony Frank Buck
Bring him back dead.	Day Keene
Bring me another corpse.	Peter Rabe
Bring the jubilee.	Ward Moore
The British navy's Air arm.	Owen Rutter
The Broadway butterfly murders.	Tip Bliss
Broadway virgin.	Lois Bull
The broken angel.	Floyd Mahannah
Broken Arrow range.	Thomas W. Blackburn
The broken body.	Floyd Mahannah
The broken doll.	Jack Webb
Broken lance.	Frank Gruber
Broken shield.	Ben Benson
The broken spur.	Dudley Dean
Broken valley.	Thomas Thompson
The broken vase.	Rex Stout
Broken wagon.	Norman A. Fox
Broken Wheel Ranch.	Wayne C. Lee
Bronc buckaroo.	J. Edward Leithead
Broncho Apache.	Paul I. Wellman
The bronze mermaid.	Paul Ernst
Brother Buffalo.	Jefferson McCall
Brother Death.	John Lodwick
Brother Juniper.	Justin McCarthy
Brother of the Cheyennes.	Max Brand
Brother of the Kid.	Paul Evan Lehman
Brother outlaw.	Lee E. Wells
Brother Sebastian.	Chon Day
The brotherhood of velvet.	David Karp
The brothers Karamazov.	Fyodor Dostoyevsky
The brothers Mad.	William M. Gaines
Brothers on the trail.	Max Brand
The brothers Rico.	Georges Simenon
Br-r-r-!	Groff Conklin
Bruegel.	Wolfgang Stechow
The bruiser.	Jim Tully
Brush rider.	Dean Owen
Brutally with love.	Edith Pope
The brute.	Guy des Cars
Brute in brass.	Harry Whittington
Bubu of Montparnasse.	Charles-Louis Philippe
The buccaneer.	R. V. Cassill
Buccaneer surgeon.	C. V. Terry
Buccaneer's blade.	Donald Barr Chidsey
Buchanan gets mad.	Jonas Ward
Buchanan says no.	Jonas Ward
The buckaroo.	Burt Arthur
Buckaroo.	Eugene Cunningham
Buckaroo's code.	Wayne D. Overholser
Buckskin brigade.	Jim Kjelgaard
Buckskin empire.	Harry Sinclair Drago
Buckskin man.	Thomas W. Blackburn
Buckskin marshal.	Will Ermine
Bucky follows a cold trail.	William MacLeod Raine
Buddenbrooks.	Thomas Mann
Buffalo Bill.	Shannon Garst
Buffalo Bill and the Wild West.	Henry Blackman Sell Victor Weybright
The buffalo box.	Frank Gruber
Buffalo wagons.	Elmer Kelton
Bugles and a tiger.	John Masters
Bugles blow no more.	Clifford Dowdey
Bugles in the afternoon.	Ernest Haycox
Bugles in the night.	Arthur Herbert
Bugles on the prairie.	Gordon D. Shirreffs
Bugle's wake.	Curt Brandon
Bugles west.	Frank Gruber
Build my gallows high.	Geoffrey Homes
Build my gallows high.	Roy Sparkia
The build-up boys.	Jeremy Kirk
Built for trouble.	Al Fray
Bulfinch's mythology.	Thomas Bulfinch
Bullet ambush.	William MacLeod Raine
Bullet barricade.	Leslie Ernenwein
Bullet brand.	Hal G. Evarts

C

C.O.D. death.	G. Forbes Durand
The caballero.	Johnston McCulley
Cabbage holiday.	Anthony Thorne
Cabbages and kings.	O. Henry
The cabin in the cotton.	Harry Harrison Kroll
Cabin Road.	John Faulkner
The Cabinda affair.	Matthew Head
Cactus cavalier.	Norman A. Fox
The cactus kid.	Tom West
Caesar's angel.	Mary Anne Amsbary
Cage me a peacock.	Noel Langley
Cage of darkness.	René Masson
Cage of lust.	Allan Seager
The caged.	Fan Nichols
Cain Basin.	Barry Cord
Cain's girl friend.	William Grote
Cairo intrigue.	William Manchester
Cakes and ale.	W. Somerset Maugham
Cakes and ale and other favorites.	W. Somerset Maugham
Calamity fair.	Wade Miller
Calamity Jane of Deadwood Gulch.	Ethel Hueston
Calamity range.	Paul Evan Lehman
Calamity town.	Ellery Queen
The calendar epic.	James Kubeck
Calendar model.	Gloria Gale
Calendar of crime.	Ellery Queen
Calibre.	Irving Shulman
California gunman.	William Colt MacDonald
California passage.	Cliff Farrell
Call for Michael Shayne.	Brett Halliday
Call for the Saint.	Leslie Charteris
The call girl.	Harold Greenwald
Call her savage.	Tiffany Thayer
Call it experience.	Erskine Caldwell
Call it treason.	George Howe
Call me deadly.	Hal Braham
Call me Duke.	Harry Grey
Call me killer.	Max Carter
Call me killer.	Harry Whittington
Call me lucky.	Bing Crosby
Call of the gun.	Samuel A. Peeples
Call of the range.	Arthur Henry Gooden
The call of the wild.	Jack London
Call the lady indiscreet.	Paul Whelton
The called and the chosen.	Monica Baldwin
Calling Doctor Jane.	Adeline McElfresh
The calm man.	David Cort
The calypso murders.	P. J. Mulholland
The camera clue.	George Harmon Coxe
Camille.	Alexandre Dumas fils
The camp followers.	Ugo Pirro
Campaign train.	The Gordons
Campbell's kingdom.	Hammond Innes
Campus joke book.	Eddie Davis
Campus town.	Hart Stilwell

Can can Americana.	Harold Meyers
Can you top this?	Ed Ford et al.
Canal town.	Samuel Hopkins Adams
The canary murder case.	S. S. Van Dine
Cancel all our vows.	John D. MacDonald
Cancelled in red.	Hugh Pentecos
Candidate for love.	Maysie Greig
Candide.	Voltaire
Candlemas Bay.	Ruth Moore
The candy kid.	Dorothy B. Hughes
Cannery Row.	John Steinbeck
Canterbury tales.	Geoffrey Chaucer
Canton barrier.	Andrew Geer
The canvas coffin.	William Campbell Gault
The canvas dagger.	Helen Reilly
The canyon.	Jack Schaefer
Canyon hell.	Peter Dawson
Canyon killers.	Bradford Scott
Canyon of death.	Peter Field
Canyon passage.	Ernest Haycox
The Cape Cod mystery.	Phoebe Atwood Taylor
The captain.	Russell Thacher
Captain Adam.	Donald Barr Chidsey
Captain Barney.	Jan Westcott
Captain Bashful.	Donald Barr Chidsey
Captain Blood.	Rafael Sabatini
Captain Crossbones.	Donald Barr Chidsey
Captain Cut-throat.	John Dickson Carr
Captain Ebony.	Hamilton Cochran
Captain for Elizabeth.	Jan Westcott
Captain from Castile.	Samuel Shellabarger
Captain from Connecticut.	C. S. Forester
Captain Horatio Hornblower.	C. S. Forester
Captain Ironhand.	Rosamond Marshall
Captain Judas.	F. van Wyck Mason
Captain Lightfoot.	W. R. Burnett
Captain Marooner.	Louis B. Davidson Eddie Doherty
Captain McRae.	William Herman
The captain must die.	Robert Colby
Captain Nemesis.	F. van Wyck Mason
Captain of the Medici.	John J. Pugh
Captain Rebel.	Frank Yerby
Captain Seadog.	Jefferson Cooper
Captain Whitecap.	John Clagett
"Captains courageous".	Rudyard Kipling
The captain's doll.	D. H. Lawrence
The captain's lady.	Basil Heatter
The captive.	Norman Daniels
Captive in the night.	Donald Stokes
The captive of the Sahara.	E. M. Hull
The captive witch.	Dale Van Every
The captive women.	Walter D. Edmonds
The captives of Mora Island.	Victor Canning
Car deal!	Frank O'Rourke
The caravan passes.	George Tabori
Caravan to Xanadu.	Edison Marshall

The case of the dark hero. Peter Cheyney

Case of the dark wanton. Peter Cheyney

The case of the dead divorcée. William Holder

Case of the deadly kiss. Milton K. Ozaki

The case of the demure defendant. Erle Stanley Gardner

The case of the drowning duck. Erle Stanley Gardner

The case of the drowsy mosquito. Erle Stanley Gardner

The case of the dubious bridegroom. Erle Stanley Gardner

The case of the empty tin. Erle Stanley Gardner

The case of the fan-dancer's horse. Erle Stanley Gardner

The case of the fiery fingers. Erle Stanley Gardner

The case of the forgotten murder. Erle Stanley Gardner

The case of the fugitive nurse. Erle Stanley Gardner

The case of the gilded lily. Erle Stanley Gardner

The case of the glamorous ghost. Erle Stanley Gardner

The case of the golddigger's purse. Erle Stanley Gardner

The case of the green-eyed sister. Erle Stanley Gardner

The case of the grinning gorilla. Erle Stanley Gardner

The case of the half-wakened wife. Erle Stanley Gardner

The case of the hated senator. Margaret Scherf

The case of the haunted husband. Erle Stanley Gardner

The case of the hesitant hostess. Erle Stanley Gardner

The case of the howling dog. Erle Stanley Gardner

Case of the hypnotized virgin. John Roeburt

The case of the journeying boy. Michael Innes

The case of the lady who took a bath. Alan Hynd

The case of the lame canary. Erle Stanley Gardner

The case of the lazy lover. Erle Stanley Gardner

The case of the little doctor. Hilda Lewis

The case of the lonely heiress. Erle Stanley Gardner

The case of the lucky legs. Erle Stanley Gardner

The case of the lucky loser. Erle Stanley Gardner

The case of the Mexican knife. Geoffrey Homes

The case of the moth-eaten mink. Erle Stanley Gardner

The case of the murdered madame. Henry Kane

The case of the murdered model. Thomas B. Dewey

Case of the murdered redhead. Frances Lockridge Richard Lockridge

The case of the musical cow. Erle Stanley Gardner

The case of the nameless corpse. Clarence Budington Kelland

The case of the negligent nymph. Erle Stanley Gardner

The case of the nervous accomplice. Erle Stanley Gardner

Case of the nervous nude. Jonathan Craig

The case of the one-eyed witness. Erle Stanley Gardner

The case of the perjured parrot. Erle Stanley Gardner

Case of the petticoat murder. Jonathan Craig

Case of the red box. Rex Stout

The case of the restless redhead. Erle Stanley Gardner

The case of the rolling bones. Erle Stanley Gardner

The case of the runaway corpse. Erle Stanley Gardner

The case of the seven sneezes. Anthony Boucher

The case of the shivering chorus girls. James Atlee Phillips

The case of the shoplifter's shoe. Erle Stanley Gardner

The case of the silent partner. Erle Stanley Gardner

The case of the sleepwalker's niece. Erle Stanley Gardner

The case of the smoking chimney. Erle Stanley Gardner

The case of the solid key. Anthony Boucher

The case of the strangled starlet. James Hadley Chase

The case of the stuttering bishop. Erle Stanley Gardner

The case of the substitute face. Erle Stanley Gardner

The case of the sulky girl. Erle Stanley Gardner

The case of the sun bather's diary. Erle Stanley Gardner

The case of the talking bug. The Gordons

Case of the tearless widow. John Roeburt

The case of the terrified typist. Erle Stanley Gardner

The complete stories of Erskine Caldwell.	Erskine Caldwell
Compliments of a fiend.	Fredric Brown
Compulsion.	Meyer Levin
The con man.	Ed McBain
Conan the conqueror.	Robert E. Howard
Concannon.	Frank O'Rourke
Conceived in liberty.	Howard Fast
Conception, pregnancy and birth.	J. D. Ratcliff
Concerning the Saint.	Leslie Charteris
Concho Valley.	Barry Cord
The concise treasury of great poems.	Louis Untermeyer
The concubine.	Michael East
The condemned.	Jo Pagano
Conduct unbecoming.	Charles Fenton
Conducted to a grave.	J. Jerod Chouinard
Confession.	Dorothy Les Tina
The confession and Sight unseen.	Mary Roberts Rinehart
Confessions of a princess.	H.R.H.
Confessions of Felix Krull, confidence man.	Thomas Mann
The confessions of Jean-Jacques Rousseau.	Jean-Jacques Rousseau
The confessions of St. Augustine.	Aurelius Augustinus
Confessors of the Name.	Gladys Schmitt
Confidential.	Donald Henderson Clarke
The confidential agent.	Graham Greene
The conformist.	Alberto Moravia
Congo song.	Stuart Cloete
The Congo Venus.	Matthew Head
Conjugal love.	Alberto Moravia
Conjure wife.	Fritz Leiber
A Connecticut Yankee in King Arthur's court.	Mark Twain
The conquering prince.	Gardner F. Fox
The conqueror.	John Tebbel
Conquest.	Homer Hatten
The conquest of Don Pedro.	Harvey Fergusson
The conquest of happiness.	Bertrand Russell
Conquest of the space sea.	Robert Moore Williams
Conquests of Tamerlane.	Cothburn O'Neal
Conspirator.	Humphrey Slater
The constant nymph.	Margaret Kennedy
The consul at sunset.	Gerald Hanley
Consultation room.	Frederic Loomis
The consumer's guide to better buying.	Sidney Margolius
The Continental Op.	Dashiell Hammett
The continental touch.	Josef Wechsberg
Contraband.	Cleve F. Adams
Contraband rocket.	Lee Correy
Contract bridge for everyone.	Ely Culbertson
Contrary pleasure.	John D. MacDonald
Control high blood pressure and live longer.	Herman Pomeranz
The convertible hearse.	William Campbell Gault.
Cookbook for beginners.	Dorothy Malone
Cookbook of fabulous foods for people you love.	Carolyn Coggins
Cooking for two.	Janet McKenzie Hill
Cop.	Jack Karney
Cop hater.	Ed McBain
Cop killer.	George Bagby
Copperbelt.	Nigel Sligh
Cora Potts.	Ward Greene
Coral and brass.	Percy Finch Holland M. Smith
Coral comes high.	George P. Hunt
Cornbread aristocrat.	Claud Garner
Corner boy.	Herbert Simmons
Cornered.	Louis King
Coromandel!	John Masters
Coronado's children.	J. Frank Dobie
Coroner Creek.	Luke Short
The corpse.	Carter Brown
The corpse awaits.	Owen Fox Jerome
The corpse came calling.	Brett Halliday
A corpse for Christmas.	Henry Kane
The corpse in my bed.	David Alexander
The corpse in the corner saloon.	Hampton Stone
The corpse in the green pajamas.	R. A. J. Walling
The corpse in the guest room.	Clement Wood
The corpse in the snowman.	Nicholas Blake
The corpse in the waxworks.	John Dickson Carr
The corpse next door.	John Farris
Corpse on the town.	John Roeburt
The corpse steps out.	Craig Rice
The corpse that refused to stay dead.	Hampton Stone
The corpse that spoke.	Robert H. Leitfred
The corpse that talked.	Richard Telfair
The corpse that walked.	Octavus Roy Cohen
The corpse who wouldn't die.	Eddie Doherty
The corpse with sticky fingers.	George Bagby
The corpse with the eerie eye.	R. A. J. Walling
The corpse with the floating foot.	R. A. J. Walling
The corpse with the grimy glove.	R. A. J. Walling
The corpse with the listening ear.	Laurence D. Smith

The corpse with the red-headed friend.	R. A. J. Walling
The corpse without a country.	Louis Trimble
Corpus of Joe Bailey.	Oakley Hall
The corrupters.	William Francis
Corruption city.	Horace McCoy
The corsair.	Madeleine Fabiola Kent
Cosmic manhunt.	L. Sprague de Camp
The cosmic puppets.	Philip K. Dick
The cosmic rape.	Theodore Sturgeon
Cosmopolitans.	W. Somerset Maugham
Costigan's needle.	Jerry Sohl
Cottage sinister.	Q. Patrick
Cotton country.	Hubert Creekmore
Cotton moon.	Catherine Tracy
The Cotton Road.	Frank Feuille
Count Bruga.	Ben Hecht
Count five and die.	Barry Wynne
Count me in.	Fan Nichols
The Count of Monte Cristo.	Alexandre Dumas
Counterfeit corpse.	Ferguson Findley
The counterfeit General Montgomery.	M. E. Clifton James
The counterfeit traitor.	Alexander Klein
Counterfeit wife.	Brett Halliday
Counterspy express.	A. S. Fleischman
Counterspy murders.	Peter Cheyney
The country club set.	Otis Carney
Country girl.	Richard McMullen
Country lawyer.	Bellamy Partridge
Country place.	Ann Petry
Courage and confidence from the Bible.	Walter L. Moore
Court martial.	Jack Ehrlich
The court of last resort.	Erle Stanley Gardner
The court of shadows.	Giles Jackson
The courting of Susie Brown.	Erskine Caldwell
Courtroom.	Quentin Reynolds
The courts of the Lion.	Robert W. Krepps
The covered wagon.	Emerson Hough
A cow is too much trouble in Los Angeles.	Joseph Foster
Cow kingdom.	Paul Evan Lehman
Cow thief.	William Colt MacDonald
The cow thief trail.	Bennett Foster
Cowboy.	Clair Huffaker
Cowboy.	Ross Santee
Cowboy, say your prayers!	Will Ermine
Cowdog.	Ned Andrews
Cowhand: the story of a working cowboy.	Fred Gipson
The cowl of doom.	Edward Ronns
Cowpoke justice.	William Hopson
Coyote gulch.	Peter Field
The crack in the picture window.	John Keats
Crack of doom.	Willi Heinrich
Crackers in bed.	Vic Fredericks
Cradle of the sun.	John Clagett
Crazy cartoons by VIP.	Virgil Partch
The crazy kill.	Chester Himes
The crazy mixed-up corpse.	Michael Avallone
Crazy mixed-up kids.	William Hodapp
Crazy weather.	Charles L. McNichols
Cream of the crop.	Ed Ford et al.
The creation of the universe.	George Gamow
The creative process.	Brewster Ghiselin
Creep into thy narrow bed.	Leonard Bishop
Creep, shadow, creep.	A. Merritt
The creepers.	John Creasey
The creeping shadow.	Sam Merwin Jr.
The creeping Siamese.	Dashiell Hammett
The creeps.	Anthony Abbot
Creole woman.	Gardner F. Fox
Crescent carnival.	Frances Parkinson Keyes
Crescent City.	William E. Wilson
Cress Delahanty.	Jessamyn West
Crime and punishment.	Fyodor Dostoyevsky
Crime cop.	Larry Holden
Crime d'amour.	Paul Bourget
Crime hound.	Mary Semple Scott
Crime of violence.	Rufus King
Crime without punishment.	Guenther Reinhardt
Crimes of passion.	Edward D. Radin
The criminal.	Jim Thompson
The criminal C.O.D.	Phoebe Atwood Taylor
The crimson clue.	George Harmon Coxe
The crimson feather.	Sara Elizabeth Mason
The crimson frame.	Aylwin Lee Martin
Crimson Friday.	Dorothy Cameron Disney
The crimson horseshoe.	Peter Dawson
The crimson in the purple.	Holly Roth
Crimson is the eastern shore.	Don Tracy
The crimson quirt.	William Colt MacDonald
Crisis in 2140.	John J. McGuire H. Beam Piper
Crockett's woman.	Eric Hatch
Crome yellow.	Aldous Huxley
The crooked circle.	Manning Lee Stokes
The crooked city.	Robert Kyle
The crooked frame.	William P. McGivern
The crooked hinge.	John Dickson Carr
Crooked house.	Agatha Christie
The crooked man.	Shelley Smith
The crooked mile.	Norbert Fagan
The crooking finger.	Cleve F. Adams
Cropper's cabin.	Jim Thompson
Cross me in gunsmoke.	Clement Hardin
The cross of iron.	Willi Heinrich

A crossbowman's story.   George Millar
The cross-eyed bear
  murders.   Dorothy B. Hughes
Crossfire.   Louis Trimble
Crossfire trail.   Louis L'Amour
The crossing.   Clay Fisher
Crossroads in time.   Groff Conklin
The crossroads of time.   Andre Norton
Crosstown.   John Held Jr.
Crossword puzzles.
Crossword puzzles, book
  two.
Crow killer.   Robert Bunker
                               Raymond Thorp
Crows can't count.   A. A. Fair
The crucible.   Arthur Miller
Crucible.   Ben Ames Williams
Crucibles: the story
  of chemistry.   Bernard Jaffe
The cruel dawn.   Alfred Viazzi
Cruel is the night.   Howard Hunt
The cruel sea.   Nicholas Monsarrat
The cruel tower.   William B. Hartley
The cruiser.   Warren Tute
Crusade in Europe.   Dwight D. Eisenhower
The crust of the earth.   Samuel Rapport
                               Helen Wright
The cry and the covenant.   Morton Thompson
Cry at dusk.   Lester Dent
Cry attack!   John Burgan
Cry baby killer.   Joseph Hilton
Cry blood.   H. Vernor Dixon
Cry, brother, cry.   Jack Karney
Cry, coyote.   Steve Frazee
Cry down the lonely
  night.   Milton White
Cry, flesh.   David Karp
Cry flood!   Ernest Jason
                                 Fredericks
Cry for happy.   George Campbell
Cry hard, cry fast.   John D. MacDonald
Cry horror!   H. P. Lovecraft
A cry in the night.   Whit Masterson
Cry kill.   Wenzell Brown
Cry killer!   Kenneth Fearing
A cry of children.   John Horne Burns
Cry of the flesh.   Richard Himmel
Cry of violence.   Joseph Kessel
Cry passion.   Richard Jessup
Cry plague!   Theodore S. Drachman
Cry scandal.   William Ard
Cry shame!   Katherine Everard
Cry slaughter!   E. K. Tiempo
Cry terror.   Andrew L. Stone
Cry the lonely flesh.   Jesse L. Lasky Jr.
Cry torment.   Victor H. Johnson
Cry tough!   Irving Shulman
Cry viva!   William Hopson
Cry wolf.   Marjorie Carleton
The crying sisters.   Mabel Seeley
The crystal girl.   Stephen Longstreet
Cue for murder.   Matt Bryant

Cue for murder.   Helen McCloy
Cultural patterns and
  technical change.   Margaret Mead
The cultured man.   Ashley Montagu
The Cumberland rifles.   Noel B. Gerson
The cunning and the
  haunted.   Richard Jessup
Cup of gold.   John Steinbeck
Cure your nerves
  yourself.   Louis E. Bisch
The currents of space.   Isaac Asimov
Curse of Texas gold.   Bradford Scott
The curse of the bronze
  lamp.   Carter Dickson
The curse of the Fen.   Brad Levin
Cursed be he who moves
  my bones.   Benn Towers
Curtain for a jester.   Frances Lockridge
                               Richard Lockridge
The curtain never falls.   Joey Adams
Curtains for the copper.   Thomas Polsky
Curtains for the editor.   Thomas Polsky
The curve and the tusk.   Stuart Cloete
Curve ball laughs.   Herman L. Masin
Cut me in.   Jack Karney
The cut of the ax.   Delmar Jackson
The cut of the whip.   Peter Rabe
Cutlass empire.   F. van Wyck Mason
The cycle of American
  literature.   Robert E. Spiller
Cycle of fire.   Hal Clement
Cyrano de Bergerac.   Edmond Rostand

D

The darkening door. — Bill S. Ballinger
The darker brother. — Bucklin Moon
The darker the night. — Herbert Brean
Darkness at noon. — Arthur Koestler
The darkness of love. — Harry Olive
Darkness of slumber. — Rosemary Kutak
The darkness within. — Walter Ericson
The darling buds of May. — H. E. Bates
Darling, I hate you. — T. S. Matthews
Darling, it's death. — Richard S. Prather
Darling, this is death. — Dana Chambers
Date with darkness. — Donald Hamilton
Date with death. — Leslie Ford
Date with death. — Eaton K. Goldthwaite
A date with Dr.
 Guillotine. — Ralpha Johns
Dateline: Paris. — Reynolds Packard
The daughter. — Arthur Markowitz
The daughter of Bugle
 Ann. — MacKinlay Kantor
Daughter of Fu Manchu. — Sax Rohmer
Daughter of strangers. — Elizabeth Boatwright
 Coker
Daughter of the Gold — Corey Ford
 Rush. — Klondy Nelson
The daughter of time. — Josephine Tey
Daughters of Eve.
David Copperfield. — Charles Dickens
David Harum. — Edward Noyes Westcott
Dawn on our darkness. — Emmanuel Roblès
Dawn's early light. — Elswyth Thane
The day after tomorrow. — Robert A. Heinlein
The day Christ died. — Jim Bishop
The day he died. — Lewis Padgett
The day I died. — Lawrence Lariar
Day into night. — David Westheimer
The day Lincoln was shot. — Jim Bishop
Day of infamy. — Walter Lord
Day of the dead. — Bart Spicer
Day of the .44. — Jack Barton
Day of the gun. — Richard Telfair
Day of the harvest. — Helen Upshaw
The day of the locust. — Nathanael West
Day of the outlaw. — Lee E. Wells
Day of the ram. — William Campbell
 Gault
Day of vengeance. — Chuck Martin
The day the money
 stopped. — Brendan Gill
The day the sandman came. — Benn Towers
Daybreak. — Frank G. Slaughter
Daybreak: 2250 A.D. — Andre Norton
Days in the yellow leaf. — William Hoffman
Days of my love. — Leonard Bishop
Dead ahead. — William L. Stuart
Dead and gone. — Brandon Bird
Dead and kicking. — Frank Castle
Dead as a dinosaur. — Frances Lockridge
 Richard Lockridge
Dead as a dummy. — Geoffrey Homes
Dead babes in the wood. — D. B. Olsen

The dead can tell. — Helen Reilly
Dead center. — Mary Collins
The dead darling. — Jonathan Craig
Dead dolls don't talk. — Day Keene
The dead don't care. — Jonathan Latimer
Dead fall. — Dale Wilmer
Dead for a ducat. — Helen Reilly
Dead freight for Piute. — Luke Short
Dead game. — Michael Avallone
Dead giveaway. — Hugh Lawrence Nelson
Dead in bed. — Day Keene
Dead in Texas. — Bradford Scott
Dead lion. — Emery Bonett
 John Bonett
Dead little rich girl. — Norbert Davis
Dead low tide. — John D. MacDonald
Dead man Friday. — J. F. Hutton
Dead Man Pass. — Peter Dawson
Dead man range. — Ernest Haycox
Dead man's diary and
 A taste for cognac. — Brett Halliday
Dead man's diary and
 Dinner at Dupre's. — Brett Halliday
Dead man's folly. — Agatha Christie
Dead man's gift. — Zelda Popkin
Dead man's gold. — William Colt
 MacDonald
Dead man's gorge. — E. B. Mann
Dead man's mirror. — Agatha Christie
Dead man's plans. — Mignon G. Eberhart
Dead man's range. — Tom J. Hopkins
Dead man's saddle. — L. P. Holmes
Dead man's tide. — William Richards
Dead man's trail. — Philip Ketchum
Dead man's trail. — Bradford Scott
The dead men grin. — Bruno Fischer
Dead of night. — Stewart Sterling
Dead of summer. — Dana Mosely
Dead of the night. — John Rhode
Dead on arrival.
Dead on arrival. — George Bagby
Dead on arrival. — Stephen Marlowe
Dead on the level. — Helen Nielsen
Dead or alive. — Max Brand
Dead or alive. — Patricia Wentworth
Dead pigeon. — Robert P. Hansen
Dead reckoning. — Francis Bonnamy
The dead ride hard. — Lynn Westland
The dead ringer. — Fredric Brown
Dead ringer. — James Hadley Chase
Dead, she was beautiful. — Whit Masterson
The dead-shot kid. — Philip Ketchum
Dead stop. — Doris Miles Disney
Dead storage. — George Bagby
Dead sure. — Herbert Brean
Dead sure. — Stewart Sterling
The dead tree gives no
 shelter. — Virgil Scott
Dead warrior. — John Myers Myers
Dead weight. — Frank Kane
Dead weight. — Addison Simmons

Dead wrong.	Larry Holden
Dead wrong.	Stewart Sterling
Dead yellow women.	Dashiell Hammett
Deadlier than the male.	James E. Gunn
Deadline at dawn.	William Irish
Deadline at Durango.	Allan Vaughan Elston
Deadlock.	Ruth Fenisong
Deadly beloved.	William Ard
The deadly boodle.	J. M. Flynn
The deadly chase.	Carter Cullen
The deadly climate.	Ursula Curtiss
The deadly combo.	John Farr
The deadly dames.	Malcolm Douglas
The deadly derringer.	Sam Meriwether
The deadly desire.	Robert Colby
The deadly doll.	Henry Kane
The deadly dove.	Rufus King
Deadly draw.	Lee Floren
The deadly finger.	Henry Kane
The deadly game.	Norman Daniels
Deadly image.	Edmund Cooper
Deadly is the diamond.	Mignon G. Eberhart
The deadly mermaid.	James Atlee Phillips
The deadly Miss Ashley.	Frederick C. Davis
Deadly night call.	William Irish
Deadly nightshade.	Elizabeth Daly
The deadly pavilion.	Hilda Lawrence
The deadly pay-off.	William H. Duhart
The deadly pick-up.	Milton K. Ozaki
The deadly reasons.	Edward D. Radin
The deadly streets.	Harlan Ellison
Deadly summer.	Glenn M. Barns
The deadly sunshade.	Phoebe Atwood Taylor
The deadly truth.	Helen McCloy
Deadly weapon.	Wade Miller
Deadly welcome.	John D. MacDonald
Deadwood.	Walker A. Tompkins
Dealing out death.	W. T. Ballard
Deals with the Devil.	Basil Davenport
Dear Abby.	Abigail Van Buren
Dear, deadly beloved.	John Flagg
Dear doctor.	Juliet Lowell
Dear Hollywood.	Juliet Lowell
Dear sir.	Juliet Lowell
Death about face.	Frank Kane
Death against Venus.	Dana Chambers
Death and taxes.	David Dodge
Death and the dancing footman.	Ngaio Marsh
Death--and the gilded man.	Carter Dickson
Death and the maiden.	Q. Patrick
Death and the naked lady.	John Flagg
Death at flood tide.	Louis A. Brennan
Death at sea.	Richard Sale
Death at the bar.	Ngaio Marsh
Death at the door.	Anthony Gilbert
Death be not proud.	John Gunther
Death before bedtime.	Edgar Box
Death blew out the match.	Kathleen Moore Knight
Death by moonlight.	Michael Innes
Death canyon.	Bradford Scott
Death comes as the end.	Agatha Christie
Death comes to set thee free.	Benn Towers
Death commits bigamy.	James M. Fox
Death cries in the street.	Samuel A. Krasney
The death dealers.	Isaac Asimov
Death demands an audience.	Helen Reilly
Death down East.	Eleanor Blake
Death draws the line.	Jack Iams
Death for a hussy.	Aylwin Lee Martin
Death for dear Clara.	Q. Patrick
Death for Mr. Big.	John Gonzales
Death for sale.	Henry Kane
Death from a top hat.	Clayton Rawson
Death has a past.	Anita Boutell
Death has a small voice.	Frances Lockridge
	Richard Lockridge
Death has deep roots.	Michael Gilbert
Death has many doors.	Fredric Brown
Death has three lives.	Brett Halliday
Death has two faces.	Norman Herries
Death haunts the dark lane.	A. B. Cunningham
Death hitches a ride.	Martin Weiss
Death hits the jackpot.	John Tiger
Death hits the jackpot.	Walter Wager
Death house doll.	Day Keene
Death in a white tie.	Ngaio Marsh
Death in five boxes.	Carter Dickson
Death in four colors.	Brandon Bird
Death in one-two-three.	Robert Abrahams
Death in the air.	Agatha Christie
Death in the back seat.	Dorothy Cameron Disney
Death in the blackout.	Anthony Gilbert
Death in the cards.	Ann T. Smith
Death in the deep South.	Ward Greene
Death in the desert.	Lee E. Wells
Death in the doll's house.	Lawrence Bachmann Hannah Lees
A death in the family.	James Agee
Death in the fifth position.	Edgar Box
Death in the library.	Philip Ketchum
Death in the South Atlantic.	Michael Powell
Death in the stacks.	Max Arthur
Death in the wind.	Edwin Lanham
Death is a cold, keen edge.	Earle Basinsky
Death is a gold coin.	Ruth Fenisong
Death is a lovely dame.	Matthew Blood
Death is a lovely lady.	Ruth Fenisong
Death is a round black ball.	Mike Roscoe
Death is confidential.	Lawrence Lariar
Death is like that.	John Spain
Death is my dancing partner.	Cornell Woolrich
Death is no lady.	M. E. Corne

Death is the last lover. Henry Kane
Death knell. Baynard Kendrick
Death lies deep. William Guinn
Death lifts the latch. Anthony Gilbert
Death lights a candle. Phoebe Atwood Taylor
Death likes it hot. Edgar Box
Death must wait. Don Kingery
Death of a bullionaire. A. B. Cunningham
Death of a doll. Hilda Lawrence
Death of a fool. Ngaio Marsh
Death of a ghost. Margery Allingham
Death of a man. Lael Tucker
  Wertenbaker
Death of a peer. Ngaio Marsh
Death of a postman. John Creasey
Death of a saboteur. Hulbert Footner
Death of a salesman. Arthur Miller
Death of a swagman. Arthur W. Upfield
Death of a tall man. Frances Lockridge
  Richard Lockridge
The death of a worldly
  woman. A. B. Cunningham
Death of an ad man. Alfred Eichler
The death of Hitler's
  Germany. Georges Blond
Death of my aunt. C. H. B. Kitchin
Death on a ferris wheel. Aylwin Lee Martin
Death on Scurvy Street. Ben Ames Williams
Death on the aisle. Frances Lockridge
  Richard Lockridge
Death on the double. Henry Kane
Death on the installment Louis-Ferdinand
  plan.   Céline
Death on the Nile. Agatha Christie
Death on treasure trail. Don Davis
Death over Sunday. James Francis Bonnell
Death rider. J. O. Barnwell
The death riders. Jackson Cole
Death rides the Dondrino. Roe Richmond
Death rides the night. Peter Field
Death rides the Pecos. Davis Dresser
Death sits on the board. John Rhode
Death stalks the range. Brett Rider
Death stops at a
  tourist's camp. Leslie Charteris
Death takes a bow. Frances Lockridge
  Richard Lockridge
Death takes an option. Neil MacNeil
Death takes the bus. Lionel White
Death trap. John D. MacDonald
Death turns the tables. John Dickson Carr
Death walks in marble
  halls. Lawrence G. Blochman
Death warmed over. Mary Collins
Death was the bridegroom. Charles Samuels
Death-watch. John Dickson Carr
Death watch. Alexander Wilson
  Ruth Wilson
Death wears a white
  gardenia. Zelda Popkin
The death wish. Elisabeth Sanxay
  Holding

Death's long shadow. Jay Barbette
Death's lovely mask. John Flagg
The deaths of Lora
  Karen. R. McDougald
Death's sweet song. Clifton Adams
Debutante nurse. Margaret Howe
The deceivers. John D. MacDonald
The deceivers. John Masters
Decision at Broken
  Butte. Harry Sinclair Drago
Decision at Piute
  Wells. Philip Ketchum
Decision at sundown. Michael Carder
The decks ran red. Andrew L. Stone
The decline and fall of
  practically everybody. Will Cuppy
Decoy. Michael Morgan
The decoy. Edward Ronns
Deeds of darkness. Blair Ashton
The deep end. Fredric Brown
The deep end. Owen Dudley
Deep hills. Matt Stuart
Deep is my desire. Ian Gordon
Deep is the night. James Wellard
Deep is the pit. H. Vernor Dixon
The deep range. Arthur C. Clarke
The deep six. Martin Dibner
The Deep South says
  never. John Bartlow Martin
Deep space. Eric Frank Russell
Deep summer. Gwen Bristow
Deep waters. Ruth Moore
Deep West. Ernest Haycox
The deer park. Norman Mailer
Defeat at sea. C. D. Bekker
Defeat in the East. Jürgen Thorwald
Defense will not win
  the war. W. F. Kernan
Defiance mountain. Frank Bonham
Degas. Daniel Catton Rich
Delay en route. Jerry Weil
The delicate ape. Dorothy B. Hughes
The delicate prey. Paul Bowles
Delilah. Marcus Goodrich
Delilah of the back
  stairs. Geoffrey Household
Delinquent! Morton Cooper
The delinquent ghost. Eric Hatch
Deliver us from evil. Thomas A. Dooley
The deliverance of William Brinkley
  Sister Cecilia. Sister Cecilia
Dell book of crossword
  puzzles. Kathleen Rafferty
Dell book of jokes. Frances Cavanah
  Ruth Weir
The Dell bowling Joe Falcaro
  handbook. Murray Goodman
Dell crossword puzzle
  dictionary. Kathleen Rafferty
Dell crossword puzzles. Kathleen Rafferty
Dell crossword puzzles. Rosalind Moore
  Kathleen Rafferty

Diamond Head. Houston Branch / Frank Waters
The diamond hitch. Frank O'Rourke
Diamond in the sky. Mary Orr
Diamond Lil. Mae West
Diamond River range. Eugene Cunningham
Diamonds are forever. Ian Fleming
Diana. Diana Fredericks
Diane. Herbert Best
The diary. William Ard
Diary of a chambermaid. Octave Mirbeau
Diary of a geisha girl. Kimiko Omura / William Vaneer
Diary of a nun. Oscar de Mejo
Diary of a 16-year old French girl. Colette
The diary of a young girl. Anne Frank
Diary of death. Wilson Collison
A diary of love. Maude Hutchins
Diccionario del idioma español. Edwin B. Williams
The dice of God. Hoffman Birney
The dice spelled murder. Al Fray
Dick Tracy and the Woo Woo sisters. Chester Gould
Dictators die hard. Robert A. Levey
A dictionary of American-English usage. Margaret Nicholson
Did she fall? Thorne Smith
Did you kill Mona Leeds? John Roeburt
Die by night. M. S. Marble
Die, damn you! Paul Durst
Die in the saddle. Lincoln Drew
Die, little goose. David Alexander
Die on easy street. James Howard
Die screaming. Jo Pagano
Died in the wool. Ngaio Marsh
The diehard. Jean Potts
The diehards. Dudley Dean
The Diet of Worms. Chevallier de Viande
Diet to suit yourself. Walter Ross
Dig another grave. Don Cameron
Dig me a grave. John Spain
Dig my grave deep. Peter Rabe
Dilemma of the dead lady. William Irish
The dim view. Basil Heatter
A dime a throw. Jerome Weidman
Dining out in any language. Myra Waldo
Dinner at Antoine's. Frances Parkinson Keyes
Dinner at Belmont. Alfred Leland Crabb
Diplomatic corpse. Phoebe Atwood Taylor
Dirty Eddie. Ludwig Bemelmans
The dirty shame. John R. Humphreys
The disappearance. Philip Wylie
Disaster Trail. Al Cody
Disaster valley. Frank C. Robertson
Discover your self! Stephen Lackner
discovery no. 1. John W. Aldridge / Vance Bourjaily

discovery no. 2. Vance Bourjaily
discovery no. 3. Vance Bourjaily
discovery no. 4. Vance Bourjaily
discovery no. 5. Vance Bourjaily
discovery no. 6. Vance Bourjaily
The disenchanted. Budd Schulberg
The disguises of love. Robie Macauley
The dishonest murderer. Frances Lockridge / Richard Lockridge
Dishonor. Gerald Kersh
Dishonor among thieves. Spencer Dean
Dishonorable darling. Wilson Collison
Dishonored flesh. Joseph Pennell
Disposing of Henry. Roger Bax
Disputed passage. Lloyd C. Douglas
District nurse. Faith Baldwin
Diversey. MacKinlay Kantor
The divided path. Nial Kent
Dividend on death. Brett Halliday
Divine mistress. Frank G. Slaughter
The divine passion. Vardis Fisher
The divine romance. Fulton J. Sheen
Divorce. James Warner Bellah
Do evil in return. Margaret Millar
Do it yourself. Morris Brickman
The do-it-yourself gadget hunter's guide. William Manners
Do not disturb. Helen McCloy
Do not murder before Christmas. Jack Iams
Doc Colt. Samuel A. Peeples
Dock walloper. Benjamin Appel
Dr. Anders' dilemma. Henry Lieferant / Sylvia Lieferant
The doctor at Coffin Gap. Les Savage Jr.
The doctor died at dusk. Geoffrey Homes
Doctor Faustus. Christopher Marlowe
Dr. Gatskill's blue shoes. Paul Conant
Doctor Hudson's secret journal. Lloyd C. Douglas
The doctor is a lady. Beth Myers
Doctor Jane. Adeline McElfresh
Dr. Jekyll and Mr. Hyde. Robert Louis Stevenson
Dr. John's decision. Dorothy Worley
Doctor Kim. Lucy Agnes Hancock
The Dr. Lewis affair. Lane Johnstone
Doctor No. Ian Fleming
Dr. Norton's wife. Mildred Walker
The doctor on Bean Street. Simon Kent
Doctor Paradise. Jay J. Dratler
Dr. Parrish, Resident. Sydney Thompson
Dr. Priestley investigates. John Rhode
Doctor Pygmalion. Maxwell Maltz
Dr. Thorndyke's discovery. R. Austin Freeman
Dr. Toby finds murder. Sturges Mason Schley
Doctor Two-Guns. Peter Field

Dragonwyck.   Anya Seton
Dragoon.   Nelson Wolford
  Shirley Wolford
A dram of poison.   Charlotte Armstrong
Draw and die!   Roy Manning
Draw or drag.   Wayne D. Overholser
Draw the curtain close.   Thomas B. Dewey
Drawing self-taught.   Arthur Zaidenberg
Drawn and quartered.   Charles Addams
Drawn conclusion.   W. A. Barber
  R. F. Schabelitz
Drawn to evil.   Harry Whittington
Dread journey.   Dorothy B. Hughes
Dreadful hollow.   Irina Karlova
The dreadful night.   Ben Ames Williams
The dream and the flesh.   Vivian Connell
The dream merchants.   Harold Robbins
Dream of a woman.   Jay J. Dratler
Dream of Eden.   Winston Brebner
Dream of innocence.   Turnley Walker
A dream of kings.   Davis Grubb
The dream peddlers.   Floyd Miller
Dream street.   Robert Sylvester
Dreamboat.   Rick Lucas
The dreamers.   J. Bigelow Clark
Dressed to kill.   Milton K. Ozaki
Drift fence.   Walt Coburn
The drift fence.   Zane Grey
The drifter.   Burt Arthur
The drifters.   Allan R. Bosworth
Drink and be merry.   Lester Grady
Drink to yesterday.   Manning Coles
Drink with the dead.   J. M. Flynn
The drinker.   Hans Fallada
Drinkers of darkness.   Gerald Hanley
Drive to victory.   Robert S. Allen
Driven.   Richard Gehman
The driven flesh.   Lawrence Easton
Droll stories.   Honoré de Balzac
Droodles.   Roger Price
Drop dead!   Gordon Ashe
Drop dead.   George Bagby
The drowning pool.   John Ross Macdonald
The drowning wire.   Marvin Claire
A drum calls west.   Bill Gulick
Drumfire.   Tom J. Hopkins
The Drummond tradition.   Charles Mercer
Drums along the Mohawk.   Walter D. Edmonds
Drums of destiny.   Peter Bourne
Drums of empire.   Robert Carse
The drunk, the damned
  and the bedevilled.   Terence Ford
Drury Lane's last case.   Ellery Queen
Dry bones in the valley.   William MacLeod
  Raine
Drygulch trail.   William MacLeod
  Raine
Duchess Hotspur.   Rosamond Marshall
The Duchess of Malfi.   John Webster
Duel in the sun.   Niven Busch
Duel on the range.   Burt Arthur

Dufy.   Alfred Werner
Duke.   Hal Ellson
Duke Herring.   Maxwell Bodenheim
The duke's temptation.   Paula Batchelor
The dummy murder case.   Milton K. Ozaki
The Duncan Hines
  dessert book.   Duncan Hines
The Dunwich horror.   H. P. Lovecraft
Dupree blues.   Dale Curran
The durable fire.   Howard Swiggett
Dust in the sun.   Jon Cleary
Dust of the trail.   Bennett Foster
Dusty wagons.   Matt Stuart
The Dutch shoe mystery.   Ellery Queen
Dwellers in the mirage.   A. Merritt
The dying earth.   Jack Vance
The dynamics of Soviet
  society.   W. W. Rostow
Dynasty of death.   Taylor Caldwell

E

E pluribus unicorn.	Theodore Sturgeon
ESPer.	James Blish
Each bright river.	Mildred Masterson McNeilly
Each life to live.	Richard Gehman
The eagle and the wind.	Herbert E. Stover
Eagle at my eyes.	Norman Katkov
Eagle in the bathtub.	Jule Mannix
Eagle in the sky.	F. van Wyck Mason
Eagle on his wrist.	Homer Hatten
Early to rise.	Arnold E. Grisman
Earth and high heaven.	Gwethalyn Graham
An earth gone mad.	Roger Dee
The earth in peril.	Donald A. Wollheim
Earth is room enough.	Isaac Asimov
The earth is the Lord's.	Taylor Caldwell
An earth man on Venus.	Ralph Milne Farley
Earth satellites and the race for space superiority.	G. Harry Stine
Earth woman.	Edwin Becker
The earthbreakers.	Ernest Haycox
Earthlight.	Arthur C. Clarke
Earthly creatures.	Charles Jackson
Earthman, come home.	James Blish
Earthshaker.	Robert W. Krepps
East of Eden.	John Steinbeck
East side General.	Frank G. Slaughter
Eastern love.	Edward Powys Mathers
Eastern shame girl and other stories.	
Easy living.	Terence Ford
Easy money.	Frank Peace
Easy to kill.	Agatha Christie
Eat and reduce.	Victor H. Lindlahr
Eat dog or die!	C. William Harrison
Echo in the skull.	John Brunner
Echo of a bomb.	Mark Derby
Echo of evil.	Manuel Komroff
Economics in one lesson.	Henry Hazlitt
Ecstasy girl.	Jack Woodford
Edgar Cayce, mystery man of miracles.	Joseph Millard
Edge of beyond.	James B. Hendryx
The edge of doom.	Leo Brady
Edge of panic.	Henry Kane
Edge of the city.	Frederik Pohl
The edge of the sea.	Rachel L. Carson
Edge of the world.	Vincent McHugh
Edge of time.	David Grinnell
The edge of tomorrow.	Thomas A. Dooley
Edge of twilight.	Paula Christian
The education of a French model.	Kiki
The Eel Pie murders.	David Frome
The egg and I.	Betty MacDonald
The Egyptian.	Mika Waltari
The Egyptian cross mystery.	Ellery Queen
Eight great comedies.	Sylvan Barnet et al.
Eight great tragedies.	Sylvan Barnet et al.
The eight of swords.	John Dickson Carr
The eighth circle.	Stanley Ellin
The eighth day of the week.	Marek Hłasko
The eighth Mrs. Bluebeard.	Hillary Waugh
The 8th Pocket book of crossword puzzles.	Margaret Petherbridge Farrar
The 85 days.	R. W. Thompson
Eisenhower was my boss.	Kay Summersby
Either is love.	Elisabeth Craigin
El Greco.	John F. Matthews
El Paso.	W. Edmunds Claussen
Electronics for everyone.	Monroe Upton
Element of risk.	Mark Derby
Element of shame.	Cicely Schiller
Elephant Bill.	J. H. Williams
Eleven blue men.	Berton Roueché
Eleven of diamonds.	Baynard Kendrick
The eleventh hour.	Robert B. Sinclair
Elinda.	Frances Clippinger
Elisa.	Edmond de Goncourt
Elizabeth and Essex.	Lytton Strachey
The Elkhorn feud.	Philip Ketchum
Ellen Rogers.	James T. Farrell
Ellery Queen's awards: tenth series.	Ellery Queen
Elmer Gantry.	Sinclair Lewis
The eloquence of Winston Churchill.	Winston Churchill
Embarrassment of riches.	Marjorie Fischer
Embezzled heaven.	Franz Werfel
The embezzler.	James M. Cain
Emerson.	Ralph Waldo Emerson
Emerson: the basic writings of America's sage.	Ralph Waldo Emerson
Emma.	Jane Austen
Emma: my Lord Admiral's mistress.	F. W. Kenyon
Emperor Fu Manchu.	Sax Rohmer
The Emperor's physician.	J. R. Perkins
The emperor's snuff-box.	John Dickson Carr
The empire--and Martin Brill.	George deMare
Empire in the changing world.	W. K. Hancock
Empire of the atom.	A. E. van Vogt
Empress of Byzantium.	Helen A. Mahler
Empty saddles.	Al Cody
The empty trap.	John D. MacDonald
The enchanted cup.	Dorothy James Roberts
The enchanted heart.	Marjorie Worthington
Enchanted oasis.	Faith Baldwin
Encore for love.	Katharine Dunlap
End as a man.	Calder Willingham
The end is known.	Geoffrey Holiday Hall
End of a call girl.	William Campbell Gault
End of a war.	Edward Loomis

Eye in the sky.   Philip K. Dick
Eye witness.   George Harmon Coxe
Eyeless in Gaza.   Aldous Huxley

F

The FBI in action.	Ken Jones
F.B.I. story.	The Gordons
The FBI story.	Don Whitehead
F.O.B. murder.	Bert Hitchens
	Dolores Hitchens
Fabia.	Olive Higgins Prouty
The fabulous buccaneer.	Robert Carse
The fabulous clipjoint.	Fredric Brown
The fabulous Finn.	Dan Cushman
Fabulous gunman.	Wayne D. Overholser
Face in the abyss.	A. Merritt
A face in the crowd.	Budd Schulberg
The face in the shadows.	Peter Ordway
Face of a hero.	Louis Falstein
The face of evil.	John McPartland
The face of innocence.	William Sansom
The face of the deep.	Jacob Twersky
The face of time.	James T. Farrell
Faces in the dust.	Paul Evan Lehman
Fact detective mysteries.	W. A. Swanberg
Facts of life and love for teen-agers.	Evelyn Millis Duvall
Fahrenheit 451.	Ray Bradbury
The fair and the bold.	Donn O'Hara
Fair game.	Karl Kramer
Fair in love and war.	Denton Whitson
Fair prey.	Will Duke
A fair wind home.	Ruth Moore
Fair wind to Java.	Garland Roark
Fairoaks.	Frank Yerby
Falcons of France.	James Norman Hall
	Charles Nordhoff
Fall girl.	Richard Deming
The fall guy.	Joe Barry
The fall of night.	Giose Rimanelli
The fall of Suzanne Swift.	V. A. McMillen
The fall of valor.	Charles Jackson
The fallen sparrow.	Dorothy B. Hughes
Falling through space.	Richard Hillary
The falling torch.	Algis Budrys
False face.	Leslie Edgley
False night.	Algis Budrys
The false rider.	Max Brand
False to any man.	Leslie Ford
False witness.	Helen Nielsen
A family affair.	Roger Eddy
Family affair.	Ione Sandberg Shriber
Family honeymoon.	Homer Croy
The family of man.	Edward Steichen
A family party.	John O'Hara
A family romance.	Elizabeth Pollet
Famous American plays of the 20's.	Kenneth MacGowan
Famous artists and their models.	Thomas Craven
Famous Chinese short stories.	Lin Yutang
Fancies and goodnights.	John Collier
The fancy dress party.	Alberto Moravia

Fannie Farmer's handy cook book.	Fannie Farmer
Far and away.	Anthony Boucher
The far call.	Jackson Gregory
The far command.	Elinor Chamberlain
The far country.	Nevil Shute
The far cry.	Fredric Brown
Far, far the mountain peak.	John Masters
Far from customary skies.	Warren Eyster
Far from home.	Richard Mason
The far shore.	Gordon Webber
Fare prey.	Laine Fisher
Fare thee well.	Robert Spafford
Farewell, my lovely.	Raymond Chandler
Farewell, my young lover.	Glenn Scott
A farewell to arms.	Ernest Hemingway
Farewell to sport.	Paul Gallico
The farm.	Louis Bromfield
Farm girl.	William Brown Meloney
Farmer takes a wife.	John Gould
The farmer's bride.	Robert Hazel
The Farmers Hotel.	John O'Hara
The farmhouse.	Helen Reilly
The Faro Kid.	Leslie Ernenwein
The fascinating insect world of J. Henri Fabre.	Edwin Way Teale
The fascination.	Jean Pedrick
The fascinator.	Theodora Keogh
The fashion in shrouds.	Margery Allingham
Fashioned for murder.	George Harmon Coxe
Fast and loose.	Speed Lamkin
The fast buck.	Bruno Fischer
The fast buck.	Ross Laurence
Fast company.	Marco Page
Fast gun.	Walt Coburn
Fast on the draw.	Gordon Young
Fast one.	Paul Cain
Faster reading self-taught.	Harry Shefter
The fastest gun.	Dan Cushman
The fastest gun in Texas.	C. J. LaRoche
	J. H. Plenn
The fastest man alive.	Frank K. Everest Jr.
	John Guenther
The fat boy's book.	Elmer Wheeler
The fatal caress.	Richard Barker
The fatal cast.	Curtiss T. Gardner
The fatal decisions.	Seymour Freidin
	William Richardson
Fatal descent.	Carter Dickson
	John Rhode
The fatal foursome.	Frank Kane
Fatal in furs.	James M. Fox
The fatal kiss mystery.	Rufus King
Fatal step.	Wade Miller
The fate of the immodest blonde.	Patrick Quentin
Father and son.	James T. Farrell

Fire mission.	William P. Mulvihill	Flaming irons.	Max Brand
The fire that burns.	Mark Tryon	The flaming island.	Donald Barr Chidsey
Fire will freeze.	Margaret Millar	Flaming lead.	William Colt
Firebrand.	Tom Gill		MacDonald
The fires of spring.	James A. Michener	Flamingo Road.	Robert Wilder
The fires of youth.	Edward De Roo	Flash Casey, detective.	George Harmon Coxe
Fires that destroy.	Harry Whittington	Flash--hold for murder.	Paul Whelton
First affair.	Raffaele LaCapria	Flee from terror.	Martin Brett
First aid for the		Flee the angry	
ailing house.	Roger B. Whitman	strangers.	George Mandel
The first and the last.	Adolf Galland	Flee the night in anger.	Dan Keller
First blood.	Jack Schaefer	The flesh agents.	Jean Bosquet
The first Christian.	A. Powell Davies	Flesh and fire.	Georges Arnaud
First come, first kill.	Francis Allen	The flesh and Mr.	
First command.	Wade Everett	Rawlie.	Morton Cooper
The first fast draw.	Louis L'Amour	Flesh and the dream.	George Williams
First he died.	Clifford D. Simak	The flesh and the sea.	John Dobbin
The first Lady		The flesh and the	
Chatterley.	D. H. Lawrence	spirit.	Charles Shaw
First love.	Elizabeth Abell	The flesh baron.	P. J. Wolfson
	Joseph I. Greene	The flesh is real.	Irving Shulman
		The flesh merchants.	Bob Thomas
The first men in the		The flesh painter.	Ad Gordon
moon.	H. G. Wells	The flesh peddlers.	Frank Boyd
First on Mars.	Rex Gordon	The flesh was cold.	Bruno Fischer
First on the moon.	Jeff Sutton	Flight.	Edgar Jean Bracco
First on the rope.	R. Frison-Roche	Flight by night.	Day Keene
First person singular.	W. Somerset Maugham	Flight from Natchez.	Frank G. Slaughter
First steps in reading	Christine Gibson	Flight hostess.	Emily Thorne
English.	I. A. Richards	Flight into space.	Jonathan N. Leonard
The first time.	Chandler Brossard	Flight into terror.	Lionel White
First to the stars.	Rex Gordon	Flight nurse.	Adelaide Humphries
First train to Babylon.	Max Ehrlich	Flight of an angel.	Verne Chute
A first workbook of		Flight to darkness.	Gil Brewer
French.	I. A. Richards et al.	Flint.	Gil Dodge
A first workbook of	Christine Gibson	Flood.	David Dempsey
French.	I. A. Richards	Floodtide.	Frank Yerby
Fish the strong waters.	N. C. McDonald	The Florentine dagger.	Ben Hecht
Fistful of death.	Henry Kane	Flower arrangements	
Fit to kill.	Brett Halliday	anyone can do anywhere.	Matilda Rogers
Five acres and		The flower drum song.	C. Y. Lee
independence.	M. G. Kains	Flower painting by the	Margaret Fairbanks
Five against the house.	Jack Finney	great masters.	Marcus
Five alarm funeral.	Stewart Sterling	Flying colours.	C. S. Forester
Five and ten.	John K. Winkler	The flying saucers are	
5:45 to suburbia.	Vin Packer	real.	Donald Keyhoe
Five great comedies.	William Shakespeare	Flying saucers from	
Five great tragedies.	William Shakespeare	outer space.	Donald Keyhoe
Five murderers.	Raymond Chandler	The Flying U strikes.	B. M. Bower
Five nights.	Eric Hatch	The Flying U's last	
Five o'clock surgeon.	Dorothy Pierce Walker	stand.	B. M. Bower
The five pennies.	Grady Johnson	The flying Yorkshireman.	Eric Knight
Five rode West.	Lewis B. Patten	Focus.	Arthur Miller
Five sinister characters.	Raymond Chandler	Focus on murder.	George Harmon Coxe
Five soldiers.	Paul Vialar	Fog.	Dorothy Rice Sims
Five tales from tomorrow.	T. E. Dikty		Valentine Williams
Five who vanished.	Robert Levin	The fog comes.	Mary Collins
The fixers.	Willard Manus	Fog of doubt.	Christianna Brand
Flame of sunset.	L. P. Holmes	Folies-Bergère.	Paul Derval
Flame of the Osage.	Fred Grove	Folk songs of the	
Flame vine.	Helen Topping Miller	Caribbean.	James Morse
The flames of time.	Baynard Kendrick	Follow, as the night.	Pat McGerr
Flaming Canyon.	Walker A. Tompkins		

The Foxes of Harrow.	Frank Yerby
Foxfire.	Anya Seton
Fractured French.	F. S. Pearson II
	R. Taylor
Frail barrier.	Philip Gillon
Framed in blood.	Brett Halliday
Framed in guilt.	Day Keene
The Franchise affair.	Josephine Tey
Francie comes home.	Emily Hahn
Francis.	David Stern
Frankenstein.	Mary Wollstonecraft
	Shelley
Franklin Delano	
Roosevelt: a memorial.	Donald Porter Geddes
Fraulein Lili Marlene.	James Wakefield Burke
Free and easy.	June Wetherell
Free grass.	Ernest Haycox
Free-lance murder.	Vic Rodell
Free lovers.	Jack Woodford
Free ride.	James M. Fox
Free woman.	Katharine Brush
Freedom from money	Martha Patton
worries.	Price A. Patton
Freedom road.	Howard Fast
The freeholder.	Joe David Brown
French and frisky.	René Goscinny
French cartoons.	William Cole
	Douglas McKee
French doctor.	Louis-Charles Royer
French for murder.	Bernard Mara
French girls are vicious.	James T. Farrell
The French impressionists	
and their circle.	Herman J. Wechsler
French key mystery.	Frank Gruber
French postcards.	
The French powder	
mystery.	Ellery Queen
The French quarter.	Herbert Asbury
French stories and tales.	Stanley Geist
French summer.	Guy Gilpatric
French through pictures.	I. A. Richards et al.
French through pictures,	
book 1.	I. A. Richards et al.
The French touch.	Jack Iams
Frenchie.	David Charlson
The Frenchman in	
Mohammed's harem.	Mario Uchard
Frenchman's Creek.	Daphne du Maurier
Frenchman's River.	Will Ermine
Fresh and salt water	
spinning.	Eugene Burns
Fresh water fishing.	Arthur Carhart
Freud: his dream and	
sex theories.	Joseph Jastrow
Freud: his life and	
his mind.	Helen W. Puner
Friday for death.	Lawrence Lariar
Friday the fourteenth.	Benn Towers
Friend or foe?	Oreste Pinto
The friendless one.	Ray Hogan
Fright.	George Hopley
The frightened dove.	Peter Hardin

The frightened fiancée.	George Harmon Coxe
The frightened fingers.	Spencer Dean
The frightened man.	Dana Chambers
The frightened	
millionaire.	Leslie Charteris
The frightened pigeon.	Richard Burke
The frightened stiff.	Kelley Roos
The frightened wife.	Mary Roberts Rinehart
Frisco gal.	Clarkson Crane
The frogmen.	James Gleeson
	T. J. Waldron
From Eve on.	Brant House
From gags to riches.	Joey Adams
From here to eternity.	James Jones
From here to Shimbashi.	John Sack
From medicine man to	
Freud.	Jan Ehrenwald
From outer space.	Hal Clement
From Russia, with love.	Ian Fleming
From the earth to the	
moon and Round the	
moon.	Jules Verne
From the sea and the	
jungle.	Robert Carse
From this dark stairway.	Mignon G. Eberhart
Front for murder.	Guy Emery
Front office.	Herbert Lyons
Frontier.	Marvin De Vries
Frontier.	MacKinlay Kantor
Frontier feud.	Will Cook
Frontier: 150 years	
of the west.	Luke Short
Frontiers in space.	Everett F. Bleiler
	T. E. Dikty
The frontiers of	
astronomy.	Fred Hoyle
The frozen jungle.	Lawrence Earl
The frozen year.	James Blish
Fruit of desire.	Willa Gibbs
The fugitive.	Georges Simenon
The fugitive eye.	Charlotte Jay
The fugitive Romans.	William Murray
Fugitive's canyon.	Hal G. Evarts
Full of life.	John Fante
Fully dressed and in	
his right mind.	Michael Fessier
The fume of poppies.	Jonathan Kozol
Fun for the family.	Jerome S. Meyer
Fun in bed.	Frank Scully
Fun with mathematics.	Jerome S. Meyer
Fun with puzzles.	Joseph Leeming
The fundamentals of	
contract bridge.	Charles H. Goren
The fundamentals of	
fishing and hunting.	Byron Dalrymple
A funeral for Sabella.	Robert Travers
A funeral in Eden.	Paul McGuire
Funerals are fatal.	Agatha Christie
The funhouse.	Benjamin Appel
Funny business.	Charles Preston
Funny cartoons by VIP.	Virgil Partch
Funny side up.	

G

G. I. jokes.	Lou Nielsen
G. I. sketch book.	Aimée Crane
G stands for gun.	Nelson Nye
The G-string murders.	Gypsy Rose Lee
The Gabriel horn.	Felix Holt
The gadget maker.	Maxwell Griffith
Gag writer's private joke book.	Eddie Davis
Gal young 'un.	Marjorie Kinnan Rawlings
The galactic breed.	Leigh Brackett
Galactic cluster.	James Blish
Galatea.	James M. Cain
Galaxy of ghouls.	Judith Merril
Gale warning.	Hammond Innes
The Galileans.	Frank G. Slaughter
The gallery.	John Horne Burns
A gallery of Americans.	Frank Luther Mott
Gallery of women.	Bernard Glemser
Galloping broncos.	Max Brand
The gallows in my garden.	Richard Deming
Gallows trail.	Garth Davis
The gambler.	Max Brand
The gambler.	William Krasner
Gambler's gold.	Peter Field
Gambler's gun luck.	Brett Austin
Gambling man.	Clifton Adams
The gamecock murders.	Frank Gruber
Gandhi: his life and message for the world.	Louis Fischer
Gang girl.	Wenzell Brown
Gang rumble.	Edward Ronns
The gangs of New York.	Herbert Asbury
Gaptown law.	Louis Trimble
Gardening.	Montague Free
The gashouse gang.	J. Roy Stockton
Gas-house McGinty.	James T. Farrell
Gateway to elsewhere.	Murray Leinster
The gathering darkness.	Thomas Gallagher
Gauguin.	John Rewald
The gaunt woman.	Edmund Gilligan
The gay bandit of the border.	Tom Gill
Gay ghastly holiday.	Sebastian Blayne
The gelignite gang.	John Creasey
A gem of a murder.	Carleton Keith
The general.	C. S. Forester
The general.	Karlludwig Opitz
General Billy Mitchell.	Roger Burlingame
The general died at dawn.	Charles G. Booth
A general introduction to psychoanalysis.	Sigmund Freud
The general's wench.	Rosamond Marshall
Generation of vipers.	Philip Wylie
Genghis Khan.	Harold Lamb
The genius and the goddess.	Aldous Huxley
Gentle Annie.	MacKinlay Kantor
The gentle hangman.	James M. Fox
The gentle infidel.	Lawrence Schoonover

A gentle murderer.	Dorothy Salisbury Davis
The gentleman.	Edison Marshall
The gentleman in the parlour.	W. Somerset Maugham
Gentleman ranker.	John Jennings
The gentleman rogue.	Gardner F. Fox
Gentleman's agreement.	Laura Z. Hobson
Gentlemen of the jungle.	Tom Gill
Gentlemen prefer blondes.	Anita Loos
Gentlemen prefer corpses.	Max Arthur
George Washington.	W. E. Woodward
Georgia boy.	Erskine Caldwell
Georgia girl.	Bart Frame
Georgia girl.	Margaret Rebecca Lay
Georgia hotel.	Scott Laurence
Georgie May.	Maxwell Bodenheim
Geraldine Bradshaw.	Calder Willingham
The German generals talk.	B. H. Liddell Hart
The German raider Atlantis.	Wolfgang Frank Bernhard Rogge
German stories and tales.	Robert Pick
German through pictures.	I. A. Richards et al.
German through pictures, book 1.	I. A. Richards et al.
Germinie.	Edmond de Goncourt Jules de Goncourt
Gestalt psychology.	Wolfgang Köhler
Gestapo.	Edward Crankshaw
Get out of town.	Paul Connolly
The getaway.	Jim Thompson
Getting along in French.	John Fisher Mario Pei
Getting along in German.	Mario Pei Robert Politzer
Getting along in Italian.	Mario Pei
Getting along in Spanish.	Mario Pei Eloy Vaquero
A ghost at noon.	Alberto Moravia
Ghost gold.	Tom West
Ghost of a chance.	Kelley Roos
The ghost patrol and other stories.	Sinclair Lewis
A ghost town on the Yellowstone.	Elliot Paul
Ghostly hoofbeats.	Norman A. Fox
Giant.	Edna Ferber
Giant mystery reader.	
Gideon of Scotland Yard.	J. J. Marric
Gideon's month.	J. J. Marric
Gideon's night.	J. J. Marric
Gidget.	Frederick Kohner
A gift from the boys.	Art Buchwald
Gift from the sea.	Anne Morrow Lindbergh
The gift horse.	Frank Gruber
The gifted.	Roswell G. Ham Jr.
The gifted sinners.	Roswell G. Ham Jr.

Gigi and Julie de
  Carneilhan.   Colette
Gil Paust's gun book.   Gil Paust
Gilbert and Sullivan   William Schwenck
  operas.   Gilbert
                        Arthur Sullivan
The gilded hearse.   Charles Gorham
The gilded hideaway.   Peter Twist
The Gilded Rooster.   Richard Emery Roberts
The gin palace.   Émile Zola
Gina.   George Albert Glay
The ginger man.   J. P. Donleavy
Ginny.   Morton Cooper
Giovanni's room.   James Baldwin
A girl, a man and a   John Hawkins
  river.   Ward Hawkins
The girl beneath the   André Pieyre de
  lion.   Mandiargues
The girl cage.   Charles Mergendahl
A girl for Danny.   William Ard
The girl from Easy
  Street.   Richard Foster
The girl from Frisco.   William Heuman
The girl from Hateville. Gil Brewer
The girl from nowhere.   Rae Foley
The girl from Rome.   Michel Durafour
Girl from town.   Jack Sheridan
The girl he left behind. Marion Hargrove
Girl in a jam.   James Savage
A girl in every port.   Donald R. Morris
The girl in his past.   Georges Simenon
The girl in lover's lane. Charles Boswell
                        Lewis Thompson
The girl in Murder Flat. Mel Heimer
The girl in Poison   Jim Bishop
  Cottage.   Richard H. Hoffmann
The girl in the belfry.   Joseph Henry Jackson
                        Lenore Glen Offord
The girl in the cage.   Ben Benson
The girl in the cop's
  pocket.   Robert Turner
The girl in the death
  cell.   Fred J. Cook
The girl in the dogwood
  cabin.   Calder Willingham
The girl in the frame.   William Fuller
The girl in the Freudian
  slip.   William F. Brown
The girl in the house   Charles Samuels
  of hate.   Louise Samuels
Girl in the red dress.   Richard Cargoe
The girl in the red
  jaguar.   Jason Manor
The girl in the red
  velvet swing.   Charles Samuels
The girl in the spike-
  heeled shoes.   Martin Yoseloff
The girl in the   Charles Boswell
  stateroom.   Lewis Thompson
The girl in 304.   Harold R. Daniels
Girl meets body.   Jack Iams

The girl of the Roman
  night.   Dante Arfelli
The girl on Crown
  Street.   David Karp
Girl on the beach.   George Sumner Albee
The girl on the couch.   Georgiana Hunter
The girl on the gallows. Q. Patrick
The girl on the left
  bank.   Joan Shepherd
The girl on the lonely
  beach.   Fred J. Cook
Girl on the loose.   G. G. Fickling
Girl on the prowl.   G. G. Fickling
Girl on the run.   Edward S. Aarons
The girl on the Via
  Flaminia.   Alfred Hayes
Girl out back.   Charles Williams
Girl running.   Adam Knight
The girl who kept
  knocking them dead.   Hampton Stone
The girl with no place
  to hide.   Nick Quarry
The girl with the
  frightened eyes.   Lawrence Lariar
The girl with the
  glass heart.   Daniel Stern
The girl with the
  golden eyes.   Honoré de Balzac
The girl with the
  golden yo-yo.   Edmund Schiddel
The girl with the
  hungry eyes.
The girl with the   Charles Boswell
  scarlet brand.   Lewis Thompson
The girl with the
  swansdown seat.   Cyril Pearl
Les girls.   Constance Tomkinson
Girls--for men only.   John Paul Adams
The girls from
  Goldfield.   Jacquin Sanders
The girls from Planet 5. Richard Wilson
The girls in Nightmare   Charles Boswell
  House.   Lewis Thompson
The girls in 3-B.   Valerie Taylor
The girls of
  Sanfrediano.   Vasco Pratolini
Girls on parole.   Katherine Sullivan
The girls on the 10th
  floor.   Steve Allen
Give a man a gun.   John Creasey
Give a man a gun.   Leslie Ernenwein
Give and take.   Thomas H. Raddall
Give 'em the ax.   A. A. Fair
Give love the air.   Faith Baldwin
Give me a little
  something.   William L. Rohde
Give me possession.   Paul Horgan
Give me your love.   Jerome Weidman
Give the little corpse
  a great big hand.   George Bagby
Give us this day.   Sidney Stewart

Giveaway.   Steve Fisher
The gladiator.   Thames Williamson
Gladiator.   Philip Wylie
Gladiator-at-law.   C. M. Kornbluth
                                    Frederik Pohl
The gladiators.   Arthur Koestler
Glamor girls.   Don Flowers
The glass harp.   Truman Capote
The glass harp and
  A tree of night.   Truman Capote
The glass key.   Dashiell Hammett
The glass ladder.   Paul W. Fairman
The glass lady.   Asa Bordages
The glass mask.   Lenore Glen Offord
The glass playpen.   Edwin Fadiman Jr.
The glass room.   Lester Fuller
                                    Edwin Rolfe
The glass triangle.   George Harmon Coxe
The glass village.   Ellery Queen
Glitter.   A. B. Shiffrin
The glitter and the
  greed.   Robert W. Taylor
The glorious pool.   Thorne Smith
The glorious three.   June Wetherell
The glory jumpers.   Delano Stagg
The gloved hand.   Leigh Bryson
Go.   Clellon Holmes
Go down to glory.   Richard Warren Hatch
Go for the body.   Ed Lacy
Go for your gun.   Coe Williams
Go home, stranger.   Charles Williams
Go, man, go!   Edward De Roo
Go, man, go.   Edgar Williams
                                    Dave Zinkoff

Go tell it on the
  mountain.   James Baldwin
Go to sleep, Jeannie.   Thomas B. Dewey
Goat Island.   William Fuller
The goblin market.   Helen McCloy
God and my country.   MacKinlay Kantor
God has a long face.   Robert Wilder
God is late.   Christine Arnothy
God is my co-pilot.   Robert L. Scott Jr.
The god of channel 1.   Donald Stacy
The God that failed.   Richard Crossman
God wears a bow tie.   Lyle Stuart
Gods and demons.   Manuel Komroff
Gods and goddesses in
  art and legend.   Herman J. Wechsler
God's angry man.   Leonard Ehrlich
Gods, heroes and men of
  ancient Greece.   W. H. D. Rouse
God's little acre.   Erskine Caldwell
God's men.   Pearl S. Buck
God's wonderful world.   Agnes Leckie Mason
                                    Phyllis Brown Chanian
Gold.   Clarence Budington
                                      Kelland
Gold at Kansas Gulch.   Steve Frazee
Gold Brick Cassie.   David Loth
Gold brick range.   Allan Vaughan Elston
Gold comes in bricks.   A. A. Fair

Gold diggers.   Lois Bull
Gold for my fair lady.   Sidney H. Courtier
Gold for the gay
  masters.   Harriet Gray
Gold in the sky.   Max Catto
Gold Medal treasury of
  American verse.   John Gilland Brunini
Gold of Smoky Mesa.   Johnston McCulley
The gold of their
  bodies.   Charles Gorham
Gold on the hoof.   Walker A. Tompkins
Gold town gunman.   Ray Townsend
Gold under Skull Peak.   Frank O'Rourke
Golden Admiral.   F. van Wyck Mason
The golden apples of
  the sun.   Ray Bradbury
The golden Argosy.   Van H. Cartmell
                                    Charles Grayson

The golden ass of
  Apuleius.   Apuleius Madaurensis
The golden bawd.   Giles A. Lutz
The golden blade.   John Clou
The golden box.   Frances Crane
The golden couch.   Henry Lewis Nixon
The golden door.   Bart Spicer
The golden eagle.   Noel Gerson
The golden eagle.   John Jennings
Golden earrings.   Yolanda Foldes
The golden egg.   James Pollak
The golden exile.   Lawrence Schoonover
The golden frame.   Joseph Chadwick
The golden fury.   Marian Castle
Golden girl.   Kim Darien
The golden gizmo.   Jim Thompson
The golden hawk.   Frank Yerby
The golden herd.   Curt Carroll
The golden hussy.   Octavus Roy Cohen
The golden isle.   Frank G. Slaughter
The golden journey.   Agnes Sligh Turnbull
The golden jungle.   William Howard Harris
The golden kazoo.   John G. Schneider
The golden lure.   Michael Barrett
The golden ones.   C. V. Terry
The golden princess.   Alexander Baron
The golden road.   Peter Bourne
The golden salamander.   Victor Canning
The golden sleep.   Vivian Connell
The golden sorrow.   Theodore Pratt
The golden spiders.   Rex Stout
The golden spike.   Hal Ellson
The golden swan murder.   Dorothy Cameron
                                      Disney
The golden temptress.   Charles Grayson
The golden touch.   Al Dewlen
The golden treasury.   F. T. Palgrave
                                    Oscar Williams
The golden urge.   Robert Kyle
The golden violet.   Joseph Shearing
The golden widow.   Floyd Mahannah
The golden wildcat.   Margaret Widdemer
The golden woman.   Eric Hatch
The goldfish murders.   Will Mitchell

Gone to earth.   Mary Webb
Gone to Texas.   Leo Margulies
Gone to Texas.   J. W. Thomason Jr.
Gone with the wind.   Margaret Mitchell
Good deeds must be
  punished.   Irving Shulman
The good earth.   Pearl S. Buck
Good for a laugh.   Bennett Cerf
The Good housekeeping
  book of baby and
  child care.   L. Emmett Holt Jr.
Good housekeeping's
  the better way.
Good is for angels.   Christopher Clark
Good listening.   R. D. Darrell
Good luck to the corpse.   Max Murray
A good man.   Jefferson Young
A good man is hard to
  find.   Flannery O'Connor
Good morning, Miss Dove.   Frances Gray Patton
Good night, sailor.   J. Inchardi
Good night, sheriff.   Harrison R. Steeves
Good night, sweet prince.   Gene Fowler
Good reading.
The good shepherd.   C. S. Forester
The good soldier Schweik.   Jaroslav Hasek
Good-time girl.   Conrad Maine
A good time man.   E. P. Keating
Good-by to gunsmoke.   Ralph Catlin
Goodbye, Mr. Chips.   James Hilton
Goodbye to Berlin.   Christopher Isherwood
A goodly heritage.   Mary Ellen Chase
The goose is cooked.   Emmett Hogarth
Goren presents the
  Italian bridge system.   Charles H. Goren
The gorgeous ghoul
  murder case.   Dwight V. Babcock
Government is your
  business.   James Keller
Governor's choice.   Martin Mayer
The gown of glory.   Agnes Sligh Turnbull
Goya.   Frederick S. Wight
Grab your socks.   Shel Silverstein
The Gracious Lily affair.   F. van Wyck Mason
A gradual joy.   Alma Routsong
Graduate nurse.   Lucy Agnes Hancock
Graf Spee.   Dudley Pope
Grand canary.   A. J. Cronin
Grand hotel.   Vicki Baum
Grand Mesa.   Allan Vaughan Elston
The grand portage.   Walter O'Meara
The grand seduction.   Marcel Aymé
Grandfather stories.   Samuel Hopkins Adams
The grandmothers.   Glenway Wescott
Grant of kingdom.   Harvey Fergusson
Grant of land.   Lucile Finlay
The grapes of wrath.   John Steinbeck
Grass greed.   Glenn Balch
The grass is always
  greener.   George Malcolm-Smith
The grass is singing.   Doris Lessing
Grave danger.   Frank Kane

The grave gentlemen.   Ralpha Johns
The graveyard reader.   Groff Conklin
A graveyard to let.   Carter Dickson
The gray flannel shroud.   Henry Slesar
Gray wolf.   Rutherford Montgomery
Great American short   Mary Stegner
  stories.   Wallace Stegner
Great American sports
  humor.   Mac Davis
The great Balsamo.   Maurice Zolotow
Great black Kanba.   Constance Little
                                Gwenyth Little
The great captains.   Henry Treece
Great cases in
  psychoanalysis.   Harold Greenwald
Great circle.   Robert Carse
Great day in the
  morning.   Robert Hardy Andrews
The great days.   John Dos Passos
The great debauch.   Williams Forrest
Great dialogues of
  Plato.   Plato
Great dog stories.   Stanley Kauffmann
Great English short
  stories.   Christopher Isherwood
Great escapes.   Basil Davenport
Great essays.   Houston Peterson
Great essays in science.   Martin Gardner
Great expectations.   Charles Dickens
Great flying stories.   Frank W. Anderson Jr.
The great Gatsby.   F. Scott Fitzgerald
The great Houdini.   Samuel Epstein
                                Beryl Williams
The great I am.   Lewis Graham
The great impersonation.   E. Phillips Oppenheim
Great Italian short
  stories.   Pier Pasinetti
The great locomotive
  chase.   MacLennan Roberts
The great mail robbery.   Clarence Budington
                                  Kelland
The great man.   Al Morgan
The great mistake.   Mary Roberts Rinehart
The great mouthpiece.   Gene Fowler
Great murder stories.
The great ones.   Ralph Ingersoll
The great Pierpont
  Morgan.   Frederick Lewis Allen
The great Prince Shan.   E. Phillips Oppenheim
The great rascal.   Jay Monaghan
The great religions by   Tynette Hills
  which men live.   Floyd H. Ross
Great Russian short
  stories.   Norris Houghton
Great scenes from
  great novels.   Robert Terrall
Great sea stories.   Alan Villiers
Great sea stories of
  modern times.   William McFee
Great short stories.   Guy de Maupassant
The great short stories
  of John O'Hara.   John O'Hara

The great short stories of Robert Louis Stevenson. Robert Louis Stevenson
The great Smith. Edison Marshall
The great snow. Henry Morton Robinson
Great son. Edna Ferber
Great sports stories. Herman L. Masin
Great stories by Chekhov. Anton Chekhov
Great stories from the Saturday evening post. Ben Hibbs
Great stories from the Saturday evening post, 1947. Ben Hibbs
Great tales and poems. Edgar Allan Poe
Great tales of action and adventure. George Bennett
Great tales of city dwellers. Alex Austin
Great tales of fantasy and imagination. Philip Van Doren Stern
Great tales of the deep South.
Great tales of the Far West. Alex Austin
A great time to be alive. Harry Emerson Fosdick
Great true adventures. Lowell Thomas
Great western stories. William Targ
The great world and Timothy Colt. Louis Auchincloss
Great writings of Goethe. Johann Wolfgang von Goethe
The greater glory. Lester Gorn
The greatest book ever written. Fulton Oursler
The greatest faith ever known. Fulton Oursler
The greatest lover in the world. Alex Austin
The greatest story ever told. Fulton Oursler
Greek civilization and character. Arnold J. Toynbee
The Greek coffin mystery. Ellery Queen
The Greek experience. C. M. Bowra
Greek historical thought. Arnold J. Toynbee
The Greek philosophers. Rex Warner
The Greek way to western civilization. Edith Hamilton
The green bay tree. Louis Bromfield
Green centuries. Caroline Gordon
The green cockade. Frederic F. Van de Water
The green death. Brett Hutton
Green Dolphin street. Elizabeth Goudge
Green fire. Peter Rainier
The green flames. Marcos Spinelli
Green for a grave. Manning Lee Stokes
The green girl. Jack Williamson
Green hills of Africa. Ernest Hemingway
The green hills of earth. Robert A. Heinlein
Green light. Lloyd C. Douglas

Green light for death. Frank Kane
Green mansions. W. H. Hudson
The green millenium. Fritz Leiber
The green odyssey. Philip José Farmer
The green queen. Margaret St. Clair
Green shiver. Clyde B. Clason
The green turtle mystery. Ellery Queen Jr.
The green years. A. J. Cronin
The Greene murder case. S. S. Van Dine
Greenmantle. John Buchan
Greenmask. Jefferson Farjeon
Gretta. Erskine Caldwell
Gridiron challenge. Jackson Scholz
The grim canyon. Ernest Haycox
Grin and bear it. George Lichty
The Grindle nightmare. Q. Patrick
The gringo bandit. William Hopson
Gringo guns. Peter Field
The grinning gismo. Samuel W. Taylor
The groom lay dead. George Harmon Coxe
Grounds for divorce. Jack Woodford
Grounds for murder. John Appleby
A grove of fever trees. Daphne Rooke
The groves of desire. Nathaniel Norsen Weinreb
Growing up in New Guinea. Margaret Mead
The growth of physical science. James Jeans
Guadalcanal diary. Richard Tregaskis
Guaracha Trail. George Parker
Guard of honor. James Gould Cozzens
Guardians of the desert. Tom Gill
Guardians of the trail. Jackson Gregory
Guerrilla warfare. Bert "Yank" Levy
The guests of fame. Daniel Stern
Guestward ho! Patrick Dennis
                                Barbara Hooton
A guide to better living. N. H. Mager
                                S. K. Mager
Guideposts. Norman Vincent Peale
The guilty are afraid. James Hadley Chase
The guilty bystander. Mike Brett
Guilty bystander. Wade Miller
Gulf coast girl. Charles Williams
Gulf coast stories. Erskine Caldwell
Gulliver's travels. Jonathan Swift
The gun. C. S. Forester
Gun-blaze. Jackson Cole
Gun bulldogger. Eugene Cunningham
Gun chance. Ford Pendleton
Gun code. Philip Ketchum
The gun-crasher. William L. Rohde
Gun devil! W. Edmunds Claussen
Gun feud. W. C. Tuttle
Gun feud at Stampede Valley. Samuel A. Peeples
Gun fight at Horsethief range. B. M. Bower
A gun for Billy Reo. C. Hall Thompson
A gun for Honey. G. G. Fickling

Gun for sale.	Lee E. Wells
Gun hand.	Cliff Farrell
Gun hand.	Frank O'Rourke
Gun harvest.	Oscar J. Friend
Gun hawk.	Leslie Ernenwein
Gun hawk.	Ed Earl Repp
Gun hell.	Riley Ryan
The gun-hung men.	Leslie Ernenwein
Gun in his hand.	Jack Barton
A gun in his hand.	Victor Rosen
Gun in the valley.	Dudley Dean
Gun law.	Philip Ketchum
Gun law.	Bradford Scott
Gun law at Vermillion.	Matt Stuart
Gun lightning!	Steve Thurman
Gun play at the X-Bar-X.	Burt Arthur
Gun-play in Killer Canyon.	Tevis Miller
Gun proud.	Lewis B. Patten
Gun-quick.	Nelson Nye
Gun-runners.	Jackson Cole
Gun showdown.	William MacLeod Raine
Gun shy.	Dudley Dean
	Les Savage Jr.
Gun smoke showdown.	Matt Stuart
Gun smoke yarns.	Gene Autry
Gun talk.	Ernest Haycox
Gun talk at Yuma.	Frank Castle
The gun tamer.	Max Brand
Gun the man down.	Giles A. Lutz
Gun town.	Jackson Cole
The gun trail.	H. A. DeRosso
Gun trail.	Mack Saunders
Gun-whipped!	Paul Evan Lehman
Gunfight at the O.K. Corral.	
Gunfighter.	Paul Craig
Gunfighter brand.	Nelson Nye
Gunfighter breed.	Nelson Nye
Gunfighter from Montana.	Lewis Ford
Gunfighters pay.	William Hopson
Gunfighter's return.	Leslie Ernenwein
Gunfighter's return.	Ben Smith
Gunfire at Salt Fork.	William Hopson
Gunfire man.	Philip Ketchum
Gunfire men.	L. L. Foreman
Gunflame.	John S. Daniels
The gunhand.	Paul Evan Lehman
Gunhand from Texas.	William Heuman
Gunhand's pay.	Archie Joscelyn
Gunhawk harvest.	Leslie Ernenwein
Gunlock.	Wayne D. Overholser
Gunman brand.	Thomas Thompson
Gunman from Texas.	Todhunter Ballard
A gunman rode north.	William Hopson
Gunman's chance.	Luke Short
Gunman's creed.	L. P. Holmes
Gunman's gamble.	Jack M. Bickham
Gunman's gold.	Max Brand
Gunman's gold.	Johnston McCulley
Gunman's grudge.	George C. Appell

Gunman's land.	
Gunman's legacy.	Evan Evans
Gunman's spawn.	Ben Thompson
Gunmaster.	Ford Pendleton
Gunmen's grass.	Lewis Ford
Gunner Cade.	Cyril Judd
Gunning for trouble.	L. L. Foreman
Gunplay valley.	Joseph Wayne
Gunpoint!	John L. Shelley
The gunpointer.	Dean Owen
Gunpowder lightning.	Bertrand W. Sinclair
Guns along the Arrowhead.	Lee Floren
Guns along the Chisholm.	Will C. Brown
Guns along the Pecos.	Lee Floren
Guns along the Wickiup.	D. B. Newton
Guns along the Yellowstone.	Bliss Lomax
Guns and hunting.	Pete Brown
Guns at Broken Bow.	William Heuman
Guns between suns.	William Colt MacDonald
Guns blaze at sundown.	Al Cody
Guns blaze on Spiderweb range.	Walt Coburn
Guns from Powder Valley.	Peter Field
Guns in the saddle.	Peter Field
Guns in the valley.	William Byron Mowery
Guns of Abilene.	James B. Chaffin
Guns of Arizona.	Charles N. Heckelmann
Guns of Arizona.	Nelson Nye
Guns of Chickamauga.	Richard O'Connor
Guns of Circle 8.	Jeff Cochran
The guns of Fort Petticoat.	C. William Harrison
The guns of Hammer.	Barry Cord
Guns of Hell Valley.	John Prescott
Guns of Horse Prairie.	Nelson Nye
Guns of Mist River.	Jackson Cole
The guns of Navarone.	Alistair MacLean
Guns of North Texas.	Will Cook
Guns of Rio Conchos.	Clair Huffaker
Guns of the Arrowhead.	Gordon Young
Guns of the Barricade bunch.	Philip Ketchum
Guns of the frontier.	William MacLeod Raine
Guns of the lawless.	Todhunter Ballard
Guns of the timberlands.	Louis L'Amour
Guns of the Tom Dee and The valley of the Rogue.	Ernest Haycox
Guns of vengeance.	Jim O'Mara
The guns of Witchwater.	Colby Wolford
Guns on the Cimarron.	Allan Vaughan Elston
Guns on the high mesa.	Arthur Henry Gooden
Guns on the Santa Fe.	Peter Dawson
Guns up.	Ernest Haycox
Gunshot empire.	Lee E. Wells
Gunshot trail.	Nelson Nye
Gunsight.	Frank Gruber
Gunsight Pass.	William MacLeod Raine

Gunsight Range.   William Colt
                            MacDonald
Gunsight showdown.   Johnston McCulley
Gunsight trail.   Alan LeMay
The gunslammer.   Lee Floren
The gunslingers.   Harry Widmer
Gunsmoke.   Leslie Ernenwein
Gunsmoke.   Don Ward
Gunsmoke and trail dust. Bliss Lomax
Gunsmoke at Buffalo
  Basin.   Paul Evan Lehman
Gunsmoke empire.   Lewis B. Patten
Gunsmoke gold.   Tom West
Gunsmoke graze.   Peter Dawson
Gunsmoke in Nevada.   Burt Arthur
Gunsmoke justice.   Louis Trimble
Gunsmoke kingdom.   Paul Evan
Gunsmoke men.   L. L. Foreman
Gunsmoke mesa.   Dan James
Gunsmoke on the mesa.   Davis Dresser
Gunsmoke over Big Muddy. Frank O'Rourke
Gunsmoke over Sabado.   Paul Evan
Gunsmoke over Texas.   Bradford Scott
Gunsmoke reckoning.   Joseph Chadwick
Gunsmoke trail.   Jackson Cole
The gunsmoke trail.   Barry Cord
Gunsmoke trail.   William MacLeod Raine
Gunsmoke vengeance.   Johnston McCulley
Gunswift.   Jack Byrne
Gunswift.   Stewart Gordon
Gunthrower.   William Hopson
The gunthrowers.   Steve Frazee
Gus the Great.   Thomas W. Duncan
The guy from Coney
  Island.   Jack Hanley
Guys and dolls.   Damon Runyon
Gypsy.   Gypsy Rose Lee
Gypsy sixpence.   Edison Marshall

H

H as in hunted.	Lawrence Treat
H is for heroin.	David Hulburd
H. M. Pulham, Esq.	John P. Marquand
H.M.S. Ulysses.	Alistair MacLean
Hag's nook.	John Dickson Carr
The hair-trigger kid.	Max Brand
Half.	Jordan Park
Half angel.	Fanny Heaslip Lea
Halfway down the stairs.	Charles Thompson
Halfway house.	Ellery Queen
Halfway to heaven.	Terrance Flair
Halfway to hell.	Harry Whittington
Halfway to timberline.	Ward West
Halo for a heel.	Mike Skelly
A halo for nobody.	Henry Kane
Halo for Satan.	John Evans
Halo in blood.	John Evans
Halo in brass.	John Evans
Hamlet.	William Shakespeare
Hammer me home.	Richard R. Werry
The Hammersmith murders.	David Frome
Hammett homicides.	Dashiell Hammett
The hand in the cobbler's safe.	Seth Bailey
The hand in the glove.	Rex Stout
The hand of the hunter.	Jerome Weidman
Hand of the mafia.	Jack Baynes
Handbook for army wives and mothers.	Catherine Redmond
The handbook of beauty.	Constance Hart
Handbook of politics and voter's guide.	Lowell Mellett
A handful of dust and Decline and fall.	Evelyn Waugh
A handful of hell.	Noah Sarlat
Handle with fear.	Thomas B. Dewey
Hands off!	Luke Short
Handsome.	Theodore Pratt
The handsome road.	Gwen Bristow
Handsome's seven women.	Theodore Pratt
Handwriting analysis.	Dorothy Sara
The handy book of gardening.	Victor A. Tiedjens / Albert E. Wilkinson
The handy home medical adviser.	Morris Fishbein
Handy legal advisor for home and business.	Samuel G. Kling
Hang by your neck.	Henry Kane
Hang my wreath.	Ward Weaver
Hang the men high.	Noel M. Loomis / Paul Leslie Peil
Hanged for a sheep.	Frances Lockridge / Richard Lockridge
The hanging heiress.	Richard Wormser
The hanging hills.	Brad Ward
Hanging judge.	Bruce Hamilton
The hanging tree.	Dorothy M. Johnson
The hangman of Sleepy Valley.	Davis Dresser
Hangman's hat.	Paul Ernst
Hangman's mesa.	Dan J. Stevens
The hangman's overture.	J. Jerod Chouinard
Hangman's range.	Lee Floren
Hangman's tie.	Christopher Hale
The hangman's tree.	Dorothy Cameron Disney
Hangman's valley.	Ray Hogan
The hangman's whip.	Mignon G. Eberhart
Hangover House.	Sax Rohmer
Hangtown.	Les Savage Jr.
Hangtree country.	Eric Allen
Hangtree range.	William Hopson
Hannibal.	Mary Dolan
The haploids.	Jerry Sohl
The happy highwayman.	Leslie Charteris
Happy marriage.	John A. O'Brien
The happy time.	Robert Fontaine
The happy valley.	Max Brand
Harbin's Ridge.	Henry Giles
Harbour.	Philip MacDonald
Hard and fast.	U. S. Andersen
The hard blue sky.	Shirley Ann Grau
The hard guys.	John B. Sanford
Hard man.	Leo Katcher
The hard man.	Philip Ketchum
Hard man with a gun.	Charles N. Heckelmann
Hard men.	Frank O'Rourke
The hard men.	Roe Richmond
Hard money.	Luke Short
Hard rock rancher.	William E. Vance
Hard rock town.	Joseph Gage
The hard sell.	David Delman
Hard to get.	Edwin Gilbert
The hard way.	Robert V. Williams
The hardboiled lineup.	Harry Widmer
The hard-boiled omnibus.	Joseph T. Shaw
The hard-boiled virgin.	Jack Woodford
Hardcase.	Matt Kinkaid
Hardcase.	Luke Short
Hardcase range.	Jackson Gregory
The harder they fall.	Budd Schulberg
Hardly a man is now alive.	Herbert Brean
Hardman.	David Karp
Hardrock.	Frank Bonham
The harem.	Louis-Charles Royer
Harlem is my heaven.	Ian Gordon
The harlot killer.	Allan Barnard
Harper's magazine reader.	
Harriet.	Elizabeth Jenkins
Harrison High.	John Farris
Harry Black.	David Walker
Harry of Monmouth.	A. M. Maughan
Harvard has a homicide.	Timothy Fuller
The Harvey girls.	Samuel Hopkins Adams
Harvey Kurtzman's jungle book.	Harvey Kurtzman
Hashknife of Stormy River.	W. C. Tuttle
Hasty wedding.	Mignon G. Eberhart
Hate alley.	Martin Weiss

The hostile hills.	E. E. Halleran
The hostiles.	Richard Ferber
Hot.	Frederick Lorenz
The hot and the cool.	Edwin Gilbert
Hot cargo.	G. H. Otis
Hot date.	Elliot Storm
Hot freeze.	Martin Brett
The hot half hour.	Robert L. Foreman
Hot iron.	Elmer Kelton
Hot leather.	Beulah Marie Dix
	Bertram Millhauser
Hot money girl.	Arlo Wayne
Hot rod.	Henry Gregor Felsen
Hot rod gang rumble.	Meyer Dolinsky
Hot spell.	Lonnie Coleman
Hot, sweet and blue.	Jack Baird
Hot town.	Frank Malachy
Hot winds of summer.	John H. Secondari
Hotel fever.	Arnold Gifford
Hotel hostess.	Faith Baldwin
The hotel murders.	Stewart Sterling
Hotel room.	Natalie Anderson Scott
Hotel Splendide.	Ludwig Bemelmans
Hotel Talleyrand.	Paul Hyde Bonner
The hotshot.	Fletcher Flora
Hound-dog man.	Fred Gipson
The hound of earth.	Vance Bourjaily
The hound of the Baskervilles.	Arthur Conan Doyle
Hour of glory.	Robert Lund
The hour of truth.	David Davidson
The hours after midnight.	Joseph Hayes
A house in Naples.	Peter Rabe
A house in Peking.	Robert Payne
House in Shanghai.	Emily Hahn
A house in the uplands.	Erskine Caldwell
A house is not a home.	Polly Adler
The house next door.	Lionel White
House of darkness.	Allan MacKinnon
House of deceit.	Rae Loomis
House of dolls.	Ka-tzetnik 135633
House of evil.	Clayre Lipman
	Michel Lipman
The house of exile.	Nora Waln
House of flesh.	Bruno Fischer
House of fury.	Felice Swados
House of hate.	W. Craig Thomas
A house of her own.	Robert F. Mirvish
The house of Madame Tellier.	Guy de Maupassant
The house of numbers.	Jack Finney
House of storm.	Mignon G. Eberhart
The house of the dead.	Fyodor Dostoyevsky
The house of the seven gables.	Nathaniel Hawthorne
The house on Q Street.	Robert Dietrich
The house on the beach.	E. L. Withers
A house on the Rhine.	Frances Faviell
The house on the roof.	Mignon G. Eberhart
House party.	Virginia Rowans
The house without a door.	Thomas Sterling
The house without a key.	Earl Derr Biggers
The house without the door.	Elizabeth Daly
Houseboy.	Walton Fairbank
A houseful of love.	Marjorie Housepian
The householder's manual.	Richard Kent
The housekeeper's daughter.	Donald Henderson Clarke
The housewarming.	George Sklar
How brave we live.	Paul Monash
How cheap can you get?	Martin Abzug
How fares it with the happy dead?	Benn Towers
How green was my sex life.	Lawrence Lariar
How green was my valley.	Richard Llewellyn
How I became a girl reporter.	Hyman Goldberg
How I made a million.	Noah Sarlat
How I pick winners.	Ken Kling
How life began.	Irving Adler
How like a god.	Rex Stout
How rough can it get?	Joe Weiss
How Russia prepared.	Maurice Edelman
How sharp the point.	P. J. Wolfson
How the great religions began.	Joseph Gaer
How the Jap army fights.	
How to be a better member.	Horace Coon
How to build and operate a model railroad.	Marshall McClintock
How to buy stocks.	Louis Engel
How to develop self-confidence.	Dale Carnegie
How to draw and paint.	Henry Gasser
How to draw the human figure.	John R. Grabach
How to eat better for less money.	Sam Aaron / James A. Beard
How to get rich in Washington.	Blair Bolles
How to help your child in school.	Lawrence K. Frank / Mary Frank
How to help your doctor help you.	Walter C. Alvarez
How to help your husband get ahead.	Mrs. Dale Carnegie
How to know American antiques.	Alice Winchester
How to know and enjoy New York.	Carl Maas
How to know and predict the weather.	Robert Moore Fisher
How to know the American mammals.	Ivan T. Sanderson
How to know the birds.	Roger Tory Peterson
How to know the minerals and rocks.	Richard M. Pearl

How to know the wild flowers. — Alfred Stefferud
How to land the job you want. — Jules Z. Willing
How to live with your heart. — Peter J. Steincrohn
How to live with yourself and like it. — Henry Clay Lindgren
How to live without liquor. — Ralph A. Habas
How to make a success of your marriage. — Eustace Chesser
How to make more money. — Marvin Small
How to make psychology work for you. — Abraham P. Sperling
How to make your emotions work for you. — Dorothy C. Finkelhor
How to overcome nervous stomach trouble. — Joseph F. Montague
How to pick a mate. — Clifford R. Adams / Vance Packard
How to play canasta. — Richard Frey
How to play samba. — Richard Frey
How to play winning checkers. — Millard Hopper
How to play with your child. — A. F. Arnold
How to retire and enjoy it. — Ray Giles
How to spell and increase your word power. — Horace Coon
How to stop killing yourself. — Peter J. Steincrohn
How to stop smoking. — Herbert Brean
How to stop worrying and start living. — Dale Carnegie
How to succeed in business without really trying. — Shepherd Mead
How to succeed with women without really trying. — Shepherd Mead
How to survive an atomic bomb. — Richard Gerstell
How to take better pictures. — Joseph C. Keeley
How to understand music. — Oscar Thompson
How to understand your dreams. — Wilhelm Stekel
How to use premiums in your business to increase your sales and profits.
How to use the power of prayer. — Harold Sherman
How to win and hold a mate. — Samuel G. Kling
How to win friends and influence people. — Dale Carnegie
How to work with tools and wood. — Fred Gross

How to write and speak effective English. — Edward Frank Allen
How you can forecast the weather. — Eric Sloane
How you can take better photos. — Simon Nathan
The howls of ivy. — Henry Boltinoff
Hoyle's rules of games. — Albert H. Morehead / Geoffrey Mott-Smith
Huckleberry Finn. — Mark Twain
The hucksters. — Frederic Wakeman
Hugger-mugger in the Louvre. — Elliot Paul
Human? — Judith Merril
The human angle. — William Tenn
The human beast. — George Milburn / Émile Zola
The human beast. — Émile Zola
The human body. — Logan Clendening
The human body and how it works. — Elbert Tokay
Human breeding and survival. — Guy I. Burch / Elmer Pendell
The human comedy. — William Saroyan
Human destiny. — Pierre Lecomte du Noüy
The human side of animals. — Vance Packard
Human types. — Raymond Firth
The humbug digest. — Harvey Kurtzman
The humming box. — Harry Whittington
The humorous side of Erskine Caldwell. — Erskine Caldwell
Humorous stories and anecdotes.
The hunchback of Notre Dame. — Victor Hugo
The hunchback of Notre Dame, volume 1. — Victor Hugo
The hunchback of Notre Dame, volume 2. — Victor Hugo
The hunger and other stories. — Charles Beaumont
The hunger and the hate. — H. Vernor Dixon
Hunger fighters. — Paul deKruif
Hunger Mountain. — William R. Scott
The hungering shame. — R. V. Cassill
Hungry hill. — Daphne du Maurier
The hungry house. — Lilian Lauferty
Hungry men. — Edward Anderson
The hungry years. — Annabel Johnson
Hunt the killer. — Day Keene
Hunt the man down. — William Heuman
Hunt the man down. — William Pearson
Hunt with the hounds. — Mignon G. Eberhart
Hunted riders. — Max Brand
The hunter. — James Aldridge
The hunter. — Hugh Fosburgh
Hunter. — J. A. Hunter
The hunters. — James Salter
The hurricane. — James Norman Hall / Charles Nordhoff

Hurry the darkness.	Maurice Procter
The husband.	Vera Caspary
A husband in the house.	Stuart Engstrand
The husband who ran away.	Hildegarde Dolson
Husbands and lovers.	Elizabeth Abell
	Joseph I. Greene
Husky: co-pilot of the Pilgrim.	Rutherford Montgomery
The hustlers.	Sam Ross
The hygiene of marriage.	Millard S. Everett
Hypnosis and you.	Ben Benson
	Howard D. Tawney
Hypnotism and the power within.	S. J. Van Pelt
Hypnotism comes of age.	Raymond Rosenthal
	Bernard Wolfe

I

I am a fugitive from a chain gang!	Robert E. Burns
I am a marked woman.	
I am a woman.	Ann Bannon
I am Adam.	Maxine Kaufman
I am fifteen--and I don't want to die.	Christine Arnothy
I am gazing into my 8-ball.	Earl Wilson
I am legend.	Richard Matheson
I am thinking of my darling.	Vincent McHugh
I, barbarian.	Jay Scotland
I came to kill.	Gordon Davis
I can get if for you wholesale!	Jerome Weidman
I can't stop running.	Edward Ronns
I chose freedom.	Victor Kravchenko
I, Claudius.	Robert Graves
I cried in the dark.	Ann Scott
I detest all my sins.	Jack Weeks
I die possessed.	J. B. O'Sullivan
I die slowly.	Kenneth Millar
I dive for treasure.	Harry E. Rieseberg
I drive the turnpikes-- and survive.	Paul Kearney
I escaped from Devil's Island.	René Belbenoit
I fear you not.	Ben Kerr
I flew for the Führer.	Heinz Knoke
I get what I want.	Larry Heller
I have Gloria Kirby.	Richard Himmel
I, James Dean.	T. T. Thomas
I killed Stalin.	Sterling Noel
I knew your soldier.	Pete Martin
	Eleanor "Bumpy" Stevenson
I know my love.	Fan Nichols
I leap over the wall.	Monica Baldwin
I, libertine.	Frederick R. Ewing
I like 'em tough.	Curt Cannon
I like it tough.	James Howard
I lost my girlish laughter.	Jane Allen
I love you, I love you, I love you.	Ludwig Bemelmans
I married a dead man.	William Irish
I married a hunter.	Marjorie Michael
I, mobster.	
I.O.U.--murder.	William Francis
I prefer murder.	Charles A. Landolf
	Browning Norton
I, robot.	Isaac Asimov
I saw it happen.	Lewis Gannett
I see red.	Sterling Noel
I should have stayed home.	Horace McCoy
I stole $16,000,000.	Thomas P. Kelley
	Herbert Emerson Wilson

I survived Hitler's ovens.	Olga Lengyel
I take all.	Robert Carson
I take the rap.	Gordon Shelly
I take this man.	Emilie Loring
I take this woman.	Georges Simenon
I, the executioner.	Stephen Ransome
I, the jury.	Mickey Spillane
I thought of Daisy.	Edmund Wilson
I wake up screaming.	Steve Fisher
I want out.	Tedd Thomey
I want to live!	Tabor Rawson
I was a drug addict.	David Loth
	Leroy Street
I was a house detective.	Dev Collans
	Stewart Sterling
I was a Nazi flier.	Gottfried Leske
"I was there".	Ken Jones
I worked for Lucky Luciano.	
Ice Palace.	Edna Ferber
Idaho.	Paul Evan Lehman
Ideas of the great economists.	George Soule
The idiot.	Fyodor Dostoyevsky
If a body.	George Worthing Yates
If a man be mad.	Harold Maine
If death ever slept.	Rex Stout
If he hollers let him go.	Chester B. Himes
If I die before I wake.	Sherwood King
If I forget thee.	Robert S. de Ropp
If I kill him.	John Hawkins
	Ward Hawkins
If I live to dine.	Hillary Waugh
If I should die before I wake.	William Irish
If I should murder.	Patrick Laing
If the coffin fits.	Day Keene
If this be sin.	Loren Wahl
If winter comes.	A. S. M. Hutchinson
If you are a woman.	Lee Graham
If you have tears.	John Evans
If you like Hazel.	Ted Key
The Iliad.	Homerus
I'll be right home, Ma.	Henry Denker
I'll bring her back.	Peter Cheyney
I'll bury my dead.	James Hadley Chase
I'll call every Monday.	Orrie Hitt
I'll cry tomorrow.	Lillian Roth et al.
I'll eat you last.	H. C. Branson
I'll find my love.	Joan Dirksen
I'll find you.	Richard Himmel
I'll fix you.	Hal Ellson
I'll get mine.	Thurston Scott
I'll get you yet.	James Howard
I'll kill you next!	Adam Knight
Ill met by moonlight.	Leslie Ford
I'll never go there any more.	Jerome Weidman
I'll never let you go.	Fan Nichols
I'll see you in hell.	John McPartland

I'll sing at your
  funeral.   Hugh Pentecost
I'll take what's mine.   Nard Jones
Ill wind.   James Hilton
Illusion.   Allene Corliss
The illustrated man.   Ray Bradbury
The illustrious corpse.   Tiffany Thayer
I'm Cannon--for hire.   Curt Cannon
I'm for me first.   Roger Price
I'm no good.   Peter W. Denzer
I'm Owen Harrison   James Whitfield
  Harding.   Ellison
The image and the search.   Walter Baxter
The image makers.   Bernard Dryer
Imagination unlimited.   Everett F. Bleiler
                                T. E. Dikty
The imitation of Christ.   Thomas à Kempis
Imitation of life.   Fannie Hurst
The immodest maidens.   Eleanore Browne
Immoral woman.   Jack Hanley
The immortal.   Walter Ross
Immortal poems of the
  English language.   Oscar Williams
Immortal wife.   Irving Stone
Immortality, inc.   Robert Sheckley
Impatient virgin.   Donald Henderson
                                Clarke
Imperial city.   Elmer Rice
The imperial orgy.   Edgar Saltus
Imperial woman.   Pearl S. Buck
Impossible greeting
  cards.   Len Levinson
The impotent general.   Charles Pettit
The impudent rifle.   Dick Pearce
In a dark garden.   Frank G. Slaughter
In a deadly vein.   Brett Halliday
In a lonely place.   Dorothy B. Hughes
In a summer season.   Ludwig Lewisohn
In bed we cry.   Ilka Chase
In case of emergency.   Georges Simenon
In comes death.   Paul Whelton
In hazard.   Richard Hughes
In his blood.   Harold R. Daniels
In love.   Alfred Hayes
In one head and out
  the other.   Roger Price
In savage surrender.   Whitman Chambers
In search of love.   William Fain
In the balance.   Patricia Wentworth
In the best families.   Rex Stout
In the grip of terror.   Groff Conklin
In the teeth of the
  evidence.   Dorothy L. Sayers
In the wet.   Nevil Shute
In the years of Our Lord.   Manuel Komroff
In this corner...
  Dennis the menace.   Hank Ketcham
In those days.   Harvey Fergusson
In tragic life.   Vardis Fisher
In winter light.   Edwin Corle
The incident.   Marc Rivette

Incident at Sun
  Mountain.   Todhunter Ballard
The inconvenient bride.   James M. Fox
The inconvenient corpse.   E. P. Fenwick
The incredible truth.   Chris Massie
The incredible year.   Faith Baldwin
The incurable wound.   Berton Roueché
Indian beef.   Harold Channing Wire
Indian country.   Dorothy M. Johnson
Indian-fighting army.   Fairfax Downey
Indian paint.   Glenn Balch
Indian summer.   Robert Sylvester
Indians of the Americas.   John Collier
An Indian's tale.   Jefferson McCall
Indigo.   Christine Weston
The indigo necklace
  murders.   Frances Crane
The indiscreet
  confessions of a nice
  girl.
Infamy.   Francis Carco
The Inferno.   Dante Alighieri
Infidelity.   Arthur Weigall
The infinite woman.   Edison Marshall
The informer.   Liam O'Flaherty
Ingenue.   Millicent Brower
The inhabited universe.   Derek D. Dempster
                                Kenneth W. Gatland
Inherit the night.   Robert Christie
Inland passage.   George Harmon Coxe
The Inn of the Sixth
  Happiness.   Alan Burgess
The innocent
  ambassadors.   Philip Wylie
The innocent and the
  wicked.   Phyllis Hastings
The innocent and
  willing.   Morton Cooper
The innocent at large.   Noel Langley
The innocent bottle.   Anthony Gilbert
Innocent bystander.   Craig Rice
The innocent flower.   Charlotte Armstrong
Innocent madame.   Eleanore Browne
The innocent Mrs. Duff.   Elisabeth Sanxay
                                Holding
The innocent one.   James Reach
The innocent villa.   Barnaby Conrad
The innocent voyage.   Richard Hughes
Inquest.   Percival Wilde
Inside Mad.   Harvey Kurtzman
Inside U.S.A., volume 1.   John Gunther
Inside U.S.A., volume 2.   John Gunther
The insider.   James Kelly
The insiders.   Booth Mooney
The insolent chariots.   John Keats
Inspector Maigret and
  the burglar's wife.   Georges Simenon
Inspector Maigret and
  the dead girl.   Georges Simenon
Inspector Maigret and
  the killers.   Georges Simenon

Inspector Maigret and the strangled stripper. Georges Simenon
Inspector Maigret in New York's underworld. Georges Simenon
Inspector Queen's own case. Ellery Queen
The inspirational reader. William Oliver Stevens
Intent to kill. Michael Bryan
Intimacy. Jean-Paul Sartre
The intimate Henry Miller. Henry Miller
The intimate problems of women. Henry B. Safford
The intimate stranger. William Lynch
Into Plutonian depths. Stanton A. Coblentz
Into the valley. John Hersey
Intrigue in Paris. Sterling Noel
Introducing Shakespeare. G. B. Harrison
Introduction to economic science. George Soule
An introduction to modern architecture. Elizabeth B. Mock
J. M. Richards
The intruder. Charles Beaumont
The intruder. Octavus Roy Cohen
The intruder. Helen Fowler
Intruder in the dust. William Faulkner
The intruders. Robert Bright
The invaders. Stuart Engstrand
The invaders are coming! J. A. Meyer
Alan E. Nourse
Invaders from earth. Robert Silverberg
Invaders of earth. Groff Conklin
Invasion from Mars. Orson Welles
Invasion of privacy. Harry Kurnitz
The invisible curtain. Joseph Anthony
The invisible flag. Peter Bamm
Invisible man. Ralph Ellison
The invisible man. H. G. Wells
The invisible outlaw. Max Brand
Invitation to dishonor. Eric Arthur
Invitation to live. Lloyd C. Douglas
Invitation to murder. Rex Stout
Invitation to the waltz. Rosamond Lehmann
Invitation to violence. Lionel White
Irene. Ronald Marsh
Irish stories and tales. Devin A. Garrity
The iron bronc. Will Ermine
The iron gates. Margaret Millar
The Iron King. Maurice Druon
Iron lover. Gardner F. Fox
The iron maiden. Edwin Lanham
Iron man. W. R. Burnett
The iron mistress. Paul I. Wellman
The iron spiders. Baynard Kendrick
The iron virgin. James M. Fox
The ironmaster. Anne Powers
Is another world watching? Gerald Heard
Is marriage necessary? George H. Bartlett
Is my flesh of brass? P. J. Wolfson

Is sex necessary? James Thurber
E. B. White
Islam in modern history. Wilfred Cantwell Smith
Island in the sky. Ernest K. Gann
Island in the sun. Alec Waugh
The island of Dr. Moreau. H. G. Wells
Island of the pit. Vincent James
Island victory. S. L. A. Marshall
Isle of demons. John Clarke Bowman
Isle of the damned. George John Seaton
It ain't hay. David Dodge
It happened at Thunder River. Bliss Lomax
It happens every spring. Valentine Davies
It walks by night. John Dickson Carr
Italian through pictures. I. A. Richards et al.
Italian through pictures, book 1. I. A. Richards et al.
It's a crime. Richard Ellington
It's a free country. Ben Ames Williams
It's a sin to kill. Day Keene
It's lonely being dead. Benn Towers
It's my funeral. Peter Rabe
It's never too late to love. Anna K. Daniels
It's your money--come and get it. Sidney Margolius
Ivanhoe. Walter Scott

J

July, 1863.	Irving Werstein
The jungle.	Nelson Algren
Jungle fury.	Robb White
Jungle heat.	Dale Wilmer
Jungle hunting thrills.	Edison Marshall
The jungle kids.	Evan Hunter
The jungle of love.	Robin Maugham
The jungle seas.	Arthur A. Ageton
Jungle she.	Dan Cushman
Junior miss.	Sally Benson
The junk pusher.	Robert W. Taylor
Junkie.	William Lee
Jurgen.	James Branch Cabell
Just around the corner.	Stuart Brock
Just married.	
Just so far.	Floyd Miller
Just what the doctor ordered.	Anthony Bassler
Justice comes to Tomahawk.	William MacLeod Raine
Justice, my brother!	James Keene
Juvenile delinquency.	Charles Preston
Juvenile delinquents.	Lenard Kaufman
Juvenile hoods.	Joseph Shallit
Juvenile jungle.	
Juvenile jungle.	Firth Counsel

K

KKK.	Paul Walsh
Kamikaze.	Gordon T. Allred
	Yasuo Kuwahara
The Kansan.	Richard Brister
Kansas guns.	Paul Durst
Kansas trail.	Hascal Giles
Katherine.	Anya Seton
Katrina.	Jeramie Price
Kay Manion, M.D.	Adeline McElfresh
Keats.	John Keats
Keelboats North.	William Heuman
Keep cool, Mr. Jones.	Timothy Fuller
Keep the aspidistra flying.	George Orwell
Keeper of the keys.	Earl Derr Biggers
Keeping women in line.	Mischa Richter
Kelly.	Donald Henderson Clarke
Ken Murray's giant joke book.	Ken Murray
The kennel murder case.	S. S. Van Dine
The Kentuckians.	Janice Holt Giles
Kentucky pride.	Gene Markey
Kept woman.	Viña Delmar
The key.	Patricia Wentworth
A key to death.	Frances Lockridge
	Richard Lockridge
Key to economic progress.	D. G. Kousoulas
The key to Nicholas Street.	Stanley Ellin
A key to the heavens.	Leo Mattersdorf
Key witness.	Frank Kane
The keys of the kingdom.	A. J. Cronin
Kiboko.	Daniel P. Mannix
Kick-off!	Ed Fitzgerald
The kid comes back.	John R. Tunis
The kid from Dodge City.	Bennett Foster
Kid Galahad.	Francis Wallace
The kidnap murder case.	S. S. Van Dine
The kidnaper.	Robert Bloch
Kidnapped.	Robert Louis Stevenson
The kidnappers.	Albert Ullman
Kids say the darndest things!	Art Linkletter
Kilkenny.	Louis L'Amour
The kill.	Émile Zola
Kill a wicked man.	Kyle Hunt
Kill and tell.	Howard Rigsby
Kill-box.	Michael Stark
Kill him tonight.	Jeremy Lane
Kill me if you can.	Ralpha Johns
Kill me in Shimbashi.	Earl Norman
Kill me in Tokyo.	Earl Norman
Kill me with kindness.	J. Harvey Bond
Kill my love.	Kyle Hunt
Kill once, kill twice.	Kyle Hunt
Kill one, kill two.	Robert Kelston
Kill or cure.	William Francis
Kill the beloved.	Lane Kauffmann

Kill the boss good-bye.	Peter Rabe
The killer.	Wade Miller
A killer among us.	Ben Ames Williams
The killer brand.	William Colt MacDonald
Killer by proxy.	Selwyn Jepson
Killer colt.	James Woodruff Smith
A killer comes riding.	Rod Patterson
Killer cop.	Ferguson Findley
Killer country.	Jackson Cole
Killer in silk.	H. Vernor Dixon
Killer in the house.	Borden Deal
Killer in white.	Tedd Thomey
The killer inside me.	Jim Thompson
A killer is loose.	Gil Brewer
A killer is loose among us.	Robert Terrall
The killer is mine.	Talmage Powell
Killer, take all!	James O. Causey
Killer take all.	Philip Race
Killer with a key.	Dan Marlowe
The killers.	Peter Dawson
Killers are my meat.	Stephen Marlowe
Killer's choice.	Stuart Brock
Killer's choice.	Ed McBain
Killer's choice.	Wade Miller
Killer's crossing.	Burt Arthur
Killers five.	William Hopson
Killers' game.	Edward Hudiburg
Killers in Africa.	Alexander Lake
A killer's kiss.	Hal Ellson
Killer's payoff.	Ed McBain
Killers play rough.	Adam Ring
Killer's Range.	E. B. Mann
Killer's wedge.	Ed McBain
The killing.	Lionel White
The killing ground.	Elleston Trevor
Killing the goose.	Frances Lockridge
	Richard Lockridge
The kill-off.	Jim Thompson
Kim.	Rudyard Kipling
Kind are her answers.	Mary Renault
The kind man.	Helen Nielsen
The kind of guy I am.	Robert McAllister
	Floyd Miller
Kinfolk.	Pearl S. Buck
The king and four queens.	Theodore Sturgeon
King colt.	Luke Short
The king is dead.	Ellery Queen
The king is dead on Queen Street.	Francis Bonnamy
King of Abilene.	Thomas Thompson
King of Crazy River.	William Colt MacDonald
King of Paris.	Guy Endore
King of the bush.	William MacLeod Raine
King of the range.	Max Brand
The king of Thunder Valley.	Archie Joscelyn

King Solomon's mines.   H. Rider Haggard
                         Jean Francis Webb
Kingdom of death.   Margery Allingham
Kingdom of flying men.   Frederic Nelson
                           Litten
The kingdom of Johnny
  Cool.   John McPartland
Kingdom of the spur.   Gene Markey
The kingpin.   Tom Wicker
King's arrow.   Joseph Patrick
The King's cavalier.   Samuel Shellabarger
The king's choice.   Margaret Campbell
                           Barnes
The king's general.   Daphne du Maurier
Kings go forth.   Joe David Brown
The king's mistress.   Jean Plaidy
Kings Mountain.   Florette Henri
The kings of the road.   Ken W. Purdy
King's rebel.   James D. Horan
King's rogue.   Max Peacock
Kings Row.   Henry Bellamann
Kingsblood royal.   Sinclair Lewis
Kinkaid of Red Butte.   Leslie Ernenwein
The Kipling sampler.   Rudyard Kipling
Kiss and kill.   Joe Barry
Kiss and kill.   Adam Knight
Kiss and kill.   Reed McCary
The kiss and The duel.   Anton Chekhov
A kiss before dying.   Ira Levin
Kiss her goodbye.   Wade Miller
Kiss me again, stranger. Daphne du Maurier
Kiss me, deadly.   Mickey Spillane
Kiss me hard.   Tom Brandt
Kiss me quick.   Karl Kramer
Kiss my fist!   James Hadley Chase
The kiss of death.   Eleazar Lipsky
Kiss the blood off my
  hands.   Gerald Butler
Kiss the killer.   Joseph Shallit
Kiss the night away.   C. G. Lumbard
Kiss tomorrow good-bye. Horace McCoy
The kiss-off.   Douglas Heyes
Kitten with a whip.   Wade Miller
Kitty.   Rosamond Marshall
Kitty Foyle.   Christopher Morley
Klever kid kartoons.   Harold Meyers
The knave of diamonds.   Jack Karney
Knee-deep in death.   Bruno Fischer
Kneel to the rising sun. Erskine Caldwell
The knife.   Theon Wright
Knife at my back.   Adam Knight
Knife in my back.   Sam Merwin Jr.
A knife is silent.   David Kent
Knight's gambit.   William Faulkner
The Knights of Bushido. Lord Russell
Knock and wait awhile.   William Rawle Weeks
Knock 'em dead.   Jack Karney
Knock on any door.   Willard Motley
Knocked for a loop.   Craig Rice
Know your real abilities.Charles V. Broadley
                         Margaret E. Broadley
The Kodak camera guide.

Kon-Tiki.   Thor Heyerdahl
Korea's heroes.   Bruce Jacobs
Kundu.   Morris L. West

L

The labors of Hercules. Agatha Christie
Lad: a dog. Albert Payson Terhune
Ladies in Hades. Frederic Arnold Kummer
Ladies of chance. Anthony Scott
The lady. Conrad Richter
The lady and the cheetah. John Flagg
The lady and the snake. John Farr
Lady Ann. Donald Henderson Clarke
The lady came to kill. M. E. Chaber
Lady Chatterley's lover. D. H. Lawrence
Lady, don't die on my doorstep. Joseph Shallit
Lady for love. Alan Schultz
Lady Godiva and Master Tom. Raoul C. Faure
Lady in dread. Ryerson Johnson
Lady in peril. Lester Dent
Lady in peril. Ben Ames Williams
The lady in the lake. Raymond Chandler
The lady in the morgue. Jonathan Latimer
The lady in the tower. Katharine Newlin Burt
Lady into fox and A man in the zoo. David Garnett
The lady is afraid. George Harmon Coxe
Lady killer. William M. Hardy
Lady killer. Ed McBain
The lady killers. William T. Brannon
The lady kills. Bruno Fischer
Lady, mind that corpse. Hank Janson
A lady named Lou. Donald Henderson Clarke
The lady regrets. James M. Fox
The lady said yes. George Victor Martin
Lady sings the blues. William Dufty, Billy Holiday
The lady takes a flyer. Edward Ronns
Lady, that's my skull. Carl Shannon
The lady was a tramp. Harry Whittington
Lady with the dice. Joel Townsley Rogers
The laff parade. Jerry Lieberman
Laird's choice. Rosamond Marshall
Lament for a lover. Patricia Highsmith
Lament for four virgins. Lael Tucker
Lament for the bride. Helen Reilly
A lamp for nightfall. Erskine Caldwell
The lamp of God. Ellery Queen
Lancet. Garet Rogers
Land below the wind. Agnes Newton Keith
Land beyond the law. John Callahan
Land grab. Jackson Cole
The land grabber. Peter Field
The land grabbers. John S. Daniels
Land of the lawless. Les Savage Jr.
Land of the strangers. Ray Hogan
Land of vengeance. John Jennings

Langenscheidt's German-English, English-German dictionary.
Language. Joshua Whatmough
Language for everybody. Mario Pei
Lani. Margaret Widdemer
A lantern in her hand. Bess Streeter Aldrich
Laramie rides again. Will Ermine
Laramie rides alone. Will Ermine
Laredo Road. Will C. Brown
Larousse's French-English, English-French dictionary.
The lash of desire. Marcos Spinelli
Lash of Idaho. Roe Richmond
The last angry man. Gerald Green
The last Apaches. William Hopson
The last billionaire, Henry Ford. William C. Richards
The last blitzkrieg. Walter Freeman
The last chance. Frank O'Rourke
Last chance at Devil's Canyon. Barry Cord
Last-chance range. Dean Owen
The last combat. Ralph Leveridge
The last days of Hitler. H. R. Trevor-Roper
The last days of Sodom and Gomorrah. Paul Ilton
The last enemy. Berton Roueché
The last Englishman. Hebe Weenolsen
The last express. Baynard Kendrick
The last frontier. Howard Fast
Last frontier. Richard Emery Roberts
The last hero. Peter W. Denzer
The last holdup. Sam Meriwether
The last hunt. Milton Lott
The last hurrah. Edwin O'Connor
Last in convoy. James Pattinson
The last kill. Charles Wells
The last laugh. Charles Einstein
The last night. John McPartland
The last of Mr. Norris. Christopher Isherwood
Last of the breed. Les Savage Jr.
Last of the conquerors. William Gardner Smith
Last of the great outlaws. Homer Croy
Last of the longhorns. Will Ermine
The last of the Mohicans. James Fenimore Cooper
The last of the plainsmen. Zane Grey
The last parallel. Martin Russ
The last party. Robert Lowry
The last planet. Andre Norton
The last princess. Charles O. Locke
Last race. Jon Manchip White
The last rodeo. Ernest Haycox
The last round. Frank O'Rourke
The last secret. Dana Chambers
Last seen wearing... Hillary Waugh
The last shoot-out. William Hopson

Last stage to Aspen.   Allan Vaughan Elston
Last stage West.   Frank Bonham
Last stand at Anvil Pass. Merle Constiner
Last stand at Papago
  Wells.   Louis L'Amour
Last stand at Saber
  River.   Elmore Leonard
Last summer.   Boris Pasternak
The last temptation.   Joseph Viertel
The last time I saw
  Paris.   Elliot Paul
The last trail.   Zane Grey
Last train from Gun Hill. Gordon D. Shirreffs
The last voyage of the   A. A. Hoehling
  Lusitania.   Mary Hoehling
The late George Apley.   John P. Marquand
The late lamented lady.   Marie Blizard
Late last night.   James Reach
The late Liz.   Elizabeth Burns
Latigo.   Frank O'Rourke
Laugh with Leacock.   Stephen Leacock
Laugh yourself well.   Eddie Davis
Laughing Boy.   Oliver La Farge
The laughing fox.   Frank Gruber
Laughing on the inside.   Bill Yates
Laughs around the world.
Laughter came screaming.   Henry Kane
Laughter in the dark.   Vladimir Nabokov
Laughter, incorporated.   Bennett Cerf
Laughter is legal.   Francis Leo Golden
The laughter of my
  father.   Carlos Bulosan
Laura.   Vera Caspary
The law and Jake Wade.   Marvin H. Albert
Law and order, unlimited. William Colt
                             MacDonald
The law and you.   Max Radin
The law at Randado.   Elmore Leonard
Law badge.   Peter Field
The law bringers.   Bliss Lomax
The law busters.   Bliss Lomax
A law for the lion.   Louis Auchincloss
Law for Tombstone.   Chuck Martin
Law from back beyond.   Chuck Martin
Law killer.   Richard Brister
Law man.   Lee Leighton
Law of the gun.   Max Brand
Law of the gun.   Brett Rider
Law of the trigger.   Clifton Adams
Law of the trigger.   Giles A. Lutz
Law rides the range.   Walt Coburn
The lawbringers.   William Porter
Lawless guns.   Dudley Dean
Lawless range.   Charles N. Heckelmann
Lawman without a badge.   D. L. Bonar
Lawman's feud.   Steve Frazee
Lawman's pay.   Frank C. Robertson
Lay that pistol down.   Richard Powell
Lazarus murder seven.   Richard Sale
Lazy H feud.   Ed La Vanway
Lead in his fists.   Tom West
The lead-slingers.   J. Edward Leithead

Lead with your left.   Ed Lacy
The league of
  frightened men.   Rex Stout
Leashed guns.   Peter Dawson
The leather pushers.   H. C. Witwer
Leave cancelled.   Nicholas Monsarrat
Leave her to God.   O. O. Osborne
Leave her to heaven.   Ben Ames Williams
Leave her to hell!   Fletcher Flora
Leave it to me.   George Joseph
Leave it to Psmith.   P. G. Wodehouse
Leaves of grass.   Walt Whitman
Left bank of desire.   R. V. Cassill
                           Eric Protter
The left hand of God.   William E. Barrett
The left leg.   Alice Tilton
Leg artist.   Gene Harvey
The legacy.   Nevil Shute
Legacy of a spy.   Henry S. Maxfield
The legal encyclopedia
  for home and business.   Samuel G. Kling
Legend in the dust.   Frank O'Rourke
Legend of the lost.   Bonnie Golightly
The legion of the
  damned.   Sven Hassel
Lend-lease: weapon for   Edward R.
  victory.   Stettinius Jr.
The lenient beast.   Fredric Brown
Lenin.   David Shub
Leopard in the grass.   Desmond Stewart
Lesson in love.   Émile Zola
The lessons of love.   W. Carroll Munro
Lest we forget thee,
  earth.   Calvin M. Knox
Let it come down.   Paul Bowles
Let me alone.   Donald Windham
Let me kill you,
  sweetheart.   Fletcher Flora
Let no man write my
  epitaph.   Willard Motley
Let the guns roar!   Charles N. Heckelmann
Let the night cry.   Charles Wells
Let the sky fall.   Roger Dee
Let them eat bullets.   Howard Schoenfeld
The lethal sex.   John D. MacDonald
Let's explore your mind.   Albert Edward Wiggam
Let's go naked.   Donald A. Wollheim
Let's make Mary.   Jack Hanley
Letter from Peking.   Pearl S. Buck
Letter to five wives.   John Klempner
Liability limited.   John A. Saxon
Liana.   Martha Gellhorn
Liberty laughs.   Frances Cavanah
                           Ruth Weir
The lie.   Peggy Goodin
Lie down in darkness.   William Styron
Lie down, killer.   Richard S. Prather
Lie down with lions.   Marvin H. Albert
Lie like a lady.   C. S. Cody
Lieutenant Hornblower.   C. S. Forester
Life among the savages.   Shirley Jackson

A lover would be nice.   F. Hugh Herbert
The lovers.   Mitchell Wilson
The lovers.   Kathleen Winsor
Lovers and libertines.   Cliff Howe
Lovers are losers.   Howard Hunt
Lovers in the sun.   Robert Payne
Lovers in torment.   Gordon Merrick
Lover's point.   C. Y. Lee
Love's lovely
  counterfeit.   James M. Cain
Loves of Goya.   Marion Chapman
The loves of Liberace.   Leo Guild
The loves of Lucrezia.   Francesca Wright
The loving and the
  daring.   Françoise Mallet
The loving and the dead.   Carter Brown
The loving and the lost.   James Lord
The loving couple.   Virginia Rowans
The low calorie diet.   Marvin Small
Low company.   Mark Benney
Low level mission.   Leon Wolff
Low man on a totem pole.   H. Allen Smith
Lowdown.   Richard Jessup
Low-down.   Reynolds Packard
Lower than angels.   Walter Karig
The loyalty of free men.   Alan Barth
The Luciano story.   Sid Feder
                            Joachim Joesten
Lucinda.   Howard Rigsby
Lucky Larribee.   Max Brand
The lucky stiff.   Craig Rice
Lucky to be a Yankee.   Joe Di Maggio
Lucy Crown.   Irwin Shaw
Luisita.   Rae Loomis
Lulie.   Joan Sherman
Lummox.   Fannie Hurst
Lures of death.   Paul Whelton
The lurking fear and
  other stories.   H. P. Lovecraft
The lurking man.   Gerald Butler
Lust for life.   Irving Stone
The lust of Private
  Cooper.   James Gordon
Lust to live.   Peter W. Denzer
A lust to live.   E. B. Garside
The lustful ape.   Bruno Fischer
The lustful ape.   Russell Gray
Lustful summer.   R. V. Cassill
The lusting drive.   Ovid Demaris
Lusty conquest.   Lee Richards
The lusty men.   William R. Cox
Lusty wind for Carolina.   Inglis Fletcher
The lute player.   Norah Lofts
Luther.   Roy Flannagan
Lydia Bailey.   Kenneth Roberts
The lying days.   Nadine Gordimer
The lying ladies.   Robert Finnegan
Lyle Brown's sports quiz.   Lyle Brown
Lyn Darling, M.D.   Ray Dorien
Lynch law.   Paul Evan
Lynch-rope law.   Davis Dresser
Lysander.   F. van Wyck Mason

M

The macabre reader.	Donald A. Wollheim
Macamba.	Lilla van Saher
MacArthur--man of action.	Frank Kelley
	Cornelius Ryan
Macbeth.	William Shakespeare
Machines that built America.	Roger Burlingame
The Mackenzie raid.	Red Reeder
The Mackerel Plaza.	Peter De Vries
Mad Baxter.	Wade Miller
The mad hatter mystery.	John Dickson Carr
The mad marshal.	William Colt MacDonald
The Mad reader.	Harvey Kurtzman
Mad River.	Donald Hamilton
Mad strikes back.	Harvey Kurtzman
Madam is dead.	Robert Terrall
Madame Bovary.	Gustave Flaubert
Madame Buccaneer.	Gardner F. Fox
Madame Curie.	Eve Curie
Madame de Pompadour.	Nancy Mitford
Madame Serpent.	Jean Plaidy
Madball.	Fredric Brown
Made up to kill.	Kelley Roos
Madeleine.	
Mademoiselle de Maupin.	Théophile Gautier
Mademoiselle Fifi and other stories.	Guy de Maupassant
Madigan's women.	John Conway
Madison Avenue, U.S.A.	Martin Mayer
Madonna of the sleeping cars.	Maurice Dekobra
Madwoman?	Emily Harvin
Mafia.	Ed Reid
Maggie Cassidy.	Jack Kerouac
Maggie--her marriage.	Taylor Caldwell
Maggie now.	Betty Smith
Magic house of numbers.	Irving Adler
Magic, myth and medicine.	D. T. Atkinson
The magician.	W. Somerset Maugham
The magician.	Georges Simenon
The magnate.	John Harriman
The magnificent bastards.	Lucy Herndon Crockett
The magnificent courtesan.	Lozania Prolé
The magnificent female.	Cecil Saint-Laurent
The magnificent Moll.	John Gonzales
Magnificent obsession.	Lloyd C. Douglas
The magnificent rascal.	Thomas Sancton
Magnus the Magnificent.	Leslie Turner White
Maharaja.	Richard Cargoe
Maid for murder.	Milton K. Ozaki
Maidens in the midden.	Oliver Anderson
Maigret travels south.	Georges Simenon
Main line.	Livingston Biddle Jr.
Main Street merchant.	Norman Beasley
Mainsprings of civilization.	Ellsworth Huntington
Major Barbara.	George Bernard Shaw
Make each day count.	James Keller
Make me an offer.	Charles Gorham
Make mine love.	Faber Birren
Make mine murder.	Robert Sidney Bowen
Make mine vengeance.	Robert Colby
Make my bed in hell.	John B. Sanford
Make my coffin strong.	William R. Cox
Make way for murder.	A. A. Marcus
Making of a mistress.	Susan Morley
Malay woman.	A. S. Fleischman
Male and female.	Margaret Mead
Male and female.	Jack Woodford
Malenkov.	Robert Frazier
Malice aforethought.	Francis Iles
Malice in Wonderland.	Nicholas Blake
The Maltese falcon.	Dashiell Hammett
Mama's bank account.	Kathryn Forbes
Mamba.	Stuart Cloete
Mambo to murder.	Dale Clark
Mamie Brandon.	Jack Sheridan
Mamma's boarding house.	John D. Fitzgerald
A man against fate.	Frank Canizio
	Robert Markel
Man against nature.	Charles Neider
Man alone.	William Doyle
	Scott O'Dell
Man and man: the social philosophers.	Saxe Commins / Robert N. Linscott
Man and spirit: the speculative philosophers.	Saxe Commins / Robert N. Linscott
Man and superman.	George Bernard Shaw
Man and the state: the political philosophers.	Saxe Commins / Robert N. Linscott
Man and the universe: the philosophers of science.	Saxe Commins / Robert N. Linscott
A man called Destiny.	Lan Wright
A man called Spade.	Dashiell Hammett
A man can love twice.	Robert Paul Smith
Man divided.	Dean Douglas
Man drowning.	Henry Kuttner
A man escaped.	André Devigny
The man from Andersonville.	Brad Ward
The man from Bar 20.	Clarence E. Mulford
The man from Boot Hill.	Dean Owen
The man from Brazil.	E. B. Garside
The man from Idaho.	Dan Temple
The man from Laramie.	T. T. Flynn
The man from Mesabi.	Sarah Lockwood
The man from Missouri.	Frank Gruber
The man from Nazareth.	Harry Emerson Fosdick
Man from nowhere.	T. T. Flynn
The man from nowhere.	T. V. Olsen
The man from Paris.	Louis-Charles Royer
The man from Riondo.	Dudley Dean
The man from Salt Creek.	Archie Joscelyn
The man from Scotland Yard.	David Frome
The man from Stony Lonesome.	Jay Albert
The man from Texas.	H. A. DeRosso

The man from Texas.	Jackson Gregory
The man from the Badlands.	Paul Evan Lehman
The man from Thief River.	Peter Field
The man from tomorrow.	Wilson Tucker
The man from Wyoming.	R. M. Hankins
The man from yesterday.	John S. Daniels
The man from Yuma.	Hal G. Evarts
A man gets around.	John McNulty
Man: his first million years.	Ashley Montagu
The man I killed.	Shel Walker
The man in lower ten.	Mary Roberts Rinehart
The man in the brown suit.	Agatha Christie
The man in the gray flannel suit.	Sloan Wilson
Man in the modern world.	Julian Huxley
The man in the moonlight.	Helen McCloy
The man in the net.	Patrick Quentin
The man in the queue.	Josephine Tey
Man in the saddle.	Ernest Haycox
Man in the shadow.	Harry Whittington
The man inside.	M. E. Chaber
Man into woman.	Niels Hoyer
Man makes himself.	V. Gordon Childe
Man missing.	Mignon G. Eberhart
The man next door.	Mignon G. Eberhart
The man nobody knows.	Bruce Barton
The man nobody saw.	Peter Cheyney
A man obsessed.	Alan E. Nourse
Man of Ablemarle.	Inglis Fletcher
A man of affairs.	John D. MacDonald
The man of cold rages.	Jordan Park
Man of earth.	Algis Budrys
Man of many minds.	E. Everett Evans
Man of Montmartre.	Ethel Longstreet / Stephen Longstreet
A man of parts.	Vivian Connell
Man of the West.	Will C. Brown
Man of the West.	Philip Yordan
Man of the world.	Stanley Kauffmann
Man on a rope.	George Harmon Coxe
Man on fire.	Owen Aherne
The man on the blue.	Luke Short
Man on the buckskin.	Peter Dawson
Man on the couch.	Mischa Richter
Man on the run.	Charles Williams
Man on the tightrope.	Neil Paterson
Man-size.	William MacLeod Raine
Man story.	
Man the beast and The wild, wild women.	Virgil Partch
Man tracks.	Bennett Foster
The man who broke things.	John Brooks
The man who came to dinner.	Moss Hart / George S. Kaufman
The man who could cheat death.	Barre Lyndon / Jimmy Sangster
The man who could not shudder.	John Dickson Carr
The man who didn't exist.	Geoffrey Homes
The man who had everything.	Louis Bromfield
The man who had too much to lose.	Hampton Stone
The man who held five aces.	Jean Leslie
The man who japed.	Philip K. Dick
The man who killed Lincoln.	Philip Van Doren Stern
The man who killed Tex.	Edwin Booth
The man who lived forever.	Anna Hunger / R. DeWitt Miller
The man who mastered time.	Ray Cummings
The man who murdered Goliath.	Geoffrey Homes
The man who murdered himself.	Geoffrey Homes
The man who never was.	Ewen Montague
The man who paid his way.	Walt Sheldon
The man who rode alone.	Lewis B. Patten
The man who said no.	Walt Grove
The man who shot Quantrill.	George C. Appell
The man who sold the moon.	Robert A. Heinlein
The man who upset the universe.	Isaac Asimov
The man who watched the trains go by.	Georges Simenon
The man with my face.	Samuel W. Taylor
The man with one talent.	Josiah E. Greene
The man with the golden arm.	Nelson Algren
The man with the lumpy nose.	Lawrence Lariar
The man with three faces.	Hans-Otto Meissner
The man with two wives.	Patrick Quentin
The man within.	Graham Greene
The man without a face.	John Eugene Hasty
Man without a gun.	Hal G. Evarts
Man without a star.	Dee Linford
A man without friends.	Margaret Echard
The manatee.	Nancy Bruff
Mandingo.	Kyle Onstott
Maneaters of Kumaon.	Jim Corbett
Manet.	S. Lane Faison Jr.
Manhattan.	Seymour Krim
Manhattan nights.	Faith Baldwin
Manhattan transfer.	John Dos Passos
Manhunt.	Donald MacKenzie
Manhunt.	Philip Van Doren Stern
Manhunt west.	Walker A. Tompkins
The manhunter.	Matthew Gant
The manhunter.	Paul Evan Lehman
Maniac rendezvous.	Marc Brandel
Mankind on the run.	Gordon R. Dickson
A man's affair.	Dawn Powell
Man's emerging mind.	N. J. Berrill

Mansion of evil.	Joseph Millard
Mantrap.	Duane Yarnell
Manuela.	William Woods
Many a monster.	Robert Finnegan
Many loves have I.	William Brown Meloney
Many rivers to cross.	Steve Frazee
A many-splendored thing.	Han Suyin
The mapmaker.	Frank G. Slaughter
Maracaibo.	Sterling Silliphant
The Maras affair.	Eliot Reed
Marauders' moon.	Luke Short
The marble fawn.	Nathaniel Hawthorne
The March Hare murders.	E. X. Ferrars
The march up country: Xenophon's Anabasis.	Xenophon
The marching morons.	C. M. Kornbluth
Marcia Blake, publicity girl.	Nancy Webb
Marcia, private secretary.	Zillah K. MacDonald
Mardios Beach.	Oakley Hall
Margaret.	Caroline Slade
Margin of terror.	William P. McGivern
Marianne.	Rhys Davies
The Maricopa trail.	Noel M. Loomis
Marie Antoinette.	Stefan Zweig
Marie of the Isles.	Robert Gaillard
Marihuana.	William Irish
The marijuana mob.	James Hadley Chase
Marilyn Monroe as The Girl.	Sam Shaw
The Marina Street girls.	Rae Loomis
Marital blitz.	Janice Berenstain
	Stanley Berenstain
Marjorie Morningstar.	Herman Wouk
The mark.	Charles Israel
Mark it for murder.	Douglas Sanderson
Mark it with a stone.	George Victor Martin
Mark Kilby solves a murder.	Robert Caine Frazer
Mark of the hunter.	Gene Caesar
The mark of the moon.	Francis Gérard
The mark of Zorro.	Johnston McCulley
Mark Twain.	Mark Twain
Marked down for murder.	Spencer Dean
Marked for murder.	Brett Halliday
Marked for murder.	John Ross Macdonald
The marked men.	Allan Vaughan Elston
Market for murder.	Frank Gruber
Marmaduke.	Brad Anderson
	Phil Leeming
Marmaduke rides again.	Brad Anderson
	Phil Leeming
Marriage and morals.	Bertrand Russell
The marriage bed.	H. Vernor Dixon
A marriage manual.	Abraham Stone
	Hannah Stone
The marriage racket.	Viña Delmar
Marriage, sex and family problems and how to solve them.	J. J. Anthony
Married to murder.	Harry Whittington

Marry for money.	Faith Baldwin
The Mars monopoly.	Jerry Sohl
Marsha.	Margaret Maze Craig
The marshal.	Frank Gruber
The marshal from Deadwood.	John Hunter
Marshal of Deer Creek.	Al Cody
The marshal of Medicine Bend.	Brad Ward
Marshal of Sundown.	Jackson Gregory
Marshal without a badge.	Ray Hogan
Martha Crane.	Charles Gorham
Martha Logan's meat cook book.	Thora Campbell
	Beth Bailey McLean
The Martian chronicles.	Ray Bradbury
The Martian way and other stories.	Isaac Asimov
Martians, go home.	Fredric Brown
Martin Eden.	Jack London
Martinis and murder.	Henry Kane
The Marx brothers.	Kyle Crichton
Mary.	Sholem Asch
Mary Anne.	Daphne du Maurier
Mary Hallam.	Susan Ertz
Marye Dahnke's salad book.	Marye Dahnke
The mask.	Stuart Cloete
A mask for murder.	Henry Kane
Mask of evil.	Charlotte Armstrong
Mask of glass.	Holly Roth
Mask of glory.	Dan Levin
A mask of guilt.	Sigrid de Lima
Masquerade in blue.	Glenn M. Barns
Masquerade into madness.	Russ Meservey
Massacre.	James Warner Bellah
The massacre at San Pablo.	Lewis B. Patten
Massacre at White River.	Lewis B. Patten
Massacre canyon.	Jackson Cole
Massacre creek.	Gordon D. Shirreffs
Massacre trail.	George C. Appell
Master-at-arms.	Rafael Sabatini
Master of life and death.	Robert Silverberg
Master of the world.	Cothburn O'Neal
Masterpiece in murder.	Richard Powell
Masters of deceit.	J. Edgar Hoover
Masters of evolution.	Damon Knight
Matador.	Barnaby Conrad
The matchmaker.	Georges Simenon
Mathematician's delight.	W. W. Sawyer
The mating call.	Wilene Shaw
The mating cry.	Frank Daniels
Mating manual.	Reamer Keller
Matisse.	Clement Greenberg
A matter of morals.	Joseph Gies
A matter of policy.	Sam Merwin Jr.
Matthew Steel.	Mildred Masterson McNeilly
Maupassant.	Guy de Maupassant
Maverick.	Verne Athanas
Maverick empire.	Lewis Ford

A midsummer's night's
dream. William Shakespeare
Midway. Mitsuo Fuchida
Masatake Okumiya
The Midwich cuckoos. John Wyndham
The midwife of Pont
Clery. Flora Sandström
Mig alley. Robert Eunson
Might as well be dead. Rex Stout
The mighty blockhead. Frank Gruber
Mildred Pierce. James M. Cain
Miles to go before
you sleep. Benn Towers
The mill on the Floss. George Eliot
The miller and the
mayor's wife. Pedro de Alarcón
Millie. Donald Henderson
Clarke
Millie's daughter. Donald Henderson
Clarke
Million dollar murder. Thomas Black
Million dollar murder. Edward Ronns
Millions for love. Colette Roberts
Mima. Tom Hanlin
Mimi. Robert W. Taylor
The mind cage. A. E. van Vogt
Mine own executioner. Nigel Balchin
Mine to avenge. Thomas Wills
Mingo Dabney. James Street
The ministry of fear. Graham Greene
Mink coat. Kathleen Norris
Minute for murder. Nicholas Blake
Minute mysteries. Austin Ripley
A minute of prayer. Christopher Cross
Mirabelle: woman of
passion. Ellen Caren
The mirabilis diamond. Jerome Odlum
Miracle gardening. Samm Sinclair Baker
The miracle of growth. Arnold Sundgaard
The miracle of language. Charlton Laird
The miracle of Lourdes. Ruth Cranston
The miracle of the bells. Russell Janney
Miracle on 34th Street. Valentine Davies
Miri. Peter Sourian
Mirror for man. Clyde Kluckhohn
A mirror for observors. Edgar Pangborn
Mirror, mirror on the
wall. Mona Kent
Mirror of your mind. Joseph Whitney
Mischief. Charlotte Armstrong
Miss Agatha doubles
for death. H. L. V. Fletcher
Miss Dilly says no. Theodore Pratt
Miss Jill from Shanghai. Emily Hahn
Miss Lonelyhearts. Nathanael West
Miss Pinkerton. Mary Roberts Rinehart
Missing. Egon Hostovský
The mission. Dean Brelis
Mission: danger. Dod Orsborne
Mission for vengeance. Peter Rabe
Mission: interplanetary. A. E. van Vogt
Mission of gravity. Hal Clement

The mission of
Jeffery Tomaly. Darwin L. Teilhet
Mission to Moscow. Joseph E. Davies
Mission to murder. Richard Glendinning
Mission to the stars. A. E. van Vogt
Mississippi flame. Ryerson Johnson
The Missouri maiden. C. William Harrison
Mr. Ace. Helen Christy
Mr. Adam. Pat Frank
Mr. and Mrs. Cugat. Isabel Scott Rorick
Mr. and Mrs. North and Frances Lockridge
a pinch of poison. Richard Lockridge
Mr. and Mrs. North and Frances Lockridge
the poisoned playboy. Richard Lockridge
Mr. and Mrs. North Frances Lockridge
meet murder. Richard Lockridge
Mr. Angel comes aboard. Charles G. Booth
Mr. Arkadin. Orson Welles
Mr. Blandings builds
his dream house. Eric Hodgins
Mister Glencannon. Guy Gilpatric
Mr. Littlejohn. Martin Flavin
Mr. Midshipman
Hornblower. C. S. Forester
Mr. Parker Pyne,
detective. Agatha Christie
Mr. Pinkerton at the
Old Angel. David Frome
Mr. Pinkerton finds a
body. David Frome
Mr. Pinkerton goes to
Scotland Yard. David Frome
Mr. Pinkerton grows a
beard. David Frome
Mr. Pinkerton has the
clue. David Frome
Mr. Polton explains. R. Austin Freeman
Mister Roberts. Thomas Heggen
Mister Smith. Louis Bromfield
Mr. Smith's hat. Helen Reilly
Mr. Taxicab. James Maresca
Mr. Trouble. William Ard
The mistress. H. C. Branner
The mistress. Carter Brown
The mistress. Theodora Keogh
Mistress Glory. Susan Morley
Mistress murder. Peter Cheyney
Mistress of Horror
House. William Woody
Mistress of rogues. Rosamond Marshall
Mistress Wilding. Rafael Sabatini
Mitsou. Colette
Mittee. Daphne Rooke
The mob says murder. Albert Conroy
Moby Dick. Herman Melville
Mocambu. Marcos Spinelli
Model for murder. Robert Kyle
Model for murder. Stephen Marlowe
Model railroading.
Modern American
painting and sculpture. Samuel Hunter
Modern battle. Paul W. Thompson

The mountain and the
  valley.   Ernest Buckler
Mountain boy.   Felix Holt
The mountain boys.   Paul Webb
The mountain cat
  murders.   Rex Stout
Mountain girl.   Cord Wainer
The mountain is young.   Han Suyin
Mountain meadow.   John Buchan
The mountain men.   Bill Gulick
Mountain pony.   Henry V. Larom
Mountain pony and the
  pinto calf.   Henry V. Larom
The mountains have
  no shadow.   Owen Cameron
Mourn the hangman.   Harry Whittington
Mourned on Sunday.   Helen Reilly
Mourning after.   Thomas B. Dewey
A mouse is born.   Anita Loos
The mouse that roared.   Leonard Wibberley
Move along, stranger.   Frank Castle
The moving finger.   Agatha Christie
The moving target.   John Ross Macdonald
Mrs. Candy and
  Saturday night.   Robert Tallant
Mrs. Craddock.   W. Somerset Maugham
Mrs. Homicide.   Day Keene
Mrs. McGinty's dead.   Agatha Christie
Mrs. Mike.   Benedict Freedman
     Nancy Freedman
Mrs. Miniver.   Jan Struther
Mrs. Murdock takes a
  case.   George Harmon Coxe
Mrs. Parkington.   Louis Bromfield
Much loved books,
  volume I.   James O'Donnell
     Bennett
Mud on the stars.   William Bradford Huie
The mudlark.   Theodore Bonnet
The mugger.   Ed McBain
Mugs, molls and Dr.
  Harvey.   George Malcolm-Smith
Mum's the word for
  murder.   Brett Halliday
Murder after hours.   Agatha Christie
Murder all over.   Cleve F. Adams
Murder among friends.   Lange Lewis
Murder and the
  married virgin.   Brett Halliday
Murder and the
  wanton bride.   Brett Halliday
Murder as a fine art.   Francis Bonnamy
Murder at Arroways.   Helen Reilly
Murder at Cambridge.   Q. Patrick
Murder at Hazelmoor.   Agatha Christie
Murder at midnight.   Richard Sale
Murder at midnight.   R. A. J. Walling
Murder at nightfall.   Edna Sherry
Murder at the Vicarage.   Agatha Christie
Murder at the White Cat.   Mary Roberts Rinehart
Murder bait.   Duane Yarnell
Murder begins at home.   Delano Ames
Murder by an aristocrat.   Mignon G. Eberhart

Murder by latitude.   Rufus King
Murder by magic.   Amelia Reynolds Long
A murder by marriage.   Robert George Dean
Murder by prescription.   Jonathan Stagge
Murder by the book.   Rex Stout
Murder by the clock.   Rufus King
Murder by the dozen.   Hugh Wiley
Murder by the pack.   Carl G. Hodges
Murder can't stop.   W. T. Ballard
Murder can't wait.   Manning Lee Stokes
Murder challenges
  Valcour.   Rufus King
Murder charge.   Wade Miller
Murder cheats the bride.   Anthony Gilbert
Murder city.   Oakley Hall
Murder comes calling.   Malcolm Douglas
Murder comes first.   Frances Lockridge
     Richard Lockridge
Murder doll.   Milton K. Ozaki
Murder enters the   W. A. Barber
  picture.   R. F. Schabelitz
Murder for charity.   Owen Dudley
Murder for madame.   Adam Knight
Murder for the asking.   George Harmon Coxe
Murder for the bride.   John D. MacDonald
Murder for the holidays.   Howard Rigsby
Murder for two.   George Harmon Coxe
Murder! Great true
  crime cases.   Alan Hynd
Murder has many faces.   William Grew
Murder in a hurry.   Frances Lockridge
     Richard Lockridge
Murder in a nunnery.   Eric Shepherd
Murder in any language.   Kelley Roos
Murder in Baracoa.   Paul Walsh
Murder in brass.   Lewis Padgett
Murder in Fiji.   John W. Vandercook
Murder in Havana.   George Harmon Coxe
Murder in Las Vegas.   Jack Waer
Murder in Lima.   Robert A. Levey
Murder in Majorca.   Michael Bryan
Murder in Manhattan.   John Roeburt
Murder in marble.   Judson Philips
Murder in Mesopotamia.   Agatha Christie
Murder in Miami.   Brett Halliday
Murder in mink.   Robert George Dean
Murder in Monaco.   John Flagg
Murder in Paradise.   Richard Gehman
Murder in Port Afrique.   Bernard Victor Dryer
Murder in red.   Frank Castle
Murder in retrospect.   Agatha Christie
Murder in Room 13.   Albert Conroy
Murder in season.   Octavus Roy Cohen
Murder in Shinbone
  Alley.   Helen Reilly
Murder in the Calais
  coach.   Agatha Christie
Murder in the family.   Leslie Charteris
Murder in the madhouse.   Jonathan Latimer
Murder in the mews.   Helen Reilly
Murder in the mist.   Zelda Popkin
Murder in the Navy.   Richard Marsten

Murders at Scandal house. Peter Hunt
Murder's end.   Robert Kelston
Murders in silk.   Mike Teagle
Murders in volume II.   Elizabeth Daly
Murder's nest.   Charlotte Armstrong
Murder's web.   Dorothy Dunn
Murdock's acid test.   George Harmon Coxe
Muscle boy.   Bud Clifton
Music and imagination.   Aaron Copland
Music for the millions.   David Ewen
Music out of Dixie.   Harold Sinclair
Musk, hashish and blood.   Hector France
Mustang.   Thomas C. Hinkle
Mustang Mesa.   Peter Field
The mustangers.   Jack Barton
The mustangs.   J. Frank Dobie
The mustard seed.   Vicki Baum
The mutant weapon.   Murray Leinster
Mutiny on the Bounty.   James Norman Hall
                            Charles Nordhoff
My best science fiction   Oscar J. Friend
  story.   Leo Margulies
My bride in the storm.   Theodore Pratt
My brother, my enemy.   Mitchell Wilson
My brother the gunman.   William Heuman
My brother's bride.   William March
My brother's keeper.   Marcia Davenport
My brother's wife.   Harry Davis
My business is murder.   Henry Kane
My Chinese wife.   Karl Eskelund
My cousin Rachel.   Daphne du Maurier
My days of anger.   James T. Farrell
My dead wife.   William Worley
My deadly angel.   John Chelton
My dear Bella.   Arthur Kober
My dearest love.   Emilie Loring
My enemy, my wife.   Allen Haden
My enemy, the world.   Guido D'Agostino
My face for the world
  to see.   Alfred Hayes
My fair lady.   Alan Jay Lerner
My father--my son.   William Dufty
                            Edward G. Robinson Jr.
My favorite football
  stories.   Red Grange
My favorite sports
  stories.   Bill Stern
My first 10,000,000
  sponsors.   Frank Edwards
My first two thousand   Paul Eldridge
  years.   George Sylvester
                              Viereck
My flag is down.   James Maresca
My flesh is sweet.   Day Keene
My forbidden past.   Polan Banks
My greatest day in
  baseball.   John Carmichael
My greatest day in   Leonard Lewin
  football.   Murray Goodman
My gun, her body.   Jeff Bogar
My gun is my law.   Will Ermine
My gun is quick.   Mickey Spillane

My husband keeps
  telling me to go
  to hell.   Ella Bentley Arthur
My kingdom for a hearse. Craig Rice
My Lady Greensleeves.   Constance
                              Beresford-Howe
My late wives.   Carter Dickson
My life and hard times. James Thurber
My life as an Indian.   J. W. Schultz
My life in crime.   John Bartlow Martin
My Lord America.   Alec Rackowe
My lord what a morning. Marian Anderson
My love is violent.   Thomas B. Dewey
My love must wait.   Ernestine Hill
My love wears black.   Octavus Roy Cohen
My man Godfrey.   Eric Hatch
My mistress, death.   Robert Spafford
My name is Aram.   William Saroyan
My name is Michael
  Sibley.   John Bingham
My name is Rose.   Theodora Keogh
My name is violence.   John D. Matthews
                            Jeffrey Roche
My old man.   Richard B. Erno
My old man's badge.   Ferguson Findley
My own murderer.   Richard Hull
My private hangman.   Norman Herries
My several worlds.   Pearl S. Buck
My sister Eileen.   Ruth McKenney
My sister, goodnight.   Gordon McDonell
My sister, my beloved.   Edwina Mark
My sister, my bride.   Merriam Modell
My six convicts.   Donald Powell Wilson
My son, the murderer.   Patrick Quentin
My ten years in a
  quandary.   Robert Benchley
My true love lies.   Lenore Glen Offord
The Mycenaid.   C. Everett Cooper
The mysterious affair
  at Styles.   Agatha Christie
Mysterious Mickey Finn. Elliot Paul
The mysterious Mr. Quin. Agatha Christie
Mystery at Spanish
  hacienda.   Jackson Gregory
The mystery companion.   A. L. Furman
Mystery house.   Kathleen Norris
Mystery in blue.   Gertrude E. Mallette
The mystery of Batty
  Ridge.   Alan Gregg
Mystery of Hidden
  Village.   Annette Turngren
The mystery of
  Hunting's end.   Mignon G. Eberhart
The mystery of the
  Baghdad chest.   Agatha Christie
The mystery of the
  blue train.   Agatha Christie
The mystery of the
  crime in Cabin 66.   Agatha Christie
The mystery of the
  dead police.   Philip MacDonald

N

The NBC book of stars.	Earl Wilson
N or M?	Agatha Christie
N.Y., N.Y.	Will Oursler
Nadia.	Assia Djebar
Naked acre.	Francis Mitchell
Naked and alone.	Michael Lawrence
The naked and the damned.	Robert Shafer
The naked and the dead.	Norman Mailer
The naked and the guilty.	Ralph Ingersoll
The naked and the lost.	Franklin M. Davis Jr.
The naked angel.	Jack Webb
Naked canvas.	Warwick Scott
The naked city.	Sterling Silliphant
Naked ebony.	Dan Cushman
The naked eye.	Gita Lewis
	Henriette Martin
The naked fear.	Carl Offord
Naked fury.	Day Keene
The naked heart.	John Lee Weldon
Naked Hollywood.	Mel Harris
	Weegee
The naked hours.	Wenzell Brown
The naked hunter.	William Woolfolk
The naked I.	Roy Chanslor
Naked in the dark.	Gene Paul
Naked in the night.	Jon Cleary
Naked in the streets.	Ryerson Johnson
The naked jungle.	Harry Whittington
The naked land.	Lee E. Wells
The naked maja.	Samuel Edwards
Naked morning.	R. V. Cassill
The naked night.	Dan Brennan
Naked on roller skates.	Maxwell Bodenheim
The naked range.	Steven C. Lawrence
The naked rich.	Vivian Connell
Naked sin.	Gordon Clark
The naked spur.	Rolfe Bloom
	Allan Ullman
Naked spurs.	Larry Lawson
The naked storm.	Simon Eisner
The naked streets.	Vasco Pratolini
The naked sword.	Donald Barr Chidsey
The naked sword.	Anthea Mitchell
The naked sun.	Isaac Asimov
Naked tide.	Roderic Hastings
Naked to mine enemies.	Susan Yorke
Naked to my past.	Frederic Wakeman
Naked to my pride.	Howard Rigsby
The naked year.	Philip Atlee
The name is Archer.	John Ross Macdonald
The name is Chambers.	Henry Kane
The name is Malone.	Craig Rice
The name is Mary.	Fannie Hurst
Name your poison.	Helen Reilly
The name's Buchanan.	Jonas Ward
Nana.	Émile Zola
Nana's mother.	Émile Zola
Nancy Ross, private secretary.	Jeanne Judson
Naomi Martin.	Clarkson Crane
Napoleon.	Emil Ludwig
Narcotic agent.	Maurice Helbrant
The narrow cell.	Dale Clark
The narrow corner.	W. Somerset Maugham
The narrowing circle.	Julian Symons
The Narrows.	Ann Petry
The Natchez woman.	Alice Walworth Graham
National Velvet.	Enid Bagnold
Native girl.	Harry Whittington
Native son.	Richard Wright
Native stone.	Edwin Gilbert
The natural.	Bernard Malamud
Natural child.	Calder Willingham
The natural way to better golf.	Jack Burke
The nature of living things.	Robert K. Enders / C. Brooke Worth
The nature of love.	H. E. Bates
The nature of the non-western world.	Vera Micheles Dean
The nature of the universe.	Fred Hoyle
Naughty 90's joke book.	Harold Meyers
Nautilus 90 north.	William R. Anderson / Clay Blair Jr.
Navajo Canyon.	Thomas W. Blackburn
The navigator.	Jules Roy
The Navy Colt.	Frank Gruber
The Nazarene.	Sholem Asch
The neat little corpse.	Max Murray
The Necronomicon.	
Nectar is a sieve.	Kamala Markandaya
Negative of a nude.	Charles E. Fritch
The Negro in American culture.	Margaret Just Butcher
The neighbors' kids.	George Clark
Neither five nor three.	Helen MacInnes
Nell Gwyn: royal mistress.	John H. Wilson
Nellie the nurse.	Kaz
The neon jungle.	John D. MacDonald
The neon wilderness.	Nelson Algren
Nerves.	Lester del Rey
The nester.	John S. Daniels
The net.	Edward Ronns
Net of cobwebs.	Elisabeth Sanxay Holding
Nevada.	Zane Grey
Nevada killing.	Duke Montana
Never bet your life.	George Harmon Coxe
Never come morning.	Nelson Algren
Never kill a cop!	Mel Colton
Never kill a cop.	Lee Costigan
Never kill on Sundays.	Ralpha Johns
Never leave me.	Harold Robbins
Never look back.	Mignon G. Eberhart
Never love a stranger.	Harold Robbins
Never plead guilty.	Bernard Averbuch / John Wesley Noble
Never say die.	Milton K. Ozaki
Never say love.	Pierre Sichel

Never say no to a killer. Jonathan Gant
Never smile at children. E. T. French
Never so few. Tom T. Chamales
Never the same again. Gerald Tesch
Never too young. Joseph Weeks
Never victorious,
  never defeated. Taylor Caldwell
Never walk alone. Rufus King
The new adventures of
  Ellery Queen. Ellery Queen
The New American guide
  to colleges. Gene R. Hawes
The New American handy Albert H. Morehead
  college dictionary. Loy Morehead
New American Roget's
  college thesaurus in
  dictionary form.
The New American
  Webster dictionary.
The new art of selling. Elmer G. Leterman
New Avon bedside
  companion.
New campus writing. Nolan Miller
New campus writing,
  no. 2. Nolan Miller
The new Crest crossword
  puzzle book. James Freeman
The new Dell modern
  American dictionary. Jess Stein
A new desire. Stanley Kauffmann
The new Hammond-Dell
  world atlas.
New handbook of the Hubert J. Bernhard
  heavens. et al.
The new Italian cook
  book. Rose L. Sorce
The new Jimmy Hatlo book. Jimmy Hatlo
New Orleans lady. Viña Delmar
The new Peter Arno
  Pocket book. Peter Arno
The new Pocket anthology
  of American verse. Oscar Williams
The new Pocket quiz book. Louise Crittenden
  Rosejeanne Slifer
New poems by American
  poets. Rolfe Humphries
New poems by American
  poets no. 2. Rolfe Humphries
The new quiz book. Albert H. Morehead
  Geoffrey Mott-Smith
New short novels. Mary Louise Aswell
New short novels no. 2.
New soldier's handbook.
A new southern harvest. Albert Erskine
  Robert Penn Warren
New standard book of
  model letters for all
  occasions. Leo J. Henkin
New stories for men. Charles Grayson
New tales of space
  and time. Raymond J. Healy
The New testament.

The new veteran. Charles G. Bolte
New voices: American
  writing today. Don M. Wolfe
The new way to eat and
  get slim. Donald G. Cooley
New ways to greater Roger B. Goodman
  word power. David Lewin
New world writing no. 1.
New world writing no. 2.
New world writing no. 3.
New world writing no. 4.
New world writing no. 5.
New world writing no. 6.
New world writing no. 7.
New world writing no. 8.
New world writing no. 9.
New world writing
  no. 10.
New world writing
  no. 11.
New world writing
  no. 12.
New world writing
  no. 13.
New world writing
  no. 14.
New world writing
  no. 15.
New worlds of modern
  science. Leonard Engel
New York call girl. Robert Lowry
New York confidential. Jack Lait
  Lee Mortimer
New York 22. Ilka Chase
The newest Jimmy Hatlo
  cartoon book. Jimmy Hatlo
The next development
  in man. Lancelot Law White
The next Germany.
Next time is for life. Paul Warren
Nice guys finish dead. Albert Conroy
Nice guys finish last. Robert Kyle
Nigger heaven. Carl Van Vechten
Nigger John. Sam Meriwether
Night after night. Leonard Nathan
Night after night. Steve Thurman
The night air. Harrison Dowd
Night and the city. Gerald Kersh
The night and the naked. Gordon Merrick
Night at the Mocking
  Widow. Carter Dickson
Night at the Vulcan. Ngaio Marsh
The night before
  Chancellorsville. Shelby Foote
The night before dying. Robert M. Coates
The night before murder. Steve Fisher
Night boat to Paris. Richard Jessup
The night-branders. Walt Coburn
Night bus. Samuel Hopkins Adams
Night cry. William L. Stuart
Night extra. William P. McGivern

Night fell on Georgia.	Charles Samuels
	Louise Samuels
Night fire.	Edward Kimbrough
Night flight.	Antoine de Saint
	Exupéry
A night for treason.	John Jakes
Night has a thousand	
eyes.	William Irish
The night horseman.	Max Brand
Night in Bombay.	Louis Bromfield
Night in Manila.	John Langdon
The night is mine.	David Davidson
The night is my undoing.	Delmar Jackson
The night is so dark.	Robert M. Coates
The night it happened.	Martin Manners
Night lady.	William Campbell
	Gault
The night life of the	
gods.	Thorne Smith
Night light.	Douglass Wallop
Night man.	Lucille Fletcher
	Allan Ullman
Night never ends.	Frederick Lorenz
Night of fire and snow.	Alfred Coppel
Night of flame.	Warren Desmond
The night of the coyotes.	Philip Ketchum
The night of the hunter.	Davis Grubb
Night of the Jabberwock.	Fredric Brown
Night of the quarter	
moon.	Franklin Coen
Night of violence.	Louis Charbonneau
A night out.	Basil Heatter
Night passage.	Norman A. Fox
Night raid.	Frank Bonham
Night raider of the	
Atlantic.	Terence Robertson
The night raiders.	Hal G. Evarts
Night rider.	Robert Penn Warren
Night shift.	Maritta Wolff
The night thorn.	Ian Gordon
A night to remember.	Walter Lord
Night unto night.	Philip Wylie
Night walker.	Donald Hamilton
Night ward.	Noah Gordon
The night was made	
for murder.	Will Cotton
The night watch.	Thomas Walsh
The night winds.	Brian Talbot Cleeve
A night with Mr.	
Primrose.	Whitfield Cook
Night without sleep.	Elick Moll
Night without stars.	Winston Graham
Nightfall.	David Goodis
Nightmare.	Guy Endore
Nightmare.	William Irish
Nightmare alley.	William Lindsay
	Gresham
Nightmare at noon.	Stewart Sterling
Nightmare in Manhattan.	Thomas Walsh
Nightmare town.	Dashiell Hammett
Nightrider deputy.	Ralph R. Perry
Nightrunners of Bengal.	John Masters

Nights of love and	
laughter.	Henry Miller
Nightshade.	John N. Makris
The Nightshade Ring.	Lindsay Hardy
The nightwalkers.	Beverley Cross
Nikki.	Stuart Friedman
Nina.	Donald Henderson
	Clarke
Nine--and death makes	
ten.	Carter Dickson
Nine days to Mukalla.	Frederic Prokosch
The nine lives of	
Michael Todd.	Art Cohn
Nine miles to Reno.	Jill Stern
Nine stories.	J. D. Salinger
The nine tailors.	Dorothy L. Sayers
Nine times nine.	H. H. Holmes
Nine to five.	W. H. Prosser
The nine waxed faces.	Francis Beeding
The nine wrong answers.	John Dickson Carr
1984.	George Orwell
The 1955 baseball	
almanac.	Hy Turkin
The 1955 Pocket almanac.	George Gallup
The 1954 Pocket almanac.	George Gallup
The 1959 pro football	
handbook.	Don Schiffer
The 1956 baseball	
almanac.	Don Schiffer
The 1956 Pocket almanac	
of facts.	George Gallup
1953 racing almanac.	Rowland Barber
	John I. Day
1919.	John Dos Passos
Nineteen stories.	Graham Greene
19 tales of terror.	Hallie Burnett
	Whit Burnett
Ninth Avenue.	Maxwell Bodenheim
The ninth hour.	Ben Benson
The 9th Pocket book of	Margaret Petherbridge
crossword puzzles.	Farrar
The ninth wave.	Eugene Burdick
No angels for me.	William Ard
No bed of her own.	Val Lewton
No bed of her own.	Cicely Schiller
No benefit of law.	Brett Rider
No blade of grass.	John Christopher
No bones about it.	Ruth Sawtell Wallis
No boundaries.	Henry Kuttner
	C. L. Moore
No bugles, no glory.	Fred Grove
No bugles tonight.	Bruce Lancaster
No business for a lady.	James Rubel
No but I saw the movie.	Peter De Vries
No coffin for the	
corpse.	Clayton Rawson
No crime for a lady.	Zelda Popkin
No down payment.	John McPartland
No entry.	Manning Coles
No good from a corpse.	Leigh Brackett
The no-gun fighter.	Nelson Nye
No halo for me.	Jason Manor

No hands on the clock. Geoffrey Homes
No head for her pillow. Sam S. Taylor
No hiding place. Beth Day
No highway. Nevil Shute
No letters for the dead. Gale Wilhelm
No luck for a lady. Floyd Mahannah
No man is an island. Thomas Merton
No marriage in paradise. Myron Brinig
No mask for murder. Andrew Garve
No money down--36 months
  to pay! Charles Preston
No mourners present. Frank G. Presnell
No narrow path. Catharine Whitcomb
No nice girl. Gale Wilhelm
No orchids for Miss
  Blandish. James Hadley Chase
No other white men. Julia Davis
No people like show
  people. Maurice Zolotow
No place on earth. Louis Charbonneau
No place to hide. David Bradley
No pockets in a shroud. Horace McCoy
No private heaven. Faith Baldwin
No range is free. E. E. Halleran
No star is lost. James T. Farrell
No surrender. Martha Albrand
No survivors. Will Henry
No tears for Hilda. Andrew Garve
No time at all. Charles Einstein
No time for sergeants. Mac Hyman
No time like the future. Nelson Bond
No time like tomorrow. Brian W. Aldiss
No time to kill. George Harmon Coxe
No trumpet before him. Nelia Gardner White
No vacation for Maigret. Georges Simenon
No villain need be. Vardis Fisher
No wings on a cop. Cleve F. Adams
No world of their own. Poul Anderson
Nobody cares for me. Sara Harris
Nobody dies in Paris. Jerry Weil
Nobody heard the shot. Donald Barr Chidsey
Nobody lives forever. W. R. Burnett
Nobody wore black. Delano Ames
Nobody's in town. Edna Ferber
Nonce. Michael Brandon
None but the lethal
  heart. Carter Brown
A noose for the
  desperado. Clifton Adams
Nora Meade, M.D. Elizabeth Wesley
North from Rome. Helen MacInnes
North of 36. Emerson Hough
The North Star. Will Henry
North to Texas. Noel M. Loomis
The northern light. A. J. Cronin
The Norths meet murder. Frances Lockridge
  Richard Lockridge
Not as a stranger. Morton Thompson
Not for a curse. Karl Kramer
Not quite dead enough. Rex Stout
Not so evil as Eve. John Creighton
Not this August. C. M. Kornbluth

Not too narrow...not
  too deep. Richard Sale
Not with my neck. Ben Kerner
  Tom Van Dycke
Not yet... Tereska Torres
Notched guns. William Hopson
Nothing but the night. James Yaffe
Nothing can rescue me. Elizabeth Daly
Nothing in her way. Charles Williams
The nothing man. Jim Thompson
Nothing more than
  murder. Jim Thompson
Nothing so strange. James Hilton
Nothing to lose but
  my life. Louis Trimble
Notorious. Day Keene
Now I lay me down to
  sleep. Ludwig Bemelmans
Now I'll tell one. Harry Hershfield
Now is the time. Lillian Smith
Now it's my turn. M. E. Chaber
Now sleeps the beast. Don Tracy
Now, voyager. Olive Higgins Prouty
Now, will you try for
  murder? Harry Olesker
Now you see me, now
  you don't. Roy Michaels
Nude croquet.
Nude in mink. Sax Rohmer
Nudist cartoons. Harold Meyers
Number one. John Dos Passos
The nun's story. Kathryn Hulme
Nurse Fairchild's
  decision. Zillah K. MacDonald
A nurse for Galleon Key. Ethel Hamill
Nurse Howard's
  assignment. Virginia Roberts
Nurse into woman. Marguerite Mooers
  Marshall
Nurse Kathy. Adeline McElfresh
Nurse Landon's
  challenge. Adelaide Humphries
Nurse on location. Virginia Roberts
Nurse with wings. Marguerite Mooers
  Marshall
The nutmeg tree. Margery Sharp
The nymph and the lamp. Thomas H. Raddall

O

The O.S.S. and I.	William J. Morgan
Oath of seven.	George Albert Glay
Obit deferred.	Louis Trimble
Obit delayed.	Helen Nielsen
The obsessed.	Gertrude Schweitzer
Occam's razor.	David Duncan
Occasion of sin.	Robert William Taylor
Octagon House.	Phoebe Atwood Taylor
The October country.	Ray Bradbury
The octopus.	Frank Norris
Odd girl out.	Ann Bannon
Odd man out.	F. L. Green
The odd ones.	Edwina Mark
Odd woman out.	Joseph Linklater
Odds against tomorrow.	William P. McGivern
Odor of violets.	Baynard Kendrick
The Odyssey.	Homerus
The Oedipus plays of Sophocles.	Sophocles
Oedipus the King.	Sophocles
Of a strange woman.	James Wakefield Burke
Of all my sins.	Thomas Rourke
Of all possible worlds.	William Tenn
Of former love.	Emma Laird
Of human bondage.	W. Somerset Maugham
Of love forbidden.	Anna Elisabet Weirauch
Of mice and men.	John Steinbeck
Of missing persons.	David Goodis
Of sin and the flesh.	Robert De Vries
Of tender sin.	David Goodis
Of the imitation of Christ.	Thomas à Kempis
Off limits.	Hans Habe
Off on a comet.	Jules Verne
Off the beaten orbit.	Judith Merril
Off the cuff.	Jerry Lieberman
The office encyclopedia.	N. H. Mager
	S. K. Mager
Office laffs.	Charles Preston
Office nurse.	Adelaide Humphries
The office wife.	Faith Baldwin
Office wife.	Jerry Weil
Officers' plot to kill Hitler.	Constantine FitzGibbon
The official American Medical Association book of health.	W. W. Bauer
The Ogden Nash Pocket book.	Ogden Nash
Oh, doctor!	Charles Preston
Oh, murderer mine.	Norbert Davis
Oh, promised land.	James Street
Oh, what a wonderful wedding.	Virginia Rowans
Oh, you Tex!	William MacLeod Raine
O'Halloran's luck.	Stephen Vincent Benét
Oil for the lamps of China.	Alice Tisdale Hobart
Ol' man Adam an' his chillun.	Roark Bradford
The old battle ax.	Elisabeth Sanxay Holding
The old blood.	Edgar Mittelholzer
Old bones.	Herman Petersen
The old copper collar.	Dan Cushman
The old dark house.	J. B. Priestley
The old goat.	Tiffany Thayer
Old lover's ghost.	Leslie Ford
The old man.	William Faulkner
The old man's place.	John B. Sanford
The old Santa Fe Trail.	Stanley Vestal
Old soldiers never die.	Wolf Mankowitz
Old Yeller.	Fred Gipson
Oliver Twist.	Charles Dickens
Olivia.	Olivia
Olympic cavalcade of sports.	John V. Grombach
O'Malley's nuns.	Bill O'Malley
Omar Khayyam.	Harold Lamb
O'Mara.	Laurence Greene
Omnibus of American humor.	Robert N. Linscott
On an odd note.	Gerald Kersh
On becoming a woman.	Irene Kane
	Mary McGee Williams
On borrowed time.	Lawrence Edward Watkin
On ice.	Robert George Dean
On life and sex.	Havelock Ellis
On love, family and the good life.	Plutarchus
On my own.	Eleanor Roosevelt
On the beach.	Nevil Shute
On the dodge.	William MacLeod Raine
On the hook.	Richard Powell
On the midnight tide.	Don Tracy
On the prod.	Ernest Haycox
On the road.	Jack Kerouac
On the spot.	Edgar Wallace
On to Santa Fe.	William Heuman
On understanding science.	James B. Conant
Once a fighter...	Les Savage Jr.
Once a widow.	Lee Roberts
Once in Vienna.	Vicki Baum
Once off guard.	J. H. Wallis
One against a bullet horde.	Walker A. Tompkins
One against eternity.	A. E. van Vogt
One against Herculum.	Jerry Sohl
One against the odds.	Norbert Fagan
One angel less.	H. W. Roden
One basket.	Edna Ferber
One by one.	Fan Nichols
One deadly dawn.	Harry Whittington
One foot in heaven.	Hartzell Spence
One for hell.	Jada M. Davis
One for the road.	Fredric Brown
One for the road.	Robert Dietrich
One got away.	Harry Whittington

P

Peabody's mermaid.	Constance Jones
	Guy Pearce Jones
Peace marshal.	Frank Gruber
Peace of mind.	Joshua Loth Liebman
Peace of soul.	Fulton J. Sheen
Peace with God.	Billy Graham
The peacemaker.	Richard Poole
The peacock feather murders.	Carter Dickson
The pearl.	John Steinbeck
Pebble in the sky.	Isaac Asimov
The peddler.	Douglas Ring
The Pedlocks.	Stephen Longstreet
Peeping Tom.	Jack Woodford
The Peeping Tom murders.	Jack Baynes
Peggy covers the news.	Emma Bugbee
Pemmican.	Vardis Fisher
Pencil points to murder.	W. A. Barber
	R. F. Schabelitz
The Penguin book of sonnets.	Carl Withers
The Penguin guide to California.	Carl Maas
The Penguin Hoyle.	Albert H. Morehead
	Geoffrey Mott-Smith
Penguin Island.	Anatole France
The Pennycross murders.	Maurice Procter
Peony.	Pearl S. Buck
The people against O'Hara.	Eleazar Lipsky
The people maker.	Damon Knight
People minus X.	Raymond Z. Gallun
The pepper tree.	John Jennings
Père Goriot.	Honoré de Balzac
Perelandra.	C. S. Lewis
The perennial boarder.	Phoebe Atwood Taylor
The perfect frame.	William Ard
The perfect hostess.	Maureen Daly
Perfect 36.	Ed Spingarn
The perfect victim.	James McKimmey
Peril at End house.	Agatha Christie
Perilous passage.	Arthur Mayse
The Perma cross word puzzle dictionary.	Frank Eaton Newman
The Perma quiz book.	Joseph Nathan Kane
The Perma X-word puzzle book.	Alexander Field
Persephone.	Thomas Skinner Willings
The Persian cat.	John Flagg
The persistent image.	Gladys Schmitt
The personality of animals.	H. Munro Fox
Perversity.	Francis Carco
The Peter Arno Pocket book.	Peter Arno
Pets--including women.	Charles Preston
Peyton Place.	Grace Metalious
The phantom canoe.	William Byron Mowery
The phantom emperor.	Neil H. Swanson
The phantom filly.	George Agnew Chamberlain
Phantom fortress.	Bruce Lancaster
Phantom lady.	William Irish
The phantom of the opera.	Gaston Leroux
The Phantom Pass.	William Colt MacDonald
The Philadelphia murder story.	Leslie Ford
The Philadelphia story.	Philip Barry
The Philadelphian.	Richard Powell
The philanderer.	Stanley Kauffmann
Philosopher's holiday.	Irwin Edman
Philosophy for pleasure.	Hector Hawton
Philosophy in a new key.	Susanne K. Langer
Phyllis.	Ted Key
The physiology of love.	Rémy de Gourmont
The physiology of sex.	Kenneth Walker
Picaroon.	Ernest Dudley
Picasso (blue and rose periods).	William S. Lieberman
Pick your victim.	Pat McGerr
Pickup alley.	Edward Ronns
Pick-up on Noon Street.	Raymond Chandler
Picnic.	William Inge
The picture of Dorian Grey.	Oscar Wilde
Picture quiz book.	John Paul Adams
Pierre's woman.	Jacques de Bout
Pigboats.	Theodore Roscoe
The pigskin bag.	Bruno Fischer
Pikes peek or bust.	Earl Wilson
Pilgrimage to earth.	Robert Sheckley
Pilgrim's inn.	Elizabeth Goudge
The pilgrim's progress.	John Bunyan
Pillars of the sky.	Will Henry
Pillow talk.	Marvin H. Albert
A pinch of poison.	Frances Lockridge
	Richard Lockridge
The pink camellia.	Temple Bailey
The pink hotel.	Patrick Dennis
	Dorothy Erskine
The pink umbrella murder.	Frances Crane
The Pinkerton case book.	Alan Hynd
Pinocchio.	Carlo Collodi
Pioneer loves.	Ernest Haycox
The pioneers.	Courtney Ryley Cooper
The pioneers.	Jack Schaefer
Pipeline to battle.	Peter Rainier
The pipes are calling.	Donald Barr Chidsey
Piping hot.	Émile Zola
Pirate wench.	Frank Shay
Pirates of the range.	B. M. Bower
The pirates of Zan.	Murray Leinster
Pissarro.	John Rewald
Pistol law.	Paul Evan Lehman
Pistol pardners.	William MacLeod Raine
Pistol passport.	Eugene Cunningham
Pistol Pete.	Frank Eaton
Pistolman.	Steve Frazee
Pistols on the Pecos.	Paul Evan Lehman

Pitcairn's Island.   James Norman Hall
                           Charles Nordhoff
Pitchman.   Robin Moore
The pitfall.   Jay Dratler
Pius XII: Eugenio   Oscar Halecki
  Pacelli, Pope of peace. James F. Murray Jr.
Pivot man.   Dick Friendlich
A place called
  Estherville.   Erskine Caldwell
The place of jackals.   Ronald Hardy
The plague and I.   Betty MacDonald
The Plague court murders. Carter Dickson
Plague ship.   Andrew North
Plain murder.   C. S. Forester
The planet explorer.   Murray Leinster
A planet for Texans.   John J. McGuire
                           H. Beam Piper
Planet in peril.   John Christopher
The planet killers.   Robert Silverberg
Planet of no return.   Poul Anderson
Planet of the dreamers.   John D. MacDonald
Platoon.   Adam Singer
Play a lone hand.   Luke Short
Play for keeps.   Harry Whittington
Play it cool.   Jack Gerstine
Play it yourself.   Jack Bassett
                           Norman Monath
Playgirls, U.S.A.   Eddie Davis
Playthings of desire.   J. Wesley Putnam
Pleasant Valley.   Louis Bromfield
Please don't eat the
  daisies.   Jean Kerr
Please send me
  absolutely free!   Arkady Leokum
Pleasure Island.   William Maier
The pleasures of the
  jazz age.   William Hodapp
The plot against earth.   Calvin M. Knox
A plot for murder.   Fredric Brown
Plunder.   Benjamin Appel
Plunder of the sun.   David Dodge
Plunder range.   Homer Hatten
Plunder valley.   Nelson Nye
The plundered land.   Coe Williams
The plunderers.   L. P. Holmes
Plus blood in their
  veins.   Robert Paul Smith
The Plymouth adventure.   Ernest Gebler
Pnin.   Vladimir Nabokov
The Pocket Aristotle.   Aristotle
The Pocket Atlantic.   Edward Weeks
The Pocket aviation
  quiz book.   Milton Figen
Pocket battleship.   H. J. Brennecke
                           Theodor Krancke
The Pocket Bible.
The Pocket book magazine. Franklin Watts
The Pocket book magazine
  no. 2.   Franklin Watts
The Pocket book magazine
  no. 3.   Franklin Watts

The Pocket book of   Philip Van Doren
  adventure stories.   Stern
The Pocket book of   Philip Van Doren
  America.   Stern
The Pocket book of
  American poems.   Louis Untermeyer
The Pocket book of baby
  and child care.   Benjamin Spock
The Pocket book of
  basic English.   I. A. Richards
The Pocket book of
  boners.
The Pocket book of
  cartoons.   Bennett Cerf
The Pocket book of
  crossword puzzles.   Margaret Petherbridge
The Pocket book of dog
  stories.   Harold Berman
The Pocket book of
  Erskine Caldwell
  stories.   Erskine Caldwell
The Pocket book of
  Esquire cartoons.
The Pocket book of
  etiquette.   Margery Wilson
The Pocket book of
  famous French short
  stories.   Eric Swenson
The Pocket book of
  Father Brown.   G. K. Chesterton
The Pocket book of
  flower gardening.   Montague Free
The Pocket book of
  games.   Albert H. Morehead
The Pocket book of   Philip Van Doren
  ghost stories.   Stern
The Pocket book of
  great detectives.   Lee Wright
The Pocket book of
  great drawings.   Paul J. Sachs
The Pocket book of   Henry Simon
  great operas.   Abraham Veinus
The Pocket book of
  Greek art.   Thomas Craven
The Pocket book of
  home canning.   Elizabeth Beveridge
The Pocket book of
  household hints.   Holly Cantus
The Pocket book of
  humorous verse.   David McCord
The Pocket book of
  jokes.   Bennett Cerf
The Pocket book of
  modern American plays.   Bennett Cerf
The Pocket book of
  modern American short   Philip Van Doren
  stories.   Stern
The Pocket book of
  modern verse.   Ted Malone
The Pocket book of
  mystery stories.   Lee Wright

The Pocket book of O. Henry prize stories.   Herschel Brickell
The Pocket book of O. Henry stories.   O. Henry
The Pocket book of Ogden Nash.   Ogden Nash
The Pocket book of old masters.   Herman J. Wechsler
The Pocket book of quotations.   Henry Davidoff
The Pocket book of Robert Frost's poems.   Robert Frost
The Pocket book of science-fiction.   Donald A. Wollheim
The Pocket book of short stories.   M. E. Speare
The Pocket book of story poems.   Louis Untermeyer
The Pocket book of the war.   Quincy Howe
The Pocket book of true crime stories.   Anthony Boucher
The Pocket book of true stories.   Ernest Heyn
The Pocket book of vegetable gardening.   Charles Nissley
The Pocket book of verse.   M. E. Speare
The Pocket book of war humor.   Bennett Cerf
The Pocket book of western stories.   Harry E. Maule
The Pocket companion.   Philip Van Doren Stern
The Pocket cook book.   Elizabeth Woody
The Pocket entertainer.   Shirley Cunningham
A pocket full of rye.   Agatha Christie
The Pocket guide to birds.   Allan D. Cruickshank
A Pocket guide to the trees.   Rutherford Platt
The Pocket guide to the wildflowers.   Samuel Gottscho
The Pocket history of American painting.   James Thomas Flexner
The Pocket history of the second world war.   Henry Steele Commager
The Pocket history of the United States.   Henry Steele Commager / Allan Nevins
The Pocket history of the world.   H. G. Wells
The Pocket household encyclopedia.   N. H. Mager / S. K. Mager
The Pocket mystery reader.   Lee Wright
The Pocket quiz book.   Louise Crittenden / Rosejeanne Slifer
The Pocket reader.   Philip Van Doren Stern
Pocket self-pronouncing dictionary and vocabulary builder.   William J. Pelo
The Pocket stamp album.   H. E. Harris

The Pocket treasury.   Louis Untermeyer
The Pocket treasury of American folklore.   B. A. Botkin
The Pocket week-end book.   Philip Van Doren Stern
Poe.   Edgar Allan Poe
Poems for men.   Damon Runyon
Poetry: a modern guide to its understanding and enjoyment.   Elizabeth Drew
Point counter point.   Aldous Huxley
Point of a gun.   Dean Owen
The point of honour.   W. Somerset Maugham
Point of no escape.   Mel Colton
Point of no return.   John P. Marquand
Point of peril.   Edward Ronns
Point Ultimate.   Jerry Sohl
Point Venus.   Susanne McConnaughey
Poirot investigates.   Agatha Christie
Poirot loses a client.   Agatha Christie
Poison for one.   John Rhode
Poison in jest.   John Dickson Carr
The poisoned chocolates case.   Anthony Berkeley
Poisons unknown.   Frank Kane
Poker according to Maverick.
Polikushka and Two Hussars.   Leo Tolstoy
Polish nights.   Wldyslawa Chojnowska
Politics is murder.   Edwin Lanham
The ponder heart.   Eudora Welty
Popular book of cartoons.   Ned L. Pines
Popular book of western stories.   Leo Margulies
A popular history of music.   Carter Harman
Popularity plus.   Sally S. Simpson
Porgy.   Du Bose Heyward
Pork Chop Hill.   S. L. A. Marshall
Pornography and the law.   Eberhard Kronhausen / Phyllis Kronhausen
Port Afrique.   Bernard Victor Dryer
Port of call.   Maxwell Griffith
Port Orient.   Dan Cushman
Port Royal.   Noel B. Gerson
Portrait in smoke.   Bill S. Ballinger
Portrait of a man with red hair.   Hugh Walpole
Portrait of a marriage.   Pearl S. Buck
Portrait of a mobster.   Harry Grey
Portrait of a woman.   John Hyde Preston
A portrait of Jennie.   Robert Nathan
Portrait of Lisa.   William Brothers
Portrait of Rene.   Harry Davis
Portrait of the artist as a young man.   James Joyce
Portrait of the damned.   Richard McKaye
Position unknown.   Ian Mackersey
Posse from hell.   Clair Huffaker
Possess me not.   Fan Nichols

Possessed.	Anne Chamberlain
Possessed.	June Wetherell
Possession.	Louis Bromfield
Possible worlds of science fiction.	Groff Conklin
The postman.	Roger Martin du Gard
The postman always rings twice.	James M. Cain
Post-mark homicide.	A. A. Marcus
Postmark murder.	Mignon G. Eberhart
The powder burn.	Frank C. Robertson
Powder burn.	Bradford Scott
Powder burns.	Al Cody
Powder mission.	Herbert E. Stover
Powder smoke.	Jackson Gregory
Powder Valley pay-off.	Peter Field
Powder Valley showdown.	Peter Field
Powdersmoke feud.	William MacLeod Raine
Powdersmoke range.	William Colt MacDonald
The power.	Frank M. Robinson
The power and the glory.	Graham Greene
The power and the prize.	Howard Swiggett
The power gods.	Bud Clifton
Power golf.	Ben Hogan
The power of negative thinking.	Charles Preston
The power of people.	Charles P. McCormick
The power of positive living.	Douglas Lurton
The practical way to a better memory.	Bruno Furst
Prairie guns.	Will Cook
Prairie guns.	Ernest Haycox
Prairie marshal.	Walker A. Tompkins
Prairie reckoning.	Paul Durst
Prairie terror.	Rod Patterson
Pray love, remember.	Stephen Wendt
Precious bane.	Mary Webb
Pregnancy and birth.	Alan F. Guttmacher
Prelude to a certain midnight.	Gerald Kersh
Prelude to murder.	Sterling Noel
Prelude to space.	Arthur C. Clarke
Prelude to victory.	James B. Reston
Prescription for murder.	Hannah Lees
Presenting Lily Mars.	Booth Tarkington
Presidential year.	C. M. Kornbluth Frederik Pohl
Pressure.	Charles Francis Coe
Prettiest girl in town.	Thomas Fall
Previews of entertainment.	Gilbert Seldes
Prey by night.	Malcolm Douglas
The preying streets.	Ledru Baker Jr.
The price is right.	Jerome Weidman
The price of courage.	Curt Anders
The price of murder.	John D. MacDonald
The price of salt.	Claire Morgan
Pride and prejudice.	Jane Austen
Pride of innocence.	David Buckley
Pride's castle.	Frank Yerby
The priest.	Joseph Caruso
A primer of Freudian psychology.	Calvin S. Hall
The primitive.	Chester Himes
The prince.	Niccolò Machiavelli
The prince and the showgirl.	Terence Rattigan
Prince Bart.	Jay Richard Kennedy
Prince of Egypt.	Dorothy Clarke Wilson
The prince of foxes.	Samuel Shellabarger
Princess of the atom.	Ray Cummings
Prison girl.	Wenzell Brown
Prison nurse.	Louis Berg
The prisoner ate a hardy breakfast.	Jerome Ellison
Prisoner in paradise.	Garet Rogers
The prisoner of Zenda.	Anthony Hope
Prisoner's base.	Rex Stout
The prisoners of Combine D.	Len Giovannitti
The private affairs of Bel Ami.	Guy de Maupassant
Private duty.	Faith Baldwin
The private eye.	Cleve F. Adams
Private eyeful.	Henry Kane
A private killing.	James Benét
The private life of Helen of Troy.	John Erskine
A private party.	William Ard
The private practice of Michael Shayne.	Brett Halliday
A private stair.	David Loughlin
Prize articles of 1954.	Llewellyn Miller
The problem of the green capsule.	John Dickson Carr
The problem of the wire cage.	John Dickson Carr
Proceed at will.	Burke Wilkinson
The prodigal gun.	Barry Cord
Prodigal shepherd.	Al Hirshberg Robert Pfau
The prodigal women.	Nancy Hale
The producer.	Richard Brooks
The professional.	W. C. Heinz
Professional lover.	Maysie Greig
Profiles in courage.	John F. Kennedy
The promise.	Pearl S. Buck
Promise of love.	Mary Renault
The promising young men.	George Sklar
The promoters.	Stephen Longstreet
The prophet.	Sholem Asch
The proposition.	Hunt Collins
The prosecuter.	Bernard Botein
The proud diggers.	William O. Turner
Proud land.	Logan Forster
Proud new flags.	F. van Wyck Mason
The proud ones.	Verne Athanas
The proud retreat.	Clifford Dowdey
The proud sheriff.	Eugene Manlove Rhodes
Proud youth.	Alexander Eliot
The proving flight.	David Beaty
Prowl cop.	Gregory Jones

Q

Q as in quicksand.	Lawrence Treat
Q.B.I.	Ellery Queen
The quaking widow.	Robert Colby
Quality.	Cid Ricketts Sumner
Quantrill's raiders.	Frank Gruber
Quartet.	W. Somerset Maugham
Quartet in "H".	Evan Hunter
The queen and the corpse.	Max Murray
The queen bee.	Edna Lee
Queen of Sheba.	Gardner F. Fox
Queen of the East.	Alexander Baron
Queen of the flat-tops.	Stanley Johnston
The Queen's awards:	
eighth series.	Ellery Queen
Queen's blade.	Nicholas Gorham
Queen's caprice.	George Preedy
The Queen's cross.	Lawrence Schoonover
Queen's gift.	Inglis Fletcher
Queen's own.	George C. Appell
Queer patterns.	Lilyan Brock
The quest.	O. O. Osborne
The questing sword.	Jefferson Cooper
A question of proof.	Nicholas Blake
Questions and answers	
from the Book of	
knowledge.	E. V. McLoughlin
The quick and the loving.	Clifford Irving
The quick brown fox.	Lawrence Schoonover
The quick cook book.	Lois S. Kellogg
Quick draw.	Curtis Bishop
Quick on the shoot.	George C. Appell
Quick service.	P. G. Wodehouse
Quick-trigger country.	Clem Colt
Quick trigger law.	Jim O'Mara
Quick triggers.	Eugene Cunningham
Quicksand.	William Brinkley
The quiet American.	Graham Greene
Quiet horror.	Stanley Ellin
Quietly my captain waits.	Evelyn Eaton
Quintet.	
Quo vadis?	Henryk Sienkiewicz

R

The race of giants.	Matt Kinkaid
Race to the stars.	Oscar J. Friend
	Leo Margulies
The racer.	Hans Ruesch
Rachel Cade.	Charles Mercer
Radigan.	Louis L'Amour
The raft.	Robert Trumbull
Raft of despair.	Ensio Tiira
A rag and a bone.	Hillary Waugh
Rag top.	Henry Gregor Felsen
A rage at sea.	Frederick Lorenz
Rage in heaven.	James Hilton
Rage in Texas.	Howard Rigsby
Rage in the wind.	Boyd Cochrell
Rage of desire.	Charles Mergendahl
Rage of the soul.	Vincent Sheean
Rage on the bar.	Geoffrey Wagner
A rage to die.	Richard Jessup
A rage to kill.	B. E. Lovell
A rage to live.	John O'Hara
Rage to love.	Frank Tilsley
The ragged ones.	Burke Davis
The raging tide.	Ernest K. Gann
The raid.	John Brick
Raid at Dieppe.	Quentin Reynolds
The raiders.	Richard Ferber
The raiders.	Will Henry
Raiders of the rimrock.	Luke Short
Rails West.	Logan Stewart
Railtown sheriff.	Stuart Brock
Rain.	W. Somerset Maugham
Rain in the doorway.	Thorne Smith
Rain of terror.	Malcolm Douglas
The rainbow.	D. H. Lawrence
The rainbow and the rose.	Nevil Shute
Rainbow in the royals.	Garland Roark
Rainbow road.	Davenport Steward
The rainmaker.	N. Richard Nash
The rains came.	Louis Bromfield
Raintree County.	Ross Lockridge Jr.
Raising demons.	Shirley Jackson
The rake's progress.	Philip Lindsay
Raleigh's Eden.	Inglis Fletcher
Rally round the flag, boys!	Max Shulman
Ralph 124C41+.	Hugo Gernsback
Rambling top hand.	William Hopson
Rampage.	Leslie Ernenwein
Rampart Street.	Everett Webber
	Olga Webber
Ramrod.	George C. Appell
Ramrod.	Luke Short
Ramrod from hell.	Leslie Ernenwein
Ramrod from hell.	Ernie Wayne
Ramrod vengeance.	William Hopson
Ranch cat.	William Hopson
Ranchero.	Stewart Edward White
Rancher's revenge.	Max Brand
Rand McNally-Pocket world atlas.	

Randall and the river of time.	C. S. Forester
Random harvest.	James Hilton
Range beyond the law.	William MacLeod Raine
Range boss.	D. B. Newton
Range boss.	Gordon Young
The range bum.	Kenneth Fowler
The range buster.	William Heuman
The range doctor.	Oscar J. Friend
Range drifter.	Thomas Thompson
The range grabbers.	Sidney Stewart
The range kid.	William Colt MacDonald
Range king.	J. E. Grinstead
The range maverick.	Oscar J. Friend
Range pirate.	L. P. Holmes
Range rebel.	Gordon D. Shirreffs
Range rider.	W. H. B. Kent
The range terror.	Bradford Scott
Range war.	Tom J. Hopkins
The rangemaster.	Robert McCaig
Ranger man.	William Colt MacDonald
The ranger way.	Eugene Cunningham
Ranger's luck.	William MacLeod Raine
Ranger's revenge.	Nelson Nye
Rap sheet--my forty years outside the law.	Blackie Audett
The rapist.	Samuel A. Krasney
Raquel.	Lion Feuchtwanger
The rascal's guide.	Bruce Jay Friedman
Rascals in paradise.	A. Grove Day
	James A. Michener
Rashomon and other stories.	Ryunosuke Akutagawa
The rasp.	Philip MacDonald
The rat began to gnaw the rope.	C. W. Grafton
The rat race.	Alfred Bester
Rate yourself.	Pauline Arnold
Raton Pass.	Thomas W. Blackburn
Ratoons.	Daphne Rooke
Rats, lice and history.	Hans Zinsser
Ravaged range.	Peter Field
The raw edge.	Benjamin Appel
Raw land.	Luke Short
Raw wind in Eden.	Ed Robinson
Rawhide and Bob-wire.	Luke Short
The rawhide breed.	John Callahan
Rawhide gunman.	Todhunter Ballard
Rawhide guns.	Frank Bonham
Rawhide Range.	Ernest Haycox
Rawhide rider.	Thomas Thompson
Rawhide river.	Cliff Farrell
Rawhide summons.	Brett Austin
The rawhide years.	Norman A. Fox
Rawhider from Texas.	Dean Owen
Rawhiders.	Tom Roan
The razor's edge.	W. Somerset Maugham
Reach for tomorrow.	Arthur C. Clarke
Reach for your guns.	Curtis Bishop
Reach to the stars.	Calder Willingham

The reader is warned.	Carter Dickson
The reader's companion to world literature.	Lillian Herlands Hornstein et al.
Readings from world religions.	Selwyn Gurney Champion
	Dorothy Short
The real cool killers.	Chester Himes
A real gone guy.	Frank Kane
The real story of Lucille Ball.	Eleanor Harris
A really sincere guy.	Robert Van Riper
Really the blues.	Mezz Mezzrow
	Bernard Wolfe
Realm of the Incas.	Victor W. Von Hagen
Reap the whirlwind.	Jean Hougron
Reap the wild wind.	Thelma Strabel
Rear guard.	James Warner Bellah
Rebecca.	Daphne du Maurier
Rebecca's pride.	Donald McNutt Douglass
Rebel basin.	Harry Sinclair Drago
Rebel gun.	Arthur Steuer
Rebel raider.	Joseph Chadwick
Rebel ranger.	William Colt MacDonald
Rebel ranger.	S. E. Whitman
Rebel road.	Frank Gruber
Rebel wench.	Gardner F. Fox
Rebel yell.	Leslie Ernenwein
The rebellion of Leo McGuire.	Clyde Brion Davis
The rebellious stars.	Isaac Asimov
Rebels and redcoats.	Hugh F. Rankin
	George Scheer
Rebel's roundup.	W. Edmunds Claussen
Rebirth.	Thomas Calvert McClary
Re-birth.	John Wyndham
Recipe for homicide.	Lawrence G. Blochman
Reckless passion.	Gordon Sample
The reckless years.	Virginia Oakey
Reckoning at Yankee Flat.	Will Henry
Reclining figure.	Marco Page
Recoil.	Jim Thompson
Reconstruction in philosophy.	John Dewey
Recruit for Andromeda.	Milton Lesser
Red.	Richard Vincent
Red alert.	Peter Bryant
The red and the black.	Stendhal
The red badge of courage.	Stephen Crane
Red blizzard.	Clay Fisher
Red bone woman.	Carlyle Tillery
The red box.	Rex Stout
The red bull.	Rex Stout
Red canvas.	Marcel Wallenstein
The red carnation.	Elio Vittorini
Red carpet for Mamie Eisenhower.	Alden Hatch
The red dress.	John Watson
The red gate.	LaSelle Gilman
Red Harvest.	Dashiell Hammett

Red hot ice.	Frank Kane
The red house.	George Agnew Chamberlain
The red house mystery.	A. A. Milne
The Red knight of Germany.	Floyd Gibbons
The red lamp.	Mary Roberts Rinehart
The red law.	Jackson Gregory
The red lily.	Anatole France
Red Lion Inn.	Robert Payne
Red man's range.	Al Cody
The red pony.	John Steinbeck
Red range.	Eugene Cunningham
The red rider of Smoky Range.	William Colt MacDonald
The red right hand.	Joel Townsley Rogers
Red River.	Borden Chase
The red room.	Françoise Mallet
Red runs the river.	William Heuman
Red rust.	Cornelia James Cannon
The red sands of Santa Maria.	Bill Murphy
The red scarf.	Gil Brewer
Red sky at midnight.	Robert F. Mirvish
Red snow at Darjeeling.	Leslie Charteris
The red sombrero.	Nelson Nye
The red tassel.	David Dodge
Red threads.	Rex Stout
The red widow murders.	Carter Dickson
The redhead from Chicago.	Louis-Charles Royer
The redhead from Sun Dog.	W. C. Tuttle
Red-headed woman.	Katharine Brush
The reef.	Keith Wheeler
Re-enter Fu Manchu.	Sax Rohmer
Reflections in a golden eye.	Carson McCullers
The reformed gun.	Marvin H. Albert
The regatta mystery.	Agatha Christie
The regenerate lover.	Donald Henderson Clarke
Rehearsal for love.	Faith Baldwin
Reincarnation--the whole startling story.	R. DeWitt Miller
Relativity for the layman.	James A. Coleman
Relentless.	Kenneth Perkins
Relentless gun.	Giles A. Lutz
Religion and the rise of capitalism.	R. H. Tawney
Religion without revelation.	Julian Huxley
The religions of man.	Huston Smith
The reluctant gun.	Howard Rigsby
Reluctant gunman.	William MacLeod Raine
Reluctant millionaire.	Maysie Greig
Rembrandt.	Wilhelm Koehler
Remember me to God.	Myron S. Kaufmann
Remembered death.	Agatha Christie
Remembering laughter.	Wallace Stegner
The Renaissance.	Walter Pater

Rogue's honor.   Anne Powers
Rogue's march.   Maristan Chapman
Rogue's yarn.   John Jennings
Roll back the sky.   Ward Taylor
Roll the wagons.   William Heuman
Rolling stone.   Patricia Wentworth
A Roman affair.   Ercole Patti
The Roman and the
   slave girl.   John Medford Morgan
The Roman hat mystery.   Ellery Queen
The Roman spring of
   Mrs. Stone.   Tennessee Williams
Roman tales.   Alberto Moravia
The Roman way to
   western civilization.   Edith Hamilton
Romance for sale.   Maysie Greig
Romance in the first
   degree.   Octavus Roy Cohen
Rome haul.   Walter D. Edmonds
Romelle.   W. R. Burnett
Romeo and Juliet.   William Shakespeare
Rommel, the desert fox.   Desmond Young
Room at the top.   John Braine
Room clerk.   Herbert Gold
Room for a stranger.   Constantine FitzGibbon
Room for murder.   Thomas B. Dewey
A room in Berlin.   Günther Birkenfeld
A room in Paris.   Peggy Mann
The room in the
   Dragon Inn.   Joseph S. Le Fanu
A room on the route.   Godfrey Blunden
Room to swing.   Ed Lacy
The room upstairs.   Mildred Davis
Rooming house.   Berton Roueché
Roosevelt and Hopkins,
   volume 1.   Robert E. Sherwood
Roosevelt and Hopkins,
   volume 2.   Robert E. Sherwood
Root of evil.   James Cross
Root of evil.   Eaton K. Goldthwaite
The root of his evil.   James M. Cain
The roots of heaven.   Romain Gary
Roots of the trouble
   <u>and</u> The black record
   of Germany.   Lord Vansittart
Rope.   Alfred Hitchcock
The rope began to hang
   the butcher.   C. W. Grafton
Rope law.   Lewis B. Patten
A rope of sand.   Francis Bonnamy
The rose and the flame.   Jonreed Lauritzen
The rose tattoo.   Tennessee Williams
Rouault.   Jacques Maritain
The rough and the smooth.   Robin Maugham
Rough justice.   Ernest Haycox
A rough shoot.   Geoffrey Household
Roughly speaking.   Louise Randall
    Pierson
Roughneck.   Jim Thompson
Roughshod.   Norman A. Fox
Round the bend.   Nevil Shute

The round-the-world
   cook book.   Myra Waldo
Roundup.   Todhunter Ballard
The round-up.   Oscar J. Friend
Roundup on the
   Picketwire.   Allan Vaughan Elston
Route 28.   Ward Greene
The roving eye.   Michael Wells
Roxana.   Marian Castle
Roy Bean: law west of
   the Pecos.   C. L. Sonnichsen
The royal box.   Frances Parkinson
    Keyes
Royal Gorge.   Peter Dawson
The royal road to
   romance.   Richard Halliburton
Royal scandal.   Philip Lindsay
The royal vultures.   Hillel Black
    Sam Kolman
Royalist.   Edward Grierson
The Rubáiyát of Omar
   Khayyám.   Omar Khayyám
The rubber band.   Rex Stout
Rubens.   Julius S. Held
Ruby.   Viña Delmar
Ruby.   Frederick Lorenz
Ruby McCollum.   William Bradford Huie
Rue Pigalle.   Francis Carco
Ruggles of Red Gap.   Harry Leon Wilson
The rule of the
   pagbeasts.   J. T. McIntosh
Ruler of the range.   Peter Dawson
The ruling passion.   George deMare
Rumble.   Harlan Ellison
Rumble on the docks.   Frank Paley
Rumor, fear and the
   madness of crowds.   J. P. Chaplin
Run, brother, run!   Tom Brandt
Run by night.   Hammond Innes
Run, Chico, run.   Wenzell Brown
A run for the money.   Dale Clark
Run for your life.   Bruno Fischer
Run for your life!   Sterling Noel
Run for your life.   Michael Stark
Run from the hunter.   Keith Grantland
Run, killer, run.   William Campbell
    Gault
Run, killer, run!   Lionel White
Run...run...run...   Frank Taubes
Run silent, run deep.   Edward L. Beach
Run the river gauntlet.   John Clagett
Run the wild river.   D. L. Champion
Run, thief, run.   Frank Gruber
Run to death.   Patrick Quentin
Run while you can.   William Woolfolk
Runaway black.   Richard Marsten
The runaways.   Carl Bottume
The running man.   Ben Benson
Running target.   Steve Frazee
Runyon à la carte.   Damon Runyon
Runyon first and last.   Damon Runyon

Russia.	Bernard Pares
Russia and America: dangers and prospects.	Henry L. Roberts
The Russian revolution.	Alan Moorehead
Rustler of the owlhorns.	Jim O'Mara
The rustlers.	Luke Short
Rustlers' Bend.	Will Ermine
Rustlers' canyon.	E. E. Halleran
Rustlers' Gap.	William MacLeod Raine
Rustlers' moon.	Will Ermine
Rustlers of Beacon Creek.	Max Brand
Rustlers of the Rio Grande.	Paul Evan Lehman
Rustlers' range.	Bradford Scott
Rusty Desmond.	Steve January
Rusty guns.	Bliss Lomax
The ruthless men.	Lewis B. Patten
Rutledge trails the ace of spades.	William MacLeod Raine
The Rynox murder mystery.	Philip MacDonald

S

S-F: the year's greatest science-fiction and fantasy.	Judith Merril
SF: the year's greatest science-fiction and fantasy 2nd annual volume.	Judith Merril
S-F: the year's greatest science-fiction and fantasy 3rd annual volume.	Judith Merril
SF: the year's greatest science-fiction and fantasy 4th annual volume.	Judith Merril
S.S. murder.	Q. Patrick
S.S. San Pedro.	James Gould Cozzens
Sabotage.	Cleve F. Adams
The sabotage murder mystery.	Margery Allingham
Sabrina Kane.	Will Cook
The sacrilege of Alan Kent.	Erskine Caldwell
Sad cypress.	Agatha Christie
Saddle and ride.	Ernest Haycox
Saddle Bow Slim.	Nelson Nye
The saddle bum.	Philip Ketchum
Saddle by starlight.	Luke Short
Saddle hawks.	Bliss Lomax
Saddle justice.	Steven C. Lawrence
Saddle-man.	Matt Stuart
Saddle the storm.	Harry Whittington
Saddle tramp.	Todhunter Ballard
Saddle up for sunlight.	Allan Vaughan Elston
The saddle wolves.	Lee Floren
Saddlebow rancher.	Ray Townsend
Saddlebum.	William MacLeod Raine
Safari to dishonor.	Edmund Schiddel
Safe conduct.	Boris Pasternak
The saga of Billy the Kid.	Walter Noble Burns
The sagebrush bandit.	Bliss Lomax
Said the spider to the fly.	Richard Shattuck
Said with flowers.	Anne Nash
Saigon singer.	Van Wyck Mason
Sail the dark tide.	Davenport Steward
Sailor, take warning!	Kelley Roos
Sailor town.	Paul Fox
Sailor's choice.	Carl Bottume
Sailor's leave.	Brian Moore
Sailor's luck.	Basil Heatter
The Saint and Mr. Teal.	Leslie Charteris
The Saint and the last hero.	Leslie Charteris
The Saint and the sizzling saboteur.	Leslie Charteris
The Saint around the world.	Leslie Charteris
The Saint at the thieves' picnic.	Leslie Charteris
The Saint cleans up.	Leslie Charteris
Saint errant.	Leslie Charteris
The Saint-Fiacre affair.	Georges Simenon
The Saint goes on.	Leslie Charteris
The Saint goes West.	Leslie Charteris
The Saint in action.	Leslie Charteris
The Saint in England.	Leslie Charteris
The Saint in Europe.	Leslie Charteris
The Saint in Miami.	Leslie Charteris
The Saint in New York.	Leslie Charteris
The Saint intervenes.	Leslie Charteris
Saint Joan.	George Bernard Shaw
The Saint meets his match.	Leslie Charteris
The Saint meets the Tiger.	Leslie Charteris
The Saint on guard.	Leslie Charteris
The Saint on the Spanish Main.	Leslie Charteris
Saint overboard.	Leslie Charteris
The Saint sees it through.	Leslie Charteris
The Saint steps in.	Leslie Charteris
The Saint--the brighter buccaneer.	Leslie Charteris
The Saint--the happy highwayman.	Leslie Charteris
The Saint vs. Scotland Yard.	Leslie Charteris
The Saint--wanted for murder.	Leslie Charteris
Saint's getaway.	Leslie Charteris
A Saki sampler.	Saki
Salambô.	Gustave Flaubert
The Salem frigate.	John Jennings
Salome.	Paul Eldridge George Sylvester Viereck
Salome, the princess of Galilee.	Henry Denker
Sam Snead's natural golf.	Sam Snead
Samurai!	Martin Caidin et al.
San Francisco murders.	Joseph Henry Jackson
The San Quentin story.	Clinton T. Duffy Dean Jennings
Sanctuary.	William Faulkner
Sanctuary and Requiem for a nun.	William Faulkner
The sands of Karakorum.	James Ramsey Ullman
Sands of Mars.	Arthur C. Clarke
Sandy.	John B. Thompson
Sangaree.	Frank G. Slaughter
Santa Fe passage.	Clay Fisher
Sappho.	Alphonse Daudet
The Saracen blade.	Frank Yerby
Saratoga mantrap.	Dexter St. Clare
Saratoga trunk.	Edna Ferber
Sargasso of space.	Andrew North

Sartoris. William Faulkner
Saskia. Claude Marais
Satan is a woman. Gil Brewer
Satan takes the helm. Calvin Clements
Satan was a man. Edward Hale Bierstadt
Satan's gal. Carolina Lee
Satan's Rock. Carl D. Burton
Satchmo. Louis Armstrong
Satellite! William Beller
Erik Bergaust
Satellite E One. Jeffery Lloyd Castle
Satellites, rockets
  and outer space. Willy Ley
Satin straps. Maysie Greig
The Saturday evening
  post cartoons. John Bailey
The Saturday evening
  post fantasy stories. Barthold Fles
The Saturday evening
  post sport stories. Red Smith
The Saturday evening
  post western stories. Barthold Fles
Saturday mountain. Nathaniel Jones
Saturday night. James T. Farrell
Saturday night town. Harry Whittington
The Saturday review
  reader.
Saturday review reader,
  no. 2.
Saturday review reader,
  no. 3.
Saturday's harvest. Paul Shelley
The savage. Mikhail Artzybasheff
The savage. Noel Clad
The savage affair. Virgil Scott
Savage breed. Joseph Chadwick
Savage bride. Cornell Woolrich
Savage cavalier. Noel B. Gerson
The savage chase. Frederick Lorenz
The savage city. Jean Paradise
Savage conqueror. Davenport Steward
The savage gentleman. Philip Wylie
Savage holiday. Richard Wright
Savage interlude. Dan Cushman
Savage night. Jim Thompson
The savage place. Leon Arden
Savage range. Luke Short
The savage soldiers. Harold Waters
Aubrey Wisberg
Savage star. Lewis B. Patten
The savage streets. Floyd Miller
Savage stronghold. Logan Stewart
Savage triangle. Louis-Charles Royer
Savage valley. Barry Cord
The savage warriors. Henry Treece
The savages. Peter Dawson
Save them for violence. James M. Fox
Sawdust and sixguns. Evan Evans
The Saxon charm. Frederic Wakeman
Say, darling. Richard Bissell
Say it with bullets. Richard Powell
Say it with murder. Edward Ronns

Say yes to murder. W. T. Ballard
The sayings of
  Confucius. Confucius
Sayonara. James A. Michener
Scalpel. Horace McCoy
Scandal. Robert W. Taylor
Scandal in Troy. Eva Hemmer Hansen
The scandal of Father
  Brown. G. K. Chesterton
Scandals of Clochemerle. Gabriel Chevallier
The scapegoat. Daphne du Maurier
The scarab murder case. S. S. Van Dine
Scaramouche. Rafael Sabatini
Scarecrow. Eaton K. Goldthwaite
The scarf. Robert Bloch
Scarf of passion. Robert Bloch
Scarface. Andre Norton
Scarlet angel. Dorene Clark
The scarlet circle. Jonathan Stagge
Scarlet Cockerel. Garald Lagard
The scarlet cord. Frank G. Slaughter
The scarlet guidon. Ray Toepfer
The scarlet letter. Nathaniel Hawthorne
The scarlet letters. Ellery Queen
The scarlet patch. Bruce Lancaster
The scarlet petticoat. Nard Jones
The Scarlet pimpernel. Baroness Orczy
Scarlet sister Mary. Julia Peterkin
The scarlet slippers. James M. Fox
The scarlet spade. Eaton K. Goldthwaite
Scarlet starlet. Doug Warren
The scarlet sword. H. E. Bates
The scarlet treasury
  of great confessions. Whit Burnett
The scarlet Venus. Chalmers Green
The scattered seed. Stuart Engstrand
Scent of cloves. Norah Lofts
Scent of mystery. Kelley Roos
The scented flesh. Robert O. Saber
Scheherezade: tales
  from The 1001 nights.
Schifferes' family
  medical encyclopedia. Justus J. Schifferes
The Schirmer
  inheritance. Eric Ambler
Schnozzola. Gene Fowler
Science and surgery. Frank G. Slaughter
Science and the Alfred North
  modern world. Whitehead
Science and the moral
  life. Max Otto
The science book of Harold Leland
  space travel. Goodwin
The science book of
  the human body. Edith E. Sproul
The science book of
  wonder drugs. Donald G. Cooley
Science fiction Fredric Brown
  carnival. Mack Reynolds
Science fiction omnibus. Groff Conklin
Science fiction terror
  tales. Groff Conklin

The shadow and the glory. John Jennings
The shadow and the peak. Richard Mason
The Shadow and the
  voice of murder.   Maxwell Grant
Shadow at noon.   Harry White
Shadow of a gunman.   Gordon D. Shirreffs
Shadow of a hero.   Allan Chase
Shadow of a killer.   William Mole
Shadow of a star.   Elmer Kelton
Shadow of madness.   Hugh Pentecost
Shadow of the butte.   Thomas Thompson
Shadow of the mafia.   Louis Malley
Shadow of the moon.   M. M. Kaye
Shadow of the rope.   Ray Gaulden
Shadow of tomorrow.   Frederik Pohl
Shadow on the border.   George C. Appell
Shadow on the range.   Norman A. Fox
The shadow rider.   William Colt
                             MacDonald
Shadow riders of the
  Yellowstone.   Les Savage Jr.
Shadow valley.   Gordon D. Shirreffs
The shadowed trail.   Arthur Henry Gooden
Shadows in the sun.   Chad Oliver
Shadows move among them.   Edgar Mittelholzer
Shadows of shame.   John Taylor
The shadowy third.   Marco Page
Shady lady.   Cleve F. Adams
A shady place to die.   John Savage
Shag.   Thomas C. Hinkle
Shake hands with the
  devil.   Rearden Conner
Shake well before using.   Bennett Cerf
Shakedown.   Richard Ellington
Shakedown.   Ben Kerr
Shakedown.   Roney Scott
Shakedown for murder.   Ed Lacy
Shakedown hotel.   Ernest Jason
                             Fredericks
Shakespeare without
  tears.   Margaret Webster
The shame.   Richard Himmel
Shame.   Émile Zola
The shame of Mary Quinn.   Clifton Cuthbert
Shameless.   James M. Cain
Shameless honeymoon.   Thomas Stone
The shameless ones.   Uberto Quintavalle
Shane.   Jack Schaefer
Shanghai Flame.   A. S. Fleischman
Shanghai incident.   Steve Dodge
Shannahan's feud.   Archie Joscelyn
Shannon's way.   A. J. Cronin
Shanty boat girl.   Kirk Westley
The shape of tomorrow.   George Soule
The shaping of the
  modern mind.   Crane Brinton
Sharks and little fish.   Wolfgang Ott
Sharon.   Harriett H. Carr
The sharp edge.   Richard Himmel
Sharp the bugle calls.   Steve Frazee
She.   H. Rider Haggard
                             Don Ward

She asked for murder.   Edna Sherry
She ate her cake.   Blair Treynor
She-devil.   Harry Hervey
She died a lady.   Carter Dickson
She faded into air.   Ethel Lina White
She loves me not.   Edward Hope
She posed for death.   Russell Gordon
She screamed blue
  murder.   Kelliher Secrist
She shall have murder.   Delano Ames
She shark.   John Farr
She walks alone.   Helen McCloy
She woke to darkness.   Brett Halliday
The she-wolf.   Saki
Shear the black sheep.   David Dodge
The sheik.   E. M. Hull
She'll be dead by
  morning.   Dana Chambers
Shell game.   Richard Powell
Shell of death.   Nicholas Blake
The sheltering night.   Steve Fisher
The sheltering sky.   Paul Bowles
The shepherd of the
  hills.   Harold Bell Wright
The sheriff.   Forrest Covington
Sheriff of Big Hat.   Barry Cord
The sheriff of Painted
  Post.   Tom Gunn
The sheriff of San
  Miguel.   Allan Vaughan Elston
Sheriff on the spot.   Peter Field
Sheriff wanted!   Peter Field
Sheriff's revenge.   Peter Field
The sheriff's son.   William MacLeod Raine
The Sherlock Holmes
  Pocket book.   Arthur Conan Doyle
Shield for murder.   William P. McGivern
Shiloh.   Shelby Foote
The shining mountains.   Dale Van Every
The shining tides.   Win Brooks
The ship.   C. S. Forester
Ship ahoy.
The ship of Ishtar.   A. Merritt
The ship without a crew.   Howard Pease
Ship's company.   Lonnie Coleman
The shipwrecked.   Graham Greene
Shipyard diary of a
  woman welder.   Augusta H. Clawson
The shivering bough.   Noel Burke
Shock treatment.   James Hadley Chase
The shocking secret.   Holly Roth
Shoe the wild mare.   Gene Fowler
The shook-up generation.   Harrison E. Salisbury
Shoot a sitting duck.   David Alexander
Shoot the works.   Richard Ellington
Shoot the works.   Brett Halliday
Shoot to kill.   Wade Miller
Shootin' man.   Bradford Scott
Shootin' Melody.   E. B. Mann
Shooting star.   Robert Bloch
The shoot-out at
  Sentinel Peak.   Richard Brister

The skeleton in the clock.	Carter Dickson
Skeleton key.	Lenore Glen Offord
Ski patrol.	Montgomery Atwater
The skin.	Curzio Malaparte
Skin and bones.	Thorne Smith
The sky block.	Steve Frazee
The sky is red.	Giuseppe Berto
Sky-pilot cowboy.	Walt Coburn
The sky tramps.	Dennison O'Hara
Skycruiser.	Howard M. Brier
The Skylark of space.	E. E. Smith
Skyline riders.	Francis W. Hilton
Skyscraper.	Faith Baldwin
The skyscraper murder.	Samuel Spewack
Slab happy.	Richard S. Prather
Slade.	Ad Gordon
Slan.	A. E. van Vogt
The slander of witches.	Richard Gehman
Slant of the wild wind.	Garland Roark
The slasher.	Ovid Demaris
Slattery's hurricane.	Herman Wouk
Slattery's range.	Richard Wormser
Slaughter street.	Louis Falstein
The slaughtered lovelies.	Don Stanford
Slave ship.	Frederik Pohl
Slaves of the Klau.	Jack Vance
Slay ride.	Frank Kane
Slay ride for a lady.	Harry Whittington
Slay the loose ladies.	Patrick Quentin
Slay the murderer.	Hugh Holman
The sledge patrol.	David Howarth
Sleep, my love.	Robert Martin
Sleep no more.	Sam S. Taylor
Sleep till noon.	Max Shulman
Sleep with strangers.	Dolores Hitchens
Sleep with the devil.	Day Keene
The sleeper.	Holly Roth
The sleeping sphinx.	John Dickson Carr
The sleepless moon.	H. E. Bates
Slice of hell.	Mike Roscoe
Slick on the draw.	Tom West
A slight case of scandal.	Jack Iams
Slim.	William Wister Haines
The sling and the arrow.	Stuart Engstrand
Slippery hitch.	Gerald Butler
Slipping beauty.	Jerome Weidman
Slogum House.	Mari Sandoz
The slot.	John Clagett
The small back room.	Nigel Balchin
Small beer.	Ludwig Bemelmans
Small talk.	Syms
Small town D.A.	Robert Traver
Smart guy.	William MacHarg
Smash-up.	Theodore Pratt
A smattering of ignorance.	Oscar Levant
The smell of money.	Matthew Head
The smell of murder.	S. S. Van Dine
The smell of trouble.	Louis Trimble
The smiler with the knife.	Nicholas Blake
Smiling desperado.	Max Brand
The smiling rebel.	Harnett T. Kane
Smoke among the plains.	Vingie Roe
Smoke Bellew.	Jack London
Smoke in the valley.	Steve Frazee
Smoke of the gun.	John S. Daniels
Smoke up the valley.	Monte Barrett
Smoke wagon kid.	Clem Colt
The smoking iron.	Peter Field
Smoking-room jokebook.	Harold Meyers
Smoky Range.	E. E. Halleran
Smoky river.	Tom Roan
The smoky trail.	Matt Stuart
Smoky Valley.	Donald Hamilton
The smoldering fire.	Harry Harrison Kroll
The smoldering sea.	U. S. Andersen
Smooth and deadly.	Quentin Reynolds
The smuggled atom bomb.	Philip Wylie
The snake in the grass.	James Howard Wellard
The snake pit.	Mary Jane Ward
The snake stomper.	Joseph Wayne
Snaketrack.	Frank Bonham
The snatch.	Harold R. Daniels
The snatchers.	Lionel White
Snow fury.	Richard Holden
The snow was black.	Georges Simenon
The snows of Ganymede.	Poul Anderson
Snowslide.	Carl Jonas
So big.	Edna Ferber
The so blue marble.	Dorothy B. Hughes
So cold, my bed.	Sam S. Taylor
So dead my love!	Harry Whittington
So dead, my lovely.	Day Keene
So deadly fair.	Gertrude Walker
So dear to my heart.	Sterling North
So evil my love.	Joseph Shearing
So fair, so evil.	Paul Connolly
So far from spring.	Peggy Simson Curry
So help me God.	Felix Jackson
So I'm a heel.	Mike Heller
So it doesn't whistle.	Robert Paul Smith
So little time.	John P. Marquand
So love returns.	Robert Nathan
So lovely to kill.	Harrison Wade
So low, so lovely.	Curtis Lucas
So many doors.	Oakley Hall
So many steps to death.	Agatha Christie
So nude, so dead.	Richard Marsten
So rich, so dead.	Gil Brewer
So rich, so lovely, and so dead.	Harold Q. Masur
So soon to die.	Jeremy York
So strong a flame.	Bernice Kavinoky
So sweet, so cruel.	Julian Farren
So well remembered.	James Hilton
So wicked my love.	Bruno Fischer
So young a body.	Frank Bunce
So young, so cold, so fair.	John Creasey
So young, so wicked.	Jonathan Craig
The soft arms of death.	Richard Hayward
Soft shoulders.	Peter Shelley

Soft touch. John D. MacDonald
The soft voice of
  the serpent. Nadine Gordimer
Solar lottery. Philip K. Dick
Soldier of democracy. Kenneth S. Davis
Soldier of fortune. Ernest K. Gann
Soldiers' daughters
  never cry. Audrey Erskine
   Lindop
Soldiers' pay. William Faulkner
Soldiers three. Humphrey Slater
Soldier's weekend. Hansford Martin
Soldiers' women. Stan Smith
Sole survivor. Louis Falstein
Solomon and Sheba. Jay Williams
Some came running. James Jones
Some day I'll kill you. Dana Chambers
Some die slow. William E. Heber
Some die young. James Duff
Some faces in the crowd. Budd Schulberg
Some inner fury. Kamala Markandaya
Some like it hot. I. A. L. Diamond
   Billy Wilder
Some like it tough. Jack Karney
Some must die. Gil Brewer
Some women won't wait. A. A. Fair
Somebody loves me. Nancy Morgan
Somebody up there likes Rowland Barber
me. Rocky Graziano
Someday, boy. Sam Ross
Someone called Maggie
 Lane. Frances Shelley Wees
Someone from the past. Margot Bennett
Someone is bleeding. Richard Matheson
The Somerset Maugham
 Pocket book. W. Somerset Maugham
Something about a
 soldier. Mark Harris
Something about midnight. D. B. Olsen
Something foolish, Glen Sire
 something gay. Jane Sire
Something for nothing. H. Vernor Dixon
Something for nothing. P. D. Kappan
Something of value. Robert Ruark
Something to live by. Dorothea S. Kopplin
Something wonderful
 to happen. Darwin L. Teilhet
Something's got to give. Marion Hargrove
Something's rotten in
 the State of Texas. Benn Towers
Sometime, never.
Somewhere in this house. Rufus King
Somewhere they die. L. P. Holmes
Son of a hundred kings. Thomas B. Costain
A son of Arizona. Charles Alden Seltzer
Son of Egypt. James Busbee Jr.
Son of Haman. Louis Cochran
Son of Mad. William M. Gaines
The Son of man. Emil Ludwig
Son of the Flying Y. Will F. Jenkins
Son of the giant. Stuart Engstrand
The son of the grand
 eunuch. Charles Pettit

Sonata with bullets. J. Jerod Chouinard
The song of Bernadette. Franz Werfel
The song of God:
 Bhagavad-gita.
The song of Ruth. Frank G. Slaughter
The Song of Songs.
Song of the gun. Dudley Dean
Song of the whip. Evan Evans
Song without sermon. James Woolf
Sonnets from the Elizabeth Barrett
 Portuguese. Browning
Sons and lovers. D. H. Lawrence
Sons of the saddle. William MacLeod Raine
Sons of the sheik. E. M. Hull
Sophie. Geoffrey Wagner
Sorority house. Jordan Park
Sorry, wrong number. Lucille Fletcher
   Allan Ullman
A sort of a saga. Bill Mauldin
The sound and the fury. William Faulkner
Sound of gunfire. Frank Bonham
Sound of revelry. Octavus Roy Cohen
The sound of thunder. Taylor Caldwell
The sound of white
 water. Hugh Fosburgh
South by Java Head. Alistair MacLean
South moon under. Marjorie Kinnan
   Rawlings
South of Cancer. John Hersey
South of Rio Grande. Max Brand
South of the sun. Wade Miller
South sea cartoons. Harold Meyers
South sea stories. W. Somerset Maugham
South sea tales. Jack London
South Street. William Gardner Smith
South to Santa Fé. George Kilrain
South wind. Norman Douglas
The southern cook book. Marion Brown
The Southern Cross. Peter French
Southern daughter. Daniel White
Southern territory. Robert Tallant
Southpaw. Donal Hamilton Haines
The southpaw. Mark Harris
Southways. Erskine Caldwell
Southwest. John Houghton Allen
Sow the wild wind. John Vail
The space-born. E. C. Tubb
The space frontiers. Roger Lee Vernon
The space merchants. C. M. Kornbluth
   Frederik Pohl
Space on my hands. Fredric Brown
The space plague. George O. Smith
Space platform. Murray Leinster
Space Station No. 1. Frank Belknap Long
Space tug. Murray Leinster
The space willies. Eric Frank Russell
The Spanish cape
 mystery. Ellery Queen
The Spanish cave. Geoffrey Household
The Spanish gardener. A. J. Cronin
Spanish Ridge. E. E. Halleran

Spanish stories and tales.	Harriet de Onís
Spanish through pictures.	I. A. Richards et al.
Spanish through pictures, book 1.	I. A. Richards et al.
Spark of life.	Erich Maria Remarque
Speak better--write better--English.	Horace Coon
Speak no evil.	Mignon G. Eberhart
The spear.	Louis de Wohl
Spearhead.	Franklin M. Davis Jr.
Special nurse.	Lucy Agnes Hancock
Special nurse.	Margaret Howe
Speed demon.	Jim Bosworth
Speedy.	Max Brand
The spell.	Gustav Breuer
Spencer Brade, M.D.	Frank G. Slaughter
Spendthrift.	Eric Hatch
Spider house.	F. van Wyck Mason
The spider in the cup.	Norman Hales
The Spider King.	Lawrence Schoonover
The spider lily.	Bruno Fischer
Spiderweb.	Robert Bloch
Spiderweb trail.	Eugene Cunningham
The spiked heel.	Richard Marsten
Spill the jackpot.	A. A. Fair
Spin the glass web.	Max Ehrlich
The spiral road.	Jan de Hartog
The spiral staircase.	Ethel Lina White
The spirit of the border.	Zane Grey
The spitfires.	Beril Becker
The spitting image.	Michael Avallone
Splendid quest.	Edison Marshall
The splintered man.	M. E. Chaber
The spoiled children.	Philippe Hériat
Sponger's jinx.	Bert Sackett
Sporting lady.	Gene Gauntier
Sports laughs.	Herman L. Masin
Sports shorts.	Mac Davis
Spotlight.	Helen Topping Miller
The spotted horse.	John Dillon
The spring begins.	Helen Rich
Spring fire.	Vin Packer
Spring harrowing.	Phoebe Atwood Taylor
Spring in Fialta.	Vladimir Nabokov
Spring of desire.	Louis Falstein
Spring riot.	Jay Presson
Spur to the smoke.	Steve Frazee
Spurs west!	Joseph T. Shaw
The spy.	Vincent Brome
Spy catcher.	Oreste Pinto
A spy in the house of love.	Anaïs Nin
The spy trap.	William Gilman
Square in the middle.	William Campbell Gault
Square shooter.	William MacLeod Raine
The squealer.	Edgar Wallace
The squeeze.	Gil Brewer
Squelches.	Brant House
The squirrel cage.	Edwin Gilbert
Stab in the dark.	Joe Rayter
Stab in the dark.	Louis Trimble
Stag gags.	Sandy Nelkin
	Pat Untermeyer
Stag night.	Phillips Rogers
The stag party.	William Krasner
Stag stripper.	Jack Hanley
Stage door canteen.	Delmer Daves
Stage road to Denver.	Allan Vaughan Elston
Stage to Painted Creek.	Vechel Howard
Stagecoach kingdom.	Harry Sinclair Drago
Stagecoach to Hellfire Pass.	Paul Evan Lehman
Stagecoach West.	William Heuman
Stages South.	Robert Steelman
The Stagline feud.	Peter Dawson
The stainless steel kimono.	Elliott Chaze
Staircase 4.	Helen Reilly
Stairway to an empty room.	Dolores Hitchens
Stairway to death.	Bruno Fischer
Stairway to murder.	Leslie Charteris
Stairway to nowhere.	Hal Ellson
The staked plain.	Frank X. Tolbert
The stakes are high.	Brent Ashabrannar
Stalingrad.	Theodor Plievier
Stalk the hunter.	Mitchell Wilson
Stamped for death.	Emmett McDowell
Stamped for murder.	Ben Benson
Stampede.	E. B. Mann
Stampede.	Chad Merriman
Stampede.	Yukon Miles
Stampede at Blue Springs.	Gene Olson
Stampede Canyon.	Robert J. Hogan
The stampeders.	James B. Hendryx
Stand up and die.	Frances Lockridge
	Richard Lockridge
The standard bartender's guide.	Patrick Gavin Duffy
The standard bartender's guide.	James A. Beard
	Patrick Gavin Duffy
Star born.	Andre Norton
Star bridge.	James E. Gunn
	Jack Williamson
Star guard.	Andre Norton
Star lust.	Jack Hanley
Star money.	Kathleen Winsor
The star of life.	Edmond Hamilton
Star of Macedon.	Karl V. Eiker
Star science fiction stories.	Frederik Pohl
Star science fiction stories no. 2.	Frederik Pohl
Star science fiction stories no. 3.	Frederik Pohl
Star science fiction stories no. 4.	Frederik Pohl
Star science fiction stories no. 5.	Frederik Pohl
Star science fiction stories no. 6.	Frederik Pohl

Star shine.	Fredric Brown	A stir of echoes.	Richard Matheson
Star short novels.	Frederik Pohl	Stir up the dust.	William Colt
Star spangled summer.	Janet Lambert		MacDonald
Star ways.	Poul Anderson	The stirrup boss.	Peter Dawson
Starbuck valley winter.	Roderick L. Haig-	Stirrups in the dust.	Burt Arthur
	Brown	The stockade.	Kenneth Lamott
Starburst.	Alfred Bester	The stolen squadron.	Charles Leonard
Starhaven.	Ivar Jorgenson	The stolen stallion.	Max Brand
Starlight Basin.	Giff Cheshire	Stolen woman.	Wade Miller
Starlight pass.	Tom Gill	Stone cold blonde.	Adam Knight
Starlight rider.	Ernest Haycox	Stone cold dead.	Richard Ellington
The stars.	Irving Adler	Stone dead.	Patrick Laing
The stars are ours.	Andre Norton	A stone for Danny	
Stars in my crown.	Joe David Brown	Fisher.	Harold Robbins
The stars in the making.	Cecilia Payne-	The stone of chastity.	Margery Sharp
	Gaposchkin	The stoneware monkey.	R. Austin Freeman
The stars look down.	A. J. Cronin	Stool pigeon.	Louis Malley
The stars, my		Stop dieting! Start	
destination.	Alfred Bester	losing!	Ruth West
Stars on the sea.	F. van Wyck Mason	Stop this man.	Peter Rabe
The stars spell death.	Jonathan Stagge	Stopover for murder.	Floyd Mahannah
Stars still shine.	Lida Larrimore	Stopover: Tokyo.	John P. Marquand
State Department murders.	Edward Ronns	Stories for here and	Elizabeth Abell
State fair.	Phil Stong	now.	Joseph I. Greene
State of siege.	Eric Ambler	Stories for stags.	Eddie Davis
The state vs. Elinor	Mary Roberts	Stories for the dead	
Norton.	Rinehart	of night.	Don Congdon
The statesman.	Henry Taylor	Stories for tonight.	
Station in space.	James E. Gunn	Stories from	
Station West.	Luke Short	Shakespeare.	Marchette Chute
Stay away, Joe.	Dan Cushman	Stories in the modern	
Steamboat Gothic.	Frances Parkinson	manner.	
	Keyes	Stories of famous	Harold Vincent
Steamboat round the bend.	Ben Lucien Burman	operas.	Milligan
Steel horizon.	Edward Churchill	Stories of scarlet	
The steel mirror.	Donald Hamilton	women.	
The steel noose.	Arnold Drake	Stories of sudden truth.	Elizabeth Abell
Steel to the south.	Wayne D. Overholser		Joseph I. Greene
Steel to the sunset.	Allan R. Bosworth	Stories of the Foreign	
The steel web.	Thomas Thompson	Legion.	Percival C. Wren
Steele of the Royal		Stories of the great	
Mounted.	James Oliver Curwood	operas.	Milton Cross
The steep ascent.	Anne Morrow Lindbergh	Stories of venial sin.	John O'Hara
The steeper cliff.	David Davidson	The stork didn't bring	
The Steinbeck Pocket		you.	Lois Pemberton
book.	John Steinbeck	Storm.	George R. Stewart
Stella.	Jan de Hartog	The storm and the	
Stella and Joe.	Lester Cohen	silence.	David Walker
Step in the dark.	Ethel Lina White	Storm centre.	Robert Standish
Step right up!	Daniel P. Mannix	Storm fear.	Clinton Seeley
Step to the music.	Phyllis A. Whitney	Storm haven.	Frank G. Slaughter
Stephana.	Joseph Foster	Stormy in the West.	Norman A. Fox
The Stephen Vincent	Stephen Vincent	Stormy present.	Hope Field
Benét Pocket book.	Benét	Stormy range.	Dwight Bennett
Stepsons of Terra.	Robert Silverberg	The story of America.	Hendrik Willem
Steve Yeager.	William MacLeod Raine		van Loon
Stevenson.	Robert Louis	The story of Edgar	
	Stevenson	Cayce.	Thomas Sugrue
Stiffs don't vote.	Geoffrey Homes	The story of Ernie Pyle.	Lee Miller
Stigma for valor.	Williams Forrest	The story of Esther	
A stillness at		Costello.	Nicholas Monsarrat
Appomattox.	Bruce Catton		

The story of human birth.   Alan F. Guttmacher
The story of jazz.   Marshall Stearns
The story of mankind.   Hendrik Willem van Loon
The story of Mrs. Murphy.   Natalie Anderson Scott
The story of my psychoanalysis.   John Knight
The story of philosophy.   Will Durant
The story of Sandy.   Susan Stanhope Wexler
The story of the Bible.   Hendrik Willem van Loon
The story of the Brooklyn Dodgers.   Ed Fitzgerald
The story of the world.   John Van Duyn Southworth
The story of Wake Island.   James P. S. Devereux
The story of Walt Disney.   Pete Martin Diane Disney Miller
The story Pocket book.   Whit Burnett
Story poems.   Louis Untermeyer
The strain.   Kenneth E. Shiflet
A strange affair.   Felix Jackson
Strange are the ways of love.   Lesley Evans
Strange as it seems.   Elsie Hix
Strange bargain.   Harry Whittington
Strange barriers.   J. Vernon Shea
The strange bedfellow.   Evelyn Berckman
The strange brigade.   John Jennings
Strange brother.   Blair Niles
Strange but true.
The strange case of Lucile Clery.   Joseph Shearing
The strange case of Miss Annie Spragg.   Louis Bromfield
The strange co-ed.   Bart Frame
Strange conquest.   Alfred Neumann
Strange courage.   Evan Evans
Strange customs of courtship and marriage.   William J. Fielding
Strange desires.   J. Vernon Shea
Strange desires.   Len Zinberg
Strange friends.   Agnete Holk
Strange fruit.   Lillian Smith
Strange fulfillment.   Denys Val Baker
A strange innocence.   Charles Mergendahl
The strange land.   Ned Calmer
Strange lovers.   Armando Meoni
The strange path.   Gale Wilhelm
Strange ports of call.   August Derleth
Strange sisters.   Fletcher Flora
The strange story of our earth.   A. Hyatt Verrill
Strange witness.   Day Keene
The strange woman.   Ben Ames Williams
The stranger.   Lillian Bos Ross
Stranger and alone.   J. Saunders Redding
Stranger at home.   George Sanders
Stranger at the door.   Gil Meynier
Stranger from Arizona.   Norman A. Fox

Stranger from Texas.   Ray Townsend
The stranger in boots.   Scott Leslie
A stranger in Eden.   Desmond Stewart
Stranger in flight.   Mignon G. Eberhart
A stranger in my arms.   Robert Wilder
Stranger in our midst.   Robert Carson
Stranger in Paris.   W. Somerset Maugham
Stranger in Sundown.   Ben Smith
Stranger in the land.   Colby Wolford
Stranger in town.   Brett Halliday
Stranger in town.   Howard Hunt
Stranger with a gun.   Bliss Lomax
The strangers.   William E. Wilson
Strangers and lovers.   Edwin Granberry
Strangers in love.   Viña Delmar
Strangers in my bed.   Allen O'Quinn
Strangers in paradise.   Howard Otway
Strangers in the desert.   Alice D. Russell
Strangers in the house.   Georges Simenon
Strangers in the universe.   Clifford D. Simak
Strangers may kiss.   Ursula Parrott
Strangers on a train.   Patricia Highsmith
Strangers on Friday.   Harry Whittington
Strangers when we meet.   Evan Hunter
Strangle hold.   Mary McMullen
The strangled witness.   Leslie Ford
Stranglehold.   John Creighton
Strangler's serenade.   William Irish
The strategy of terror.   Edmond Taylor
Straw boss.   E. E. Halleran
Straw man.   Doris Miles Disney
Strawberry roan.   Clem Colt
Straws in the wind.   W. C. Tuttle
The strawstack murders.   Dorothy Cameron Disney
The stray lamb.   Thorne Smith
The streak.   Paul Darcy Boles
The streak.   Max Brand
The street.   Ann Petry
Street music.   Theodora Keogh
Street of no return.   David Goodis
Street of painted lips.   Maurice Dekobra
Street of the barefoot lovers.   Joseph Foster
Street of the lost.   David Goodis
Street rod.   Henry Gregor Felsen
A streetcar named Desire.   Tennessee Williams
Stretch Dawson.   W. R. Burnett
A stretch on the river.   Richard Bissell
Strictly business.   Dale McFeatters
Strictly for laughs.   Joey Adams
Strike heaven on the face.   Charles Calitri
Strikeout story.   Bob Feller
Strip for murder.   Richard S. Prather
Strip for violence.   Ed Lacy
Strip street.   Jack Hanley
Strip the heart.   Jacquin Sanders
Stripped for murder.   Bruno Fischer
The strong city.   Taylor Caldwell

Sword of Casanova.	James Kendricks
Sword of fortune.	Noel B. Gerson
The sword of Rhiannon.	Leigh Brackett
The sword of Satan.	H. M. Mons
Swords for Charlemagne.	Mario Pei
The swordsman.	Jefferson Cooper
Sybil.	Louis Auchincloss
Sylvia.	Edgar Mittelholzer
The Syndic.	C. M. Kornbluth
Syndicate girl.	Frank Kane
The synthetic man.	Theodore Sturgeon

T

T as in trapped.	Lawrence Treat
TNT for two.	James Byron
TVA: democracy on the march.	David E. Lilienthal
TV movie almanac and ratings, 1958-1959.	Steven H. Scheuer
Taboo.	James Wakefield Burke
Tacey Cromwell.	Conrad Richter
Taffy.	Philip B. Kaye
Taggart.	Louis L'Amour
Take a murder, darling.	Richard S. Prather
Take a number.	Armando T. Perretta
Take a step to murder.	Day Keene
Take all you can get.	Steve Fisher
Take it easy.	Damon Runyon
Take it out in trade.	Walter Whitney
Take me as I am.	William H. Fielding
Take me as I am.	Loren Wahl
Take me home.	Fletcher Flora
Take my face.	Peter Held
Take off your mask.	Ludwig Eidelberg
Take your last look.	Matt Brady
Takeoff.	C. M. Kornbluth
Taking a turn for the nurse.	Kaz
A tale for midnight.	Frederic Prokosch
A tale of poor lovers.	Vasco Pratolini
A tale of two cities.	Charles Dickens
Tale of two lovers.	Henry Morton Robinson
A talent for murder.	Anna Mary Wells
The talented Mr. Ripley.	Patricia Highsmith
Tales for salesmen.	Francis Leo Golden
Tales from the Arabian nights.	
Tales from the Decameron.	Giovanni Boccaccio
Tales from the White Hart.	Arthur C. Clarke
Tales of Chinatown.	Sax Rohmer
Tales of fair and gallant ladies.	Abbé de Brantôme
Tales of gooseflesh and laughter.	John Wyndham
Tales of love and fury.	
Tales of midsummer passion.	
Tales of outer space.	Donald A. Wollheim
Tales of piracy, crime and ghosts.	Daniel Defoe
Tales of the south Pacific.	James A. Michener
Tales of Wells Fargo.	Frank Gruber
Tales out of (night) school.	Hy Gardner
Talk of the town.	Charles Williams
The talking clock.	Frank Gruber
The tall captains.	Bart Spicer
Tall, dark and dead.	Kermit Jaediker
Tall, dark and deadly.	Harold Q. Masur
The tall dark man.	Anne Chamberlain
The tall Delores.	Michael Avallone

Tall in the saddle.	Chuck Martin
Tall in the saddle.	Gordon Young
Tall in the West.	Vechel Howard
Tall man riding.	Norman A. Fox
The tall men.	Clay Fisher
The tall stranger.	Louis L'Amour
The tall T.	
Tall Wyoming.	Dan Cushman
Tallulah.	Tallulah Bankhead
Tambay gold.	Samuel Hopkins Adams
Tamerlane.	Harold Lamb
The taming of Carney Wilde.	Bart Spicer
The taming of the shrew.	William Shakespeare
Tangled trail.	Roy Manning
The tank destroyers.	Lawrence H. Kahn
Tap roots.	James Street
Taps for Private Tussie.	Jesse Stuart
Tarawa.	Robert Sherrod
Target in taffeta.	Ben Benson
Tarzan and the lost empire.	Edgar Rice Burroughs
Tarzan in the forbidden city.	Edgar Rice Burroughs
Tasker Martin.	Diana Gaines
A taste for cognac.	Brett Halliday
A taste for honey.	H. F. Heard
A taste for murder.	H. F. Heard
A taste for violence.	Brett Halliday
A taste of brass.	Robert Donald Locke
A taste of murder.	Joanna Cannan
A taste of sin.	R. V. Cassill
The tattooed heart.	Theodora Keogh
Tattooed man.	Howard Pease
Tavern girl.	Glen Watkins
Tawny.	Donald Henderson Clarke
Tawny.	Thomas C. Hinkle
Taxi.	Abraham Bernstein
Tea and sympathy.	Robert Anderson
Teach me to love.	Jack Woodford
Teacher's pet.	Fay Kanin
	Michael Kanin
The teachings of the compassionate Buddha.	Edwin A. Burtt
The Teahouse of the August Moon.	Vern Sneider
Tears are for angels.	Paul Connolly
Tears for the bride.	Robert Martin
Teen-age cartoons and jokes.	Harold Meyers
The teen-age diet book.	Ruth West
Teen-age gangs.	Madeline Karr
	Dale Kramer
Teen-age jungle.	Harry Whittington
Teen-age mafia.	Wenzell Brown
The teen-age manual.	Edith Heal
Teen-age mobster.	Benjamin Appel
Teen-age terror.	Wenzell Brown
Teen-age vice!	Courtney Ryley Cooper
Tejanos!	K. R. G. Granger
Tejas country.	Frank Miller

The telephone booth
  Indian.   A. J. Liebling
Tell it on the drums.   Robert W. Krepps
Tell me about women.   Harry Reasoner
Tell me, doctor.   Henry B. Safford
Tell them nothing.   Hal Ellson
Tempered blade.   Monte Barrett
Tempest.   R. V. Cassill
The temple of gold.   William Goldman
Temptation.   John Pen
Temptation in a
  southern town.   William L. Heath
Temptation in Paris.   Honoré de Balzac
The temptation of
  Roger Heriott.   Edward Newhouse
Temptations of Valerie.   Harry Whittington
The temptress.   Rosamond Marshall
Ten against Caesar.   K. R. G. Granger
The Ten commandments.   A. Powell Davies
Ten days in August.   Bernard Frizell
10 days to a successful   Joyce Brothers
  memory.   Edward P. F. Eagan
Ten days' wonder.   Ellery Queen
Ten droll tales.   Honoré de Balzac
Ten holy horrors.   Francis Beeding
Ten nights of love.
Ten North Frederick.   John O'Hara
Ten roads to hell.   Robert Travers
Ten seconds to hell.   Lawrence Bachmann
10,000 eyes.   Richard Collier
The tender age.   Russell Thacher
Tender is the night.   F. Scott Fitzgerald
Tender mercy.   Lenard Kaufman
The tender poisoner.   John Bingham
Tender to danger.   Eliot Reed
Tender victory.   Taylor Caldwell
The tenderfoot.   Max Brand
The tenderfoot.   W. H. B. Kent
The tenderfoot kid.   Peter Field
The tent of the wicked.   Robert Switzer
A tent on Corsica.   Martin Quigley
The 10th Pocket book   Margaret Petherbridge
  of crossword puzzles.   Farrar
Tequila.   Margaret Page Hood
Teresa.   Les Savage Jr.
The terrible game.   Dan Tyler Moore
The terrible night.   Peter Cheyney
The terrible swift sword. Arthur Steuer
Terror at night.   Herbert Williams
Terror at Tres Alamos.   Samuel A. Peeples
Terror comes creeping.   Carter Brown
Terror in the night.   Sebastian Blayne
Terror in the night.   Robert Bloch
Terror in the streets.   Howard Whitman
Terror in the sun.   Richard Glendinning
Terror in Times Square.   Alan Handley
Terror is my trade.   Stephen Marlowe
The terror of the
  leopard men.   Juba Kennerley
Terror on Broadway.   David Alexander
Terror over London.   Gardner F. Fox
The terror package.   Robert Chavis

Terror rides the range.   Allan K. Echols
Terror tournament.   J. M. Flynn
Terry.   Harriet T. Comstock
Terry and the Pirates
  in the adventures of
  the jewels of jade.   Edward J. Boylan Jr.
Tess of the
  D'Urbervilles.   Thomas Hardy
Tex.   Clarence E. Mulford
The Texan.   Burt Arthur
The Texan.   Scott Leslie
The Texan.   Herbert Shappiro
A Texan came riding.   Frank O'Rourke
Texan-killer.   Gene Austin
Texan on the prod.   Philip Ketchum
Texas badman.   Bradford Scott
Texas, blood red.   Shepard Rifkin
Texas breed.   William MacLeod Raine
A Texas cowboy.   Charles A. Siringo
Texas fists.   Jackson Cole
Texas fury.   John Callahan
Texas fury.   Jackson Cole
The Texas gun.   Leslie Ernenwein
The Texas gun.   Philip Ketchum
Texas guns.   Leslie Ernenwein
The Texas hawk.   Bradford Scott
Texas heller.   E. M. Parsons
Texas hellion.   J. H. Plenn
The Texas kid.   William MacLeod Raine
Texas manhunt.   Jackson Cole
Texas men.   Paul Evan Lehman
Texas outlaw.   Richard Jessup
The Texas pistol.   James Keene
Texas pride.   Chuck Martin
Texas rawhider.   Jack Barton
Texas revenge.   Archie Joscelyn
Texas sheriff.   Eugene Cunningham
Texas spurs.   J. L. Bouma
The Texas terror.   Bradford Scott
Texas tornado.   Jackson Cole
The Texas tornado.   Nelson Nye
Texas triggers.   Eugene Cunningham
Texas vengeance.   Paul Evan Lehman
Texas vengeance.   Bradford Scott
Thank you, Mr. Moto.   John P. Marquand
Thanks to the Saint.   Leslie Charteris
That French girl.   Joseph Hilton
That girl from Memphis.   Wilbur Daniel Steele
That girl on the river.   Ted Fox
That Jane from Maine.   Marvin H. Albert
That kind of woman.   Robert Lowry
That Mrs. Renney.   Donald Henderson
                             Clarke.
That none should die.   Frank G. Slaughter
That Randall girl.   Samuel Edwards
That winter.   Merle Miller
That's my baby.   Josef A. Schneider
Theatre.   W. Somerset Maugham
Their ancient grudge.   Harry Harrison Kroll
Their guns were fast.   Harry Sinclair Drago
Theme for ballet.   Vicki Baum
Then came Mulvane.   William Heuman

This is murder, Mr. Herbert.	Day Keene
This is murder, Mr. Jones.	Timothy Fuller
This is my body.	
This is my funniest.	Whit Burnett
This is my night.	Robert Lowry
This is my story.	Eleanor Roosevelt
This is Russia-- uncensored.	Edmund Stevens
This is temptation.	James Ronald
This is the navy.	Gilbert Cant
This is the West.	Robert West Howard
This kill is mine.	Dean Evans
This man and this woman.	James T. Farrell
This naked love.	Helga Moray
This range is mine.	Dean Owen
This side of innocence.	Taylor Caldwell
This side of paradise.	F. Scott Fitzgerald
This spring of love.	Charles Mergendahl
This thing called love.	Harvey Breit
	Marc Slonim
This time for keeps.	John MacCormac
This, too, is love.	Sam Ross
This very earth.	Erskine Caldwell
This way out.	James Ronald
This woman.	Pietro di Donato
This woman.	Albert Idell
This woman is mine.	Harry Whittington
This woman is mine.	P. J. Wolfson
This'll slay you.	Alan Payne
Thomas Alva Edison.	G. Glenwood Clark
Thomas Jefferson on democracy.	Thomas Jefferson
The thorn in the flesh.	D. H. Lawrence
The Thorndike-Barnhart handy pocket dictionary.	Clarence Barnhart
The thoroughbred and the tramp.	Burgess Leonard
Those about to die.	Daniel P. Mannix
Those barren leaves.	Aldous Huxley
Those devils in baggy pants.	Ross Carter
Those idiots from earth.	Richard Wilson
Those without shadows.	Françoise Sagan
Thread of evil.	Charles Jackson
Three blind mice.	Agatha Christie
Three bright pebbles.	Leslie Ford
The three coffins.	John Dickson Carr
Three complete western novels.	Luke Short
Three comrades.	Erich Maria Remarque
Three day pass--to kill.	James Wakefield Burke
	Edward Grace
Three-day terror.	Vin Packer
Three doors to death.	Rex Stout
Three faces of time.	Sam Merwin Jr.
Three for the chair.	Rex Stout
Three for the gallows.	Emmett McDowell
Three for the money.	Joe Barry
Three for the money.	James McConnaughey
Three from out there.	Leo Margulies
Three gorgeous hussies.	Jack Woodford
Three great Irishmen.	Arland Ussher
Three great plays of Euripides.	Euripides
Three harbours.	F. van Wyck Mason
Three hostages.	John Buchan
Three hundred Pillsbury prize recipes.	
300 tricks you can do.	Howard Thurston
Three loves had Margaret.	James Hilton
Three loves had she.	Mark Schorer
Three men and Diana.	Kathleen Norris
Three men out.	Rex Stout
Three minutes a day.	James Keller
The three musketeers, volume 1.	Alexandre Dumas
The three musketeers, volume 2.	Alexandre Dumas
Three musketeers and a lady.	Tiffany Thayer
Three must die!	Dan Gregory
Three-Notch Cameron.	William Colt MacDonald
Three of a kind.	P. J. Wolfson
Three plays.	Thornton Wilder
Three plays by Ibsen.	Henrik Ibsen
The three roads.	Kenneth Millar
Three secrets.	Margaret Lee Runbeck
Three short biers.	Jimmy Starr
Three sinners in Paris.	Toni Howard
Three thirds of a ghost.	Timothy Fuller
3,000 years.	Thomas Calvert McClary
Three times a victim.	F. L. Wallace
Three times infinity.	Leo Margulies
Three to conquer.	Eric Frank Russell
Three to get married.	Fulton J. Sheen
Three trails.	George C. Appell
Three violent people.	Leonard Praskins
	Barney Slater
3 weeks to a better memory.	Brendan Byrne
The three wise guys.	Damon Runyon
Three witnesses.	Rex Stout
Three women in black.	Helen Reilly
Three's a shroud.	Richard S. Prather
Threshold of eternity.	John Brunner
The thrill kids.	Vin Packer
Through a glass, darkly.	Helen McCloy
Thruway west.	Lee Floren
Thunder at Harper's Ferry.	Allan Keller
Thunder below.	Thomas Rourke
Thunder Creek Range.	Paul Evan
Thunder in the dust.	Alan LeMay
Thunder in the heart.	John Lee Weldon
Thunder in the sun.	Frank O'Rourke
Thunder in the wilderness.	Harry Hamilton
Thunder mountain.	Theodore Pratt
Thunder of hoofs.	Tex Holt

The town that God forgot.	William Colt MacDonald
A town to tame.	Joseph Chadwick
The townsman.	Pearl S. Buck
The track of the cat.	Walter Van Tilburg Clark
Tracked down.	Leslie Edgley
Tragedy in the hollow.	Freeman Wills Crofts
The tragedy of Hamlet, Prince of Denmark.	William Shakespeare
The tragedy of Julius Caesar.	William Shakespeare
The tragedy of King Lear.	William Shakespeare
The tragedy of Macbeth.	William Shakespeare
The tragedy of Othello, the Moor of Venice.	William Shakespeare
The tragedy of X.	Ellery Queen
The tragedy of Y.	Ellery Queen
The tragedy of Z.	Ellery Queen
Tragedy trail.	Max Brand
Tragic ground.	Erskine Caldwell
The trail.	Logan Stewart
Trail boss.	Peter Dawson
Trail boss of Indian beef.	Harold Channing Wire
Trail drive.	Bill Gulick
The trail driver.	Zane Grey
Trail end.	Tom J. Hopkins
Trail from Needle Rock.	Peter Field
The trail from Texas.	Dale Homer
Trail of a tramp.	Nick Quarry
The trail of danger.	William MacLeod Raine
Trail of the damned.	Jack Barton
Trail of the Macaw.	Eugene Cunningham
Trail of the restless gun.	Will Hickok
Trail partners.	Max Brand
Trail rider.	Lynn Westland
Trail smoke.	Ernest Haycox
Trail South from Powder Valley.	Peter Field
The trail to Tomahawk.	Edwin Booth
Trail town.	Ernest Haycox
Trail town marshal.	Todhunter Ballard
Trails by night.	Tom J. Hopkins
Trail's end.	Edison Marshall
Trail's end.	William MacLeod Raine
The train from Pittsburgh.	Julian Farren
The traitor.	William L. Shirer
The tramplers.	Jason Manor
The transcendent man.	Jerry Sohl
The transposed man.	Dwight V. Swain
Trap.	George E. Jones
Trapped.	Richard Hayward
Trapped!	Jean Hougron
Treachery at Rock Point.	Peter Dawson
Treachery in Trieste.	Charles Leonard
Treasure book of fairy tales.	Ann McGovern
Treasure Island.	Robert Louis Stevenson

The treasure of Pleasant Valley.	Frank Yerby
Treasure of the brasada.	Les Savage Jr.
The treasure of the Sierra Madre.	B. Traven
A treasury of Asian literature.	John D. Yohannan
A treasury of faith.	Leon McCauley
A treasury of folk songs.	John Kolb Sylvia Kolb
A treasury of ribaldry, volume 1.	Louis Untermeyer
A treasury of science fiction.	Groff Conklin
A treasury of short stories.	Rudyard Kipling
A treasury of True.	Charles N. Barnard
A treasury of wisdom and inspiration.	David St. Leger
A tree grows in Brooklyn.	Betty Smith
A tree of night.	Truman Capote
The trees.	Conrad Richter
Trees die at the top.	Edna Ferber
The trembling earth.	Dale Van Every
Trent's last case.	E. C. Bentley
Trent's own case.	H. Warner Allen E. C. Bentley
Trespass.	Eugene Brown
Trial.	Don M. Mankiewicz
Trial and error.	Anthony Berkeley
Trial by darkness.	Charles Gorham
Trial by fire.	Charles Elliott
Trial by fury.	Craig Rice
Trial by gunsmoke.	Jim O'Mara
Trial by marriage.	Vereen Bell
Trial by perjury.	John Creighton
Trial by terror.	Paul Gallico
The trial of Mary Dugan.	Bayard Veiller William Almon Wolff
The tribe that lost its head.	Nicholas Monsarrat
Trigger gospel.	Harry Sinclair Drago
Trigger justice.	Leslie Ernenwein
Trigger kid.	Bennett Foster
Trigger law.	Jackson Cole
Trigger man.	Burt Arthur
Trigger mortis.	Frank Kane
Trigger talk.	Bradford Scott
Trigger trail.	Todhunter Ballard
Trigger vengeance.	B. M. Bower
Triggerman.	Frank Austin
Trinity in violence.	Henry Kane
Trio.	Dorothy Baker
Trio.	W. Somerset Maugham
The triple cross.	Joe Barry
Triple jeopardy.	Rex Stout
Triple slay.	Adam Knight
Trish.	Margaret Maze Craig
The triumph of time.	James Blish
The triumph of Willie Pond.	Caroline Slade
Troopers West.	Forbes Parkhill

Tropic moon.   Georges Simenon
Tropical passions.
Trouble at Borrasca Rim.   Mark Owen
Trouble at Breakdam.   Ben Smith
Trouble at Moon Dance.   A. B. Guthrie Jr.
Trouble at the JHC.   W. C. Tuttle
Trouble comes double.   Robert P. Hansen
Trouble follows me.   Kenneth Millar
Trouble in July.   Erskine Caldwell
Trouble in the saddle.   Arthur Henry Gooden
Trouble in Tombstone.   Tom J. Hopkins
Trouble in triplicate.   Rex Stout
Trouble is my business.   Raymond Chandler
Trouble is my name.   Stephen Marlowe
Trouble on Big Cat.   Glenn Corbin
Trouble on Crazyman.   Sam Allison
Trouble on the border.   Gordon Young
Trouble on the Brazos.   Will C. Brown
Trouble on the Massacre.   Todhunter Ballard
Trouble rider.   Thomas Thompson
Trouble rides tall.   William Hopson
Trouble shooter.   Jackson Cole
Trouble shooter.   Ernest Haycox
Trouble shooter.   Robert Traver
Trouble town.   Burt Arthur
Trouble trail.   Coe Williams
The trouble trailer.   W. C. Tuttle
Trouble valley.   Ward West
The trouble with
  fidelity.   George Malcolm-Smith
The trouble with murder.   Roger Bax
The troubled air.   Irwin Shaw
The troubled midnight.   Rodney Garland
Troubled range.   E. B. Mann
Troubled spring.   John Brick
Troubling of a star.   Walt Sheldon
The true believer.   Eric Hoffer
Trumpet in the dust.   Gene Fowler
Trumpet to arms.   Bruce Lancaster
The trumpet unblown.   William Hoffman
Trumpets of Company K.   William Chamberlain
Trumpets to the West.   Will Cook
Trumpets West!   Luke Short
The truth about Belle
  Gunness.   Lillian De La Torre
Try and stop me.   Bennett Cerf
Tubie's monument.   Peter Keveson
Tuck's girl.   Marcel Wallenstein
Tucson.   Paul Leslie Peil
The Tuesday Club murders.   Agatha Christie
Tuesday to bed.   Francis Wickware
Tugboat Annie.   Norman Reilly Raine
Tumbling Range woman.   Steve Frazee
The tumult and the
  shouting.   Grantland Rice
The tunnel escape.   Eric Williams
The tunnel of love.   Peter De Vries
Turn back the river.   W. G. Hardy
Turn left for murder.   Stephen Marlowe
Turn of the table.   Jonathan Stagge
Turn on the heat.   A. A. Fair
Turn the tigers loose.   Walt Lasly

Turnabout.   Thorne Smith
The turning wheels.   Stuart Cloete
The turquoise.   Anya Seton
The turquoise shop.   Frances Crane
Tutt and Mr. Tutt.   Arthur Train
Twelfth night.   William Shakespeare
12 against crime.   Edward D. Radin
12 against the law.   Edward D. Radin
12 Chinamen and a woman.   James Hadley Chase
12 Chinks and a woman.   James Hadley Chase
The twelve disguises.   Francis Beeding
Twelve o'clock high.   Sy Bartlett
                                Beirne Lay Jr.

12 stories they
  wouldn't let me
  do on TV.   Alfred Hitchcock
21st century sub.   Frank Herbert
25 great ghost stories.
The 24th horse.   Hugh Pentecost
Twenty grand short
  stories.   Ernestine Taggard
20 great ghost stories.
Twenty-one.   Jack Barry
The 27th day.   John Mantley
26 men and a girl.   Maxim Gorky
23 women.
The 22 brothers.   Dana Sage
Twice in time.   Manly Wade Wellman
Twice upon a time.   Charles L. Fontenay
Twilight for the gods.   Ernest K. Gann
Twilight men.   André Tellier
The twilighters.   Noel M. Loomis
Twin mavericks.   William Hopson
Twist of the knife.   Victor Canning
Twist the knife slowly.   Kate Clugston
The twisted ones.   Vin Packer
The twisted trail.   Paul Evan Lehman
Twisted trail.   Tom West
Twisted trails.   W. C. Tuttle
The twittering bird
  mystery.   H. C. Bailey
Two adolescents.   Alberto Moravia
Two and the town.   Henry Gregor Felsen
Two beds for Roxane.   Stephen Longstreet
Two-bit rancher.   Charles N. Heckelmann
Two clues.   Erle Stanley Gardner
Two deaths must die.   Richard Himmel
Two-edged vengeance.   Todhunter Ballard
Two faces West.   T. T. Flynn
Two-gun deputy.   William Colt
                                  MacDonald
Two-gun devil.   Jackson Cole
Two-gun fury.   Chuck Martin
Two-gun law.   Clifton Adams
Two-gun man.   Gordon Young
Two-gun Rio Kid.   Don Davis
Two-gun Texan.   Burt Arthur
Two guns for hire.   Neil MacNeil
Two if by sea.   Roger Bax
The two lives of Dr.
  Stratton.   Russell Boltar
Two loves.   Elliott Arnold

U

U-boat killer.   Donald Macintyre
U-boat 977.   Heinz Schaeffer
U-boats at war.   Harald Busch
The U.P. trail.   Zane Grey
U.S. foreign policy.   Walter Lippmann
The U.S. marines on
  Iwo Jima.
The ugly duchess.   Lion Feuchtwanger
The ultimate invader.   Donald A. Wollheim
The unafraid.   Gerald Butler
Unarmed killer.   C. William Harrison
The unbearable
  Bassington.   Saki
Uncle Dynamite.   P. G. Wodehouse
Uncle Good's girls.   John Faulkner
Uncle Sagamore and his
  girls.   Charles Williams
Uncle Tom's children.   Richard Wright
The uncomplaining
  corpses.   Brett Halliday
Unconquered.   Neil H. Swanson
The unconscious witness.   R. Austin Freeman
The undaunted.   John Harris
Under cover of night.   Manning Lee Stokes
The under dog and other
  mysteries.   Agatha Christie
Under northern stars.   William MacLeod Raine
Under the badge.   C. Hall Thompson
Under the mesa rim.   Chandler Whipple
Under the sea wind.   Rachel L. Carson
Under the skin.   Phyllis Bottome
Underdog.   W. R. Burnett
Understanding chemistry.   Lawrence P. Lessing
Understanding human
  nature.   Alfred Adler
Understanding other
  people.   Stuart Palmer
Understanding surgery.   Robert E. Rothenberg
The underworld.   Ira Wolfert
Underworld U.S.A.   Joseph F. Dinneen
The undiscovered self.   C. G. Jung
Undressed to kill.   Peter Cheyney
The undying fire.   Fletcher Pratt
Uneasy lies the head.   William L. Rohde
Uneasy street.   Wade Miller
Uneasy virtue.   Dana Wilson
The unexpected.   Bennett Cerf
Unexpected night.   Elizabeth Daly
Unfaithful.   John Baxter
Unfaithful.   Frank S. Caprio
The unfaithful lady.   Charles Pettit
The unfaithful wife.   Jules Roy
Unfinished business.   Cary Lucas
Unfinished crime.   Helen McCloy
The unforeseen.   Dorothy Macardle
The unforgiven.   Alan LeMay
An unfound door.   Al Hine
The unfulfilled.   W. G. Hardy
The ungilded lily.   Morton Cooper
Unhappy hooligan.   Stuart Palmer

Unholy flame.   Olga Rosmanith
The unholy lovers.   Paul Monash
The unholy three and
  other stories.   Louis Auchincloss
The unholy wife.   John Roeburt
Unhurrying chase.   Morris Markey
The unicorn murders.   Carter Dickson
Unidentified woman.   Mignon G. Eberhart
The uninvited.   Dorothy Macardle
Uninvited corpse.   Paul Whelton
The United Nations and
  how it works.   David Cushman Coyle
United States book of
  baby and child care.
The United States
  political system and
  how it works.   David Cushman Coyle
Universe.   Robert A. Heinlein
The universe and Dr.
  Einstein.   Lincoln Barnett
Universe maker.   A. E. van Vogt
The University of
  Chicago Spanish-English,
  English-Spanish   Carlos Castillo
  dictionary.   et al.
The unknown--is it   Eric J. Dingwall
  nearer?   John Langdon-Davies
The unknown Lincoln.   Dale Carnegie
The unknown path.   Anne Meredith
The unknown quantity.   Mignon G. Eberhart
The unknown soldier.   Väinö Linna
The unleashed will.   Christopher Clark
Unmarried couple.   Maysie Greig
The unpleasantness at
  the Bellona Club.   Dorothy L. Sayers
The unpossessed.   William H. Fielding
The unquiet corpse.   William Sloane
Unrepentant sinners.   Louis-Charles Royer
The unscrupulous Mr.
  Callaghan.   Peter Cheyney
The unsuspected.   Charlotte Armstrong
The untamed.   Max Brand
Untamed.   Warner Hall
Untamed.   Helga Moray
The untamed breed.   Jack Barton
Untamed darling.   Jack Woodford
The untamed wife of
  Louis Scott.   W. Carroll Munro
Untidy murder.   Frances Lockridge
        Richard Lockridge
Until you are dead.   Henry Kane
Untouched by human hands.   Robert Sheckley
The unvanquished.   Howard Fast
The unvanquished.   William Faulkner
The unwanted.   Dante Arfelli
Up a winding stair.   H. Vernor Dixon
Up at the villa.   W. Somerset Maugham
Up from slavery.   Booker T. Washington
Up front.   Bill Mauldin
Up jumped the devil.   Cleve F. Adams
Up to her neck.   John Newton Chance
The Upanishads.

V

V.I.P.	William L. Rohde
VOR.	James Blish
V-2: the Nazi rocket.	Walter Dornberger
Valcour meets murder.	Rufus King
Valerie.	Jordan Park
Valiant is the word for Carrie.	Barry Benefield
The valiant Virginians.	James Warner Bellah
Valley of angry men.	Matthew Gant
The valley of dry bones.	Arthur Henry Gooden
The valley of fear.	Arthur Conan Doyle
The valley of God.	Irene Patai
Valley of guns.	Wayne D. Overholser
The valley of hunted men.	Paul Evan Lehman
The valley of love.	H. E. Bates
Valley of the shadow.	Charles M. Warren
Valley of the tyrant.	Dick Pearce
Valley of vanishing herds.	W. C. Tuttle
Valley of vanishing men.	Max Brand
Valley of violence.	Louis Trimble
Valley of violent men.	Lewis B. Patten
Valley of wild horses.	Zane Grey
Valley thieves.	Max Brand
The valley vixen.	Ben Ames Williams
Valley vultures.	Max Brand
Van Gogh.	Robert Goldwater
Vanguard from Alpha.	Brian W. Aldiss
Vanish in an instant.	Margaret Millar
The vanishing gun-slinger.	William Colt MacDonald
Vanishing ladies.	Richard Marsten
The vanishing vixen.	Roy B. Sparkia
Vanity fair.	William Makepeace Thackeray
Vanity Row.	W. R. Burnett
The vanquished.	Alan Marcus
A vaquero of the brush country.	J. Frank Dobie
The variable man and other stories.	Philip K. Dick
The varieties of religious experience.	William James
A variety of weapons.	Rufus King
Various temptations.	
Vegas, gunman marshal.	William Hopson
The vehement flame.	Ludwig Lewisohn
Vein of iron.	Ellen Glasgow
Velázquez.	Margaretta Salinger
The velvet ape.	David C. Holmes
The velvet doublet.	James Street
The velvet fleece.	Lois Eby
	John Fleming
The velvet well.	John Gearon
The velvet whip.	Leonard Snyder
Venables.	Geoffrey Wagner
Venetian adventurer: Marco Polo.	Henry Hart
Vengeance is mine.	Mickey Spillane
The vengeance riders.	Jack Barton
Vengeance trail.	Max Brand
Vengeance trail.	Ernest Haycox
Vengeance trail.	Charles N. Heckelmann
The vengeance trail.	Paul Evan Lehman
Vengeance trail.	Chuck Martin
Vengeance under law.	Frank Castle
Vengeance valley.	Allan K. Echols
Vengeance Valley.	Paul Evan Lehman
Vengeance valley.	Roy Manning
Vengeance valley.	Luke Short
The vengeful men.	Ray Gaulden
The vengeful virgin.	Gil Brewer
Venture in the East.	Bruce Lancaster
Venturous lady.	George Harmon Coxe
The Venus death.	Ben Benson
Venus in Sparta.	Louis Auchincloss
Venus of the counting house.	Émile Zola
Venus on wheels.	Maurice Dekobra
Vera.	Robert Scott Taylor
Verdict in dispute.	Edgar Lustgarten
Verdict of twelve.	Raymond Postgate
Veronica's veil.	Jefferson Cooper
Vertigo.	Pierre Boileau Thomas Narcejac
Very cold for May.	William P. McGivern
A very silent symphony.	J. Jerod Chouinard
The vicar of Wakefield.	Oliver Goldsmith
Vice girl.	Sim Albert
Vice, inc.	Joachim Joesten
The vice net.	Michael Carey
Vice squad cop.	Michael Carey
The vice trap.	Elliott Gilbert
The victim.	Carter Brown
The victim was important.	Joe Rayter
Victorine.	Frances Parkinson Keyes
Victory in the dust.	Arthur Phillips
The view from Pompey's Head.	Hamilton Basso
View from the air.	Hugh Fosburgh
Vigilante.	Richard Summers
The viking.	Edison Marshall
Vile bodies.	Evelyn Waugh
The villain and the virgin.	James Hadley Chase
The violated.	Vance Bourjaily
The violators.	Israel Beckhardt Wenzell Brown
Violence at sundown.	Frank O'Rourke
Violence in the night.	Alan Hynd
Violence in velvet.	Michael Avallone
Violence is golden.	C. H. Thames
Violence is my business.	Stephen Marlowe
Violence valley.	William Heuman
Violent city.	John Hawkins Ward Hawkins
The violent hours.	Frank Castle
Violent hours.	Robert Walsh

W

Waterfront cop. William P. McGivern
A way home. Theodore Sturgeon
Way of a buccaneer. Davenport Steward
Way of a wanton. Richard S. Prather
The way of all flesh. Samuel Butler
The way of life. Lao-tzu
Way of the wicked. William Woolfolk
The way of woman. Johnson E. Fairchild
The way of Zen. Alan W. Watts
The way some people die. John Ross Macdonald
Way station west. William E. Vance
Way to happiness. Fulton J. Sheen
The way to inner peace. Fulton J. Sheen
The way we live now. Warren Miller
The way west. A. B. Guthrie Jr.
A way with women. William Gwinn
Wayward angel. Verne Chute
The wayward blonde. John Creighton
The wayward bus. John Steinbeck
The wayward ones. Sara Harris
The wayward widow. William Campbell
 Gault

We all killed Grandma. Fredric Brown
We are betrayed. Vardis Fisher
We are not alone. James Hilton
We are the living. Erskine Caldwell
We are the public
 enemies. Alan Hynd
We burn like candles. Bernice Kavinoky
We burn like fire. Will Cook
We claim these stars. Poul Anderson
We dare you to solve
 this! John Paul Adams
We die alone. David Howarth
We fished all night. Willard Motley
We never called him Harry Bennett
 Henry. Paul Marcus
We too are drifting. Gale Wilhelm
We too must love. Ann Aldrich
We took to the woods. Louise Dickinson Rich
We walk alone. Ann Aldrich
We were strangers. Robert Sylvester
We who survived. Sterling Noel
The weapon shops of
 Isher. A. E. van Vogt
Wear a fast gun. John Jakes
The weather. Raymond Bush
 George Kimble
The web of days. Edna Lee
Web of destiny. Muriel Elwood
The web of evil. Lucille Emerick
Web of gunsmoke. Will Hickok
The web of life. John H. Storer
Web of murder. Harry Whittington
Web of passion. Edward D. Radin
Webster's new world
 dictionary of the
 American language. David B. Guralnik
The wedding journey. Walter D. Edmonds
Wedding ring. Beth Brown
Week-end marriage. Faith Baldwin
Weekend with death. Patricia Wentworth

Weep for a blonde. Brett Halliday
Weep for a wanton. Lawrence Treat
Weep for me. John D. MacDonald
The weeper and the
 blackmailer. Richard H. Rovere
The weeping and the
 laughter. Vera Caspary
The weight of the cross. Robert O. Bowen
Weird shadow over
 Innsmouth. H. P. Lovecraft
The weird sisters. Douglas M. Alver
The well of loneliness. Radclyffe Hall
The wench and the flame. Robert L. Trimnell
The wench is dead. Fredric Brown
The werewolf of Paris. Guy Endore
West of Abilene. Vingie Roe
West of Devil's Canyon. Richard Poole
West of justice. John Hunter
West of quarantine. Todhunter Ballard
West of Texas law. Walker A. Tompkins
West of the law. Al Cody
West of the law. William MacLeod Raine
West of the Pecos. Paul Evan
West of the rimrock. Wayne D. Overholser
West of the river. Charlton Laird
West of the Wolverine. Paul Evan Lehman
West side jungle. Jason Ridgway
West to the sun. Noel M. Loomis
Western roundup! Arnold Hano
Western stories. Gene Autry
Western stories. William MacLeod Raine
Western triggers. Arnold Hano
Westport Landing. Homer Hatten
Westward the drums. L. A. Hearne
Westward the river. Dale Van Every
Wetback. William O'Farrell
Wharf girl. William Manners
What a body! Alan Green
What a man wants. Harvey Fergusson
What am I doing here? Abner Dean
What are the odds? Leo Guild
What became of Anna
 Bolton? Louis Bromfield
What d'ya know for sure? Len Zinberg
What fools these mortals
 be. Benn Towers
What happened in history. V. Gordon Childe
What hath God rot. G. Forbes Durand
What mad universe. Fredric Brown
What makes Sammy run? Budd Schulberg
What Mrs. McGillicuddy
 saw! Agatha Christie
What price murder. Cleve F. Adams
What really happened. Brett Halliday
What rhymes with murder? Jack Iams
What, then, is love. Emilie Loring
What to do till the Donald B. Armstrong
 doctor comes. Grace T. Hallock
What to listen for in
 music. Aaron Copland
What to tell your
 children about sex. Adie Suehsdorf

The wings of the dove.	Henry James
Winner take all.	James McKimmey
Winston Churchill.	Robert Lewis Taylor
Winter ambush.	E. E. Halleran
Winter harvest.	Norah Lofts
Winter kill.	Steve Fisher
Winter meeting.	Ethel Vance
Winter of the Sioux.	Robert Steelman
Winter range.	Alan LeMay
The winter's tale.	William Shakespeare
Winter's tales.	Isak Dinesen
Wintertime.	Jan Valtin
The Winthrop woman.	Anya Seton
Wiped out.	John D. Newsom
The wire.	David Walker
The wire god.	Jack Willard
Wire in the wind.	Matt Stuart
Wired for scandal.	F. L. Wallace
Wiretap!	Charles Einstein
The wisdom and ideas of Plato.	David Appel / Eugene Freeman
Wise blood.	Flannery O'Connor
Wisteria Cottage.	Robert M. Coates
Wit from overseas.	Roy Hoopes Jr.
The witch diggers.	Jessamyn West
Witch doctor.	N. C. McDonald
The witch finder.	Thomas L. O'Brien
Witch of Salem.	Benjamin Siegel
The witch of spring.	William Shore
The witches.	Jay Williams
The witching night.	C. S. Cody
The witching pool.	Robert Presnell Jr.
Witch's moon.	Giles Jackson
The witch's thorn.	Ruth Park
With murder for some.	H. C. Huston
With naked foot.	Emily Hahn
With sirens screaming.	Ernest Booth
With this ring.	Mignon G. Eberhart
Without armor.	James Hilton
Without magnolias.	Bucklin Moon
The witness for the prosecution.	Agatha Christie
Witness this woman.	Gardner F. Fox
Witness to death.	Leslie Charteris
Wives and husbands.	David Duncan
Wives and lovers.	Alex Austin
Wives to burn.	Lawrence G. Blochman
Wolf dog range.	Will Watson
Wolf dogs of the north.	Jack Hines
Wolf in man's clothing.	Mignon G. Eberhart
Wolf song.	Harvey Fergusson
The wolf streak.	Richard Brister
The wolf that fed us.	Robert Lowry
Wolf whistle and other stories.	William Bradford Huie
Wolfbane.	C. M. Kornbluth / Frederik Pohl
The woman and the prowler.	Stuart Friedman
Woman and the puppet.	Pierre Louÿs
The woman aroused.	Ed Lacy
A woman called desire.	Richard Marshe
A woman called Fancy.	Frank Yerby
A woman called Trouble.	P. A. Hoover
Woman doctor.	Hannah Lees
A woman for Henry.	Allen O'Quinn
A woman in Berlin.	
The woman in black.	Leslie Ford
Woman in love.	Lucy Cores
The woman in red.	Anthony Gilbert
A woman in the house.	Erskine Caldwell
The woman in the picture.	John August
The woman in the woods.	Lee Blackstock
Woman obsessed.	John Mantley
A woman of Bangkok.	Jack Reynolds
Woman of Cairo.	John Flagg
Woman of Egypt.	Kevin Matthews
A woman of forty.	Desmond Hall
Woman of Kali.	Gardner F. Fox
Woman of Paris.	Guy des Cars
A woman of Paris.	André Tellier
Woman of property.	Mabel Seeley
The woman of Rome.	Alberto Moravia
A woman of Samaria.	James Wesley Ingles
Woman of the Avalon.	L. L. Foreman
Woman of the night.	Robert Carse
Woman of the world.	W. Somerset Maugham
Woman on her way.	Faith Baldwin
A woman on the place.	Harry Whittington
The woman on the roof.	Helen Nielsen
The woman racket.	Gil Lawrence
Woman soldier.	Arnold Rodin
Woman surgeon.	Else K. LaRoe
The woman who rode away.	D. H. Lawrence
The woman with claws.	Williams Forrest
Woman without love.	André Maurois
Woman without love.	Roswell Williams
Woman's doctor.	Russell Boltar
A woman's heart.	Guy de Maupassant
A woman's life.	Guy de Maupassant
Woman's medical problems.	Maxine Davis
Women.	A. M. Krich
Women and children first.	Paul Steiner
Women and Thomas Harrow.	John P. Marquand
Women and vodka.	Mark Merrill
Women are like that.	Alice Elinor Lambert
The women in his life.	Eleanor Nash
Women in love.	D. H. Lawrence
Women in prison.	Joan Henry
Women in the shadows.	Ann Bannon
Women in trouble.	James Donner
Women must weep.	Ruth Adams Knight
The women of Champion City.	Doris Davis
Women on the wall.	Marshall McClintock
Women to love.	Sinclair Drago
Women will be doctors.	Hannah Lees
Women without men.	Alex Austin
Women without men.	Reed Marr
Women's barracks.	Tereska Torres
The wonderful country.	Tom Lea
A wonderful world for children.	Peter Cardozo

X Y Z

X marks the shot.	G. Forbes Durand
The X-ray murders.	M. Scott Michel
Yaller gal.	Carolina Lee
Yama, the hell-hole.	Alexandre Kuprin
A Yank on Piccadilly.	C. L. McDermott
Yankee from Olympus.	Catherine Drinker Bowen
Yankee mariner.	James Busbee Jr.
Yankee pasha.	Edison Marshall
Yankee storekeeper.	R. E. Gould
Yankee stranger.	Elswyth Thane
Yankee trader.	Stanley Morton
Yankee woman.	Eric Baume
Yanqui's woman.	George McKenna
Year of consent.	Kendell Foster Crossen
Year of the gun.	Giff Cheshire
The year of the tempest.	Peter Matthiessen
The year the Yankees lost the pennant.	Douglass Wallop
Year 2018!	James Blish
Yell bloody murder.	Joseph Shallit
Yellow Hair.	Clay Fisher
Yellow Kid Weil.	William T. Brannon "Yellow Kid" Weil
The yellow overcoat.	Frank Gruber
The yellow room.	Mary Roberts Rinehart
Yellow rope.	Lincoln Drew
The yellow taxi.	Jonathan Stagge
The yellow turban.	Charlotte Jay
The yellow violet.	Frances Crane
Yellowhorse.	Dee Brown
Yellowstone Kelly.	Clay Fisher
Yellowstone passage.	Coe Williams
Yellowstone scout.	William Marshall Rush
Yesterday's love.	James T. Farrell
Yesterday's madness.	Marian Cockrell
Yesterday's murder.	Craig Rice
Yonder.	Charles Beaumont
Yorktown.	Burke Davis
You and music.	Christian Darnton
You and the atom.	Gerald Wendt
You and the universe.	N. J. Berrill
You and your heart.	H. M. Marvin
You asked for it.	Ian Fleming
You belong to me.	Sam Ross
You can change the world.	James Keller
You can live after death.	Harold Sherman
You can't catch me.	Lawrence Lariar
You can't do business with Hitler.	Douglas Miller
You can't keep the change.	Peter Cheyney
You can't live forever.	Harold Q. Masur
You can't see around corners.	Jon Cleary
You can't stop me.	William Ard
You got to stay happy.	Robert Carson
You live once.	John D. MacDonald
You must relax.	Edmund Jacobson
You only hang once.	H. W. Roden
You play the black and the red comes up.	Richard Hallas
You shall know them.	Vercors
You tell my son.	Rex Pratt
You'll die next!	Harry Whittington
You'll get yours.	Thomas Wills
You'll never see me again.	William Irish
Young.	Miriam Colwell
Young Ames.	Walter D. Edmonds
Young and deadly.	Leo Margulies
The young and hungry-hearted.	James Aswell
The young and violent.	Vin Packer
Young and wild.	Morton Cooper
Young awakening.	Robert Fontaine
The young Caesar.	Rex Warner
Young Claudia.	Rose Franken
Young Doctor Galahad.	Elizabeth Seifert
Young Doctor Kildare.	Max Brand
Young Doctor Randall.	Adeline McElfresh
The young don't cry.	Richard Jessup
The young killers.	Willard Wiener
The young life.	Leo Townsend
The young lions.	Irwin Shaw
Young Lonigan.	James T. Farrell
The young lovers.	Julian Halevy
The young lovers.	Meyer Levin
Young man of Manhattan.	Katharine Brush
Young man of Paris.	Henri Calet
Young man with a horn.	Dorothy Baker
The young manhood of Studs Lonigan.	James T. Farrell
Young Mr. Keefe.	Stephen Birmingham
The young punks.	Leo Margulies
Young sinner.	Elisabeth Gill
The young Texan.	Paul Evan Lehman
The young who sin.	John Haase
Young widow.	Clarissa Fairchild Cushman
The young wolves.	Edward De Roo
Youngblood.	John O. Killens
Younger sister.	Kathleen Norris
Your adolescent at home and in school.	Lawrence K. Frank Mary Frank
Your body and its care.	Richard E. Winter
Your body and your mind.	Frank G. Slaughter
Your child and you.	Sidonie Gruenberg
Your child from 2 to 5.	Morton Edwards
Your daughter Iris.	Jerome Weidman
Your guide to financial security.	Sidney Margolius
Your key to happiness.	Harold Sherman
Your legal advisor.	Samuel G. Kling
Your life in the atom world.	John Houston Craige
Your most intimate problems.	Lawrence Gould
Your own beloved sons.	Thomas Anderson

www.ingramcontent.com/pod-product-compliance
Lightning Source LLC
Chambersburg PA
CBHW080323270326

41927CB00014B/3086